AF832514

The Manasseh Hill Country Survey

Culture and History of the Ancient Near East

Founding Editor

M.H.E. Weippert

Editor-in-Chief

Jonathan Stökl

Editors

Eckart Frahm
W. Randall Garr
B. Halpern
Theo P.J. van den Hout
Leslie Anne Warden
Irene J. Winter

VOLUME 21.5

The titles published in this series are listed at *brill.com/chan*

The Manasseh Hill Country Survey

Volume V: The Middle Jordan Valley, from Wadi Fasael to Wadi 'Aujah

By

Adam Zertal Z"l
Shay Bar

BRILL

LEIDEN | BOSTON

The Library of Congress Cataloging-in-Publication Data is available online at http://catalog.loc.gov.
LC record available at https://lccn.loc.gov/2004045595

Translated by Amatsia Halevi
English language editing by John Tresman
Graphic Design by Sapir Haad

Typeface for the Latin, Greek, and Cyrillic scripts: "Brill". See and download: brill.com/brill-typeface.

ISSN 1566-2055
ISBN 978-90-04-40084-9 (hardback)
ISBN 978-90-04-40086-3 (e-book)

Copyright 2019 by Koninklijke Brill NV, Leiden, The Netherlands.
Koninklijke Brill NV incorporates the imprints Brill, Brill Hes & De Graaf, Brill Nijhoff, Brill Rodopi, Brill Sense, Hotei Publishing, mentis Verlag, Verlag Ferdinand Schöningh and Wilhelm Fink Verlag.
All rights reserved. No part of this publication may be reproduced, translated, stored in a retrieval system, or transmitted in any form or by any means, electronic, mechanical, photocopying, recording or otherwise, without prior written permission from the publisher.
Authorization to photocopy items for internal or personal use is granted by Koninklijke Brill NV provided that the appropriate fees are paid directly to The Copyright Clearance Center, 222 Rosewood Drive, Suite 910, Danvers, MA 01923, USA. Fees are subject to change.

This book is printed on acid-free paper and produced in a sustainable manner.

1. The Manasseh Hill Country Survey team, March 2012. From left to right: Isaac Bejerano, Noga Goldring, Amatsia Halevi, Shoshi Lotan, Meir Adar, Shraga Hashman, Osnat Gadir, Adam Zertal and Oren Cohen. Missing: Leah Tremer and Moshe Einav (Shay Bar).

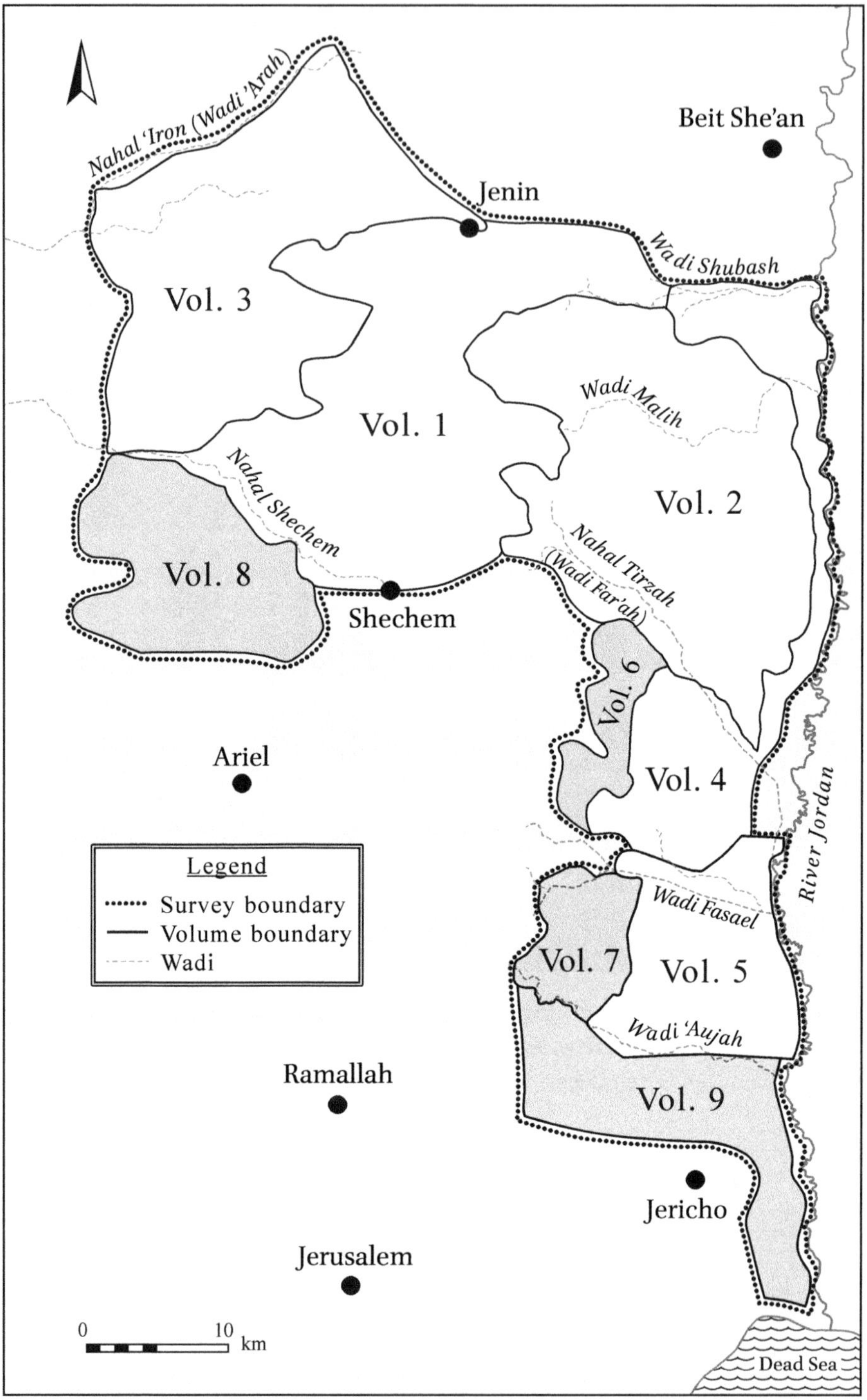

2. The Manasseh Hill Country Survey: Publication volumes.

CONTENTS

ABBREVIATIONS

a.m. - above-mentioned
a.s.a. - above surrounding area
a.s.l. - above sea level
BCE, B. C. E. - Before Common Era
blk - black
BP - before present
br - brown
b.s.a. - below surrounding area
b.s.l. – below sea level
Byz - Byzantine period
CE, C. E. - Common Era
Chal, CH - Chalcolithic period
CP - cooking pot
CTE - Core trimming element
dec - decorated, decoration
dk - dark
EA - el-Amarna
EB, EBA - Early Bronze Age
EM - Early Moslem period
EP, E. P. - elevation point
ER - Early Roman period
gr - grey
ha - hectare
Hel - Hellenistic period
HM - holemouth (jar)
IA - Iron Age
IBA - Intermediate Bronze Age
IDF - Israeli Defense Forces
Kh. - Khirbeh (t)
km - kilometre
LB, LBA - Late Bronze Age
LR - Late Roman period
lt - light
LU/L.U. - landscape unit/s
m - metre, metres
MA - Middle Ages, Medieval period
Mam - Mamluk
MB, MBA - Middle Bronze Age
MHCS - Manasseh Hill Country Survey
misc - miscellaneous
mod - modern
Nd - not defined
NE/Neo - Neolithic
no., nos - number, numbers
Ott - Ottoman period
PEF - Palestine Exploration Fund
Per/Pers - Persian period
PPN - Pre-Pottery Neolithic period
rd - red
Rom - Roman
sq. km - square kilometres
sq. m - square metres
wh - white
yel - yellow
Chron - Chronicles
Deut - Deutronomy
Josh - Joshua
Kgs – Kings
Numb - Numbers

PREFACE

Only a year has elapsed since Volume 4 of the Manasseh Hill Country Survey appeared in English. We are happy to introduce Volume 5 in the series to researchers, students and interested members of the public.

The preceding volumes have long been an important document and database for the study of Israel/Palestine, and a fundamental component in the knowledge of Judea and Samaria. They are based on detailed data from each site, the new regions previously unexplored, the methodology of the survey, and the detailed synthesis of the history of the region and the different periods of occupation.

Volume 5 is an organic continuation of Volume 4 (From Nahal Bezeq to the Sartaba – Zertal and Bar 2017), and expands the study of the Jordan Valley to the south. The Middle Jordan Valley starts in the north in Wadi Ahmar, extending south from the broad Fasael Valley to Nahal Yitav (Wadi 'Aujah).

The Jordan Valley spreads transversely, from the foot of the eastern range of Samaria in the west to the Jordan Valley in the east. For the sake of publication, we have divided it into three longitudinal sections: north – from Nahal Bezeq to the Sartaba (included in Volume 4); middle – from Wadi Fasael to Wadi 'Aujah (in this volume); and south – from Wadi 'Aujah to the Dead Sea (future Volume 9).

In contrast to Volume 4, in which the landscape units are diverse, the current volume is homogeneous. The middle and southern Jordan Valley, from Wadi Ahmar south of the Sartaba to the northern shore of the Dead Sea, is a broken flat plain, made of Lisan marl near the River Jordan and stony-desert soils at the foot of the mountains. The natural division into landscape units is obvious here, based on the floodplains of the wadis flowing down to the River Jordan, resulting in the division of the 161 sites in this volume into three landscape units. The area of about 150 sq. km between two streams (which flowed in the past, before being diverted for irrigation): Nahal Fasael (Wadi Rashash) in the north and Nahal Yitav (Wadi 'Aujah) in the south. Both have prominent floodplains (deltas), chosen to serve as the natural boundaries of this volume. Another division of the Middle Jordan Valley, separate from the transverse strips, is into four longitudinal strips. These, from north to south, are: the eastern mountainous step of Samaria and the foothills; the marl plains; the upper *Ghor*; and the *Zor*.

Due to our method of survey, the region was not surveyed in sequence. The work commenced in the 1990s, and continued sporadically. Additional work was done in 2014-2016 as part of the final preparation of the publication of this fully-revised and updated English version (An earlier version in Hebrew was published in 2012).

Within the Survey framework, almost the entire area was systematically investigated on foot, except for minefields and the cliffs of the wadis. The survey began in the west, at the foot of the eastern Samaria Mountains and in the wadis draining them. This strip of land is very rich in settlements, compared to the next one to the east with its marl plains, which includes most of the area surveyed. In the last transverse strip the ancient sites are scarce, and only in later times (from the Hellenistic period onwards) did the settlement of the region begin. In the Bronze and Iron Ages there were no human habitations in the marl plains, the salinas and the broken zones close to the River Jordan.

As in the previous volumes, the area included in this one was almost unexplored. Former surveys and excavations were sporadic, offering little information about the region.

This volume includes varied information about the region: historical (history of research; historical sources), geographical (geology and geomorphology; climate, water, soil and vegetation; road systems), details of the different landscape units, an analysis of the settlements according to period, and a summary of the history of the region based on archaeological information. Another important section is the research of the geographical-historical identifications.

All the sites are then presented in detail (see Volume 1 – Zertal 2004: chapters 1 and 2, for the methodology of the survey and the format of the site presentation). Most of the sites were measured and the plans are attached. Apart from photographs taken in the field, in certain places aerial photographs have also been introduced.

Additional information appears in the Appendices and Indices. These begin with the important research of the flint finds (by Winter). Complementing Winter's work is the summary of earlier prehistoric surveys in the Middle Jordan Valley by myself. We also include a rare South-Arabian tomb inscription, the first of its kind found west of the River Jordan (by Zertal and Gruntfest). A great deal of work was invested in the study and mapping of the aqueducts of Wadis Fasael and 'Aujah: these appear in Appendix D (by Zertal).

All these important contributions are followed by the indices of the book that include a list of water sources, a list of roads, a large list of agricultural installations and other features, a site index, and a list of sites by period.

The participants in the survey of the Middle Jordan Valley were: Shoshi and Meir Adar-Lotan, Ron Be'eri, Isaac Bejerano, Dror Ben-Yosef, Haim Cohen, Oren Cohen, Gil Cooper, Moshe Einav, David Eitam, Osnat Gadir, Noga Goldring, Amatsia Halevi, Shraga Hashman, Gilad Itach, Rafi Kimhi, Yael Leder, Ari Levi, the late Nivi Mirkam, Michal Oren, Murad Tabber, Leah Tremer, Dafna

Ullman, and others. We wish to emphasise that the most essential component for over 40 continuous years of effort in carrying out the survey is our loyal and dedicated team.

Thanks are due to those who created and arranged this volume: Oren Cohen, who engaged in the laborious tasks of gathering and arranging the finds and the data and proofreading the text; Amatsia Halevi, who translated from Hebrew; John Tresman, who edited the English; Osnat Gadir, who drew some of the maps; Sapir Haad, who drew other maps and the pottery and paginated the book. Most of the field photos were taken by Moshe Einav and myself. Thanks are also due to Asaf Solomon and Nitzan Eshed who was the pilot for the aerial photos.

We also grateful to those who assisted by financing the survey activities and the publications: foremost to the Norwegian Organization for Israel and the Bible headed by Gro and Bruno Venske; Avraham Ben-Naftali and the Pedagogica Foundation; the late Dani Barak; the Jordan Valley Regional Council; the Hecht Fund; and others.

We also thank our dear friends in the Jordan Valley: the Cooper family of Argaman and the Leiba family of Fasael.

The Zinman Archaeological Institution in the University of Haifa serves us as scientific home.

We shall always remember the late Professor Adam Zertal. Adam initiated this project in 1978, and was its main researcher and driver for 38 years. Adam passed away in November 2015, and we continue his life's project in his memory.

Most importantly, thanks go to our families who endured our many days of absence from home.

Shay Bar, July 2018

PART ONE

INTRODUCTION

CHAPTER ONE

GEOGRAPHICAL AND SETTLEMENT DATA

A. HISTORY OF RESEARCH AND HISTORICAL SOURCES[1]

1. Ancient sources

The Middle and Southern Jordan Valley, from Wadi Ahmar to the Dead Sea, appears on a few occasions in Roman period sources and onwards. The main reason for its appearance in these texts is its proximity to Jericho, and Herod's feats of construction. In the writings of Josephus Flavius, much space is dedicated to the River Jordan and its environs (and see section E below). Some places in the region are mentioned in the 4th century CE Onomasticon of Eusebius (Notley and Safrai 2005): Gilgal (no. 311), Jordan (no. 527), Naarah (no. 732), and Zin (no. 824). In the Madaba Map, the names of Corae, Archelais, and maybe that of Phasaelis, may have been preserved in the Middle Jordan Valley (Avi-Yonah 1953). However, the marks of fortified city or village for Archelais or Phasaelis have not been preserved (Avi-Yonah 1953: 135).

Burchard of Mount Sion, a traveller in Crusader times, whose account appeared in 1280, tells the following: "Four leagues to the east of Emon, at the going down of Mount Ephraim, on the plain, two leagues from Jordan, is the village of Phesech, at the place where the brook Cherith runs down from the mountain. Here Elijah abode, when the ravens brought him food in the morning and in the evening." (Stewart 1896: 56).

Almost the same description is given by the Italian Crusader period historian, Marino Sanuto, writing: "... Fasael, three leagues distant from the Jordan, in the plain country, where the brook Cherith comes down from the mountain, in which place Elijah dwelt when the ravens brought him meat (I Kgs 22)." (Stewart 1896: 14).

Beyer (1940: 189), in his comprehensive work on the region of Neapolis (Shechem) in the Crusader period, states that Burchard of Mount Sion calls Phesech "casal" (fortress), associating it with the region of Neapolis. The region later became the property of the King of Jerusalem (Beyer 1940: 201).

---

1 All references accompanied by a number refer to the site numbers in this volume. To simplify the discussion, we use the following abbreviations: Volume 2 = Zertal 2008; Volume 4 = Zertal and Bar 2017.

2. *Travellers, explorers and archaeologists in the 19th and 20th centuries*

There were two groups of visitors to the Jordan Valley: travellers in the 19th and the beginning of the 20th centuries, and archaeologists who investigated from 1967 onwards. We have already noted the researchers of the first group (Zertal and Bar 2017: 11): the British Survey, Victor Guérin, Felix Marie Abel, William Foxwell Albright, and others. The explorers of the River Jordan itself who explored the Middle Jordan Valley have been discussed in detail in Ben-Yosef's dissertation (2007: 45-53).

The identification of Phesech with Phasaelis, originating in the Middle-Ages, was repeated by many (for instance Guérin 1874: 231-232). The identification of Nahal Fasael (Wadi Rashash) with biblical Nahal Cherith (the brook of Cherith) was also repeated in these later sources.

Van de Velde visited the region in 1851-2, providing a detailed description of Nahal Fasael. He went down from Shechem to Aqrabeh (Van de Velde 1854: 306ff), and from there to the village of Majdal Bani Fadil. He noted that the Arabic name *Majdal* is derived from the Hebrew *Migdal* (tower). He noted that the village of Majdal has a fine view of the Jordan Valley, and added that it is the last one before the *Ghor*. He also described the prominence of Qarn Sartaba in the landscape. Later he arrived at the village of Daumeh (Dumah). When the guide went to get information regarding the descent to the Jordan valley, the traveller noted "I had heard much about a ruin called el-Aujeh, which by some has been identified with the fortress of Archelaus." (Van de Velde 1854: 308). From Dumah they went eastwards in a "steep and rocky track of more than a thousand feet descent had we to follow." (Van de Velde 1854: 308-309). After a strenuous walk they arrived at 'Ein Fasael (Van de Velde 1854: 310, Site 12), and repeated the narrative of Nahal Cherith and the dispute regarding its location (the other option indicates Wadi Qelt, to the south, near Jericho). Van de Velde notes that from Fasael Springs is three-quarters of an hour's walk east to the wadi outlet, mentioning the great many natural caves in the sides of the wadi. His guide remarked that: "In these, the Bedouins dwell during the winter season, in order to find shelter from the rains" (Van de Velde 1854: 312). The traveller saw in the wadi valley "The cucumber gardens were yet green, but the wheat harvest was over" (Van de Velde 1854: 312). He called the small tell in the wadi outlet (Tell esh-Sheikh Diyab, Site 23) Tell Fasael, and considered it (mistakenly) to be the acropolis of the city of the same name, built by Herod. "A few yards to the south", he noted the remains of a small site (probably el-Hisha, Site 26), and there he identified the city of Phasaelis (again mistakenly). Finally, he noted the remnants of the aqueduct on the slope south of the stream. From Phasaelis the traveller returned to Dumah.

Lynch, an American naval officer who sailed the River Jordan and the Dead Sea in 1847, travelled with his party along the west bank of the river. He described the land south of the Damia crossing as follows: "Moreover, from the plateau behind our camp, we could see nothing towards the south but rough and barren cliffs, sweeping into the purple haze of the lower *Ghor*. And the rolling sand-hills, which form the surface of the upper plain, stretched far along the bases of the mountains without a mark of cultivation, or the shelter of a tree. Heretofore, we had seen patches of grain, but there were none now visible, and all before us was the bleakness of desolation." (Lynch 1849: 251). Later he wrote: "In ten minutes after leaving the camping-ground this morning, the caravan struck upon the plain and crossed the wady Faria, pursuing a south-west course... The high peak of "Kurn Surtabeh" - horn of the rhinoceros, bore west from that point... Beyond Wady el Aujeh, the soil bore a scanty crop of grass, now much parched; and to the right, where the mountains receded from the plain, there were extensive fields of low, scrubby bushes, powdered with clay-dust of the soil; on the left, was a blank desert, with one or two oases, and a waving line of green, where the Jordan betrayed itself, at times, by a glitter like the sheen from bright metal." (Lynch 1849: 255-258).

Tristram came to the region in January 1864, while travelling in the southern Jordan Valley. After a detailed description of Kh. es-Samrah (Tristram 1865: 236-237), he expressed his wish to visit Fasael. On the way, he spoke about "...a perfect, but waterless aqueduct..." (Tristram 1865: 235).

Edward Robinson did not mention the Middle Jordan Valley.

Victor Guérin (1874: 225-232) crossed the region on his way from Jericho to Wadi Far'ah in April 1870. He left 'Ein Sultan near Jericho, and briefly described the route to Wadi 'Aujah. On his way, he saw a site north of Wadi 'Aujah (probably Kh. Beiyudhat – Archelais, Site 111), mistakenly identifying it with Na'aran. In that year Wadi 'Aujah flowed abundantly in its channel and the aqueducts could not cope with the flow of water. He described a site named Kharbet El-Maskarah (part of Kh. Beiyudhat, Site 111), Kh. Fusayil (Site 34) and Nahal Fasael in detail. The water reservoir near Tell esh-Sheikh Diyab was blocked at the time of his visit, thus he encamped inside it. Guérin suggested that the tell was the base for a fort, and he also noticed the earth rampart east of the tell.

In Thomson's book (1880: 359) only a journey from Damia Bridge south to Jericho is mentioned. Trying to explain why the region is called "dryness" or "desolation" by the European explorers, he described the marl plain as: "... I could not obtain a drop of water until I reached 'Ain es Sultan, six hours' rapid riding. The whole plain is either absolutely bare or overrun with a tangled mass of low bushes impossible to penetrate".

In the British Survey (Conder and Kitchener 1879: map 15; 1882: 380-404) the information concerns both the mountainous country and the Jordan Valley, the latter being described on p. 383, with data on the streams Fasael and 'Aujah and the area between them. In their historical and descriptive account are mentioned: Archelais (Site 111), Phasaelis (Site 34), Qanat el-Musa aqueduct (Site 147), 'Aujah et-Tahtah (Site 146), 'Aujah el-Foqa (Site 143), and Kh. Beiyudhat (Site 111). In Archelais they identified only two watch towers, but not the city itself. They identified Kh. Fusayil correctly as Phasaelis: and concentrated on it, rather neglecting descriptions of other nearby places.

Felix Marie Abel visited the region in February 1910 (Abel 1913: 235), during his research expedition to the Jordan Valley. After visiting the opening of Wadi Fasael he identified Tell esh-Sheikh Diyab (Site 23), its reservoir and the nearby aqueducts. Abel also mentioned the presence of the region in the Madaba map, noting the data about Phasaelis. He also noted that the region was also a place of importance in the Byzantine period.

3. New publications

In the Emergency Survey of 1967-1968 (Kochavi 1972) the area defined as "The Jericho and Jordan Valley wilderness as far as Damia Bridge" was investigated (Bar-Adon 1972). Due to limitations and the short time available, the mountainous country east and south from Aqrabeh was united with the Jordan Valley. In the Middle Jordan Valley, the area covered by this volume, only a few sites were found. The Emergency Survey map (Bar-Adon 1972) shows fewer than 20 sites, some of which are Roman roads. The surveyors focused mainly on Wadi 'Aujah, in which about half of the sites were found. Bar-Adon's group, noteworthy for the numerous plans they published, did not deal with geographical-historical identifications. Porath, in his later addition to the original Emergency Survey (1968, unpublished manuscript), added some information, mainly about Wadi Far'ah.

Ilan's book (1973) included additional important information concerning the Jordan Valley. The author synthesized the previous sources, and published them with the archaeological material from the Emergency Survey. The archaeological data are not up to date, due to circumstances, but the historical chapters are of value.

From the later researches we note Porath's dissertation (1985b), where he investigated and summed up the ancient irrigation systems in the region. He based his study on the fieldwork he conducted in the 1970s: the Fasael and 'Aujah aqueducts were published with illustrations and plans. This pioneering dissertation on the subject was carried out when most the systems were intact (many of the architectural remains no longer exist).

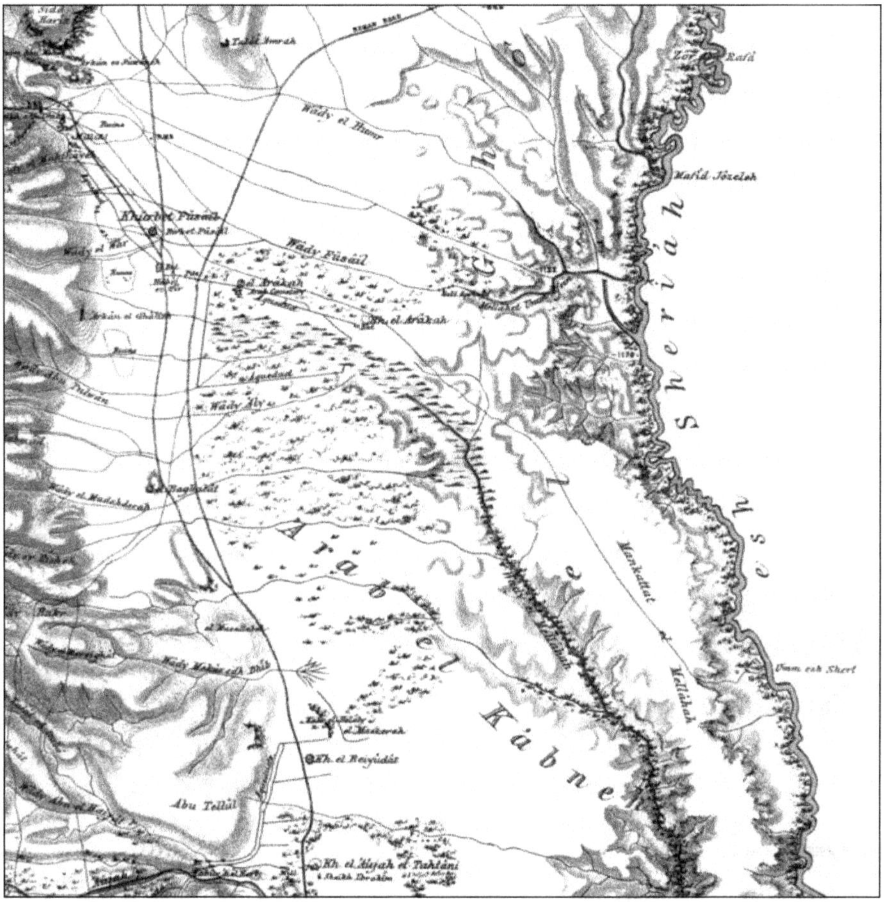

3. Section from the British Survey map (sheet XV) presenting the territory in this volume.

In the late 1980s an expedition from Braunschweig University (Garbrecht and Netzer 1991) worked on the Wadi 'Aujah aqueducts. Their work was published under the auspices of the Hebrew University, and we made use of it for comparisons.

Spanier (1992) partially surveyed sections of the region in the late 1980s. In the hill country he surveyed 15 sites, but their descriptions are somewhat laconic and without plans or drawings of sherds.

Various researchers of the Judea and Samaria Archaeology Staff Officer conducted sporadic surveys and excavations, some published (Hizmi 1993; 2003; 2008a; 2008b; 2012; Kagan 2009; Peleg 2000a; 2000b; 2006; 2009; Peleg and Hameiri 2002), and others not yet published (e.g. The monastery at Kh. Umm Zaqumeh - Site 150; the Silo Site [1] – Site 81; 'Aujah el-Foqa Village – Site 143 [1], and 'Aujah Fortress, Site 140).

Two PhD dissertations dealt with the Middle Jordan valley. Ben-Yosef (2007) worked on the Iron Age I period, and conducted excavations in two foot-shaped enclosures: Bedhat esh-Sha'ab and Yafit (3). Bar (2008) worked on the Chalcolithic and Early Bronze I sites of the region, and conducted excavations in three sites: Fasael (2), Fasael (7) and Tell esh-Sheikh Diyab (2); Sites 19, 24 and 21 respectively (Bar 2013a; 2013b; 2014; Bar and Winter 2010; Bar et al. 2011; 2013a). Later he expanded the research and excavated the sites of Fasael (1) Fasael (4) and Fasael (5) (Sites 14, 18 and 22 respectively; Bar et al. 2012; 2014; 2015).

Additionally, excavations at the Iron Age site of Tell esh-Sheikh Diyab (Site 23) were conducted by Zertal (Zertal et al. 2012), and at the Roman-Byzantine city of Phasaelis – Site 34, by Hizmi (2012).

In 2017 a new excavation project was initiated by Ben-Shlomo and Hawkins (2017) in the site of el-Mastarah (1) (Site 113).

B. THE GEOGRAPHY OF THE MIDDLE JORDAN VALLEY

1. Boundaries

The boundaries of the Middle Jordan valley are simple to define, being identical to the natural limits, which are: Wadi Ahmar in the north (the southern limit of the territory in the previous Volume 4); The River Jordan in the east; the foothills of the eastern Samaria mountain range in the west; and Nahal Yitav in the south. All of these require further explanation:

a. **Wadi Ahmar:** The riverbed is a clear border line. The broad valley north of the channel (Wadi Ahmar) was presented in Volume 4. For practical reasons we used the new road from Fasael junction to Ma'ale Ephraim, which is adjacent to the south of Wadi Ahmar, as an actual border line.

b. **The River Jordan** is a well-defined narrow land-strip; however, the geopolitical circumstances prevented a complete survey down to the river itself. The Israeli border fence system and the minefields were an obstacle; however, most of the land to the east of it was surveyed. The fence and adjacent minefields occupy a strip 2–3 km wide between the River Jordan and the upper shoulder of the *Ghor*. This low western strip of the *Zor*, in which the river flows, was almost all omitted from the survey under the circumstances. Thanks to the current process of clearing the minefields and conversion of the land to agriculture, mainly date palms, we succeeded in surveying many parts in the upper shoulder, the *Ghor*, east of the border fence. Following are the fully surveyed areas east of the fence and minefields:

   b1. Large areas in the northern Nahal Tirzah nature reserve (Israel map, 1:50.000, between latitude 168 north, and 162 in the south). There are areas of cut up marl hills without sites. About 8 sq. km were surveyed.

b2. Large areas in the southern Nahal Tirzah nature reserve (Israel map 1:50.000 between latitude 163 and 157). Here also large areas of the marl hills were explored on foot to no avail. About 15 sq. km were surveyed.

b3. Extensive sections of the Wadi Malha eastern nature reserve, across the border fence (Israel map 1:50,000, between latitude 156 and 148). About 12 sq. km have been surveyed, and the only site found was Kh. Umm esh-Shughut (Site 73).

The River Jordan remains the eastern border, and the extensive survey of parts of the cut up marl areas of the *Ghor* did not yield any settlements. A similar result was obtained in the western Wadi Malha reserve (see below), and all these areas were empty. This conclusion was derived from surveying about 70% of the entire area.

c. **The eastern range of Samaria Mountains:** this is a conspicuous morphological line, clearly tilting with sharp slopes descending and joining with the Jordan Valley plain. For various reasons the lower eastern step of this ridge, the border of which now exists as an unpaved road along its entire length, has been included in this volume. In the north the step begins in Nahal Fasael, continues southward along unpaved road no. 5530 in the 1:50,000 map, then further south crosses Wadis Sansileh, Dabal and el-'Imri. From coordinates 1898/1596 it becomes an asphalted road skirting to contain Jebel Fusayil. After crossing the transverse road 5626, both the road and border extend further south along road 5629. From the unpaved road junction next to E.P. 60 (coordinates 1892/1544) the border continues south along the road, and crosses Wadis Baqer, Hamam, Nabiris and Haiyat to reach Wadi 'Aujah, west of Yitav. The total area of the step is about 15 sq. km.

The criteria for deciding the western border were: in the lower step were many sites, mostly in the floodplains of the wadis; whose subsistence was based on both the Jordan Valley and the ridge above them. Customary agriculture in the Jordan Valley was cultivation in winter and grazing, for which the upper hill country served. The upper hill country included the area from E.P. 30 to the north via Fusayil and the ridges between Wadis Sha'ab el-Bir and Tal'at Zghararah, through the area between Wadis Baqer and 'Aujah. There was almost no settlement in the whole area.

The connection between the 'low step' at the foot of the Jordan Valley begins from the Fasael–Ma'ale Ephraim road in the north; descending along the Jordan Valley main drainage channel to Tell esh-Sheikh Diyab. The line continues along the unpaved road ascending south along the ridge to road 5530 next to Kh. Fusayil. This road passes west of the settlements Tomer, Gilgal and Netiv Hagdud, reaching west of Niran. From its meeting point with road 5526 it continues south to become road no. 5629. In the vicinity of Niran a long ridge, called et-Tulul, extends east, reaching the Beit She'an–Jericho road (B10). Here the western border touches Wadi 'Aujah (Nahal Yitav) and the southern border. All the data and road names have been taken from Israel map 1:50,000 (track and trail-marking map: Jordan Valley and Eastern Samaria, no. 5-6, Survey of Israel and The Society for Protection of Nature in Israel).

d. **Nahal Yitav** (Wadi 'Aujah): the head of the stream is in Kh. es-Samia in the west; however, the current volume commences at eastern 'Ein 'Aujah. In order to complete the 'area-cell' we have chosen to move the boundary south of Wadi 'Aujah channel, and to include the valley up to the road from Rimonim Junction to Jericho. The ridges south and east of the '54 Memorial' (a memorial of a 1977 helicopter crash) have not been included in this volume, and the border reaches the River Jordan along Wadi 'Aujah.

2. *Geology and Geomorphology*

The Middle Jordan Valley is a continuation of the northern one, separated by Wadi Ahmar. The extent of the 150 sq. km area dealt with in this volume is an alluvial Lisan marl floodplain and other types of soils, washed by the wadis entering from the west. The geological review is partially based on the data gathered by Ilan (1973), and data gathered from various sources by Ben-Yosef (2007: 7-22).

The Jordan Valley is part of the Great Syrian-African Rift Valley. It is about 105 km long from the Sea of Galilee to the Dead Sea. The breadth of the Middle Jordan Valley west of the river varies from 8 to 16 km. In the west it is confined by the foot of the eastern Samaria Mountains, and in the east by the *Zor*.

The Rift Valley was created by geological movements, and later was filled by sedimentary rocks resulting from terrestrial and maritime erosion. According to Belitzky (1999), the Jordan Valley and northern Aravah were covered by the saline water of Lake Lisan about 70,000 years ago. The water level at that time was -180 m. When the water receded, the present plain, gradually sloping from -200 m in the Lake of Galilee vicinity down to -400 m around the Dead Sea, was exposed. The ravines of the Lisan marl landscape were formed by sedimentation processes and erosion by the River Jordan.

The *Zor* is a narrow strip, several hundred metres wide, through which the river flows. The *Zor* banks are relatively steep on both sides, with a terrace between the *Zor* and the *Ghor* (Nir and Ben-Arieh 1965).

After the retreat of Lake Lisan new structures of folding and fracture were formed in the Jordan Valley, as a result of later activity of fracture and

4. The *Zor* in the area of Wadi Malha, looking north. Note the white cliffs of the *Ghor* and the dense forest of the *Zor* (S. Bar).

5. The ravines of the Lisan marl landscape in the Nahal Tirzah reserve, 2008 (N. Eshed).

reversed fractures, influencing the morphology (Belitzky 1999: 441-442). These fractures are longitudinal, characterizing the mid-section of the area between the Succoth Valley in the east and the Dead Sea in the south. The sea water, which penetrated as a result of these fractures during the Pliocene Epoch (Horowitz 2001; Horowitz and Zak 1968), formed the Jericho syncline in which a great deal of sediments accumulated. This mechanism formed the fold constructions (diapirs), of which one is Zaharet el-Qurqin, about 27 km north of the Dead Sea opposite Fasael. The Jordan Valley in this region is about 16 km wide and is asymmetric. There are also other diapirs.

The *Ghor* and the *Zor*: these zones, briefly previously discussed (Vol. 4: 18-19; Ben-Yosef 2007: 15-16), are defined as parallel longitudinal strips. The River Jordan flows in the *Zor*, while the *Ghor* is the 'shoulder', bordering the *Zor* on both sides.

6. Geological structures in Wadi Nabiris caused by the constant fractures and reverse fractures in the region, 2005 (S. Bar).

3. *Climate, Water, Soil, and Vegetation*

In this aspect there is great resemblance to Volume 4 of the Survey. A semi-arid (Irano-Turanian) climate prevails in the Middle Jordan Valley: a long hot summer with high temperatures and continuous steady winds. The winds blow in the afternoon from west to east, mainly along the valleys of Wadis Ahmar, Rashash, Tal'at Zagharah and 'Aujah. The average winter temperatures are 25°C during the day and 15°C at night. The average precipitation from November to April is lower than the aridity threshold (Ilan 1973: 38). In the rainy seasons of 1970 and 1971, the average measured rainfalls were 183 mm in Argaman and 95 mm in Fasael. The average annual rainfall in Jericho from 1921 to 1950 was 143 mm.

The water sources are divided into interconnected springs and flowing streams. Nahal Fasael (Wadi Rashash) commences its course at Fasael Springs (see aqueduct review in Appendix D and Site 10). The water flow of these springs ranges from 30 cu. m/hour in summer to 150 cu. m/hour in winter and spring. The spring water was taken by aqueducts in ancient times (Roman-Herodian period). No springs have been recorded along a 12 km line from Fasael Springs to Wadi 'Aujah, and the settlements of the region relied on the two flowing wadis, wells, and collection and storage of water.

7. Ein 'Aujah, winter 2012 (S. Bar).

8. Water flow in the modern aqueduct from 'Ein 'Aujah to 'Aujah et-Tahtah village and its fields, 2007 (M. Einav).

The 'Ein 'Aujah water source (coordinates 1868/1514, Site 131) emerges where the wadi is fairly wide. The water flow of 'Ein 'Aujah was 9.5 million cu. m/year (1973), and part of the flow was already utilized in the Roman era, or even earlier. The aqueducts led from here to Jericho (the southern aqueduct), to Archelais (the north-eastern aqueduct), and for watering the vicinity.

The main areas of cultivated and irrigated land were in the floodplains of Wadi Fasael and Wadi 'Aujah. Between them lay the bottom mountain terrace, the marl plains and the ravine land by the River Jordan.

The soil is of several types, based on origin and agrarian value. In the Middle Jordan Valley the plain is 4 to 10 km wide, broader than the area north of it, and is suitable for cultivation, being made of Pleistocene Lisan marl. On top of the marl (covering the *Ghor* and the *Zor*) is chalky silt from the Samaria fringes (the Samarian desert). On the silt layer are fan-shaped tracts of stony-desert soil, with many pebbles, which also cover the marl areas. The fan-shaped silt, in which are also integrated Brown-Forest and Terra-Rossa fertile soils, is rather ancient, originating in fluvial times. Later on the silt soils were cut by ravines resulting from flash floods.

The main soil types are:
1. Alluvial brown (= brown forest), covers the *Ghor* from the foothills and to the east, brought down by the streams in the floodplains. It contains many stones close to the hills, diminishing in the direction of the River Jordan. These soils, which contain 20% to 40% chalk, originate mostly from the upper eastern Samaria mountain ranges. Their fertility is moderate to high if irrigated.
2. The marl soils contain a great deal of chalk, gypsum and salts. They lie in the eastern *Ghor* area and in the *Zor*, mostly cut and creviced by floods.
3. Salinas: these are marl soils with high concentrations of salts due to the lack of drainage. Large areas are present in the salinas of Nahal Tirzah (in the north) and Wadi Malha (centre and south). The salinas soils do not allow cultivation without thorough flushing with fresh water. During winter time impassable marshes are formed in them.

The flora of the Middle Jordan Valley is divided into the following phytogeographical zones: Saharo-Sinadian, tropical (Sudano-Deccanian) and semi-arid (Irano-Turanian).

The principal floral groups which influenced the ancient population are (from east to west):
1. The *Zor* was known in the biblical traditions for its thick forest (Jeramiah 49: 19; Zacharias 11: 3) and predators (lions, among others). This strip of land, up to 2 km wide, is covered by a thicket with three main species: Euphrates poplar, Jordan tamarisk and willow (Sabah 1992: 55). The forest is watered by the River Jordan water and is difficult to cross. It appears that the region has not been cultivated and served only for some logging (although the timber is not really good for construction – II Kgs 6: 2-4). Beneath the wood there is undergrowth and thickets of cane, reed-grass, *Lycium*, asparagus, saltbush and screw bean (*Prosopsis*).
2. In the areas of the salinas flooded in winter, the flora which have been recorded are mainly *Salsola*, saltbush, *Anabasis*, statice or sea lavender, *Nitraria*, asphaltic sea blight (*Suaeda asphaltica*), and *Arthrocnemum*. Among the annual plants (Therophyte) are prominent carpets of *Aizoon hispanicum* (Sabah 1992: 54). According to the Survey, the salinas areas were uninhabited: perhaps they served for grazing, but even nowadays the Bedouins occasionally graze there.
3. In the marl plains is a strip of semi-arid Irano-Turanian vegetation. This includes groups of Christ's thorn Jujube, Sodom Apple (*Calotropis procera*) and *Retama*, accompanied by carpets of annual plants in rainy years.
4. In the zone of the geologically folded layers in the eastern part of the Samaria Mountains (the closest ridge to the east to the Jordan Valley plain) are groups of rock vegetation, mostly *Chilladenus iphionoides* and *Teucrium*

9. Christ's thorn Jujube, at right and Sodom Apple (*Calotropis procera*), at left, on the banks of Wadi 'Aujah, 2006 (S. Bar).

capitatum. The *Retama raetam* forms the flora of the desert fringe *garigas* (Sabah 1992: 53). *Rhustri partita* and asphaltic sea blight grow over south- and east-facing surfaces.

4. Roads

The principal land road, B10 in our terminology, runs from Beit She'an to Jericho, the northern part of which has been dealt with in Volume 4 (Zertal and Bar 2017). The first direct testimony about it is in the *Tabula Peutingeriana*, in which is marked a road 36 Roman miles long from Scythopolis to Herichonte (Jericho), divided into three 12-mile sections: the first station from the north is Coabis, and the second is Archelais. Zertal (1991) proposed to identify Coabis with 'Iraq Abu Hasish, but this proposition has serious drawbacks. The fort is not near the road and its construction was not finished. Another option, somewhat more likely, is the identification with Kh. Khiraf (Volume 2: Site 266) but the distance from Beit She'an is slightly too far. It seems preferable to leave the place unidentified at present.

Regarding the road remains, the situation has changed since its first description some 150 years ago. Van de Velde mentions, after passing from Qaraweh to Damia Bridge: "...remains of the great Roman highway through the *Ghor*..." (de

Velde 1854: 321). In the British Survey map, sheet XV (Conder and Kitchener 1879) are noted the remnants of the road from Beit She'an as far as north of Fasael. Its continuation is the Roman road to Neapolis, ascending in a straight line from Jericho to Phasaelis (Kh. Fusayil, Site 34). Near Kh. es-Saleh (Volume 4: Site 44), Glueck (1951: 420) found the 6 m-wide remains of this road in 1943. Bar-Adon's party described it in the Emergency Survey (Bar-Adon 1972: Site 14) as: "Remains of a Roman road, marked in maps, with forts on both sides: one north of the road and another one south of it.". Despite our efforts we could not trace it, and it seems that the road was completely destroyed by modern construction and agriculture.

Pompey descended along this route from Corea to Jericho, after negotiating with Aristobulus (War I, vi: 5-6). Afterwards Vespasian travelled it, coming from Neapolis to Corea and onward to Jericho (War IV, viii: 1). It is certain that the route, although not necessarily paved, was in use during the Early Roman period, and possibly earlier. This supposition is based on the topography which forced all routes to transverse the marl plains, between the *Ghor* and the foothills. The three Roman cities of Corea, Phasaelis and Archelais, mark the route. The first of the three is Corea – Tell es-Simadi (Volume 4: Site 84), founded in the Early Bronze Age, and existing almost continuously until the Middle Ages. The lower city by the tell, Corea itself, was founded in the Roman period. The earliest sherds in Kh. Fusayil (Site 34) are Hellenistic, suggesting that the place was populated then. King Herod founded the city (anew?) (War I, xxi: 9) by the road. The same applies to Archelais – Kh. Beiyudhat (Site 111). Iron Age II sherds were found in the site, but a real settlement existed there only from the Hellenistic period onwards. In this case also, the city was re-established by Herod.

The establishment of the cities and their prolonged existence testifies to a principal road interconnecting them. The use of the road from Beit-She'an to Jericho also lasted through the Ottoman and British times. The historical evidence is scanty. Yelin (1972: 331), tells of renewal of use of the Jericho–Beit She'an road by donkey owners. According to him: "[A person] will travel from Jerusalem to Jericho and from there will directly transverse the Jordan Plain from south to north to reach Tiberias within sixteen hours. And the road is straight and there are no obstacles in it and not the paths of terror which the traveller meets while going via Shechem."

General Archibald Wavell, in his book *The Palestine Campaigns*, on the First World War, relates the following about a Turkish road: "...the greater portion of the Seventh Army...had set out from Nablus ...by a motor-road which the Turks had made down the Wadi Fara to Beisan and the Jordan."(Wavell 1941: 213). In another place in the book he relates: "...so as to gain control of as many as possible of the routes into the Jordan Valley...On the right of the XX Corps, the 60th Division, in the Jordan Valley, was to drive the enemy north of the Auja and to occupy the high ground about Abu Tellul and Musallabeh, which secured the water supply of the River 'Aujah and commanded the Beisan-Jericho road, one of the principal routes into the valley from the north." (Wavell 1941: 178). It is not difficult to understand the exact intent; obviously that route was used.

Should the foundation of the road be related to the Iron Age? In the absence of direct historical sources[2] one has to refer to a certain degree to the period's forts. It is not certain whether these served mainly for the protection of the roads or for other purposes (presence?). The Roman era forts indicate a similar tendency.

Five Iron Age forts have been discovered along the road: two are east of the Sartaba, and three other round ones by the roads leading from across the River Jordan to the regions of Shechem and Samaria. The forts east of the Sartaba (Volume 4: Sites 98, 99), Tell 'Abeid [1] and [2]), resemble each other in their oval form and period of existence. Both were established during Iron Age Ic (11th–10th centuries BCE), and they were occupied mostly in Iron Age II (54% and 50% of the sherds respectively). Both forts raise queries, due to their proximity (about 200 m apart) and the absence of other such forts between Beit She'an and Jericho. Their closeness to the road and their dominance of it, suggest a link between the forts and the road.

The three round forts of the 'Rujm el-Malfuf' type, almost identical in shape and dimensions, were built at the beginnings of the three main roads, within the bounds of the Jordan Valley from the Beit She'an–Jericho road, leading westward: Wadi Malih, Wadi Far'ah and the road to Majdal Bani Fadil. Zertal (1988; 1995) proposed that this array of forts guarded the approach roads to the centre of the Israelite kingdom. The two excavated forts (Yeivin 1974; 1992), have been dated to the 9th–8th centuries BCE.

Another Roman road (our C40-C41) goes from Jericho to Neapolis (Roman Shechem). It is discussed in Volume 4: 28, and has been dealt with by Ilan and Damati (1975: map on p. 44). The British Survey members described it as follows: "The Roman road is very perfect near this ruin (Khurbet Fusayil, A. Z.), it consists of three parallel lines of stones, about 1 foot square, forming the sides and central rib of the road, 9 feet apart, giving 18 feet for the width of the road. There seems to have been no foundation or drainage, but the central rib is higher than the sides, so that the road had a section of two inclined planes. The part between the ribs is filled in with a sort of cobble of stones of irregular size, covered with smaller metalling. The central rib consists of two lines of

2 A direct source regarding the roads of the Jordan Valley is available in Deut 11: 30, in which "The land of the going down of the sun" is defined. It has been identified by Zertal (Volume 2: 28) as the Nahal Tirzah road. No other references contain defined routes.

stones, the outer wall, or curb-stone, of a single line each side." (Conder and Kitchener 1882: 392-393).

No remnants have survived from that section of the road. From Kh. Fusayil, Roman Phasaelis, the road branched into two: one, our C40, and no. 2 in Ilan and Damati (1975), ascends north-north-west via Wadi Ahmar valley and reaches 'Ein Haffirah: here it turns to Wadi Ahmar and climbs to Neapolis via Sahel Afjeam, Wadi Qarad and Tana et-Tahta. From this branch an intact section of constructed road has been preserved, climbing to E.P.105 (Volume 4: Site 168). A section of the road (Volume 4: Site 177), includes the steep slope and the relatively level part over the spur which is built and paved (Volume 4: figs. 351 and 352).

The other branch, C41 in our terminology (no. 1 in Ilan and Damati [1975]), ascends north-west from Kh. Fusayil over the extension south of Ma'ale Ephraim. The 1960-1970s 'old road' also climbs over the same extension. The Roman road went up in the direction of Majdal Bani Fadil, passing the site at Rujm Abu Mukheir (Site 5; Bar-Adon 1972: Site 10). A section of it, which appears in Bar-Adon's plan of the round fort, is still visible.

Two or three other such roads, not traced in the field, certainly existed during ancient times. Certainly, such a road or path existed along Nahal Fasael (C47), at least to the springs. Such a road was essential for the maintenance of the various aqueducts and for reaching the springs. A similar road probably also existed along Wadi 'Aujah (C48), probably climbing west over the ridge. Indirect evidence of it lies in the foundation and upkeep of the city at Kh. 'Aujah el-Foqa (Site 143). In our opinion, the place served as the central administrative city in the southern Jordan Valley in the days of the Kingdoms of Israel and Judea. This branch was obviously connected to the main Beit She'an–Jericho road (B10), and apparently westwards up the Samaria Mountains.

C. THE LANDSCAPE UNITS

The three landscape units included in this volume stretch from north to south. A division into longitudinal strips was also considered, but for numerous reasons the transverse one has been chosen. The area is practically formed of the two wide floodplains of Wadis Fasael (Rashash) and Yitav ('Aujah) with the intermediate areas. To these is added the southern part of the Wadi Ahmar floodplain.

The three units are: Landscape Unit 31 – Nahal and Fasael Valley; Landscape Unit 32 – from Nahal Fasael to Nahal Yitav (Wadi 'Aujah); and Landscape Unit 33 – Nahal Yitav (Wadi 'Aujah) and its tributaries.

Landscape Unit 31 – Nahal and Fasael Valley

The area of Landscape Unit 31 is about 24 sq. km, consisting of the valley of Nahal Fasael (Wadi Rashash), its surrounding ridges and the floodplain down to the River Jordan. The unit is divided into three sub-districts:

A. Nahal Fasael: slightly less than 3 km from the springs to Tell esh-Sheik Diab. The valley in which it flows is 100 to 300 m wide. Nahal Fasael starts in the area of the springs at the confluence of two deep wadis: a) Wadi Zannanir, which starts at Kh. Bani Fadil and descends from the north-west, and is about 4 km long to the confluence; and b) Wadi Rashash which descends from the south-south-west, from the area of 'Ein Duma, and is about 3.5 km long. Both streams are deep and narrow with high ridges around them.

In the vicinity of the springs the wadi broadens to form a small valley,

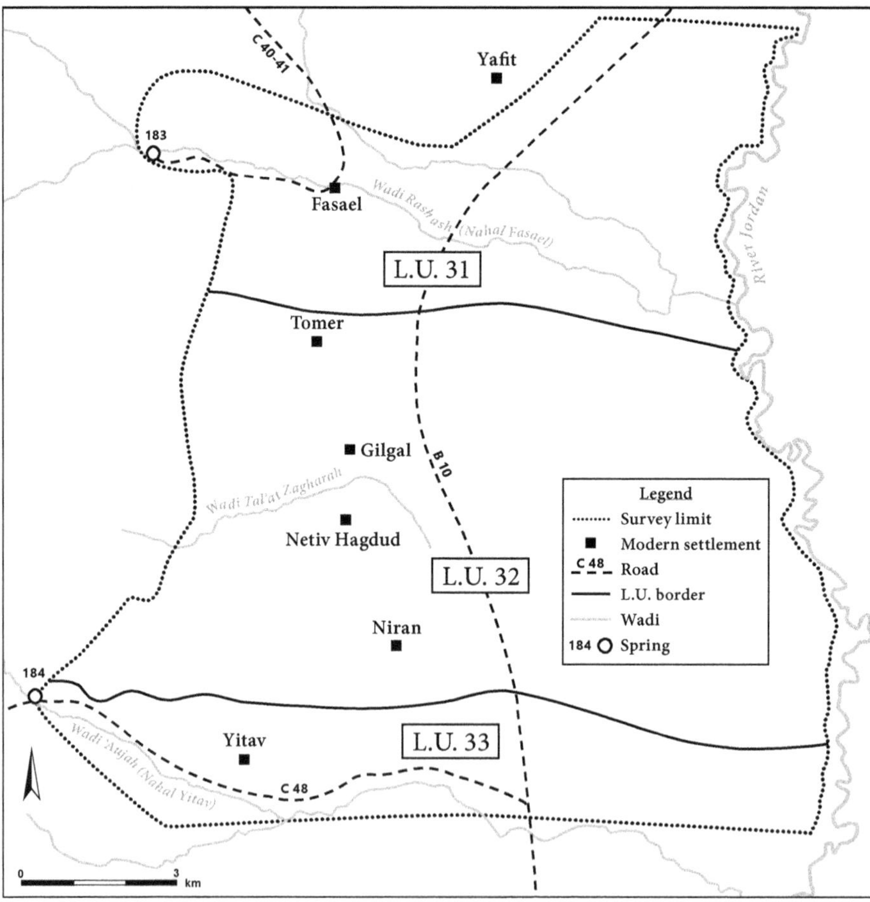

10. The landscape units, roads and springs in the Middle Jordan Valley.

with caves in the slopes (Sites 6–8, 13). The stream empties into its floodplain opposite Tell esh-Sheikh Diyab (Site 23).

In the stream valley itself there are no historical period settlements, except for the caves and aqueducts. About ten prehistoric sites, mainly Middle, Upper and Epipalaeolithic, were found in the survey conducted by Goring-Morris in the 1970s (Appendix B). The dwellers in ed-Duqaneh caves (Sites 7, 8, 13) from the Iron Age onward were mostly shepherds.

The aqueducts along the southern bank functioned with intervals from the Roman period to the present. Their dating is discussed in Appendix D.

B. Also included in this landscape unit is the broad ridge north-west of the stream, running north-west to south-east. Three roads ascend the ridge, leading from the Jordan Valley in the east towards modern Ma'ale Ephraim. The roads were in use during the Iron Age, Roman period and modern times. From the Jordan Valley they ascended west to the first mountainous stage, the location of the modern Ma'ale Ephraim junction and the nearby sites (Volume 4: Site 174). On the ridge is a small Iron Age I-II and Hellenistic-Roman site (Site 3), possibly linked to the road. Also noteworthy is the Iron Age II round fort (Rujm Abu Mukheir, Site 5) and the nearby roads. Zertal (1988: 86; 1995: 265–266) proposed identifying it with the site of 'Migdal', number 58 in Shoshenq's List. The identification is based on the plan of the site and the preservation of the name in the vicinity (in the modern village name of Majdal Bani Fadil).

C. The floodplain: A little east of Tell esh-Sheikh Diyab the narrow wadi widens to become the broad alluvial fan of Nahal Fasael, stretching to the River Jordan. This is a large triangle, with its base, about 3 km long, along the current Jordan Valley road. The floodplain includes the following parts:

1. The western alluvial fan is a triangle, covered by arable Mediterranean soil: Brown-Forest and Terra-Rossa, irrigated in the past with the water of Fasael Springs. This is the most populated area in this landscape unit, and one of the most densely settled in eastern Samaria and the Jordan Valley. The concentration of Chalcolithic and Early Bronze Age I sites is significant. Excavations of some of the sites by Bar (2008; 2013a; 2013b; 2014) indicate a new view of habitation at the final phase of the Chalcolithic Period.

   The Chalcolithic sites (Fasael [2], [5] and [7], Sites 19, 22 and 24 respectively) are present on the northern side of the alluvial fan and within it.

   In the following period the settlements 'ascended' to the first topographic step above the stream (Sheikh Diyab [2] and Fasael [4], Sites 21 and 18 - see the discussion on settlement in Section D).

   The intensive habitation in the alluvial fan also continued in some of the subsequent periods. Iron Age enclosures were discovered in the fan's southern part (Sites 31–33), and also the complex of Tell esh-Sheikh Diyab (Site 23): the tell itself, the water reservoir and the aqueducts (Appendix D).

The city of Phasaelis (Site 34) was founded in the southern part of the alluvial fan in the Herodian period (end of the 1st century BCE), and was one of the main Roman cities in the Jordan Valley. The city planners based it on a large area and the abundance of water. The city has been investigated and measured by the Manasseh Hill Country Survey. It is suffering a fast process of ruination by the inhabitants of Kh. Fusayil, and archaeological excavations have begun only lately (Hizmi 2012).

The habitation in the region also continued in the Byzantine and Early Moslem periods. The unique ceramic ware ('sugar vessels') is evidence of a cane-sugar processing plant at el-Hisha (Site 26). According to the Arab traveller Yaqut, sugar production also continued into the Middle Ages. During the Ottoman period the habitation dwindled, with most of the settlements deserted and the irrigation systems abandoned.

The ancient agricultural activity has been investigated by Porath (1985b), who noted the chain of well-like shafts (qanat-tunnels) and the division of land into irrigation plots (Porath 1985b: 29-45).

2. The rectangular marl plains extend at about 275 m below sea level from the Jordan Valley Memorial in the north to Tomer in the south, and from

11. Wadi Fasael, view to the west, 2012 (A. Solomon).

the Jordan Valley road in the west to the border fence in the east. The 5 sq. km area (5,000 dunams) is now mostly cultivated and planted. The plains here are covered by a thin layer (40–50 cm) of fertile alluvial soil. These areas are well levelled, and are drained by a network of shallow wadis – the streams of Fasael and Ahmar and their tributaries.

The intensive cultivation prevented a complete survey, and only about 80% of the area has been surveyed. It was concluded from the search that the region was relatively devoid of settlement. Only two sites were found: the 'Salvadora farm' (Site 36), excavated in the 1970s by Porath, and lately by Peleg (unpublished), and Kh. ed-Dashe (Site 38), which has not yet been surveyed due to minefields.

3. Nahal Tirzah nature reserve is a large (about 16 sq. km) and ravine-cut zone, stretching from Wadi Ahmar in the north to E.P. -326 in the south. The ravines and salinas of the reserve have been deeply eroded by Wadis Ahmar, Malha, Dashe and their tributaries. The grooving and slotting of the soft marl soil result from the ferocity of floods. Noteworthy also are the large saline areas. The region, which is a nature reserve, has been systematically surveyed, without discovering any major sites. Also absent are prehistoric flint scatters, and as said before, the area was almost devoid of human activity.

Landscape Unit 32 – from Nahal Fasael to Nahal Yitav (Wadi 'Aujah)

Landscape Unit 32 is a passage between the floodplains of the two main streams – Fasael and Yitav ('Aujah). The unit boundaries are the village of Tomer in the north; a line from Tomer eastward via Kh. ed-Dashe to the River Jordan (latitude 159/659); the River Jordan in the east; the mountain step in the west (longitude 191/241); and the Wadi 'Aujah alluvial fan in the south. The southern boundary runs diagonally to the north-east from coordinates 150/650 to coordinates 193/243 to el-Maskarah, and from there in a straight line to the River Jordan (latitude 153/653). This area includes the city of Beiyudhat-Archelais (Site 111). As for the previous landscape unit, we have adopted the division into three longitudinal strips.

The total area of the unit is about 95 sq. km, and it is divided to three sub-districts:

A. The lower step of the ridge; about 10 km long by 2.5 km wide on the average; including the ridges and sites in the wadis. Following are the parts:

A.1. The first land-block north, Umm Suwei'ad, is a large ridge between Nahal Fasael and Wadi Sansileh, and is about 1 sq. km (1,000 dunams) in area. A paved road (no. 5530) enters it along Wadi ed-Dabl to the south.

A.2. The second land-block is Jebel Fasil, about 3 sq. km in area, drained by Wadis el-Butem, Sa'ad and Abu Mahmud. Another paved road, no. 5526, enters the Jebel via Wadi Abu Mahmud.

A.3. The area of the third land-block, marked in the map by E.P. -11 and E.P. 71, is about 5 sq. km. It is crossed by Wadis Sha'ab el-Bir and Tal'at Zagharah, and its southern boundary is the large Wadi et-Baqar which has numerous tributaries.

A.4. The fourth land-block is the largest area between latitudes 154 and 151; its total area is about 13 sq. km and it is drained by Wadis Hamam, Maqor ed-Dib, Nabiris and Haiyat. Here the topography is gentler, with low hills and wide valleys. The advantages of the region made it the richest settlement in this landscape unit.

B. The longitudinal north-south strip runs from the village of Tomer in the north to the ridge west of the modern village of 'Aujah (et-Tullul, E.P. -170) in the south.

It is about 8.5 km long by 2 km wide on the average, and its area is about 18 sq. km. Most of the ancient settlements, the modern settlements (Tomer, Gilgal and Netiv Hagdud), and the Arab villages (et-Fusayil and 'Aujah et-Tahtah) are concentrated in this strip.

This part of the landscape unit is a marl plain covered by alluvium, which forms a stretch of arable land. The plain is cut and grooved by numerous wadis descending from the western ridge. The deep ravines diverted the roads by a kilometre and more eastward. Next to the entries of the wadis to the plain are soil surfaces with many stones, rendering passage and cultivation difficult. Below is an account of the alluvial fans of the wadis, from north to south:

B.1. Wadi Sansileh and Wadi Ahmar enter the southern part of Nahal Fasael fan. The city of Fasaelis, one of the two Herodian cities in the Mid-Jordan Valley, was established in this large plain. In the same plain there are several Iron Age enclosures (Sites 31–33), testifying to habitation and flock grazing. A narrow asphalt road was paved in the 1970s along Wadi Sansileh, from which a bad unpaved road leads to Kh. Jibeit, just west of the Alon road.

B.2. Wadi Butum empties into the Jordan Valley plain opposite Tomer. In the wadi is a two-period site: Chalcolithic and next to it, Middle Bronze Age II (Site 37). Between Wadi Butum and Wadi Sa'ad floodplains existed an affluent habitation, most of whose sites (mainly Tomer [2]–[6]) are situated in the eastern lower step of the ridges. In the western part of the wadi is Wadi Sa'ad (2) (Site 48), which is situated on a narrow high shoulder surrounded by deep streams. At the entry of the wadis to the

Jordan Valley plain, extensive date-palm plantations were planted, perhaps obliterating other ancient sites.

B.3. Wadi Abu Mahmud and its tributaries enter the Jordan Valley between Tomer and Gilgal. Road 5526 was built along this route. Here also, the sites are situated at the edge of the plain; among these are the important complex Iron Age sites, such as Gilgal (5), Site 60. This habitation is dealt with in section D, below.

B.4. Close to Wadi Tal'at Zagharah's entry into the Jordan Valley are important enclosure sites, including Wadi Tal'at Zagharah (2) (Site 65). Near the south-western corner of Netiv Hagdud an Iron Age fort and enclosures (Site 72) stand on a Neolithic site.

B.5. Wadi el-Baqar, one of the largest in the region, drains the area north of the watershed between Wadis Nabiris and Baqar: it also drains the extensive plateau land west of Netiv Hagdud. Apart from its tributaries and their drainage basins, the wadi forms a fairly large valley (Salibiya) between Niran and Netiv Hagdud. This valley has many prehistoric excavated and surveyed sites; including the 'grain-silos' and 'cup-mark' sites, testifying to an ancient agricultural area (Appendix B).

B.6. Wadis Maqor edh-Dhib, Hamam, Haiyat and Nabiris drain a large area of low hills north of Wadi 'Aujah. The intensity of the settlement is thoroughly discussed in section D.

12. The cultivated marl plains of the Middle Jordan Valley, 2005. In the background is the Sartaba ridge and fortress (M. Einav).

C. The marl plains: In this large area, approximately 50 sq. km, are included marl plains (mostly planted with date-palms) and areas of salinas (Wadi Malha badlands and Wadi Malha Nature Reserve). To these the *Zor*, which was only partially surveyed, has been annexed.

The marl plains and the vast salinas were almost uninhabited in the past, as nowadays, caused by lack of water sources, particularly poor soil and the danger of floods and landslides. These soils are arable only after thorough fresh water washing, and must be constantly irrigated (see below about the alluvial fans of Wadi Fasael and Wadi 'Aujah).

The subject of pasture is not entirely clear. 19th-century travellers described the marl plains as a totally desolate region with occasional stunted vegetation. Tristram (1865: 227) writes about the marl plains: "On either side, before or behind, not a tree or a blade of grass was visible, save the oasis of Jericho in the rear, and the fringe of the Jordan in front." He writes about the irrigation which nurtured the region in ancient times (the Fasael springs). On his way north from Jericho he remarks: "For many miles up, the width of the plain cannot have been less than ten miles, a desert, but only so by man's neglect." (Tristram 1865: 238). Lynch (1849: 184-185) also noted that the plain was covered by poor grass cover. From information provided to us by modern Bedouin, today also there are few areas fit for pasture .

Landscape Unit 33 – Nahal Yitav (Wadi 'Aujah) and its tributaries

Landscape Unit 33 is a relatively narrow strip, north and east of Nahal Yitav (Wadi 'Aujah). Its boundaries are 'Ein 'Aujah in the west; the line from Yitav to Archelais to the River Jordan in the north; and latitude 147 in the south. Not all of the boundaries are natural. In the north, included in the strip are parts of Wadi Nabiris and Wadi el-Haiyat valleys, and in the south – the line north of the '54 Memorial' hills. The total area of this landscape unit is nearly 32 sq. km.

Nahal Yitav was once one of the more important rivers in eastern Samaria. It is about 15 km long from Wadi 'Aujah down to the Jordan estuary, divided into several secondary divisions. As in Nahal Fasael, the aqueducts from 'Ein 'Aujah and the sites linked to them are of great significance (see Appendix D).

Landscape Unit 33 is divided into three sub-districts:

A. 'Ein 'Aujah and the valley to the east: 'Ein 'Aujah flows from a small step in the narrow section of the channel (coordinates 1868/1514). The aqueduct, which survives only partially, starts here and runs to the east. Three enclosure sites were discovered next to the streambed and the spring (Sites 131–133). Other settlements here are linked to the aqueducts, discussed in

Appendix D; included among them is the 'Aujah mill (Site 142). Two noteworthy sites are found next to the stream channel: 'Aujah Fortress and Villa 'Aujah (Sites 140 and 139 respectively). The first should be especially noted because of its unusual triangular shape. It was founded in the Iron Age, and later a Byzantine monastery was built on it.

The most important site in the region is the fortified city of Kh. 'Aujah el-Foqa (Site 143). Geographical and historical analyses suggest identification with 'Ataroth – an administrative city either in the Kingdom of Israel or Judah in the 9th–8th centuries BCE (Josh 16: 7). The 'Aujah fortress by the wadi riverbed was apparently connected to the city above it – 'Aujah el-Foqa. The considerable density of sites in the region undoubtedly relied on the abundant water source of Wadi 'Aujah. It appears that the Israelite city of 'Ataroth was intended to protect and defend it, among other purposes.

B. Mid-Wadi 'Aujah is located between Sub-unit A in the west and the modern village of 'Aujah et-Tahtah in the east. The rocky blockage of the valley from the south is not particularly high (its top is in E.P. -69, coordinates 1931/1492), but it dominates the plain. The wadi and the path bypass this ridge from the north. This part of LU 33 includes the plain south of the wadi, between latitudes 150 and 151. This is a fairly flat plain with low hills in its eastern side, crossed by the tributaries of Wadi 'Aujah: Wadis el-Mubarah, Taibet el-Asam and others. The valley is 1 km wide, 4 km long, with an area of about 400 ha (4,000 dunams). In spite of the readily cultivated land and its proximity to the stream, the habitation remains are relatively poor. In the western part, south of the modern water channel and the road junction at coordinates 1888/1504, there are several enclosures. In the centre of the valley are several sites, but in comparison to the abundant resources in the valley, it is empty of settlements. Modern construction activities have erased large areas of the stream plain in the south-western area, in which perhaps there were sites. Another possible reason for the sparse habitation could be a population move to the nearby cities: Jericho, 'Ataroth ('Aujah el-Foqa), and Archelais.

C. The marl plains east of the village of 'Aujah. These extensive plains stretch north and south of the wide riverbed of the wadi. Over their western part lies the village of 'Aujah and its fields, which spread east to the border fence. The survey here, executed on foot, was almost complete, except for the built-up areas. As in the marl plains further north, the settlement was rather poor. Two Chalcolithic sites on the banks of the wadi and its tributaries have been surveyed: Site 152, noted already by Glueck; and Site 154, which was discovered during our survey. The ravine area around the wadi streambed was found to be empty of settlement. To the east, in the vicinity of Malhaqa el-Wadian, the remains of a Byzantine monastery and enclosure (Sites 151

13. The western section of Wadi 'Aujah, 2008. Note the village of Yitav, the modern aqueduct and road, and the wide floodplain with its tropical fauna (N. Eshed).

14. The modern aqueduct of Wadi 'Aujah, looking west, 2006. In the photo are D. Ulman, D. Ben-Yosef and O. Cohen (S. Bar).

and 157) have been surveyed, both already noted by the Emergency Survey. Otherwise, the eastern part was found to be almost devoid of settlement. In the areas surveyed on foot across the border fence, including the ravines and the salinas, no settlements have been found.

D. THE SETTLEMENT BY PERIODS

The Middle Jordan Valley is a geographical and habitation bridge between the north part of the Jordan Valley, described in Volume 4, and the smaller southern bridge to the Dead Sea. The survey provides preliminary and previously unknown information about habitation and its spread in the various periods. The results are presented both individually, and for comparison with the data in the previous volumes.

The review in this volume is based on the 161 prehistoric and historic sites surveyed and published here. The prehistoric sites discovered in the same area by other scholars appear in Appendix B. Like the situation before the beginning of our survey in Samaria and the Jordan Valley, this region also has been scantily investigated, and more than 75% of the sites published here are new.

The general settlement pattern: As already seen in the discussion about the landscape units, the sites in this volume are scattered in a triangle, the vertex of which is Nahal Fasael (Wadi Rashash) and its base is along Nahal Yitav (Wadi 'Aujah). The sites are located in a narrow north-south strip (up to 2 km wide on average) at the foot of the eastern escarpment of the Samaria mountains. This pattern changes only in the Mastarah-Nabiris zone; from where is an opening to the east, and a ring of sites is located around the ridges of Niran and el-Musalabah.

This settlement pattern raises some interesting questions. The focal one is, again, as to why the alluvium soils and marl plains to the east were not settled. These plains comprise about 70% of the total area, and ostensibly there is no reason to leave them vacant. However, the fact is that in all periods only the hilly area between the bottom of the escarpment and the Jordan Valley plain was settled. It appears that this area best suited the requirements of the settlers, while the marl plains did not offer any advantage.

1. Prehistory

The prehistoric information concerning the sites we visited is presented in Appendix A. The previous surveys in the area are presented and discussed in Appendix B. Noteworthy are the clusters of prehistoric sites in Nahal Fasael and the Netiv Hagdud–Salibiya Basin area.

2. The Chalcolithic Period (4800-3800 BCE)

The 30 sites with Chalcolithic finds represent 18.6% of the total number of sites in this volume; however, there is no resemblance in the types of the settlements and their scatter.

There is a concentration of settlement in the alluvial fan of Nahal Fasael, comprising six sites (14, 19, 20, 22, 24 and 30) situated east of the entry of the stream to the Jordan Valley plain. Bar (see below) proposes considering most of them to have been one large spread settlement. This had been proposed by Porath (1985a), but our survey and Bar's excavations produced a new and more detailed picture. This is a cluster of unwalled very Late Chalcolithic settlements, relatively large and scattered, with gaps between them, over an area of 14 ha (140 dunams); of which the sites of Fasael (1), (2), (5) and (7) (Bar 2013; 2014; Bar et al. 2013; 2015) have been or are now being excavated. Prominent here are the large habitation complexes including broadrooms with very large courtyards attached. These sites exhibit a rich pottery assemblage typical of the latest phases of the Chalcolithic alongside rich stone tool (Cohen-Klonymus and Bar 2016) and copper assemblages. In the flint repertoire an important discovery is that the Cananean technology was first introduced in the Chalcolithic period, earlier than previously known (Bar and Winter 2010). The largest roofed structure from the period was exposed in the excavations of Fasael (7) (Bar 2013b: chapter 6; Bar 2014: chapter 11).

Other sites in the region are not as large and complex as the settlement in the Fasael region. There are a few enclosure sites and sherd scatters.

In the vicinity of Wadi ʿAujah (Nahal Yitav), there are a number of other small settlements (Sites 128, 134, and 136). Site 128 in Yitav was excavated by Hizmi (2003), and a dwelling structure with a large courtyard was found. This type of site is more common in the Fasael Valley.

The soil and water potential in the valley of Nahal Yitav should have created a more impressive settlement concentration; however, the number of sites and their dimensions do not compare with those in Nahal Fasael. The reason for the relative scarcity of settlements is unclear.

The sites of Nahal Fasael belong to the type of large settlements in the

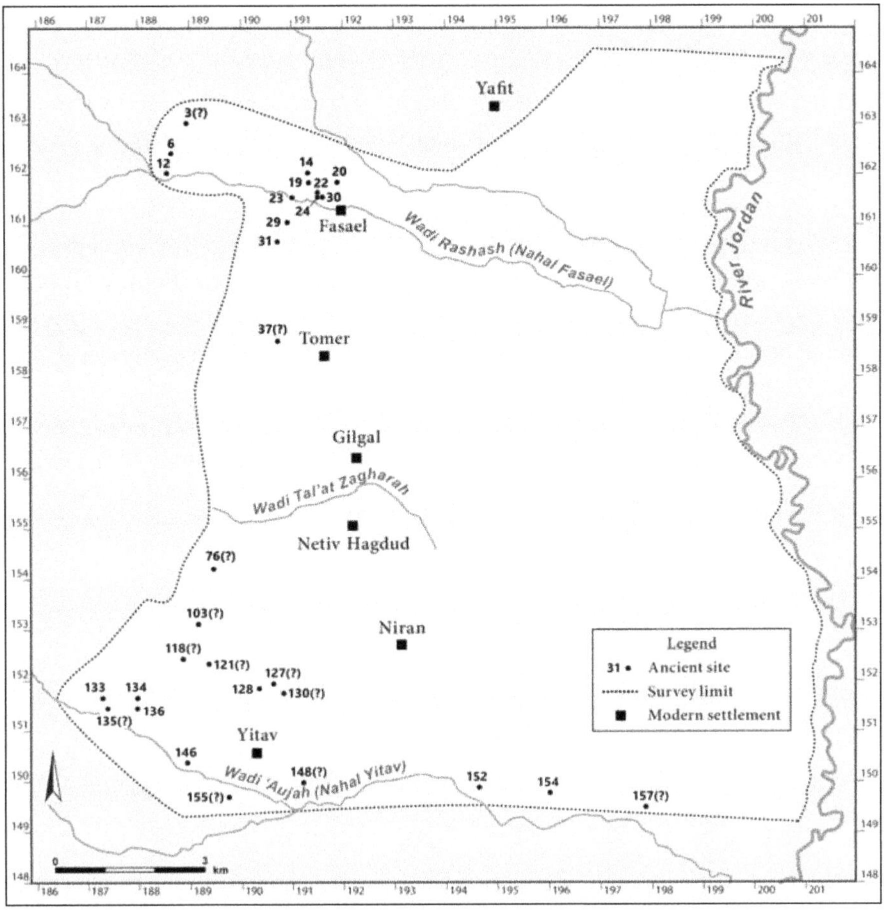

15. Map of the Chalcolithic Period sites.

alluvial plains, such as the clusters in the southern Beit She'an Valley and Wadi Far'ah (Volume 4: 50-52).

For a detailed study of the Chalcolithic period in the Middle Jordan Valley see Bar 2014.

For a detailed report of the excavations of the cluster of sites in the Fasael Valley see Bar 2013b.

3. The Early Bronze Age I (*3800-3050 BCE*) *and the Early Bronze Age in general* (*3800-2500 BCE*)

This period has been investigated much more deeply by Bar, and part of the conclusions are derived from his work.

Only in 11 sites, representing 6.8% of the total number of sites in this volume, have EBA I sherds been found, representing a sharp decrease of about a third from the previous period. The region is practically devoid of habitation, apart from the two large settlements partially excavated: Fasael (4) (Bar et al. 2012) and Tell esh-Sheikh Diyab (2) (Bar et al. 2011). Large planned rural settlements were exposed in both of these. Particularly prominent is the village at Sheikh Diyab (2) - Site 21.

Site 21 is located on a narrow spur descending to Nahal Fasael. Fairly impressive architectural complexes have been discovered in it, with curved walls enclosing structures and courtyards, and alleyways between them. Well-built silos were exposed in the dwelling complexes, indicating stockpiling of cereals. Animal bones (cattle, sheep and goats), indicating a grazing economy supplement the picture.

Another excavation, Site 18, in a settlement of the same period, located north of Nahal Fasael in Fasael (4), has been started. Especially notable here are the

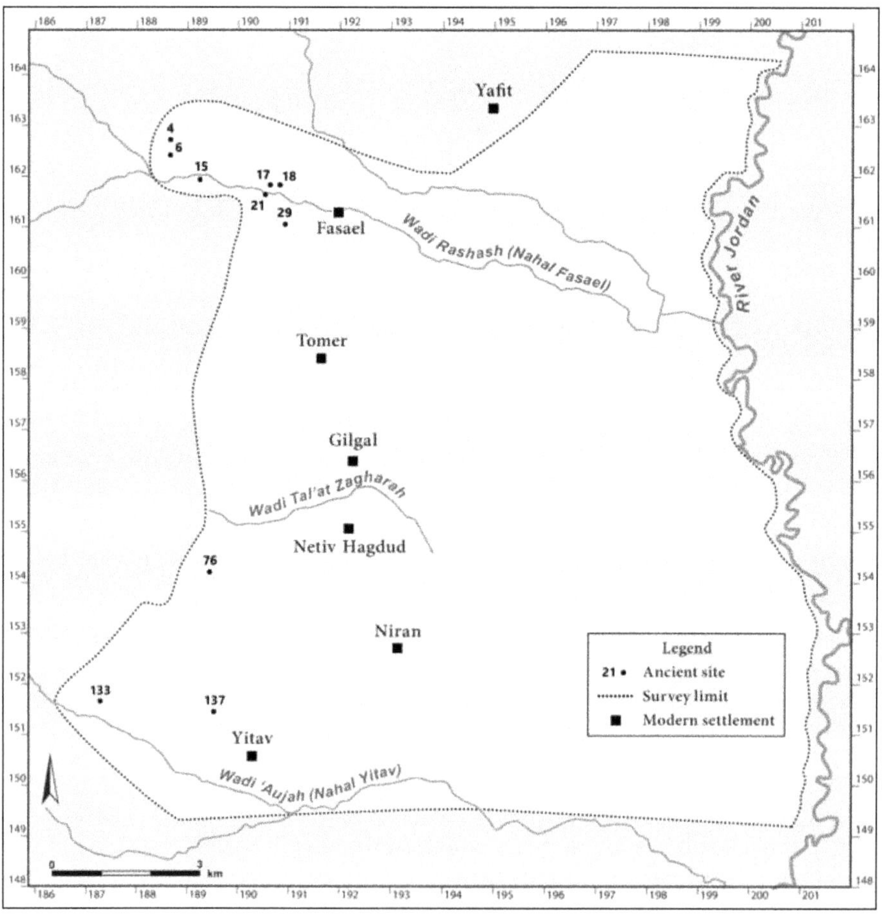

16. Map of the Early Bronze Age I Period sites.

clusters of round silos, resembling those of the former site. New insights are hoped for during the excavation.

The decline of habitation in the Early Bronze I period is similar to that discovered in the northern Jordan valley (Volume 4: 52-54 and fig. 18). In both, the review of the period in Volume 4 and in Bar's work (2014: 96-133), it seems that a population movement from the Valley plains to eastern Samaria occurred, mainly to a series of tells, fortified in the Early Bronze Age II. According to Bar's review the region underwent changes at the end of EBA I. Almost all the central settlements in the western Jordan Valley were abandoned or destroyed, and others declined. The assumptions regarding the reasons, in the absence of historical sources, are very problematic. Little evidence and no solid proof have been found that the destruction strata were caused by man, and not by natural causes. It is quite possible that the destruction resulted from

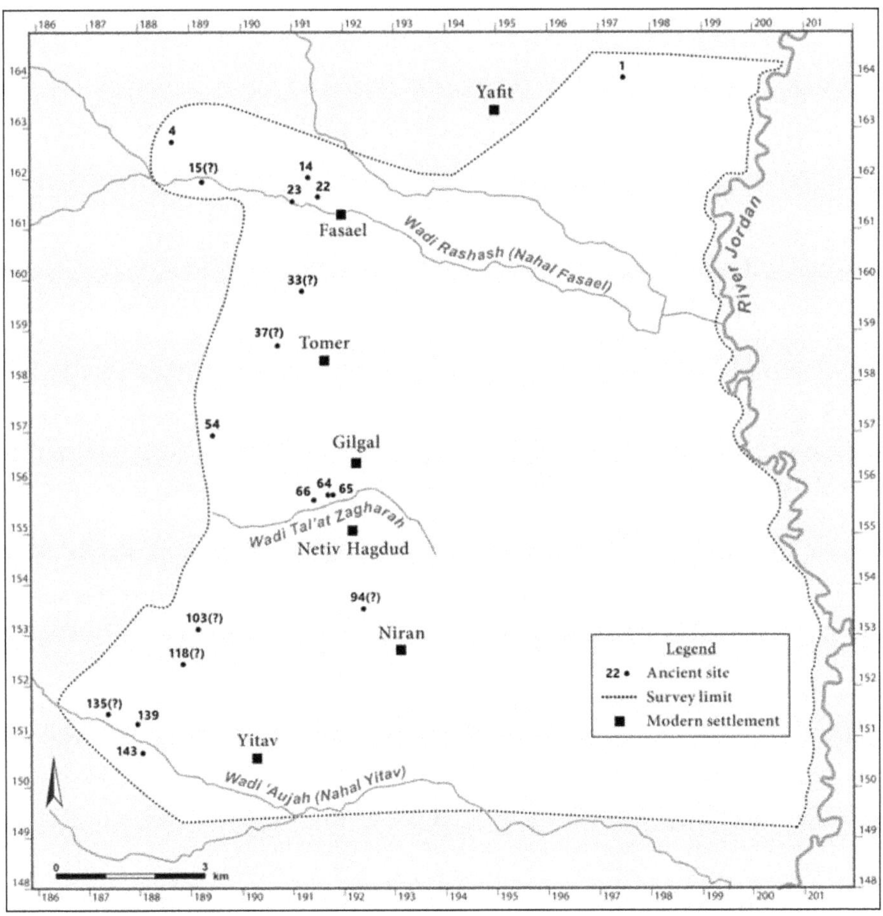

17. Map of sites generally attributed to the Early Bronze Age.

struggles between "power hubs resembling city-states". The rate of change in the mode of settlement was enhanced also by climatic factors: the decrease in precipitation at the end of the 4th millennium can explain the abandonment of settlements based on growing cereals, ascending to the moister mountain zone, suitable for plantations.

Another aspect in Bar's work is the analysis of the 'Umm-Hammad Ware' pottery, typifying the EB IB in our region (Bar 2010; 2014: 179-194).

Another group of 19 EBA sites was not related to a specific sub-period. It appears that some of these sites belong to the EBA I, and others to later stages. There are hints of almost total abandonment of the region in EBA II-III, while in the north, in the Wadi Far'ah region, and in the south, in the Jericho area, a developed settlement continued.

For a detailed study of the Early Bronze Age I period in the Middle Jordan Valley see Bar 2014.

For a detailed report of the excavations of the sites in the Fasael Valley see Bar 2013.

4. The Intermediate Bronze Age (MBA I/EBA IV) (2500-2000 BCE)

In this period also the region was relatively empty. The sherds of this period in the six sites discovered (representing 3.7% of the total number of sites in this volume) did not exceed 15%, rendering it difficult to draw conclusions. Apsidal houses found in Site 118 may be related to the IBA.

In comparison to the considerable settlement concentrations in the southern Beit She'an Valley (Volume 4: 54, 56 and fig. 19), in Wadi Malih (Volume 2: 75-78, and fig. 26), in Wadi Far'ah (Volume 4: 56), and in the northern Buqei'a (Volume 2: fig. 26) – the area here is almost empty. The conclusion is that in the Middle Jordan Valley, south of the regions mentioned above, there was no IBA settlement.

Unique types of sites have been excavated by Bar north of the Survey region: In Elevation Point -167 in the Wadi Ahmar Valley (to the north of Fasael in the area covered by Volume 4 of the Survey), where large stone structures and courtyards were exposed. The paucity of small finds (pottery, flint and organic) brought the excavator to the conclusion of partial nomadism. The radiometric dates indicate a period from 2400 to 2200 BCE (Bar 2017a); In Wadi Malih (in the area covered by Volume 2 of the Survey), the fortified site of Kh. el-Meiyiteh (Bar et al. 2013b) surrounded by a 2 m-thick stone wall was probed.

To the south of the Survey region, in Jericho, Kenyon (1993: 679) found a very rich IBA cemetery, with a poor settlement on the tell.

Despite the suitable environmental potential, particularly the extensive grazing plains, the population did not reach that of the Middle Jordan Valley

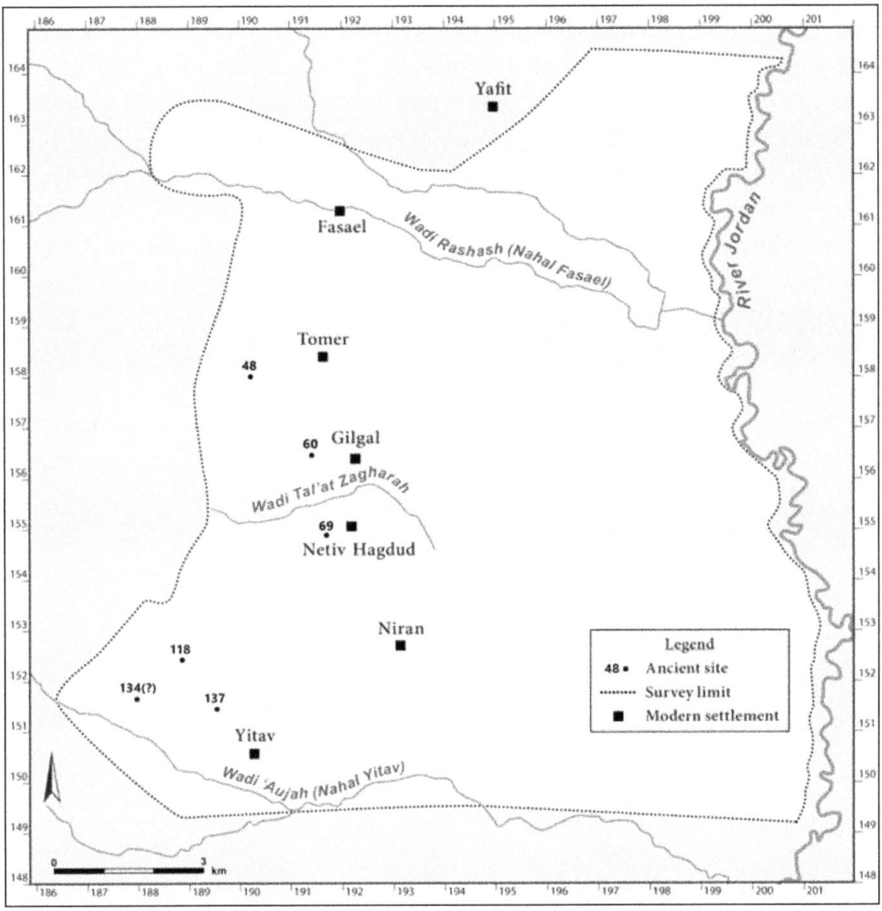

18. Map of the Intermediate Bronze Age Period sites.

in this period. This suggests that habitation considerations were only partially dependent on the natural potential (water, soil), but to large extent were linked to human factors (society, tribe).

5. *The Middle Bronze Age II* (2000-1550 *BCE*)

The number of settlements is not large, but a certain degree of recovery is seen. In 32 sites (19.8% of the total) sherds of the period were found; but only in two was the settlement proper established.

The Middle Bronze Age settlements are almost evenly spread over the region. Most of the sites are sherd scatters, and not a single large site or fortified tell from the period was found.

Along Nahal Fasael were found seven sites, some of them in caves (Mughur ed-Duqhaneh); in all of which the number of sherds is small. Outstanding is Site 37 at the entrance to Wadi el-Butum. Here (Tomer [7]) a small village was found, with a support wall for protection from floods and small structures built of very large stones, similar to the construction style in the Gittit-Ma'ale Ephraim Junction areas (e.g. site 160 in Volume 4). A slightly higher than average percentage of sherds was found in Site 85 – Niran (1) in the Salibiya Basin. Here a cluster of rock-cut cup-marks and basins was found, an outstanding example of its type in the surveyed area. Next to the cup-marks is a small enclosure with sherds from the period.

In the east of Samaria (Volumes 2 and 6 [Bar and Zertal 2016]) is an MBA II settlement influx, the population of which adjusted itself to the conditions in the fringes of the desert. In another place (Volume 2: 78) is written that: "The population of the period settled in East Manasseh almost as much as in the

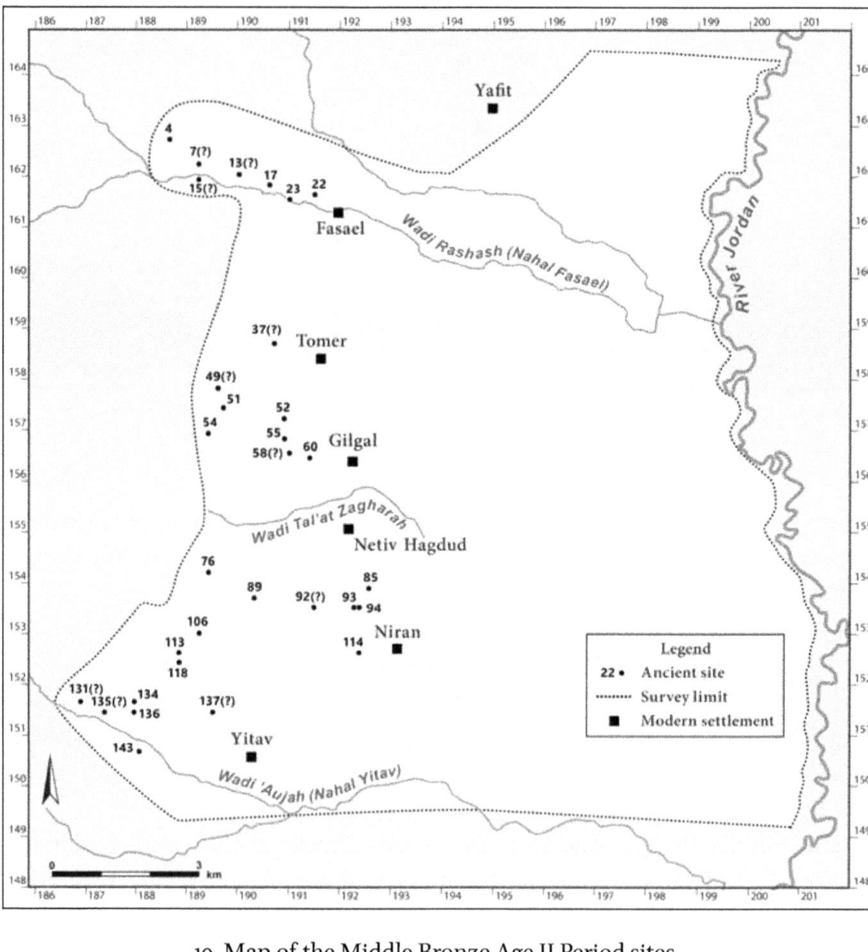

19. Map of the Middle Bronze Age II Period sites.

Mediterranean zone". This is the situation in this area, and to a much lesser degree in the north of the Jordan Valley; where, as noted: "It seems as if the settlement wave of the MBA IIb had stopped short in the eastern valleys and in the areas west of the Jordan Valley, resulting in a modest dispersion of sites." (Volume 4: 56).

In comparison to concentrations of the period's settlements in the fringes of Samaria and in the Mediterranean zone, the Middle Jordan Valley is almost devoid of habitation, and the settlement presence is small and sporadic.

6. The Late Bronze Age (1550-1200 BCE)

In this period the area was completely empty of inhabitants. Only in Tell esh-Sheikh Diyab (Site 23) and Kh. 'Aujah el-Foqa (Site 143) were Late Bronze sherds found. In the excavations at the first site no Bronze Age architecture or even additional sherds were found.

Therefore there is a question about the origin of the sherds found in the survey at the tell. Be'eri and Cohen (2008), who published an article about the burials of Late Bronze traders in the site of Huzuq Musa (site 47 in Volume 4), noted the commerce routes in the region. It is quite possible that this also happened here to a certain degree.

7. The Iron Age I (1200-1000 BCE)

During this short period of about 200 years, a habitation revolution occurred in the region, already referred to several times in earlier publications (Volume 4: 58-63; Ben-Yosef 2007: 215-228). Iron Age I sherds were found in 66 sites (41% of the total). A substantial portion of these settlements were established on virgin soil during this period. Many of the sites survived in their original form, thus enabling a thorough examination.

Distribution: the Iron Age I sites are spread along the narrow strip west of the escarpment. As in the other periods, here also the settlers avoided the marl plains, the ravine-cut land and the salinas. The easternmost of the settlements (Sites 123, 144) are west of Niran. The large area from there to the River Jordan was possibly exploited only for grazing.

Clustering: most of the settlements are gathered into five compact groups, 0.5–1 km apart. These groups comprise:

1. The Nahal and Fasael Valley (12 sites). Six enclosure sites were found at the south of the valley. The most prominent one is Site 33 – Fusayil (2), composed of a large enclosure and settlement remains. The proximity to the stream did not necessarily attract the settlers, and their sites were established all over the area.

2. The Tomer-Gilgal group (12 sites): includes some of the more important new sites have been found here. Together with the definite dominance of the enclosure-site type of settlement amongst the settlements (Discussion in Volume 4: 61-62), appears a new type of settlement – the complex enclosure. At least two such sites were discovered: Site 60 - Gilgal (5) and Site 65 - Wadi Tal'at Zagharah (2), see discussion below.
3. The el-Mastarah group (11 sites): in the el-Mastarah Valley and its environs is an outstanding concentration of Iron Age I-II sites. Some were established during Iron Age I, and all continued into the IA II.

   These sites are a transition stage from the nomad 'world of enclosures', characteristic of IA I, to the IA II village. Two contrasting elements are present in this case: on one hand are the enclosure courtyards, and on the other

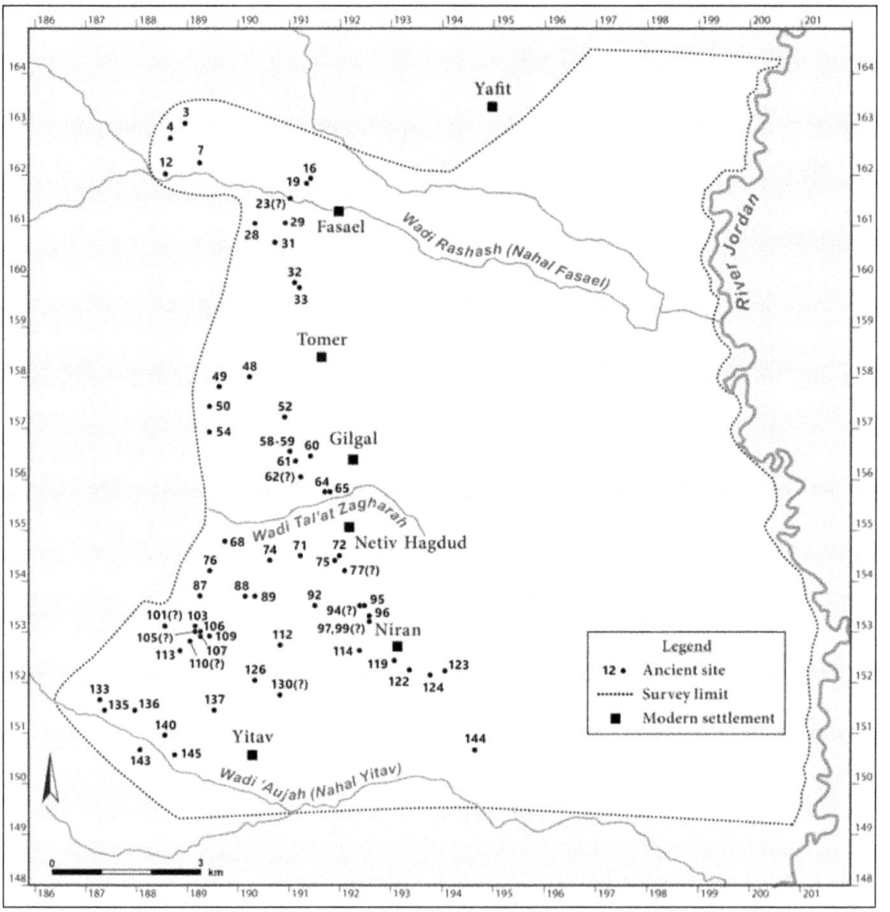

20. Map of the Iron Age I Period sites.

is the permanent construction, which on some occasions is rather impressive.
4. The Niran group (9 sites): around the ridges of Niran and el-Musalabah is another group of enclosure sites, all of the usual design.
5. The Wadi 'Aujah group (5 sites): among these are included the settlement nuclei in the city of 'Aujah el-Foqa (Site 143), 'Aujah Fort (Site 140) and others. There is no doubt about the sites being already settled in Iron Age I and afterwards were developed in the following period.

The layout of all groups and the similarity in the form of the sites suggests grouping or gathering in clans.

Types of settlements

The **simple enclosure** was the commonest: a round courtyard or pen 20-40 m in diameter, usually surrounded by a double wall built from large stones. It is reasonable to suggest that on top of the pen foundation wall was a fence of perishable materials – mainly faunal, such as the common Christ's thorn Jujube (*Zizyphus spina-christi*) (Volume 4: 61), and around it stood tents or simple constructions.

The **composite enclosure**: the two relatively large composite enclosures mentioned (Sites 60 and 65), are built as a complex of courtyards and enclosures of eight to eleven such units connected by walls. The sites are not fortified, but around them was an enclosing wall. Both sites were found in the Jordan Valley plain, on slightly elevated locations, not far from the bottom of the ridge, and far from the riverbeds to avoid flooding. The architecture is relatively developed, and remnants of additional structures are also to be found. Although the IA I pottery in these sites does not exceed half of the total, and the sites are multi-period (34% Iron Age I in Site 60 and 40% in Site 65; see the problem of dating such sites in Ben-Shlomo and Hawkins 2017: 71*-76*), some assumptions can be derived:

1. Continuity is a significant factor; in both sites the decisive majority of the find is from Iron Age I. The excavations of the 'Gilgals' at Bedhat esh-Sha'ab (Ben-Yosef 2007: 228-278; 2017a; Zertal and Ben-Yosef 2009) and Yafit (3) (Ben-Yosef 2007: 279-315; 2017b) proved that the sites survived, with minor changes, from Iron Age I through the following period. In light of the fact that the Gilgals were sites of worship, sweeping comparisons should be avoided, but it appears that the Iron Age I construction style survived, with changes, even later.
2. There is a certain evolution of the enclosure/pen concept. The linkage between nomadism and the sheepfold has been recognized and accepted. Elsewhere (Zertal 1994: 58-59) we have pointed out the process of ascending

westward up to the Samarian Mountain country from the east, simultaneously with the transition from nomadism to permanent settlement. By clustering a number of pens to a composite enclosure, such as in these sites, is also a social evolvement: consideration of density factors, passage between the pens, ownership of land, etc. The vicinity of the sites is also important because there must have been sufficient grazing to feed the herds of livestock.

3. In order to manage such a site, a sort of tribal hub, some local leadership is required.
4. It should be pointed out that up to now no similar sites have been found, in our survey or elsewhere. Adding the Gilgal sites (Zertal and Ben-Yosef 2009), it has been concluded that the Gilgals and the composite enclosures are connected to organization and tribal leadership, and there is a significant difference between them and the individual encampments scattered around the area. Architectonically, the construction style retains the curved round lines. There are no sharp angles, undoubtedly resulting from the Iron Age I pens/Gilgals construction tradition.

In comparison to nearby areas, continuation and increase of the Iron Age I settlement influx can be noted. The process of nomad settlement in the Jordan Valley and in the fringes of the desert has already been mentioned in the previous volumes: in Volume 2 47 sites are noted over a much larger area (469 sq. km, Volume 2: 83-85) and in Volume 4 69 sites are noted over an area of 250 sq. km (Volume 4: 58). It is obvious that the density of Iron Age I sites in the Middle Jordan Valley (66 sites over an area of 150 sq. km) reached its peak in comparison to the data presented in the previous volumes.

8. The Iron Age II (1000-722 BCE)

This is one of the peak periods in settlement in the region: sherds of this period have been identified in 92 sites (57.1% of the total). This is the period in which the Northern Kingdom of Israel flourished. Indeed, the conclusions of the previous volume are repeated here: this is a period of thriving settlement, a result of the stable regime in the capital Samaria. The kings of the Omride Dynasty and the successor kings maintained a policy of developing the border regions (Zertal 2001: detailed settlement analysis).

The distribution of sites and their characteristics are very much like those in the previous period, and the map shows the clear continuity between the periods (56 sites, 61% of the total, continuing from the Iron Age I). The Iron Age II was, on one hand, a continuing culture (the population continued living in the same settlements), and on the other was also a time of expansion, when

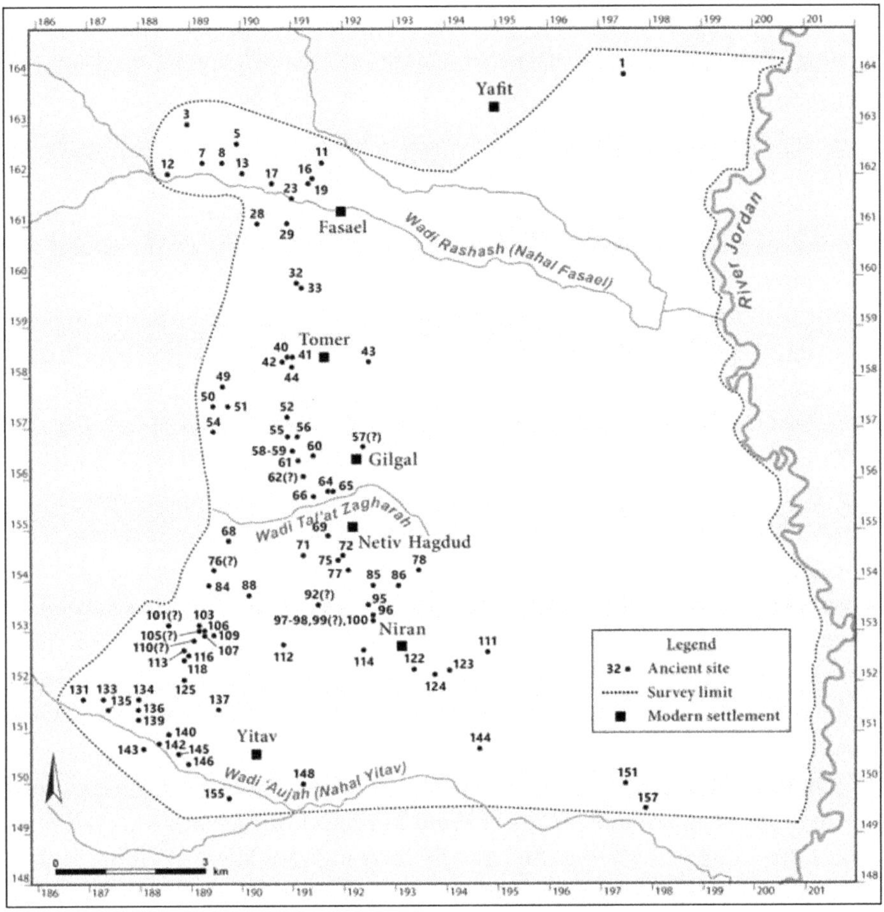

21. Map of the Iron Age II Period sites.

20 new sites were established on virgin soil.

Types of settlements

Enclosures: Although a substantial portion of the settlements were permanent sites, the special character of the Jordan Valley was retained in the enclosure type phenomenon. About half the sites are enclosures, showing that the nomad element continued to be an important component in the fringes of the Iron Age II Israelite society.

Tells: In almost every floodplain of a stream in East Samaria is a small tell; such as several sites in the southern Beit She'an Valley: Tell el-Hilu in Wadi Malih (Volume 2: site 96), Tell es-Simadi in Wadi Far'ah (Volume 4: Site 84) and Tell esh-Sheikh Diyab in Nahal Fasael (this volume). These are not real cities, and it has been proposed (Volume 4: 64, 284) that these served as podia for forts built on them. In Tell esh-Sheikh Diyab at least this proposition has been verified by excavation.

In eastern Samaria and the Jordan Valley the characteristic rural settlement of nomads and permanent settlers did not evolve into city-tells as in the Mediterranean zones. There were only a few sites in locations extremely rich in water sources: Beit She'an and Rehov in the Beit She'an Valley and Tell es-Sultan in the oasis of Jericho.

Fortresses: the importance of the Jordan Valley as a transit zone and road junction motivated the relative increase in the number of forts. Five such forts have been published in Volume 4 (Volume 4: 64-65), and in this volume there are three (apart from Tell esh-Sheikh Diyab, which is described separately).

The first is Rujm Abu Mukheir (Site 5), a fort of the Rujm el-Malfuf type. This is a round tower, about 20 m in diameter, with three concentric inner stone-built circles, with the spaces between them divided into rooms. This type, possibly Ammonite in origin, was first identified by Glueck (1939: 166). This fort had been discovered during the Emergency Survey, and excavated by Yeivin (1992). Zertal (1988; 1995: 261-265; Volume 2: 62) proposed that the three similar forts of this type were situated on the crossroads from the Jordan Valley to the centre of the Israelite Kingdom: in Wadi Malih (Volume 2: Site 82), Wadi Far'ah (Yeivin 1974; 1992) and Rujm Abu Mukheir.

The second fort is the site at Thor el-Walad (Site 51). The site is on a plateau enclosed by deep streams north of Wadi Mahmud. In the site is a well-built square structure resembling the Israelite forts in Wadi Malih (Volume 2: sites 83, 91) and those described in Volume 4 (Sites 73, 86, 154). As none of the latter have been excavated, Site 51 is doubtful in this respect.

The third fort is 'Aujah Fortress (Site 140). This large structure on the north bank of Nahal Yitav is fortified by casemate walls and has a triangular shape unknown elsewhere. A Byzantine monastery was built above and on top of it, with numerous water facilities. This fortress is not easy to understand, but it can be assumed that it was related to the nearby city at 'Aujah el-Foqa (Site 143).

Unique phenomena: to these belong the sites at Tell esh-Sheikh Diyab (Site 23) and 'Aujah el-Foqa (Site 143).

Tell esh-Sheikh Diyab (Site 23) has been excavated and seems to have been an artificial Iron Age II podium. Such a podium for a superstructure of this nature, built of thick walls with earthen filling layers, was previously unknown to us. The archaeological data are relatively clear, but the fact that the superstructure (fortress?) did not survive renders understanding of the site difficult. The location and shape of the site suggest a structure guarding both the Nahal

Fasael water system, and perhaps the agricultural land, already established at that period.

'Aujah el-Foqa (Site 143) is a well-planned fortified city on a hill south of the outlet of Wadi 'Aujah to the Jordan Valley plain. We identified it as 'Ataroth (Josh 16: 7; see chapter 2). The importance of 'Aujah el-Foqa is its strategic location, its protective location of the Wadi 'Aujah water sources, its planning, and its state of preservation. We suggest that it was an administrative-military city of the Kingdoms of Israel and Judah.

9. The Iron Age III (*722-586 BCE*)

This period, coinciding with the Assyrian and Babylonian rule over the Kingdom of Israel, has been identified in the area of Samaria (Zertal 1989) thanks to the wedge-shaped decorated bowl. This vessel was discovered in excavations during the first half of the 20th century, but its significance had been overlooked. Its geographical distribution and Mesopotamian origin enabled its presentation as a leading '*fossil directeur*' of the Cuthean (Samaritan) populace transferred to the Kingdom of Israel by the Assyrians. In later research, Itach (2015) has shown that this bowl was also used in the early Persian period, making it less distinctive than previously assumed.

In two previous volumes (Volume 2: 89-90; Volume 4: 67) we noted the decline in population in the Kingdom of Israel after the destruction of Samaria, resulting from the exile of the Israelite population. The foreign population settled in Samaria was located, also according to the distribution of these bowls, in the eastern valleys of Samaria.

Almost no finds from Iron Age III are noted in this volume. Yeivin dated the tower in Site 5 to Iron Age III without clear reasoning; the rim of a wedge-shaped bowl was found in Fasael – 6 (Site 17), and a similar bowl fragment was found in Tell esh-Sheikh Diyab (Site 23). These are the only examples found in the region surveyed, suggesting a decline in settlement in the Jordan Valley plains in this period.

10. The Babylonian and Persian Periods (*586-332 BCE*)

After the emptiness of the former period, there was some growth in the Persian period (12 sites, 7.4% of the total, none of them established during this period). The presence in all the sites did not exceed 10% of the pottery retrieved. The difference between the Persian and Hellenistic periods could not always be recognized, and both have been defined together in some places.

In the previous volumes it was noted that settlement in the Persian period was concentrated in the Mediterranean zones of Samaria, the Galilee and the Mediterranean coastal plain. The fringes of the desert areas, the Jordan Valley and the Negev were almost devoid of settlement (Volume 2: 90-92).

From these periods only 23 sites have been found over a very large area in the eastern valleys and the fringes of the desert (Volume 2); and only 20 sites in the Northern Jordan Valley are noted (Volume 4: 67). From this aspect the Middle Jordan Valley described in the current volume is in line with the other areas.

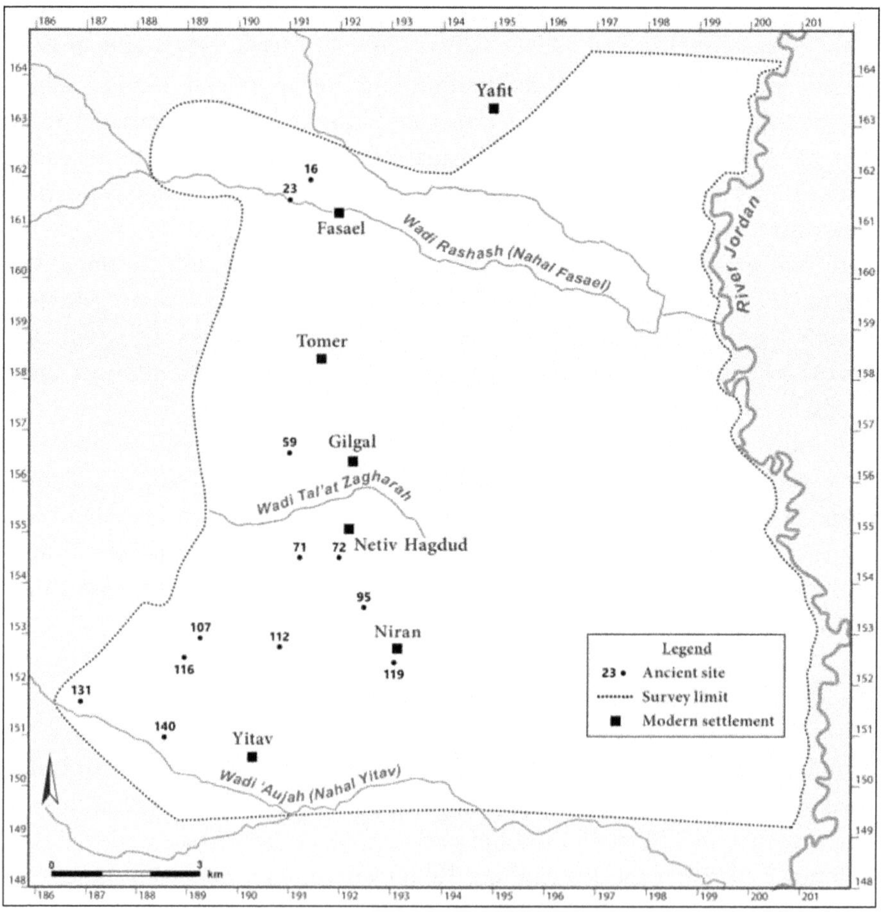

22. Map of the Persian Period sites.

11. *The Hellenistic Period (332-63 BCE)*

The 26 sites of this period (16.1% of the total) are a leap in settlement – more than double the Persian period. There is an explanation for this leap in the historical sources.

The historical introduction (Section E) shows that the kings of the Hasmonean Dynasty, particularly Alexander Jannaeus, considered the Jordan Valley as an important region for two reasons: a convenient place for the cultivation of date palms and balsam trees in the King's estates, and at the same time as a strategic border land in the wars against the Nabateans. Both Phasaelis and Archelais have a Hellenistic nucleus, indicating that they were founded prior to the rule of Herod. Noteworthy also is the important fortress erected by

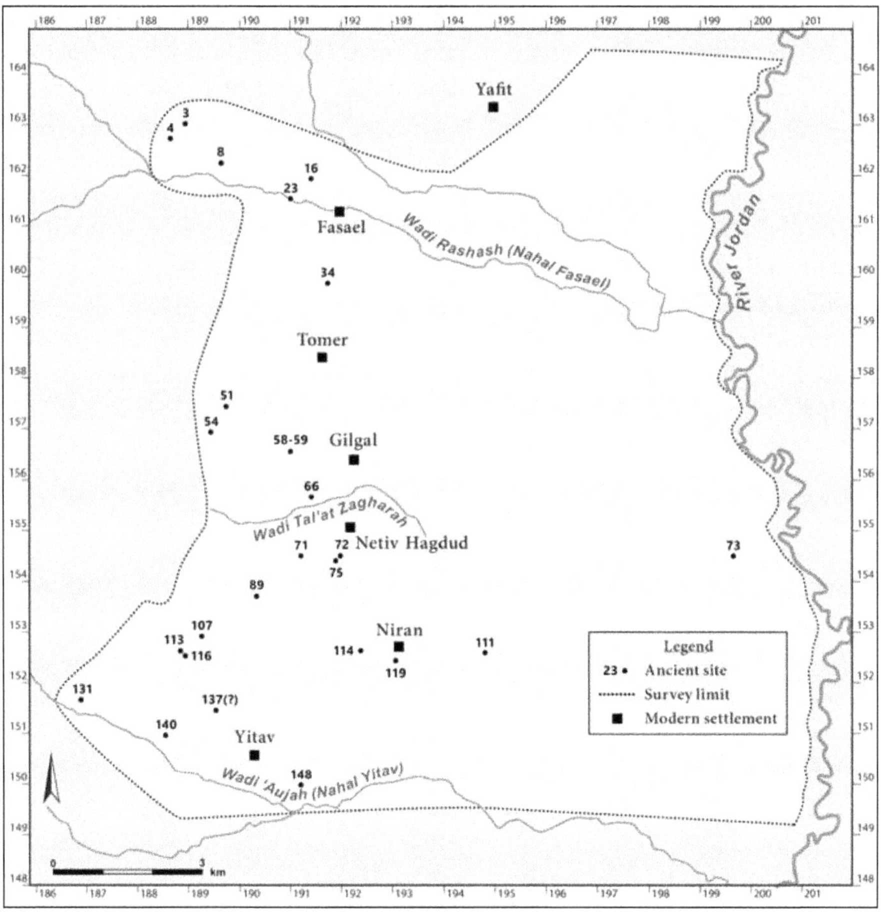

23. Map of the Hellenistic Period sites.

Jannaeus, which is near these sites in the Sartaba-Alexandrion (Volume 4: Site 173). For maintaining a fortress of such magnitude a settlement and logistic infrastructure was required in the area, an element deduced from the noticeable growth and development of the sites.

In a few of the 26 sites of the period included here only Hellenistic pottery was found, and in many of them the period has been determined as Persian-Hellenistic or Hellenistic-Early Roman. The find has been determined for both periods with continuity from one to the other, a conclusion derived from the absence of imported Attic pottery, stamped Rhodian handles (Hellenistic import) and/or other vessels which could be attributed to a single period. The variable range in the various sites is wide, and could derive from one of the periods or from both.

In this case, as in the Persian period, most of the diagnostic pottery does not exceed 10% of the total number of sherds in each site. Two alternatives are offered as an explanation: either the settlements were founded at that period, but mostly settled in later times; or that in this period there was no decisive presence in this region.

In the eastern valleys and the fringes of the desert, included in Volume 2, 24 sites were found, equalling the number in the current volume, but over a much larger area. Historically it has been suggested as follows: "The settlement of the Persian period in East Manasseh seems not to have been adversely affected by the Greeks..." (Volume 2: 93).

Despite a certain settlement recovery in the Persian period, the Jordan Valley in the Hellenistic Period is still defined as rather poor, especially in regard to the area dealt with in this Volume.

12. The Early Roman – Herodian Period (63 BCE-73 CE)

A considerable increase in the number of sites in this period (48, 29.8% of the total) compared to the previous one, was probably caused by the change in settlement policy during the rule of Herod.

Some of the sites are noteworthy: the Rampart Site (Site 11), which possibly served as a fort on the road ascending to Ma'ale Ephraim, similarly to the function of Tell esh-Sheikh Diyab (Site 23) and Rujm Abu Mukheir (Site 5) during earlier periods.

The group of seven nearby settlements close to Kibbutz Gilgal (Sites 56, 58-61, 65, and perhaps 72), resemble a similar Iron Age I group within the same region (above). In the unique site at Wadi Nabiris (Site 2), were structures built from very large stones over a rocky spur. At the centre of the settlement is a 10 m diameter circular tower with concentric stone circles. Although the site was founded in the Iron Age, the Herodian presence is clear.

The city of Archelais (Site 111) was built, according to the pottery collected, on a much smaller Iron Age and Hellenistic nucleus. The city of Phasaelis was also built at the same time. Also interesting is Villa 'Aujah (Site 139), where a large, fine and well preserved structure was discovered.

In our opinion, the historical evidence from the Herodian period is more substantial than the results of the survey. The information from Josephus' books, *Antiquities* and *War*, describing Herod's great investment in the Jordan Valley, is not necessarily apparent in the field. The reason is obvious: the settlement in the following periods – Late Roman and Byzantine –mostly covered the ancient nuclei, in part or completely. Therefore a certain distortion in the results of the survey should be taken into account.

A settlement increase was also recorded in regions close to the Middle Jordan Valley: in Volume 2, 35 Herodian period sites are included, with a large

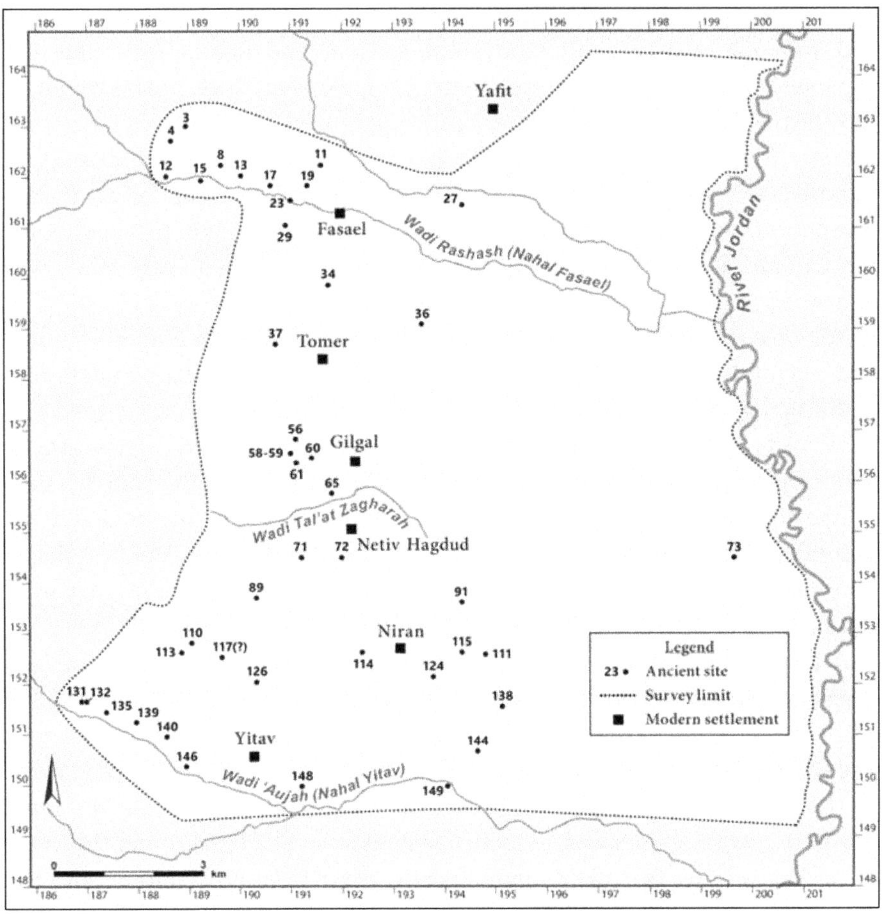

24. Map of the Early Roman Period sites.

portion of them having been established then. In Volume 4 (38 sites) there is also some increase compared to the Hellenistic period.

Finally, the historical account of the transfer of the King's Estates in the Middle Jordan Valley, from one Emperor to another, or to the Emperor's wife or elsewhere, testifies to the value of the distinctive agriculture of the region (for details see Section E).

13. The Late Roman Period (73-313 CE)

This is a period of settlement climax: the period's sherds were found in 119 sites (73.9% of the total), almost three times more than in the former period. The wealth and prosperity of the settlement are shared by the entire region, and the two large cities, Archelais and Phasaelis, enjoyed great influence over their environs.

Historically, the agricultural production in which the Jordan Valley excelled and won fame: date palm cultivation, balsam and balm, continued and expanded. For these lucrative products, meticulous cultivation was required, together with the use of sophisticated irrigation systems. In Appendix D we propose that the water systems in Fasael and Wadi 'Aujah, which existed for hundreds of years, were begun in the Herodian period. In the following Byzantine period, lasting about 250 years, their use and improvement was continued. Most of the Jordan Valley settlements of the period apparently relied and depended on that water support and irrigated agriculture.

We have estimated the area of Phasaelis to have been 500 dunams (50 ha), and calculating cautiously, based on 300 souls per ha, it had a population of about 15,000. Such a large number, by ancient world standards, suggests two facts: a), a great portion of the population practiced specialized agriculture, as learnt from the extent of the cultivated areas and their planning; and b), such a large population required a food supply, mainly cereals and livestock-derived products. Theoretically it was possible to import such products in exchange for the income from the dates and balsam, but it is more likely that they were grown and produced in nearby sites.

Architectonically, the courtyard fortress at Phasaelis was dated to the Late Roman period, based on its similarity to other courtyard fortresses (see Site 34). The rest of the structures could not be dated by means of the survey only, and we hope that the new excavation at the site will yield more data.

The division of the rural settlement into two is deduced from the map: one part was theoretically connected to Phasaelis (Sites 3–66) and the other to Archelais (Sites 67–155). Geographically, Wadi Tal'at Zagharah divides the settlement strip at the foot of the escarpment into two: they are not equal in size, but this division suits the linkage to the two big cities. The leap in the number of settlements, almost three times the number in the Herodian period, testifies to the general prosperity. The numerous enclosures indicate the nomadic life of part of the population, and the marketing of livestock-derived produce to the cities. A nearby market can favourably influence the economic viability of flock husbandry.

Archelais (Site 111) was mainly settled in the Late Roman and Byzantine periods. The population of this large city of 35 ha (350 dunams) would have been about 10,000 souls. A sophisticated aqueduct system was found (see Appendix D), including four systems of aqueducts on the ridge supplying the city to the west (et-Tulul), and another main aqueduct carrying water for irrigation eastward to the plain, a distance of 1 km and more.

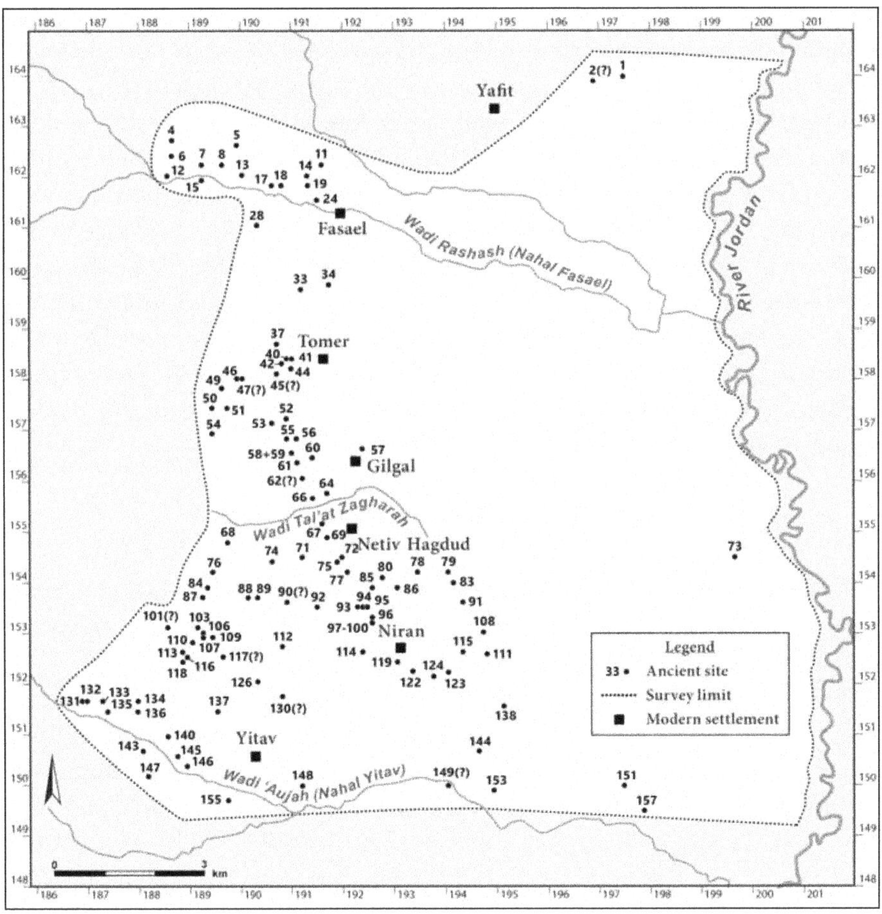

25. Map of the Late Roman Period sites.

This city should also be linked to the sites of Archelais North-West (Site 108), Archelais-West (Site 115) and the probable Archelais-Cemetery of the city (Site 91). The city outskirts at the north were defended by a small fort (el-Maskarah).

All the nomadic or semi-nomadic Niran group of sites (Sites 69-124, not in sequence); and the el-Mastarah group of sites (Sites 101-120, also not in sequence), and others, continued to exist around Archelais.

According to Avi-Yonah (Section E), the Jewish settlement in the Jordan Valley also continued after the destruction of the Temple and the various exiles, thanks to its expertise in the special agricultural products. No archaeological evidence for this suggestion was discovered, except for the probable source of the Kh. ed-Dasha (Site 38) menorah (candelabrum) relief.

The prosperity during the Late Roman Period has been mentioned in the previous volumes. In the eastern valleys and in the fringes of the desert 70 sites were discovered, a number similar to that of the peak of the Iron Age II period. In the region were also townships founded in areas not previously containing large settlements (Volume 2: 95-96). As in the area to the north of this region, the settlement multiplied almost four-fold during the Late Roman period, compared to the former one. Regarding this issue it has been written: "As to the LR period, we are inclined to link the process to the importance with which the Trajan-Herodian rulers regarded the Jordan Valley. Evidence of this is shown in the well-developed military infrastructure we discovered along the Valley, the focus of which is the camp at Kh. es-Suweideh (Zertal 2008: site 239). The historical background to this setup is as yet unclear; possibly it was linked to the military actions during the Bar-Kochba uprising in 132–135 CE, or perhaps it represents the strengthening of the *limes* system along the borders of the province." (Volume 4: 73).

14. The Byzantine Period (313-632 CE)

A significant decline in settlement occurred in this period. Byzantine sherds have been found in 70 sites (43.5% of the total). In about half of them the period has been termed Roman-Byzantine.

The Byzantine period is a continuation of the former one, with one exception – the gradual conversion of the Roman Empire to Christianity. Among other characteristics, the large settlements were distinguished as Byzantine by the presence of churches. One such church was found and excavated in Archelais (Site 111), and another is currently being excavated at Phasaelis (Hizmi 2012).

Byzantine characteristics have been found in two more places: a bowl fragment decorated with a cross from Site 34 (Phasaelis), and a synagogue lintel decorated with a menorah in Site 38, probably a Byzantine period example.

The existence of the two large cities continued, but their areas were slightly reduced. In the Madaba Map the area between the cities appears as empty, although this does not necessarily testify to a lack of settlement.

Monasteries: the region was influenced by the proximity to Jericho, making it an international hub for Christian pilgrimage. Clues to this exist in several places in the south of the region, where monasteries or churches were located. Their locations along the banks of Nahal Yitav (Wadi 'Aujah), which perhaps hint at ecclesiastical estates or monastery holdings, are:

- Kh. Umm Zaqumeh, Site 150 – the site has not been excavated, but it is similar in essence and name to Site 153, which was excavated and where remains of a Byzantine monastery were found.

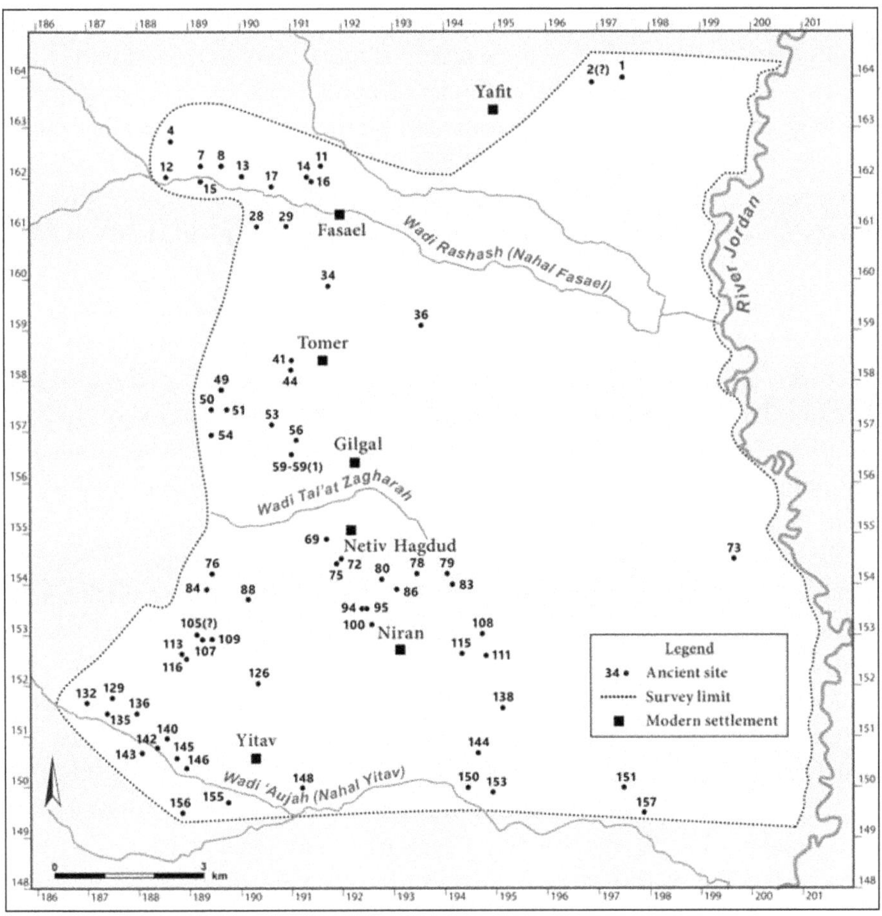

26. Map of the Byzantine Period sites.

- Kh. Umm Zaqum, Site 153 – A church with mosaics, pools, a central structure and bell-shaped cistern. These structures are typical of the numerous monasteries in the area of Jericho (for example see Patrich and Cohen 1993).
- Malhaqa el-Wadian, Site 157 – distinct remnants of a monastery, including a colourful mosaic, a bell-shaped cistern and others. Not far away are remnants of a large reservoir built for irrigation.
- 'Aujah Fortress, Site 140 – this is a large structure on the north bank of Nahal Yitav, with a Byzantine monastery inside it, with many water installations. The structure has been excavated recently and is not yet published.
- Another monastery was recently excavated at Phasaelis (Hizmi 2012: 165).

The Jericho monasteries have been much investigated (Hirschfeld 1992; Sion 1996): apparently, as already observed, here is the northern boundary of this 'monastery land'.

In Volume 2 is an account of the settlement in the Byzantine period, reaching an unprecedented climax in the desert fringes of Samaria, continuing from the Late Roman period. In the summary (Volume 2: 96–98) is a discussion of the large cities (Scythopolis and Neapolis) and their influence over the vicinity and also in the towns and villages. In Volume 4, as in the present one, a settlement decline is noted. Here also (Volume 4: 75) it is suggested that Scythopolis attracted part of the population, and the decline affected all the Jordan Valley.

15. The Early Moslem Period (632–1099 CE)

There is a certain enigma in this case. The historical data tell of the development of the Jordan Valley by the Umayyad Sultans, after a period of decline. Porath (1985b: 184) proposed that the Fasael aqueduct system was founded in this period. However, the data from the survey indicate a much poorer settlement than in the previous period.

Sherds from this period, which lasted some 400 years (the Umayyad, Fatimid and Abbasid dynasties), were found in only 28 sites, 17.4% of the total. It shows a drastic decrease in the number of settlements compared to the Byzantine period.

Regarding the size of sites, the two large cities continued to exist, but seem to have shrunk in size. There is no mention by the excavators of the discovery of a mosque.

According to the data it appears that the settlement mode underwent a considerable change: the Umayyad Sultans emphasized large estates and palaces, together with sugar production projects. One of these is Kh. Mafjar (Hisham's Palace), near Jericho (Hamilton 1959; 1993). Another, supposed estate is Kh. ed-Dasha (Site 38), not investigated by us due to minefields. In other sources the place is described as: "The centre of the 'farm', or the management of the arable areas, likewise was in Kh. ed-Dasha...south-west of it and the highway are remains of a large pool, apparently used for the settlement at Kh. ed-Dasha. The northernmost of the aqueducts from the springs led to this pool. The pool is 12.5×12.5 m and its original height was about 4 m. In three of its corners were found stones: the springs of arches, showing that the pool was originally covered by a domed roof. It contained about 600 cu. m of water. West of the pool is an ancient lime kiln. It is difficult to determine the function of the settlement at Kh. Ed-Dasha, in which was found a large square public structure with numerous rooms. Apparently it was a luxury building founded in the Umayyad period – the main building of the farm for its owner or manager on behalf of the regime" (Ilan 1973: 278).

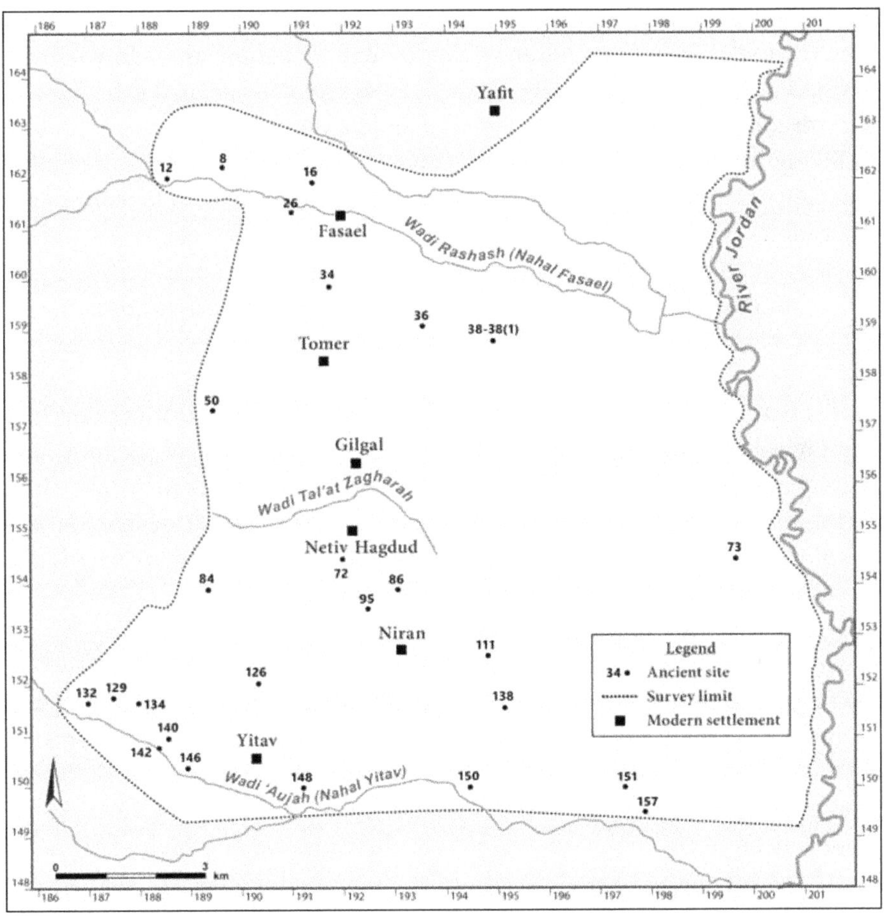

27. Map of the Early Moslem Period sites.

Porath (1985b: 42) described: "a big square structure (65 m by 65 m) built of ashlars." At its corners and along its outer walls were towers. He dated the sherds to the Early Moslem period (7th-8th centuries CE). Glass fragments and plastered water installations were also found. According to him, this was a palace built during the Umayyad period.

It can be assumed that at least two centres were built – estates and/or palaces. They served as managerial and economic hubs, accommodating high-ranking officials, and occasionally even the sultan himself. There was probably a sugar processing centre at Kh. el-Hisha (Site 26). The rest of the rural settlement shrank in both area and number of sites; and the population probably moved to central sites.

A similar decline has been recorded in the eastern valleys and in the desert fringes. Here the settlement was reduced by two-thirds compared to the Byzantine period (Volume 2: 98). The decline was characterized by the lack of new sites, shrinkage of settlements and abandonment of certain areas. In Volume 4 it is stated: "...the severity of the decline in this region is surprising, because of the considerable development in Jericho and its vicinity." (Volume 4: 75).

Taking into account the above separately authored summaries, including the one concerning the palaces, the settlement decline should be considered as a general process.

16. The Middle Ages – The Crusaders and Mamluk Periods (1099-1516 CE)

In this period, which also lasted about 400 years, there is a distinct development in settlement. MA sherds were found in 59 sites, 36.6% of the total, and slightly more than double the previous period. Two factors are to be taken into account: a). there is a distinct division between the Crusader regime and the Mamluk one, which has to be considered; and b), painted Mamluk sherds can be easily identified, perhaps increasing the number of sites.

Several aspects and insights are noteworthy:

1. The cities of Phasaelis and Archelais were almost totally deserted. In Phasaelis absolutely no pottery of the period was found, and in Archelais only 4% Mamluk sherds were traced. These cities are also not mentioned in the historical sources of the MA. If the cities were abandoned it is reasonable that the greater part of the irrigation systems, if not all of them, would have been neglected or abandoned. In the Crusader and Mamluk sources only Jericho and Qaraweh in Wadi Far'ah are mentioned. The first served as a sugar, indigo and balm cultivation centre, and sugar was grown in the other.

This fact raises two questions at least: why did the cultivation and irrigation of large tracts of land not last under the Crusaders and Mamluks, and did they settle solely for the Jericho oasis? Why were a great portion of the irrigation systems abandoned? A likely answer rests in the shortage of manpower in the Crusader Kingdom, which depended on the Moslem peasantry. As to the weak Mamluk rule, it seems that it did not allocate resources and attention to the region. However, this issue requires additional research.

2. There is a recovery of the rural settlement. Quite a few sites, nonexistent in the former period, were re-established, in the MA. This was probably linked to the settlement projects of the Mamluk Sultan al-Nasir Muhammad ibn Qala'un (1270-1290) who settled these regions.

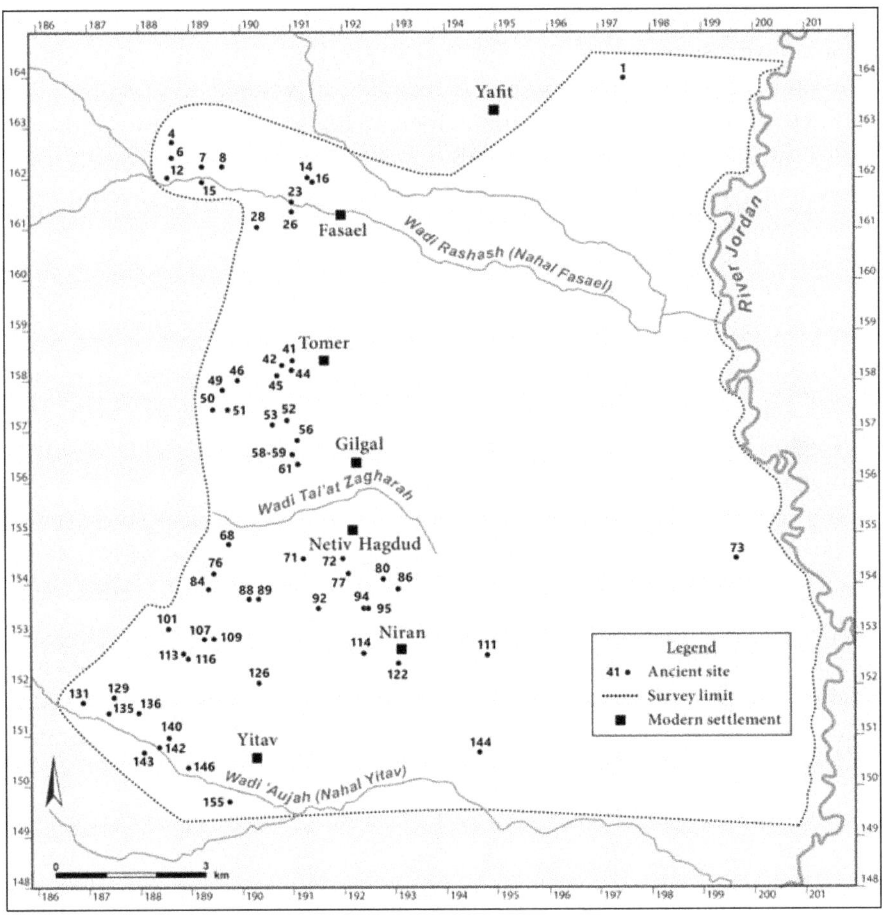

28. Map of the Middle Ages sites.

3. More than half the sites with MA pottery are enclosures, a fact that testifies to an enhancement of the typical Bedouin settlement. In the latter phases of this period (the 16th century), the Bedouin tribes Qays and Yaman intruded into the Jordan Valley and the Samaria Mountain country, and the Islamization of the population was almost completed.
4. The power of the Bedouin in the Jordan Valley increased to the extent of capturing the Mamluk governor of Jerusalem in 1479. This fact also fits the settlement situation as we interpret it.

The recovery of habitation is also notable in the area of Volume 2 – the desert fringes of Samaria to the north of the region researched here. The 69 sites found there represent a 20% increase compared to the previous period. As in the Middle Jordan Valley, the establishment of new sites and the return to cultivation of abandoned tracts of land occurred in the north (Volume 2: 101). New enclosure sites appear in the east of the Buqei'ah, corresponding to the situation we discovered.

A similar simultaneous process is recorded in Volume 4. 84 sites of the period were located and their number increased in every one of the landscape units (Volume 4: 77). Coinciding with this state of affairs, 'sugar vessels' were also found in the southern Beit She'an Valley, and the enclosure sites continued to exist along the Beit-She'an-Jericho road.

17. The Ottoman Period (1516-1918 CE)

The settlement crisis also reached this region in this long period. In 41 sites, 25.5% of the total, Ottoman sherds were found, a decline compared to the MA. The region lost its built-up nature, and only tent encampments and enclosures testify to a Bedouin habitation.

The state of settlement fits well with the historical sources (see Section E): the region lost all significance, being ruled by relatively powerful Bedouin tribes; and Jericho completely lost its centrality, as European travellers testified. In the Ottoman inhabitant's census of 1596 (Hütteroth and Abdulfattah 1977), only Bedouin tribes appear in the region. This situation continued into modern times until 1967, when new Israeli settlement changed the Jordan Valley entirely. A similar situation is also recorded in Volume 2 (Volume 2: 101).

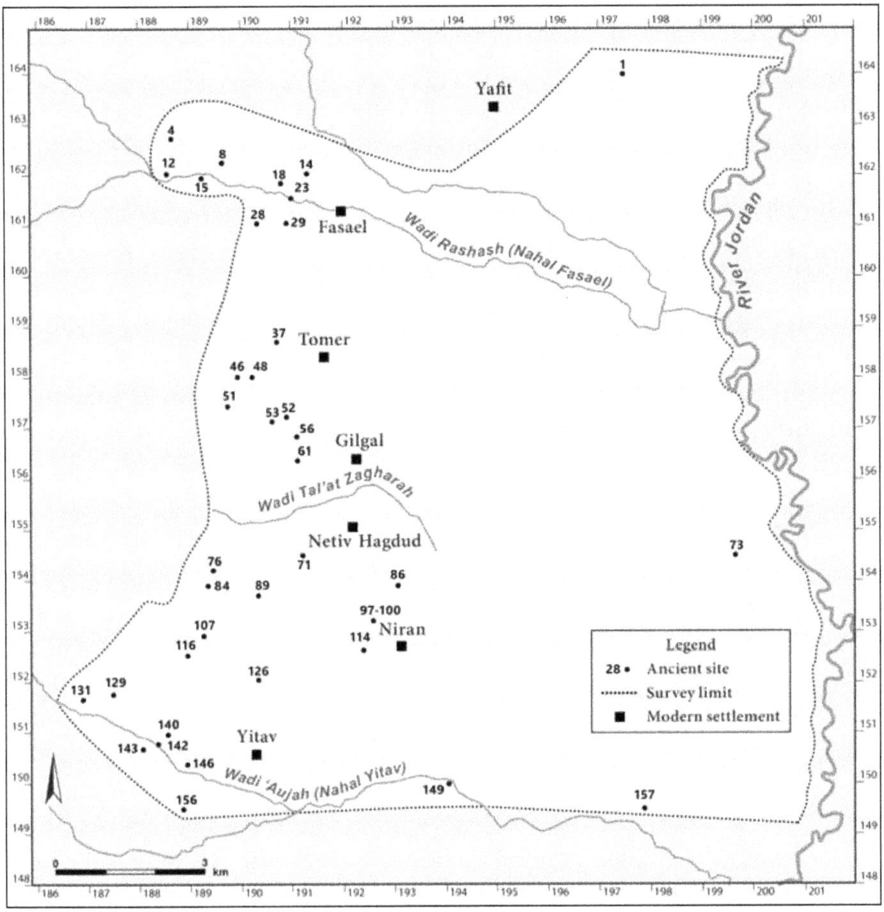

29. Map of the Ottoman Period sites.

E. OUTLINE OF THE HISTORY OF THE REGION

The history summarized in this volume is part of that of the Jordan Valley in general, but the partition of the Valley into three units necessitates discussion of each one.

1. **The Bronze Age.** From the Early Bronze Age to the Late Bronze Age – from the 4th millennium BCE until the end of the 2nd millennium BCE – settlement in the Jordan Valley was rather scanty, except in the Early Bronze I (Bar 2014). There were few fortified cities, and the rural settlement was sparse. The reasons for this are discussed in the previous section. There are also few historical sources. In the Execration Texts and the Story of Sinuhe, the written Egyptian sources about the Land of Israel in the Middle Bronze Age

II, there is no direct mention of the Jordan Valley (see Discussion in Volume 4: 80-81).

2. **Iron Age I.** The settlement around the region is intensive and extensive, as in the entire Jordan Valley. The 35 new settlements founded on virgin soil in the region, and the other 31 sites that were reinhabited after a settlement gap, are part of the settlement influx of Iron Age I, recorded all over the region. The Biblical traditions related to this settlement influx: the passage of the tribes across the northern Jordan Valley (Deut 11: 29-30; 27: 1-9), the Great Altar tradition in Josh 22, pursuing the Midianites, etc. are discussed in the previous volume (Volume 4: 84ff).

   The biblical source does not differentiate between the various parts of the Jordan Valley; therefore we have to distinguish the various aspects relevant to the region.

   2.1. The road 'where the sun sets' has been identified by Zertal (2000: 240-259; 2008: 28) with the ancient road from the River Jordan to Shechem along Nahal Tirzah (Wadi Far'ah – Volume 4: 30). In his deliberations regarding the book of Josh, Koifman (1970: 130-131) routes Deut 11: 30's The Road 'where the sun sets', directly from Jericho to the mountains of Ebal and Gerizim. According to Koifman's map (Koifman 1970: map 5) the road begins east of the Dead Sea and ascends north via Jericho to a spot south of the Sartaba; from there it ascends in two branches along Wadi Far'ah and Wadi Ahmar to the vicinity of Shechem. There is no evidence whatsoever in the field in support of Koifman's opinion that the traditional source was at Mount Nebo near the Dead Sea. It deserves mention only because of the definition: "... in the land of the Canaanites who live in the Arabah," (Deut 11: 30), according to which the Jordan Valley is the biblical Arabah. The issue has been dealt with (Zertal 2000: 254), and it is reasonable to suggest that the Middle Jordan Valley is part of the Biblical Arabah.

   2.2. The taking of Jericho and Ai are described in Josh 6-8, and have been vastly deliberated in research. However, as in other cases, the geographical and archaeological reality is missing. Wadi 'Aujah is 8 km north of Tell es-Sultan, which has been identified as ancient Jericho. The marl plains spread between them also fit the definition of Arabah in the geographical-botanical sense. However, the extent of the Jericho Arabahs is undetermined: where is their boundary in the north, and do they reach the shore of the Dead Sea in the south? Apparently, they included the Wadi 'Aujah region as well.

   The realistic and chronological basis of the expeditions from Jericho to the Ai (Josh 7, 8) is difficult to substantiate, but it cannot be invalidated offhand. Even if the text was edited after the events, it is reasonable that the author knew the topography well. There are two identifications of the site of the Ai: the traditional one (at et-Tell – Grintz 1969, in which is a detailed discussion and references) and the new one at Kh. Marjameh (Ben-Nun 1993). Both are reached from Jericho via Wadi 'Aujah, which has abundant water. The definition of the Ai with Beit-Aven, east of Beth-El (Josh 7: 2) drew numerous arguments (Grintz 1969); and the approach to the Ai from Jericho, is always an 'ascent' (Josh 7: 2, 4; 8: 1). Topographically speaking, the ascent west is possible north of Wadi 'Aujah, along the route of the modern road no. 5660 (Map of Israel, 1:50,000, sheet 5-6). Another alternative is via the route of Tariq Abu George, ascending from the south of 'Aujah Valley to modern Rimonim. The first road reaches the Samiya Valley almost directly, and Kh. Marjameh and/or the other site of the Ai – et-Tell. Water is available along all the route. The other road is longer and there is no water along it.

It is certainly feasible that along Wadi 'Aujah was an ancient road with an ascent, linking to the high Ephraim plateau. This route is possibly the one mentioned in II Kgs 2: 23, when Elisha went up from Jericho to Beth-El. Either way, the complete discussion will follow after completing the survey of the mountain block west and north of Wadi 'Aujah (future Volume 7), and a review regarding the location of Ai, based on additional information.

3. **Iron Age II – the Israelite and Judean Kingdoms.** Here also are several traditions concerning the subject region.
   3.1. The Manasseh – Ephraim boundary and the location of 'Ataroth: the arguments for the identification of 'Ataroth (Josh 16: 7) with Kh. 'Aujah el-Foqa, Site 143 are:
      3.1.1. The boundary between Ephraim and Manasseh went more or less in a straight line, from the Michmethath east of Shechem to Jericho and the Dead Sea. If Thaanath- Shiloh was in the sites of Tana (Khirbet Tana et-Tahtah, see Bar 2017b), and Janoah is in Kh. Yanon, then the site should be located on that same south-east oriented boundary, reaching Jericho.
      3.1.2. The proposals of Alt (1927), Elliger (1930: 279) and Kallay (1971), identifying 'Ataroth with Tell es-Simadi, do not fit the terrain. They force an unnatural boundary with several curves and turns, ascending from Kh. Yanon to Wadi Far'ah and onward to Jericho. The tells of es-Simadi and esh-Sheik Diyab, which are the alternative suggestions, do not fit the description of a city built on a mountain summit (Hebrew: *Atarah* – crown).
      3.1.3. Some researchers have shown that *Atarah* or *Ataroth* are biblical

names for rounded (and fortified?) places on top of a mountain or hill summit. These are some of the topographical definitions for a place of settlement, such as *Geva, Giv'ah* (hill) and likewise; *Ramah* and *Ramoth* (high place/places); *Mitzpeh* (lookout post); *Beit-Ha'emeq* (house in the valley); *Afeq* and *Afiq* (riverbed) and many more (see also Aharoni 1979: 109).

3.1.4. The city is situated at a boundary between the Manasseh and Benjamin tribal allotments and the territories of the Kingdoms of Israel and Judea at a later stage. Typical elements in the pottery of the site are characteristic of the northern and southern kingdoms alike (Zertal et al. 2009: 116-117).

Thus, the boundary between Ephraim and Manasseh ran along the ancient road along which the modern Alon north to south road runs. Ben-Nun (1993: 49ff), discussed this route, logically proposing to consider it to have been the route of the Assyrian army described in Isaiah 10: 28-32: "He has come to Aiath; he has passed through Migron; at Michmash he stores his baggage; they have crossed over the pass; at Geba they lodge for the night; Ramah trembles; Gibeah of Saul has fled. Cry aloud, O daughter of Gallim! Give attention, O Laishah! O poor Anathoth! Madmenah is in flight; the inhabitants of Gebim flee for safety. This very day he will halt at Nob; he will shake his fist at the mount of the daughter of Zion, the hill of Jerusalem"[3].

This road may have been used in Shishak's expedition in 925 BCE. The Egyptian king ascended from Beit Horon to the Jordan Valley, bypassed Jerusalem and the Gibeon road (no. 23 in Shishak's list) and Migdal (no. 58 in that list), and then reached Zemaraim (no. 57), Adamah (no. 56 – the Damiya ford?) and Succoth (no. 55). There are those who arranged the list in the *boustrophedon* method (lines reading alternately left to right and right to left) (for example: Mazar 1980: 236-237), but the site sequence remains logical when the extremes – Beit-Horon and Succoth – are well identified.

Zertal (1988: 85-86) proposed to identify the tower fortress at Rujm Abu Mukheir, Site 5, with Migdal in Shishak's list. The identification rests on the form and location of the site, and supports the attitude of the earlier researchers who did not have a site to refer to. Zemaraim remains unknown despite several proposals.

The Manasseh-Ephraim boundary (Josh 16) ran, then, along the convenient route of the ancient road. From Kh. Yanon and Kh. Tana the

3 There is a snag in Ben-Nun's proposal, according to which this route is theoretical (1993: note 42). It is preferable to assume that this was a real route, although it is difficult to link it particularly to Sennacherib's expedition in 701 BCE.

30. The Iron Age II city at Khirbet 'Aujah el-Foqa (Site 143), identified with biblical 'Ataroth, 2012 (A. Solomon).

boundary went north-south, left the main road, and descended to the Wadi 'Aujah Valley where the region's main city of 'Ataroth was built.

3.2. Nahal Cherith: in I Kgs 17: 2-8, tells the story of Elijah hiding in Nahal (brook) Cherith which is east of the Jordan, where he drank from its water and was fed by ravens. This tradition belongs to the narrative of miracles of the prophet, and in our case the hiding and the location of the brook are significant.

The hiding places for escapees from the authorities – robbers and outlaws, debtors and bankrupts, prophets and intellectuals – are known from King David's time and even earlier. The vast eastern desert fringes, along with the deep wadis and the water sources helped concealment. This reality continued during the Second Temple period (Wadi ed-Daliya in the Persian-Hellenistic periods, and in other regions during the Great Revolt and the Bar-Kochba's rebellion, see Spanier 1997). The area near the River Jordan was a convenient place for escapees from the settled areas of the northern Kingdom of Israel. Elijah's tradition is part of this, as described in the narratives in I Kgs 18: 13; 19: 3ff; II Kgs 2: 1, 4-8. The identification of the region, whether east or west of the River Jordan (for details: Younker 1992) is fairly clear: Elijah prophesied near Samaria and not east of the river. In I Kgs 17: 3 it is said: "Depart from here and turn eastward and hide yourself by the brook Cherith". The command mentioned escape eastward and hiding by the River Jordan, therefore it is necessary to identify the areas of refuge and some of the brooks. Significant are the lexical usages in the Bible (for example the discussion in Zertal 2000: 226-227) and the discussion in the verse "on the face" (of the Jordan), which appears frequently. The varied usage in the phrase begins in "on the face of the field" (strewn in the field – II Kgs 9: 37) and continue by "on the face of Egypt" and "on the face of the desert". The geographical term relates mainly to "observe at", "look at", "looked down", such as in Genesis 18: 16, and elsewhere. From these arise the three stipulations for the identification of Nahal Cherith: it should preferably be within the bounds of the Kingdom of Israel, it flows all year round (except during an extreme drought) and it can be closely observed from the River Jordan. The proposed Jordan Valley streams; Fasael and Qelt do not fit, unlike Wadi 'Aujah. The first two enter the valley plain and branch into many streams; their sources are in the mountains far from the River Jordan, and there are not many hiding places in them. Unlike them, Wadi 'Aujah flows (or flowed in the past) all year round, its channel is wide and deep and is fringed by cliffs. At its confluence with the River Jordan (coordinates 1475/2000) Wadi Malha joins it north of it, where there is a thicket of cane, which is a nesting place for an abundance of fowls. These are ideal hiding places, fitting the descriptions of Nahal Cherith.

4. **The Assyrian, Babylonian and Persian periods.** In the absence of detailed data about the 500 years from the 8th to the 4th centuries BCE, only fragments of data could be assembled. According to Lemair's (1994: 12) division, the region is at the boundaries of the Persian provinces of Samaria and Judea. During that time the region was sparsely settled, and only a *rujm* (a nomad tumulus tomb) close to Yafit (Magen 2004) was found.

Groups of Samaritans hid in the caves of Wadi ed-Daliyeh, which are near the western boundary of the area in this Volume. They escaped with their belongings from Samaria, the provincial capital, in fear of the Macedonian conqueror in 334 BCE (Lapp 1993). This is additional evidence about Iron Age 'areas of hiding'. During the survey a stone was found with two letters apparently in Aramaic script (Site 63). Their style resembles that of the Persian period, but this is uncertain.

Among the returnees to Zion the book of Nehemiah (7: 36, 38) mentions people from Jericho and Senaah. The last name belongs to a family from Binyamin returning from the Babylonian exile with Zerubbabel (Ezra 2: 35). Researchers linked this to the settlement of Magdal Senna of Eusebius, some 10 km north-west of Jericho (Notley and Safrai; 2005, no. 824). However, there are other opinions (Bergdall 1992). Avi-Yonah (1976: 80) proposed identifying it at Kh. Beiyudhat, the present location of Archelais. Kallay (1968) discussed Senaah's location at length, repeating Glueck (1951: 413) and Avi-Yonah's opinion identifying it at Beiyudaht. However, in the survey and excavation of the site no Persian period artefacts were found, and the proposition that depends on the tower at the centre of the site, which is not connected to the issue, cannot be accepted. The genealogical linkage tells of a site within the bounds of Binyamin, large enough to house several families. For now we leave this identification issue open to future research.

5. **The Hellenistic period.** Most of the information is about Jericho. Alexander III of Macedon sent a delegation to Jericho (Gutmann 1940: 278-279), and the battle between Bacchides and Jonathan took place near the city (I Maccabees 9: 43-49, and see also Alon 1976: 153-154). The fortresses guarding the Jordan Valley – Alexandrion, Tracheas and Taurus – were built by Alexander Jannaeus mainly to counter the Nabataean threat. The tradition about the Battle of Papyron (War I, vi: 3; Ant. XIV, ii: 3) is related to the location of Beit Hogla.

   Pottery from the Hellenistic Period was found in both the cities 'founded' by Herod – Phasaelis (Site 34) and Archelais (Site 111). According to the literature both were established during Herod's rule, but the percentage of Hellenistic period pottery is not negligible, and it seems that they were founded then. It is probable that Herod built these cities on top of existing settlements engaged in date and balsam cultivation. It therefore seems that the Jordan Valley was already integrated into the economic and political national system in Hasmonean times, and Herod built the cities and new projects on an existing infrastructure.

6. **The Early Roman (Herodian) period.** During the century between Herod's rise to power (37 BCE) and the Great Revolt in 66 CE the Jordan Valley enjoyed unprecedented development; there is a full description of this in War IV, viii: 2: "Jericho lies in a plain, but above it hangs a bare and barren mountain range of immense length, extending northwards as far as the territory of Scythopolis...The region enclosed between these two mountains ranges is called the Great Plain. This extends from the village of Ginnabris to the Lake Asphaltitis, and is twelve hundred furlongs in length, and a hundred and twenty in breadth; it is intersected by the Jordan...In summer the plain is burnt up, and the excessive drought renders the surrounding atmosphere pestilential; for it is wholly without water, apart from the Jordan, which, moreover, explains why the palm-groves on the banks of that river are more luxuriant and productive than those further off".

   In the description of Herod's deeds it has been mentioned that "He also gave the name of Phasaelis to another city which he built in the valley to the north of Jericho" (War I, xxi: 9). At first, Herod leased the 'land of date-palms' from Cleopatra, who received it from Antonius (War I, xviii: 5). In the trial between Archelaus and his rivals conducted before Augustus Caesar,

Archelaus received Samaria and Judaea, and Salome, Herod's sister, received Phasaelis, among other places. Upon her death she bequeathed the Phasaelis date-palm plantations to Livia Augustus' wife.

The account of the establishment of the city of Archelais includes the following: "He (Archelaus son of Herod) also rebuilt the royal palace in Jericho in splendid fashion, and diverted half the water that served to irrigate the village of Neara, leading it into a plain that had been planted by him with palm-trees. He also created a village and gave it the name of Archelais" (Ant. XVII, xiii: 1).

Another account is as follows: "...Marcus Ambivulus, during whose administration Salome, the sister of King Herod, died. To Julia she bequeathed Jamnia and its territory, together with Phasaelis, which lay in the plain, and Archelais, where palms are planted in very great numbers and the dates are of highest quality" (Ant. XVIII, ii: 2).

Pliny the Elder (1st century CE) notes that Archelais, between Jericho and Phasaelis, is famous for the quality of its fruit (Natural History XIII, ix: 44 [Rackham 1962]). Upon Julia's death in 29 CE, Archelais was passed to Caesar. Herod (Agrippa I) received it in 41 CE, and upon his death the place was put under the authority of the Roman governor in Caesarea.

The Jordan Valley was Herod's most significant agricultural and settlement project, because until then the area had not been intensively settled, and it had considerable development potential. Another incentive for this process resulted from the many ownerless or unallocated plots, which became royal estates. Two facts testify to this: a) the date-palms and balsam plantations were transferred to Caesar's ownership without claims from others, and b) the balsam orchards, after Archelais' impeachment in 6 CE, became the property of the Roman State treasury (*Fiscus*) (Ilan 1973: 86). Both these facts show the king's ownership of the land. The ground itself was agriculturally useless, and large areas were irrigated only in organized projects, with the climate encouraging the crops. Josephus Flavius praises the region: "Hard by Jericho... is a copious spring of excellent value for irrigation...this spring irrigates a larger tract than all others, irrigating a plain seventy furlongs in length and twenty in breadth, and fostering within that area the most charming and luxuriant parks. Of the date-palms watered by it there are numerous varieties differing in flavour and in medicinal properties; the richer species of this fruit when pressed under foot emit copious honey, not much inferior to that of bees...Here, too, grows the juicy balsam, the most precious of all the local products...so that it would be no misnomer to describe as "divine" this spot...it would difficult to find another region in this habitable world comparable to this; so manifold are the returns from whatever is sown. I attribute these results to the warmth of the air and the

31. The remains of the central structure, perhaps a tower, in Archelais, 2012 (A. Solomon).

bracing effects of the water, the one calling forth and diffusing the young plants, while the moisture enables them all to take firm root and supplies them with vitality in summer, when the surrounding region is so parched up, that one can scarcely venture out of doors...The country from Jericho to Jerusalem is desert and rocky; to the Jordan and the Lake Asphaltitis the ground is lower, though equally wild and barren" (War IV, viii: 3).

The description confirms that only state-organised irrigation could yield from the Jordan Valley its main produce: excellent dates and balsam (about date palm cultivation see Rosenson 1987 and London's comprehensive works: 2003; 2005. For balsam, balm – review by Porath 1985b: 177-183). The archaeological find points also to such projects: the irrigation projects of Nahal Fasael (Appendix D and Porath 1985b: 29-45), which irrigated hundreds of dunams in the wadi floodplain, were founded and maintained in connection to the city of Phasaelis; while those of Wadi 'Aujah were initiated on behalf of Archelais and its watered areas (Porath 1985b: 45-57). Hence, the irrigation projects were constructed simultaneously along the foundation of the cities and their development, the fruit of the state-run initiative.

The balsam (Ilan 1973: 86-87; Felix 1957: 246-248, 256-258) is described in numerous sources as a fragrance and medicinal plant, which the Jews were expert in raising. During the Great Revolt against Rome (66-73 CE) Titus conducted a military expedition in the Jordan Valley, aimed at the protection of the precious plantations from destruction by Jewish rebels (Stern 1968: 217).

Avi-Yonah (1970: 22-23) notes that after the destruction of the Bar-Khochba revolt Jews survived in the Jordan Valley thanks to their knowledge of balsam cultivation. Rabi Yossi of the 2nd century CE called them "... balsam gatherers from En Gedi to Ramah" (Bavli Shabat II.8A [Neusner 1992: 89]). According to Avi-Yona, who fails to give the reference, about a dozen Jewish settlements remained in the Jordan Valley.

Netzer's maps (2006: maps 3 and 4) of his survey of the Valley of Jericho, only partially include the areas north of the city. In his opinion the south and middle of the valley, from Fasael to Jericho, were integrated into the comprehensive Herodian period development project.

7. **The Late Roman and Byzantine periods.** With the continuation and expansion of the development project, the habitation reached its climax, testified by the considerable archaeological finds in Phasaelis and Archelais (see these cities in this volume and in Hizmi 1993; 2008a; 2008b). The rural habitation also expanded, mainly during the Late Roman period . In the Talmud the Jordan Valley is considered to excel in the cultivation of balsam (for example Yerushalmi 43: 71; Shabbat 26: 71; Tosefta Sheviyit 7: 10-12; Bavly Yomah 39: 2). The continued usage of the irrigation systems is a sign of the continuation of habitation. The phases of the various aqueducts (Appendix D) with several plaster layers and repairs, testify to a usage of hundreds of years.

32. The aqueducts near ancient Phasaelis, near the modern village of Fusayil, 2011 (S. Bar).

With the beginning of Christianity, in 27 CE, John the Baptist began calls to rependence and baptised people in the River Jordan, Jesus of Galilee among them (John 29: 28-34). In Eusebius' Onomasticon (Notley and Safrai 2005) the sites appearing in the district are Gilgal (no. 311), Jordan (no. 527), Naarah (no. 732), and Zin (no. 824), which is noted as: "A boundary of Judaea. Magdalsenna is now at the eighth mile north of Jericho".

The Madaba map (Avi-Yonah 1953: leaf 1), shows the symbols of Corea, Archelais, and perhaps Phasaelis, all in the Middle Jordan Valley. Avi-Yonah (1953: 140) identifies Phasaelis by the preceding name in the map (Archelais), but the issue is not clear. Also unexplained is the conjunction of the names by a colon. It is also feasible that another place altogether is being referred to. The signs of a fortified city or a village have not been preserved for either site (Avi-Yonah 1953: 135). The identification of the site of Galgala (defined as the place of the twelve stones) has been suggested as the Samara Quarry (future Volume 8).

The Jordan Valley area appears in the Madaba map rather empty of settlements, apart from the cities. The rural settlement, the date-palms and balsam plantations are not shown, as in comparison to the dense Judea allotment (Avi-Yonah 1953: leaf 8), or the vicinity of Jerusalem (Avi-Yonah 1953: leaf 7). However, this tendency is general in the map, and the description focuses on the identified Biblical, religious and historical places.

After the major crisis of the Jewish settlement in the 3rd century (200-260 CE), Avi-Yonah (1970: 15) notes that rural settlement in the Jordan Valley remained stable. He refers to the list of settlement places known from the various sources (Avi-Yonah 1970: 114).

The names of 43 Jewish settlements are known from the end of the Byzantine rule – 31 villages and 12 cities (Avi-Yonah 1970: 208), "...several villages (of them) still remained in the Jordan Valley." This is testimony to the stability of the Jewish habitation in the region, stability which depended and relied on cultivation of balsam.

Pilgrimage to Jericho and its environs developed in the Byzantine period, mainly to the baptism site in the River Jordan. The progressive agriculture and livelihood resources, including European pilgrimage, attracted population to settle in the region. The Jordan Valley, in a broader essence, is not mentioned in the sources, but information about Jericho itself in this period may be found in the journal of the Pilgrim of Bordeaux (333 CE), describing ruined Jericho. In contrast, in 381 CE the pilgrim Egeria tells of a church and pilgrims' hostel in Jericho. The anonymous pilgrim of Piacenza (570 CE) describes Jericho as a centre for pilgrimage to Christian holy places. He also tells about the wealth of the city and the region, bearing two crops a year. The great productivity of Jericho seemed to the pilgrims to be a miracle (for references see Grabois 1983: 51-52). In a document published by Russell (1980: 50), is an account of a major earthquake in the region in 363 CE.

8. **The Early Moslem, Crusade and Middle Ages periods.** About 100 years after the Moslem conquest in 637 CE, the Jordan Valley, and particularly Jericho and its vicinity, again became an important hub. At first the Moslem conquest caused the destruction of Jericho, which was abandoned by the Christian population. The pilgrim Arculfus (end 7th century CE) found in Jericho only "three intact houses" (Grabois 1983: 52), but recovery began rather soon.

The renewed prosperity in the 8th century onward is related to the Umayyad Caliphs. Moslem Jericho concentrated north of the present city, in the Kh. el-Mafjar area, with Hisham's Palace at the centre. An urban centre was built, and in 723 CE the pilgrim (Saint) Willibald found a flourishing settlement (Grabois 1983: 53). The magnificent Hisham's Palace (Schiller 1976; Hamilton 1959; 1993) was one of the Umayyad Caliphs' winter palaces in the deserts of the Land of Israel, Jordan and Syria.

Agriculture and sugar production: the Moslems apparently introduced the growing of woad – *Isatis tinctoria*, the source of indigo dye, and sugar cane. When the Crusaders arrived they found these plants with the date-palm plantations (Horowitz 1923: 347). The Moslem traveller Al-Mukadasi mentioned cultivation of bananas, and the traveller Yaqut the growing of woad (Le Strange 1890: 202-203). The great prosperity went together with the renewal of agricultural settlement, although not many Early Moslem period remains have been found in the area covered by this volume. Prominent are the sites at Kh. ed-Dashe (Site 38) with its nearby large agricultural plots and El-Hisha (Site 26), apparently used for sugar production.

Peled (2009) scrutinizes the history of sugar growth and production in the Jordan Valley. In her opinion, the growth of sugar began in the days of the Umayyad Dynasty in the 8th century CE. Two of her sources (Peled 2009: 16-17), tell about the irrigation projects linked to the River Jordan. It appears that these are the oases of Phasael and 'Aujah, because no irrigation project is known to have been connected to the river itself, due to the differences in elevation. Another source (Peled 2009: 18) tells of oil extraction from the Egyptian Zaqqum = Jericho Balsam (*Balanites aegyptiaca*). The traveller Yaqut (Peled 2009: 22), cites a 9th century Persian Abbassid traveller who does not mention Phasael or Fussayil, only Qaraweh (in the Wadi Far'ah floodplain) and 'Aujah.

Despite the decrease in pilgrimage, the existence of a Christian centre in Jericho and its vicinity also continued in this period. The pilgrims descended from Jerusalem to Jericho and the River Jordan. The city became Moslem (called during this time Al-Ariha), but had no administrative function during the Abbassid and Fatimid periods, and was not fortified.

Ilan (1973: 90) also notes that with the rise of Islam and the persecution of the Jews in the 7th century, Jews emigrated from the Hejaz and settled in the Jericho Valley.

General information regarding the Crusader period. Jericho (and apparently the sites around it) was devastated in the earthquake of 1031 and remained ruined until the Crusader conquest. Raymond de Saint-Gilles, one of the Crusader leaders, took control of Jericho and the region in 1099. The First Crusade ended with renewed baptism in the River Jordan (a procession and baptism holding palm branches). The city and its vicinity were given by the Crusader kings to the Latin Patriarch of Jerusalem. At this stage the region enjoyed a renewed and intensive development. Many Greek monasteries were built, and the Jericho district became a place of assembly for the Crusader leaders every year in January for mass baptism ceremonies (Grabois 1983: 53-54).

The agricultural wealth of the Jordan Valley increased the income of the feudal masters, who relied, apart from dates, on the cultivation of indigo (*Indigofera tinctoria*), sugarcane and balsam. The income from the Jericho estates was estimated by William of Tyre, the historian of the Crusade, to be 5000 gold bezants per annum (Grabois 1983: 54).

In 1112 the priest Arnulf of Chocques became Archbishop of Jerusalem, and immediately established the court of the bourgeois in Jericho, a judicial and administrative institution for the urban population in the Crusader Kingdom of Jerusalem. Arnulf transferred the legacy of Jericho as dowry to his niece, who married Garnier, the Master of Caesarea, but the transfer was annulled by King Baldwin I. King Fulk/Foulque of Anjou (reigned 1131-1144) assigned the defence of the city to the Order of the Knights Templar. The Templars erected a fortress on the bank of the Jordan, close to the Monastery of John the Baptist (Grabois 1983: 54).

In 1143 Melisande, Queen of Jerusalem, bestowed Jericho and the vicinity on the Monastery of Lazarus in Many, which consequently became one of the wealthiest in the kingdom. The royal house kept some authority in its hands, such as the supervision of the court and military service (Grabois 1983: 54).

In his comprehensive work on the Neapolis (Shechem/Nablus) district during the Crusading era Beyer (1940: 189) tells that after the battle of Hittin the Moslems seized Jericho, which began to decline. From the 13th to 15th centuries European pilgrims testified to its poor state. Burchard of Mount-Zion (Stewart 1896: 56) states in 1280 that there were only eight houses in Jericho. In 1485 the traveller Soriano tells that the district had become the domicile of assassins and robbers (Schiller 1983: 55).

About Phasaelis Burchard writes: "Four leagues to the east of Emon, at the going down of Mount Ephraim, on the plain, two leagues from Jordan, is the village of Phesech, at the place where the brook Cherith runs down from the mountain. Here Elijah abode, when the ravens brought him food in the morning and in the evening." (Stewart 1896: 56). He called Phesech 'casal' (fortress), and associated it to the Neapolis district. Marino Sanuto, a well-known Italian historian who also described Acre, repeats that (Stewart 1896: 14), writing: "Fasael, three leagues distant from the Jordan, in the plain country, where the brook Cherith comes down from the mountain, in which place Elijah dwelt when the ravens brought him meat (I Kgs xxii.)." (Stewart 1896: 56). Later the district became a possession of the King of Jerusalem (Beyer 1940: 201).

Between the periods of the First and Second Crusader Kingdoms of Jerusalem the Jordan Valley was still under Ayyubid rule. Its inhabitants raised sugar in Tiberias and Beit She'an. In the area south of the latter city the produce was called "The sugar of Shechem". Yaqut tells of Qarawa in which excellent sugar is being planted (Le Strange 1890: 480). The quality of the sugar of Jericho is praised by both Yaqut and the pilgrim Thietmar in 1217 (Peled 2009: 124). Neither mention Fussayil, and it appears that the entire area was for a short period of time in the royal domain of the Crusaders. According to Peled's sources (Peled 2009: 224-225) the sugar was used by the Teutonic Order to treat sick inmates of their hospital. Jacques de Vitry (Peled 2009: 226) speaks of abundance of sugar, without geographical details. Peled (2009: 230-231) also introduces Porath's summaries concerning the ancient agriculture, and see Discussion in Appendix D.

9. **The Mamluk and Ottoman periods.** In the Mamluk period, 14th–16th centuries, the population of the Shechem mountain area mostly converted to Islam. The slow process was hastened after the victory over the Crusaders, accompanied by persecution of the Christian population. At the same time a massive influx of Bedouin tribes started, some of which settled in the Jordan Valley (Yekutieli 1971: 208-209). Members of the Qays and Yaman tribes arrived in the area, The Qays settled south of Shechem and the Yaman north of it. The disputes between them played a significant role in the history of the district.

The Russian Archimandrite Agrefenii arrived at Jericho in the 1370s, and mentioned the abundance of growing fruit, including bananas, watermelons, oranges and sugar. He also noted that all was ruined in Jericho, except for a few Arab houses (Raba 1992: 160- 161).

Rabbi Ovadiah (ben Abraham) of Bartenura who visited the region in 1485 wrote that in Jericho: "However, honey and dates I have not found here, and also have not seen any dates, and in Jericho, the city of dates, a reliable man who was present there, told me, that it is not far from Jerusalem but half a day's journey, (and) that in the whole of Jericho there are but three bad date-palms which do not bear fruit." (Ammar 1992: 233 [from Hebrew, A. H.]).

At the end of Mamluk rule the Bedouin tribes strengthened to such an extent that in 1479 they captured the Mamluk Governor of Jerusalem. Although he was later released , the event was a sign of the general anarchy in the land, and particularly of the strength of the Bedouin in the Jordan Valley (Drory 1981: 28).

Schiller (1983: 55) noted that after the era of the Crusades the region lost its importance. With the Ottoman occupation in 1516 appeared the names of Bedouin tribes: Masa'id (who settled in the *Ghor* of Wadi Far'ah and in other parts of the Jordan Valley –Yekutieli 1971: 211), and to some extent Beni-Sakhr. Samaria and the Jordan Valley belonged to the *eyalet* (Turkish – primary administrative division) of esh-Sham, which was subdivided into two *sanjaks*: Shechem (Nablus) and Jerusalem. The Jordan Valley was not a *nahiya* (secondary district) by itself, and the tribes in it were subject to the *nawahi* of the central mountain country.

In the 18th century Daher el-Omar increased his strength, establishing special relations with the Sultanate at Istanbul. He made a short-lived covenant with the Beni-Sakhr tribe, who also settled in the Jordan Valley, and made a living from raiding and robbery (Yekutieli 1971: 214). The covenant was soon violated when the Bedouin turned the people of Shechem against Daher el-Omar and his followers. In a battle in the Jezreel Valley in 1735 Daher defeated the army of the people of Shechem and Beni-Sakhr alliance, and the survivors retreated to their strongholds.

The accounts of the European travellers, some of which are quoted above, give descriptions of the situation. There are few descriptions of the Jordan Valley itself, but the information on Jericho is an indication of the general state of affairs. According to this the population of Jericho was very poor, lived in miserable hamlets, and subsisted on looting (Schiller 1983: 55).

Ibrahim Pasha destroyed the district before returning to Egypt in 1840. In 1876 the Baedeker Guide describes Jericho as: "Jericho. The Inn, situated on the left at the entrance to the village, is a dirty mud-hut surrounded by hedges. The beds are bad, the rooms small and close, and vermin abundant… Modern Jericho consists of a group of squalid hovels inhabited by about sixty families. Like the other inhabitants of the S. part of the Jordan valley, those of Jericho appear to be a degenerate race, as the hot and unhealthy climate has an enervating effect. The villagers usually crowd round travelers with offers to execute a 'fantasia', or dance accompanied by singing, but the performance is tedious and uninteresting" (Baedeker 1876: 261-262).

The region during World War I. Erlich (1987: 57-70) accumulated data on the Jordan Valley front in 1918. Two battalions (nos. 38 and 39) of the Jewish Legion participated in the battles, holding the ridges of el-Musalabah (E.P. -191) and et-Tulul (E.P. -140), north and south of Kibbutz Niran and west of the Jordan Valley road. The first ridge appears by its name on the British map, but is not named on the 1:50,000 map (Israel). The second ridge, also from the British map, borders the Archelais complex in the west. Included in it are the sites of Archelais north-west (Site 108) and Archelais-west (Site 115). The Jewish battalions deployed east of the Wadi Malha channel and gained a foothold in the Turkish front line (Erlich 1987: 70). Several battles took place until the battalions captured Umm ash-Shurut ford (coordinates 2010/1542), enabling the crossing of the River Jordan by British troops (Erlich 1987: 66-67).

The discovery of the base and the supposed Turkish cemetery nearby at Kh. Umm esh-Shughut (Site 73), enhances the data about the August-September 1918 events. The Turkish fallen were probably buried here (although this issue requires additional proof) after the battles around the crossing to Transjordan (A-Salt and Amman), the most important crossing at the time in the south Jordan Valley.

33. The Ottoman flour mill in Wadi Fasael, looking south, 2011 (S. Bar).

CHAPTER TWO

THE GEOGRAPHICAL–HISTORICAL IDENTIFICATIONS

This chapter contains the identifications in Volume 5. Some of these are new and are suggested by us, and others have been suggested by earlier scholars, and are to be reconsidered.

Site 5: Rujm Abu Mukheir

Zertal (1988: 85-86; 1995) proposed identifying the circular fortress on the road from the Jordan Valley to the Kingdom of Israel with Migdal, no. 58 in Shishak's List. The list was published by Mazar (1980: 237), who proposed reading it as *boustrophedon* (alternate lines read from left to right and right to left). Whichever direction it is, Migdal is found on the road to the Jordan Valley, according to Shishak's route in the central hill country (according to Mazar, Sakut, no. 55 in the list, comes after Migdal). It has also been proposed that this type of circular fort is the Watchtower (*Migdal Hanozrim*) in the Bible (II Kgs 17: 9; 18: 8).

Shishak's tower was identified in the past at Majdal Beni-Fadil, which is close to Rujm Abu Mukheir (Abel 1935: 272; Mazar 1980: n. 10a). The term *Migdal* (tower) according to Mazar (1970), is the acropolis of a fortified city, a watchtower in a wall or a single tower. Therefore the site fits its description.

Site 23: Tell esh-Sheikh Diyab

The site has been identified as 'Ataroth (Josh 16: 7-8) by Glueck and Alt (see below), but after the discovery of the site at 'Aujah el-Foqa (Site 143; Zertal et al. 2009: 120-121) it seems that the identification is not correct.

'Ataroth is situated on the border between Manasseh and Ephraim, which starts east of Shechem (the Michmethath) and descends to Jericho and the River Jordan. The source of the common name 'Ataroth is in the topography – a circular wall on top of a summit (Kallay 1971: 168). According to the south-eastward route of the border 'Ataroth should have been situated between Yanoah (Kh. Yanon?) and Naaratha (Na'aran?). Alt (1926: 33) proposed identifying it at Kh. 'Aujah et-Tahtah (Site 146); The logic here results from the fact that the place is on the probable border between Manasseh and Ephraim. Later, Alt (1927: 32) and Elliger (1930: 279) switched 'Ataroth to Tell es-Simadi (Site 84 in

Vol. 4) or to Tell esh-Sheikh Diyab. Glueck (1951: 419), and Kallay (1971: 165-166) agreed with this interpretation.

However, these last propositions rested on an irrational route for the border, according to which the line descends from Shechem south-east to Kh. Yanoah, and then turns sharply eastward to Wadi Far'ah, and from there along the Jordan Valley to Na'aran. The direct line in the direction of Jericho is rational, following the topographical contours. Therefore, we propose restoring 'Ataroth to the Wadi 'Aujah area, anchoring it in a new site – Kh. 'Aujah el-Foqa.

Site 34: Kh. Fusayil-Phasaelis

The identification with the city of Phasaelis which was founded by Herod is accepted by all and confirmed (see bibliography). Below are the relevant data:

History: The information about the founding of Phasaelis appears in *The Antiquities of the Jews* by Josephus as follows: "He also built a city named after him in the valley of Jericho northward from there, and thereby made the surrounding region, formerly a wilderness, more productive through the industry of its inhabitants. And this city he called Phasaelis" (Ant. XVI, v: 2). "...Marcus Ambivulus, during whose administration Salome, the sister of King Herod, died. To Julia she bequeathed Jamnia and its territory, together with Phasaelis, which lay in the plain, and Archelais, where palms are planted in very great numbers and the dates are of the highest quality" (Ant. XVIII, ii: 2).

The data appear in *The War of the Jews* thus:

1. "He (Herod) also gave the name of Phasaelis to another city which he built in the valley to the north of Jericho" (War I, xxi: 9).
2. "Salome (Herod's sister) besides the legacy which the King had left her in his will, was declared mistress of Jamnia, Azotus and Phasaelis" (War II, vi: 3).
3. "...as for Salome, she at her death bequeathed her toparchy to Julia, the wife of Augustus, together with Jamnia and the palm-groves of Phasaelis" (War II, ix: 1).

The preservation of the name, the location and the irrigation systems support the identification. The city also appears in the Madaba map, although only partially.

Additional Bibliography: Abel 1913: 235; Alt 1927: 31; Avi-Yonah 1976: 87 (and in it additional bibliography); Hizmi 2012; Möller and Schmitt 1976: 187-188.

Site 111: Kh. el-Beiyudhat

This is a reasonable identification with the city of Archelais, established by Herod in the Jordan Valley. The sources are: Josephus Flavius, who tells of the building of the city by Archelaus, Herod's son, thus: "He (Archelaus son of Herod) also rebuilt the royal palace in Jericho in splendid fashion, and diverted half the water that served to irrigate the village of Neara, leading it into a plain that had been planted by him with palm trees. He also created a village and gave it the name of Archelais" (Ant. XVII, xiii: 1).

After the banishment of Archelaus by Augustus Caesar the city was transferred to Salome, Herod's sister. In her will she bequeathed the city to Julia, Augustus' wife, and Josephus describes it thus: "...Marcus Ambivulus, during whose administration Salome, the sister of King Herod, died. To Julia she bequeathed Jamnia and its territory, together with Phasaelis, which lay in the plain, and Archelais, where palms are planted in very great numbers and the dates are of highest quality" (Ant. XVIII, ii: 2).

Pliny the Elder (1st century CE) notes that Archelais is situated between Jericho and Phasaelis, and the place is famous for the quality of its fruit (Natural History XIII, ix: 44 [Rackham 1962]).

When Julia died Archelais became Caesar's property. Agrippa I received it in 41 CE, and after his death the place was transferred to the possession of the Roman governor in Caesarea. In the Ptolemy's Canon (VII, xvi: 5 [Nobbe 1966]) from the 2nd century CE, the place is mentioned as a settlement north of Jericho and Phasaelis. The Peutinger map (2nd century CE), recorded a distance of 12 miles between Jericho and Archelais (Miller 1962: Segmentum X: 1-2), and such is its relative location also in the Madaba map (6th century CE [Avi-Yonah 1953: 140 and pl. 5]).

A document from the beginning of the Byzantine era (Russell 1980: 50) states that the place was affected, with several other settlements, by the 363 CE earthquakes. Avi-Yonah (1976: 80) identified it mistakenly with Migdalsenna, and identified Archelais in the village of 'Aujah et-Tahtah (Russell 1980: 30).

The place was partially excavated by Hizmi (1993; 2008a; 2008b) and surveyed and remapped by our Survey team.

Additional Bibliography: Conder and Kitchener 1882: 392; Abel 1913: 236; Dalman 1913: 74; Alt 1927: 31.

Site 143: Kh. 'Aujah el-Foqa

We have identified this site as 'Ataroth of the book of Josh (16: 7-8, and see Zertal et al. 2009: 120-121). This assertion is based on the following arguments:

First, 'Ataroth is situated on the border of Manasseh and Ephraim, starting east of Shechem and descending to Jericho and the Jordan. According to the course of the border from Shechem south-eastward 'Ataroth is placed between Yanoah (Kh. Yanon?) and Naratha (Na'aran). Alt's first suggestion (Alt 1926: 33) of identifying it with Kh. 'Aujah et-Tahtah (Site 146), is reasonable because the place is situated on the probable border. On the other hand, the later propositions by Alt (1927: 32), Elliger (1930: 279), Glueck (1951: 419) and Kallay (1971: 165-166) produce an irrational route for of the border (see above in Site 23). The direct line to Jericho rests on convenient topographical routes, unlike the other proposed line. Therefore we have proposed to put 'Ataroth back into the Wadi 'Aujah vicinity and to identify it in the new site of Kh. 'Aujah el-Foqa.

Secondly, the site itself is a fortified and planned Iron Age city, located on a prominent summit (fitting the essence of its name – 'Ataroth [crown]). The place was built a priori as an impressive city for the sake of presence and government, as suggested in the detailed publication (Zertal et al. 2009: 120-121).

Thirdly, apparently the area and the city were planned as government centre, settled on the main water source at 'Ein 'Aujah. Testimony to this is the Iron Age fortress in Wadi 'Aujah (Site 140). The location is north and below the site of Kh. 'Aujah el-Foqa, and it may also be linked to the site at E.P. 44 (Site 125).

Site 146: Kh. 'Aujah et-Tahtah

Additional identification of 'Ataroth by Alt (1926: 33), is based on the fact of the place being located on the logical border between Manasseh and Ephraim: see discussion and bibliography for Site 23 – Tell esh-Sheikh Diyab.

PART TWO

DESCRIPTION OF THE SITES

CHAPTER THREE

NAHAL AND FASAEL VALLEY

LANDSCAPE UNIT 31

34. Wadi Fasael, an engraving by Van de Velde (in Schiller 1977).

Site 1: 19-16/74/1

ELEVATION POINT -290

Israel grid: 1974/1640
UTM grid: 7361/5509
Elevation: 290 m b.s.l., 10 m a.s.a.
Name: nearest place
Site type: Prehistoric
Area: 3 dunams (3000 sq. m)
Topography: low ridge
Rock type: flint conglomerate
Soil type: Lisan marl
Soil quality: 1
Cultivation: none
Cisterns: none
Water source: Nahal Tirzah (104), 1.5 km distant
Road: Beit She'an–Jericho (B10), 1.5 km distant
Visit: December 2008; 56 sherds

A site on a slope of a low ridge in the Jordan Valley plain, near the meeting point of the road to the Tirzah reservoir with the border fence, about 2 km east-north-east of Yafit.

The site has been disturbed by quarrying activity and there is much raw and worked flint in it.

No construction remains have been found. The pottery was collected from the slope.

Pottery: Early Bronze – 5%; Iron II – 4%; Late Roman-Byzantine – 52%; Medieval – 23%; Ottoman – 10%; Modern – 6%.
Flint: 111 items from the Pre-Pottery Neolithic B period (see Appendix A).
Additional surveys: none.

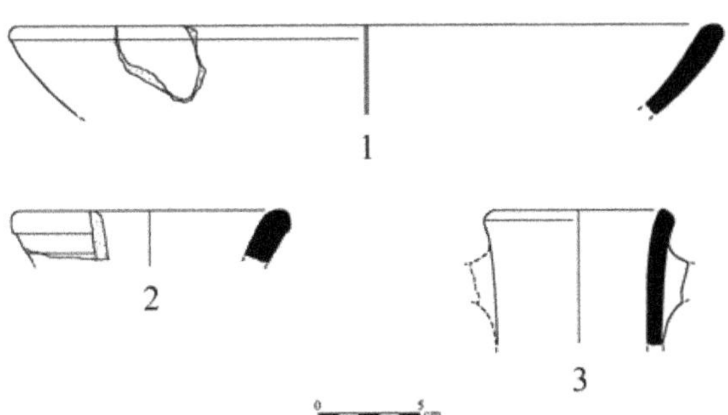

35. Pottery from **E.P.** -290: 1. Bowl, rd, MA; 2. Jar, buff, mod; 3. Jar, rd, MA.

Site 2: 19-16/63/1

EL-MARMALEH

Israel grid: 1969/1639
UTM grid: 7355/5508
Elevation: 258 m b.s.l., 0 m a.s.a.
Name: nearest place
Site type: water reservoirs
Area: 5 dunams (5000 sq. m)
Topography: uneven plain
Rock type: Dead Sea group
Soil type: Lisan marl
Soil quality: 3
Cultivation: none
Cisterns: none
Water source: Nahal Tirzah (104), 2.2 km distant
Road: Beit She'an–Jericho (B10), 500 m distant
Visit: March 2002; 10 sherds

A site of ruined water reservoirs in the Jordan Valley plain, about 500 m east of the Beit She'an–Jericho road.

A newly planted date-palm plantation covers the unpaved road leading to the site, and the area has been badly disturbed by earthmoving operations of the IDF and the valley settlers. A new earthen rampart near E.P. -258 ruined the ancient pools. The oval enclosure is about 35 m across with a recess in it – perhaps a remnant of one of the pools.

The site was first published in the Hebrew version of Volume 4 of the Survey (Zertal and Bar 2017: site 103), and has been revised after a change in the borders included in the different volumes, and after another visit to the site.

The members of the Emergency Survey (1968) report: "Remains of structures and two pools. One is round, 25 m in diameter, and the other one elliptical measuring 28×13 m. Pottery is from the Roman-Byzantine period." (Bar-Adon 1972: site 9).

Pottery: Late Roman-Byzantine – 100%; only body shards.
Additional surveys: Bar-Adon 1972: site 9.

Site 3: 18-16/83/1

ELEVATION POINT 111

Israel grid: 1888/1630
UTM grid: 7275/5498
Elevation: 111 m a.s.l., 0 m a.s.a.
Name: nearest place
Site type: courtyards
Area: 2 dunams (2000 sq. m)
Topography: slope and spur
Rock type: Judea group
Soil type: terra rossa
Soil quality: 2
Cultivation: none
Cisterns: none
Water source: Fasael Springs (183), 1.1 km distant
Road: Phasaelis-Neapolis (C41), next to the site
Visit: March 2000; 10 sherds

A site on a moderate spur, 1 km south of Ma'ale Ephraim. The older road from the Jordan Valley to the village passes close to the north.

In the northern part is a square structure 5×5 m built of large stones, now dismantled. Next to it are two rounded courtyards: the diameter of the eastern one is 12 m, and there are remains of small stone-built structures. The smaller western yard is 6 m in diameter.

The sherd scatter is small, and apparently the site is related to Iron Age and Roman period roads (see also Rujm Abu-Mukheir, Site no. 5), but the dating of the courtyards is not clear.

Pottery: Chalcolithic (?) – 7%; Iron I – 15%; Hellenistic-Early Roman – 78%.
Flint: 3 items (see Appendix A).
Additional surveys: Bar-Adon 1972: site 10b; Spanier 1992: site 22.

Site 4: 18-16/82/1

MUGHUR EL-HABLEH

Israel grid: 1885/1627
UTM grid: 7271/5495
Elevation: 40 m b.s.l., 80 m a.s.a.
Name: nearest place
Site type: small, Prehistoric
Area: 1 dunam (1000 sq. m)
Topography: shoulder above wadi
Rock type: Judea group
Soil type: stony-desert
Soil quality: 3
Cultivation: none
Cisterns: none
Water source: Fasael Springs (183), 700 m distant
Road: Phasaelis-Neapolis (C41), 700 m distant
Visits: February 2000, 2008; 80 sherds

A small site on a shoulder, north and above Fasael Springs.

It is a concentration of flint artefacts, basalt and ceramic, with remains of walls and new pens without coherent plan.

The place appears to be a seasonal encampment site with a few structures.

Pottery: Early Bronze I-II – 70%; Middle Bronze II – 6%; Iron I – 4%; Hellenistic-Early Roman – 4%; Late Roman-Byzantine – 6%; Medieval – 2%; Ottoman-Modern – 4%; Unidentified – 4%.
Flint: 148 items, Upper Palaeolithic (high probability) and EBA (possible), see Appendix A.
Additional surveys: none.
Additional bibliography: Bar 2014: site 82.

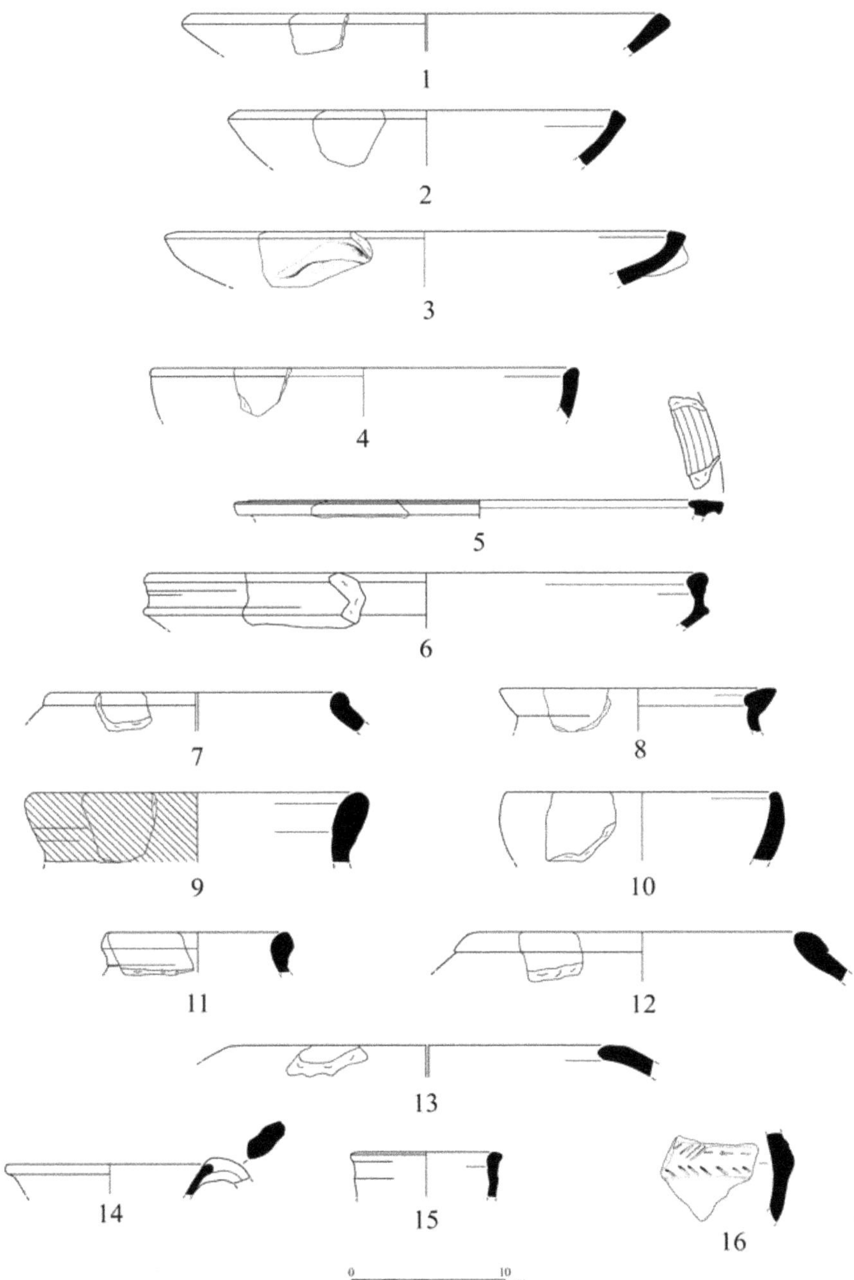

36. Pottery from **Mughur el-Hableh**: 1. Bowl, gr, EB; 2. Bowl, gr, MB II; 3. Bowl, lt br, MA; 4. Bowl, lt br, EB; 5. Bowl, lt br, Rom-Byz; 6. Bowl, gr, Ott/mod; 7. Folded rim CP, gr, MB II; 8. Jar, gr, MB II; 9. Pithos, gr, blk slip, IA I; 10. Bow-rim jar, buff, EB I; 11. Jar, lt br, Hel; 12. HM jar, rd, EB; 13. HM jar, gr, EB; 14. Jug, lt br, Hel-ER; 15. Jug, rd, Rom; 16. Sherd (CP?) herring-bone pattern dec, br, MB II.

Site 5: 18-16/92/1

RUJM ABU MUKHEIR

Israel grid: 1897/1625
UTM grid: 7284/5494
Elevation: 10 m b.s.l., 100 m a.s.a.
Name: on map
Site type: fortress
Area: 1 dunam (1000 sq. m)
Topography: spur
Rock type: Judea group
Soil type: brown forest
Soil quality: 2
Cultivation: none
Cisterns: none
Water source: Nahal Fasael (181), 700 m distant
Road: Phasaelis-Neapolis (C41), next to the site
Visits: December 2003, 2008, 2015 and more; 60 sherds

A fortress by the old road from the Jordan Valley to Ma'ale Ephraim, and about 2 km east of the settlement.

The site is on a spur with a good lookout to the east, and is about 320 m above the Jordan Valley. The place is mentioned for the first time by the British Survey (Conder and Kitchener 1882: 402) and was surveyed by the Emergency Survey (Bar-Adon 1972: site 10a). In 1975 it was excavated on behalf of the Israel Antiquities Authority, an excavation headed by Z. Yeivin (1992: 156-157).

Remains of a round tower were exposed, built with fieldstones, in the dry construction method laid over the bedrock. It had two circles: outer (17.2 m in diameter) and inner (8.7 m). The area between the circles was divided into eight cells by radial walls about 1.2 m thick. An oblique support wall 5 m high supported the tower from the outside at an incline of 70 degrees.

The cells between the circles were paved with small and medium-sized stones; storage jars were found on the paving. An entrance opened from one of the cells to the inner circle, which was bisected by a wall. Another opening in the western end connected the parts of the inner circle. No entrances were found from the outside.

The excavator dated the tower to Iron Age III, but it should be noted that Iron Age II sherds indicate its construction over a more ancient site.

During the Manasseh Hill Country Survey additional walls were found outside the tower, covered by the excavation spoil. Zertal (1995) proposed that a square structure once existed, similarly to other fortresses in the Jordan Valley (Kh. Umm Ghazal and el-Makhruq (2) [Zertal 2008: site 82 and Zertal and Bar 2017: site 73 respectively]), where towers with adjacent square structures were found. These fortresses are located by the roads from the Jordan Valley to the centre of the Kingdom of Israel (Shechem). Because similar circular towers are characteristic of Ammonite architecture, Zertal (1995: 261-265; 2008: 62)

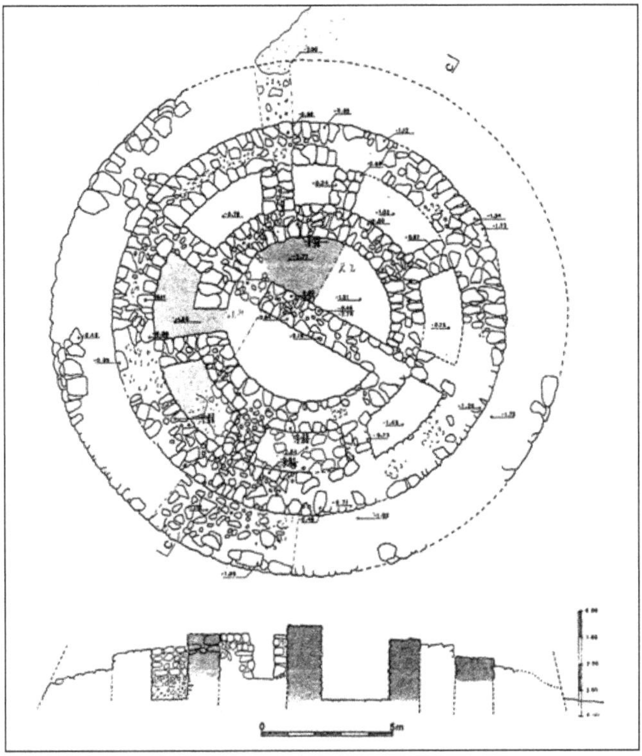

37. Plan of **Rujm Abu Mukheir** (Yeivin 1992, illustration 3).

38. Aerial view of the circular tower of the *Malfuf* type at **Rujm Abu Mukheir**, 2012. Note the circular construction and the inner division of the rooms. Such towers were discovered in the Ammonite Kingdom and in the east of the Manasseh Hill Country (A. Solomon).

proposed that their presence west of the River Jordan hints at an Ammonite penetration.

About 200 m to the south-east are remains of a structure on a hillock with a small Roman period sherd scatter. This structure may have been mentioned in the Emergency Survey (Bar-Adon 1972: site 10c).

Pottery: Iron II-III – 90%; Late Roman – 10% (in the adjacent structure).
Additional surveys: Bar-Adon 1972: sites 10a, 10c; Spanier 1992: sites 23, 24.

♦ ♦ ♦

Site 6: 18-16/82/2

ELEVATION POINT 55

Israel grid: 1885/1624
UTM grid: 7272/5493
Elevation: 50 m a.s.l., 100 m a.s.a.
Name: nearest place
Site type: small
Area: 3 dunams (3000 sq. m)
Topography: slope
Rock type: Judea group
Soil type: stony desert
Soil quality: 2
Cultivation: none
Cisterns: none
Water source: Fasael Springs (183), 500 m distant
Road: Phasaelis- Fasael springs (C47), 600 m distant
Visits: March 2000, 2007; 60 sherds

This is a site on a moderate slope at the top of the saddle of E.P. 55, north and above Nahal Fasael.

There is a scatter of flint artefacts including adzes over a small area. Remains of a constructed courtyard apparently belonged to the site. The rest of the

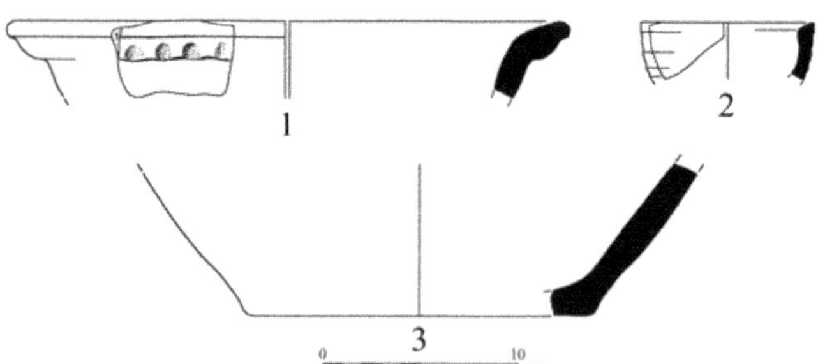

39. Pottery from E.P. 55: 1. Bowl, br, thumbed rope-ornamentation, Chal-EB; 2. Bowl, lt br, LR; 3. Jar base, gr, Chal-EB.

structures were dismantled, and now there is only a cultivated field.

The pottery find includes flat bases and rope ornamentations.

Pottery: Chalcolithic/Early Bronze I – 90%; Late Roman – 5%; Medieval – 5%.
Flint: 50 items, Chalcolithic (see Appendix A).
Additional surveys: none.
Bibliography: Bar 2014: site 85.

♦ ♦ ♦

Site 7: 18-16/82/4

MUGHUR ED-DUQANEH (1)

Israel grid: 1888/1622
UTM grid: 7275/5491
Elevation: 40 m b.s.l., 70 m a.s.a.
Name: in map
Site type: caves with sherd scatter
Area: 10 dunams (1 ha)
Topography: upper slope
Rock type: Judea group
Soil type: brown forest
Soil quality: 4
Cultivation: none
Cisterns: none
Water source: Nahal Fasael (181), 300 m distant
Road: Phasaelis- Fasael Springs (C47), 300 m distant
Visit: April 2010; 160 sherds

A site of shallow caves and rock shelters along a low cliff, on a ridge north-west above Nahal Fasael and about 2.5 km north-north-west of Fasael. An unpaved road leading to the settlement of Ma'ale Ephraim ascends from the wadi and a narrow ravine descends from the east.

The south-west to north-east cliff is about 200 m long and about 5 m in average height. The ceilings of the caves and the rock shelters collapsed in antiquity, and the accumulated soot testifies to flock husbandry and dwelling, according to the testimonies of Guèrin (1874: 229) and Van de Velde (1854, II: 312).

The courtyards which were built on the slope in front of the caves were destroyed by the track, and there is a moderate scatter of sherds there.

70 m to the east is a terrace wall made of medium-sized and large stones, with an additional small cave and two rock-hewn oval installations (30 cm across).

Similar caves sites characterize Nahal Fasael.

Pottery: Middle Bronze II – 3% (body sherds); Iron I – 1%; Iron II – 3%; Late

Roman – 50%; Byzantine – 28%; Medieval – 15%.
Stone: five basalt items, including a weight (see Fig. 42: 10-11).
Additional surveys: none.

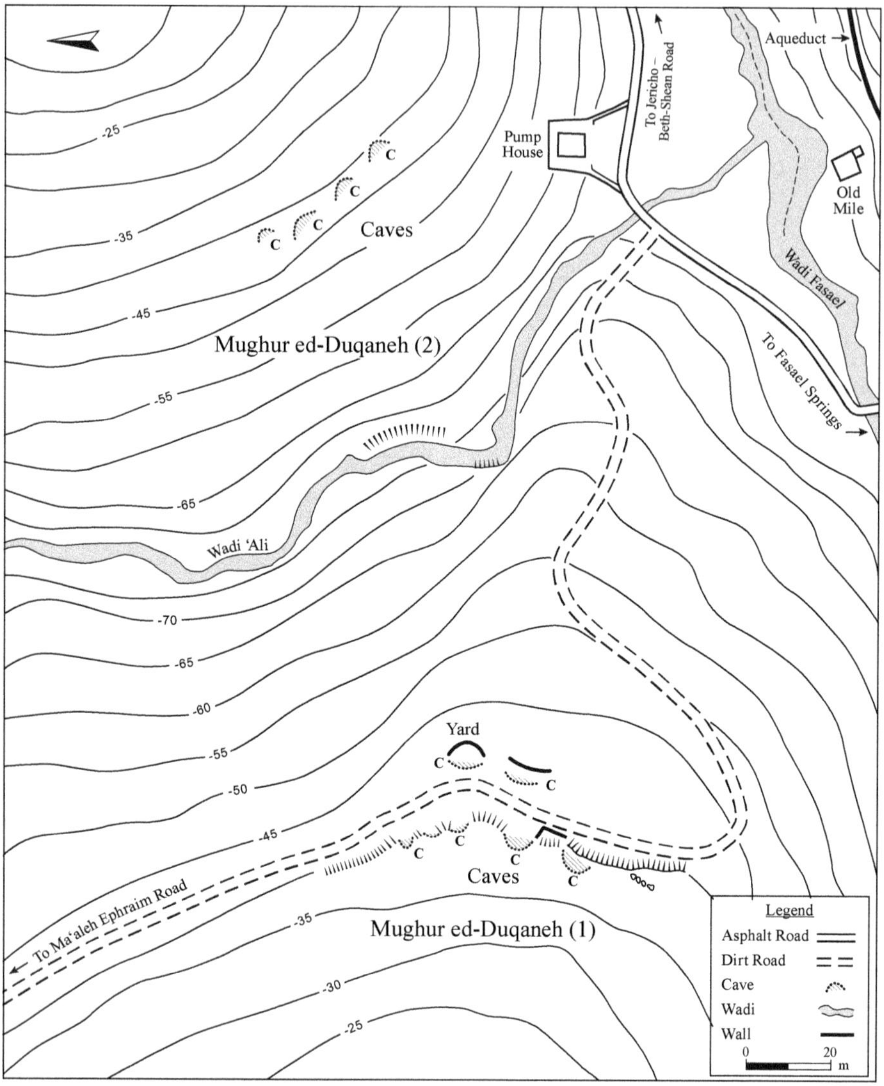

40. Plan of **Mughur ed-Duqaneh** (1) and (2).

41. Aerial view west of the caves at **Mughur ed-Duqaneh (1)**. The caves, which are practically rock shelters, are mentioned by 19th century travellers, 2012 (A. Solomon).

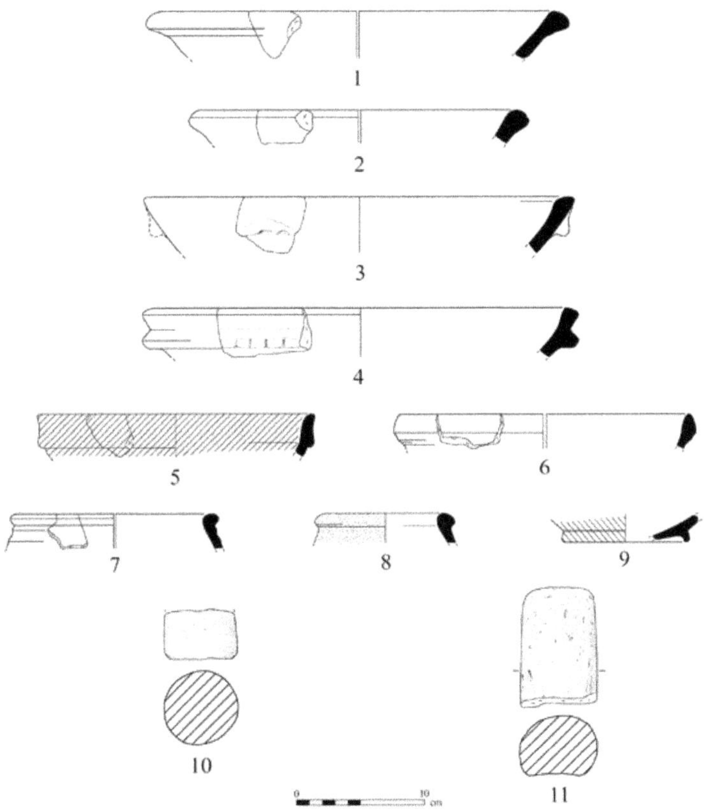

42. Finds from **Mughur ed-Duqaneh (1)**: 1. Basin, dk br, MA; 2. Basin, dk br, Byz; 3-4. Bowls, lt br, MA; 5. Bowl, gr, rd slip, LR-Byz; 6. CP, dk br, IA I-II; 7. Jar, dk br, LR (?); 8. Jug, dk br, wh wash, IA II; 9. Bowl, dk br, dk glazing (inside), purple slip (outside), MA; 10. Weight (?), basalt; 11. Pestle, basalt.

Site 8: 18-16/92/3

MUGHUR ED-DUQANEH (2)

Israel grid: 1895/1622
UTM grid: 7282/5490
Elevation: 40 m b.s.l., 50 m a.s.a.
Name: in map
Site type: caves and courtyards
Area: 1 dunam (1000 sq. m)
Topography: slope
Rock type: Judea group
Soil type: brown forest
Soil quality: 4
Cultivation: none
Cisterns: none
Water source: Nahal Fasael (181), 200 m distant
Road: Phasaelis- Fasael Springs (C47), 200 m distant
Visit: April 2010; 250 sherds

A dwelling cave on a slope on the northern bank of Nahal Fasael, north-east of Tahunet el-Fusayil (Site 15).

The cliff is about 120 m long and is 5-6 m high, descending from west to east. Along it about eight caves and rock shelters for dwelling and flock husbandry, indicated by the smoothed ceilings. After collapses the caves became rock shelters. In front of them are large stone-built terraces which supported courtyards. A modern track ascends to the site over a high wall and rockfall, and is apparently built on top of an ancient pathway. There is a considerable sherd scatter in front of the caves.

43. Aerial view north at the **Mughur ed-Duqaneh (2)**. Note the courtyards in front of the dwelling caves, 2012 (A. Solomon).

This site served a similar purpose, and may be from the same time, as Mughur ed-Duqaneh (1 [Site 7]).

According to the find, the caves were abandoned at the end of the Mamluk era, but were in partial use afterwards (Van de Velde 1854, II: 312).

Pottery: Iron II – 5%; Hellenistic-Early Roman – 2%; Late Roman – 20%; Byzantine – 56%; Early Moslem – 1%; Medieval – 12%; Ottoman – 4%.
Stone: three basalt grinding stones.
Additional surveys: none.

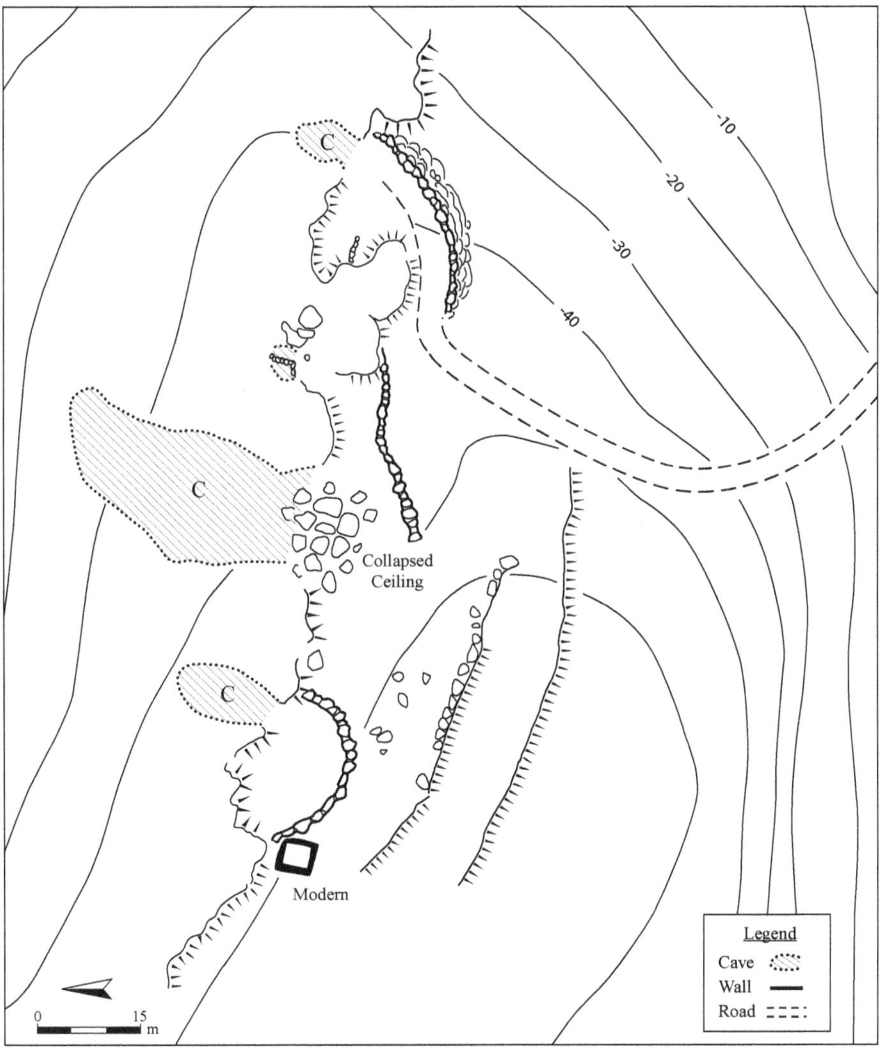

44. Plan of **Mughur ed-Duqaneh (2)**.

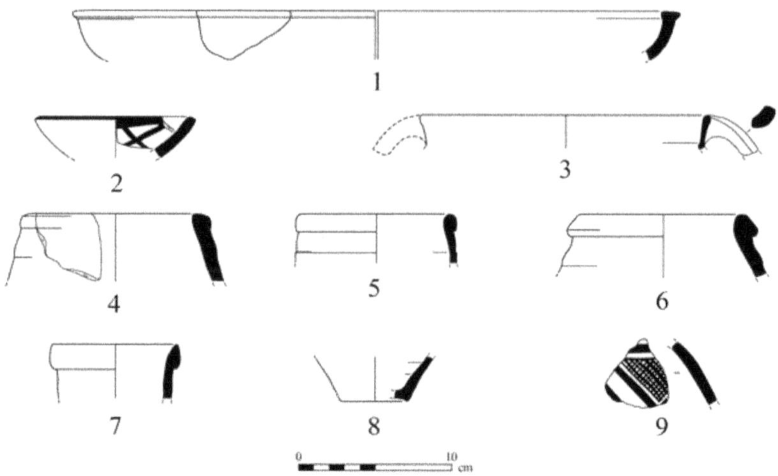

45. Pottery from **Mughur ed-Duqaneh (2)**: 1. Bowl, dk br, IA II; 2. Bowl, dk br, purple dec, MA; 3. CP, dk br, Rom; 4. Jar, lt br, IA II (?); 5. Jar, dk br, Rom-Byz; 6. Jar, gr, Hel; 7. Jug, dk br, Rom; 8. Jug base, dk br, Rom; 9. Jug (body sherd), buff, purple dec, MA.

◆ ◆ ◆

Site 9:

SURVEY OF LATE QUATERNARY SITES IN WADI FASAEL

At the end of the 1970s, A. N. Goring-Morris (1980) conducted a prehistoric survey along the banks of Nahal Fasael. The area from Fasael Springs to the outlet of the narrow ravine into the Jordan Valley opposite Fasael village was surveyed. Ten prehistoric sites have been discovered; see description in Appendix B.

◆ ◆ ◆

Site 10:

THE WATER SYSTEM OF THE FASAEL VALLEY

This is an area of built aqueducts and water reservoirs along Nahal Fasael and in the Fasael Valley, carrying water from the spring to the fields and the city of Phasaelis.

All parts of the aqueducts have been measured and redrawn.

See description and comprehensive discussion in Appendix D.

Site 11: 19-16/12/2

RAMPART SITE

Israel grid: 1915/1622
UTM grid: 7302/5490
Elevation: 210 m b.s.l., 0 m a.s.a.
Name: given by the survey
Site type: tower and courtyard
Area: 2 dunams (2000 sq. m)
Topography: plain
Rock type: alluvial plain
Soil type: marl
Soil quality: 2
Cultivation: none
Cisterns: none
Water source: Nahal Fasael (181), 1 km distant
Road: Phasaelis-Neapolis (C41), next to the site
Visits: December 2006, 2008, 2012; 26 sherds

The site includes an enclosure and tower, and is in the Nahal Fasael (Wadi Rashash) floodplain, 1 km north-north-west from the centre of Fasael. The northern part is covered by the 10-m ramp of the new road from Fasael junction to Ma'ale Ephraim. A 24×20 m enclosure or courtyard rises about 2.5 m above the surrounding plain. The southern wall extends 20 m eastwards. In the northern part of the enclosure is a rectangular structure, measuring about 10×6 m, perhaps a tower. The wall around it is built of two rows of large and medium-sized stones. Another platform raises the tower by 1.5 m above the courtyard. A piece of plaster hints at the existence of a pool or other water installation.

The site might have served a military function, such as guarding the fields in the vicinity.

This is perhaps a site from the Emergency Survey (coordinates 1914/1624; Bar-Adon 1972: site 11) partly excavated by Yosef Porath. A large enclosure and courtyard were found, together with a dwelling wing. The residence wing included two rooms paved with pebbles, one of them a pool, measuring 1.2×1.1 m, with a plastered step. The finds were dated to the 1st century BCE. An Alexander Jannaeus coin was found on the surface. The plan of the site was published in the Emergency Survey, but no plans were published from the salvage excavation.

Pottery (in our survey): Iron II (body sherds) – 4%; Early Roman – 24%; Late Roman – 57%; Byzantine – 15%.
Additional surveys: Bar-Adon 1972: site 11.
Additional Bibliography: "A site in the Fasael Area", *HA* 50 (1974: 9-10); Porath 1985b: site C1.

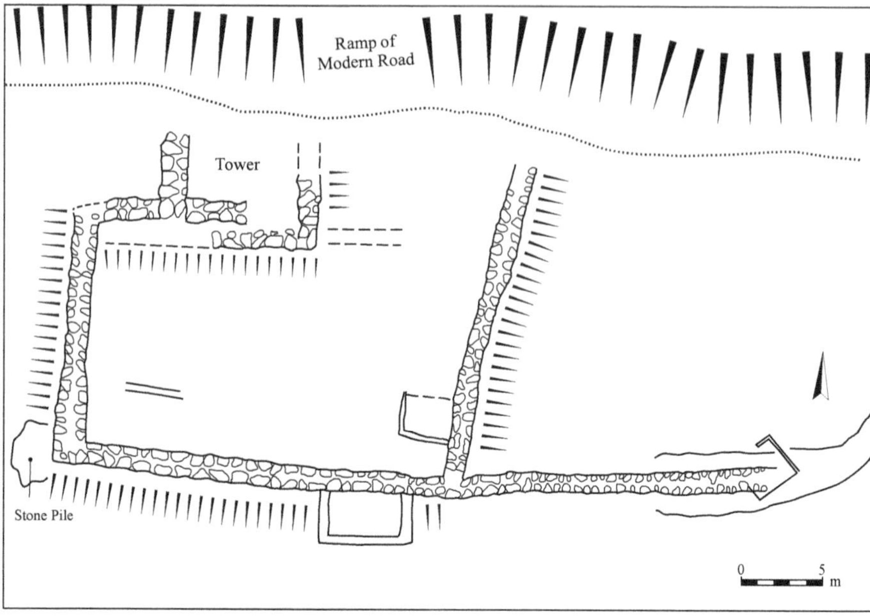

46. Plan of the **Rampart Site.**

47. The **Rampart Site:** view to the south-east from the road rampart, 2009 (M. Einav).

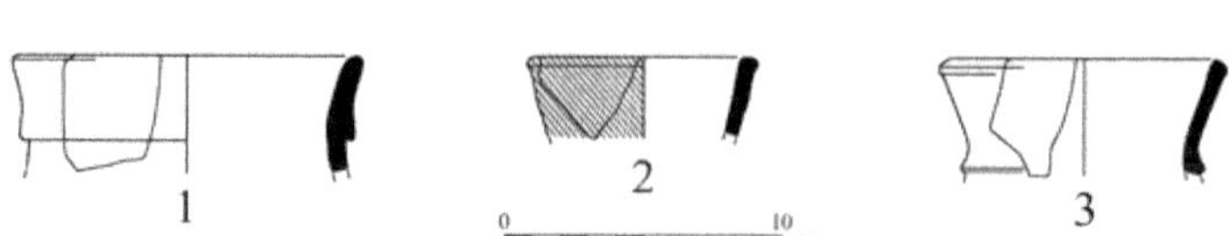

48. Pottery from the **Rampart Site:** 1, 3. Jars, buff, Rom; 2. Jug, br, blk slip, Rom-Byz.

Site 12: 18-16/82/3

FASAEL SPRINGS

Israel grid: 1884/1620
UTM grid: 7271/5488
Elevation: 50 m b.s.l., 70 m b.s.a.
Name: nearest place
Site type: cluster of sites by springs
Area: 300 dunams (30 ha)
Topography: valley
Rock type: Judea Group
Soil type: marl
Soil quality: 3
Cultivation: none
Cisterns: none
Water source: Fasael Springs (183), at the site
Road: Phasaelis- Fasael Springs (C47), next to the site
Visits: November 2008, 2012 and more; 240 sherds

A concentration of springs and caves in an inner valley at the confluence of Wadi Rashash and Wadi Zananir. Nahal Fasael (Wadi Rashash) flows eastward from the site, and the aqueducts starting from the springs and dams lead eastward to Kh. Fusayil and Tell esh-Sheikh Diyab. Below are details of the sites and structures around the valley:

1. Water springs and dam: in this area, in which sherds are scattered, the spring water was collected and fed into the various aqueducts. In the absence of settlement it is difficult to date them, but the latest one is a Jordanian or British period concrete duct. Sections of older stone ducts connecting to the main stone aqueduct leading eastward along the wadi have also been found.

   The modern dam is built of stone and cement on top of old foundations. It is about 30 m long and 1.5 m thick. Perpendicular to it to the west is a stone wall, possibly an even older dam. West of it, in the wadi channel, are two flowing springs. For a more thorough discussion see Appendix D.
2. Mughur er-Rashash: three caves, south-west and about 50 m above the springs. Their average dimensions are: opening about 8 m wide, depth about 5 m and entrance height about 2 m. Iron Age I-II, Roman, Byzantine and Early Moslem period sherds were found in the rubble in front of the caves. The charred ceilings testify to residence and flock husbandry.
3. A nearby structure: over the slope below the caves is a three-roomed structure built of cut stones. Its location on a bulge in the slope is a good lookout to the valley of the springs and its vicinity. Nearby the structure are Early Roman sherds.
4. Mughur Hableh: north-east of and opposite er-Rashash caves, across Wadi er-Rashash, in the cliffs, well up in the slope, is another cluster of caves.
5. A Neolithic-Chalcolithic site: over a small hillock, above and north of the

principal spring, are wall sections which are not sconty to allow a plan drawing. About 40 sherds were gathered, among them a ledged rim bowl, holemouth jar rims, a flat base with a mat impression and body sherds with rope decoration.

6. Prehistoric sites stretching from the springs and along the wadi (see Appendix B).

Pottery: Neolithic/Chalcolithic – 18%; Iron I-II – 5%; Roman-Byzantine – 50%; Early Moslem – 5%; Medieval – 12%; Ottoman – 10%.
Additional survey (in parts 5 and 6): Goring-Morris 1980: 8.
Bibliography: Van de Velde 1854, II: 310-312; Conder and Kitchener 1882: 392; Tristram 1865: 238-241; Abel 1913: 235; Guèrin 1874: 229; Ilan 1973: 285-287; Spanier 1992: 239; Markus 1992: 123-126; Bar 2014: site 86.

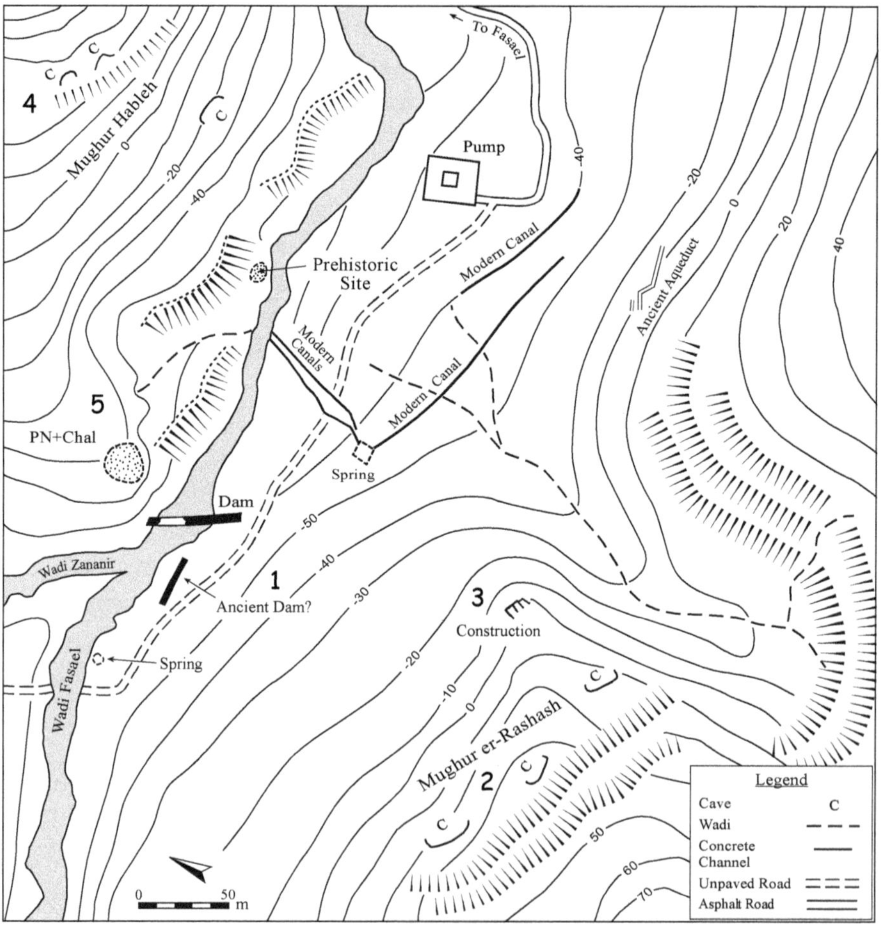

49. Plan of the vicinity of **Fasael Springs**.

50. Aerial view westward to er-Rashash Caves (south-west of Fasael springs), 2012. At the bottom right of the photo can be seen Fasael pumping station (A. Solomon).

51. View south-west of one of the fountains of **Fasael Springs**. Note the cement aqueducts (M. Einav).

Site 13: 18-16/92/4

MUGHUR ED-DUQANEH (3)

Israel grid: 1899/1620
UTM grid: 7286/5488
Elevation: 90 m b.s.l., 40 m a.s.a.
Name: in map
Site type: cave and courtyard
Area: 1 dunam (1000 sq. m)
Topography: slope
Rock type: Judea Group
Soil type: stony-desert
Soil quality: 1
Cultivation: none
Cisterns: none
Water source: Nahal Fasael (181), 200 m distant
Road: Phasaelis-Fasael Springs (C47), 200 m distant
Visit: May 2010; 53 sherds

The site is a cave and courtyard on a steep slope above and north of Nahal Fasael, about 2 km west-north-west of the centre of Fasael.

Along the steep slope bordering the stream valley is a cliff about 4 m high descending from north-west to south-east. In its centre is a medium-sized cave about 8 m deep and about 4 m wide. In front of it is an oval courtyard about 15 m across. The wall supporting the levelled yard is built of several courses of large and medium-sized stones with supports. Next to the main entrance to the cave is another smaller cave. The sherd scatter mainly testifies to years of habitation during the Early Roman and Byzantine periods. There are a few

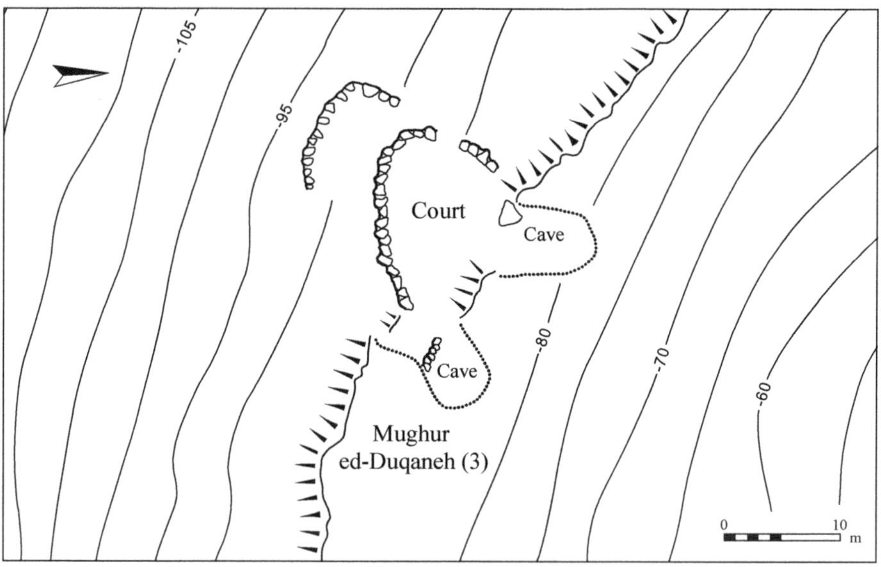

52. Plan of **Mughur ed-Duqaneh (3)**.

sherds from earlier times. This cave adds to the other complexes of Mughur ed-Duqaneh (1) and (2) (Sites 7, 8 above), situated west of the cave.

Pottery: Middle Bronze II (?) – 4%; Iron II – 3%; Early Roman – 18%; Late Roman – 56%; Byzantine – 19%.
Stone: basalt grinding stone.
Additional surveys: none.

♦ ♦ ♦

Site 14: 19-16/02/1

FASAEL (1)

Israel grid: 1909/1620
UTM grid: 7296/5488
Elevation: 200 m b.s.l., 50 m b.s.a.
Name: nearest place
Site type: large
Area: 15 dunams (1.5 ha)
Topography: slope above wadi
Rock type: Judea Group
Soil type: stony-desert
Soil quality: 3
Cultivation: none
Cisterns: none
Water source: Nahal Fasael (181), 500 m distant
Road: Phasaelis-Neapolis (C41), 300 m distant
Visits: January 2000, 2008 and many more, excavations: 2013-2014; 2800 sherds

A large site on the north bank of Nahal Fasael, about 200 m south of the Fasael reservoir.

The settlement extended over the low slopes descending southward to the wadi, disturbed in recent decades by bulldozing. Surviving structures are built of two rows of medium-sized stones. The largest surviving structure is 10×4 m. There are additional wall segments, structures and sherd scatters – mostly small fragments.

The site was one in a cluster of Chalcolithic settlements in the area, already noted by Glueck (1951: 416).

The site was excavated by Bar in 2013-2014 (Bar et al. 2014), and re-surveyed again in 2014 as part of a survey class of the University of Haifa. A four-stratum Chalcolithic site was revealed. While the cultural attribution of the basal stratum (S 4) is still obscure, the architecture and finds from the later strata attest to a Ghassulian village of the Chalcolithic period, the earliest site of this period so far noted in the Wadi Fasael floodplain.

Stratum I was the main horizon exposed. The main feature excavated was a 4×10 m broad room house, with the well preserved threshold of an entrance and a rounded corner installation. The walls were 65 cm thick, and the masonry was of two rows of medium fieldstones. The almost complete absence of additional collapsed building materials suggests that the preserved walls were stone foundations for mud brick walls that did not survive.

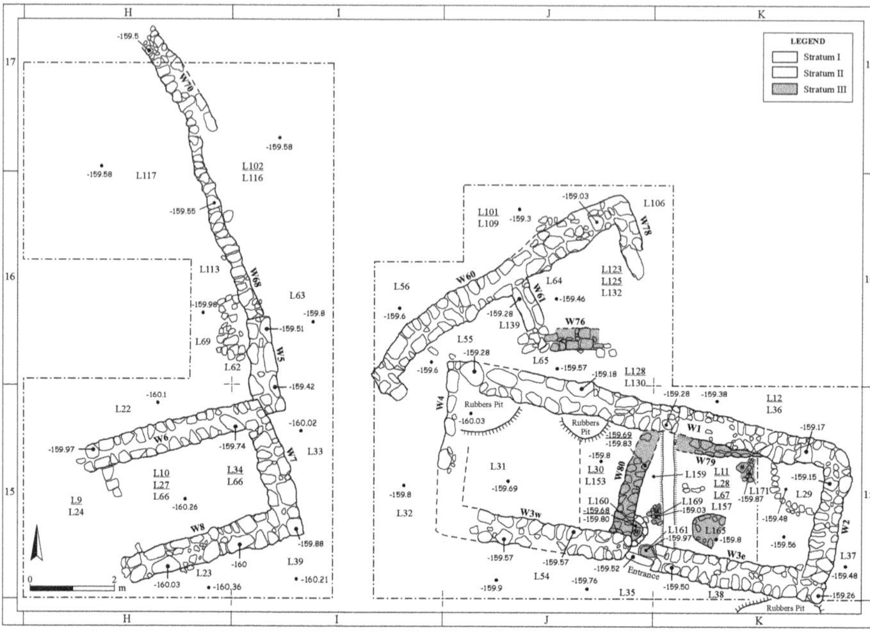

53. Plan of the excavations at **Fasael (1)** (after Bar et al. 2014: fig. 6).

54. Aerial photo of Strata I-II at **Fasael (1)** at the end of the 2013 excavation season (after Bar et al. 2014: fig. 3).

The finds from the dig were typical of the Ghassulian culture of the Chalcolithic period, and included indicative pottery and flint tools (Bar et al. 2014: 186-193).

Pottery: Chalcolithic – 94%; Early Bronze – 1%; Late Roman-Byzantine – 3%; Medieval – 1%; Ottoman – 1%.
Flint: 37 items, Chalcolithic (see Appendix A).
Additional surveys: Glueck 1951: 416.
Additional Bibliography: Bar 2014: site 87.

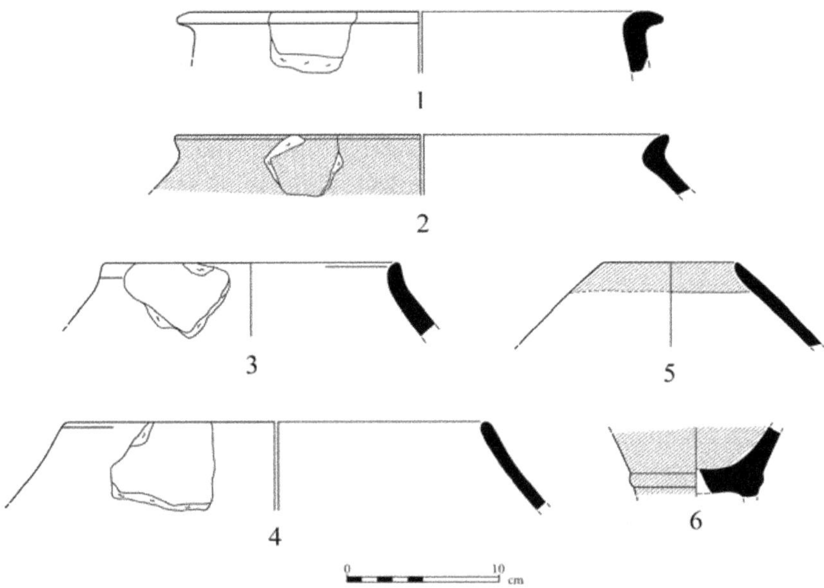

55. Pottery from the survey of **Fasael (1)**, all Chal: 1. Bowl, lt br; 2. Jar, br, rd slip; 3. Jar, br; 4. HM jar, br; 5. HM jar, lt br, rd slip; 6. Chalice, lt br, rd slip.

Site 15: 18-16/92/2

THAHUNET EL-FUSAYIL

Israel grid: 1891/1620
UTM grid: 7278/5488
Elevation: 130 m b.s.l., 0 m a.s.a.
Name: historical and in map
Site type: ancient mill
Area: 1 dunam (1000 sq. m)
Topography: stream valley
Rock type: Judea Group
Soil type: marl
Soil quality: 2
Cultivation: none
Cisterns: none
Water source: Nahal Fasael (181) , at the site
Road: Phasaelis- Fasael Springs (C47), next to the site
Visits: April 2010, 2012 and more; 60 sherds

An ancient mill at the centre of Nahal Fasael (Wadi Rashash), about 3 km west of Fasael. The mill was fed by the aqueducts along the wadi. It is built on a fairly steep slope, while the shaft rests on the slope and the halls are built on an artificial platform on the south bank of the wadi.

Plan: the building contains two halls, a shaft and water feeding duct.

The building and halls (Figs. 4.4-4.8 in Appendix D): the bottom structure length is 11.5 m, its original width was 5.4 m and the walls are about 80 cm thick. It is built of medium-sized cut stones, thickly plastered outside. Three pillars, each 1 m thick, protrude about 40 cm from the outer northern wall of the building. Two pillars or protuberances were added to the eastern wall and another strengthening pillar in the south-western corner during repairs to the south wall. Strengthening extensions have also been added at the bases of the pillars (Fig. 4.4 in Appendix D).

The structure has two vaulted entrances in the northern part of the eastern hall, one open, one blocked. The eastern, blocked, entrance is 1.5 m wide and 2 m high, and has a pointed vault. The western, open, entrance is 1.1 m wide and about 2.2 m high, and has a rounded vault. The pipe of the shaft led down to the eastern of the two halls, which is 5×4.2 m, and in the past the millstones stood there. The western hall measures 4×4 m. Both halls are roofed by a vault. The maximum height of the ceilings is 3.5 m. Both halls were lighted by small windows in the northern and western walls. The passage between the halls was also vaulted (Fig. 4.8 in Appendix D).

In the south-eastern corner of the eastern hall there is a low (30 cm) stone platform, apparently to support the millstones. A stone structure on the platform received the water flow from the shaft.

The shaft structure: This was built on the steep slope in order to receive the water from the stone aqueduct and to supply it to the mill by a channal. The original measurements of the structure, built of medium-sized cut stones, are 3.8×1.2 m on the average. In the northern part it widens slightly. The shaft structure is now completely detached from the slope and the aqueducts, standing alone as a tower. Its lower part is attached to the eastern hall.

The height of the original structure was 6.5 m from the roof of the lower building to the aqueduct (The original shaft structure rose 6.5 m above the roof of the bottom main mill building). No trace of the connection between the aqueducts and the shaft mentioned by Porath was found.

There are remains of an ancient stone structure on the north bank of Nahal Fasael, which is about 15 m wide here. This is a circle of large stones, about 6 m in diameter, with two walls projecting to east and west. The date of the structure is unknown, but it is apparent that it was connected to the ancient site in the mill area.

Porath (1985b: 39) found a stone with an unpublished Arabic inscription in the structure. According to Porath, Prof. M. Sharon dated the inscription to the Umayyad period, and particularly to the time of the learned Caliph Abd al-Malik (685-705 CE), son of Marwan I. If indeed so, the mill was probably built in the 7-8 centuries CE. However, the traveller Burchard of Mount Sion who visited Nahal Fasael at the end of the 13th century CE (the Crusader era), does not mention the mill.

In Porath's opinion (1985b: 39) in the first phase (it is not clear when, perhaps during the Umayyad period) a flour mill with a chute was erected, of the type he investigated in Wadi Qelt. In the second phase, the date of which is also unclear, a mill with a shaft was built. Porath (1985b: 184) also claims that all the flour mills in the Jordan Valley were integrated with the Early Moslem facilities. He therefore deduced that Herod, who initiated and established the agricultural arrangements in the Jordan Valley, did not make use of water power for flour milling. Porath (1985b: 39, 184) offers three possible reasons; lack of awareness and need, low water discharge of these systems, and lack of knowledge of this innovation. However, this conclusion requires re-examination.

The Survey in the mill vicinity: in April 2010 the mill area was surveyed and it appears that the original site dated from before the Roman period; a decisive majority of the sherds are from the Roman-Byzantine period, being an indirect proof of the time in which the aqueducts functioned. Sherds from the Early Moslem period, in which according to Porath, the aqueducts and the mill were built, were not found, and almost none from Medieval and later times. Despite the justified reservations from the Survey as sherds being the sole dating tool, this observation suggests earlier foundation and utilization.

Porath's description (1985b: 39-40): "An aqueduct supported by a wall in front of the mill led to the mill building. The mill was incorporated with the aqueduct without a by-pass canal. The section of the canal leading to the mill

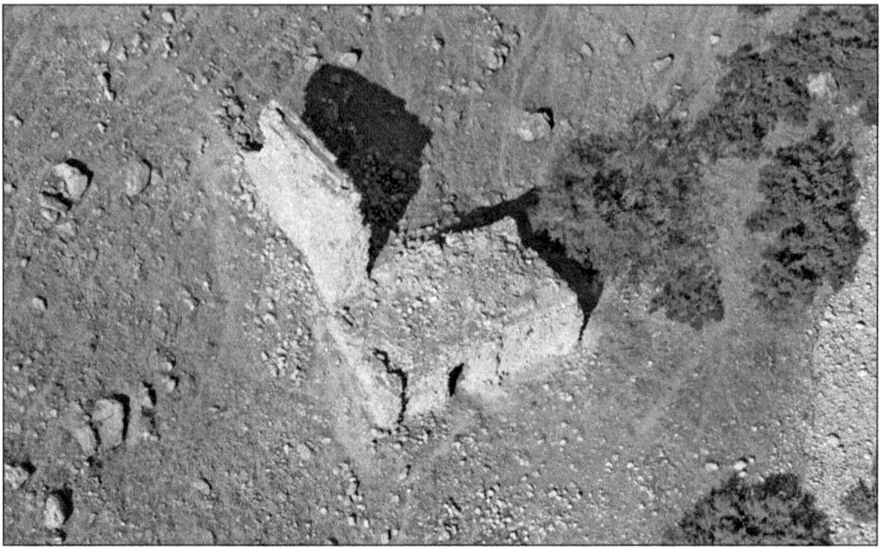

56. **Thahunet el-Fusayil**, southward aerial view, 2012 (A. Solomon).

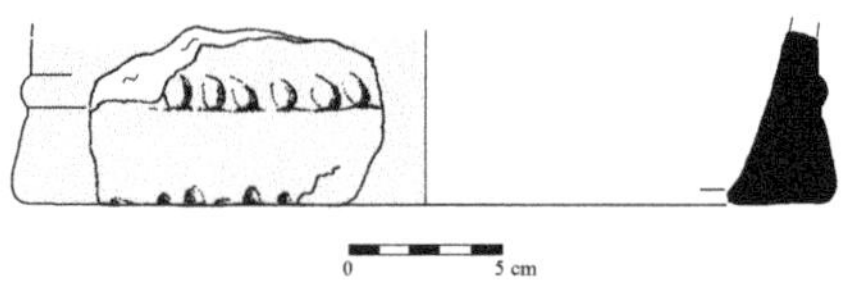

57. A find from **Thahunet el-Fusayil**: Jar base, dk br, rd slip, plastic rope dec, EB I.

was made narrower (30 cm), and in front of the wall an opening could divert the flow for maintenance. In the aqueduct section near the mill the canal was renovated by laying new plaster over the original. During the renovation the opening was blocked by stones and the new plaster covered the filling. A canal section built of stone links was exposed near the mill, but its connection to the mill had been destroyed; hence it is impossible to determine its phase and date. Two phases have been found in the mill structure: the bottom part of a rectangular structure, 2.8 m by 1.7 m with a wall 1.2 m high was from the first phase. The walls and floor were covered with plaster identical to that of the canal. In the second phase a shaft mill was built, from which remained only the bottom part of the shaft and the vaulted wheel house, although this was built in the first phase structure. In the mill floor over the vault was a circle of fieldstones which carried the bed-stone. The bed-stone was 1.8 m in diameter and the water fall height was 4.3 m. Details of the older structure did not survive to indicate its function, but its location suggests that this was a flour mill" [translated from the Hebrew].

The drawings in Porath's publication offer only partial information. In the Manasseh Hill Country Survey the mill was been measured again all around and redrawn from several perspectives. The phases found by Porath have been taken into account in the new discussion.

For complete data and thorough discussion see Appendix D.

Pottery: ancient body sherds (Early and Middle Bronze) – 5%; Early Bronze I – 2%; Roman-Byzantine – 75%; Medieval – 9%; Ottoman – 6%; Modern – 3%.
Flint: 3 items (see Appendix A).
Additional surveys: details in Appendix D.

◆ ◆ ◆

Site 16: 19-16/12/1

FASAEL (3)

Israel grid: 1913/1620
UTM grid: 7300/5489
Elevation: 180 m b.s.l., 20 m b.s.a.
Name: nearest place
Site type: caves and courtyards
Area: 2 dunams (2000 sq. m)
Topography: slope
Rock type: silicate conglomerate and Judea Group
Soil type: stony-desert
Soil quality: 2
Cultivation: none
Cisterns: none
Water source: Nahal Fasael (181), 500 m distant
Road: Phasaelis-Neapolis (C41), 300 m distant
Visit: December 2006; 50 sherds

A cave with a courtyard on a steep slope descending eastward to the Fasael Valley, about 800 m north-west of the modern agricultural village of that name. The road from Fasael junction to Ma'ale Ephraim passes about 200 m north of the site. Lower to the east is the main drainage channel of the Fasael Valley.

Shallow caves and rock shelters were located in a line of silicate conglomerate cliffs. The charred ceilings testify to residence and flock husbandry.

Over the slope in front of the caves were many finds, including sherds and modern remains (shoes, textiles, etc.). The western part of a semicircular courtyard, about 35 m in diameter, abuts the southern part of the cliff. The wall of the yard is well built of one row of three courses of large stones. A moderate number of sherds were gathered around and inside the yard.

Pottery: Iron I – 8%; Persian-Hellenistic – 4%; Byzantine – 10%; Early Moslem – 5%; Medieval – 73%.

Flint: 11 items (see Appendix A).
Additional surveys: none.

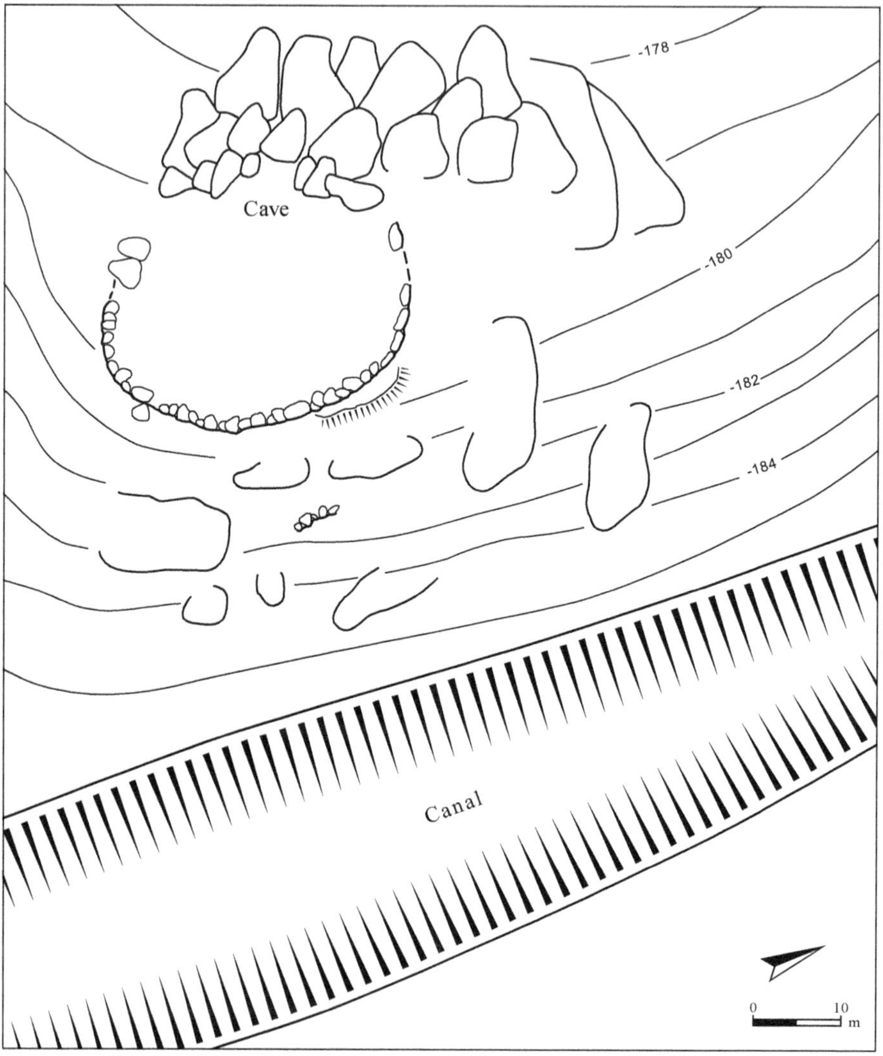

58. Plan of **Fasael (3)**.

59. An aerial view eastward of the courtyard at **Fasael (3)**, 2012 (A. Solomon).

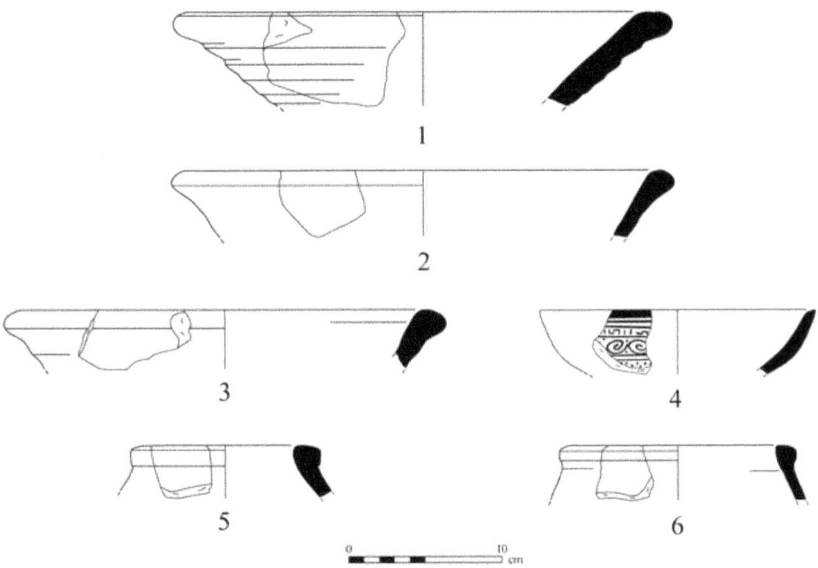

60. Pottery from **Fasael (3)**: 1-3. Basins, dk br, EM; 4. Bowl, lt br, purple dec, MA; 5-6. Jars, lt br, Hel (?).

Site 17: 19-16/01/5

FASAEL (6)

Israel grid: 1905/1618
UTM grid: 7292/5486
Elevation: 160 m b.s.l., 20 m a.s.a.
Name: nearest place
Site type: cave and courtyard
Area: 2 dunams (2000 sq. m)
Topography: slope
Rock type: Judea Group
Soil type: stony-desert
Soil quality: 1
Cultivation: none
Cisterns: none
Water source: Nahal Fasael (181), 100 m distant
Road: Phasaelis– Fasael Springs (C47), 100 m distant
Visits: November 2007, 2010; 115 sherds

A cave and courtyard on a slope north of Nahal Fasael, and about 1.5 km west-north-west of the centre of the village of Fasael. From the site there is a view of the wadi to the sites of Tell esh-Sheikh Diyab and the aqueducts.

The entrance of the shallow 5 m deep cave is 4 m wide. Southward, in front of it, over the slope, is a well-built courtyard measuring about 25×30 m. The encircling wall is built of two rows of large and medium-sized stones and is 1 m thick. The yard platform rests on an elevated rampart supported by a stone filling.

There is a moderate sherd scatter. The site borders Fasael (4) and was in use in the Early Bronze; however, the courtyard was probably built during Iron Age II.

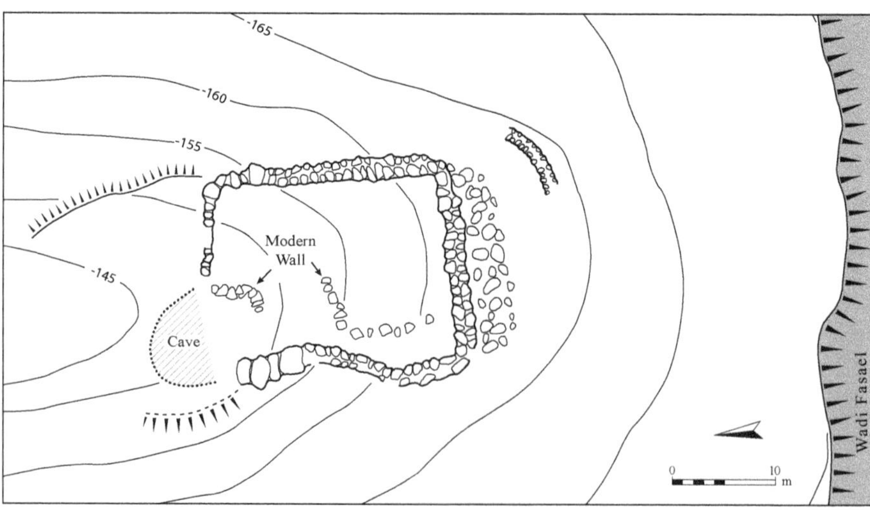

61. Plan of **Fasael (6)**.

Pottery: Early Bronze I – 18%; Middle Bronze II – 3%; Iron II – 52%; Early Roman – 7%; Late Roman-Byzantine – 20%.
Flint: 17 items (see Appendix A).
Additional surveys: none.

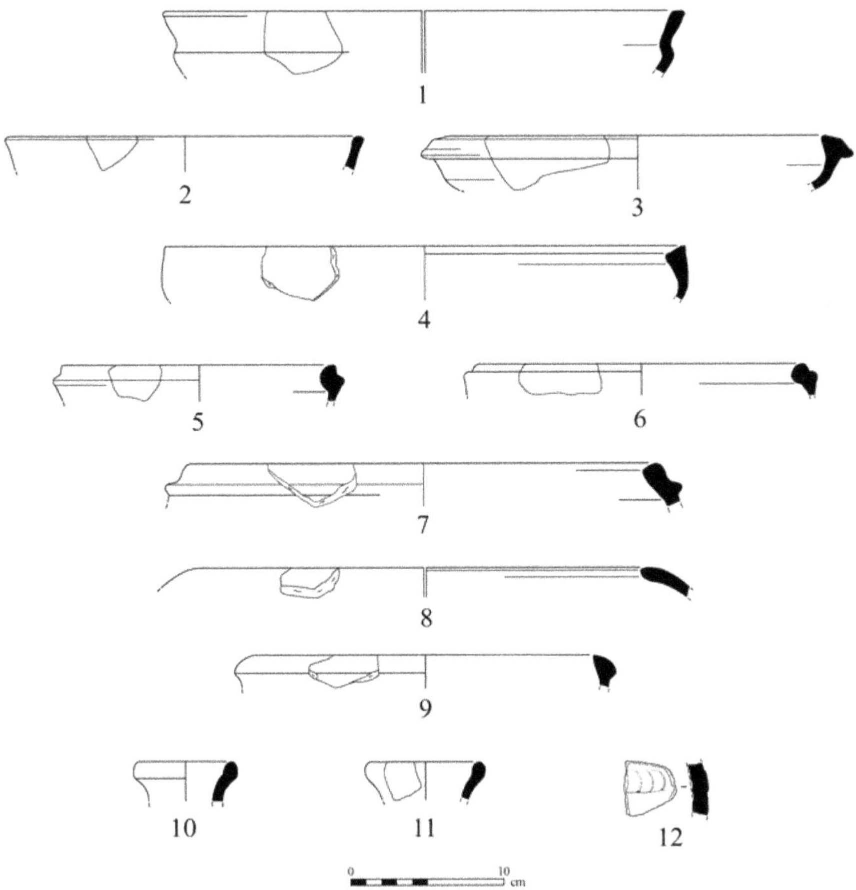

62. Pottery from **Fasael (6)**: 1. Bowl, br, MB II; 2. Bowl, br, IA II; 3. Bowl, br, IA II; 4. Bowl, lt br, EB I (?); 5-6, CP D, rd, IA II; 7. CP, rd, IA II; 8. HM jar, lt br, EB I; 9. CP (?), dk br, IA II; 10. Jug, br, IA II; 11. Jug, rd, IA II; 12. Sherd, rd, rope décor, EB I.

Site 18: 19-16/01/6

FASAEL (4)

Israel grid: 1907/1617
UTM grid: 7296/5486
Elevation: 175 m b.s.l., 30 m b.s.a.
Name: nearest place
Site type: large
Area: 30 dunams (3 ha)
Topography: stream valley edges
Rock type: Judea Group
Soil type: stony-desert
Soil quality: 2
Cultivation: none
Cisterns: none
Water source: Nahal Fasael (181), at the site
Road: Phasaelis-Neapolis (C41), next to the site
Visits: June 2008 and later, excavation 2010, 2015-2017; 330 sherds

A large settlement on the north bank of Nahal Fasael (Wadi Rashash), near the old asphalt road ascending to Ma'ale Ephraim, and about 1.2 km north-west of the centre of Fasael. In the north it borders this road, in the west with the ridge high above the site and in the south with the wadi. In the east it is open to the Jordan Valley.

Along a strip about 150 m long by about 100 m wide were located walls of many structures, currently partially silted. The thickness of the walls of two rows of stones is about 60 cm. There are about eight built circles, similar to those excavated at Tell esh-Sheikh Diyab (2), Site 21. Four of these are clustered in the western part . A single installation is located in the centre of the site, and two more in a structure in the eastern part. In the north-western part, a trench about 100 m long has been bulldozed into the mountainside. The site of Fasael (6), Site 17, is located in the western part, parallel to the new trench.

Goring-Morris (1980) conducted a limited test excavation in the site, and related the latest layer to the Chalcolithic period. His dig also revealed a prehistoric settlement (see Appendix B), but, in our opinion, the 'late' site belongs to the Early Bronze I period.

The site was partially excavated by Bar (Bar et al. 2012). These are the main results from this excavation:

The excavation focused on the group of circular and irregular buildings in the south-western part of the site (Fig. 64). A single stratum dating to the EB I, with a number of secondary phases, was identified in all excavation squares. An earlier stratum that has not yet been dated, where a rare Canaanean flint knapping work area was found (Zutovski and Bar 2017), was identified beneath a circular building (W20).

The Western Structures: These were surrounded by an 80 cm-thick wall (W1), built of two rows of medium-sized fieldstones with a core of small stones between them. The north-western building (Walls 28, 1 and 29), is an irregularly-shaped room, and seems to have been a later construction phase at the site. The walls of the room were constructed in the same manner as the perimeter wall, but they are not as well preserved. There may be a 70 cm-wide opening in the middle of the wall. Two adjacent circular structures with an

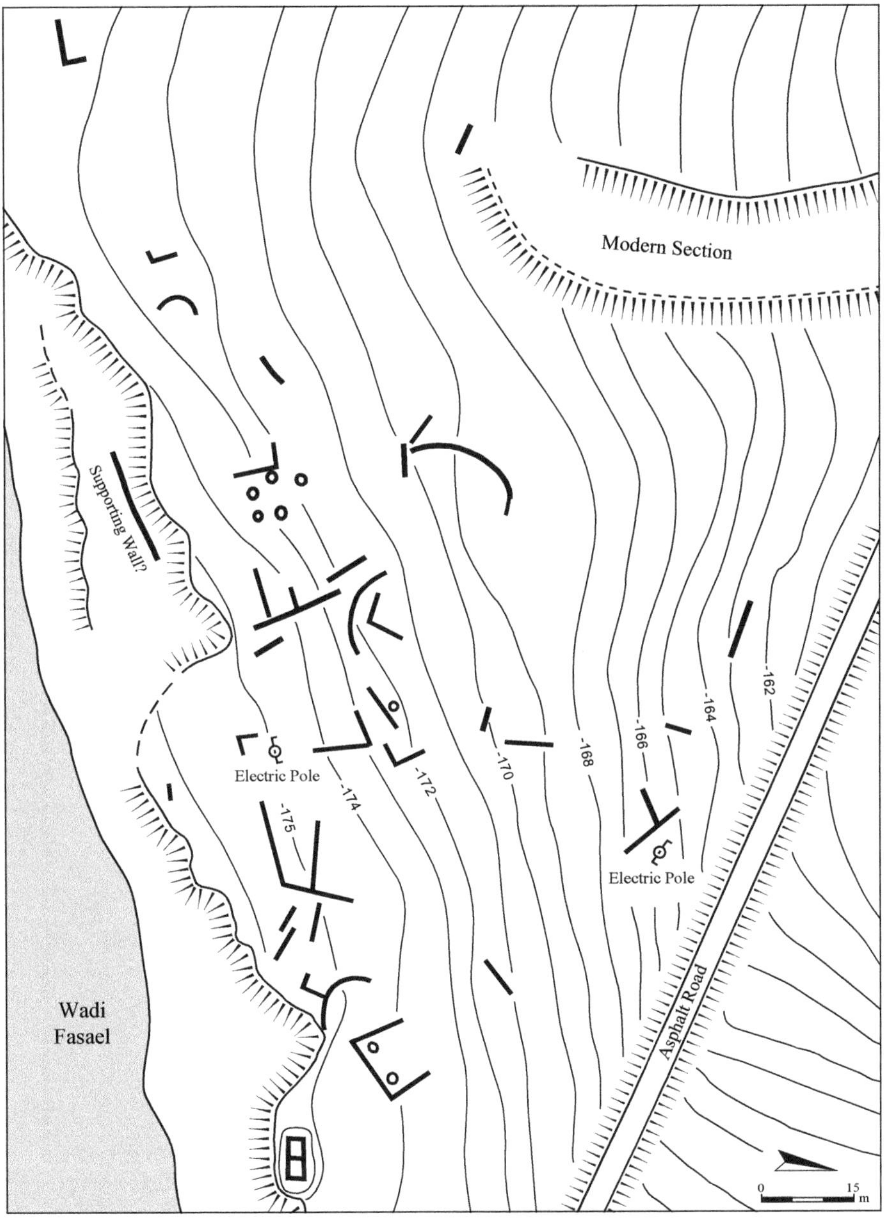

63. Plan of the survey at **Fasael (4)**.

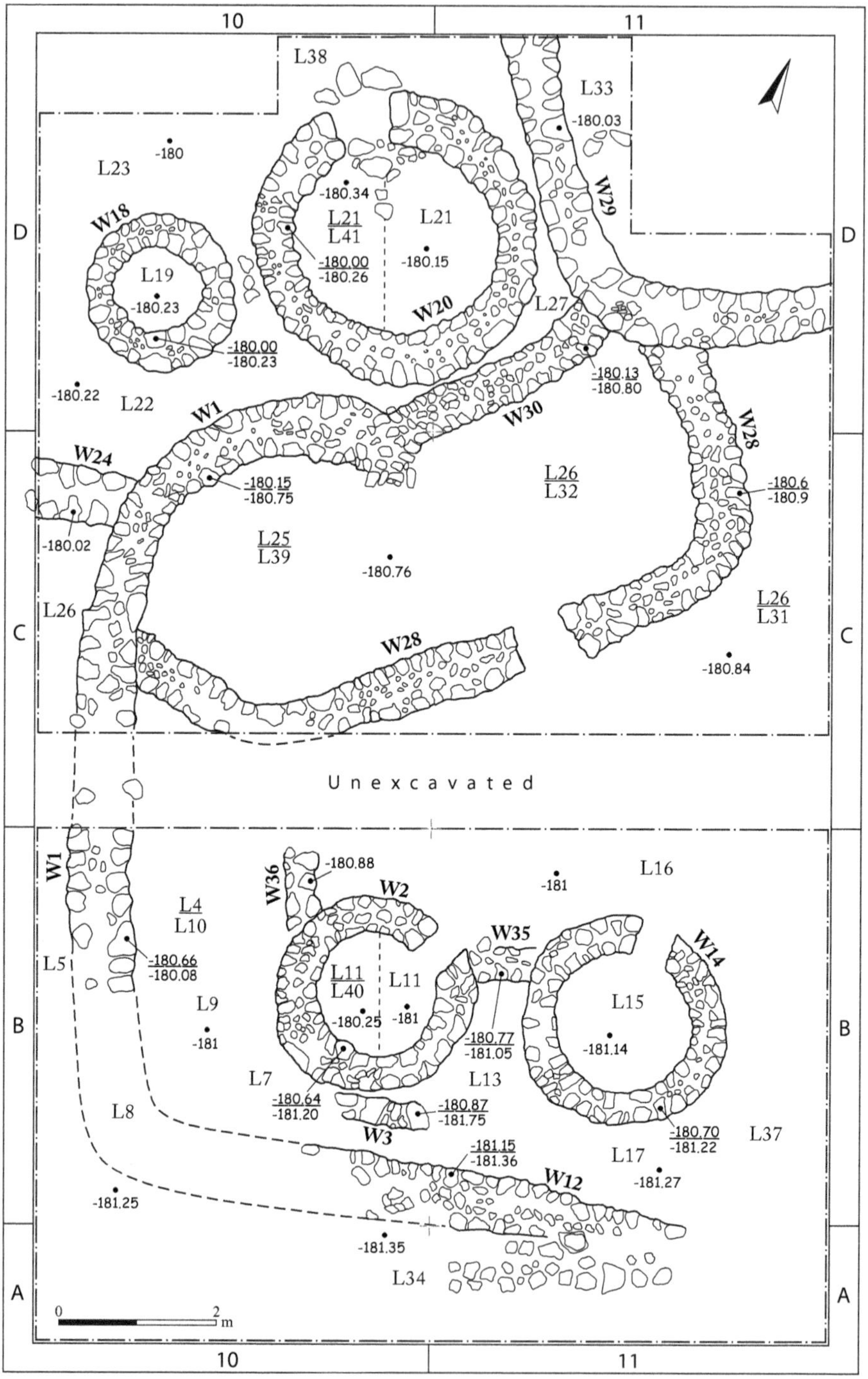

64. Plan of the excavations at **Fasael (4)** (after Bar et al. 2012: fig. 2).

inner diameter of 1.5 m were found in the southern part of the excavated area. Each was built with a wall of 55 cm average thickness, made of small and medium stones, preserved to a height of three courses. Crushed lime material that had been poured to make a horizontal surface was found inside both the buildings. This was most likely the base of the building. Both the buildings had openings that were constructed in the same manner. These faced north, and were about 60 cm wide. Although no organic material was found at the base of the buildings, it seems that they were used as silos. This supposition is primarily based on their resemblance to the built silos discovered at other EB I sites in the southern Levant (e.g. nearby Sheikh Diab 2, see Site 21), the very narrow dimensions which restricted human activity inside them, and the almost complete absence of finds of any kind. An open area, an inner courtyard, was located between all building units. Most of the stone and ceramic artefacts were discovered in the courtyard, on the ancient habitation level that consisted solely of tamped earth.

The North-Western Circular Structures: Two other circular buildings, probably silos, were discovered in the area between Walls 29, 30, 1, and 24. The larger of the structures (L21) was delimited by Wall 20 (thickness 80 cm), which was built of small and medium fieldstones, and preserved to a height of three courses. This structure had an opening 80 cm wide that faced north-north-east. A crushed lime base was also identified in this structure, which may have served as an inner pavement similar to that in the buildings to the south. The inside diameter was about 2.5 m, and unlike the other three circular

65. **Fasael (4)**, Aerial view of the excavation, view to the west, 2012 (A. Solomon).

buildings that were discovered in the excavation, one can move around inside it relatively comfortably, implying the possibility of its use as a dwelling, or for storage purposes. West of the large circular building was another smaller

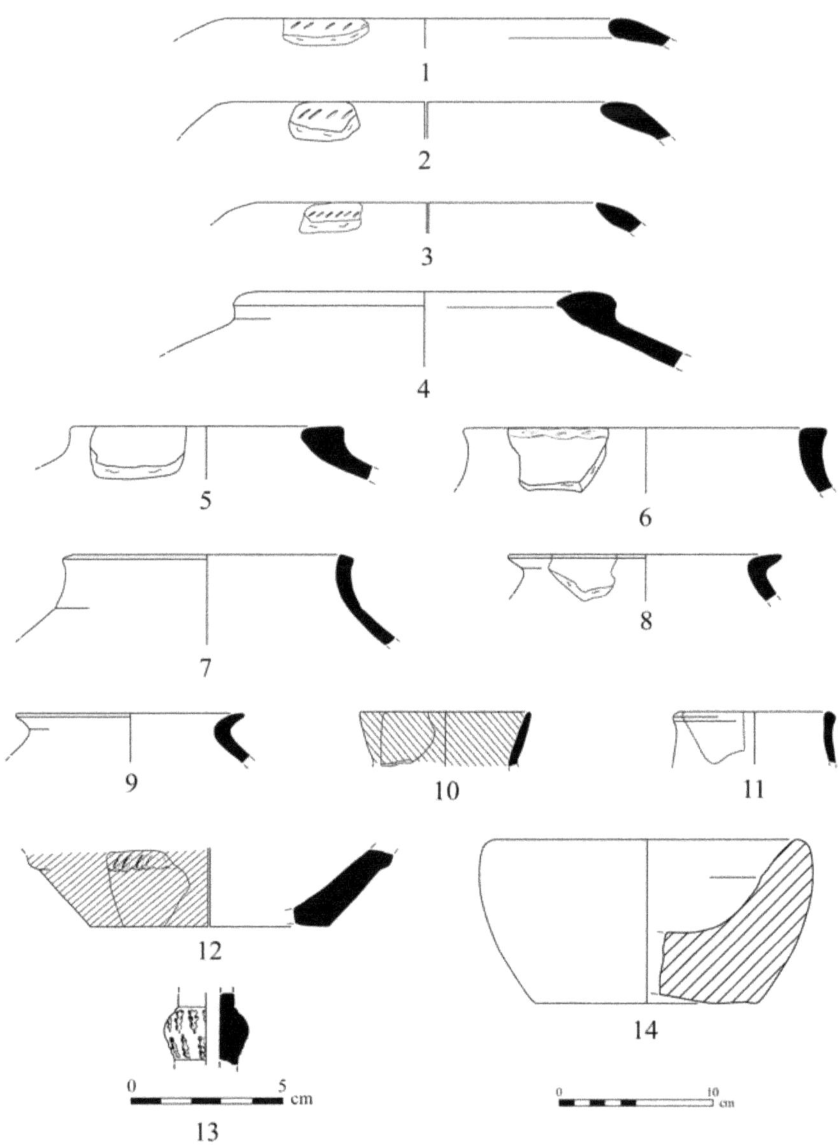

66. Finds from **Fasael (4)**, all but 11 and 13 are EBA I: 1-3. HM jars, br, engraved ornamentation; 4-5. Jars, br; 6. Jar, gr, thumbed rope dec; 7-9. Jars, lt br; 10. Jar, rd burnish; 11. Jar, rd, Rom; 12. Jar base, br, rope dec, rd slip; 13. Pipe, lt br, Ott; 14. Bowl, limestone.

round structure. Its inside diameter was 1.2 m and it was delimited by Wall 18 (thickness 50 cm), built of small and medium fieldstones. A habitation level very close to the surface was identified between the circular units. A number of crushed pottery vessels were found *in situ* on this surface.

The pottery assemblage from Fazael 4 is composed mostly of bowls and jars. The absence of kraters, jugs and juglets is interesting. In contrast, the small bowls that were used for lighting figure prominently. In most instances the vessels were fired at a low or medium temperature, and the red slip is not prevalent in the assemblage. The assemblage covers the entire time span of the EB I. It seems that the main activity at Fazael 4 was connected to storage (as testified by the quantities of pithoi and jars), most likely of grains from the nearby cultivated fields. The bowls were mainly used as oil lamps (or for cooking), and the holemouth jars were used both for storage and cooking. Based on the proximity of the site to Sheikh Diab 2, the similarity of form between the two pottery assemblages, and the architecture, it is conceivable that both sites existed, at least during the later phases of Fazael 4, at the same time.

The total quantity of flint items in the excavation (N=781) is small: however, the presence of flint items belonging to the categories of waste, semi-finished products, and retouched tools, proves the existence of a flint industry at the site. The quantity of flakes, blades, bladelets and Canaanean blades which were not shaped by a secondary treatment or retouch is considerable (N = 378, 49.6%). Retouched tools were relatively scarce, and it can therefore be assumed that at least some of the flakes or blades were the end-product, and used for various purposes. The Canaanean blades (5.2%) were probably blanks for the preparation of sickle blades. Most tools (6.6%) should be classified as ad hoc tools (a minimum of work was invested in the secondary treatment –retouching – of most of these). The relatively large number of sickle blades is indicative of an agrarian society engaged in growing grain. The relatively large quantity of notches and denticulates apparently indicates the production of artefacts made of perishable materials, such as wood or bone.

Eleven stone objects were found in the excavation. They were produced from hard stone, local limestone (10 items) and basalt (1 item). The assemblage includes six grinding stones, four small bowls, and a stone with a biconical perforation.

Pottery: Early Bronze I – 98%; Late Roman – 1%; Ottoman – 1%.
Flint (in the survey): 150 items, Epipalaeolithic Cabaren and EBA I (see Appendix A).
Additional surveys: Goring-Morris 1980: 7.
Additional Bibliography: Bar 2013b: chapter 8; Bar 2014: site 89.

Site 19: 19-16/11/2

FASAEL (2)

Israel grid: 1912/1618
UTM grid: 7299/5487
Elevation: 190 m b.s.l., 10 m b.s.a.
Name: nearest place
Site type: courtyard and village
Area: 6 dunams (6000 sq. m)
Topography: slope
Rock type: Avdat Group
Soil type: stony-desert
Soil quality: 2
Cultivation: none
Cisterns: none
Water source: Nahal Fasael (181), 200 m distant
Road: Phasaelis–Fasael Springs (C47), 200 m distant
Visits: January 2000, 2006, and many more, excavations 2007-2017; 300 sherds

A large courtyard house, part of a Chalcolithic village on a silt step at the western edge of the Fasael Valley. The unpaved road cut to the water reservoir damaged the site. In the east it is cut by the large drainage canal of the Fasael Valley. There is a fine view of the valley from the site.

The site could be divided into three parts at least:

1. A square courtyard, about 40×40 m. The perimeter wall is built of two rows of fairly large local stones. A few Late Roman sherds were found in the yard and the vicinity.

67. The Chalcolithic site **Fasael (2)** during excavation, aerial view north-east, 2012 (A. Solomon).

2. The Chalcolithic site: the location is on a hillock about 50 m south of the courtyard. In the centre there is a structure, the walls of which are built of pebbles, and around it are many Chalcolithic sherds. The site was excavated for ten seasons (see below). During the excavation it was found that a large yard is attached to the structure, and perhaps also to additional structures.
3. The 'village': east and south of the courtyard, further down the slope to the valley, were 10 to 20 scattered structures with one or more rooms, with walls built of one or two rows of local stones of varying sizes. There are support walls across the slope.

The site is a part of an extensive Chalcolithic layout in the Fasael Valley. In 2007–2017 excavations were conducted in the site headed by Bar (Bar 2008; 2013b; 2014; Bar and Winter 2010; Bar et al. 2013). Following is a description of the main finds from the dig:

The site had three strata: Stratum I was excavated at the surface level of the

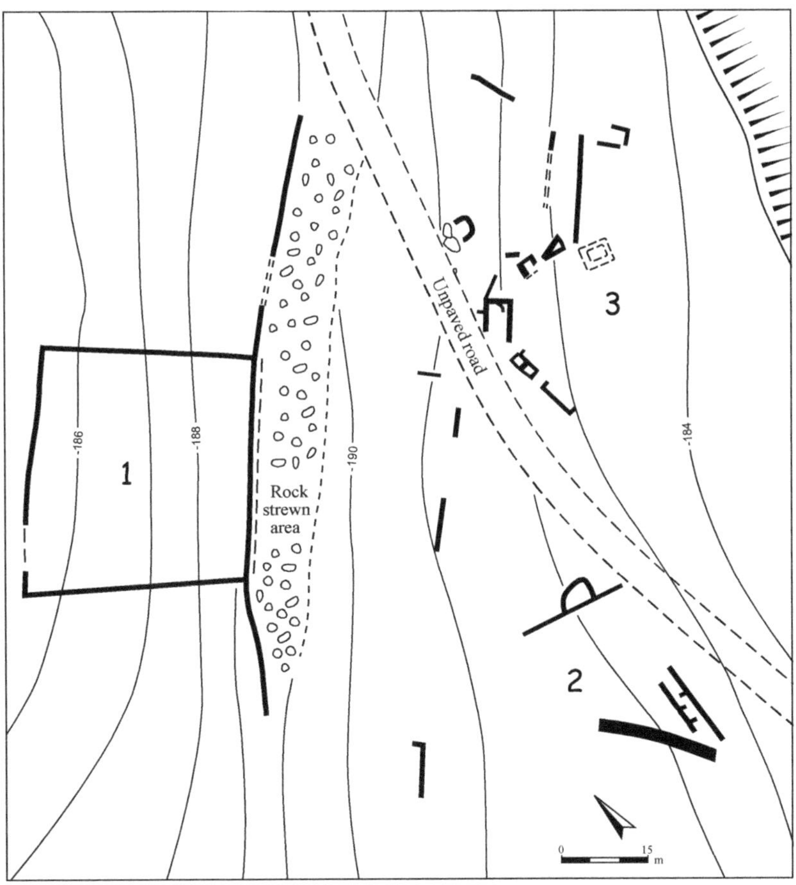

68. Plan of **Fasael (2)** and immediate vicinity.

site, and included undated rounded installations. Stratum III was excavated in small probes below Stratum II, and included mainly pits dated to the Chalcolithic period. Most of the excavation focused on Stratum II.

Stratum II should be dated late in the Chalcolithic continuum, making it important for the study of the final phases of this period before the poorly understood transition to the EBA I. The main feature discovered in Stratum II is a very large courtyard house, approximately 620 sq. m in area, containing the following main sub-structures:

69. Excavation plan of **Fasael (2)**, 2011. Note the exposed broad rooms and the large square courtyard.

1. A square courtyard: 560 sq. m in area (28×20 m), bounded by thick stone walls between 80 and 100 cm thick that survived up to a height of three courses. The masonry is of two rows of medium-sized stones with smaller stones between them. Larger fieldstones were sometimes incorporated in

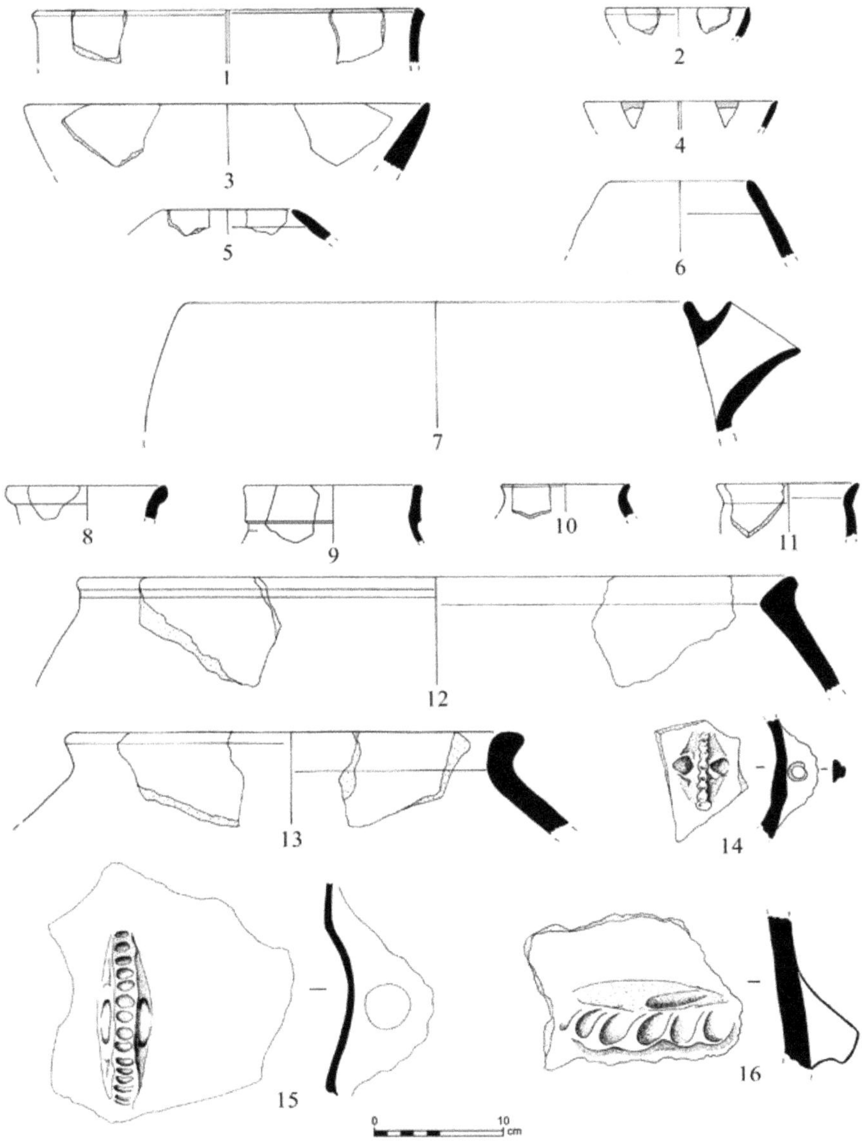

70. Pottery from **Fasael (2)**, all (except nos. 8, 9) are Chal: 1. Bowl, blk; 2, 3. Bowls, rd; 4. Bowl, rd, rd strip dec rim; 5-7. HM jars, buff; 8. Jar, gr, IA I-II; 9. Jar, lt br, ER; 10. Jar, buff; 11. Cup, rd; 12. Basin, rd; 13. Jar, rd; 14, 15. Thumb-indented lug handles, rd; 16. Thumb-indented ledge handle, rd.

the construction. Since no stone collapse was found inside the building, it seems that they were foundations for mud-brick walls that did not survive due its closeness to the surface of the site. Most of the area of the courtyard has not yet been excavated. The remains of several stone-built installations and working areas were found in the few soundings, alongside walls of additional structures and installations not yet fully excavated.

2. Two broad rooms: The first, 62 sq. m (4×15.5 m) in area, was found abutting the south-eastern section of the courtyard wall, and was completely excavated. The room was divided into two large cells, and had an entrance facing east. The masonry was identical to that of the courtyard walls. At least five successive beaten earth floors were noted abutting the walls of the room, implying a long period of habitation.

   The second broad room, in the western part of the courtyard, was partly excavated. The room was 60 sq. m (4×15 m) in area. Like the south-eastern room, it was divided into two large cells. An entrance made of two standing monoliths was found at the southern part of the room; and in the northern cell the remains of three installations were found. This broad room was built in the early phase of Stratum II, and in the later phase of the stratum it was out of use and had become part of the main courtyard.

The finds from Stratum II are typical of the later phases of the Chalcolithic period. The pottery assemblage includes V-shaped bowls with red stripes on the rims, holemouth jars, jars with inverted rims, large bowls with 'pie crust' decoration, plastic rope ornamentations on large vessels, large and small lug handles (some finger-pressed), one cornet base, etc. It is interesting to note that no churns were found, and that hemispherical and S-shaped bowls were common.

The flint assemblage included both Chalcolithic and Early Bronze Age types and technologies. While the bifacial tools, common in almost every Chalcolithic tool kit, are almost absent here, one of the commonest tools is the Canaanean blade (Bar and Winter 2010). These were found in the same loci as typical backed and truncated Chalcolithic sickle segments, suggesting that the Canaanean blade technology was already present in the later phases of the Chalcolithic period.

Other notable assemblages were:

1. A very rich assemblage of more than 35 complete and broken copper tools, including prestige items such as mace heads and fragments of crowns, and everyday tools, such as an axe and chisels;
2. A stone tool assemblage (Cohen-Klonymus and Bar 2016) included typical Chalcolithic items, such as more than 30 fragments of basalt V-shaped

bowls, fenestrated chalices, etc., alongside items of everyday use, such as grinding and pounding stones, bowlets, spindle whorls, and perforated pieces. Other prestige items included two haematite mace heads and a haematite pendant.

Radiometric dates from Stratum II living surfaces were dated to the 1st century of the 4th millennium BCE. (Bar 2008: 405).

Pottery: Chalcolithic (in the centre structure area) – 94%; Iron I-II (in the 'village' area) – 3%; Roman (around the yard) – 3%.
Additional surveys: none.
Additional Bibliography: Bar 2013: chapter 4; Bar 2014: chapter 10.

♦ ♦ ♦

Site 20: 19-16/11/3

FASAEL (11)

Israel grid: 1918/1618 UTM grid: 7305/5476

A salvage excavation by Yuval Peleg in the village of Fasael.

Remains of a square structure, measuring about 8×8 m were unearthed. The walls which were preserved up to two courses (about 1 m) high, are built of two rows of medium-sized fieldstones. The floor was made of compacted earth with small stones. A few fragments of white plaster were found. The place has been demolished.

The poor pottery find is dated to Chalcolithic.

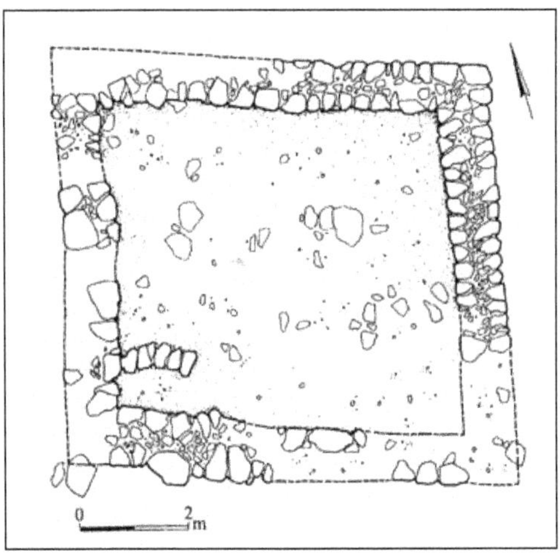

71. **Fasael (11)**, plan of excavation (Peleg 2000b: illustration 92).

Pottery: Chalcolithic – 100%.
Bibliography: Peleg 2000b; Bar 2014: site 91.

Site 21: 19-16/01/7

TELL ESH-SHEIKH DIYAB (2)

Israel grid: 1905/1615
UTM grid: 7297/5484
Elevation: 160 m b.s.l., 60 m b.s.a.
Name: nearest place
Site type: medium size
Area: 15 dunams (1.5 ha)
Topography: edge of valley
Rock type: Judea Group
Soil type: stony-desert
Soil quality: 2
Cultivation: none
Cisterns: none
Water source: Nahal Fasael (181) , at the site
Road: Phasaelis–Fasael Springs (C47), next to the site
Visits: February 2000 and later, excavation 2007–2008; 145 sherds

This site is situated on a spur and saddle descending from the south-west to Nahal Fasael (Wadi Rashash). A small wadi joins Nahal Fasael to the east, close to the site. The asphalt road to Fasael Springs passes nearby north of the site.

Ten to fifteen structures were found. Their walls are about 60 cm thick and are built of two rows of stones. The structures have been covered by silt on the slope and damaged by an abandoned army position in the lower part of the site.

There are considerable sherd and flint scatters in the area. Most of the sherds are the flat bases of coarse jars and holemouth jar rims. Rope decorations have also been found.

The site is a small village next to the water source and the agricultural area, excavated by Bar in 2007–2008 (Bar et al. 2011). Following is a description of the main finds from the dig:

The ancient remains cover an area of 1.5 ha. The site was mainly settled during the first part of the EB Ib. The buildings are spread across the middle of the site and on the slopes of a steeply sloping spur formed of chalky limestone rock and desert travertine soil. The EB I site of Fasael (4) is located across the wadi channel to the north. A large area on both sides of the wadi channel east of the site is flat, which allows agriculture and grazing. The site includes a large number of building remains, walls, and courtyards scattered across the slopes, and is covered with alluvium.

So far, about 425 sq. m have been excavated in four different areas (see plan). The entire middle of the site was cleared of sundry stone collapses in order to sketch the walls visible on the surface. The tops of the walls were cleaned so that they could be drawn, and in order to better understand their outline. The main area excavated was Complex 1 in Area G, and a description of the main architectural remains from this complex follows, representative of the nature of the entire site.

Area G (250 sq. m excavated) is located in the centre of the site, where the slope is moderate and numerous wall remains are visible at the surface level.

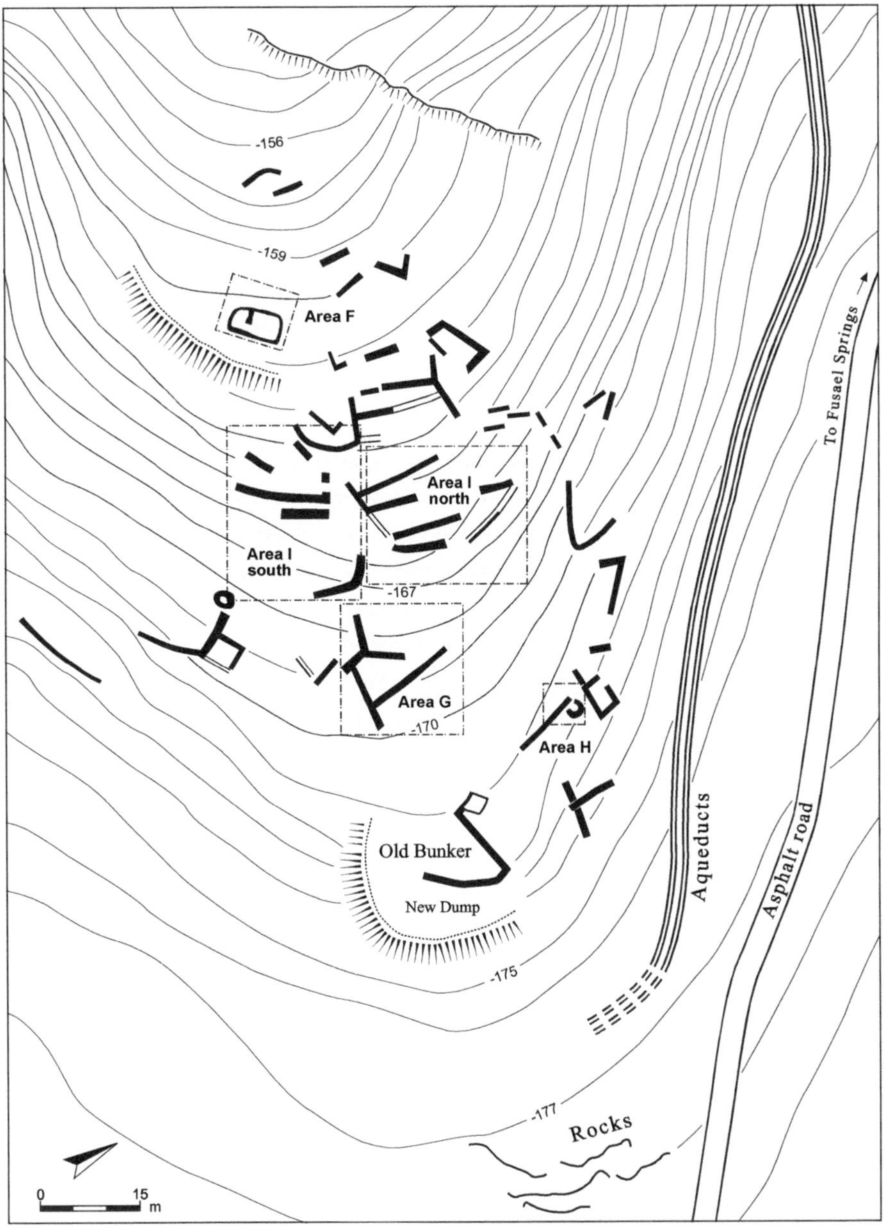

72. The survey plan of **Tell esh-Sheikh Diyab (2)**. The areas of the excavations are marked.

The main feature in this area is a residential complex (Com 1) consisting of four built units (10–13) that was completely excavated. All the ceramic artefacts recovered date to EB I.

Com 1 is a roughly circular residential complex and courtyard (140 sq. m). This complex constitutes a fine example of a residential unit at the site in the EB Ib. Com 1 was divided into four secondary units with open areas between them:

Unit 10 consists of a room 3.7×4.5 m, with an area of about 16 sq. m. It is located in the southern part of Com 1, and is delimited by Walls 103, 121 and 120s. Its northern corners are curved similarly to the traditional corners of the buildings of the EB Ib in the north of Israel. Three occupation phases were found in this unit.

Unit 11 consists of the remains of a room (Walls 146, 146n) at least 10 m wide: its exact width is not known, as its eastern wall did not survive. This is a 'sausage-shaped' residential unit, which is more characteristic of the EB Ia in the north of Israel (e.g. Braun 1997). It is abutted from the south by the courtyard's perimeter wall (W120s), which postdates the first construction phase of the unit. The courtyard's perimeter wall (W120e) abuts this unit from the east near the entrance to Com 1. It seems that an oval structure stood there, whose eastern walls were dismantled when the courtyard wall was constructed (the western wall of the building became part of the courtyard wall). The artefacts from this unit found on the bedrock belong to the latest use phase of the unit during the EB Ib, when it was part of the courtyard in the western part of Com 1. No datable material that can be associated with the earlier phase of this unit was found. The walls in this unit were preserved to a height of more than 1 m (up to seven courses in some places), and the large quantity of stone collapse attests that the walls, which rose to an even greater height, were built of stone to their entire height. The builders cut deep foundation trenches in the chalk bedrock for the walls. It should be noted that this construction method is very unusual for masonry of the EB I in the southern Levant. It was probably used because of the soft easily carved rock at the site. The north-western part of Wall 146n collapsed, and the foundation trench was exposed to a depth of at least 30 cm. The habitation level in Unit 11 was more than 1 m lower than the habitation level in Alley 138 to its west.

Unit 12 consists of the remains of a round building (W122) about 2.5 m in diameter, which was probably used for storage (silo). It was located in a depression in the natural bedrock south of the high terrace of Unit 11 and west of the covered room of Unit 10. The structure, which was not cut into the bedrock, but was erected on the surface level, was preserved to a height of 1.2 m (seven stone courses), and it seems that it was built of stone to its entire height. An opening was located in its northern part, and there was an accumulation of more than 5 cm of powdered charcoal on the bottom, indicating that it contained or was partly built of organic material.

Unit 13 consists of the remains of another round structure (W159) 50 cm in diameter, similar to Unit 12, which was apparently also used for storage. It was built in a natural depression in the bedrock next to the wall of the complex (W120e), in its north-eastern part. The structure was preserved only to a height of two stone courses.

The courtyard constitutes more than 75% of the area of Com 1, and probably

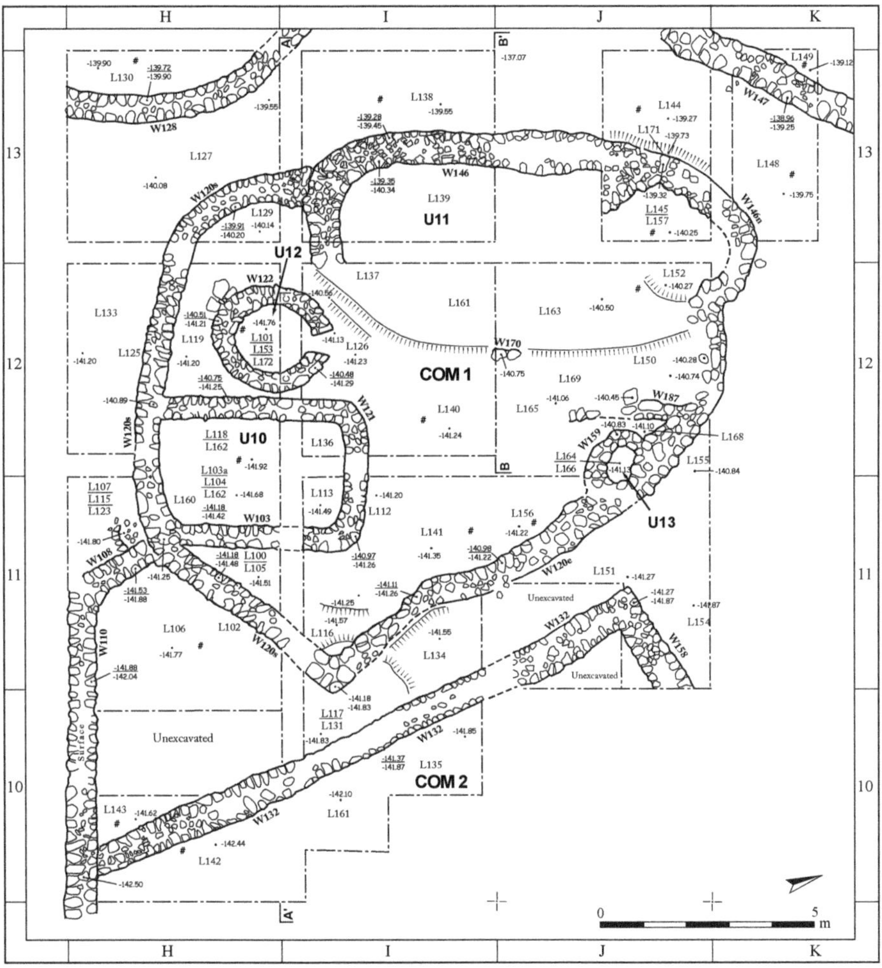

73. **Tell esh-Sheikh Diyab (2)**, plan of the Early Bronze I courtyard house in Area G. Note the yard perimeter wall, the square dwelling unit and the two circular grain silos exposed inside the yard.

served a number of purposes, including storage, animal shelter, and household activities. The courtyard did not have a roof, and the habitation level in it was situated on the natural chalk bedrock. Certain areas in the courtyard were lower than others, but unlike at the time when the walls of the courtyard were built, there is no evidence that the bedrock level was prepared at all. The courtyard wall surrounds the entire complex. This wall's main purpose was to separate the public areas (alleys, squares and open spaces) from the individual holdings

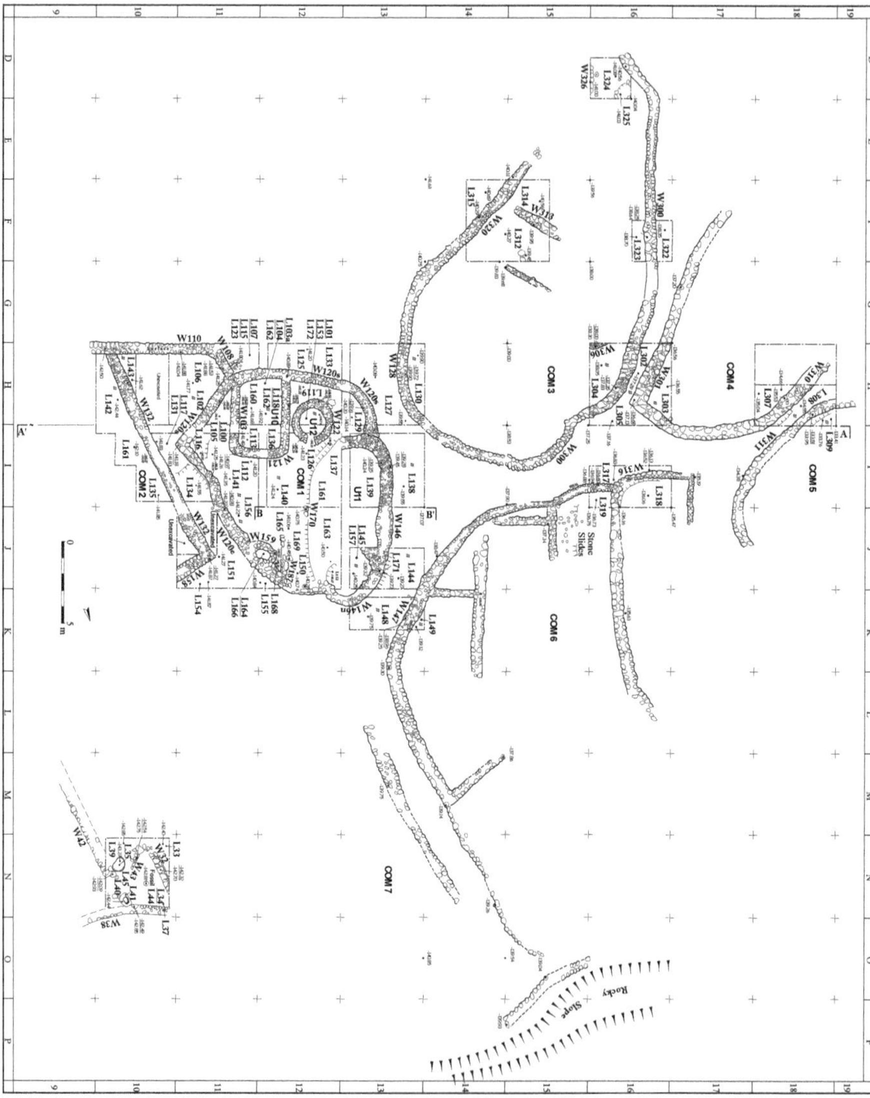

74. **Tell esh-Sheikh Diyab (2)**, plan of the Early Bronze I village at the end of the excavation.

(private spaces and property) of the residents of Com 1. The wall was built identically to the walls of the site: two rows of medium-sized fieldstones, and fill consisting of smaller stones with mud between them. The wall was 70–90 cm thick, and was preserved to a maximum height of seven courses. Its general outline was curved, and it had one perpendicular corner for which there is no structural explanation. The wall was not built as a single homogeneous unit, but rather as a collection of different segments.

Main architectural conclusions: The construction of irregularly-shaped residential complexes is one of features of the site. These consist of large oval courtyards that contain one or more covered rooms and a large open area. To date, seven complexes of this kind have been identified, and it seems that there are probably a total of 10 to 12. Thus perhaps 12 nuclear families resided there; that is to say, between 80 and 100 inhabitants. The complexes occur in different shapes and sizes; the smallest being about 150 sq. m (Com 1), and the largest about 500 sq. m (its full extent has still not been uncovered). Alleys between 1 and 2 m wide separate the residential complexes from one another. This width was sufficient for two people or animals (e.g., a donkey carrying baskets, or a file of sheep or goats) to move easily between the residential units. A main alley, from which secondary alleys branch off between the courtyards, runs through the centre of the spur. The floor of the alley is the natural chalk bedrock, which is permeable to water, and very effective in draining rainwater and sewage. The basic residential complex at the site includes typical principal elements: a roofed room or rooms and square rooms with rounded corners, which are characteristic of EB Ib in the north of Israel and earlier phases in the EB I of the Jordan Valley. In an earlier phase at the site, one unit was oval, similar to units found at sites such as Yiftah'el (Braun 1997), which typify northern Israel during the EB Ia. The rooms have an average width of about 4 m, and are 5–6 m long. No internal partitions were identified. The room was probably reserved for sleeping and storage, and occasionally for food preparation, while most of the other household activities were conducted outside in the courtyard. The courtyards range in size from 115 to 350 sq. m, and are a very important component of the residential complex. Although only a small group of vessels was found in situ on the rocky surface of the courtyards, the large size of the courtyards leads us to conclude that they were host to many activities, including animal shelter. The courtyards were floored with the natural chalk bedrock. They contained silos, as well as large ceramic containers (pithoi, kraters and jars) that were probably used by the household for storage. The different sizes of the courtyards at the site and their storage space indicate a society in which different groups of people utilized different areas. This may imply that some people had more property than others, or at least a position or way of life that required the use of a larger area.

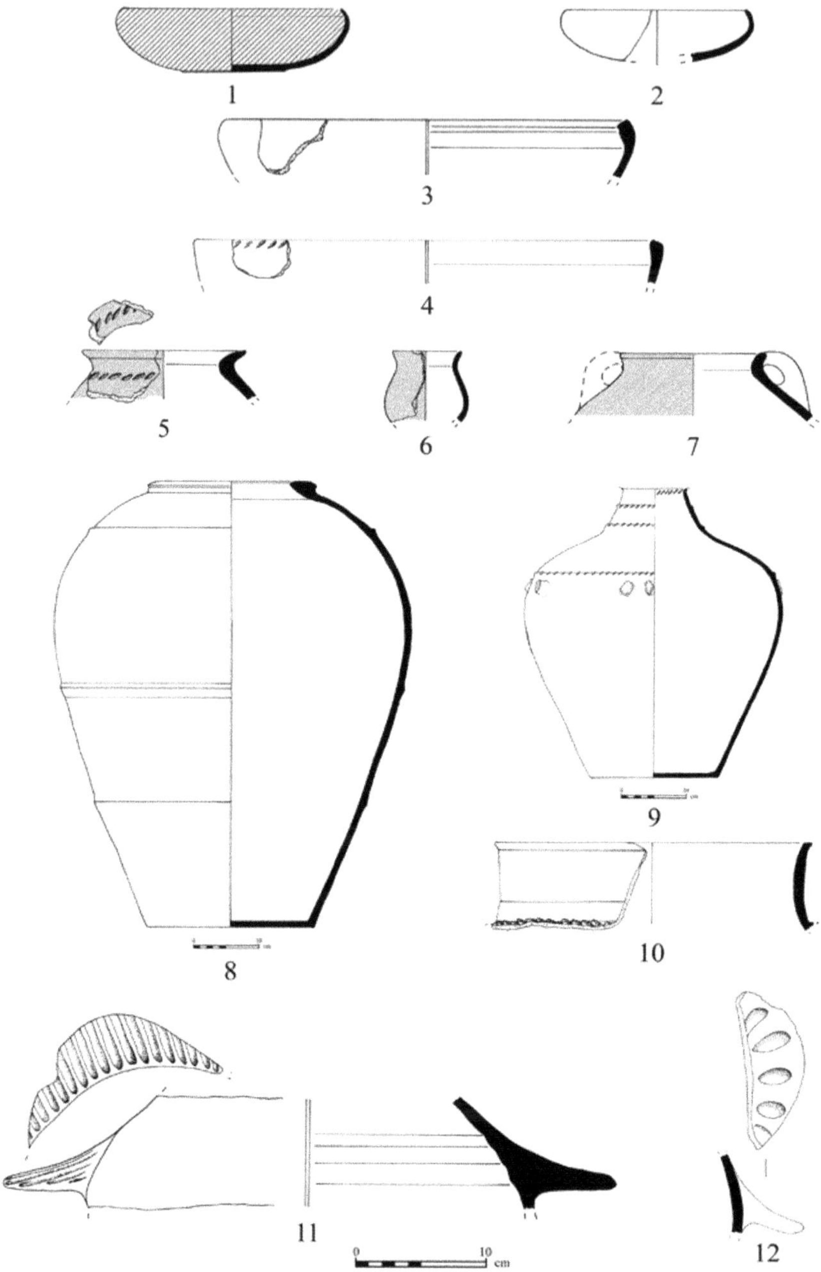

75. Pottery from the excavation at the EBA I site **Tell esh-Sheikh Diyab (2)**: 1. Bowl, rd, rd slip in and out; 2. Bowl, br; 3. Bowl, lt br; 4. Bowl, br-rd, engraved dec; 5. Amphoriskos, br-rd, engraved dec, rd slip outside; 6. Cup, lt br, rd slip out; 7. Amphoriskos, lt br, rd slip out; 8. Pithos, br-rd; 9. Jar, bright colour, rope dec; 10. Pithos, br-rd, rope dec; 11, 12. Ledge handles, br-rd, thumb indentation dec.

Additional information about the excavations is to be found in the following publications: Bar et al. 2011; Bar 2013b: chapter 7; and Bar 2014: chapter 12.

Pottery: Early Bronze I – 100%.
Flint (in the survey): 240 items, Early Bronze I (see Appendix A).
Additional surveys: none.

◆ ◆ ◆

Site 22: 19-16/11/4

FASAEL (5)

Israel grid: 1912/1615
UTM grid: 7300/5484
Elevation: 205 m b.s.l., 0 m a.s.a.
Name: nearest place
Site type: large
Area: 30 dunams (3 ha)
Topography: plain
Rock type: silt
Soil type: stony-desert
Soil quality: 2
Cultivation: none
Cisterns: none
Water source: Nahal Fasael (181), at the site
Road: Phasaelis– Fasael Springs (C47), next to the site
Visits: May 2008 and more, excavations 2009, 2012-2013; 180 sherds

A large site in the Nahal Fasael floodplain, on the north bank of the shallow channel. The location is close to the western fence of the village of Fasael, and about 700 m north-west of the settlement centre. The old asphalted road from Fasael junction to Ma'ale Ephrayim passes about 100 m to the north.

Some of the structures and various architectural elements have been well preserved; others were damaged during earth-levelling operations.

Following are descriptions of the principal parts from east to west:

1. In the eastern part is an artificially elevated road about 3-4 m wide, paved with small stones, between two walls of large stones. This road is about 20 m long, without beginning or end. In the northern section it curves, entering a round structure about 5 m in diameter, and then disappears. It is likely that the round structure stretches north in the form of a wall built from a single row of large stones.
2. West of and close to the road is a large courtyard, measuring about 40×35 m, with a bulge in the southern part. In the north-eastern corner is a room or cell, measuring 8×3 m. The yard may have been connected to Structure 3 (below).

76. Aerial view of the Chalcolithic structure (no. 4 in the plan below) at **Fasael (5)**, 2012 (A. Solomon).

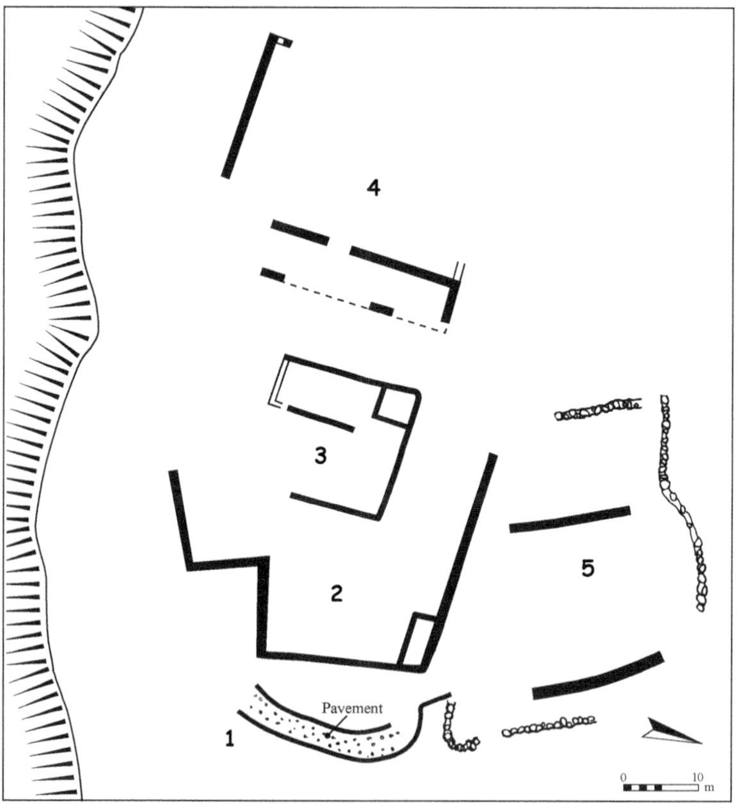

77. Plan of **Fasael (5)**.

3. West of the courtyard is a large square structure, measuring about 18×18 m. In the western side are parts of a longitudinal structure, in the northern corner of which a room, 5×5 m, has been preserved.
4. Complex 4 is situated west of structure 3, of which segments of a large courtyard, measuring about 30×30 m, and parts of the surrounding walls survived, while the rest was ruined during earth-moving operations.
5. In the northern part, sloping towards a channel or ancient ravine, were sections of an enclosing wall oriented east–west, built of a single row of large stones. Walls protruded perpendicularly from the enclosing wall, directed towards the complexes at the head of the elevation.

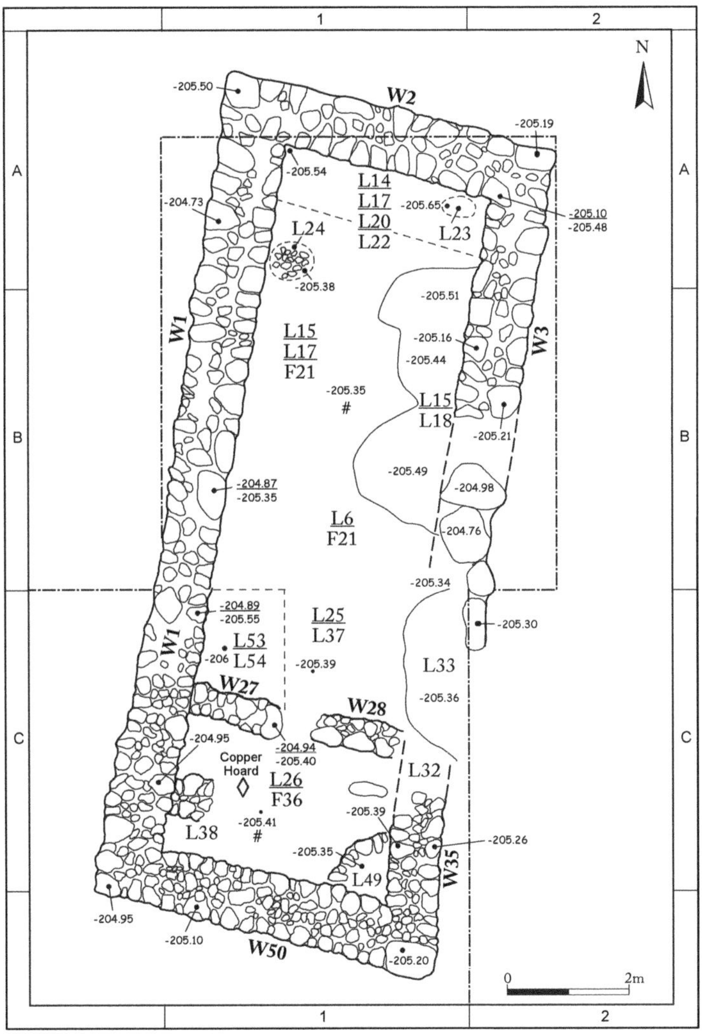

78. Plan of the excavations at **Fasael (5)** (after Bar et al. 2015: fig. 5).

Most of the walls are made of double rows of medium-sized stones, mostly pebbles; they are about 60 cm thick on the average. Other complexes of varied nature that were linked to each other did not survive.

An excavation was conducted by Bar in Complex 4 in 2009 and 2012-2014 (Bar et al. 2015), and a connection of the site to other sites of the same period in the Fasael Valley appears to be reasonable. They all apparently seem to have been parts of a large unfortified settlement on the north bank of the stream. Only small-scale excavations have carried out at this three-stratum site. In Stratum II, the main habitation level at the site, a large (14×5.5 m) broad room was exposed, and two phases were noted. In the earlier phase a rectangular broad room was built. The wall masonry was of two rows of medium-sized stones with smaller stones between them. They were 1 m thick, and survived up to a height of three courses. Beaten earth living surfaces with horizontally lying crushed pottery and stone installations abutted the outer walls, usually at the height of the upper part of the first stone course of each wall. In the later phase of this stratum an inner division was added to the broad room, creating a small cell, 2×4 m, to the south.

Although small, the pottery assemblage from the site shows many parallels to the nearby larger assemblages of Fasael (2) and (7). A small metal hoard comprising an axe, a chisel and a sceptre head, was found in the southern cell.

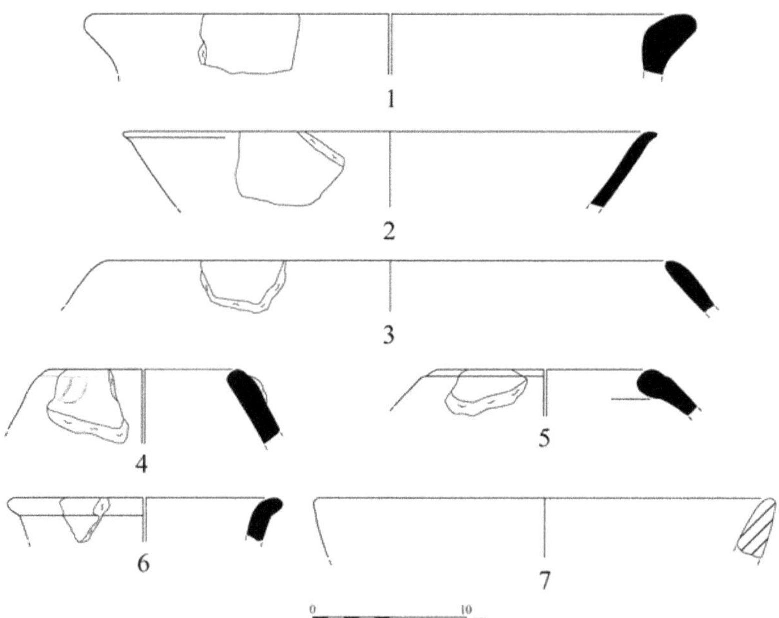

79. Chalcolithic finds from the survey of **Fasael** (5): 1. Basin, lt br; 2. Bowl, lt br; 3. HM jar, lt br; 4. HM jar, gr, thumbed rope dec; 6. Jar, lt br; 7. Bowl, basalt.

Pottery: Chalcolithic – 98%; Early Bronze – 1%; Middle Bronze II – 1%.
Flint: 32 items, Chalcolithic (see Appendix A).
Additional surveys: none.
Additional Bibliography: Bar 2013b: chapter 5.

♦ ♦ ♦

Site 23: 19-16/01/1

TELL ESH-SHEIKH DIYAB

Israel grid: 1907/1614
UTM grid: 7294/5483
Elevation: 190 m b.s.l., 10 m a.s.a.
Name: in the map
Site type: tell and reservoir
Area: 8 dunams (8000 sq. m)
Topography: edges of valley
Rock type: Judea Group
Soil type: stony-desert
Soil quality: 2
Cultivation: none
Cisterns: none
Water source: Nahal Fasael (181) and Fasael pool (171), at the site
Road: Phasaelis–Fasael Springs (C47), next to the site
Visits: February 2000 and many more, excavation 2007; 210 sherds

This is a fortified tell next to the Nahal Fasael outlet to the Jordan Valley. North of it are the wadi channel and the asphalt road alongside it, and south of it is a built pool collecting the water from the springs. The aqueducts which originate at the Fasael Springs pass close by.

The tell complex includes the following parts:

1. The conical tell rises about 10-15 m above the plain; measuring about 60×50 m, an area of about 3 dunams (3000 sq. m). In the tell's eastern part is a thick wall of large stones, about 75 m long, supporting the structures on the tell. Along the slopes are additional supporting walls and on the top of the tell are the walls of a rectangular structure, 22×18 m, with hints of inner partitions. This central structure has the characteristics of a fort. The thick walls are built of two, and occasionally more, rows of local stones. The tell has been badly disturbed by pillaging digs and mechanical earth-moving operations. Most of the pottery on the slopes is Iron Age II, and the bulk of the structures belong to that period.
2. The rampart: at the south-south-east the tell is approached by a rampart, 50 m long and about 10 m wide, built of whitish material, the top of which reaches the foundations of the tell. The relationship between the rampart and the tell is not clear: perhaps it was used for bringing building materials, or as a pathway to the structure on top, or perhaps it was a siege ramp.

80. Aerial view to south-west at **Tell esh-Sheikh Diyab** and the Fasael pool, 2008. Above the pool are seen the aqueducts which carried the water from Fasael Springs (N. Eshed).

3. The water pool abuts the south of the tell. It is a large reservoir measuring 45×45 m, and is 5 m deep. The walls are 3–3.5 m thick, built of two rows of large uncut stones with fill between them. Over the inner face of the wall is stuck a layer of well-arranged small stones covered with plaster. It is not certain that all the walls and plaster coats belong to the same phase. In the south-western corner of the pool is a staircase reaching the bottom; next to it are two plastered inner pools. Only the lower part of the plastered staircase has survived. During another visit (March 2000), the bottom of the pool was covered by water. Judging by the estimated dimensions it could contain about 15,000 cu. m of water. The owner of the land whom we met claimed to have cleaned the pool in 1972, which until then had been heavily silted. Since then the pool water has served for irrigation. It is not clear how the water entered the pool at various times, but the linkage of the pool and the aqueducts is obvious. Nowadays the pool is fed by a steel pipe originating in the Fasael Springs. For additional details about the pool see Appendix D.

Evaluation: in Tell esh-Sheikh Diyab once stood a fortified structure or fort, meant to defend the water springs and the reservoir. Although there are sherds from various periods, most of the activity in the site was in Iron Age II, and this is the presumed time of construction. The visual contact between the site and the round fort at Rujm Abu Mukheir of the same period (Site 5), which stood up the spur next to the road ascending to Majdal Bani Fadel, suggest that both were built during the Iron Age as a part of the same system. On the other hand, the irrigation systems still existing were probably built during the Roman period or later.

Previous surveys: the site is very accessible and has had a great many visitors (see descriptions by the early travellers in the Introductions).

The place appears in the British Survey map, with a very short description suggesting this might be an ancient site in the wadi entrance (Conder and Kitchener 1882: 392).

Glueck visited the site in October 1946, writing: "Tell Sheikh edh-Dhiyab (253 a), situated below the entrance of the Wadi Fusayil into the Ghor of the Jordan...with its rushing stream of water. On the S.E. side of the *tell* is a reservoir, measuring about 45 m. square. ...The small *tell*, which consists for the most part of a rocky rise, is covered with remains of foundations of walls of

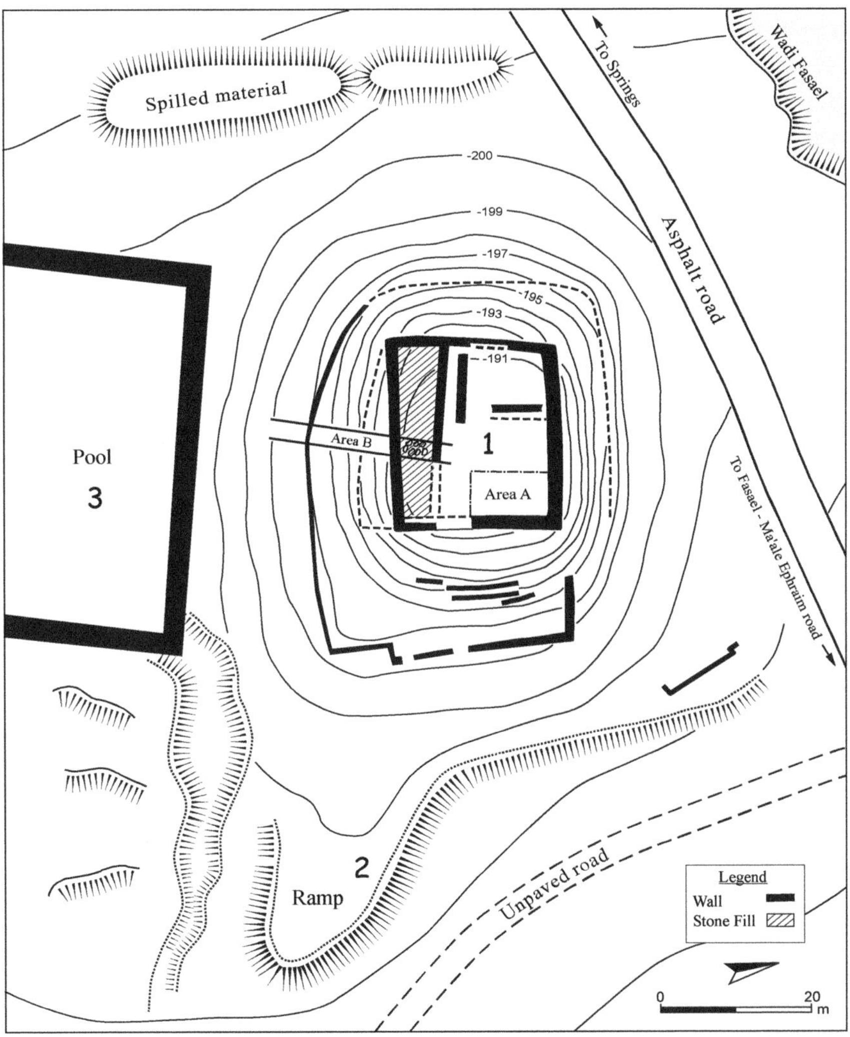

81. Plan of **Tell esh-Sheikh Diyab** and the excavation areas.

all kinds, ...Tell Sheikh edh-Dhiyab occupies an important strategic position. To judge from the considerable number of Iron Age I-II sherds found...there was a small fortress-settlement there during the period. ...Alt has suggested the possibility of identifying Tell Sheikh edh-Dhiyab with Biblical 'Ataroth... Abel, too is of the opinion that Tell Sheikh edh-Dhiyab and 'Ataroth are to be equated. We shall discuss below the reasons for rejecting this equation and for identifying 'Ataroth with Tell el-Mazar in the plain of the Wadi el-Far'ah." (Glueck 1951: 416).

Bar Adon (1972: site 13) writes: "A tell, its upper area is 25×15 m and the circumference is 50×50 m. Over the tell are seen remains of structures and foundations, close by it is a mound with a modern Arab cemetery on it. There is visual contact with Kh. Fusayil and Qurn Sartaba. South-west of the tell, at its foot, is an un-plastered structure, built of large cut stones, measuring 45×45 m. Some 20 m west of the structure are remains of aqueducts." [translation from the Hebrew].

Identification: See below Part One, Chapter Two.

In 2007 a one-week excavation in the tell was conducted by Adam Zertal under the auspices of the University of Haifa's Zinman Institute of Archaeology and the Kinneret College on the Sea of Galilee (for a detailed report see Zertal 2012: Appendix 7). The main results of this excavation are:

Two excavation areas were opened in the dig:

Area A: located at the eastern part of the tell. Here the remains of a rectangular structure, possibly a fort 22×18 m in size, were previously noted during the survey. Sections of the northern and eastern walls of the structure were exposed (walls W11002 and W11001). The walls are 1 m wide, built of two rows of medium-sized fieldstones and a fill. The fill

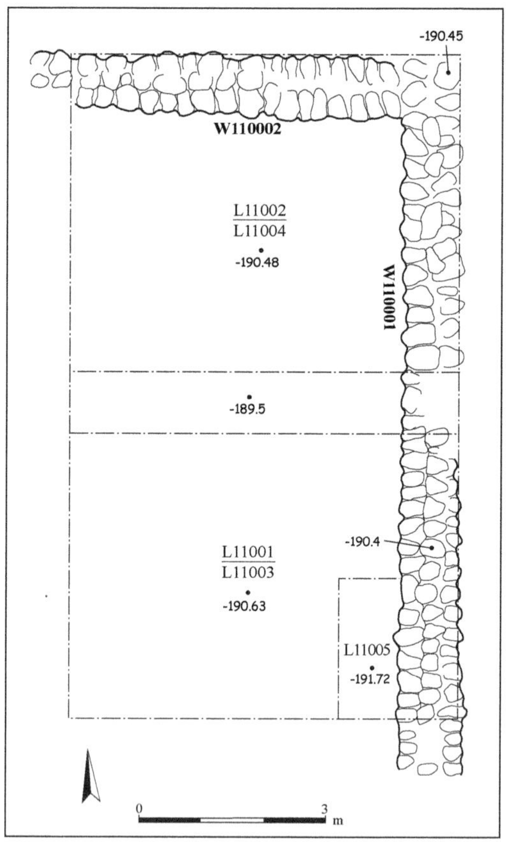

82. Plan of **Tell esh-Sheikh Diyab** Area A.

between these walls was considerably disturbed, probably in ancient times. The remains of a few Roman burials suggest that the tel became a graveyard in the Roman period. In this fill (L11001-4) pottery from all the periods of the occupation of the tel were retrieved, but none were in-situ. The burials prevented further excavation, and only a small probe adjacent to wall W11001, to research the foundation period of the wall, was executed (L11005). In this small 1×2.5 m section a 2 m-high wall was preserved. In the foundation of the wall 8–7th century BCE pottery was found, dating the construction of the large structure to Iron Age IIb.

Area B: located on the southern slope of the tel facing the large pool. Here the object of the dig was a central section 30 m long and 5 m wide. Due to time limitations only the northern and southern squares of this section were excavated.

In the northern squares the remains of two large walls were noted. W12101 is another segment of the southern wall of the large structure on the tel (the continuation of W110001 from Area A). This wall is supported on the slope by a massive boulder-built wall W12119. The entire length of both walls in the section is 4 m. A massive fill of stones was found between these walls (L12117). At first it seemed like a collapse of the upper wall, but careful inspection of the layout of the stones suggests that these inner stones were intentionally located between the walls in a stair-like manner, thus giving a glacis or pyramid shape to the outer face of the structure. Most of the pottery collected from this section was dated to Iron Age IIb, giving additional support to the dating of the large structure.

In the southern square the

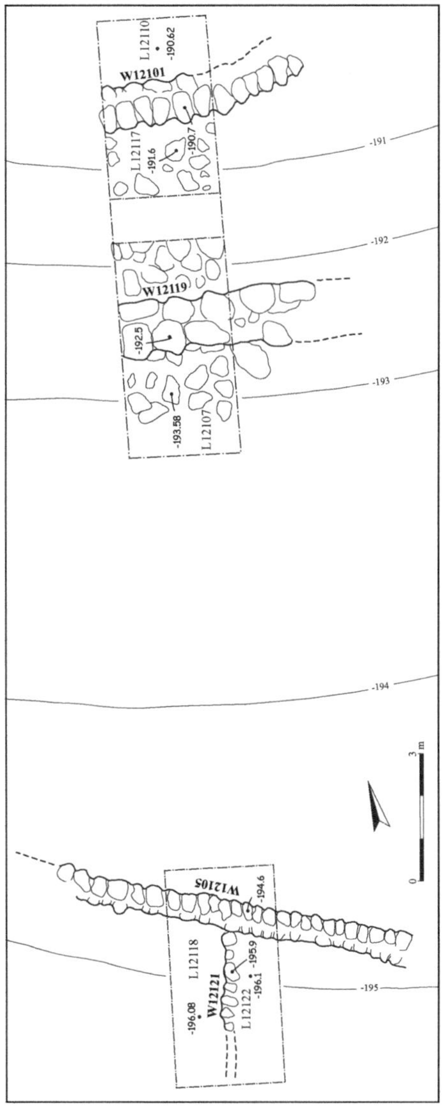

83. Plan of **Tell esh-Sheikh Diyab** Area B.

remains of the small undated wall W12105 were found at the surface level of the slope. In the section of this square four layers of different fills were noted. These are 20 to 40 cm deep, and are superimposed one above the other. Their colour varies, and includes grey, dark and light patches. All the pottery from the different fills was dated to Iron Age II.

A preliminary analysis of the two-stage construction of the Iron Age site is:

- In phase 1 the lower part of the cone of the tel was built. This was done by piling different earth layers from close by to create a step-shaped earthern construction or rampart. Small walls were incorporated in the slope's construction to increase stability.
- In phase 2 an upper structure was built. At first a very wide and robust 'stone box', intended to consolidate and support the upper part of the cone of the

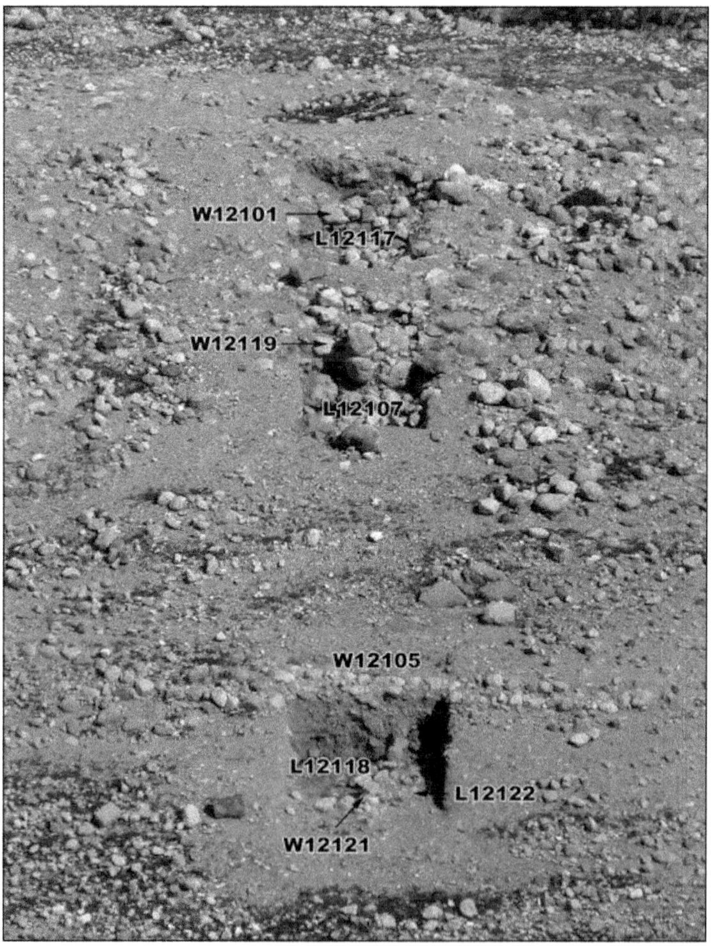

84. View to the north of **Tell esh-Sheikh Diyab**, Area B (S. Bar).

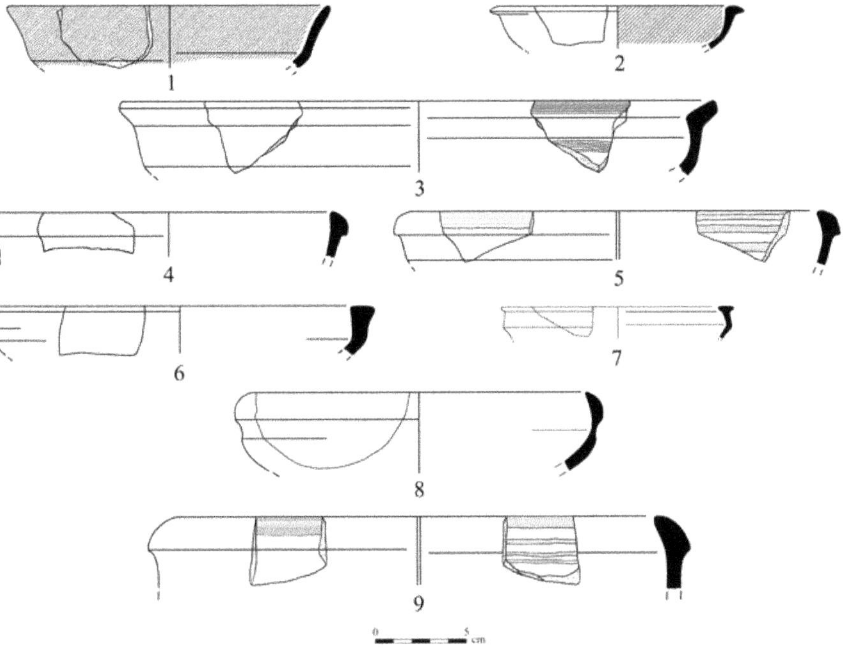

85. Iron Age II bowls from the excavation at **Tell esh-Sheikh Diyab**.

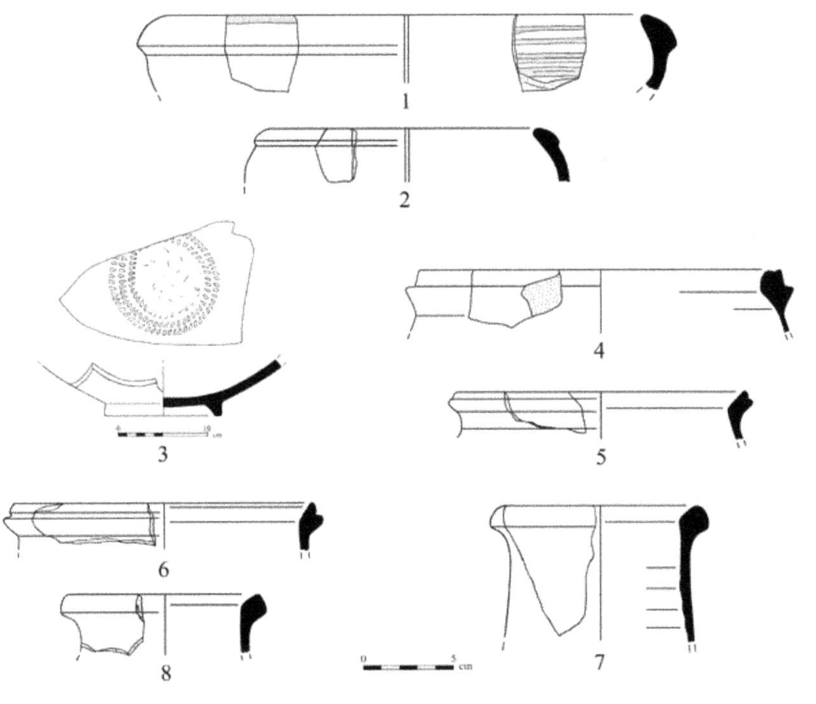

86. Iron Age II bowls, cp and jars from the excavation at **Tell esh-Sheikh Diyab**.

tel, was created. Then the large rectangular structure was built. The structure was probably intended to be a fort guarding the water and agricultural area along the banks of the wadi.

Most of the pottery from the dig originated from insecure loci. The important loci were the foundation of wall W110001 (L11005) in Area A, and the pottery from L12117 and the fills below W12105 in Area B. All the sherds from these loci were dated to the Iron Age IIb (8–7th centuries BCE). In the mixed and disrupted fills, mainly from Area A, as well as from the surface and slopes of the tel, pottery from various periods was found: Chalcolithic, Early Bronze, Middle Bronze II, Late Bronze, and possibly Iron I, pottery. This pottery could have originated from the fills brought to the site in the construction phase during Iron Age IIb. It is also possible that earlier strata from at least some of these periods are still buried below the Iron Age constructions. Only future excavations at the site will resolve this question. Pottery from the Persian, Hellenistic, Early Roman (burials), Middle Ages, and Ottoman periods represent additional later activities at the site. No architectural remains can be attributed to these periods at this stage of the research.

Most of the pottery assemblage is dated to Iron Age IIb. Many typical bowls, cooking pots and jars were retrieved from both excavation areas (see Zertal

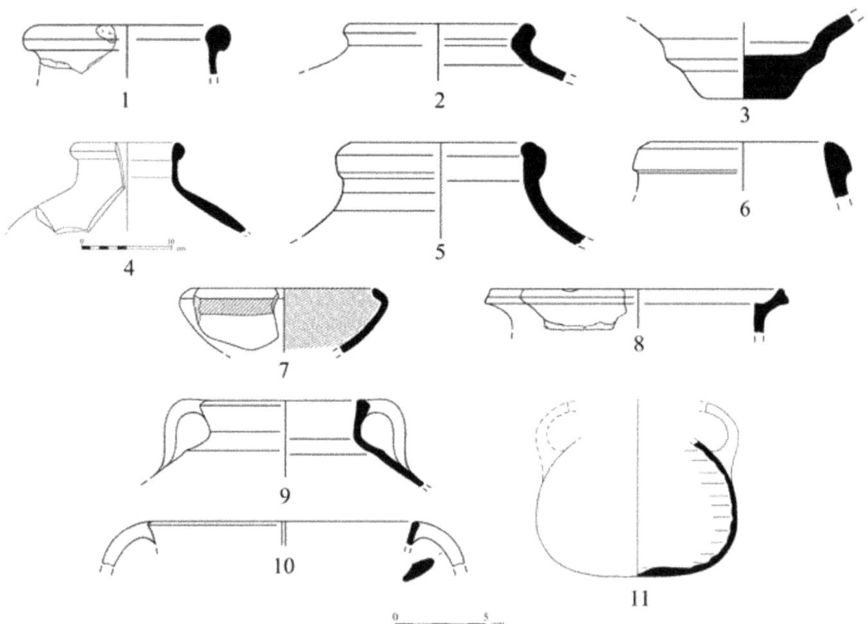

87. Pottery from the excavation at **Tell esh-Sheikh Diyab**: 1. Jar, wh, IA II; 2. Jar, br, IA II; 3. Lamp, br, IA II; 4-5. Jars, lt, Per; 6. Jar, rd-br, Per; 7. Bowl, br, Hel-ER; 8-9. CP, br, Hel-ER; 11. CP, gr, Hel-ER.

2012: Appendix 7 for additional data). Most important are typical Judaite pottery types, dated to the 7–6th centuries BCE, suggesting that the site was a border fort in the north-eastern area of Judah in the later phases of the Iron Age.

Pottery: Chalcolithic/Early Bronze – 4%; Middle Bronze II – 4%; Late Bronze – 7%; Iron I (?) – 2%; Iron II-III – 50%; Persian – 10%; Hellenistic – 8%; Early Roman – 10%; Middle Ages – 3%; Ottoman – 2%.
Additional surveys: Glueck 1951: 416; Bar-Adon 1972: site 13; Markus 1992: site 34.
Additional Bibliography: Bar 2014: site 95.

♦ ♦ ♦

Site 24: 19-16/11/6

FASAEL (7)

Israel grid: 1914/1615
UTM grid: 7302/5484
Elevation: 215 m b.s.l., 0 m a.s.a.
Name: nearest place
Site type: small
Area: 10 dunams (1 ha)
Topography: plain
Rock type: silt
Soil type: stony-desert
Soil quality: 2
Cultivation: none
Cisterns: none
Water source: Nahal Fasael (181), at the site
Road: Phasaelis-Neapolis (C41), next to the site
Visits: May 2008 and many others, excavation 2009-2017; 120 sherds

A site on a hummock west of the village of Fasael, about 500 m north-west of its centre. This is a part of the vast Chalcolithic site in Fasael Valley, separately recorded thanks to superb preservation.

There are several elements in the complex:

1. A late wall: at the top of the hummock, rising about 4 m above the plain, is a wall 12 m long, made of a single row of large stones. At both ends it turns at right angles towards the rest of the structure. This wall is built in a different orientation and should be related to a much later period than the rest of the complex (Late Roman?).
2. The Chalcolithic structure: the hillock is surrounded by a wall two rows thick of large and medium-sized stones, which belongs to the ancient intact complex. The dimensions of the large enclosure are about 45 m (northern side) and about 40 m (eastern side). The western and southern sides are similar, and are only partially preserved. In the south-western part of the

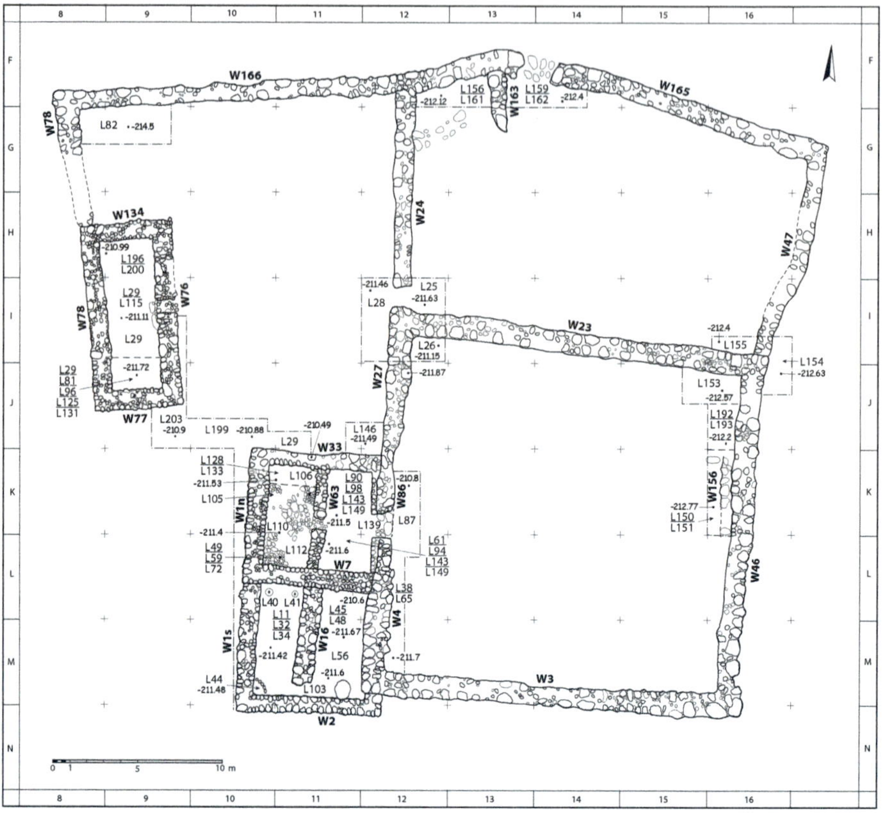

88. Plan of the excavation at **Fasael (7)**, updated, inclusive of 2016 season.

89. Aerial view north-east during the excavation at the Chalcolithic complex in **Fasael (7)**, 2012 (A. Solomon).

hillock were found remains of a longitudinal broad room structure abutting the enclosure wall. From its centre a partition wall goes southward to meet another partition wall coming from the east. This suggests that the large enclosure contained three units and remains of additional walls.

About 50 m eastward was another structure, demolished during development operations. Close to the village fence and over the entire area are scattered moderate quantities of sherds and flint items. Excavation of the site has began under the management of Bar in 2009. Here is a short summary of this ongoing excavation:

The site was excavated between 2009 and 2017 (Bar 2008; 2013b; 2014, Bar et al. 2017). It is situated to the east of Fasael (5) near the fence of the modern village of Fasael. The remains of a very large courtyard house, 1340 sq. m in area, were found. The main features of this complex include a central building surrounded by three abutting courtyards:

1. The central building: This structure (8×15 m, 120 sq. m) is one of the largest buildings in the southern Levant from the Chalcolithic period. Its massive construction included stone walls up to 1 m thick, which were preserved to a height of 1 m. The absence of any evidence indicating mudbrick construction, and the large amount of stone collapse, seem to suggest the structure was built entirely of stone. In order to span a width of 8 m, two additional walls were built along the building's longitudinal axis, which divided the structure into four units, and provided support for the roof.
2. The square courtyard: A square courtyard measuring 20×21 m (about 420 sq. m) was located west of the main building. Its walls were up to 1 m thick, built of medium and large fieldstones, and have enormous boulders incorporated in them, each of which is estimated to weigh more than 1 ton.
3. Two additional courtyards: Two other rectangular courtyards were identified on the surface, located to the north and north-west of the square courtyard. The first one, with an estimated area of about 400 sq. m, extends north of the square courtyard. The second courtyard, about 420 sq. m in area, is a continuation of the first courtyard to the west. At the western section of this courtyard a broad room was excavated. These two courtyards and the broad room were built of the same masonry as that of the central building and the square courtyard.

The finds from the site are typical of the later phases of the Chalcolithic period, and find many parallels in the nearby larger assemblage of Fasael 2. The pottery assemblage included many V-shaped bowls with red stripes on the rims, holemouth jars, jars with inverted rims, large and small lug handles, etc. The flint assemblage, similarly to Fasael (2), included both Chalcolithic and Early Bronze Age types. The bifacial tools are almost absent here, and the Canaanean blade is present. Other notable finds include a notable copper assemblage, including a mace head and a large chisel, and a typical stone tool assemblage that includes fragments of basalt V-shaped bowls, grinding and pounding stones, bowlets, spindle whorls, and perforated pieces.

Pottery: Chalcolithic – 98%; Late Roman – 2%.
Additional surveys: none.
Additional Bibliography: Bar 2013b: chapter 6; Bar 2014: chapter 11.

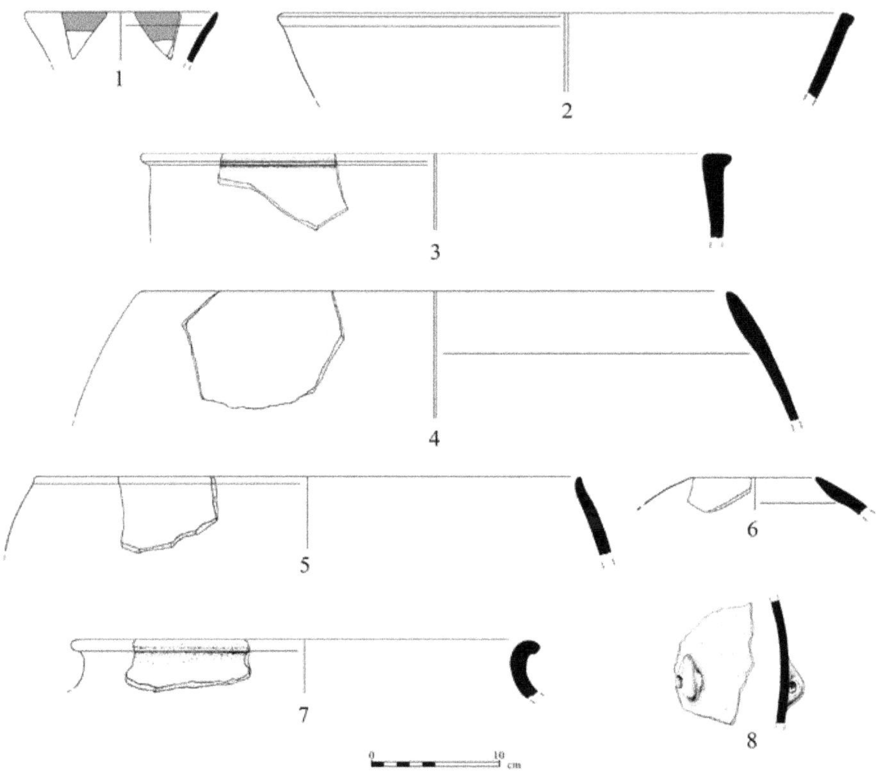

90. Pottery from the survey at **Fasael** (7), all Chal: 1. Bowl, rd, rd band dec over rim; 2. Bowl, buff; 3. Basin, buff; 4-6. HM, buff; 7. Jar, br-rd; 8. Lug handle, br-rd.

Site 25: 19-16/11/5

FASAEL (12)

Israel grid: 1915/1615
UTM grid: 7301/5484
Elevation: 200 m b.s.l., 0 m a.s.a.
Name: nearest place
Site type: prehistoric
Area: 1 dunam (1000 sq. m)
Topography: plain
Rock type: silt
Soil type: stony-desert
Soil quality: 2
Cultivation: none
Cisterns: none
Water source: Nahal Fasael (181), at the site
Road: Phasaelis-Neapolis (C41), next to the site
Visit: November 2009; 350 flint items

This is a prehistoric site adjoining site Fasael (7), Site 24, to the north.

Many flint items were collected over a limited flat area.

Flint: 350 items, Late Upper Palaeolithic (see Appendix A).
Additional surveys: none.

♦ ♦ ♦

Site 26: 19-16/01/2

EL-HISHA

Israel grid: 1909/1613
UTM grid: 7296/5481
Elevation: 200 m b.s.l., 0 m b.s.a.
Name: nearest place
Site type: structures
Area: 2 dunams (2000 sq. m)
Topography: valley edges
Rock type: Judea Group
Soil type: stony-desert
Soil quality: 3
Cultivation: none
Cisterns: none
Water source: Fasael pool (171), 200 m distant
Road: Phasaelis- Fasael springs (C47), next to the site
Visits: February 2000 and more; 160 sherds

This is a site at the margins of the Jordan Valley west of the village of Fasael, about 300 m south-west of Tell esh-Sheikh Diyab. West and above it pass the aqueducts going south from the Fasael Springs.

There are several parts to the site:

1. A large structure, about 40×40 m, badly damaged by a bulldozer. The walls are 1 m thick, built of two rows of small stones with a fill between them. In

the northern (central) unit there are three equal-sized rooms, with openings to the central corridor which contains inner partitions. The southern, parallel, unit is almost totally ruined, although it appears to be of similar design.

2. West and north-west of the central unit are two others: an elongated room with a small room attached in the north, and close by scant remnants of another room.
3. A branch of the aqueduct reaches the site, ending in a plastered pool.

Heaps of earth and stones are scattered in the area, the result of bulldozing. The quantity of sherds is particularly abundant, among them medieval 'sugar vessels'.

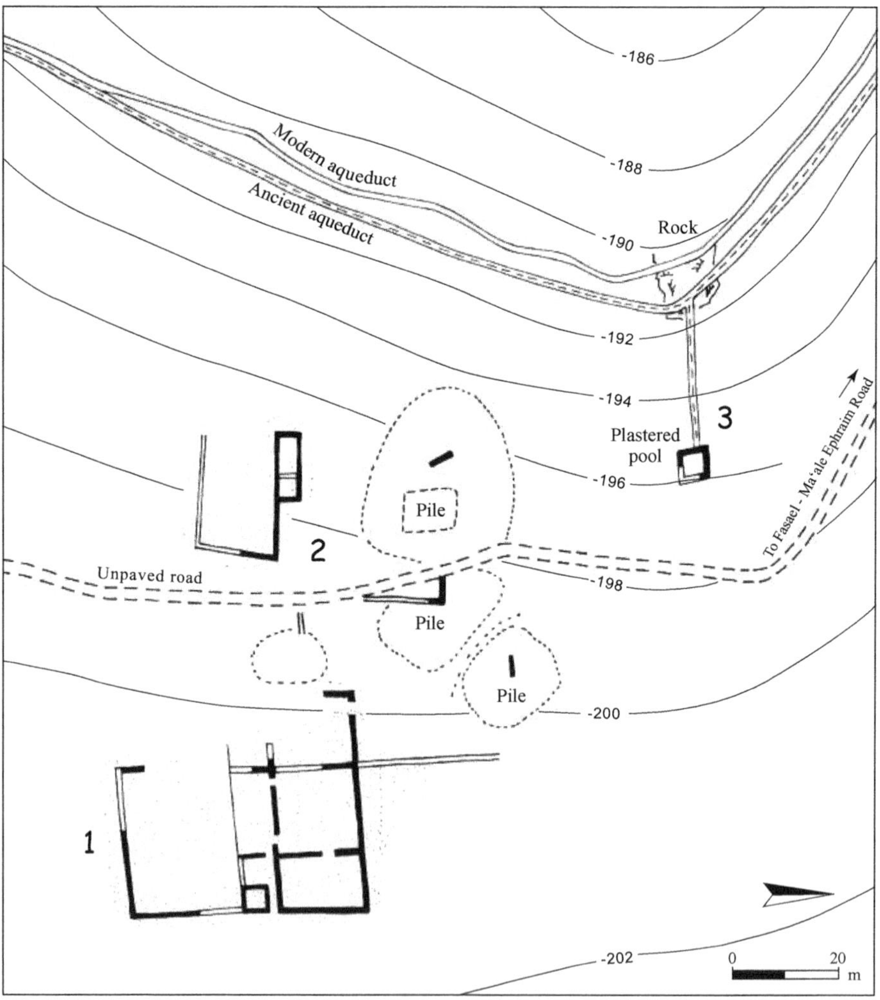

91. Plan of **el-Hisha.**

92. **El-Hisha**, an aerial view west, 2008. In the centre are seen the remains of ruined courtyards and structures. Above the site pass the unpaved road and aqueducts to Phasaelis (N. Eshed).

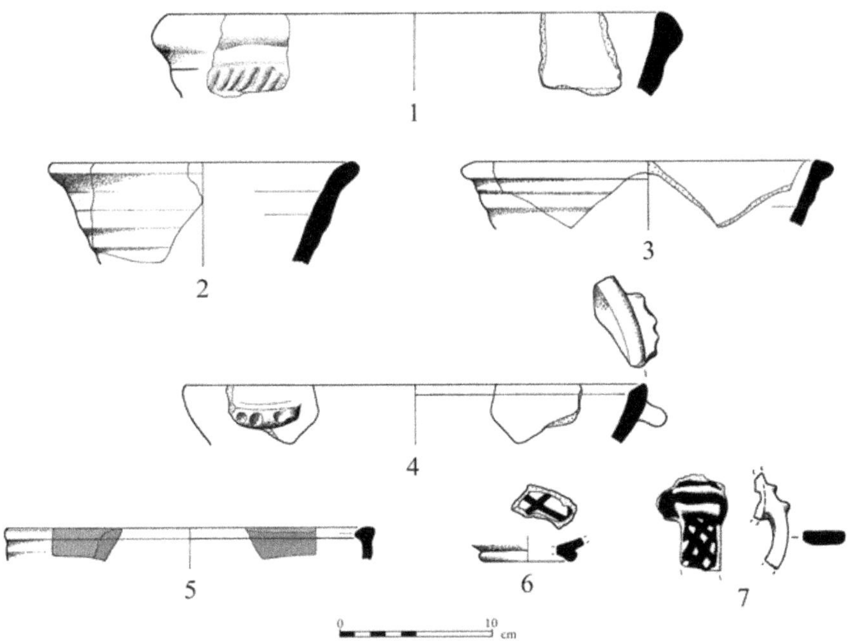

93. Pottery from **el-Hisha**: 1. Basin, rope dec, wh, EM; 2. Conical basin, buff, EM; 3. Bowl, buff, EM; 4. Bowl, thumbed ledged handle, rd, MA; 5. Bowl, green glaze, MA; 6. Bowl base, yel glaze, MA; 7. Jug handle, net pattern ornamentation, lt br, rd slip, MA.

This courtyard-type building may have been a sugar processing plant, as testified by the many thick sugar vessels. East of the site is a large agricultural area, divided by stone walls into square levelled units in a chequer pattern. A linkage between the site and the agricultural array next to it is likely.

Above the aqueducts, at coordinates 1908/1614 is a structure (does not appear in the plan) on a high shoulder, and around it are sherds identical to those in the site. This structure may have served as a watchtower.

Porath (1985b: 42), who visited when conducting his Irrigated Agricultural Survey, describes it as follows: "At the outlet of Nahal Fasael to the Jordan Valley, coordinates 1909-1612, the remains of a small settlement were surveyed. At the northern edges of the settlement is a ruined flourmill. Medieval sherds, including glazed ones, were collected." (translation from the Hebrew).

Pottery: Early Moslem – 50%; Medieval – 50%.
Flint: 3 items (see Appendix A).
Stone: a basalt grinding stone fragment.
Additional surveys: Porath 1985b: 42.

♦ ♦ ♦

Site 27: 19-16/41/1

FASAEL (EAST)

Israel grid: 1943/1614 | Site type: *rujm*
UTM grid: 7330/5483

This site is a *rujm* east of the Jordan Valley road near the village of Fasael.

In May 1998 a salvage excavation was conducted in the site by Yuval Peleg. This is his description:

"The circular *rujm* is located on the western slope of a hill, the altitude of which is 275 m below sea level, dominating its vicinity. The *rujm*, of which only the eastern part has been preserved, is built of two walls: outer (7.4 m in diameter) and inner (5.1 m). A part of the outer wall was exposed, built of large fieldstones (0.7×0.5 m on average); 1 m from it was exposed part of the inner wall, built of medium-sized stones (0.4×0.3 m on average). A box grave was found at the centre of the *rujm*, its floor made of compacted earth; the walls built of medium-sized stones plastered on the inside. The tomb's southern wall, exposed for a length of 1.78 m, has been preserved one course high, while the eastern (2.51 m long) and western walls (2.48 m) have been preserved four courses high. The finds in the tomb included several fragments of red wash decorated cooking pot, an iron arrowhead and dagger and shell splinters. The tomb has been dated based on the finds to the Early Roman period (1st Century BCE). Examination of the bones showed they were of an individual aged 30-40, but it was impossible to determine the gender." (Peleg 2000a) [translation from the Hebrew].

The site was destroyed during earth-moving operations.

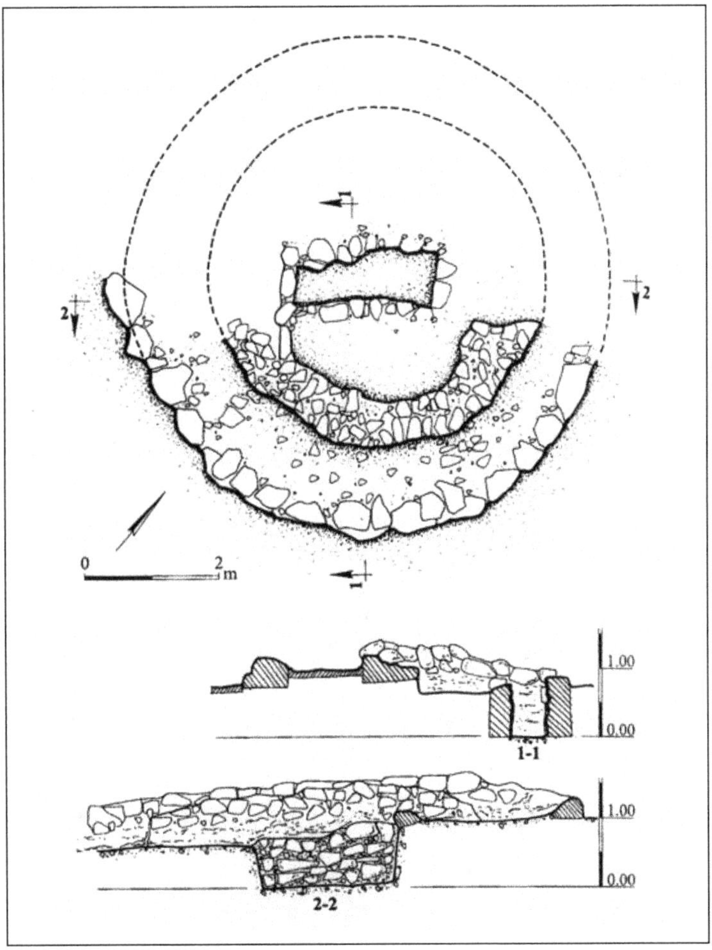

94. **Fasael (East)**, the excavation plan (Peleg 2000a: illustration 90).

Site 28: 19-16/01/3

ELEVATION POINT -85

Israel grid: 1902/1610
UTM grid: 7290/5479
Elevation: 90 m b.s.l., 20 m b.s.a.
Name: nearest place
Site type: encampment
Area: 15 dunams (1.5 ha)
Topography: saddle
Rock type: Judea Group
Soil type: stony-desert
Soil quality: 3
Cultivation: none
Cisterns: none
Water source: Fasael pool (171), 400 m distant
Road: Phasaelis- Fasael Springs (C47), 600 m distant
Visit: April 2000; 70 sherds

A large encampment site on the ridge south of Nahal Fasael and the aqueducts within, north-west of the summit of Elevation Point -85.

The site location is in a large saddle, rising to the north-east and confined in the west by a flint dyke, common in the region.

Over the surface are rough heaps of stones from clearing the area with a multi-period sherd scatter. The site is characteristic of encampment sites in the fringes of the desert, and apparently tent encampments existed here for generations.

Pottery: Iron I – 25%; Iron II – 8%; Late Roman – 21%; Byzantine – 17%; Medieval – 21%; Ottoman – 8%.
Stone: 4 fragments of basalt grinding stones.
Additional surveys: none.

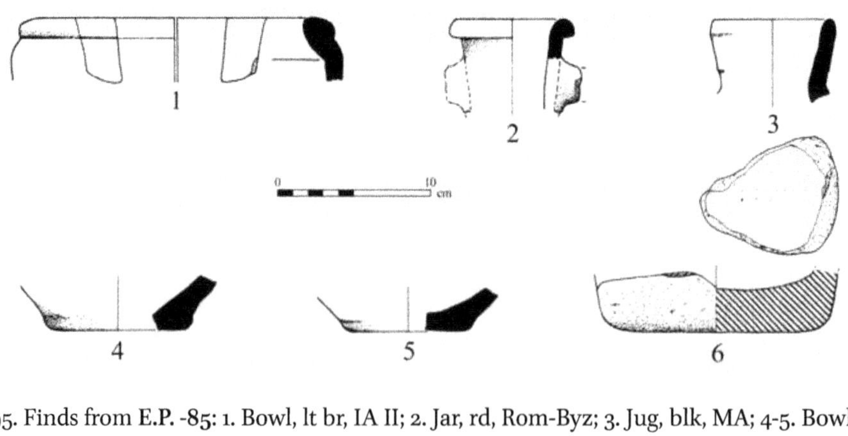

95. Finds from **E.P.** -85: 1. Bowl, lt br, IA II; 2. Jar, rd, Rom-Byz; 3. Jug, blk, MA; 4-5. Bowls bases, dk br, IA I-II; 6. Basin, basalt.

Site 29: 19-16/01/4

UMM SUWEI'AD

Israel grid: 1907/1610
UTM grid: 7295/5477
Elevation: 190 m b.s.l., 0 m b.s.a.
Name: nearest place
Site type: medium size
Area: 3 dunams (3000 sq. m)
Topography: plain in valley edge
Rock type: Judea Group
Soil type: stony-desert
Soil quality: 2
Cultivation: none
Cisterns: none
Water source: Fasael pool (171), 400 m distant
Road: Phasaelis- Fasael Springs (C47), next to the site
Visits: February 2000 and more; 125 sherds

A site on a low mound at the western edge of the Jordan Valley, and 1 km west of the village of Fasael centre. It rises about 5 m above the northern bank of Wadi ez-Zimrah channel. Nearby passes an unpaved road from Tell esh-Sheikh Diyab to el-Fusayil.

The site is a built enclosure, measuring about 45×45 m, with remains of a square structure within. The perimeter wall is built of two rows of medium-sized stones and is 70 cm thick. Large stones were laid at intervals along the walls as reinforcements.

In Porath's 1985 survey (Porath 1985b: 40) only Early Roman pottery was gathered. Our survey team collected a much more varied pottery assemblage.

Pottery: Chalcolithic/Early Bronze I – 4%; Iron I – 20%; Iron II – 30%; Early Roman – 21%; Byzantine – 20%; Ottoman – 5%.
Flint: 20 items (see Appendix A).
Additional surveys: Porath 1985b: 40.
Additional Bibliography: Bar 2014: site 99.

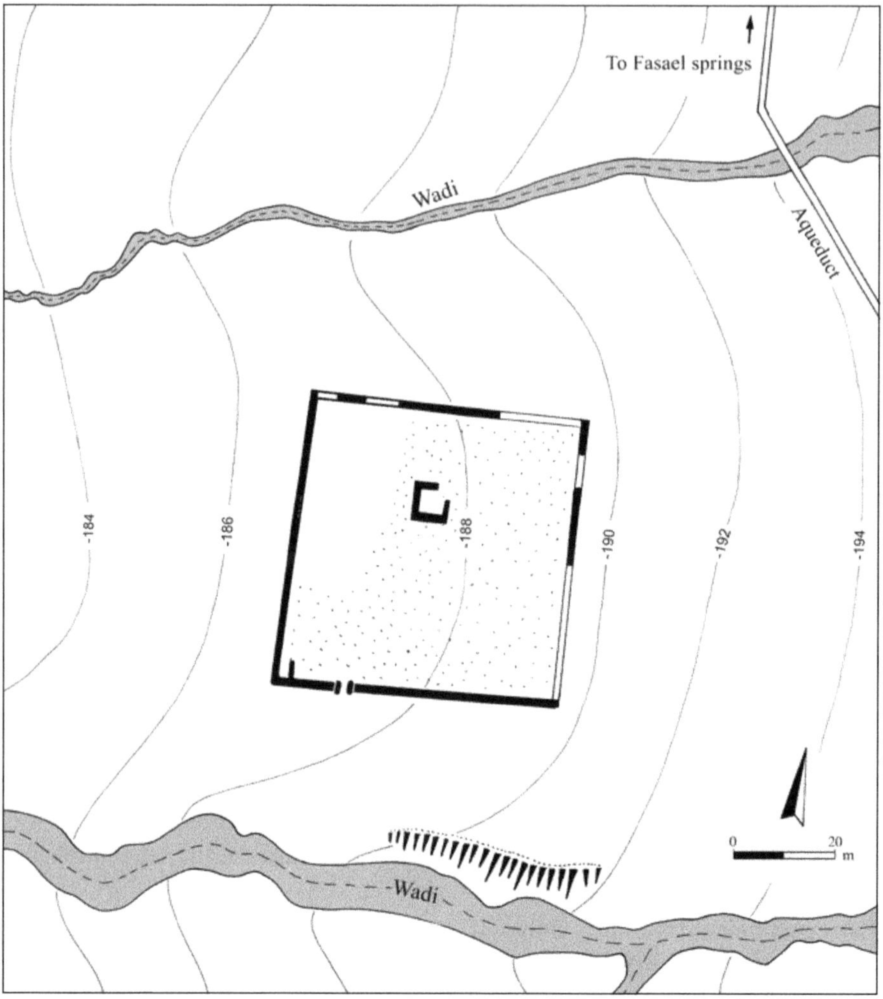

96. Plan of **Umm Suwei'ad.**

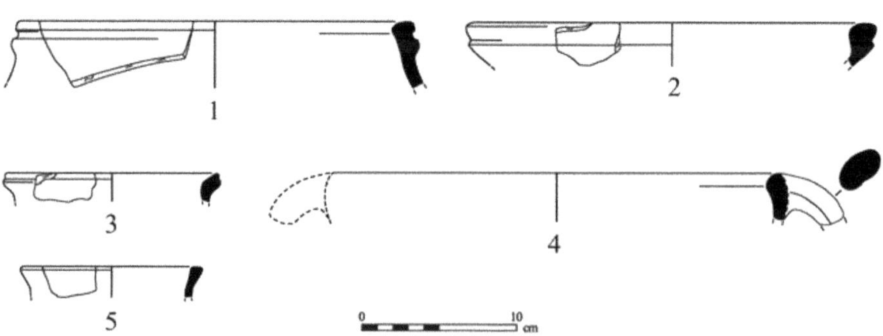

97. Pottery from **Umm Suwei'ad**: 1. CP, br, IA II; 2. CP D, br, IA II; 3-4. CP, br, IA II; 5. Jug, buff, ER (?).

Site 30: 19-16/11/1

FASAEL (10)

Israel grid: 1915/1615 UTM grid: 7303/5484

A salvage excavation in the village of Fasael, conducted by Y. Porath.

A large courtyard (16×16 m) was discovered, with a broad room structure with a central room and attached cells on both its sides in the south-western part. The measurements are: central room 7×5 m, southern cell 5×5 m and northern cell 5×4 m. The entrances to the yard and the central structure are from the east through a threshold 1 m wide with a stone socket. The room floors are made of tamped earth with pebbles.

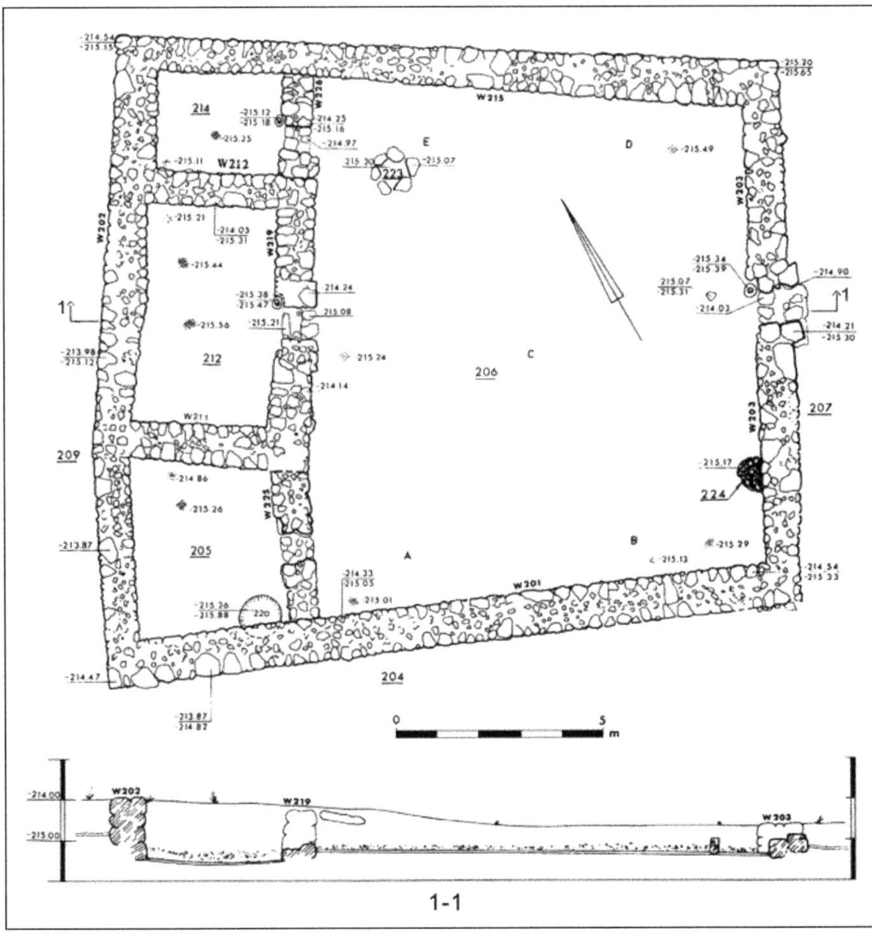

98. Y. Porath's excavation plan at **Fasael (10)** (Porath 1985a: illustration 2).

The pottery assemblage is Chalcolithic and in the stone tool assemblage are two basalt bowls with straight-sided walls, grinding stones, mortars, pestles and weights.

The site was destroyed during the construction of the modern village.

Bibliography: Porath 1973: 9-10; 1985a; Bar 2014: site 90.

♦ ♦ ♦

Site 31: 19-16/00/01

WADI EZ-ZIMRAH

Israel grid: 1906/1606
UTM grid: 7293/5474
Elevation: 150 m b.s.l., 60 m a.s.a.
Name: nearest place
Site type: enclosure and structures
Area: 2 dunams (2000 sq. m)
Topography: saddle
Rock type: Judea Group
Soil type: stony-desert
Soil quality: 1
Cultivation: none
Cisterns: none
Water source: Fasael pool (171), 1 km distant
Road: Phasaelis- Fasael Springs (C47), 400 m distant
Visits: April 2000 and more; 50 sherds

A site on a saddle, on the eastern part of the ridge of E.P. -30, 1.2 km south-west of the village of Fasael centre. The site faces north-east, and there is a fine view to the Sartaba ridge and the Fasael Valley.

The site has two parts, lower and upper:

1. In the lower part a part of a rounded enclosure has been preserved. Its wall is made of two rows of stones. Most of the wall was dismantled, and inside the enclosure were several small formless structures.
2. The upper part: about 150 m up the spur to south-west, were found remains of another ruined enclosure, and next to it at least one broad room structure. The few sherds found were Chalcolithic.

Over the entire area and the saddle is a moderate scatter of sherds.

It appears that both parts of site existed in the Chalcolithic, while during Iron Age I, only the lower part was in use.

Pottery: Chalcolithic – 50%; Iron I – 50%.
Flint: 33 items (see Appendix A).
Additional surveys: none.
Bibliography: Bar 2014: site 100.

Site 32: 19-15/19/1

ABU ZERQA

Israel grid: 1911/1591
UTM grid: 7298/5460
Elevation: 195 m b.s.l., 10 m a.s.a.
Name: nearest place
Site type: enclosure
Area: 2 dunams (2000 sq. m)
Topography: valley edge
Rock type: Judea Group
Soil type: stony-desert
Soil quality: 2
Cultivation: none
Cisterns: none
Water source: Nahal Fasael (181), 2.3 km distant
Road: Phasaelis-Neapolis (C41), 800 m distant
Visits: March 2000, 2016; 43 sherds

A site in the south-eastern edge of Fasael Valley, about 600 m north-west of the village of Tomer centre. It is located close to the asphalted road (no. 5530) leading from Tomer to the drilling sites in Wadi Senisleh. North of it passes the wide channel of Wadi Dabal and above it, on Abu Zerqa hill, is one of Tomer's water reservoirs. There is a fine lookout to Fasael Valley.

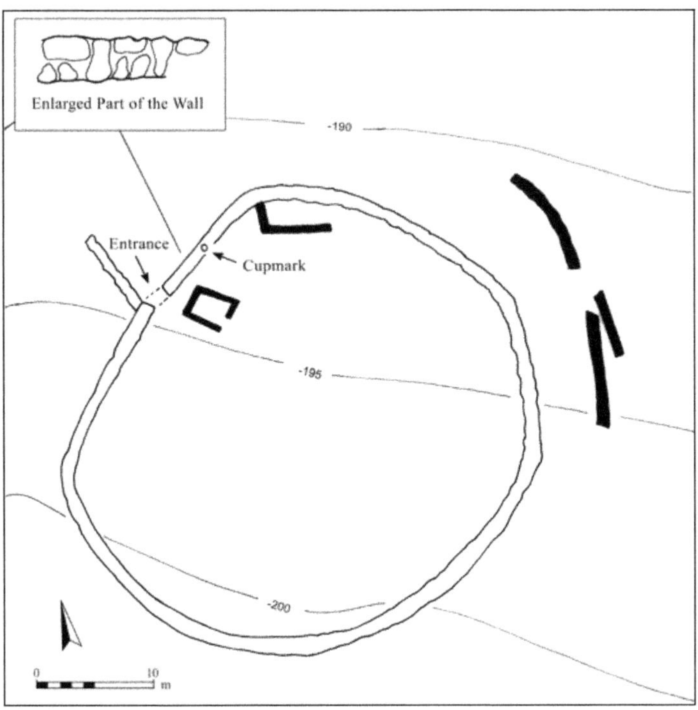

99. Plan of **Abu Zerqa.**

The enclosure served as a corral, and was built rather sharply inclined. The diameter is 35 m, encircled by a wall made of two rows of medium-sized fieldstones. In a part of it which is well preserved the construction is in the stretchers-headers pattern. In the western side is a built opening 1 m wide abutting an outer wall, 5 m long, designed to direct the flock to the pen. There is a structure inside the enclosure, next to its north wall.

There is a moderate number of sherds, more than in other similar enclosures.

Pottery: Iron I – 5%; Iron II – 95%.
Additional surveys: none.

100. **Abu Zerqa**, an aerial view south, 2008. (N. Eshed).

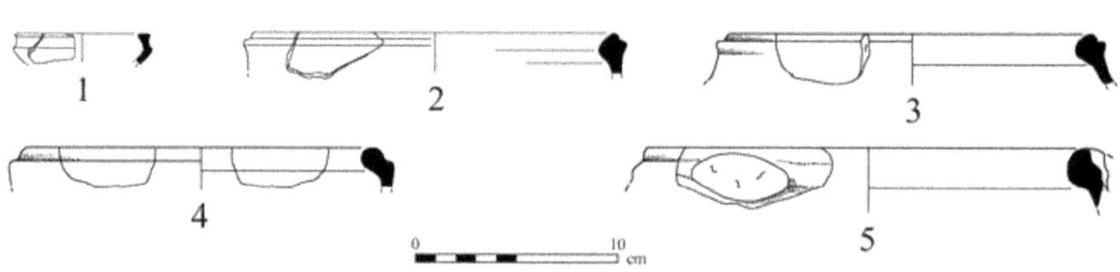

101. Pottery from **Abu Zerqa**, all IA II: 1. Bowl, br; 2-5. CP D, dk br.

Site 33: 19-15/19/2

FUSAYIL (2)

Israel grid: 1910/1598
UTM grid: 7298/5466
Elevation: 200 m b.s.l., 0 m a.s.a.
Name: nearest place
Site type: enclosure and structures
Area: 10 dunams (1 ha)
Topography: a low hillock at a valley fringe
Rock type: Judea Group
Soil type: stony-desert
Soil quality: 2
Cultivation: none
Cisterns: none
Water source: Nahal Fasael (181) 1.6 km distant
Road: Phasaelis-Neapolis (C41), 500 m distant
Visit: November 2006; 50 sherds

An enclosure and settlement on the flank of the Fasael Valley, 500 m south-west of the centre of Fasael. Both are situated on a hillock, about 20 m above

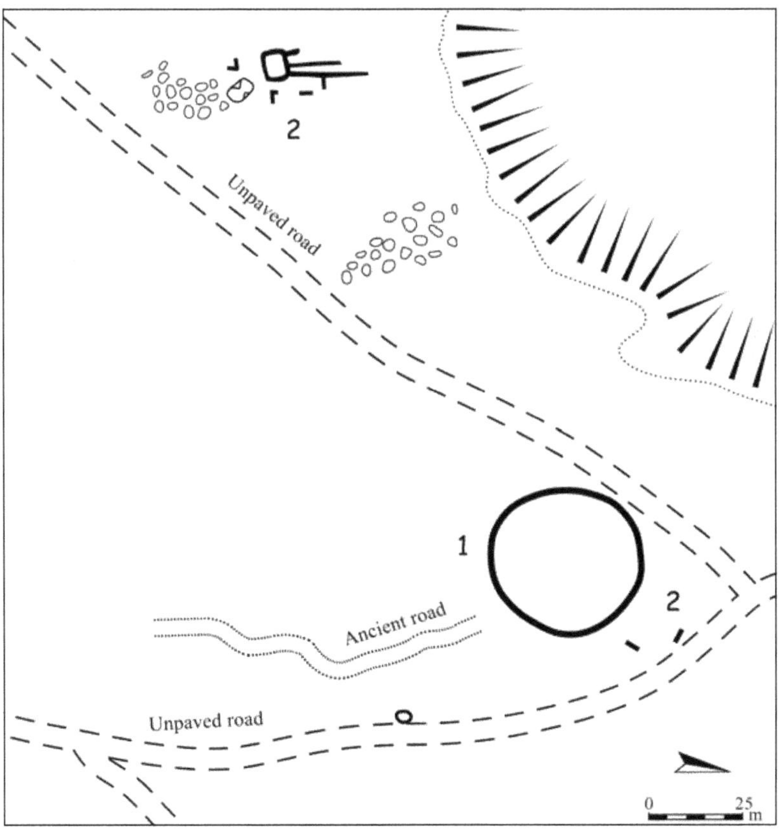

102. Plan of **Fusayil (2)**.

the surrounding vicinity and close to a Bedouin encampment. There is a good view of the expanses of the valley and the Sartaba massif. Close to the site is a junction of unpaved roads.

There are two parts to the site:

1. A large enclosure, about 42×40 m, encircled by a wall built of a single row of large stones. Some of the stones of the wall are missing, but it is obvious that it encircled the entire enclosure. Several openings were located, and various walls and structures about the enclosure wall, some possibly serving as dwellings. Remains of walls were found inside, and in the western part – a tomb, apparently modern. The site is reached by an ancient road.
2. Structures around the enclosure: near no. 1 in the plan, are remains of several structures with sections of walls. About 60 m west of it was another cluster of structures, with sections of walls and a large tumulus. Over the whole area are scattered ruined structures which cannot be measured.

Two settlements existed in the place and maybe more:
a) Ancient structures (Early Bronze?) in part no. 2;
b) The large Iron Age enclosure was built later (no. 1).
The remains of the ancient road passing by the site have not been dated.

Pottery: Early Bronze (?) – 4%; Iron I – 38%; Iron II – 48%; Late Roman – 10%.
Additional surveys: none.

103. **Fusayil (2)** the circular enclosure, aerial view south-west, 2008 (N. Eshed).

Site 34: 19-15/19/3

KHIRBET FUSAYIL (PHASAELIS)

Israel grid: 1918/1597 (centre of site)
UTM grid: 7306/5465
Elevation: 220 m b.s.l., 0 m a.s.a.
Name: ancient and in map
Site type: city
Area: 500 dunams (50 ha)
Topography: plain
Rock type: Judea Group
Soil type: stony-desert

Soil quality: 2
Cultivation: none
Cisterns: none
Water source: Nahal Fasael (181), 1.5 km distant
Roads: Phasaelis-Neapolis (C40, C41), next to the site
Visits: March 2000 and many more; 300 sherds and other finds

The remains of a large city in the centre of the Fasael Valley, 1.5 km south of the modern village of Fasael. The location is on the stream floodplain and close to the Beit She'an–Jericho road in the west. Nearby, in the south, is the modern Bedouin village of el-Fusayil. The remnants of the Roman city of Phasaelis are within the ruins.

A. The city bounds: an area of 90 dunams (300×300 m) has been measured in the city centre; but the city bounds extend further, about 200-300 m, south, north and east. The total city area is estimated by us to be about 500 dunams. On the southern part of it is the village el-Fusayil.
B. The aqueducts: the ancient aqueduct from the Fasael Springs reached the western part of the city centre, where there was a double wall with an aqueduct in the centre. A modern concrete aqueduct reaches the eastern part of the city. East of the city, in the currently cultivated fields, were additional routes of ancient aqueducts (see detailed discussion in Appendix D).
C. Constructed complexes: the high north part of the site, perhaps the acropolis or the citadel, was surveyed and investigated in detail. This suggestion is based on the fortifications discovered (no.1). A significant part of the area apparently lies beneath the present village, which is situated on the high portion of the city remnants.

At least three large built complexes have been found in the surveyed area, some of which apparently served as public buildings. They are:

1. The citadel: a fortified building, 70×70 m, about 5 dunams (5,000 sq. m) in area. It is partially built of large uncut stones, brought from the nearby mountains. The wall encircling the building is 2 m thick. There are two asymmetrical square towers in the north-western and south-eastern corners. In

the citadel centre is an inner courtyard. The well-preserved entrance is in the centre of the north side. It is about 4 m wide.

Along the outer walls were rows of rooms, some surviving until the present. There are inner partitions forming rooms or spaces, the nature of which is not clear. All the inner walls are built of pebbles and are 80-100 cm thick.

The citadel in Phasaelis is similar to the Roman courtyard fortresses of the 2nd-3rd centuries CE, which are common in Israel. Among these are also the fortresses in Kh. Khiraf (Zertal 2008: site 266), and in ʿIraq Abu Hashish (A) (Zertal 2008: site 248). A possible linkage between the founding of the city and that of the citadel, is not clear, but it is reasonable that the latter played a role in the history of the place. It may have been a link in a chain of fortresses between Beit She'an and Jericho, established during the reign of Hadrian (see also Zertal 1991).

2. A large public building: this is a complex 40 m west of the citadel. It measures about 80×70 m, an area of about 6 dunams (6,000 sq. m); the original size of which is unknown. On its western part is the football ground of the village of

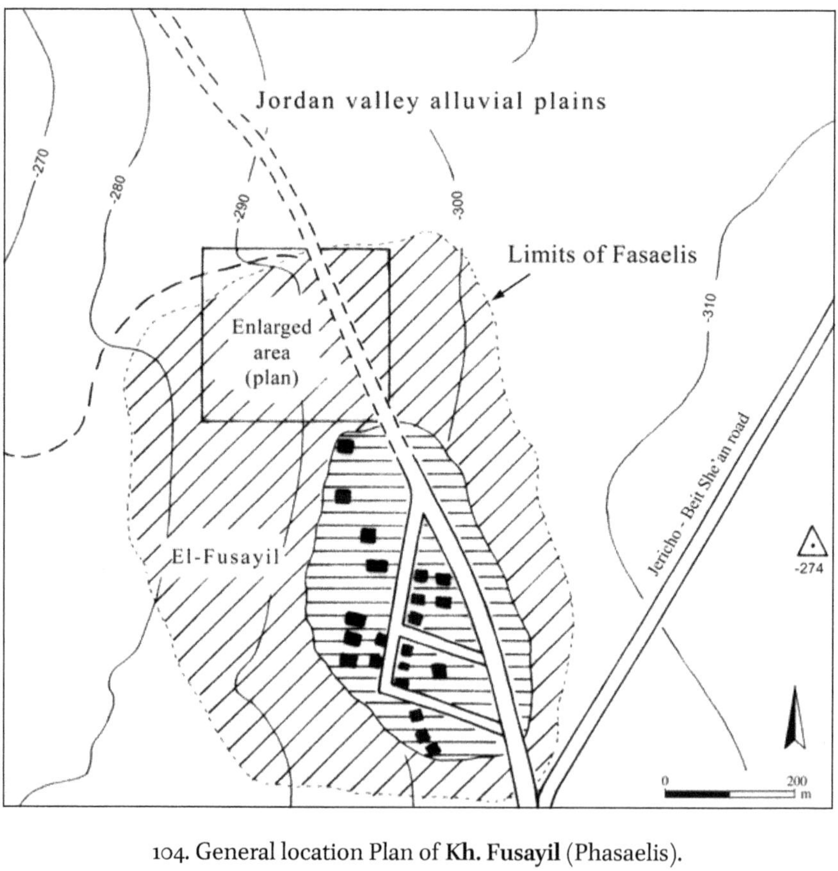

104. General location Plan of **Kh. Fusayil** (Phasaelis).

Fusayil. The structure is encircled by a wall, over 1 m thick. The eastern wall, which has a built duct in the middle, apparently served also as an aqueduct. The wall stretches in both directions, north-west and south-east. Along the wall, there was possibly a line of rooms and another along the southern wall. At the centre of the place was found a row of rooms with a wall dividing them. The complex is well planned and bears the marks of a public place.

3. Dwelling area (?): sections of structures that do not adhere to an obvious plan. The frame walls mainly remained in the northern part, with walls and

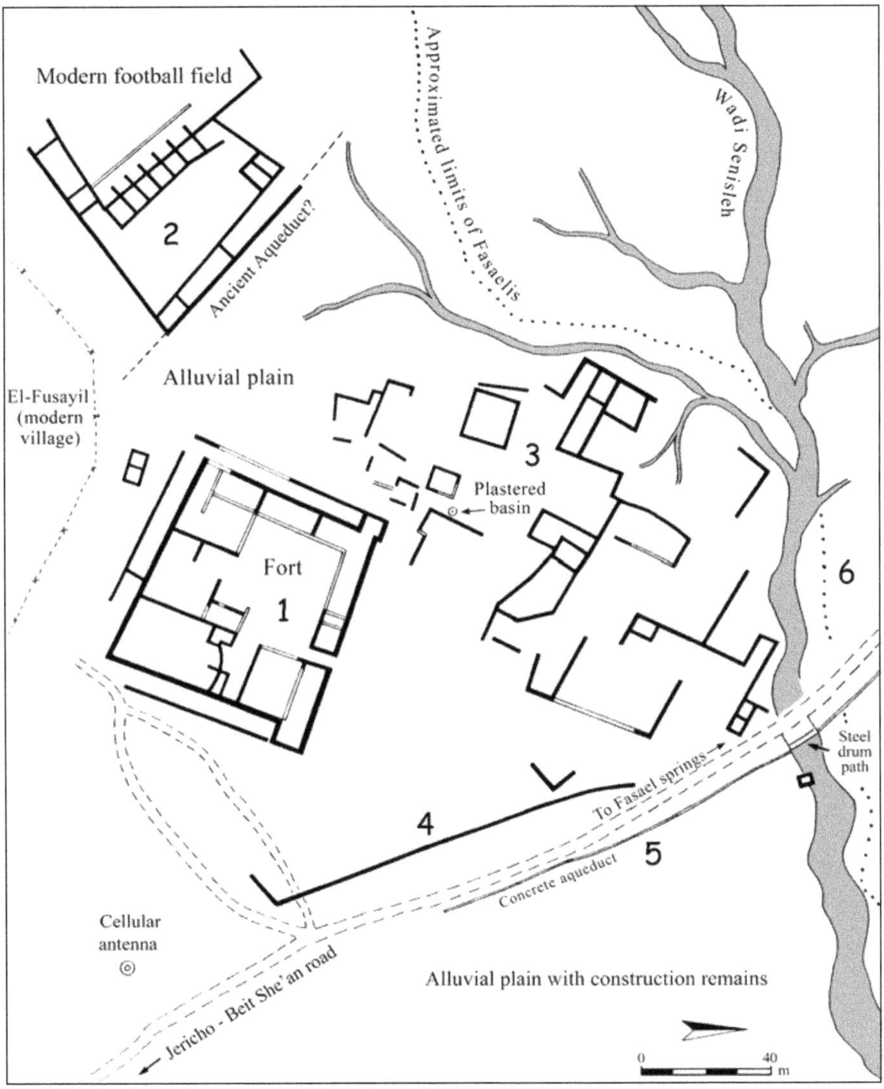

105. Detailed plan of **Kh. Fusayil.**

other elements. A plastered basin was also found in this area.
4. The enclosure wall (?): east of the citadel is 110 m long and 1 m thick. This may have been the perimeter wall of the city or citadel.
5. A modern concrete aqueduct: south of the unpaved road from the Beit She'an–Jericho road is the extension of the modern concrete aqueduct, coming from the Fasael Springs and crossing the channel of Wadi Senisleh on a bridge of steel drums (see Appendix D).
6. Other parts: north-east of the citadel and across the unpaved road is another raised area. Here were found sections of ornamented stucco plaster, belonging to villas or other structures.

It appears that the present wadi cut the city into two parts.

D. Previous surveys and history of research: the equation of Phesech with Phasaelis, originating in medieval times, was known to many, for example Guèrin (1874: 231). Van der Velde (1854: 312) named the small tell at the exit of the stream (Tell esh-Sheikh Diyab [Site 23 above]) Tell Phasaelis, and considered it to have been the acropolis of the city of Phasaelis, built

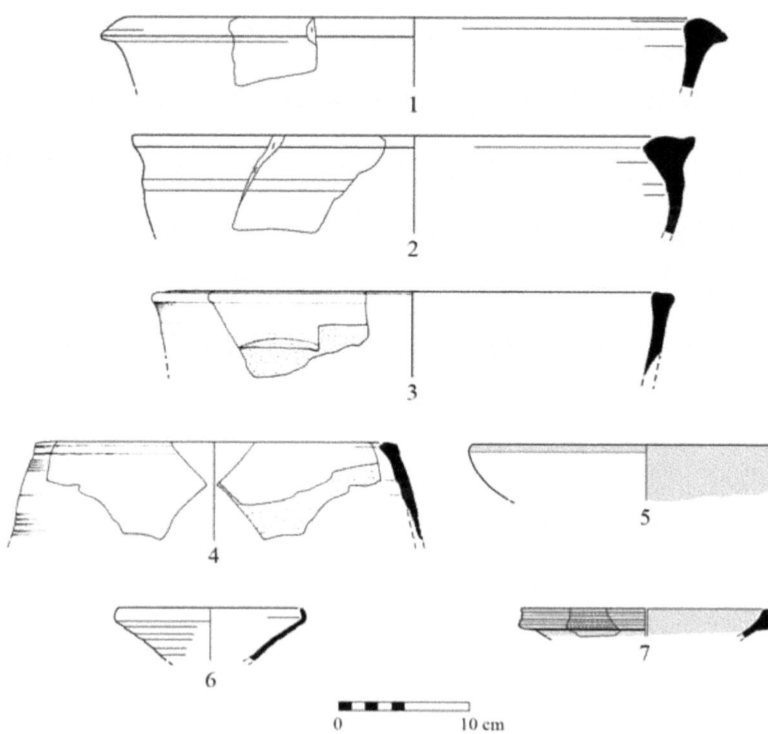

106. Pottery from **Kh. Fusayil**, part 1: 1-2. CP, blk, EM; 3. CP, buff, thumbed dec, EM; 4. CP, lt br, EM; 5. Bowl, rd slip and burnish, Hel-ER; 6. Bowl, lt br, ER; 7. Bowl, lt br, rd slip, roulette dec, Rom-Byz.

by Herod. Several yards south, the traveller saw remains of a small settlement (apparently el-Hisha [Site 26 above]), where he identified the city of Phasaelis. And finally, he noted the remains of the aqueduct on the slope south of the stream (van der Velde 1854: 312).

Tristram reached Phasaelis on January 1864, describing it as follows: "The view of the expanse was fine and exhilarating, a wide even plain, with Kurn Surtabeh and its symmetrical peak completely intersecting the *Ghor* to the

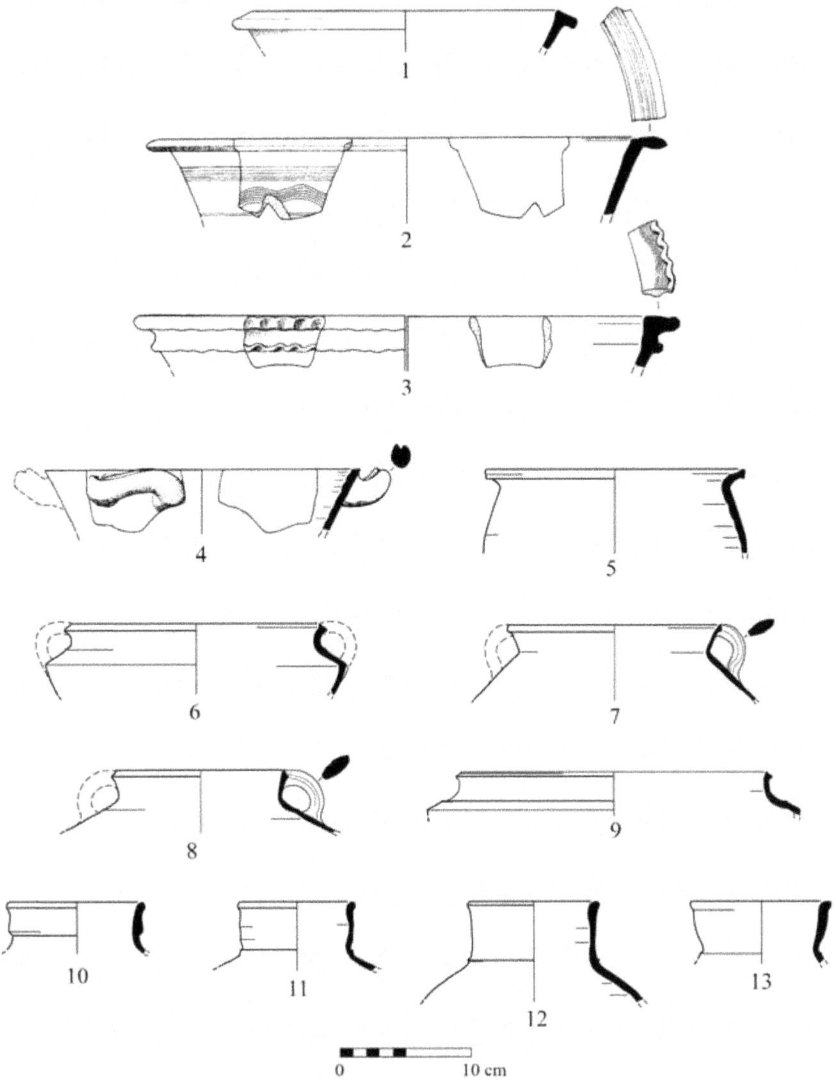

107. Pottery from **Kh. Fusayil**, part 2: 1. Bowl, rd, Rom-Byz; 2. Bowl, buff, incised dec, Byz-EM; 3. Bowl, buff, thumbed dec, EM; 4. CP, rd, Byz-EM; 5. CP, dk br, ER; 6-9. CP, rd, ER; 10-12; Jars, lt br, ER; 13. Jar, lt br, Rom-Byz.

north; ...a thicket of trees seeming to fringe the next wadi, which I took to be Fusayil...As we approached a low spur of the hills, we could discern a bright streak running down the steep side in front, but not reaching the plain – the 'Ein Fusayil. Below this, on a knoll, we could see a village of hovels perched among ruins." (Tristram 1865: 240-241).

Guèrin (1874: 228-232), mentions Kh. Fusayil and Wadi Rashash.

The British Survey described: "Khurbet Fusayil – The ruins are extensive, and occur at intervals for 2.5 miles north and south, at the edge of the hills. They consist principally of the traces of ruined garden-walls, built of unhewn stones, and there are ruined mills and aqueducts. One channel, cemented outside as well as in, is built against the side of the hill. The wall supporting

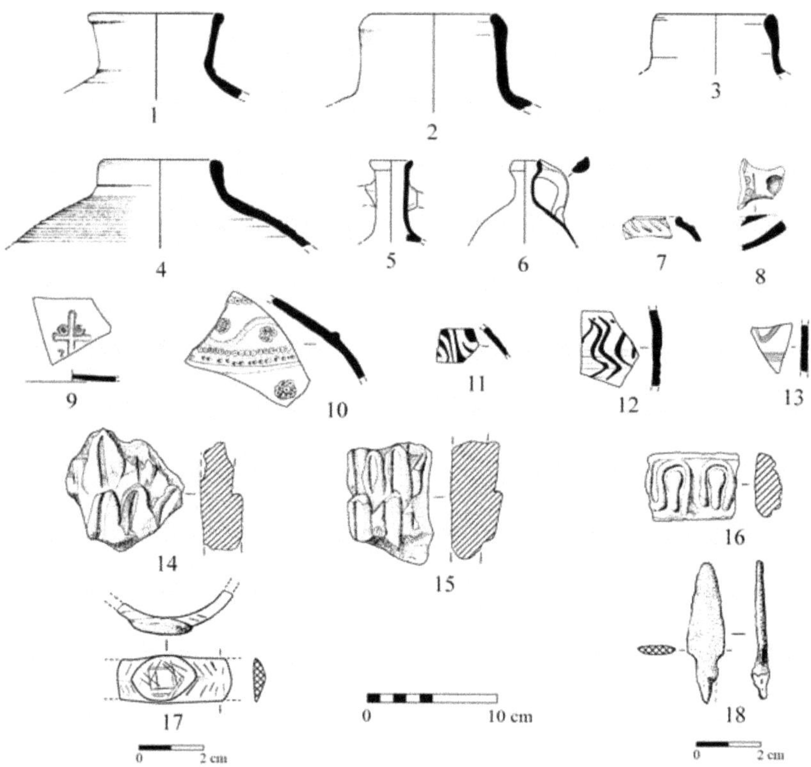

108. Finds from **Kh. Fusayil**: 1. Jar, rd, Hel-ER; 2. Jar, rd, Rom; 3. Jar, blk, Rom-Byz; 4. Jar, dk br, Byz; 5. Flask, wh, ER; 6. Juglet, lt br, ER; 7. Lamp, lt br, Byz; 8. Lamp, lt br, ER (Herodian); 9. Bowl (*Terra Sigillata*), rd, rd slip, dec of cross impression, Byz; 10. Jar (sherd), wh, incised dec and impressions, EM; 11. Sherd, lt br, blk. dec, Byz-EM; 12. Jar (sherd), blk, wh dec, Byz-EM; 13. Sherd, lt br, incised dec, Byz- EM; 14-16. Moulded dec (stucco), gypsum; 17. Ring, bronze, geometric dec, Byz (?); 18. Arrow-head, iron, Rom.

it is in places 8 feet high, and 2 feet or 3 feet thick. The stones are of all sizes, and not squared, very rudely dressed, and set in cement. This aqueduct is traceable for 5.5 miles from the 'Ein Fusayil into the *Ghor*; it supplied four tanks, and passes in one place through a line of pits at the place called Habej ez-Zir. There is also a small Tell or hillock, apparently artificial, at the mouth of the valley (Tell esh-Sheikh Diyab [Site 23 above]). The Roman road is very perfect near this ruin; it consists of three parallel lines of stones, about 1 foot square, forming the sides and central rib of the road, 9 feet apart, giving 18 feet for the width of the road. There seems to have been no foundation or drainage, but the central rib is higher than the sides, so that the road had a section of two inclined planes. The part between the ribs is filled in with a sort of cobble of stones of irregular size, covered with smaller metalling. The central rib consists of two lines of stones, the outer wall, or curb-stone, of a single line each side." (Conder and Kitchener 1882: 392-393).

Felix Marie Abel visited in the region in February 1910, while on his expedition to the Jordan Valley. Resulting from the visit to the mouth of Wadi Fasael, Abel noted the tel, the pool and the aqueducts. He mentioned that the vicinity appears in the Madaba Map and noted (on top of the common information regarding Phasaelis) that the place was also of importance in the Byzantine period (Abel 1913: 235).

The description in the Emergency Survey (Bar-Adon 1972: site 15), does not match our findings. We have tried to relate it to the measurements. Below is the text with remarks related to finds in our survey (in brackets): "Kh. Fasil (meaning Tell esh-Sheikh Diyab [Site 23], A. Z.). A small tell in the western Jordan Valley, with remains of walls on it. At the foot of the tell:

A. An aqueduct and a reservoir measuring 60×50 m – in the north (found).
B. Bath-house on top of a knoll, built of bricks – in the south (not found).
C. Aqueduct, ditches and furnace – in the west (not clear).
D. 250 m to the south – a plastered compound, possibly served as a water reservoir. Measuring 75×60 m with a line of rooms around it and in the north-western corner a tower measuring 10×9 m."

According to the dimensions the intent in D is perhaps the fortress, but this one has two towers and is not plastered. Therefore the tell should be 250 m further north, which is not the case. It is possible that the 'plastered compound' lies beneath the village. The lack of the plan and topographical notes – stream beds and likewise - hinders the understanding of the description.

During a salvage excavation by Y. Peleg (2009) in the eastern edge of the site remains of an aqueduct and a two-room structure were found. The ducts have been dated from the 1st century BCE to the 1st century

CE. The double room structure has been dated to the Early Moslem period (the second half of the 7th century CE).

E. History: the information concerning the foundation of Phasaelis appears in Josephus' Antiquity of the Jews as follows:

"He also built a city named after him in the valley of Jericho northward from there, and thereby made the surrounding region, formerly a wilderness, more productive through the industry of its inhabitants.

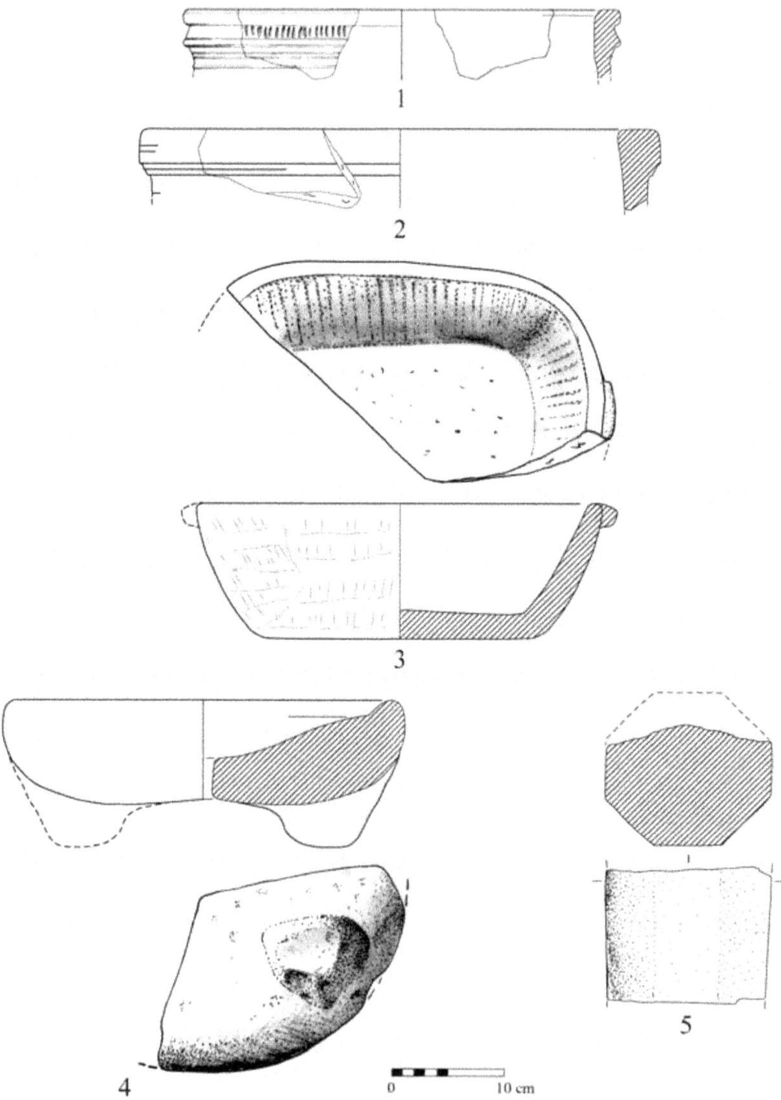

109. Stone artefacts from **Kh. Fusayil**: 1-3. Basins, limestone, ER; 4. Mortar, limestone; 5. Column link, limestone, Byz (?).

And this city he called Phasaelis" (Ant. XVI, v: 2). "…Marcus Ambivulus, during whose administration Salome, the sister of King Herod, died. To Julia she bequeathed Jamnia and its territory, together with Phasaelis, which lay in the plain, and Archelais, where palms are planted in very great numbers and the dates are of the highest quality" (Ant. XVIII, ii: 2).

The same information is included in Josephus' War of the Jews as follows:

1. "He (Herod) also gave the name of Phasaelis to another city which he built in the valley to the north of Jericho" (War I, xxi: 9).
2. "Salome (Herod's sister) besides the legacy which the King had left her in his will, was declared mistress of Jamnia, Azotus and Phasaelis" (War II, vi: 3).
3. "…as for Salome, she at her death bequeathed her toparchy to Julia, the wife of Augustus, together with Jamnia and the palm-groves of Phasaelis" (War II, ix: 1).

Pliny (Natural History XIII [Rackham 1962: 25]) tells about the date-palm plantations in the region: "But not only are these trees abundant and bear largely in Judaea, but also the most famous are found there, and not in the whole of that country but specially in Jericho, although those growing in the valley of Archelais and Phasaelis and Livias in the same country are also highly spoken of."

The monk Burchard of Mount Zion (1280) names Phasaelis for the first time Phesech: "Four leagues to the east of Emon, at the going down of Mount Ephraim, on the plain, two leagues from Jordan, is the village of Phesech, at the place where the brook Cherith runs down from the mountain." (Burchard, in Stewart 1896: 56).

F. Excavations: on July 2011 excavations at the site began under the auspices of Samaria and Judea Archaeology staff officer (Hizmi 2012). The main finds of the first published season date to the Roman and Byzantine periods. Two excavation areas were opened: Areas N and S. In Area N a very large rectangular pool, 30×41 m in size and 7 m deep, was excavated. Nearby a large Roman dwelling complex was excavated with a large 7.5×10 m hall, smaller rooms and a *miqve* (Jewish ritual bath). A small bath-house was excavated near the dwelling complex. In area S two Byzantine structures, 80 m afar, were partialy excavated: a small square 13×13 m church dated to the 5th-6th Century CE, and two adjacent courtyards partly surrounded by rooms. Both structures were interpreted as parts of a monastery. Additional results of the excavation are not published yet.

Pottery: Hellenistic-Early Roman – 10%; Late Roman – 13%; Roman-Byzantine – 52%; Byzantine – 17%; Byzantine-Early Moslem – 7%; Modern – 1%.

Flint: 22 items (see Appendix A).
Stone: pestle and a fragment of grinding board (basalt); a basin, mortar and a column link (limestone).
Other finds: shell-shaped lead weight; 15 stucco splinters.
Additional surveys: Conder and Kitchener 1882: 388, 392-393; Glueck 1951: 414; Bar-Adon 1972: site 15; Porath 1985b: 41.

◆ ◆ ◆

Site 35: 19-15/18/3

TOMER (1)

Israel grid: 1913/1588
UTM grid: 7300/5457
Elevation: 180 m b.s.l., 10 m a.s.a.
Name: nearest place
Site type: large
Area: 65 dunams (6.5 ha)
Topography: slope
Rock type: Judea Group
Soil type: stony-desert
Soil quality: 3
Cultivation: none
Cisterns: none
Water source: Nahal Fasael (181), 2.5 km distant
Road: Beit She'an–Jericho (B10), 700 m distant
Visits: January 2002, 2016; 2 sherds

A very large site over a broad spur, descending eastward from the summit of Elevation Point -48 towards Kh. Fusayil. Some 250 m north of it passes the road from the village of Tomer to the drilling places in Wadi Senisleh.

There are two bands of structures in the site. In the upper one, located on a rocky terrace, are two partly preserved round enclosures of diameter, 20-30 m encircled by a wall built of a single row of stones.

In the lower band are two clusters of enclosures and various structures built far from each other. These are built of local stones. It appears that additional structures once stood here, but it is very difficult to locate them at present. South of the deep stream bed enclosing the settlement at the south is another enclosure, about 20 m in diameter.

In some places were found archaeologically excavated squares of an unpublished excavation and unknown researcher.

Despite our thorough survey we failed to find indicative sherds.

This site is one of a unique group of well-built settlements lacking dateable material.

Pottery: 2 non-indicative sherds.
Flint: 23 items (see Appendix A).
Additional surveys: none.

♦ ♦ ♦

Site 35 (1): 19-15/18/2

TOMER (10)

Israel grid: 1912/1589
UTM grid: 7300/5458
Elevation: 200 m b.s.l., 10 m a.s.a.
Name: nearest place
Site type: enclosure
Area: 1 dunam (1000 sq. m)
Topography: valley edge
Rock type: hard limestone
Soil type: stony-desert
Soil quality: 3
Cultivation: none
Cisterns: none
Water source: Nahal Fasael (181), 2.5 km distant
Road: Beit She'an–Jericho (B10), 1 km distant
Visit: February 2016; 1 sherd

A composite enclosure site in a valley fringe, near Elevation Point -48 ridge, 600 m northwest of Tomer.

This rectangular enclosure is divided into two equal parts, each 10×15 m. In the northern corner is a built cell 1×2 m. Another wall protrudes from the dividing wall of the structure northwards. The walls are built of medium-sized stones, one stone wide. The walls survived only to one course.

Two modern excavation squares were noted at the place. These are the remains of an excavation that has not yet been published (similar to the remains of an excavation found in nearby Site 35).

This site is part of a group of well-built sites found west of Tomer containing meagre non-indicative finds.

Pottery: 1 sherd, not indicative.
Additional surveys: none.

Site 36: 19-15/39/1

SALVADORA FARM

Israel grid: 1935/1590
UTM grid: 7321/5459
Elevation: 280 m b.s.l., 0 m a.s.a.
Name: given by the survey
Site type: small
Area: 1 dunam (1000 sq. m)
Topography: plain
Rock type: none
Soil type: Lisan marl and brown-forest
Soil quality: 6
Cultivation: plantations
Cisterns: none
Water source: Nahal Fasael (181), 1.5 km distant
Road: Beit She'an–Jericho (B10), 1.5 km distant
Visit: November 2009; 50 sherds

A small site at the heart of a large agricultural plain within cultivated fields and greenhouses. It is 1 km east of the village of Tomer and 800 m east of the Jordan Valley road.

The site consists of a central structure and a perimeter wall west of it. The central structure, measuring 6×5 m, is encircled by a 1 m-thick wall built of local pebbles. Three walls project eastward from the courtyard in the centre of the site, forming two rooms whose eastern ends are unknown. There is another parallel wall 3 m west of the centre of the structure. These are probably the remains of a western room.

About 12 m west of the structure is an enclosing wall about 12 m long preserved in sections generally oriented north-south. The design is similar to that of the other walls. This could be a perimeter wall around the structure.

An unpaved agricultural road passes north of the site.

The sherd scatter is moderate.

Porath calls the place Kh. Yarcha, placing it at coordinates 1933/1591 (Porath 1985b: 41-42). According to him the enclosure excavated by him was attached to the north of the eastern cultivated plot. In the excavation were found EM period sherds (7th-8th centuries CE), a mosaic floor, remains of red painted plaster, and fragments of glass vessels.

A salvage excavation was conducted in the site by Y. Peleg and has not yet been published. The remains of at least eight excavation squares were found in the site. The excavator suggested that there was a bathhouse at the site (personal communication).

Pottery (by our survey): Early Roman – 10%; Byzantine – 40%; Early Moslem – 50%.

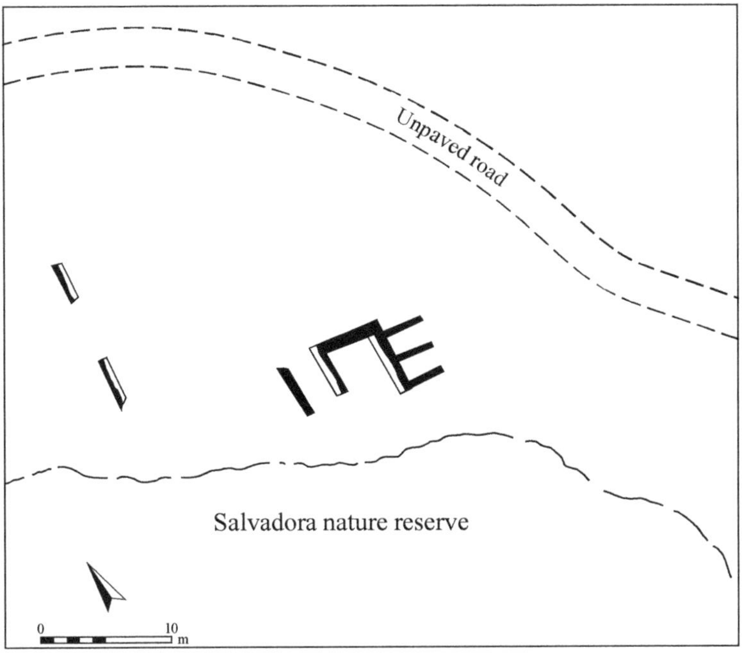

110. Plan of the **Salvadora farm.**

111. Pottery from the **Salvadora farm:** 1. bowl, wh, EM; 2. jar, br, Byz.

CHAPTER FOUR

FROM NAHAL FASAEL TO NAHAL YITAV (WADI 'AUJAH)

LANDSCAPE UNIT 32

112 . **The Jordan Valley**, engraving by Van de Velde (in Schiller 1977).

Site 37: 19-15/08/2

TOMER (7)

Israel grid: 1906/1586
UTM grid: 7294/5455
Elevation: 140 m b.s.l., 50 m b.s.a.
Name: nearest place
Site type: medium and enclosure
Area: 3 dunams (3000 sq. m)
Topography: narrow gorge
Rock type: Judea Group
Soil type: stony-desert
Soil quality: 2
Cultivation: none
Cisterns: none
Water source: Nahal Fasael (181), 2.8 km distant
Road: Beit She'an–Jericho (B10), 1 km distant
Visit: February 2002; 40 sherds (no. 1) and 25 sherds (no. 2)

The site is on the south bank and the north slope of Wadi el-Butem, near the eastern exit of the wadi from the narrow gorge.

Two main parts have been located:

1. A site, possibly dated to the MBA II, with a support wall along the south bank of the wadi and settlement remains. The support wall is 100 m long, built of very large stones (1-1.5 m), and apparently was meant as protection from floods and supporting structures.

   The settlement, with structures in it, extends south of the support wall. The walls of the houses are built of a single row of large stones, the average dimensions of which are about 70 cm. Several rooms are attached to the support wall, each 3×3 m on average. Some of the stones are standing, protruding from the ground. Many of the jambs and openings have been preserved.

   A moderate sherd scatter has accumulated over the area and the wadi, mostly body sherds of the MBA II. South of the support wall and the ancient settlement is an area of Bedouin tent encampments, with a few Late Roman and Ottoman period sherds.

   In Wadi el-Butem, about 300 m west of the site, were found the ruined remains of a dam built of very large stones; possibly serving to catch some of the floodwater in the wadi.

2. On a steep spur descending from the north to the wadi channel is a round enclosure about 20 m in diameter. Above and around it, over an area of 3 dunams (3000 sq. m) are the remains of many structures. The walls are built of medium-sized stones of the *Mishash* (Campanian) formation, which crumbles easily. The form of the structures has been almost totally lost due to erosion and disintegration. However, it appears that they are broad rooms.

Only body sherds have been found, maybe Chalcolithic (?)

Pottery: part 1: Middle Bronze II – 85% (body sherds); Roman – 10%; Ottoman – 5%; part 2: Chalcolithic/Early Bronze (?) – 100% (body sherds).
Flint: 7 items (see Appendix A).
Additional surveys: none.
Bibliography: Bar 2014: site 101.

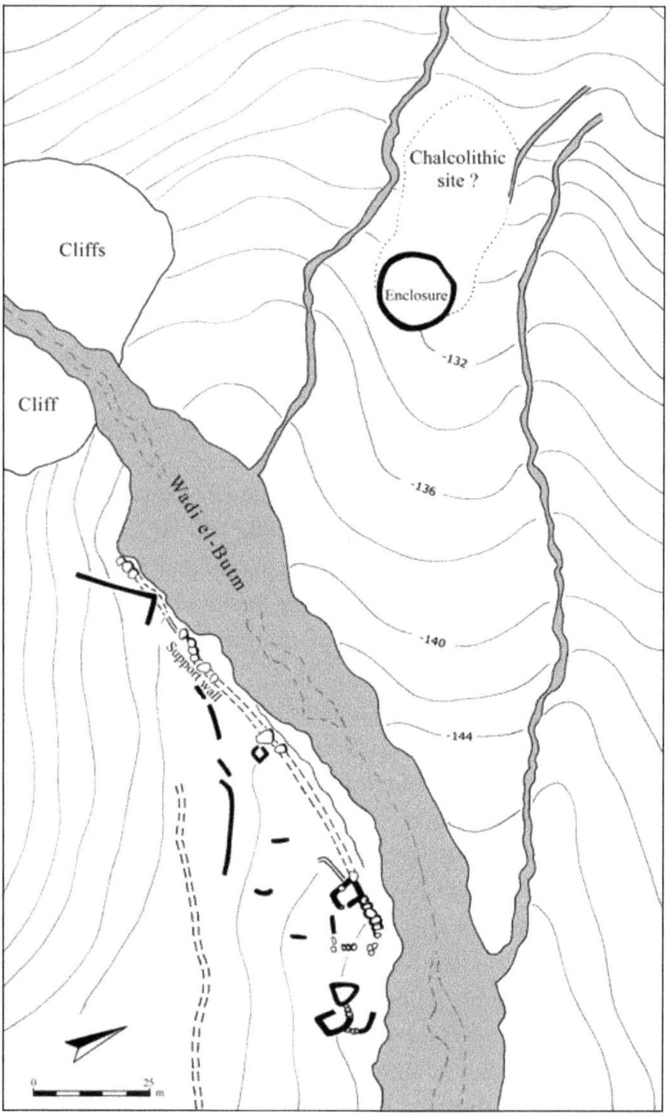

113. Plan of **Tomer** (7).

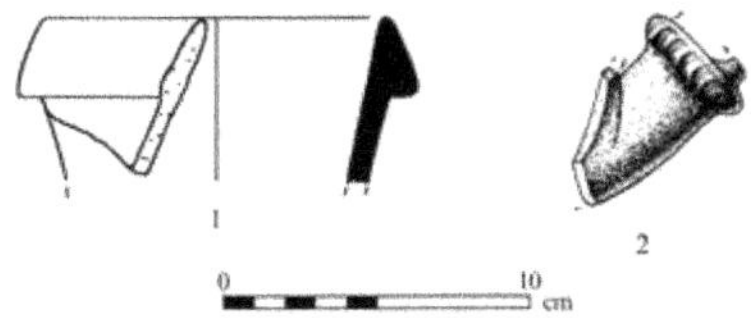

114. Pottery from **Tomer** (7): 1. Jug, lt gr, Rom; 2. Pipe, gr, Ott.

♦ ♦ ♦

Site 38: 19-15/48/1

KHIRBET ED-DASHE

A site in Israel grid: 1949/1587 (UTM grid: 7337/5456), surveyed in the Emergency Survey (1968) and currently within a minefield in the Border System Fence limits.

The description in the Emergency Survey is as follows (Bar-Adon 1972: site 17):

"Remains of a water pool, the stones of which have been removed and taken for secondary use. Remains of an aqueduct carrying water to the pool. Pottery find is from the Roman-Byzantine period only." (translation from the Hebrew).

Ilan's (1973: 278) description, which apparently relies on Porath's survey:

"The hub of the 'farm', or the cultivation management, etc. was at Kh. ed-Dashe… south-west of it and of the roadway are found remains of a large water pool, which apparently served the needs of the settlement of Kh. ed-Dashe. The pool was reached by the northernmost of the spring aqueducts. The dimensions of the pool are 12.5×12.5 m and its original height was about 4 m. In three of its corners were found the springs of the arches, showing that hence the pool was originally covered by a domed roof. It contained about 600 cu. m of water. West of the pool is an ancient lime kiln."

Porath (1985b: 42), who conducted a survey in the region of Fasael, describes a large square structure (65×65 m) built of ashlars. At its corners and along its outer walls were towers. He dated the sherds to the Early Moslem period (7th–8th centuries CE). Glass fragments and plastered water installations were also found. According to him, this is a palace built during the Umayyad Caliphate.

It is difficult to understand the purpose of the settlement at Kh. ed-Dashe, which contained a large square public building with many rooms. Apparently it was a magnificent structure in the Umayyad era. As previously mentioned, it was the hub of the farm or the owner or the manager's palace on behalf of the government.

115. Aerial view looking south at the large courtyard of **Kh. ed-Dashe**. Note the array of rooms around the yard. Porath's opinion is that the place served as a palace or large farm during the Umayyad Caliphate. The border fence (at bottom) and an unpaved military road (top), cut through the site, 2012 (A. Solomon).

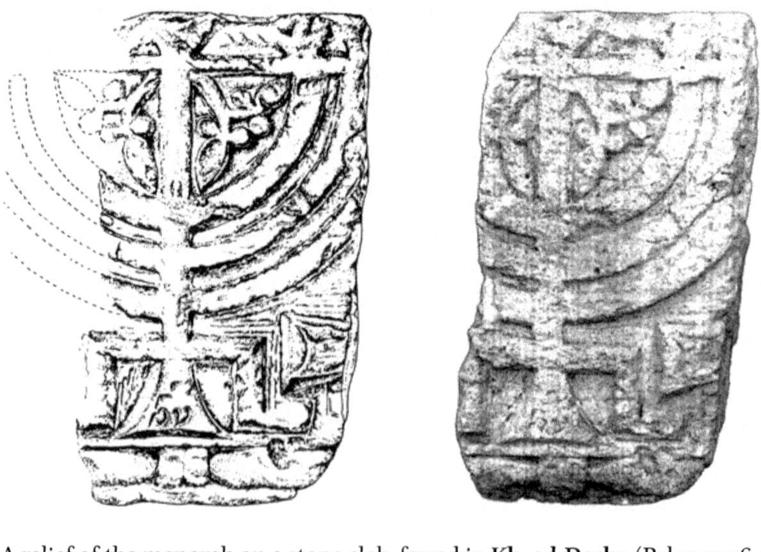

116. A relief of the menorah on a stone slab, found in **Kh. ed-Dashe** (Peleg 2006: 122).

In 1977 a stone with a relief of a menorah was found in secondary use. Y. Peleg (2006) assumed that the relief was a fragment of a lintel of a Jewish synagogue from an unknown location in the Byzantine period.

Despite our efforts, we were not able to reach the site, as it was in a minefield.

Pottery: Roman, Byzantine, Early Moslem.
Additional surveys: Bar-Adon 1972: site 17; Ilan 1973: 278; Porath 1985b: 42.

♦ ♦ ♦

Site 38 (1): 19-15/48/2

WADI MALHA

Israel grid: 1949/1582
UTM grid: 7336/5451
Elevation: 295 m b.s.l., 0 m a.s.a.
Name: nearest place
Site type: gate in long agricultural walls
Area: 0.1 dunam (100 sq. m)
Topography: plateau
Rock type: Lisan
Soil type: Lisan
Soil quality: 1
Cultivation: none
Cisterns: none
Water source: River Jordan (112), 4.3 km distant
Road: Beit She'an–Jericho (B10), 3 km distant
Visit: February 2016; 60 sherds

A gate structure in a very long well-built stone wall, 500 m south of Kh. ed-Dashe (Site 38), 2 km south-east of the Salvadora Farm (Site 36), and 3.2 km east of Tomer. The site and the wall are located in the Wadi Malha swamp nature reserve.

This site is part of the very large Early Moslem agricultural complex well described by Porath (1985b: 31-45). It includes remains of a very long wall traced for over 1.5 km on a north-south axis. The wall is usually two to three stones in width (75 cm wide). The well-built gate was partly excavated by Porath (1985b: fig.7b). It is 9.5 m long and 9.2 m wide, and the entrance is 3.3 m wide, built of drafted stones and ashlars. This gate and wall were the eastern borders of a very large agricultural area estimated by Porath to be more than 2000 dunams (200 ha) in area. Most of the walls and water channels noted by Porath (1985b: fig. 5) no longer exist due to extensive modern agricultural activities in the region.

The entire agricultural system belongs to the Early Moslem period, and is probably connected to the large farm sites from this period in Kh. ed-Dashe (Site 38), and the Salvadora Farm (Site 36).

Pottery: Early Moslem – 100%.
Additional surveys: Porath 1985b: 30-31.

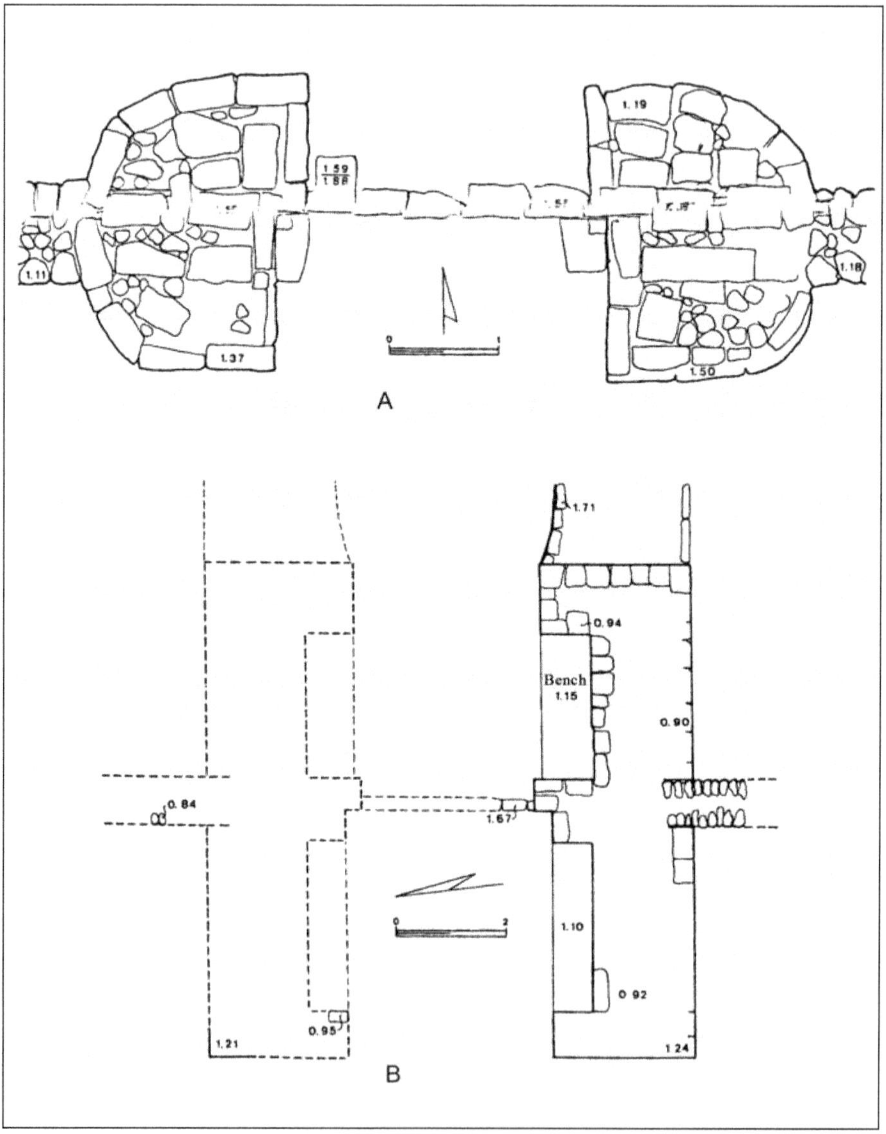

117. Plan of **Wadi Malha** (after Porat 1985b: fig. 7b).

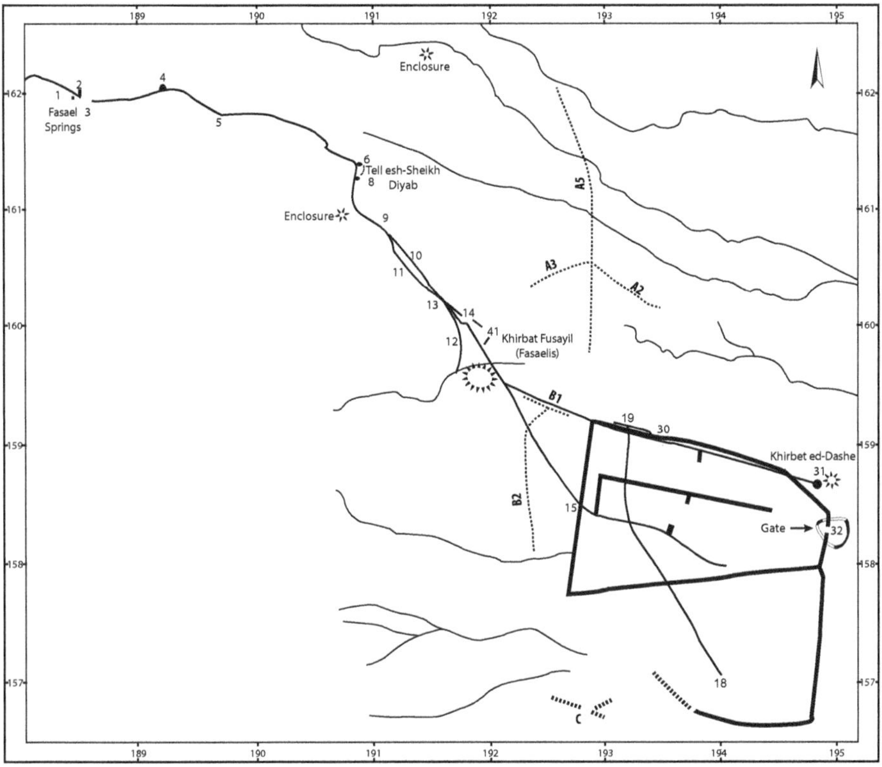

118. The large Early Moslem agricultural system east of Tomer. The gate of **Wadi Malha** is in the eastern section of this complex (after Porath 1985b: fig. 5).

◆ ◆ ◆

Site 39: 19-15/18/1

TOMER (3)

Israel grid: 1911/1584
UTM grid: 7299/5453
Elevation: 200 m b.s.l., 5 m a.s.a.
Name: nearest place
Site type: large
Area: 10 dunams (1 ha)
Topography: valley edge
Rock type: Judea Group
Soil type: stony-desert
Soil quality: 3
Cultivation: none
Cisterns: none
Water source: Nahal Fasael (181), 3 km distant
Road: Beit She'an–Jericho (B10), 200 m distant
Visit: January 2002; 10 sherds

A large site at the south-eastern edge of the ridge, east of the summit of Elevation Point -48. Parts of it have been excavated by Kagan (2009).

The settlement is in a lower part of a moderate slope descending towards the fence of the village of Tomer. Its southern part is bordered by the channel

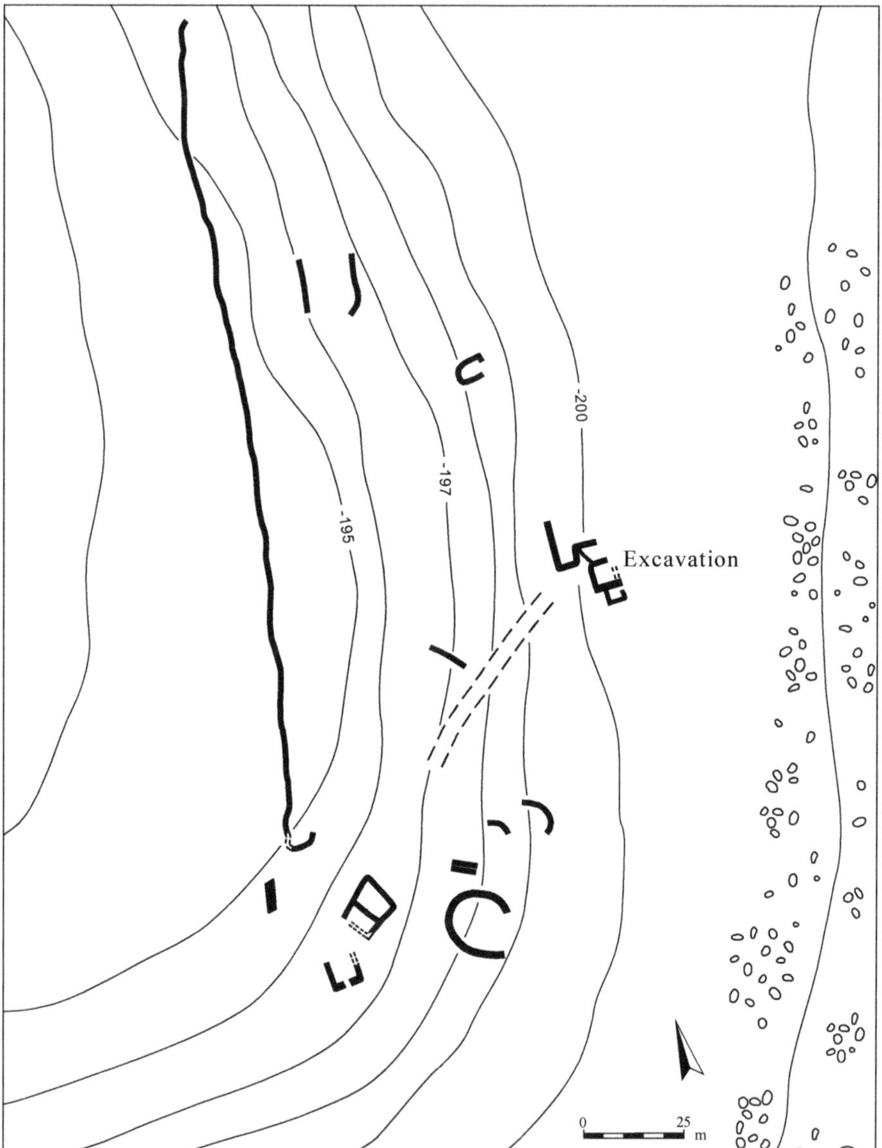

119. Plan of **Tomer** (3).

of Wadi Tal'at Zagharah. In the western upper part is a north-south wall 600 m long, two stones thick (about 80 cm).

Structures of various types are scattered in the lower part, containing one room or more, with an adjacent courtyard. The construction is of local partially worked stones.

During our survey only few undatable sherds were found.

In the salvage excavation (Kagan 2009) no datable finds have been found, and the excavator assumed that these are the poor remnants of corrals and seasonal dwelling structures.

Pottery: not diagnostic.
Additional surveys: none.
Additional Bibliography: Bar 2014: site 102.

120. **Tomer (3)**, structure remains, view to north, 2010 (S. Bar).

Site 40: 19-15/08/4

TOMER (5)

Israel grid: 1908/1582
UTM grid: 7296/5450
Elevation: 180 m b.s.l., 10 m a.s.a.
Name: nearest place
Site type: village
Area: 10 dunams (1 ha)
Topography: valley edge
Rock type: Judea Group
Soil type: stony-desert
Soil quality: 3
Cultivation: none
Cisterns: none
Water source: Nahal Fasael (181), 3.3 km distant
Road: Beit She'an–Jericho (B10), 500 m distant
Visit: January 2002; 40 sherds

A medium-sized site at the edge of the north spur of Jebel Fasil and in the valley west of the settlements of Tomer and Gilgal, 500 m west of the first one. North of it passes the deep channel of Wadi el-Butem.

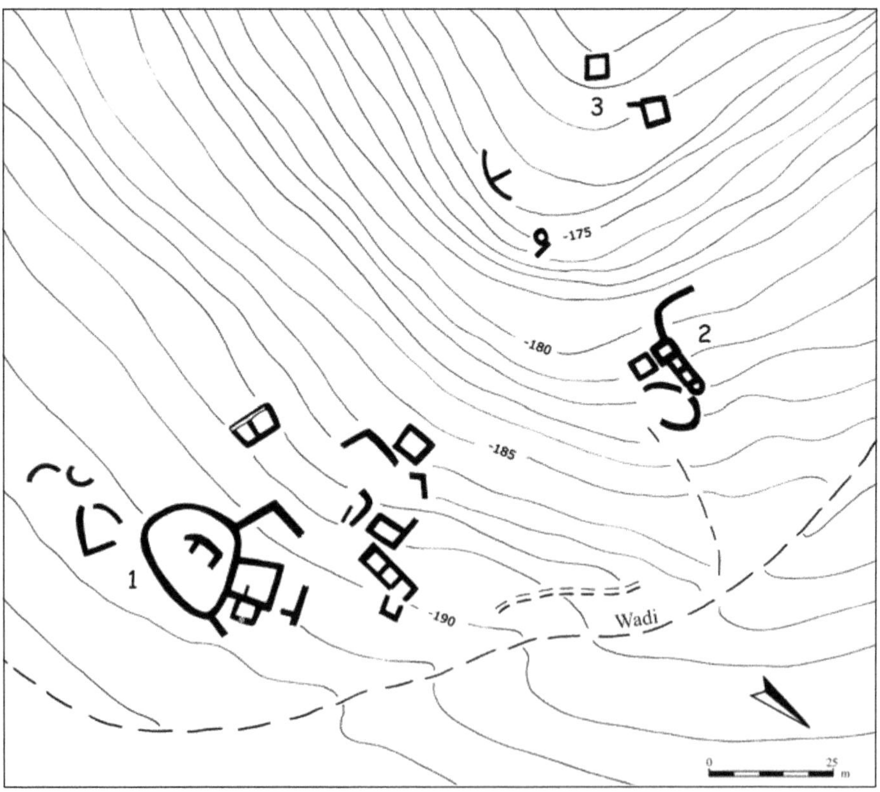

121. Plan of **Tomer** (5).

The site includes three parts: Eastern (no.1), Northern (no. 2) and Upper (no. 3):

1. The eastern part is the largest and most important one in the site. Its area is about 5 dunams (5000 sq. m), and in the centre of it is a large irregular courtyard about 20 m in diameter. The wall around it is built of two rows of large stones and is about 1 m thick. A structure measuring 10×10 m is attached to it at the north, and a small room with an opening is attached to it in the east. Up the slope to the west is another cluster of structures with rooms, badly damaged by bulldozers. Some of the openings and jambs are still visible. Most of the sherds found come from this location.
2. The northern part: about 100 m west of no. 1 are square structures next to a rounded courtyard. Their average dimensions are 6×5 m. There are traces of other structures, demolished by bulldozers.
3. The upper part is over a saddle above the other parts. There is a lookout to the Tomer Valley and to the other parts of the site. Only a few structures survived, built of thin walls of small stones. The entire plan is not clear, but it is clear that the structures were square here as well.

   Below, east of the site, are modern drainage canals on top of ancient channels.

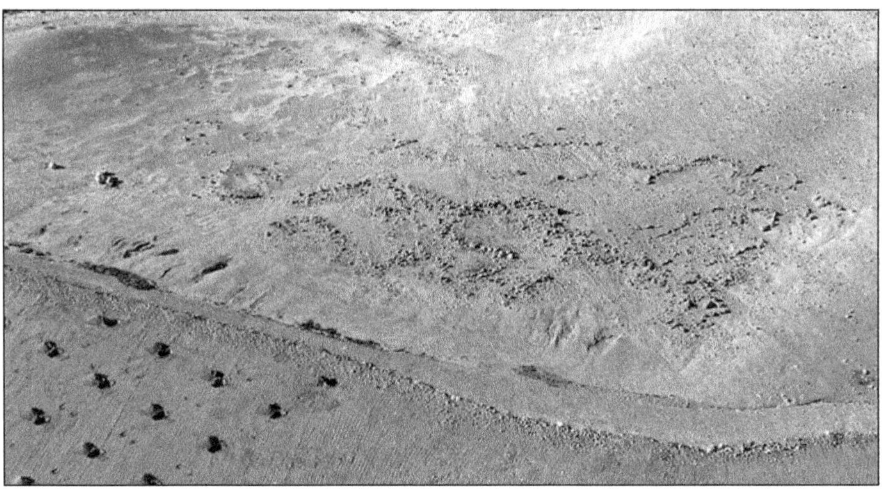

122. Aerial view of the eastern part of **Tomer (5)**, 2008 (N. Eshed).

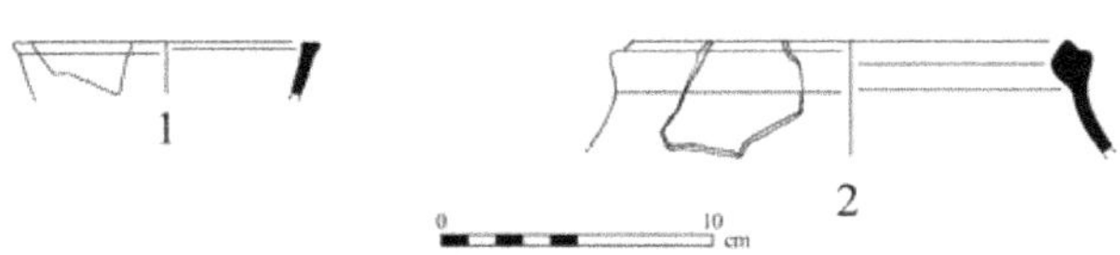

123. Pottery from **Tomer (5)**: 1. Bowl, rd, LR; 2. CP D, br, IA II.

There are at least three distinct overlapping construction stages: an ancient Iron Age stage and the others are apparently Roman period.

Pottery: Iron II – 40%; Late Roman – 60%.
Flint: 10 items, Iron Age (see Appendix A).
Additional surveys: none.

♦ ♦ ♦

Site 41: 19-15/08/1

TOMER (2)

Israel grid: 1908/1580
UTM grid: 7296/5449
Elevation: 163 m b.s.l., 20 m a.s.a.
Name: nearest place
Site type: cave and courtyard
Area: 2 dunams (2000 sq. m)
Topography: slope
Rock type: Judea Group
Soil type: stony-desert
Soil quality: 2
Cultivation: none
Cisterns: none
Water source: Nahal Fasael (181), 3.3 km distant
Road: Beit She'an–Jericho (B10), 800 m distant
Visits: January 2002 and more; 40 sherds

A cave with a courtyard in front of it, on a ridge descending eastward from the summit of Elevation Point -48 to the village of Tomer. There is a fine outlook from it to Fasael Valley.

The depth of the cave is about 10 m, and the width of the opening is 4 m. The height of the entrance is 1.5 m.

In front of the cave is a terraced courtyard, 30 m in diameter, descending eastward along the slope. The wall encircling the yard is of two rows of stones rising two to three courses.

Pottery: Iron II – 53%; Late Roman – 18%; Byzantine – 10%; Medieval – 19%.
Flint: 5 items, Iron Age (see Appendix A).
Additional surveys: none.

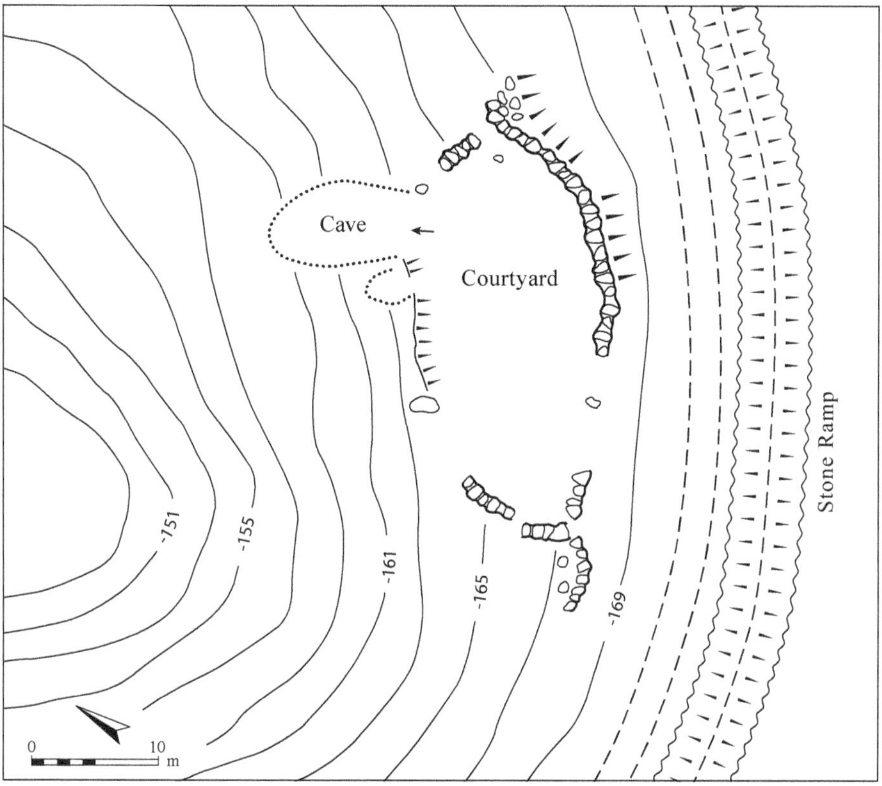

124. Plan of **Tomer (2)**.

125. Aerial view to south-west at the enclosure of **Tomer (2)**, 2012 (A. Solomon).

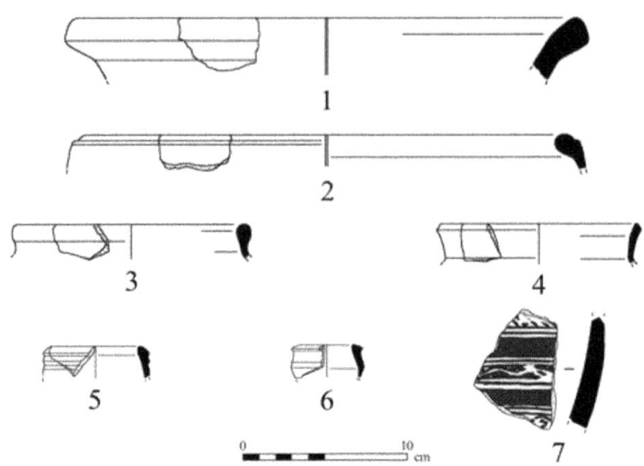

126. Pottery from **Tomer (2)**: 1. CP, rd, MA; 2. CP D, br, IA II; 3. Jar, lt gr, IA II; 4. CP, rd, Rom; 5-6. Jugs, br, Rom; 7. Sherd, purple dec over wh, MA.

♦ ♦ ♦

Site 42: 19-15/08/5

TOMER (9)

Israel grid: 1907/1582
UTM grid: 7295/5449
Elevation: 110 m b.s.l., 40 m b.s.a.
Name: nearest place
Site type: encampment
Area: 2 dunams (2000 sq. m)
Topography: stream channel
Rock type: Judea Group
Soil type: stony-desert
Soil quality: 2
Cultivation: none
Cisterns: none
Water source: Nahal Fasael (181), 3.5 km distant
Road: Beit She'an–Jericho (B10), 800 m distant
Visits: March 2002, 2016; 35 sherds

A small encampment site on the south flank of Wadi el-Butem, surrounded by a secondary channel of the wadi. The location is on a plain above the channel, about 700 m west of the village of Tomer centre.

At the centre of the site is a support wall of large stones which perhaps served as part of a courtyard. Near it are other walls. In the centre of the plain south of the wall is a stone circle, 2 m in diameter.

About 30 m to the west there are remains of a modern Bedouin tent encampment over ancient walls.

In a further visit to the site (2016) it was found that it had been destroyed in preparation for a new palm plantation.

Pottery: Iron II – 25%; Late Roman – 50%; Medieval – 10%; unidentified – 15%;
Stone: two grinding stones.
Additional surveys: none.

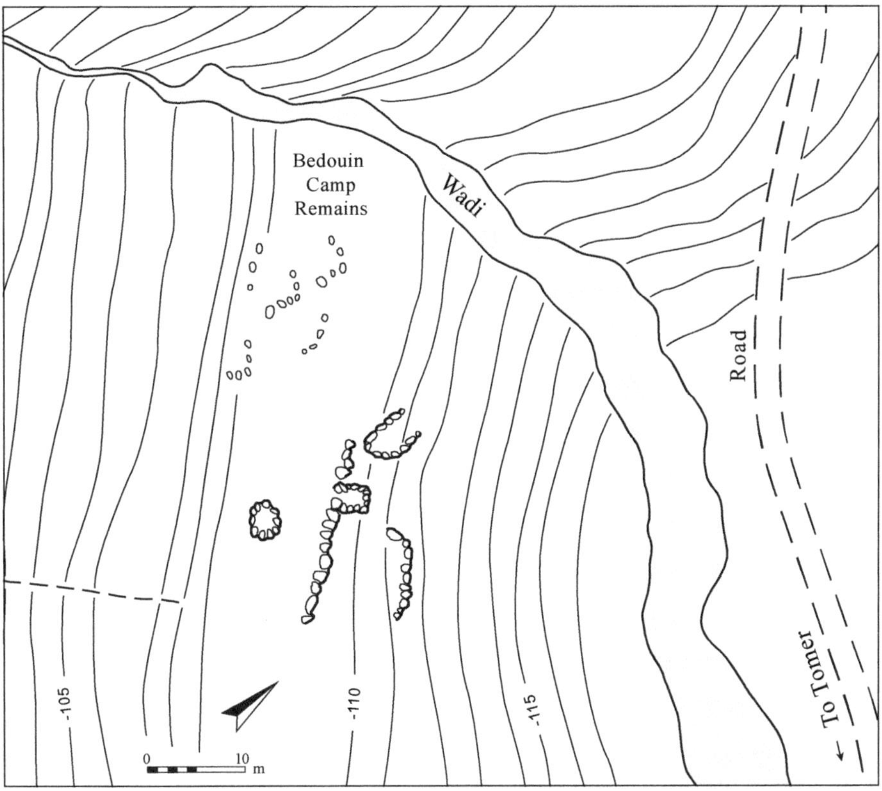

127. Plan of **Tomer (9)**.

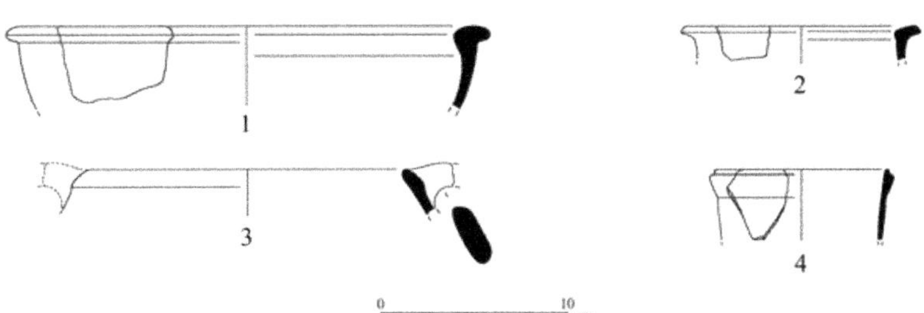

128. Pottery from **Tomer (9)**: 1-2. CP, blk, MA.; 3. CP, br, IA II; 4. Jug, gr, Rom.

Site 43: 19-15/28/1
TOMER (8)

Israel grid: 1924/1582 UTM grid: 7312/5451

Y. Porath exposed an Iron Age structure in the site. His description follows:

"The structure has been exposed in an area designated for agriculture, east of the Jericho–Beit She'an road. It contains a single rectangular room (4.5×3.75 m), situated at the centre of a courtyard encircled by an oval wall (17×10 m maximum dimensions). Only the bottom course, built of large fieldstones, has been preserved. The few sherds found are from the Israelite II period, apparently the end of the 8th century BCE." (Porath 1973: 10).

The structure was not found in a repeat visit by our survey team, and seems to have been destroyed during extensive agricultural development in the area.

♦ ♦ ♦

Site 44: 19-15/07/3
TOMER (4)

Israel grid: 1907/1579
UTM grid: 7295/5448
Elevation: 200 m b.s.l., 5 m a.s.a.
Name: nearest place
Site type: enclosures
Area: 3 dunams (3000 sq. m)
Topography: slope and valley edge
Rock type: Judea Group
Soil type: stony-desert
Soil quality: 2
Cultivation: none
Cisterns: none
Water source: Nahal Fasael (181), 3.4 km distant
Road: Beit She'an–Jericho (B10), 800 m distant
Visits: January 2002, 2006; 40 sherds

An enclosure on the northern flank of the valley, west of the settlements of Tomer and Gilgal. The location is between two channels of Wadi el-Butem and an extension of Wadi Sa'ad, and close to an unpaved road passing at the foot of the mountains.

The enclosure is about 40 m long and up to about 30 m wide. It has an irregular rhombus-like form, and is surrounded by a 1 m thick wall, built of large local stones. The construction is rather uneven. Attached to its east side is another straight wall 12 m long, which meets a stone circle – perhaps a storeroom.

129. Plan of **Tomer (4)**.

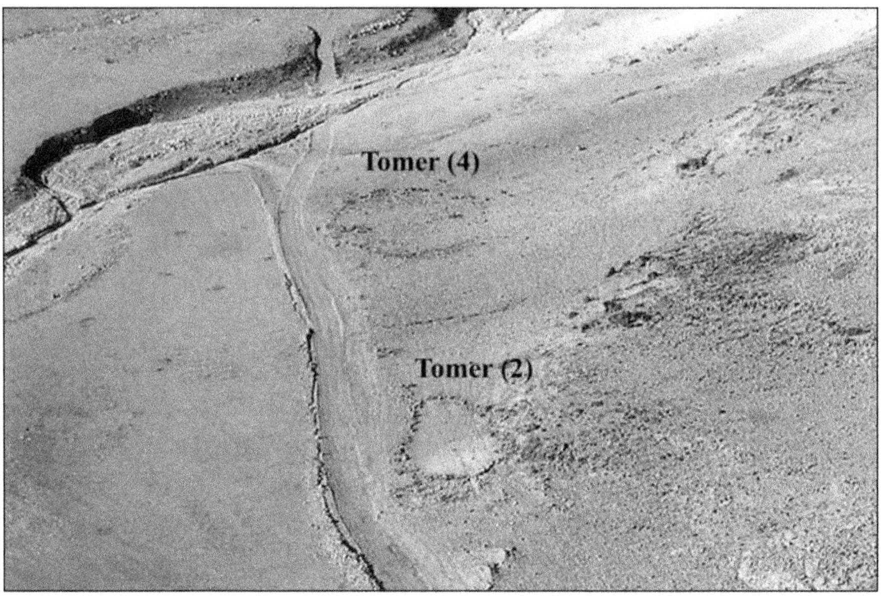

130. Aerial view south at the enclosures of **Tomer (2)** and **Tomer (4)**. At the left corner is the channel of Wadi Sa'ad, 2012 (A. Solomon).

Inside and around the enclosure are remains of rooms and structures of uncertain purpose. To the east of this enclosure are remains of another poorly preserved enclosure.

Pottery: Iron II – 63%; Late Roman – 18%; Byzantine – 10%; Medieval – 9%.
Flint: 7 items, Iron Age (see Appendix A).
Additional surveys: probably this is a section of a larger site discovered during the Emergency Survey (Bar-Adon 1972: site 18).

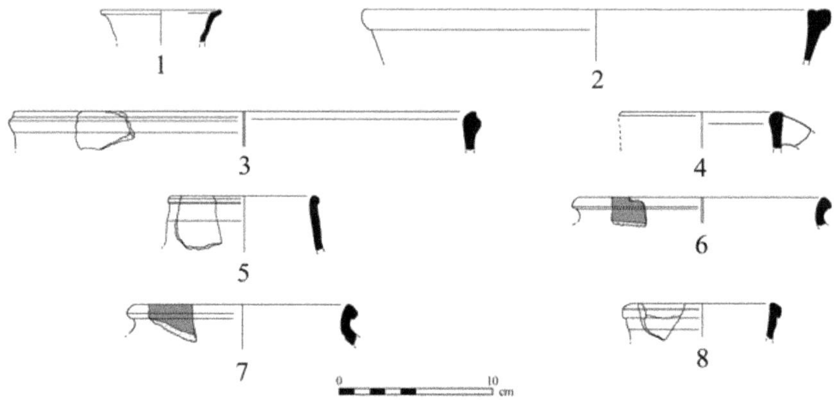

131. Pottery from **Tomer (4)**: 1. Bowl, rd, Rom; 2. CP, buff, MA; 3. CP D, br, IA II; 4. Jug, br, IA II; 5. Jar, rd, Rom; 6-7. Jugs, br, rd slip, IA II; 8. Jug, lt gr, Rom-Byz.

♦ ♦ ♦

Site 45: 19-15/08/3

TOMER (6)

Israel grid: 1906/1580
UTM grid: 7294/5449
Elevation: 110 m b.s.l., 5 m a.s.a.
Name: nearest place
Site type: medium size
Area: 6 dunams (6000 sq. m)
Topography: valley edge
Rock type: Judea Group
Soil type: stony-desert
Soil quality: 2
Cultivation: none
Cisterns: none
Water source: Nahal Fasael (181), 3.5 km distant
Road: Beit She'an–Jericho (B10), 1 km distant
Visit: January 2002; 2 sherds

A site at the flank of the valley west of the settlements Tomer and Gilgal, on a slope in the lower part of Jebel Fasil extensions descending eastward above the deep channel of Wadi Sa'ad.

There are poor remains of walls and minimal sherd scatter. A single structure, measuring 5×4 m, survived in the north part; it is built of very large boulders in one row and one course high.

Pottery: Late Roman and Medieval – a single sherd from each period.
Flint: 12 items (see Appendix A).
Additional surveys: none.

♦ ♦ ♦

Site 46: 18-15/97/2

WADI SA'AD (4)

Israel grid: 1898/1579
UTM grid: 7286/5447
Elevation: 100 m b.s.l., 40 m b.s.a.
Name: nearest place
Site type: enclosure
Area: 1.5 dunam (1500 sq. m)
Topography: shoulder above wadi
Rock type: Judea Group
Soil type: brown-forest
Soil quality: 2
Cultivation: none
Cisterns: none
Water source: Nahal Fasael (181), 4 km distant
Road: Beit She'an–Jericho (B10), 1.7 km distant
Visit: March 2008; 33 sherds

A small site on a flat shoulder on the south slope of Wadi Sa'ad, 1.7 km southwest of the village of Tomer. A currently impassable unpaved road crosses the channel of the wadi close by to the west.

There is a round enclosure in the site, about 16 m in diameter, the perimeter wall of which is built of one row of large and medium-sized stones. Outside the eastern side of the perimeter wall is attached a square partitioned structure, measuring 5×4 m.

At the time of our visit the site was covered by vegetation and additional walls could not be observed.

Pottery: Late Roman – 79%; Medieval – 10%; Ottoman – 5%; unidentified – 6%.
Additional surveys: none.

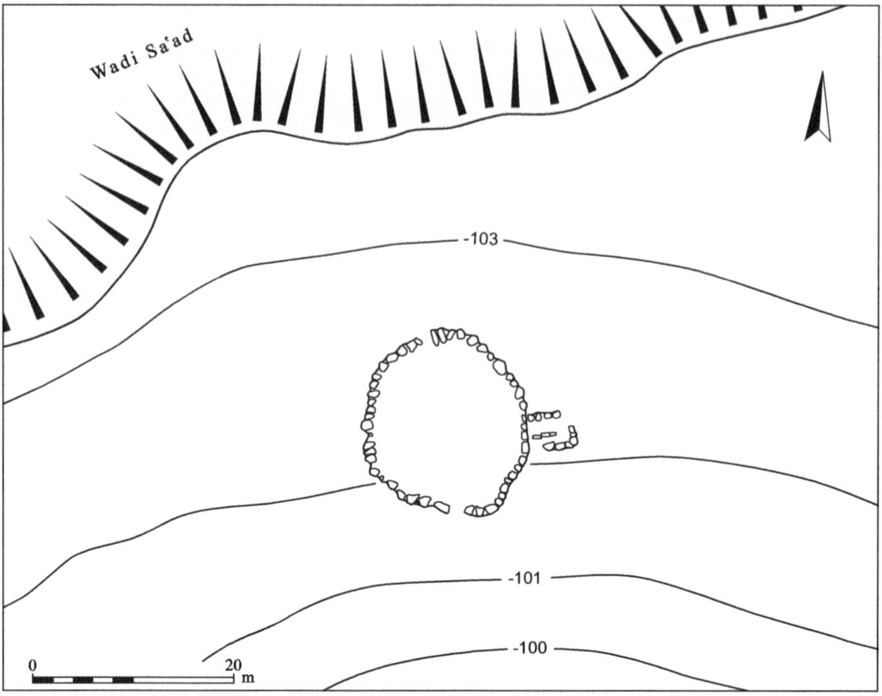

132. Plan of **Wadi Sa'ad (4)**.

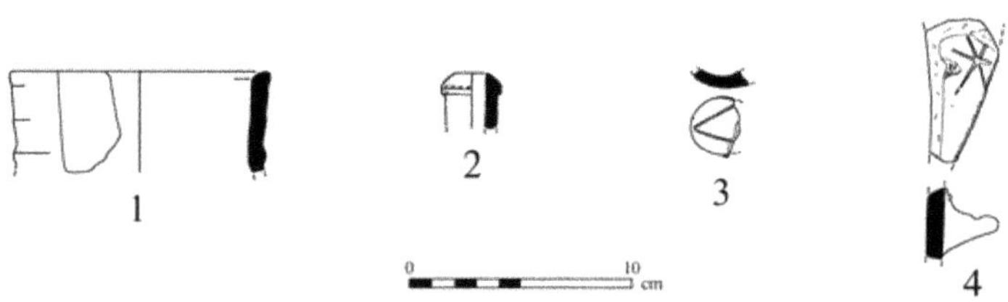

133. Pottery from **Wadi Sa'ad (4)**: 1. Jar, buff, LR; 2-3. Pipes, gr, Ott; 4. Ledge handle, dk br, incised and moulded decor, MA (?).

Site 47: 18-15/97/1

WADI SA'AD (1)

Israel grid: 1899/1579
UTM grid: 7287/5448
Elevation: 120 m b.s.l., 40 m b.s.a.
Name: nearest place
Site type: structure
Area: 0.5 dunam (500 sq. m)
Topography: shoulder above wadi
Rock type: Judea Group
Soil type: brown-forest
Soil quality: 2
Cultivation: none
Cisterns: none
Water source: Nahal Fasael (181), 4 km distant
Road: Beit She'an–Jericho (B10), 1.5 km distant
Visit: March 2008; 3 sherds

A small site on a shoulder on the steep north slope of Wadi Sa'ad, about 1.3 km south-south-west of the village of Tomer.

There is a square structure in the site, measuring 9×9 m, well-built of large unworked stones. The east and west walls have survived almost intact, while the north and south ones have been mostly washed away. The average sizes of the stones of the outer walls are about 80×70 cm.

From the western wall protrudes a small square cell, measuring 1.5×1.5 m. To the inner side of the eastern wall is attached a room measuring 4×3 m, well-built of large elongated stones. The inner partition of the structure is conjectural. From the north-eastern corner a short slightly curved wall protrudes into the structure.

At the time of the visit the site was covered by vegetation, and only a few body sherds were found. The period identification is uncertain.

Further down from the site, along the north bank of the wadi, are scattered circles of stones, apparently remains of Bedouin tent encampments.

Pottery: Late Roman – 100% (body sherds).
Additional surveys: none.

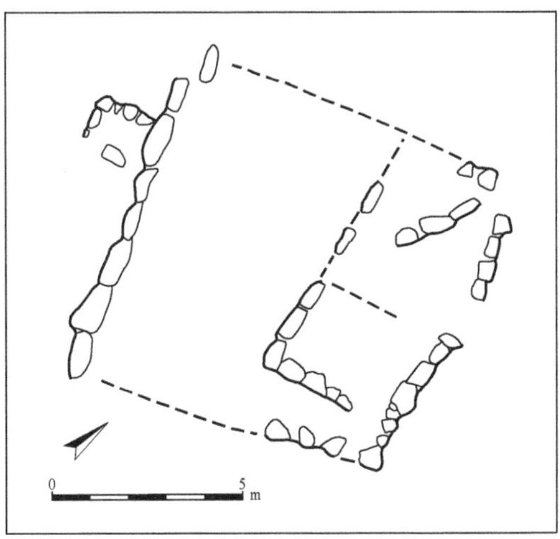

134. Plan of **Wadi Sa'ad (1)**.

Site 48: 19-15/07/2

WADI SA'AD (2)

Israel grid: 1901/1579
UTM grid: 7289/5447
Elevation: 120 m b.s.l., 40 m b.s.a.
Name: nearest place
Site type: small
Area: 10 dunams (1 ha)
Topography: spur between wadis
Rock type: Judea Group
Soil type: brown-forest
Soil quality: 2
Cultivation: none
Cisterns: none
Water source: Nahal Fasael (181), 3.8 km distant
Road: Beit She'an–Jericho (B10), 1.2 km distant
Visit: April 2006; 50 sherds

A small site on a high isolated shoulder, where tributaries of Wadi Sa'ad meet to form one channel, about 1.5 km west-south-west from the village of Tomer centre. The site location is in the deep channel of the wadi, with steep slopes all around it and a summit above it.

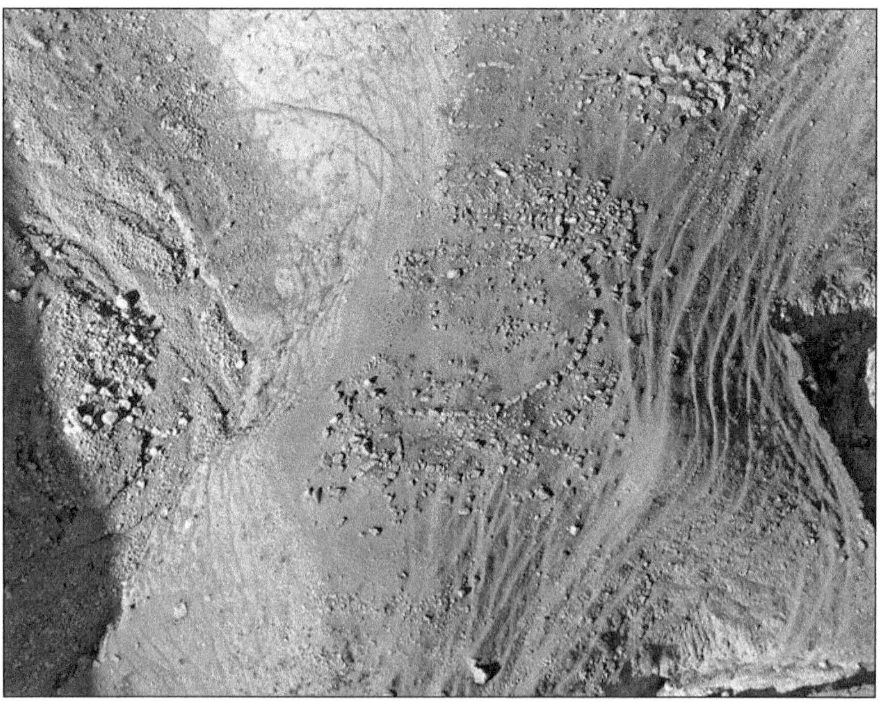

135. Aerial view west at **Wadi Sa'ad (2)**. The enclosure is immaculately built with a structure above it. 2008 (N. Eshed).

In the centre is an oval enclosure with a maximum diameter of 17 m, built of one row of medium-sized squarish slightly worked stones. The southern part of the enclosure has been washed away down the wadi. East and adjacent to the enclosure have been traced remains of another structure, the eastern part of which survived as a parallel line of stones in the steep slope. The construction is particularly aesthetic and symmetrical.

A structure with two broad rooms, one inside the other, is attached to the enclosure in the west. Above it are parts of another structure, most of which did not survive.

Judging from the location of the enclosure, defence considerations may have played a role in the establishment of the place.

Pottery: Intermediate Bronze – 15%; Iron I – 50%; Ottoman – 5%; unidentified – 30%.
Flint: 3 items (see Appendix A).
Additional surveys: none.

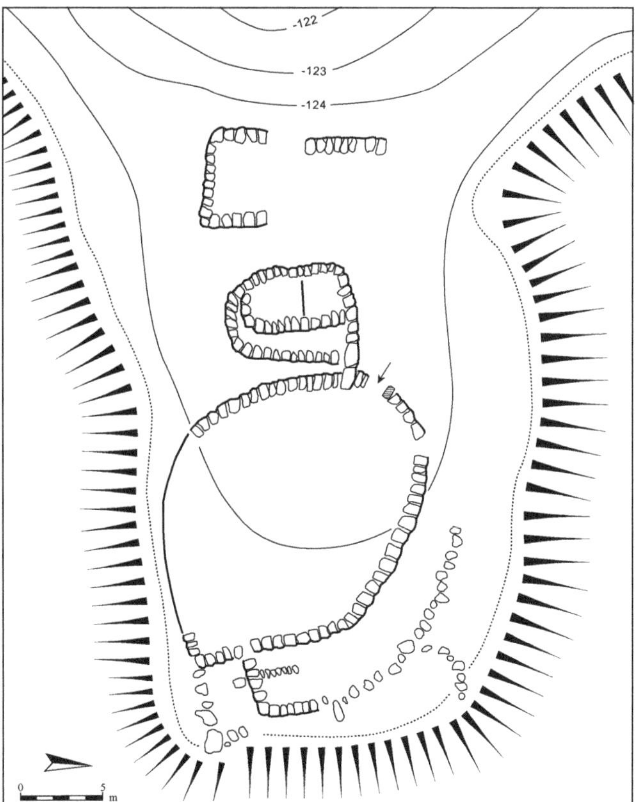

136. Plan of **Wadi Sa'ad (2)**.

137. Area plan of **Wadi Sa'ad (2)**.

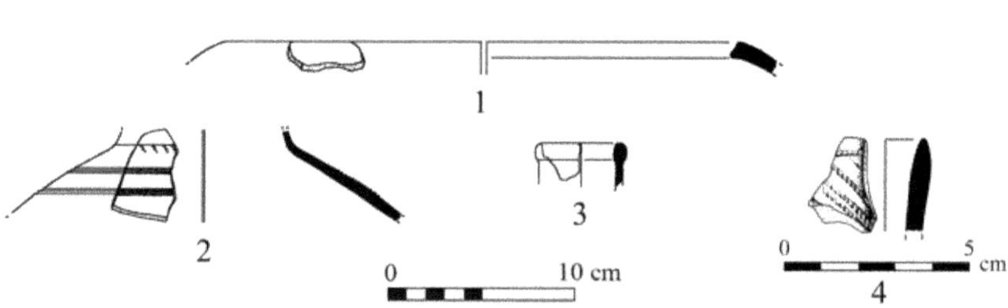

138. Pottery from **Wadi Sa'ad (2)**: 1. HM, rd, IBA; 2. Jar, lt br, IBA; 3. Jug, br, IA I; 4. Pipe, lt br, Ott.

Site 49: 18-15/97/3

WADI SA'AD (3)

Israel grid: 1895/1577
UTM grid: 7283/5445
Elevation: 22 m b.s.l., 30 m b.s.a.
Name: nearest place
Site type: enclosure
Area: 1 dunam (1000 sq. m)
Topography: shoulder between wadis
Rock type: Judea Group
Soil type: brown-forest
Soil quality: 2
Cultivation: none
Cisterns: none
Water source: Nahal Fasael (181), 4.2 km distant
Road: Beit She'an–Jericho (B10), 2 km distant
Visit: March 2008; 47 sherds

A small site on a flat shoulder, surrounded by the deep tributaries of Wadi Sa'ad. Close by and east of it passes an impassable unpaved road (not on plan) leading from the 'Well Site' (Site 54) to Jebel Abu Zarqa. The place is 2 km south-west of the village of Tomer.

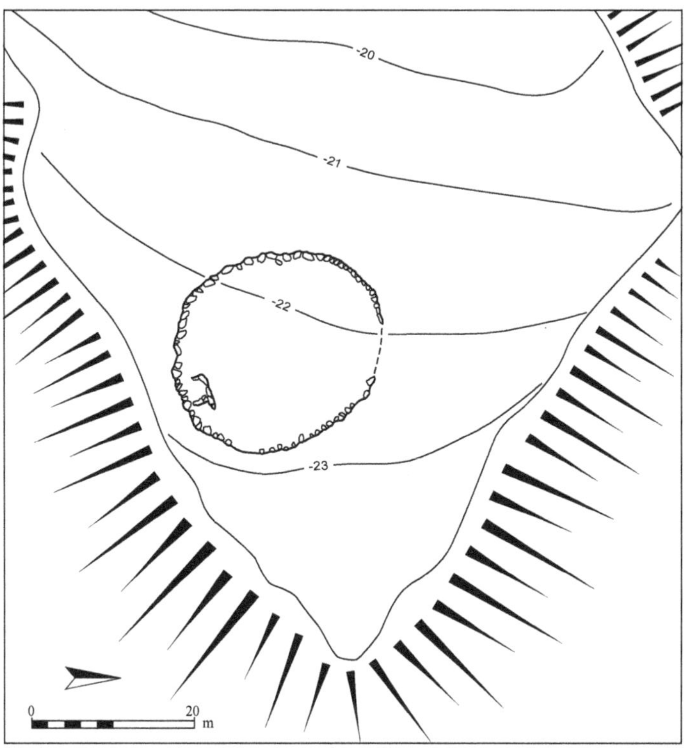

139. Plan of **Wadi Sa'ad (3)**.

Over the shoulder and near the southern earth cliff is a slightly irregular round enclosure about 24 m in diameter, built of one row of large and medium-sized stones. The stones of the wall are in disorder and some of them have been moved. In the south side is small structure, measuring about 2×2 m, built inward.

During the visit the place was covered by vegetation.

Pottery: Middle Bronze II (?) – 26%; Iron I-II – 34%; Late Roman – 32%; Byzantine – 6%; Medieval – 2%.
Flint: 3 items (see Appendix A).
Additional surveys: none.

140. Pottery from **Wadi Sa'ad (3)**: 1. Jar, rd, MA; 2. Jug, lt gr, Rom-Byz.

♦ ♦ ♦

Site 50: 18-15/97/5

JEBEL FASIL

Israel grid: 1893/1577
UTM grid: 7284/5441
Elevation: 0 m a.s.l., 15 m b.s.a.
Name: nearest place
Site type: cave and courtyard
Area: 0.5 dunam (500 sq. m)
Topography: steep slope above wadi
Rock type: Judea Group
Soil type: stony-desert
Soil quality: 1
Cultivation: none
Cisterns: none
Water source: Nahal Fasael (181), 4.6 km distant
Road: Beit She'an–Jericho (B10), 2.3 km distant
Visit: January 2011; 100 sherds

A cave with a courtyard in front, on the north bank of one of the tributaries of Wadi Abu Mahmud, 3 km north-west of Kibbutz Gilgal.

The gap of the current opening is about 10 m. The depth of the cave is about 15 m, and there are natural cavities 2 m deep on average. The ceiling is charred and apparently the place is still in use.

In front of the cave is a semicircular courtyard, the maximum radius of which is 8 m. The yard is partially built on a podium of four courses of medium-sized stones. In the stone collapse at least two dressed stones were found. The pottery was collected mainly from the slope south-east of the cave.

Pottery: Iron I-II – 10%; Late Roman-Byzantine – 70%; Early Moslem-Medieval – 20%.
Flint: 4 items (see Appendix A).
Additional surveys: none.

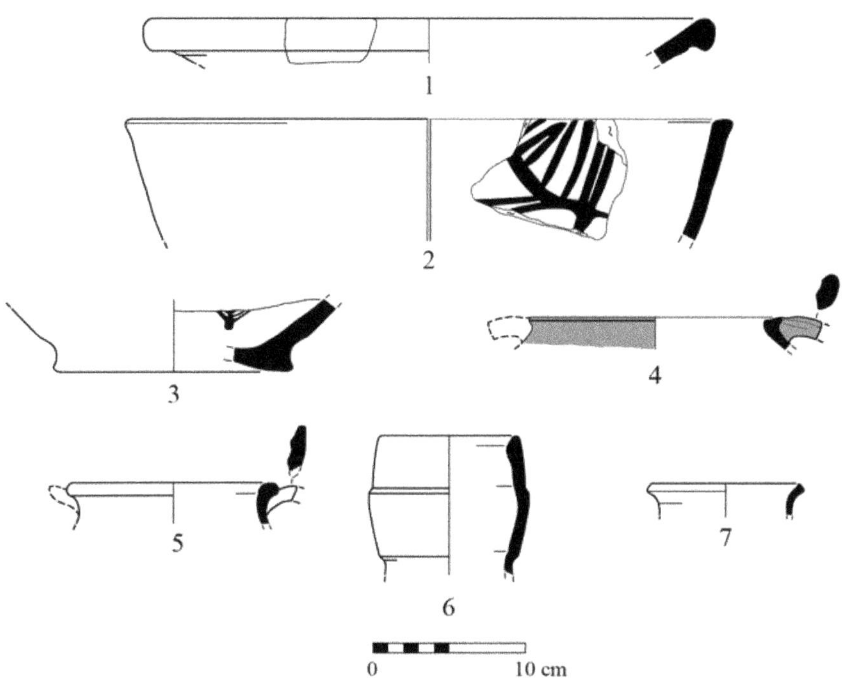

141. Pottery from **Jebel Fasil**: 1. CP, lt br, MA (?); 2-3. Bowls, lt br, amber dec, MA; 4. CP, dk br, blk slip, Byz-EM (?); 5. Cooking jug (?), dk br, Rom-Byz; 6. Jar, lt br, EM; 7. Jug, lt br, Rom-Byz.

Site 51: 18-15/97/4

THOR EL-WALAD

Israel grid: 1896/1573
UTM grid: 7284/5442
Elevation: 66 m b.s.l., 50 m b.s.a.
Name: local
Site type: fort (?) and settlement
Area: 5 dunams (5000 sq. m)
Topography: spur between wadis
Rock type: Judea Group
Soil type: stony-desert
Soil quality: 1
Cultivation: none
Cisterns: none
Water source: Nahal Fasael (181), 4.3 km distant
Road: Beit She'an–Jericho (B10), 2.2 km distant
Visit: January 2011; 140 sherds

Structures on a spur between wadis 2.5 km west-north-west of Kibbutz Gilgal. The site is in a mountainous zone, surrounded by high ridges and is separated from its vicinity by steep wadis, the tributaries of Wadi Abu Mahmud; the location is on a flat high spur and there is a fine lookout.

On the triangular spur is a large well-built square courtyard, measuring about 25×24 m. The perimeter wall is built of two rows of medium-sized stones, and is about 1 m thick, while the eastern side is supported by an embankment of small stones. In the western corner of the courtyard there is a room or cell.

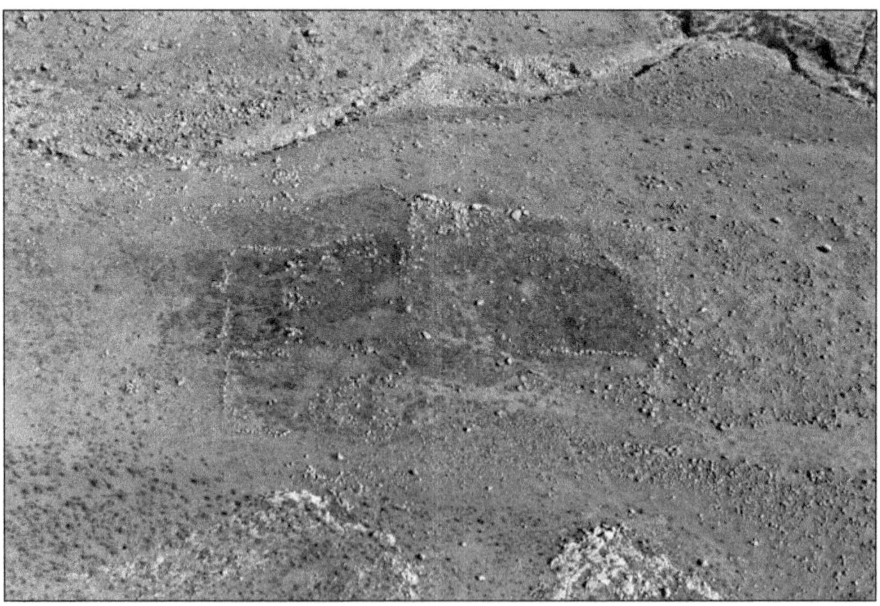

142. An aerial view north at **Thor el-Walad**, 2012 (A. Solomon).

Apparently there were structures inside the yard, but nowadays it is difficult to see their walls. The construction in general is good, and is not characteristic of the construction of grazing enclosures in the Jordan Valley.

East of the last structure and down the spur are walls and a stone scatter. Apparently, dwelling structures stood in this area. Beyond the channel west of the courtyard there are remains of more walls which were connected to the central site.

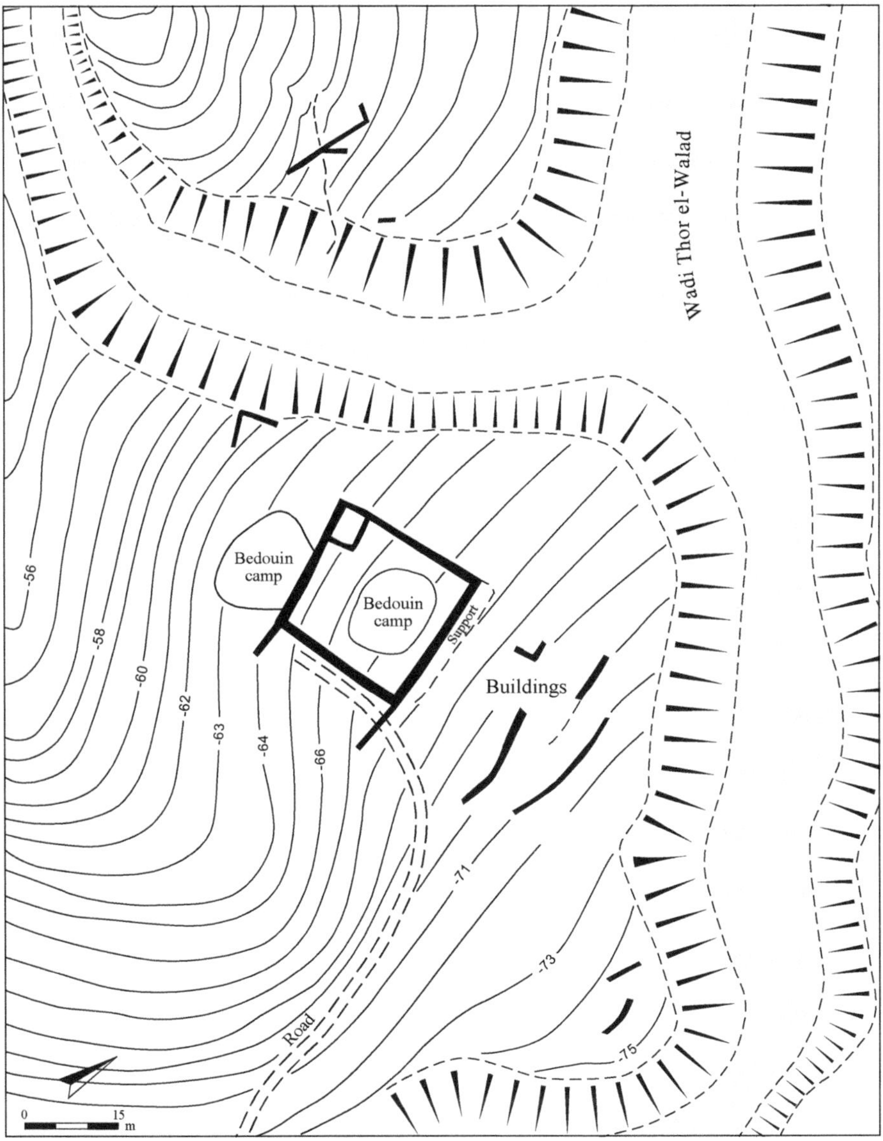

143. Plan of **Thor el-Walad.**

There is also a contemporary Bedouin tent encampment.

After careful consideration, it is considered possible that this was an Iron Age II fortress with a small settlement nearby. Similar forts have been found in Wadi Malih (Zertal 2008: site 91) and near Netiv Hagdud (Site 72).

Pottery: Middle Bronze II – 2%; Iron I – 2%; Iron II – 21%; Hellenistic – 2%; Late Roman – 51%; Byzantine – 5%; Medieval – 14%; Ottoman-Modern – 3%.
Flint: 4 items (see Appendix A).
Additional surveys: none.

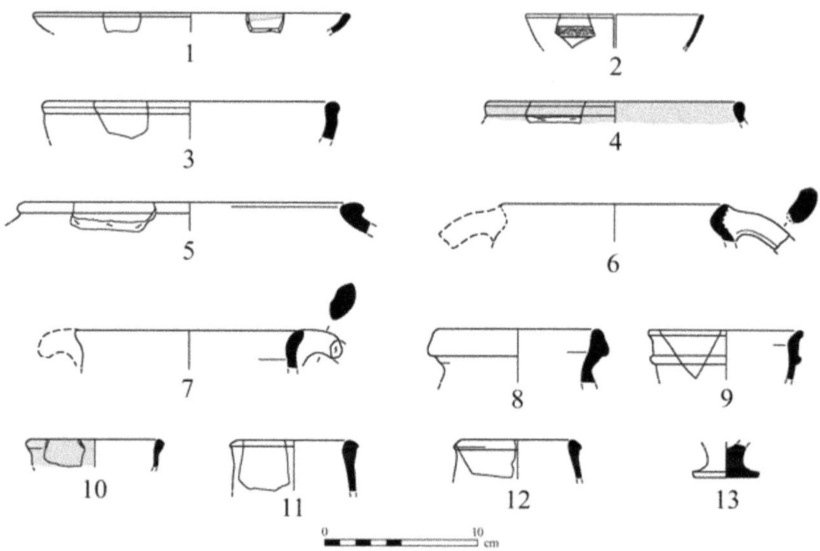

144. Pottery from **Thor el-Walad**: 1. Bowl, lt br, rd slip, Rom-Byz; 2. Tea-cup, porcelain, floral décor, Mod; 3. Bowl, lt br, Rom-Byz; 4. Bowl, dk br, rd slip, Rom-Byz; 5. CP, lt br, MB II (?); 6-7. CP, dk br, Rom-Byz; 8. Jar, lt br, IA II; 9. Jug, dk br, IA II (?); 10. Jug, dk br, rd slip (?), Rom-Byz; 11-12. Jugs, dk br, IA II; 13. Base of an unguentarium, blk, Hel.

Site 52: 19-15/07/1

ELEVATION POINT -178

Israel grid: 1907/1571
UTM grid: 7295/5439
Elevation: 170 m b.s.l., 40 m b.s.a.
Name: nearest place
Site type: structures and encampments
Area: 4 dunams (4000 sq. m)
Topography: slope
Rock type: Judea Group
Soil type: stony-desert
Soil quality: 2
Cultivation: none
Cisterns: none
Water source: Nahal Fasael (181), 4.2 km distant
Road: Beit She'an–Jericho (B10), 500 m distant
Visits: February 2002, 2011; 80 sherds

A site on a moderate slope descending from the west to the Jordan Valley, a little north of the Gilgal–Wadi Abu Mahmud road, and 1.5 km south-south-west of the village of Tomer.

There are three types of remains in the site:

1. Rectangular structures, measuring about 5×3 m, with walls one stone thick, apparently dwellings.
2. About 50 accumulations of stones, *rujms* or tomb-like, with thin scatters of sherds among them. Most of the *rujms* are oval or rectangular. The stones are of medium size and are somewhat arranged.
3. Tent encampments.

During a repeat visit to the site in January 2011, the remains of a round courtyard with an attached cell paved with small stones were found in its southern part, close to the north bank of Wadi Abu Mahmud. The yard is about 10 m diameter,

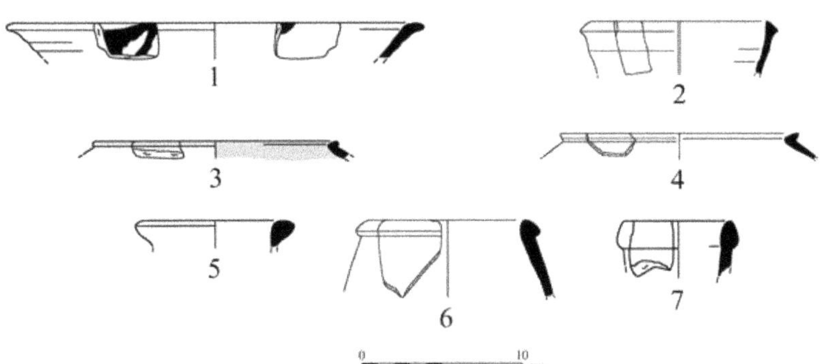

145. Pottery from **EP -178**: 1. Bowl, buff, green glaze, MA; 2. Bowl, rd, LR; 3. Bowl, rd, rd slip, LR; 4. CP, rd, LR; 5. Jar, lt br, MB II; 6. Jar, rd, LR; 7. Jug, dk br, IA I-II.

built of medium-sized stones. The round cell, which is built of medium-sized standing stones, is about 3 m diameter. Medieval and Ottoman sherds were found in the courtyard, including a fragment of an Ottoman pipe and an iron horseshoe.

The site served for encampment, cemetery and perhaps for dwelling. The variety of pottery hints at continuous activity over a long time.

Pottery: Middle Bronze II – 1%; Iron I-II – 12%; Late Roman – 45%; Medieval – 37%; Ottoman – 5%.
Additional surveys: none.

♦ ♦ ♦

Site 53: 19-15/07/4

WADI ABU MAHMUD

Israel grid: 1905/1571
UTM grid: 7293/5440
Elevation: 160 m b.s.l., 15 m b.s.a.
Name: nearest place
Site type: enclosures
Area: 1 dunam (1000 sq. m)
Topography: estuary of a wadi
Rock type: Judea Group
Soil type: stony-desert
Soil quality: 1
Cultivation: none
Cisterns: none
Water source: Nahal Yitav (182), 4.3 km distant
Road: Beit She'an–Jericho (B10), 1.3 km distant
Visit: January 2002; 58 sherds

An enclosure site next to an unpaved road, north of the channel of Wadi Abu Mahmud and close to its exit to the Jordan Valley. It is located 2 km west-northwest of Kibbutz Gilgal.

The site overlooks a narrow plain. There are two rounded enclosures about 20 m apart, carelessly built and about 12 m in diameter.

Pottery: Late Roman – 26%, Byzantine – 8%; Medieval (Mamluk) – 35%, Ottoman – 18%; Modern – 13%.
Additional surveys: none.

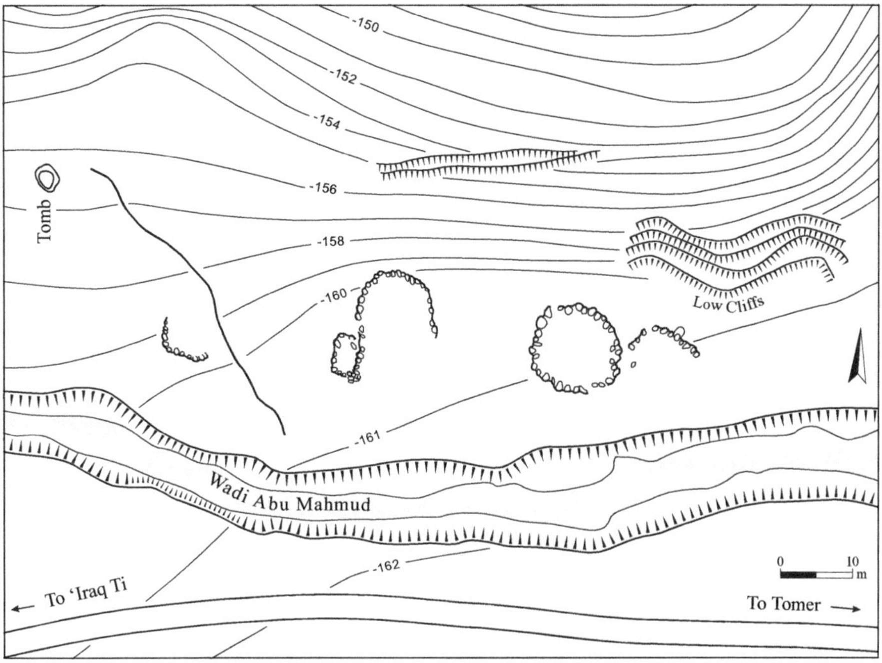

146. Plan of **Wadi Abu Mahmud**.

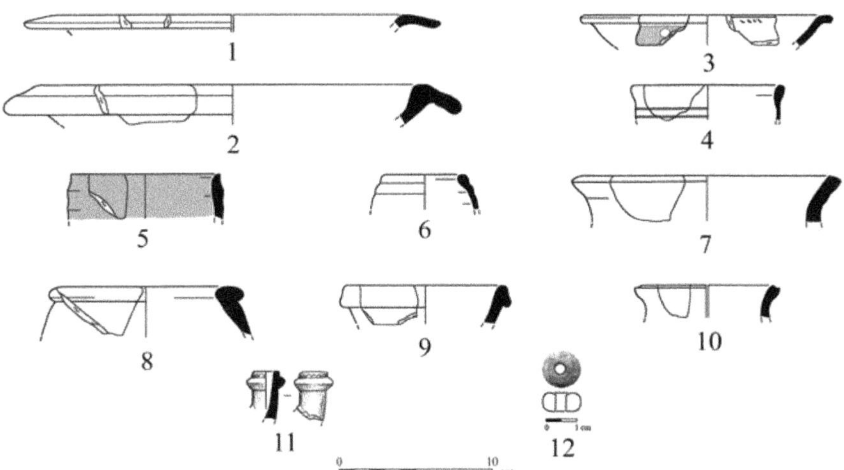

147. Finds from **Wadi Abu Mahmud**: 1. CP, amber, Rom-Byz (?); 2. CP, blk, Byz; 3. Bowl, rd, blk slip, yel glaze, MA; 4. Bowl (?), buff, Rom-Byz; 5. Bowl, rd, rd slip, MA; 6. Bowl (?), amber, Rom-Byz; 7. Jar, lt br, MA; 8. Jar, lt br, Rom-Byz; 9. Jug, blk, Ott-Mod (?); 10. Jug, rd, Rom-Byz (?); 11. Pipe, lt br, rd slip, incision dec, Ott; 12. Bead, soft limestone.

Site 54: 18-15/96/1

THE 'WELL SITE'

Israel grid: 1893/1567
UTM grid: 7282/5436
Elevation: 54 m b.s.l., 50 m b.s.a.
Name: given by the survey
Site type: enclosures
Area: 2 dunams (2000 sq. m)
Topography: shoulder between wadis
Rock type: Judea Group
Soil type: stony-desert
Soil quality: 2
Cultivation: none
Cisterns: none
Water source: Nahal Fasael (181), 5 km distant
Road: Beit She'an–Jericho (B10), 2.5 km distant
Visits: December 2002 and more; 75 sherds

A small enclosure on a high shoulder in a narrow wadi, 2.5 km west of Gilgal. On the slope above and west of it passes an asphalted road from Gilgal to a new well in the inner part of the wadi which is named 'Iraq et-Ti in the map.

The shoulder on which the site rests is flat and oval, cut off on all sides by deep wadis. The riverbed surrounding it, Wadi Abu Mahmud, is very active and parts of the site, especially the southern one, have been eroded and washed away.

148. View south at the **'Well Site'**, 2002.

There is a round enclosure about 40 m in diameter, encircled by a double wall of large stones. Inside the enclosure, a room is attached to the west side of the wall; there are also several other inner walls.

About 25 m north of the site is another round enclosure, 12 m across. The enclosures are separated by a deep ravine. Above the site there are cave entrances.

The number of sherds is relatively high for such a site.

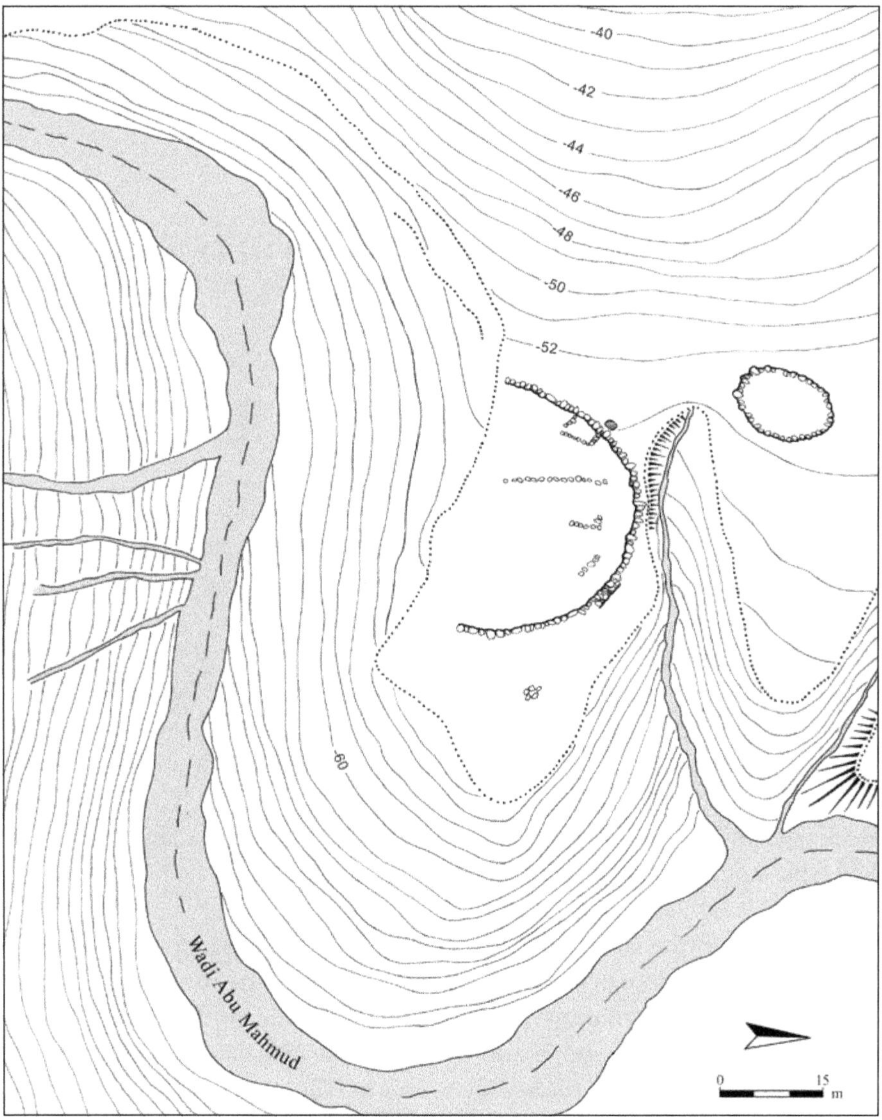

149. Plan of the **'Well Site'**.

Pottery: Early Bronze – 2%; Middle Bronze II – 4%; Iron I – 20%; Iron II – 20%; Hellenistic – 4%; Late Roman – 27%; Byzantine – 13%; unidentified – 10%.
Flint: 9 items (see Appendix A).
Additional surveys: none.
Bibliography: Bar 2014: site 103.

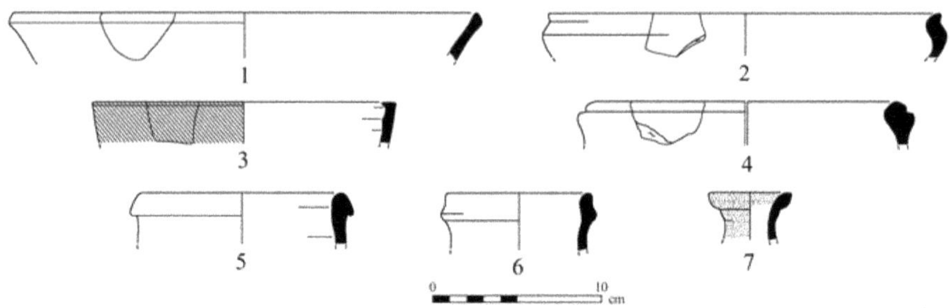

150. Pottery from the **'Well Site'**: 1. Bowl, gr, IA (?); 2. Bowl, rd, IA I-II; 3. Bowl, lt br, blk slip, Rom-Byz; 4. CP D, br, IA II; 5. Jar, dk br, Rom; 6. Jug, br, IA I-II; 7. Juglet, rd, wt slip, Rom.

♦ ♦ ♦

Site 55: 19-15/06/1

GILGAL (1)

Israel grid: 1908/1567
UTM grid: 7297/5435
Elevation: 200 m b.s.l., 50 m b.s.a.
Name: nearest place
Site type: enclosures
Area: 3 dunams (3000 sq. m)
Topography: moderate slope
Rock type: Judea Group
Soil type: stony-desert

Soil quality: 3
Cultivation: none
Cisterns: none
Water source: Nahal Fasael (181), 4.8 km distant
Road: Beit She'an–Jericho (B10), 500 m distant
Visits: November 2002 and more; 31 sherds

An enclosure in the west side of the Jordan Valley floodplain and below the escarpment descending eastwards. North of it passes the road from Gilgal to Iraq et-Ti; at the east, an unpaved road to the east leads south towards Niran.

At the centre of the site is an elongated enclosure raised 2 m above the plain, divided into three, measuring 60×24 m. The perimeter wall, about 80 cm thick, is built of two attached rows of stones. The inner walls form three sub-enclosures with cells and openings along them. There are similar cells or

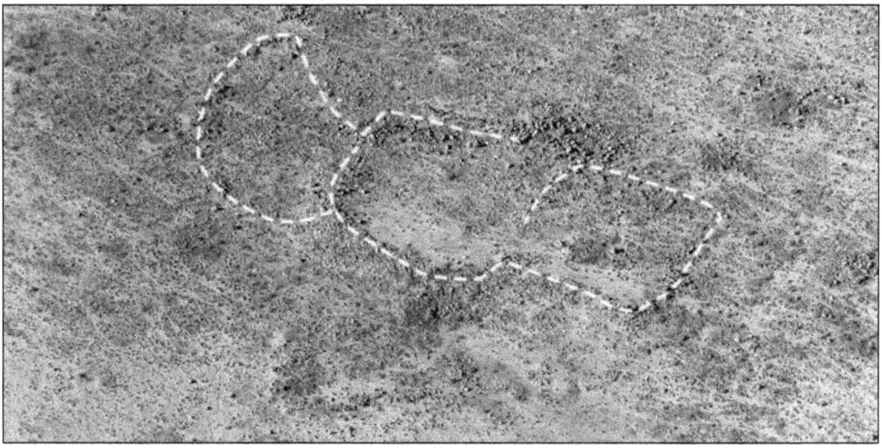

151. Aerial view south-west at the **Gilgal (1)**, 2008. The enclosure parts which are practically filled by silt are marked by a dashed line (N. Eshed).

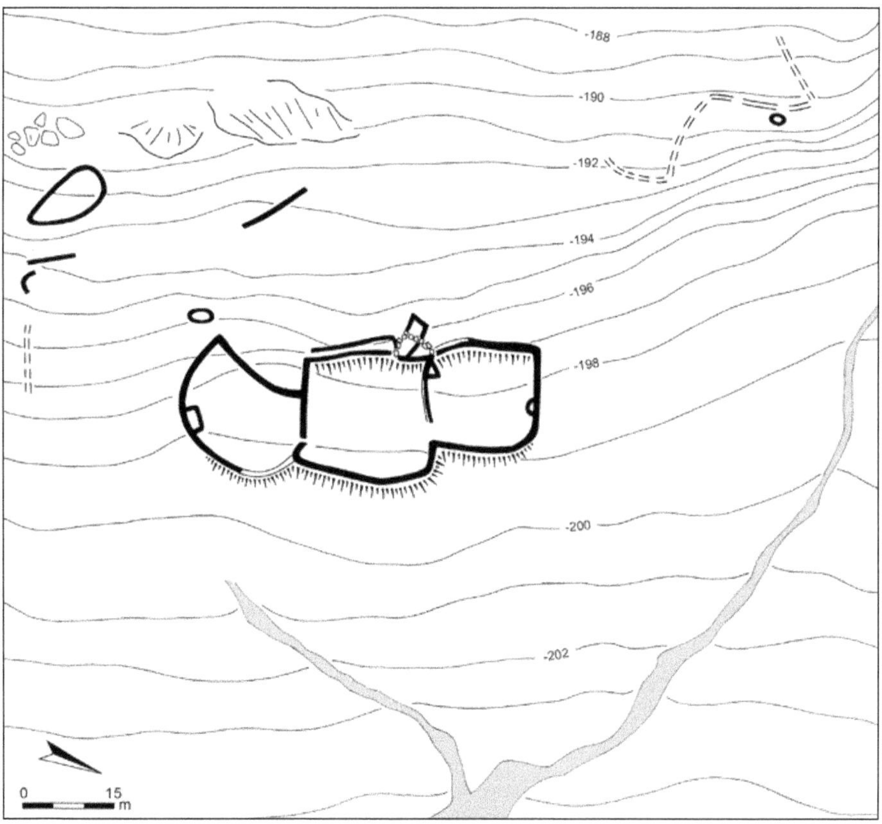

152. Plan of **Gilgal (1)**.

small rooms, built of large stones, west of the central enclosure. Some of the building stones stand upright.

Various walls are visible south-east and north-west of the centre of the site, perhaps terraces designed to prevent erosion.

About 40 m north-west of the enclosures is a 80 m-long plastered wall, built in a zig-zag pattern along the slope; apparently used as a duct to collect rain water.

There is a sparse sherd scatter over the whole area.

Pottery: Middle Bronze II – 3%; Iron II – 17%; Late Roman – 80%.
Additional surveys: none.

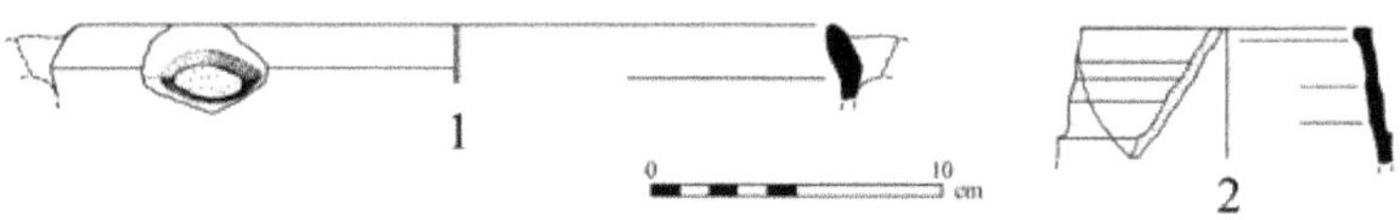

153. Pottery from **Gilgal (1)**: 1. CP, rd, IA II; 2. Jar, br, LR.

♦ ♦ ♦

Site 56: 19-15/06/2

GILGAL (6)

Israel grid: 1909/1567
UTM grid: 7297/5435
Elevation: 195 m b.s.l., 50 m b.s.a.
Name: nearest place
Site type: tents encampments
Area: 5 dunams (5000 sq. m)
Topography: Jordan Valley plain
Rock type: Judea Group
Soil type: stony-desert

Soil quality: 1
Cultivation: none
Cisterns: none
Water source: Nahal Fasael (181), 4.8 km distant
Road: Beit She'an–Jericho (B10), 500 m distant
Visit: January 2011; 100 sherds

An encampment site where the eastern Samaria ridges meet the Jordan Valley plain, 1.2 km west of Gilgal. Its location is close to the junction of an asphalt road and a unpaved road.

Over the plain are spread numerous remains of modern and ancient encampments. There are walls of mostly rounded stones, one stone thick. Occasionally there are walls of different types and also tombs in the form of small stone mounds.

154. Round encampments in **Gilgal (6)**, 2010 (S. Bar).

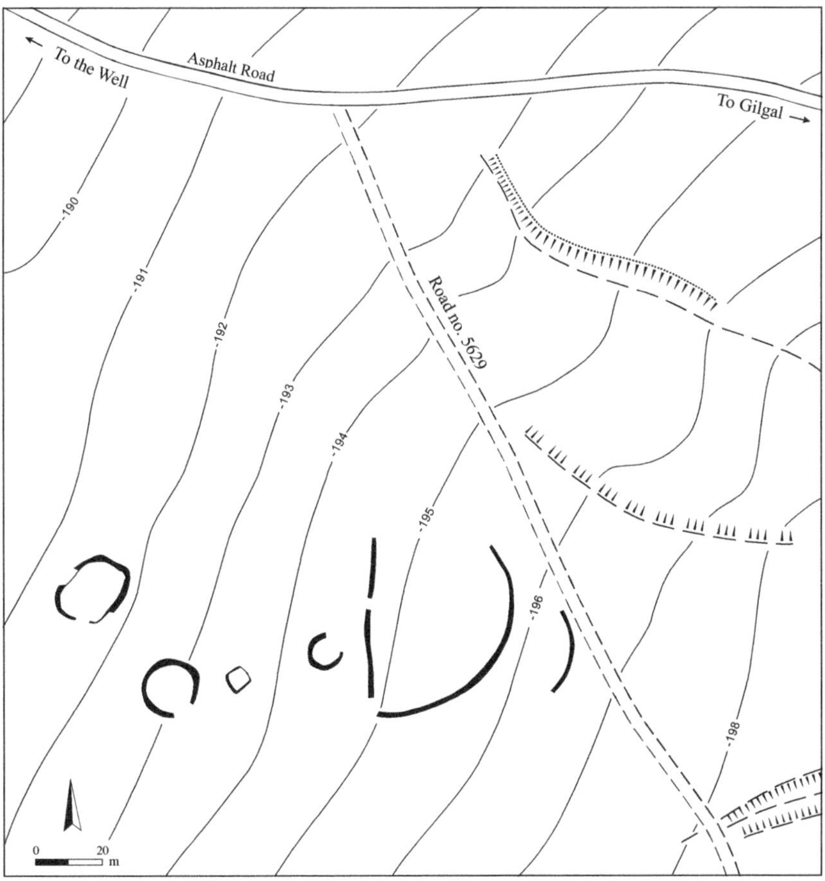

155. Plan of **Gilgal (6)**.

Unlike the poor architecture, the abundance of sherds points to a longlasting use of the place as an encampment site over many periods.

Pottery: Iron II – 4%; Early Roman – 5%; Late Roman – 30%; Byzantine – 30%; Medieval – 10%; Ottoman – 15%; Modern – 6%.
Additional surveys: none.

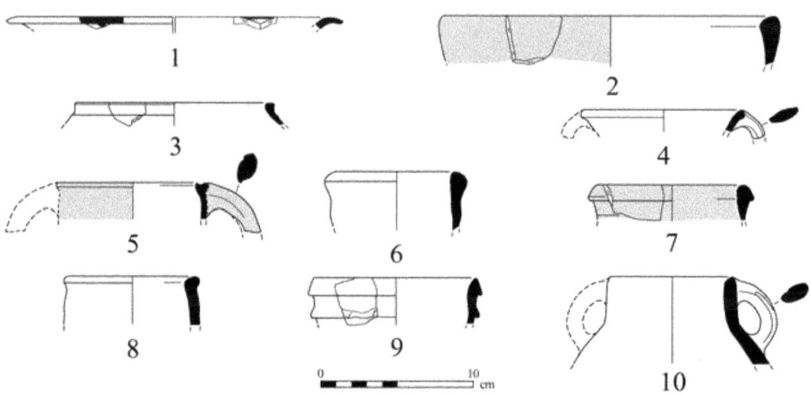

156. Pottery from **Gilgal (6)**: 1. Bowl, lt br, green glaze, MA; 2. Bowl, lt br, dk br slip, MA; 3. CP, rd, Rom-Byz; 4. CP, rd, Rom; 5, 7. Jugs, lt br, rd slip, Rom-Byz; 6. Jug (?), lt br, IA II; 8. Jug (?), dk br, IA (?); 9. Jug, dk br, Rom-Byz; 10. Cooking jug, dk br, IA II.

♦ ♦ ♦

Site 57: 19-15/26/1

GILGAL (3)

Israel grid: 1923/1565
UTM grid: 7311/5433
Elevation: 230 m b.s.l., 50 m a.s.a.
Name: nearest place
Site type: structure and sherd scatter
Area: 1 dunam (1000 sq. m)
Topography: hillock
Rock type: flint conglomerate
Soil type: stony-desert
Soil quality: 2
Cultivation: none
Cisterns: none
Water source: Nahal Fasael (181), 4 km distant
Road: Beit She'an–Jericho (B10), 200 m distant
Visits: November 2009 and more; 20 sherds

A sparse scatter of sherds and stractural remains on an elongated hillock in the centre of Kibbutz Gilgal. The site, ruined by modern construction works, dominates the Jordan Valley plain.

The site seems to have been surveyed in the Emergency Survey of 1968. Bar-Adon (1972: site 19) describes a Roman fort, measuring 8.5×7.5 m and walls 1.2 m thick, built of large flint stones.

In our visit in 2009 we found scanty remnants of a dismantled structure. Around it were found strewn displaced flint building stones. In addition to Roman sherds, IA II body sherds were found in the hilltop area.

Pottery: Iron II (body sherds) – 30%; Late Roman – 70%.
Additional surveys: Bar-Adon 1972: site 19.

◆ ◆ ◆

Site 58: 19-15/06/3

GILGAL (4)

Israel grid: 1909/1564
UTM grid: 7297/5433
Elevation: 210 m b.s.l., 0 m a.s.a.
Name: nearest place
Site type: enclosure
Area: 3 dunams (3000 sq. m)
Topography: plain
Rock type: Judea Group
Soil type: stony-desert
Soil quality: 3
Cultivation: none
Cisterns: none
Water source: Nahal Fasael (181), 5 km distant
Road: Beit She'an–Jericho (B10), 500 m distant
Visit: February 2004; 50 sherds

A small site in the floodplain, close to the ridge escarpment of eastern Samaria, 1.2 km west of Kibbutz Gilgal, and 1.8 km north-west of Netiv Hagdud. South of it is Wadi Sha'ab el-Qubur.

There are remains of the south and part of the western side of an oval enclosure of about 30 m maximum diameter, built of medium-sized stones. The northern and eastern parts of the enclosure have been washed away or dismantled.

The enclosure wall is built of one row of stones, and abutting it from the outside are rectangular and rounded rooms, the diameters of which vary from 3 to 6 m. Two longer walls project from this central wall. In the centre of the enclosure is a round well-built structure about 4.5 m in diameter. A wall projects out of it to the north, and a small room is attached to it in the west.

Around the enclosure were traces of several walls; 50 m south of it there are a few remains of another enclosure.

157. The **Gilgal (4)** enclosure, view north. In the background are seen the Jordan Valley plains; in the distance the water pool of Tomer and the Sartaba ridge (in haze), 2012 (N. Goldring).

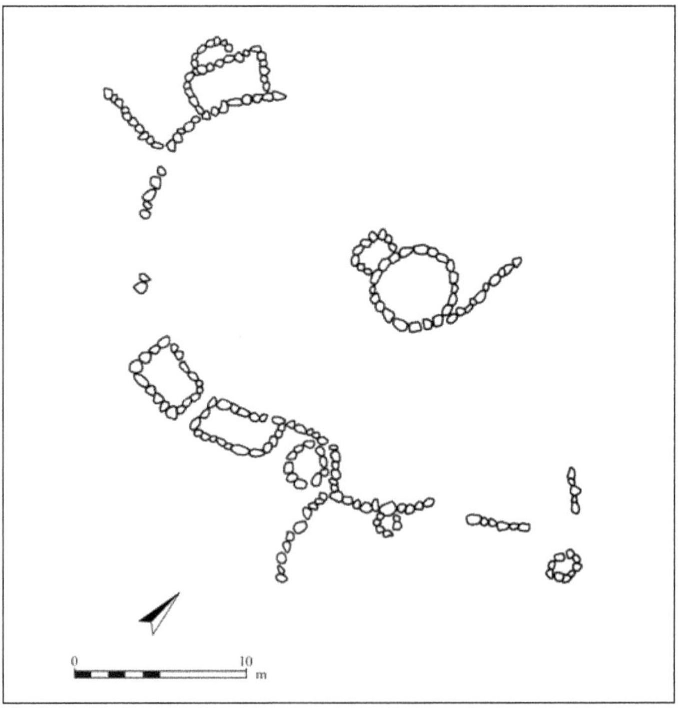

158. Plan of **Gilgal (4)**.

The uniqueness of the place is in the rooms and cells of the casement-like enclosure wall.

Pottery: Middle Bronze II (?) – 2%; Iron I-II – 46%; Hellenistic – 17%; Roman – 35%.
Flint: 6 items (see Appendix A).
Additional surveys: none.

159. Pottery from **Gilgal (4)**: 1. Jug, rd, Rom; 2. Base, rd, Hel-ER.

♦ ♦ ♦

Site 59: 19-15/06/4

NETIV HAGDUD (6)

Israel grid: 1908/1564
UTM grid: 7297/5432
Elevation: 195 m b.s.l., 10 m a.s.a.
Name: nearest place
Site type: enclosure
Area: 1 dunam (1000 sq. m)
Topography: plain
Rock type: Judea Group
Soil type: stony-desert

Soil quality: 1
Cultivation: none
Cisterns: none
Water source: Nahal Fasael (181), 4.9 km distant
Road: Beit She'an–Jericho (B10), 800 m distant
Visits: January 2011, 2016; 62 sherds

A small site where the Jordan Valley plain meets the foot of the Samaria Mountains.

There are remains of an enclosure, a slightly curved wall extending from the structure and parallel to it, built of large stones, adjacent to a low cliff to the east; 5 m further on are another wall and the probable remains of rooms. Other walls extend eastward from the main enclosure. Further south is an elongated room and wall remains, with a small structure measuring about 2×2 m.

Pottery: Iron I – 4%; Iron II – 16%; Persian-Hellenistic – 4%; Early Roman – 8%; Late Roman – 56%; Byzantine – 12%.
Additional surveys: none.

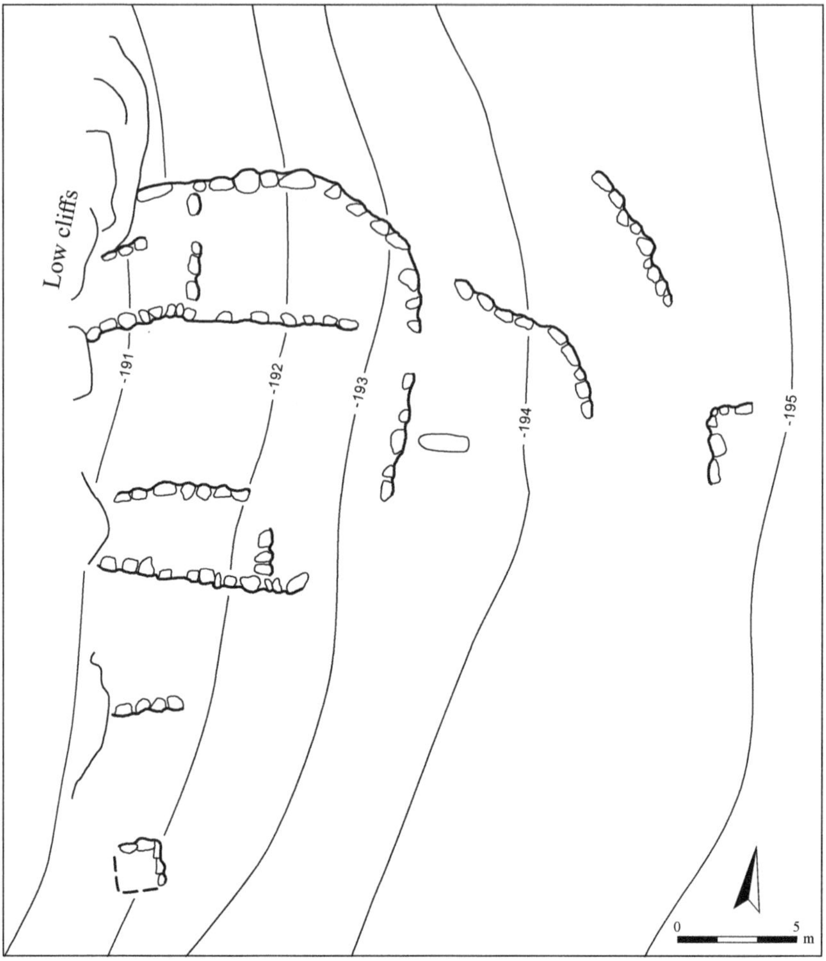

160. Plan of **Netiv Hagdud (6)**.

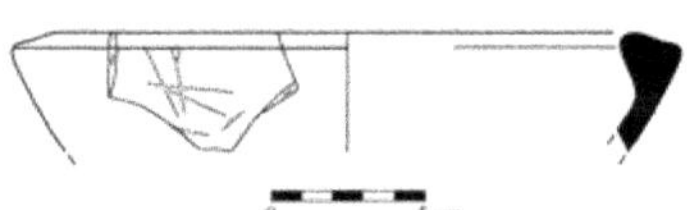

161. A sherd from **Netiv Hagdud (6)**: Bowl, lt br, incisions, Pers-Hel (?).

Site 59 (1): 19-15/06/5

GILGAL (7)

Israel grid: 1909/1565
UTM grid: 7297/5434
Elevation: 200 m b.s.l., 10 m a.s.a.
Name: nearest place
Site type: enclosures
Area: 3 dunams (3000 sq. m)
Topography: valley edge
Rock type: Yehuda Group
Soil type: stony-desert
Soil quality: 1
Cultivation: none
Cisterns: none
Water source: Nahal Fasael (181), 4.9 km distant
Road: Beit She'an–Jericho (B10), 500 m distant
Visit: February 2016; 40 sherds

An enclosure site on the edge of a valley 1.2 km west of the centre of Gilgal, and 1.9 km north-west of the centre of Netiv Hagdud. East of the site an unpaved road runs along the seam between the Jordan Valley and the slopes of the Samaria Mountains. South of the site are Site 59 and Wadi Sha'ab el-Bir.

A very large, 16×36 m, rectangular enclosure, was found. Its walls are 0.8 m wide (two stones wide), built of medium-sized stones. The masonry is good.

South of the rectangular enclosure are the remains of an earlier, badly preserved, enclosure. Only the southern wall and parts of the western wall survive. The masonry is similar to the well-preserved enclosure. A structure 1×2 m was found near this enclosure, either a cell or small tumulus. Additional walls were noted to the west of both enclosures.

This is part of the widespread Late Roman-Byzantine agricultural activity in the Jordan Valley plain.

Pottery: Late Roman-Byzantine – 95%; Medieval– 5%.
Additional surveys: none.

Site 60: 19-15/16/1

GILGAL (5)

Israel grid: 1913/1563
UTM grid: 7297/5432
Elevation: 215 m b.s.l., 0 m a.s.a.
Name: nearest place
Site type: enclosures
Area: 12 dunams (1.2 ha)
Topography: plain
Rock type: Judea Group
Soil type: marl and stony

Soil quality: 3
Cultivation: none
Cisterns: none
Water source: Nahal Fasael (181), 4.7 km distant
Road: Beit She'an–Jericho (B10), 500 m distant
Visit: October 2011; 170 sherds

A large site in the Jordan Valley floodplain, between the tributaries of Wadi Sha'ab el-Qubur. The place borders a date-palm plantation located about 1 km west of the centre of Kibbutz Gilgal.

The site is a complex of at least eight connected enclosures. The majority are oval or irregular. All the enclosures have internal sub-divisions.

In the centre of the site there is an elongated courtyard, with a constructed entrance in the west. Next to it is a casement-like wall – a double wall divided into cells. Additional enclosures are connected to this courtyard from east, north and west. The long axis of most of them is north-south. Two elongated enclosures with inner divisions are attached to the east of the yard. Several

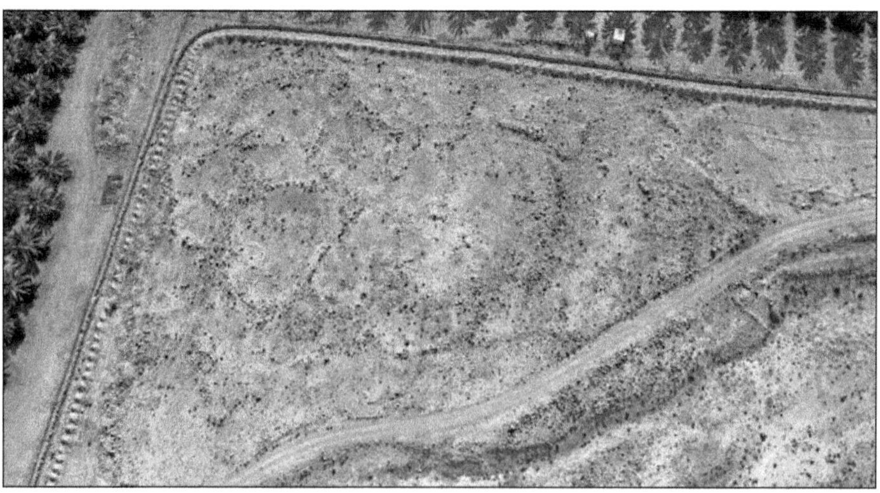

162. Aerial view east at **Gilgal (5)**. In the site is an array of attached enclosures, 2012 (A. Solomon).

enclosures, partially ruined, have been built to the south.

There are four unattached longitudinal structures around the central site; apparently there were other similar structures. It is likely that they served as dwellings.

All the walls are of two rows of medium-sized stones combined with boulders, mostly of flint conglomerate.

An unpaved road with two channels adjacent to it passes the site to the west. There are other small round enclosures between the channels.

The site, which was a central site in the Iron Age, was badly damaged during preparations for the date-palm plantation.

Pottery: Intermediate Bronze – 1%; Middle Bronze II – 1%; Iron I – 34%; Iron II – 15%; Early Roman – 11%; Late Roman – 23%; unidentified – 15%.
Flint: 57 items. Pre-Pottery Neolithic B and Iron Age (see Appendix A).
Additional surveys: none.

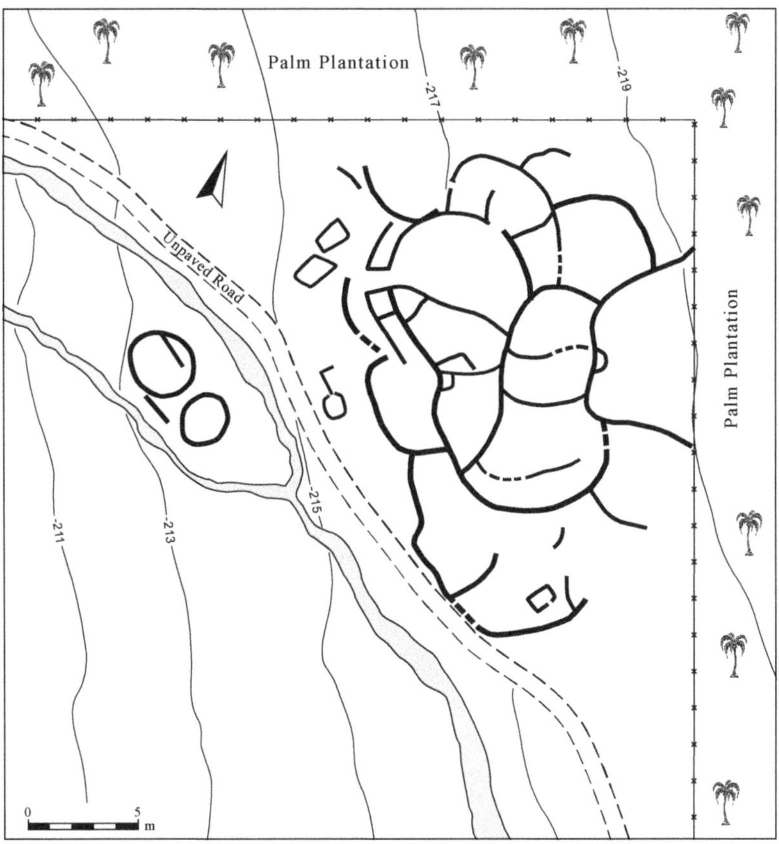

163. Plan of **Gilgal** (5).

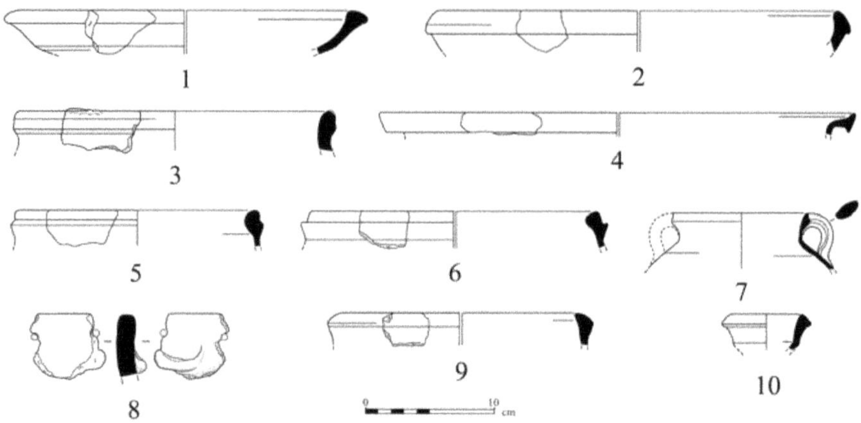

164. Pottery from **Gilgal (5)**: 1-2. Bowls, br, IA II; 3. CP, dk br, IA I; 4. CP A, dk br, IA I; 5-6. CP D, dk br, IA II; 7. CP, rd, ER; 8. Perforated cp, lt br, MB II; 9. Jug, br, IA I; 10. Jug, br, IA II.

♦ ♦ ♦

Site 61: 19-15/16/2

ZHAHRET EL-KHAIYES

Israel grid: 1910/1562
UTM grid: 7299/5430
Elevation: 195 m b.s.l., 50 m b.s.a.
Name: nearest place
Site type: encampments and enclosures
Area: 3 dunams (3000 sq. m)
Topography: plain
Rock type: Judea Group
Soil type: stony-desert
Soil quality: 1
Cultivation: none
Cisterns: none
Water source: Nahal Fasael (181), 4.8 km distant
Road: Beit She'an–Jericho (B10), 500 m distant
Visit: January 2011; 117 sherds

Enclosures and encampment remains on the south bank of Wadi Sha'ab el-Qubur, near its exit eastward from the Samaria Mountains ridge. It is located about 1.2 km west of Kibbutz Gilgal.

This is a complex array of interconnected enclosures, built from one row of local medium-sized stones laid next to each other on the ground, without a foundation trench. This is the type of construction typical of the Medieval period at the earliest in this region, or even during the Ottoman period, over the remains of an earlier site.

In the south there are two parallel enclosures built of one row of stones as above, with rooms and stone circles linked to the enclosure wall. The main wall turns north, connecting north-west to another courtyard.

Inside the channel of nearby Wadi Sha'ab el-Qubur, about 100 m north-west from the centre of the site is another enclosure, about 20 m in diameter, built from a double row wall of medium-sized stones, surrounded by a sherd scatter identical to that in the central site. The width of the wadi channel here is 40–50 m, and in its north part goes through the internal narrow gulley. Bedouin still live at the site.

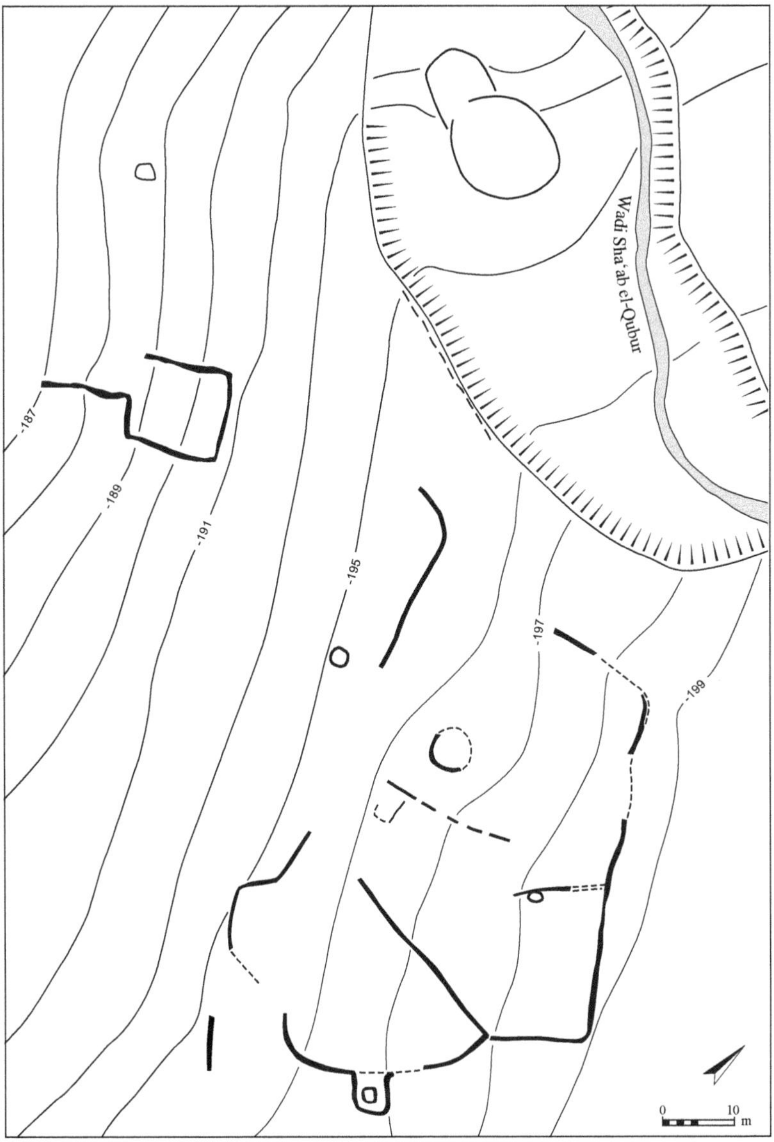

165. Plan of **Zhahret el-Khaiyes.**

Pottery: Iron I – 10%; Early Roman – 13%; Late Roman – 51%; Medieval – 17%; Ottoman – 9%.
Additional surveys: none.

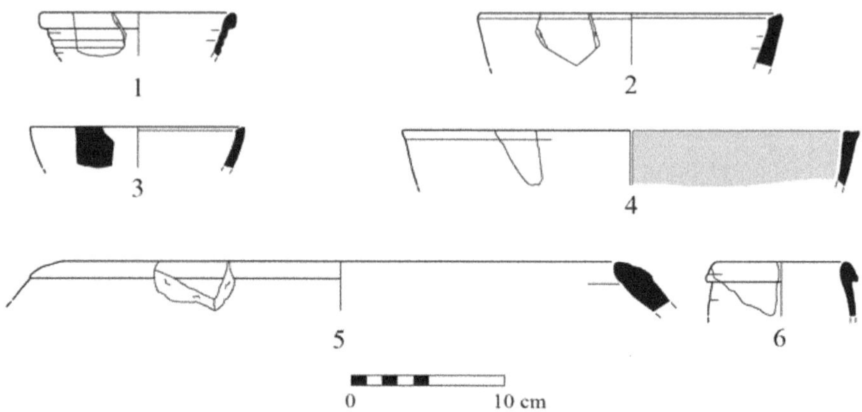

166. Pottery from **Zhahret el-Khaiyes**: 1. Bowl, rd, Rom; 2. Bowl, lt br, Rom; 3. Cooking bowl, lt br, blk slip, Rom; 4. Bowl, lt br, rd slip, Rom; 5. HM jar, lt br, MA; 6. Jar, rd, Rom (?).

♦ ♦ ♦

Site 62: 19-15/15/4

WADI SHA'AB EL-QUBUR

Israel grid: 1911/1559
UTM grid: 7299/5427
Elevation: 200 m b.s.l., 50 m b.s.a.
Name: nearest place
Site type: enclosure
Area: 2 dunams (2000 sq. m)
Topography: plain
Rock type: Judea Group
Soil type: stony-desert
Soil quality: 1
Cultivation: none
Cisterns: none
Water source: Nahal Fasael (181), 5.2 km distant
Road: Beit She'an–Jericho (B10), 500 m distant
Visit: January 2011; 4 sherds

This site, in the meeting place of the bottom of the east Samaria ridge with the Jordan Valley plain, contains structures and parts of an enclosure. It is 1 km south-west of the village of Gilgal.

The site includes at least four structures with oval rooms built of large stones. Each room measures 4×3 m on average. In the southern part is a corner of an enclosure with a double wall built of two rows of medium-sized stones. The relationship between the structures themselves and the enclosure wall is not clear. The structures are 20–30 m apart, but the manner of construction is the same.

Pottery: Iron I-II – three body sherds; Late Roman – one body sherd.
Additional surveys: none.

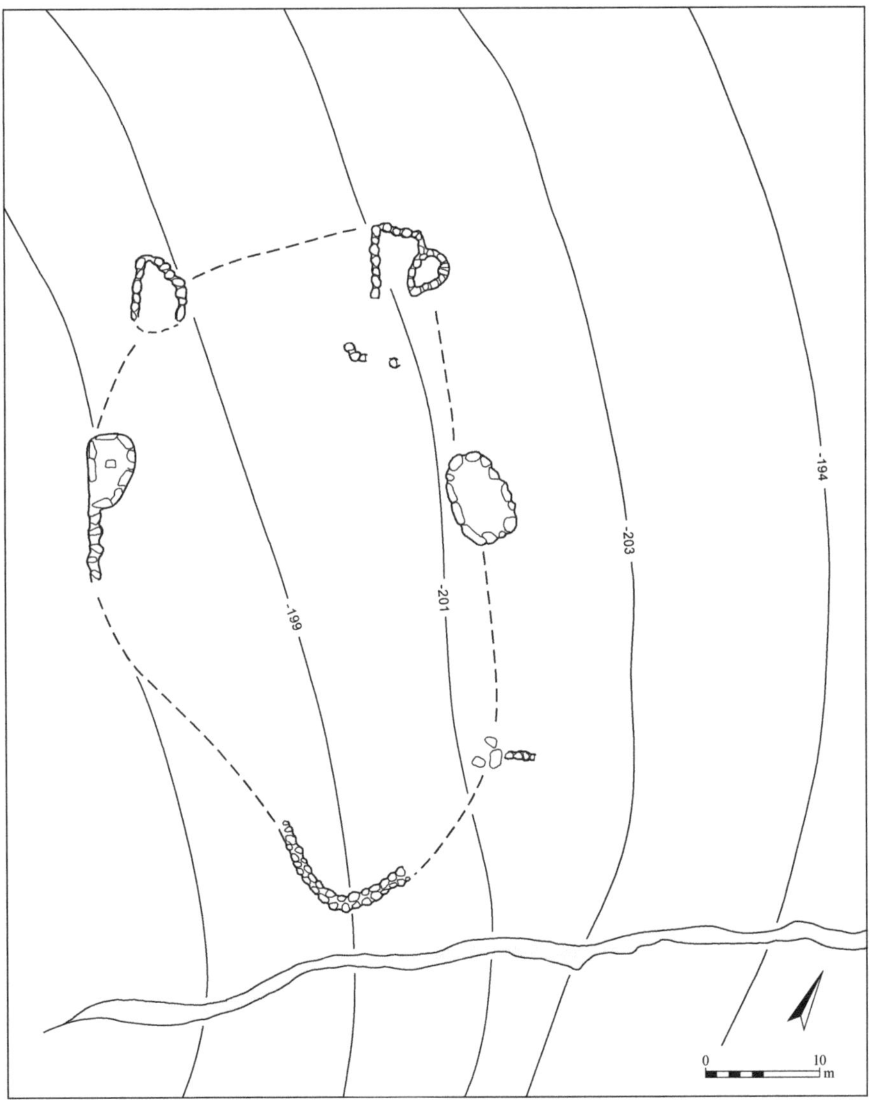

167. Plan of **Wadi Sha'ab el-Qubur**.

Site 63: 19-15/05/1

INSCRIPTION (?) ON A STONE FROM WADI TAL'AT ZAGHARAH

Israel grid: 1911/1559 UTM grid: 7299/5427

In the course of the survey in February 2003 a stone with possible remnants of an incised inscription was found. The stone was found out of context without linkage to any site, near the summit of Elevation Point -11, overlooking the Jordan Valley plain.

The stone is 40×30×15 cm. On the dressed and smoothed surface are two shallow cavities next to each other, each about 5 cm in diameter. In the centre of the stone are incised the letters "ש" and perhaps the letter "ע" in Aramaic characters. Other readings of the characters are also possible.

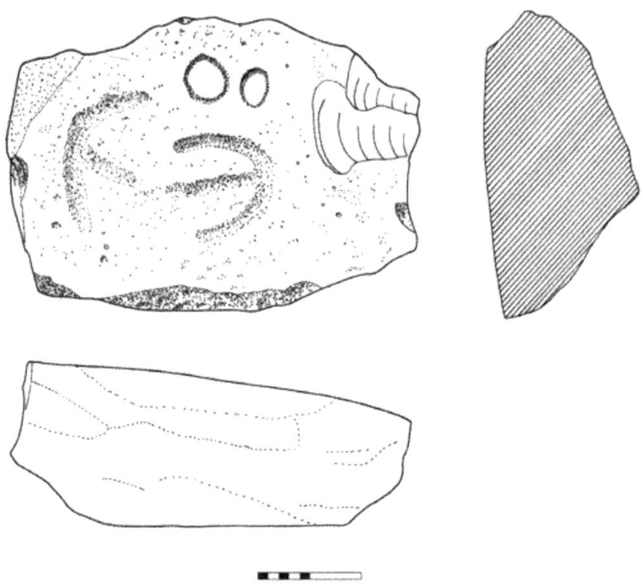

168. Stone, found near E.P. -11, with inscription or incisions: "ש" and possibly "ע".

Site 64: 19-15/15/2

WADI TAL'AT ZAGHARAH (1)

Israel grid: 1914/1555
UTM grid: 7302/5423
Elevation: 205 m b.s.l., 0 m a.s.a.
Name: nearest place
Site type: enclosures
Area: 4 dunams (4000 sq. m)
Topography: plain
Rock type: Judea Group
Soil type: marl
Soil quality: 3
Cultivation: none
Cisterns: none
Water source: Nahal Fasael (181), 5.5 km distant
Road: Beit She'an–Jericho (B10), 1.2 km distant
Visit: December 2002; 50 sherds

Two enclosures north of Wadi Tal'at Zagharah close to the north-western corner of Netiv Hagdud. Large parts of the Jordan Valley plain in this area have been levelled by bulldozers; therefore the existence of other demolished sites in the vicinity is likely. There is a view from the site to the Sartaba summit.

The enclosures are situated in the Jordan Valley plain. The channel of Wadi Tal'at Zagharah, whose northern side has been blocked by an earth rampart, passes nearby to the north. An unpaved road crosses the rampart.

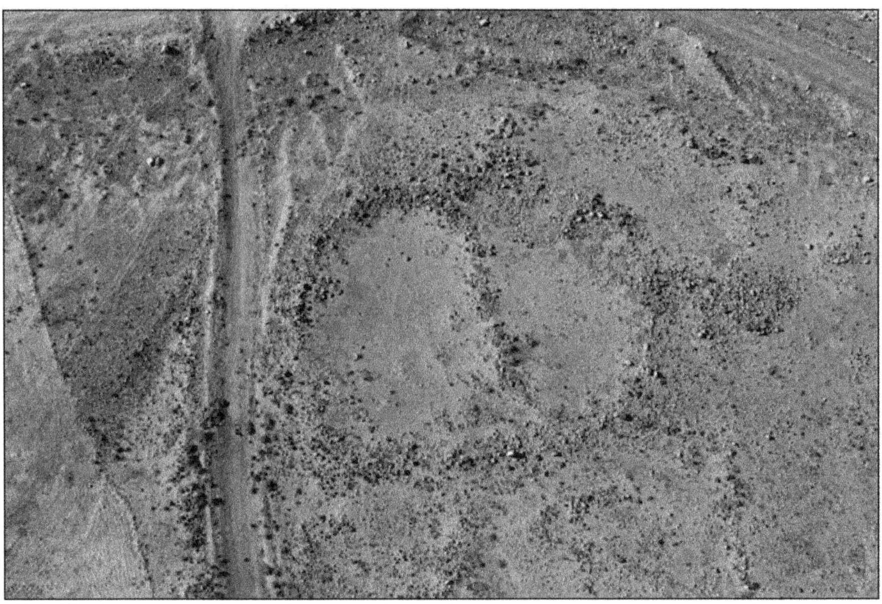

169. **Wadi Tal'at Zagharah (1)**, Aerial view north-west at the enclosures, 2012 (A. Solomon).

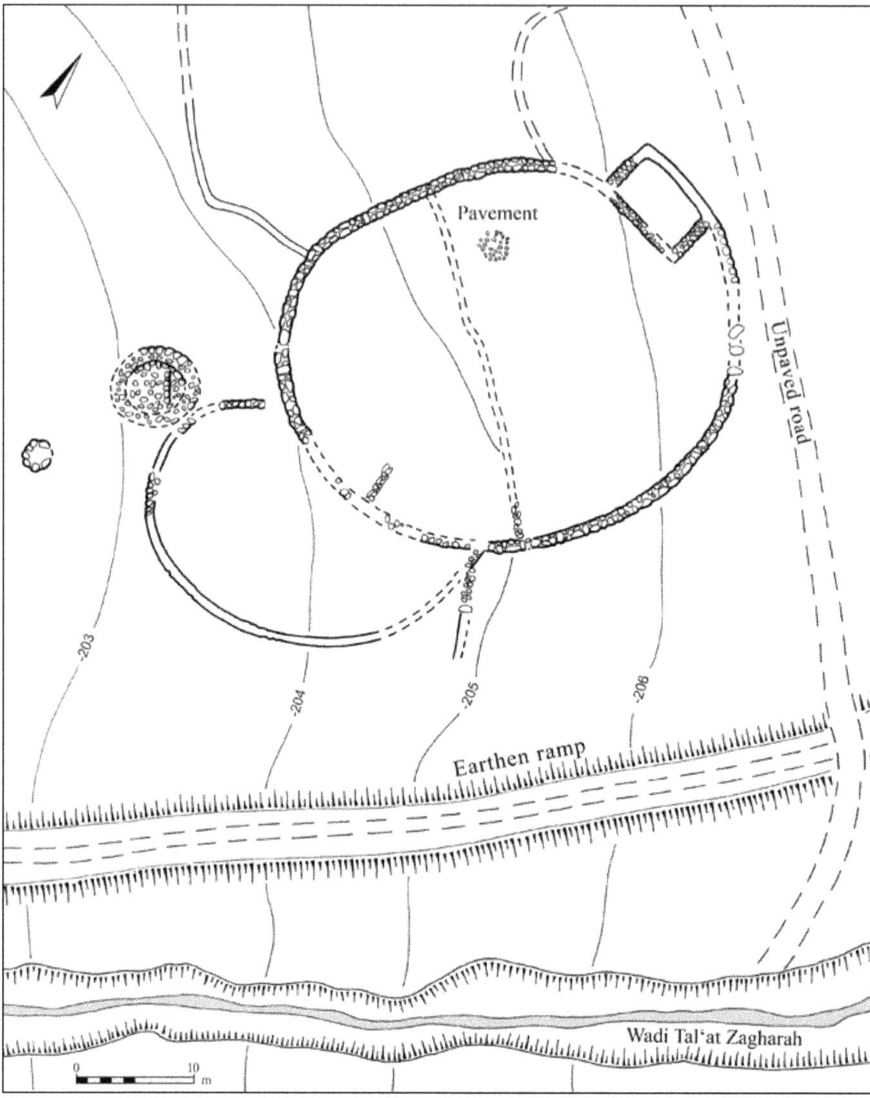

170. Plan of **Wadi Tal'at Zagharah (1)**.

171. Pottery from **Wadi Tal'at Zagharah (1)**: 1-2. HM jars, gr, EB.

The central enclosure, the northernmost of the two, is almost circular, and is 34 m in diameter. The encircling wall is built of two rows of large stones embedded in the ground, mostly horizontally placed, but some upright. The stones are of local origin, taken from the wadi bed.

In the northern part of the enclosure is a structure measuring 9×6 m incorporated in the enclosure wall. It appears that the structure is contemporary with the enclosure and is part of it. Remains of paving were found in the northern part of the enclosure.

Parts of another less preserved smaller enclosure about 25 m in diameter are attached to the south side of the larger enclosure. Near its western wall is a raised round structure ('stage') 7 m in diameter. The wall surrounding it is of two rows of large stones. In its centre is a straight wall and a fill of large stones.

The site is outstanding for its fine planning and construction, as well as for the intriguing round 'stage'.

Pottery: Early Bronze – 20%; Iron I – 15%; Iron II – 40%; Late Roman – 15%; unidentified – 10%.
Flint: 2 items (see Appendix A).
Additional surveys: none.

♦ ♦ ♦

Site 65: 19-15/15/3

WADI TAL'AT ZAGHARAH (2)

Israel grid: 1917/1555
UTM grid: 7305/5424
Elevation: 220 m b.s.l., 0 m a.s.a.
Name: nearest place
Site type: enclosures
Area: 7 dunams (7000 sq. m)
Topography: plain
Rock type: Judea Group
Soil type: silt

Soil quality: 3
Cultivation: none
Cisterns: none
Water source: Nahal Fasael (181), 5.5 km distant
Road: Beit She'an–Jericho (B10), 500 m distant
Visits: January 2003 and more; 65 sherds

A large and complex enclosure site at the western edge of the Jordan Valley plain, near the north-western corner of the village of Netiv Hagdud. Wadi Tal'at Zagharah, exiting from the eastern mountains ridge west of the site, passes close to the north of the site.

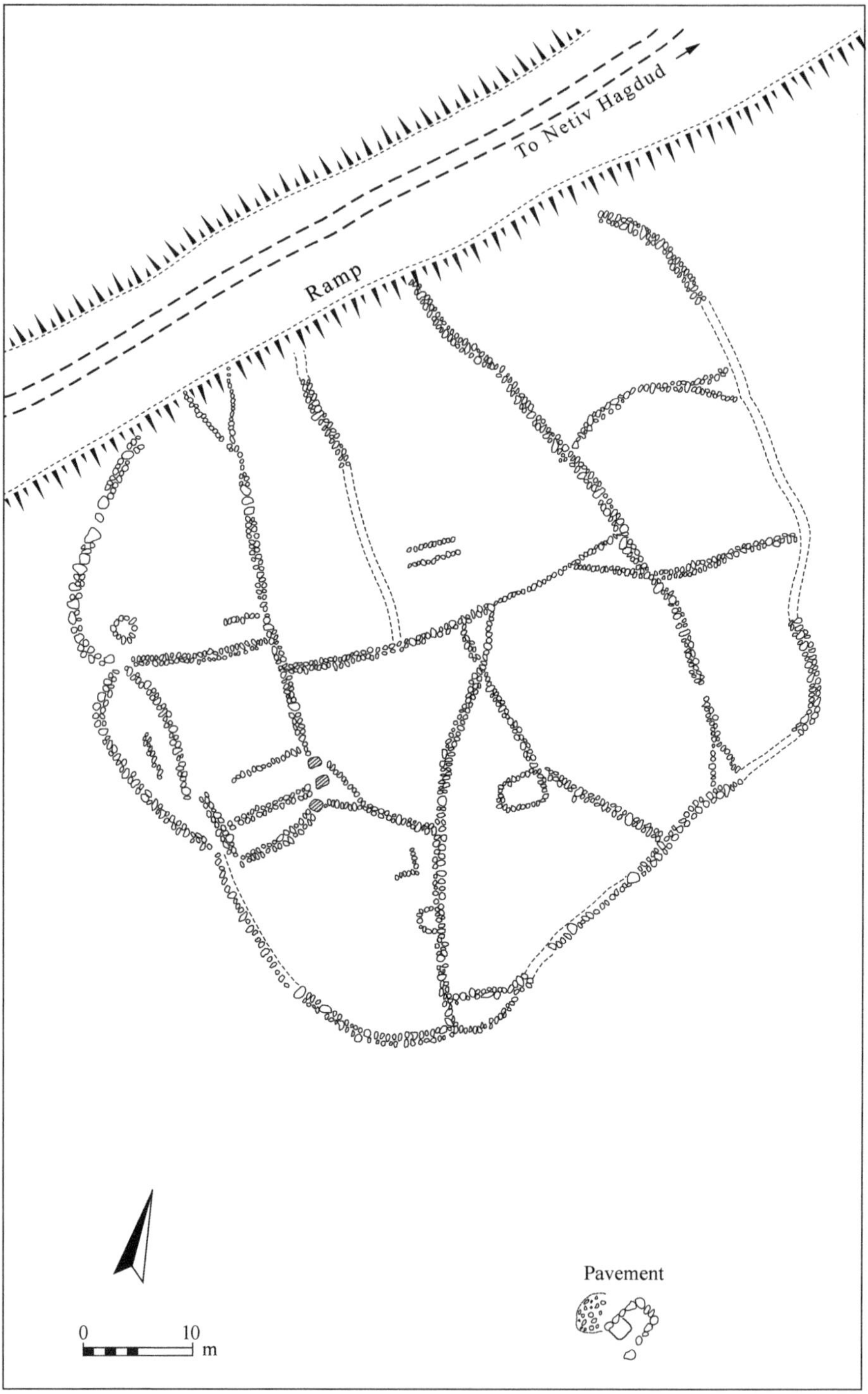

172. Plan of **Wadi Tal'at Zagharah (2)**.

There are about eleven interconnected enclosures or courtyards in the site, of area 0.2–0.7 dunam (200–700 sq. m) each. Their walls, which are well built, are of two main types:

1. A double wall of two rows of medium-sized fieldstones, well-adjusted to each other.
2. Walls of a single row of stones with large boulders placed in various places longitudinally.

The openings between the yards were built with jamb stones of white chalk.

In the courtyards there are construction remains: structures and walls, meant for human dwelling and not as pens, at least during certain periods. The connections of the walls are triangular, in a construction method unknown elsewhere.

About 40 m south of the site is a small structure, measuring 5×3 m, built of large stones with a paved area next to it.

About 200 m west of the former is the site of Wadi Tal'at Zagharah (1): probably there was a linkage between the two.

The site is outstanding in size, the special construction method and its complexity. Apparently it was an important place in the area during several periods. Changes occurring during the span of its existence are noticeable: many of the walls have been altered, and several phases of construction are visible.

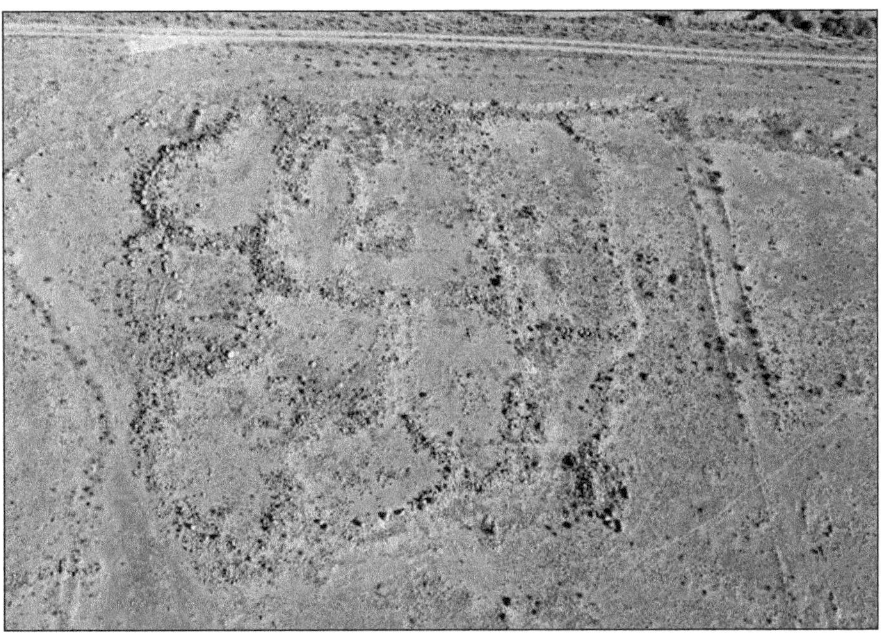

173. Aerial view east at **Wadi Tal'at Zagharah (2)**, 2012 (A. Solomon).

Pottery: Early Bronze – 4%; Iron I – 40%; Iron II – 8%; Early Roman – 48%.
Additional surveys: none.

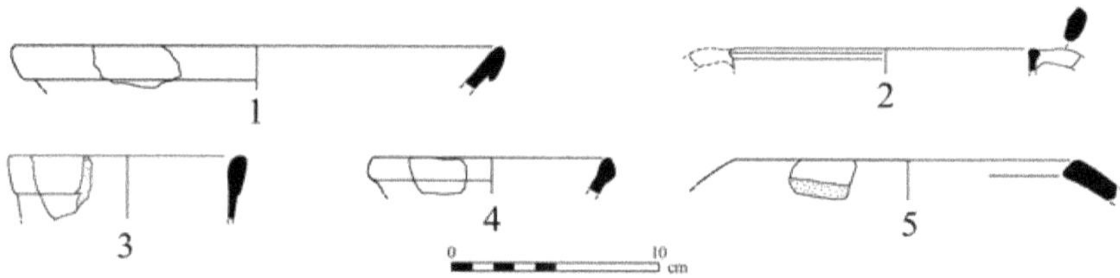

174. Pottery from **Wadi Tal'at Zagharah (2)**: 1. CP, br, IA I; 2. CP, br, ER; 3. Jar, br, ER; 4. Jug, br, IA I; 5. HM jar, br, EB.

♦ ♦ ♦

Site 66: 19-15/15/1

GILGAL (2)

Israel grid: 1912/1555
UTM grid: 7300/5423
Elevation: 180 m b.s.l., 0 m a.s.a.
Name: nearest place
Site type: enclosures
Area: 2 dunams (2000 sq. m)
Topography: edge of valley
Rock type: Judea Group
Soil type: stony-desert
Soil quality: 3
Cultivation: none
Cisterns: none
Water source: Nahal Fasael (181), 5.5 km distant
Road: Beit She'an–Jericho (B10), 1.5 km distant
Visit: December 2002; 51 sherds

Two coupled enclosures in the eastern side of the Jordan Valley, near to and north of the exit from the Wadi Tal'at Zagharah channel from the mountains to the Jordan Valley plain, 1 km north-west of the village of Netiv Hagdud.

Both enclosures are filled up and surrounded by a partly ruined wall. The larger of the two, measuring 30×25 m, is rectangular with rounded corners. In the north abutting it is a smaller oval enclosure, measuring about 20×15 m.

About 80 m to the east are parts of small round enclosures of flat stones.

There is a small sherd scatter.

Two small Epipalaeolithic complexes have been surveyed east of the site, on the north bank of the wadi and close to its exit from the narrow gorge to the Jordan Valley: Kebaran and Geometric Kebaran (Goring-Morris 1980: 10-11, and see Appendix B).

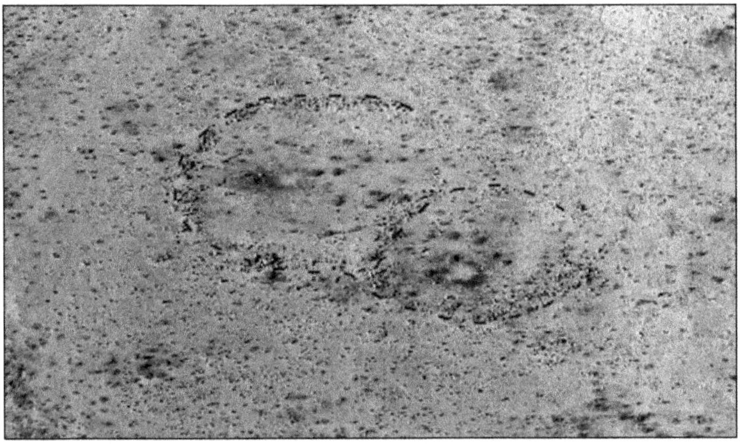

175. **Gilgal (2)**, Aerial view west at the enclosures, 2008 (N. Eshed).

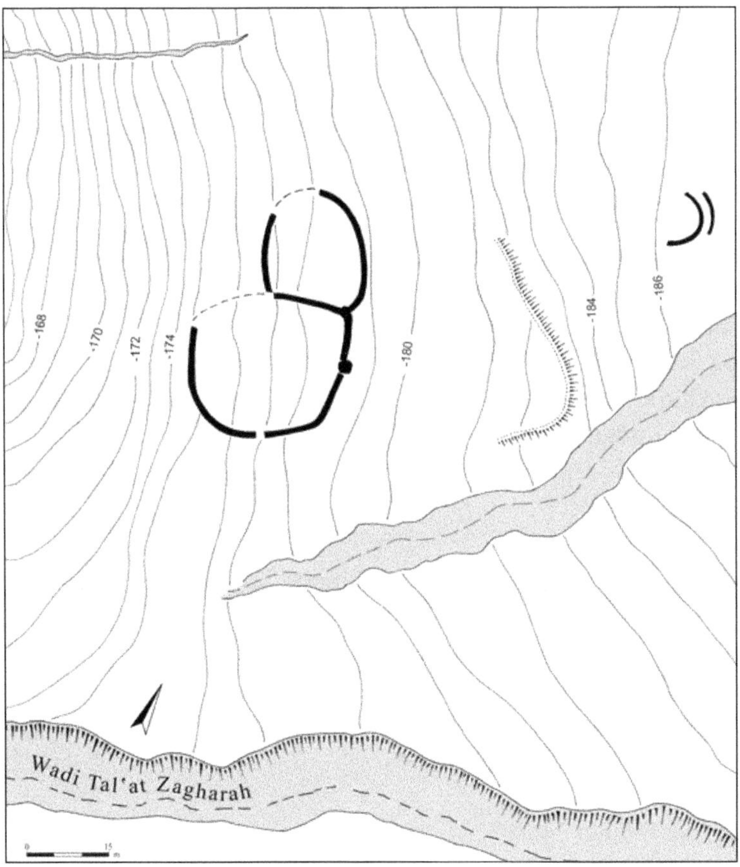

176. Plan of **Gilgal (2)**.

Pottery: Early Bronze – 4%; Iron II – 18%; Hellenistic – 8%; Late Roman – 70%.
Additional surveys: none.

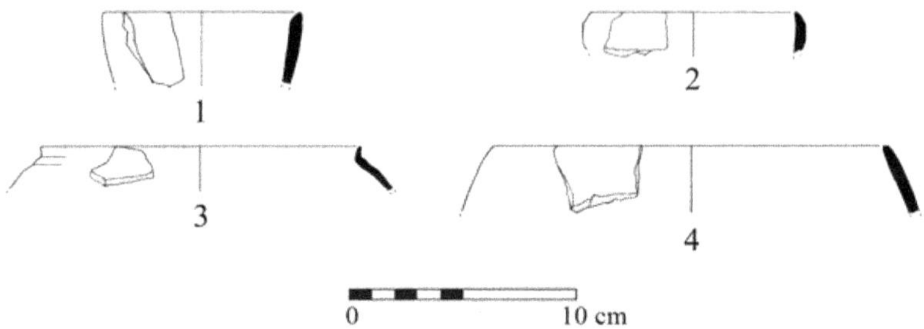

177. Pottery from **Gilgal (2)**: 1-2. Bowls, lt br, Hel; 3. CP, rd, LR; 4. HM jar, br, EB.

♦ ♦ ♦

Site 67: 19-15/15/5

NETIV HAGDUD (4)

Israel grid: 1915/1550
UTM grid: 7303/5418
Elevation: 190 m b.s.l., 50 m b.s.a.
Name: nearest place
Site type: enclosure
Area: 0.5 dunam (500 sq. m)
Topography: Jordan Valley plain
Rock type: Judea Group
Soil type: stony-desert
Soil quality: 1
Cultivation: none
Cisterns: none
Water source: Nahal Yitav (182), 5 km distant
Road: Beit She'an–Jericho (B10), 1.2 km distant
Visits: January 2011, 2016; 4 sherds

A small enclosure where the eastern Samaria ridge meets the Jordan Valley plain, 500 m west of Netiv Hagdud. Nearly 50 m east of it is the western fence of the village.

The enclosure is 10 m in diameter. It is built of one row of large stones, placed next to each other, but not attached. Outside the southern side of the enclosure wall is a small room, 3×2 m.

Pottery: Late Roman – 100%.
Additional surveys: none.

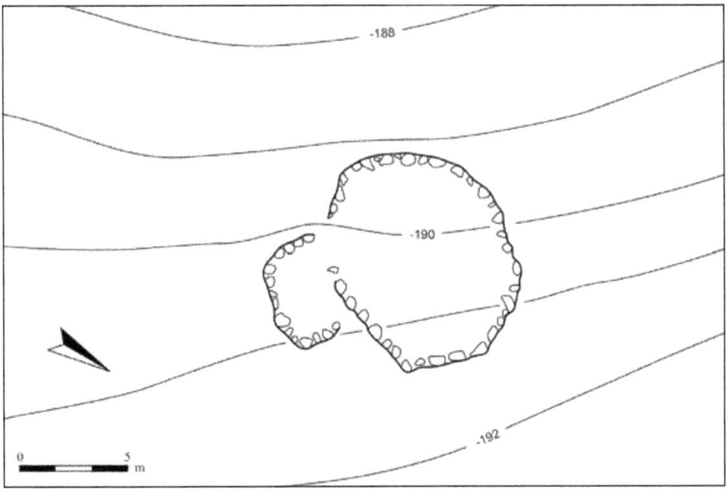

178. Plan of **Netiv Hagdud (4)**.

♦ ♦ ♦

Site 68: 18-15/94/2

ELEVATION POINT 60

Israel grid: 1896/1546
UTM grid: 7284/5414
Elevation: 25 m a.s.l., 0 m a.s.a.
Name: nearest place
Site type: sherd scatter
Area: 2 dunams (2000 sq. m)
Topography: shoulder and saddle
Rock type: Judea Group
Soil type: stony-desert
Soil quality: 2
Cultivation: none
Cisterns: none
Water source: Nahal Yitav (182), 4 km distant
Road: Beit She'an–Jericho (B10), 3.3 km distant
Visit: June 2011; 50 sherds

An encampment site on a high plateau between the deep streams Wadi el-Baqar in the north and Wadi Tal'at Zagharah in the south, 2.5 km west of Netiv Hagdud.

Over the saddle is a considerable sherd scatter, without construction remains. There are sporadic cleaned rock surfaces, possibly for tents.

It appears that the place served as a shepherds' encampment for many generations.

Pottery: Iron I – 12%; Iron II – 20%; Late Roman – 48%; Medieval – 20%.
Additional surveys: none.

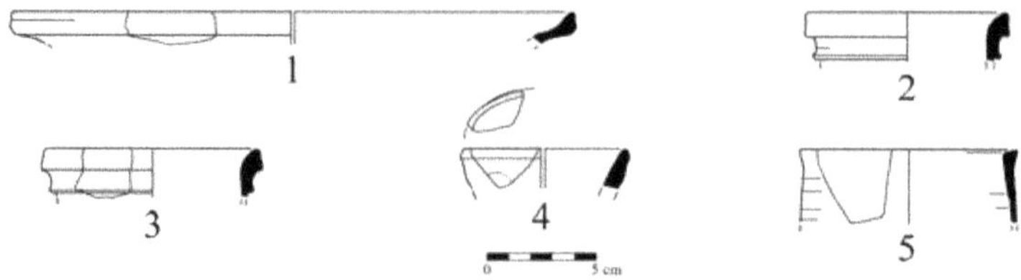

179. Pottery from E.P. 60: 1. Bowl (?), lt br, IA II (?); 2-3. Jars, lt br, LR; 4. Jar, lt br, Mod (?); 5. Jug, lt br, LR.

♦ ♦ ♦

Site 69: 19-15/14/4

NETIV HAGDUD (3)

Israel grid: 1916/1547
UTM grid: 7304/5415
Elevation: 185 m b.s.l., 50 m b.s.a.
Name: nearest place
Site type: enclosure
Area: 1.5 dunam (1500 sq. m)
Topography: wadi estuary
Rock type: Judea Group
Soil type: stony-desert
Soil quality: 1
Cultivation: none
Cisterns: none
Water source: Nahal Yitav (182), 4.5 km distant
Road: Beit She'an–Jericho (B10), 1.5 km distant
Visit: January 2011; 80 sherds

A round enclosure where the eastern Samaria ridge and the Jordan Valley plain meet, 500 m south-west of Netiv Hagdud.

The enclosure is 25 m in diameter, built from one row of large stones, which has formed a prominent platform over time. North of it are remains of a structure.

The location of the site is unusual because it is located at the wadi mouth and is subject to floods.

The pottery dates to different periods, suggesting habitation at the site for a long time.

Pottery: Intermediate Bronze – 15%; Iron II – 2%; Late Roman – 70%; Byzantine – 13%.
Additional surveys: none.

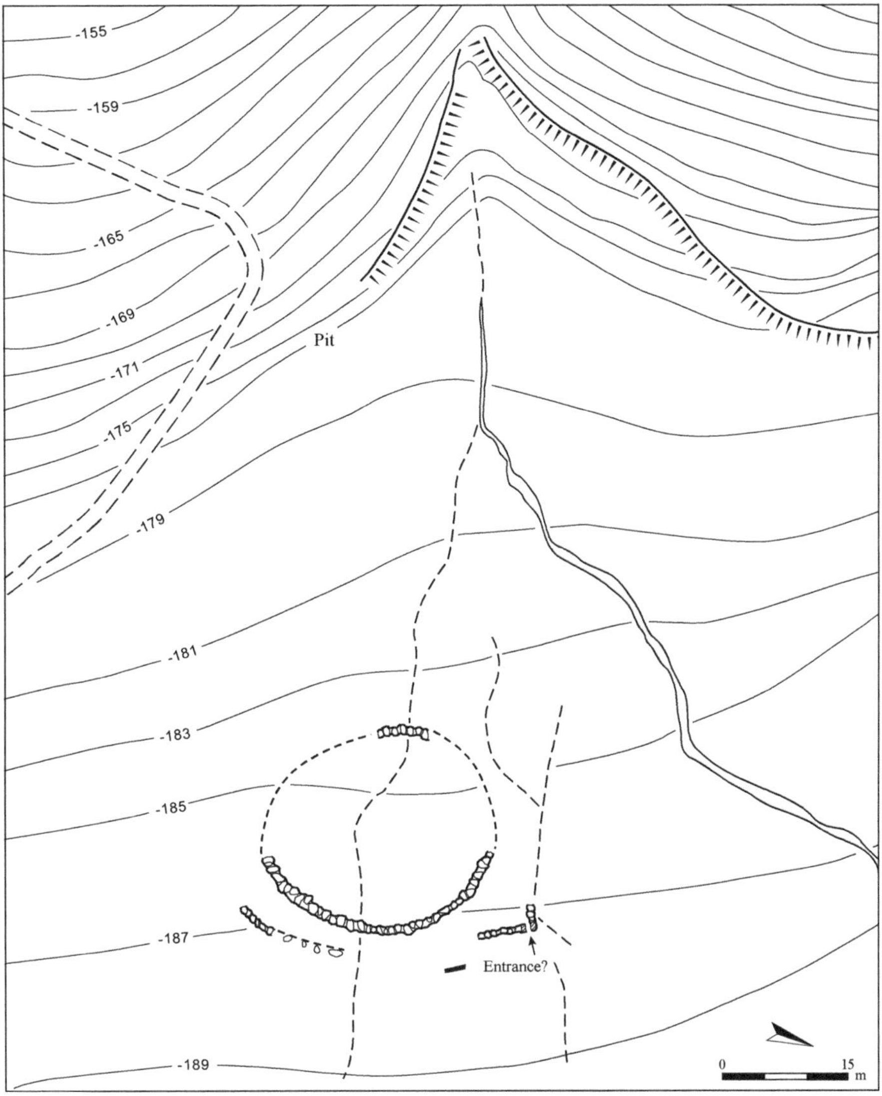

180. Plan of **Netiv Hagdud (3)**.

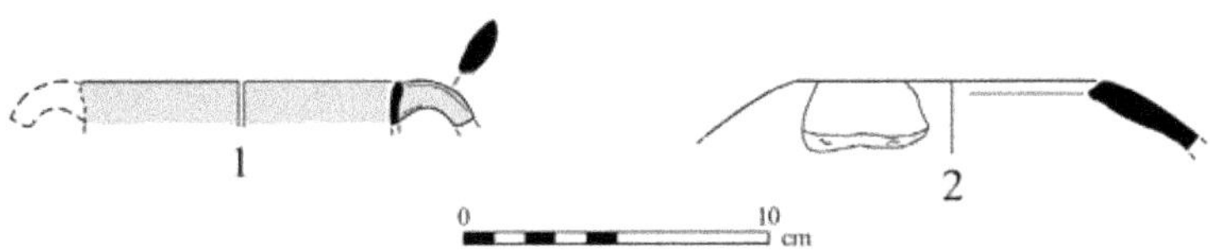

181. Pottery from **Netiv Hagdud (3)**: 1. CP, rd, rd slip, LR; 2. HM jar, lt br, IBA.

Site 70: 19-15/34/1

GILGAL

Israel grid: centre of a group of sites 1933/1547
UTM grid: 7321/5416
Elevation: 225 m b.s.l. (Gilgal I, II, IV). Elevation 230–240 m b.s.l. (Gilgal III, V)
Name: given by the survey/excavation expedition
Site type: prehistoric

Topography: ridge (Gilgal I, II, IV); plain (Gilgal III, V)
Cultivation: none
Cisterns: none
Water source: Nahal Yitav (182), 4.5 km distant
Road: Beit She'an–Jericho (B10), 300 m distant

This entry deals with a group of sites in the Salibyia basin (Gilgal III, V) and along the ridge separating it from the Jordan Valley plain (Gilgal I, II, IV) nearby to the east of Netiv Hagdud.

Systematic excavations were conducted in Gilgal I, and probe pits were dug in the other sites.

The sites Gilgal I, III and IV have been dated to the Pre-pottery Neolithic A period, and the others belong to the Late Natufian culture. The excavations were headed by Tamar Noy during the 1970s and 1980s.

Below are the main results:

Gilgal I:

In the site, the area of which is about 4 dunams (4000 sq. m), two principal strata have been identified, and 13 structures – varying in diameter from 3 to 6 m, were exposed. The walls were built of fieldstones, with mud bricks apparently laid above. On the well pressed bright earth floors of the structures were exposed hearth remains, grinding and crushing stones and stone tools made from limestone, basalt and flint. Among the latter are polished axes, long sickle blades, knives, arrow-heads, drills and awls. Bone implements and jewellery were also found in small numbers.

In a silo found in one of the structures was a large quantity of oats and barley seeds and also acorns and terebinth tree seeds. The botanical variety is evidence of year-round habitation. Close to the silo were found three human clay figurines and a bird figurine made from limestone. According to the excavator, these ritual artefacts should be linked to the granary and its contents.

The dates obtained from ^{14}C analysis of the silo contents were 8100±150 to 7710±70 BCE. The local inhabitants fed, in addition to a vegetal diet, upon crustaceans, turtles, deer and fowl.

Gilgal II:
In this site, north of Gilgal I, crater-tubes, about 70 cm deep, and flint tools from the late phase of the Natufian culture have been identified.

A stone human statuette, 30 cm tall, was found on the western slope of the site. According to the excavator it does not belong to the Natufian culture.

Gilgal III (Salibiya IX):
In this site were found el-Khiam points, a mortise chisel, drills, lunates and microliths, and bone implements, stone and shell beads and stone grinding tools. Particularly notable is a human-form stone figurine.

In the lower stratum was a Late Natufian phase.

Bibliography: Schuldenrein 1983: 14, 452-455; Noy 1993; *NEAEHL* 5: 2095 (for additional bibliography).

♦ ♦ ♦

Site 71: 19-15/14/1

WADI EL-BAQAR (4)

Israel grid: 1911/1542
UTM grid: 7300/5411
Elevation: 150 m b.s.l., 50 m b.s.a.
Name: nearest place
Site type: encampment
Area: 4 dunams (4000 sq. m)
Topography: a platform above wadi
Rock type: Judea Group
Soil type: stony-desert
Soil quality: 2
Cultivation: none
Cisterns: none
Water source: Nahal Yitav (182), 4 km distant
Road: Beit She'an–Jericho (B10), 2 km distant
Visit: April 2011; 85 sherds

An encampment site in the lower eastern part of Wadi el-Baqar, 600 m west of its exit to the Jordan Valley and 1.2 km south-west of Netiv Hagdud.

On the shoulder south of the wadi channel is a large encampment site. The shoulder is the result of erosion of the wadi. The place is vulnerable to floods.

No distinct architecture has been detected; however, modern Bedouin structural remains and tent foundations have been identified.

The sherds found indicate a multi-period encampment site of nomads and semi-nomads. It appears that some of the ancient structures were dismantled and stones taken for use in the modern tent encampments.

Pottery: Iron I – 6%; Iron II – 19%; Persian-Hellenistic – 12%; Roman – 44%; Medieval/Ottoman – 19%.
Additional surveys: none.

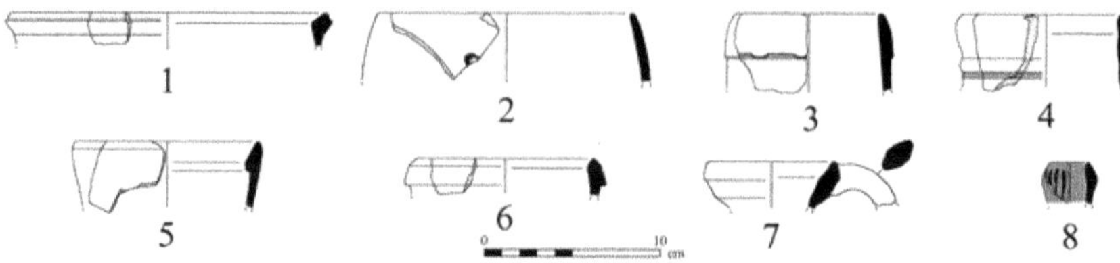

182. Pottery from **Wadi el-Baqar (4)**: 1. CP, rd, IA II; 2. Bowl, rd, Hel-Rom; 3. Jar, rd, Hel-Rom;4. Jar, dk gr, MA (?); 5. Jug, rd, MA; 6. Jug/jar, blk, IA II (?); 7. Jug, lt br, Pers (?); 8. Pipe, rd slip, Ott.

♦ ♦ ♦

Site 72: 19-15/14/2

NETIV HAGDUD (2)

Israel grid: 1919/1543
UTM grid: 7307/5412
Elevation: 190 m b.s.l., 0 m a.s.a.
Name: nearest place
Site type: prehistoric and fort
Area: fort – 2 dunams (2000 sq. m); prehistoric site – 15 dunams (1.5 ha)
Topography: plain
Rock type: Judea Group
Soil type: stony-desert
Soil quality: 3
Cultivation: none
Cisterns: none
Water source: Nahal Yitav (182), 4 km distant
Road: Beit She'an–Jericho (B10), 1.2 km distant
Visits: February 2003 and more; 134 sherds

A large site, near the outside of the south-western corner of the village of Netiv Hagdud, 1.8 km north-west of Niran. It is situated north-east of the exit of Wadi el-Baqar from the desert fringe ridges to the Jordan Valley plain. The site is crossed by a local unpaved road, passing over a rampart built parallel to the wadi bed.

There are two parts to the site:

1. The fort: at the centre of the prehistoric site and on top of its round structures was a square fort, measuring 25×25 m. Two of its walls extend south-east out of the square, while the earth rampart conceals their further extension. Possibly these were a courtyard or another hall.

The fort walls are 1 m thick, built of two rows of medium-sized stones. The construction is good, and there are two openings at least: in the south-west corner, and at the centre of the eastern leg. In each of the openings are two jamb stones standing upright and threshold stones between them.

Adjacent to the western, northern and eastern walls of the fort is a strengthening glacis made of small stones. There is a similar reinforcement on the inner side of the northern leg. The date of these additions is unknown. At the centre and west of the inner yard a large rounded section of paving with large stones survives.

There is a large sherd accumulation in and around the fort, dating it well.

2. The prehistoric site and the excavation: many walls made of small stones, and round and oval structures, were found before the excavation in the area. The site was excavated by O. Bar-Yosef, N. Goring-Morris and A. Gopher in 1977–1981 and 1983–1986 (Gopher 1993; Tchernov 1994; Bar-Yosef and Gopher 1997; *NEAEHL* 5: 2105).

Here is a summary of the published data:

In the central western part of the site were 25 structures built of large and medium-sized stones. The structures are round or oval, and the majority of them have an opening. Some of them are attached to each other, forming a complex. The date of the structures, spread over nearly 15 dunams (1.5 ha)

183. The complex of sites in **Netiv Hagdud (1-2)**, aerial view to the south-west. In the upper left part are the enclosures (Site 75). At the centre is the square Iron Age fort, and to the left are the excavated remains of the Neolithic site (Site 72), 2008 (N. Eshed).

is the Pre-Pottery Neolithic A (9th–8th millennia BCE). 14C tests yielded the following dates: 8320± 300 to 7840±380 BCE.

In the eastern part of the site (Israel coordinates 1918/1539) an excavation was conducted in an area of 30×30 m; and a multi-period site covered by silt, with only its upper parts protruding, has been exposed. The ancient site is oval; and the depth of the archaeological strata is nearly 4 m.

Round, 3-4 m in diameter, and oval, 9×4–5 m, structures with several construction phases were exposed. Their foundations are built of fieldstones and the walls solely of bricks or bricks and stones. The bricks are loaf-shaped, with a flat or convex cross-section. The walls were coated with white or amber-red plaster. In the tightly pressed floors are sunk stone blocks with cup-marks and stone-built installations.

All structures have a single space, except one that was divided into two by an inner wall. In the courtyards next to the structures were found storage, cooking, crushing and grinding facilities. Two round silos have been also exposed, 1.2 m and 1.6 m in diameter, built of bricks. The storage installations, about 50 cm in depth and diameter, are built of standing upright stone slabs and are stone paved. A cooking stove built of stone slabs was discovered with a considerable amount of charcoal and charred bones. The additional diverse concentrations of charred stones and ash testify to the presence of hearths.

A burial of a single individual, laid on his left side, was exposed below a house floor. As in other sites of the period, the skulls of buried adults were removed and taken elsewhere. In one of the structures three skulls were found on the floor. The state of preservation of the skeletons is poor.

The assemblage of small finds contains flint and stone tools: axes, awls, drills, sickle blades and grinding and crushing utensils. The latter include basalt pestles, grinding bowls, limestone grinding slabs and stones with cup-marks. A small assemblage of bone artefacts, conches and shells and two clay human figurines was also found. The zoological and botanical find indicates the diet: the minority of animal bones indicates no husbandry of domesticated animals. Proof for a diet of cereals, legumes, figs and pistachio was gathered.

The inhabitants of the place, defined by the excavators to have been a village, lived in separate units. Each unit contained one or more structures, an accompanying courtyard and various installations. The area of such a unit exceeded 150 sq. m.

Pottery: (in the fort): Iron I – 11%; Iron II – 11%; Persian-Hellenistic – 3%; Early Roman – 19%; Late Roman – 45%; Byzantine-Early Moslem – 7%; Medieval – 4%.

Additional surveys: none.

Additional Bibliography: *NEAEHL* 3: 1152; 5: 2105.

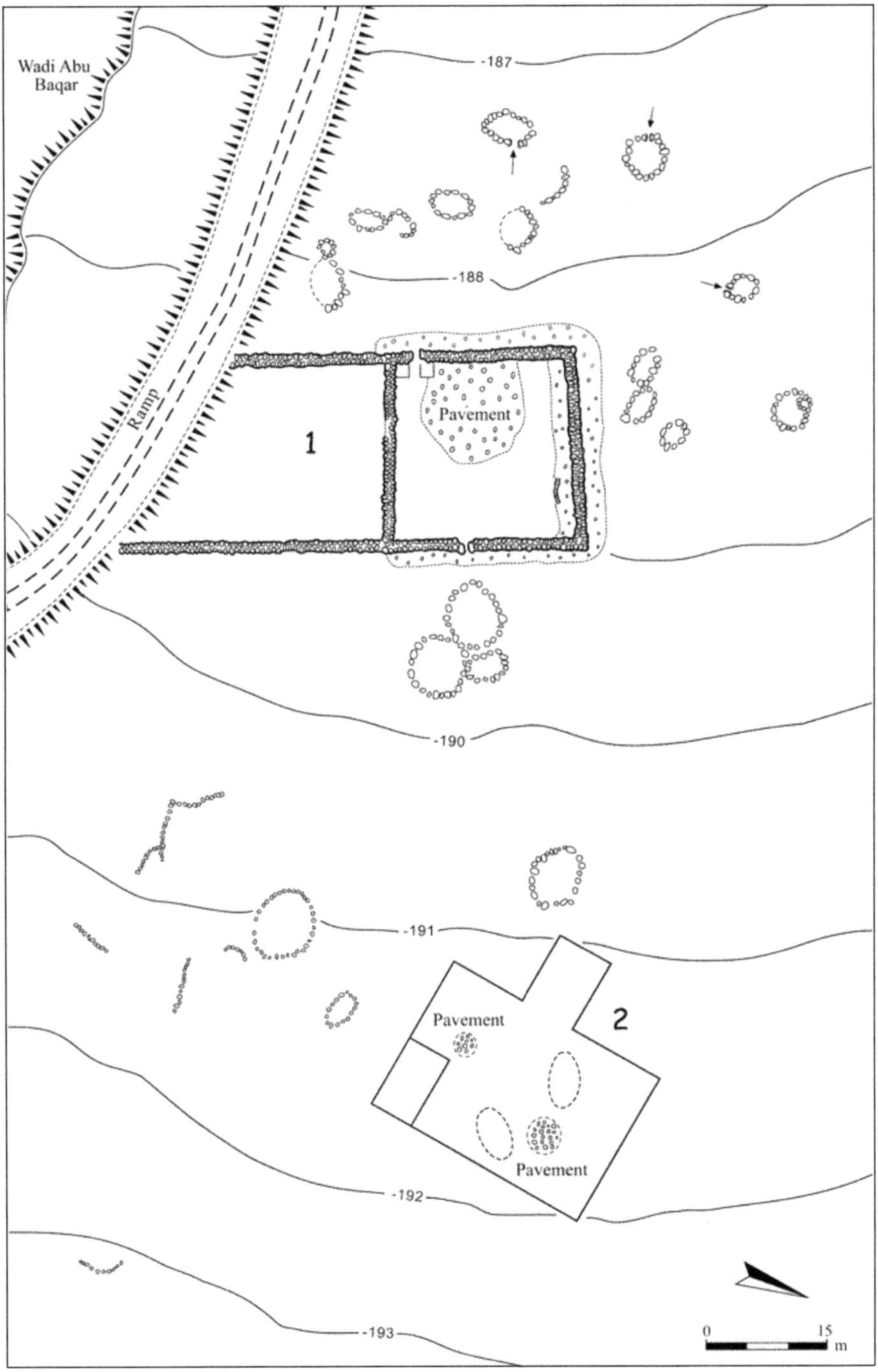

184. Plan of **Netiv Hagdud (2)**.

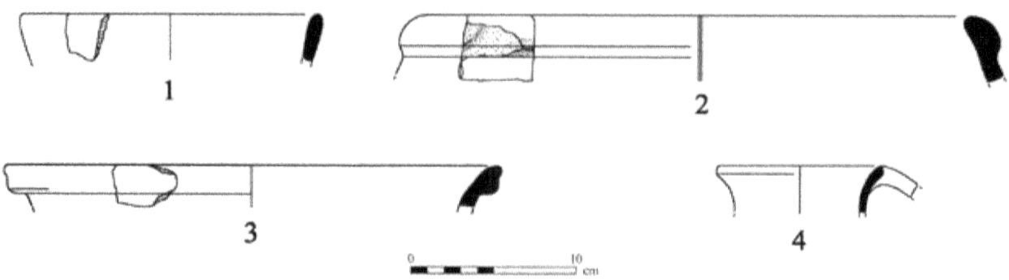

185. Pottery from **Netiv Hagdud (2)**: 1. Bowl, br, IA I-II; 2. CP, br, IA II; 3. CP A, br, IA I; 4. Jug, blk, Rom.

◆ ◆ ◆

Site 72 (1): 19-15/24/1

NETIV HAGDUD (7)

Israel grid: 1925/1545
UTM grid: 7313/5414
Elevation: 215 m b.s.l., 0 m a.s.a.
Name: nearest place
Site type: structure and enclosure
Area: 0.5 dunam (500 sq. m)
Topography: plateau
Rock type: Yehuda Group
Soil type: stony-desert
Soil quality: 3
Cultivation: none
Cisterns: none
Water source: Nahal Yitav (182), 4.2 km distant
Road: Beit She'an–Jericho (B10), 900 m distant
Visit: February 2016; 5 sherds

A structure on an unpaved road surrounding Netiv Hagdud, 400 m southwest of the centre of the settlement.

A well-built building stood here, 8×11 m. Its walls were built of small stones, 40 cm wide. The internal division is visible: in the middle is a hallway 2 m wide; on both sides of the hallway are square rooms, two on each side.

30 m southeast of the structure are the partial remains of an enclosure built of medium-sized stones. Its diameter is about 25 m and the southern part is ruined.

Pottery: not indicative.
Additional surveys: none.

Site 73: 19-15/94/1

KH. UMM ESH-SHUGHUT

Israel grid: 1998/1542
UTM grid: 7387/5412
Elevation: 310 m b.s.l., 0 m a.s.a.
Name: in the map
Site type: command post (?) and military cemetery
Area: 75 dunams (7.5 ha)
Topography: marl plain
Rock type: Lisan marl
Soil type: Lisan marl
Soil quality: 2
Cultivation: none
Cisterns: none
Water source: River Jordan (112), 800 m distant
Road: Beit She'an–Jericho (B10), 5.5 km distant
Visits: March 2008, 2011; 145 sherds

A site of structures and a cemetery in the marl plain near the Jordan River, 8 km east of Netiv Hagdud, and 800 m west of the Umm esh-Shughut river crossing.

The site is about 0.5 km long, oriented north-south, and about 150 m wide. There are 12 structures of local clay bricks, some of the walls surviving to their full height of about 2.5 m. The rest of the walls have collapsed and appear nowadays as clay mounds. Most of the structures are of a single unit measuring 5×5 m, and four of them are of two or three units each of the same dimensions. Wood and iron items have been preserved within the structures, indicating a relatively modern construction. The structures are arranged, although not in a straight line, along the unpaved road leading to Umm esh-Shughut.

At the southern end of the site, west of the unpaved road and adjacent to the southernmost structure, is an especially large cemetery. There are about 200 graves, arranged in straight rows and the grave mounds are also similar to others. Most of the mounds are about 2 m long on average, and about 50 cm high. At the grave heads are wooden posts (most of them have rotted away with time) or stone slabs without inscriptions. The pattern of burial indicates a central, fairly large military cemetery.

Close by, west of the site, an aerial bomb of unknown date is buried in the ground.

It is probable that the area served as a base and cemetery for the Turkish-German troops during their World War I holding battles against the advancing British army in August–September 1918.

The site described above was built on an earlier site.

The Emergency Survey (Bar-Adon 1972: site 20) found: "…ruins of new structures. The sherd find (singles) are from the Byz and EM periods."

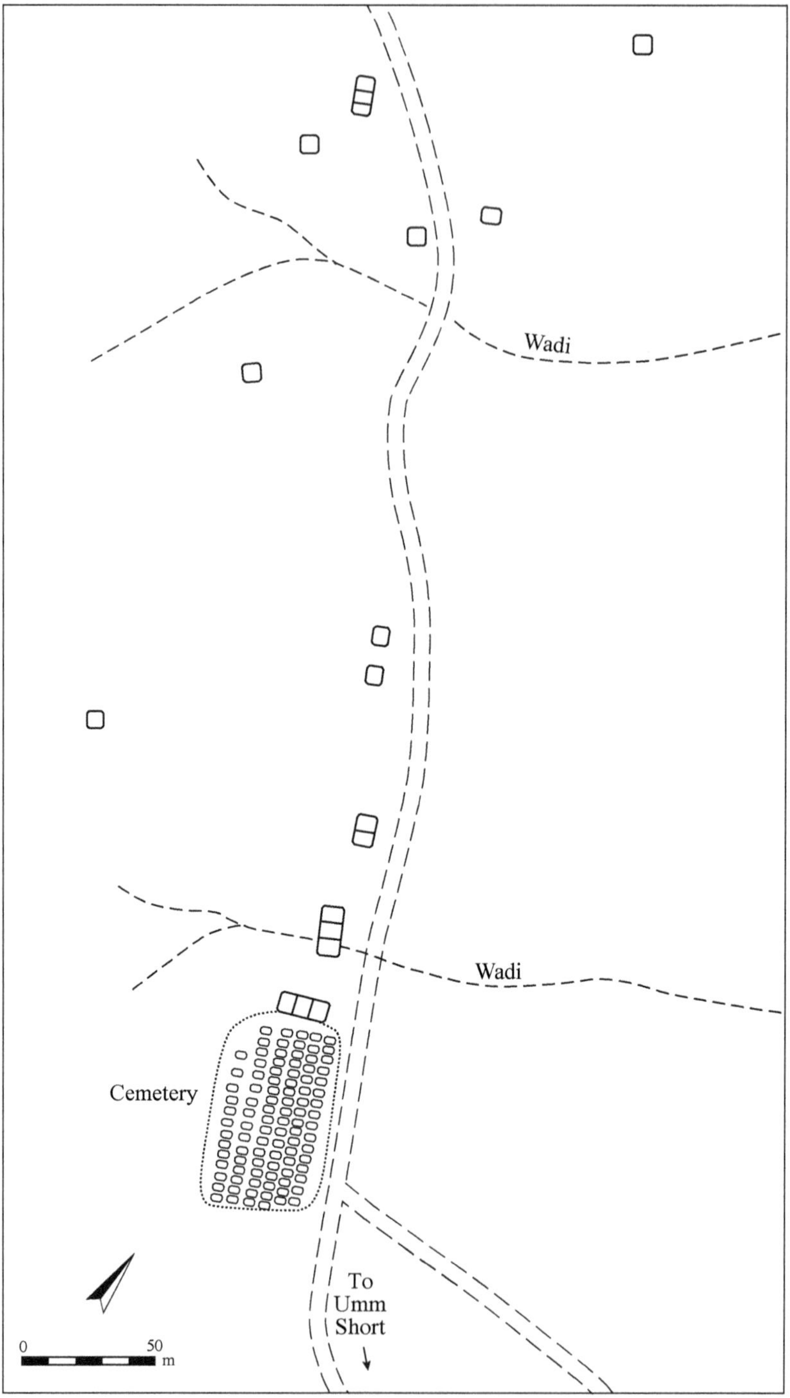

186. Plan of **Kh. Umm esh-Shughut.**

187. **Kh. Umm esh-Shughut**: remains of hamlets built of clay bricks in the Turkish army base (?), 2011 (S. Bar).

188. **Kh. Umm esh-Shughut**: view south-west at the large cemetery, 2011. The hundreds of graves have been related by the surveyors to the battles between the Turkish and the British armies in the summer of 1918 (M. Einav).

Pottery: Hellenistic – 3%; Roman-Byzantine – 14%; Early Moslem – 6%; Medieval – 3%; Ottoman-Modern – 48%; unidentified – 26%.
Miscellaneous find: two musket balls; a Tyre coin (Hellenistic); parts of a door lock; three fragments of handicraft tinted glass perfume bottles in Art Deco style from the beginning of the 20th century; a senior officer's epaulette cord interwoven with gold thread; rifle cartridges bearing the date markings "15" (1915) and "17" (1917).
Additional surveys: Bar-Adon 1972: site 20.
Additional Bibliography: Ilan 1973: 265-269; Erlich 1987: 57-72.

◆ ◆ ◆

Site 74: 19-15/04/1

WADI EL-BAQAR (3)

Israel grid: 1905/1542
UTM grid: 7294/5411
Elevation: 110 m b.s.l., 0 m a.s.a.
Name: nearest place
Site type: enclosures
Area: 1.5 dunam (1500 sq. m)
Topography: shoulder above wadi
Rock type: Judea Group
Soil type: stony-desert
Soil quality: 2
Cultivation: none
Cisterns: none
Water source: Nahal Yitav (182), 4 km distant
Road: Beit She'an–Jericho (B10), 2.7 km distant
Visit: April 2007; 40 sherds

A site on a flat shoulder, north and above Wadi el-Baqar, 2 km west-south-west from the centre of Netiv Hagdud.

There are several structures with a likely enclosure of medium-sized stones.

Later interferences, mainly Bedouin construction, uprooted many of the stones, obscuring the original layout of the site almost completely.

Pottery: Iron I – 80%; Late Roman – 20%.
Additional surveys: none.

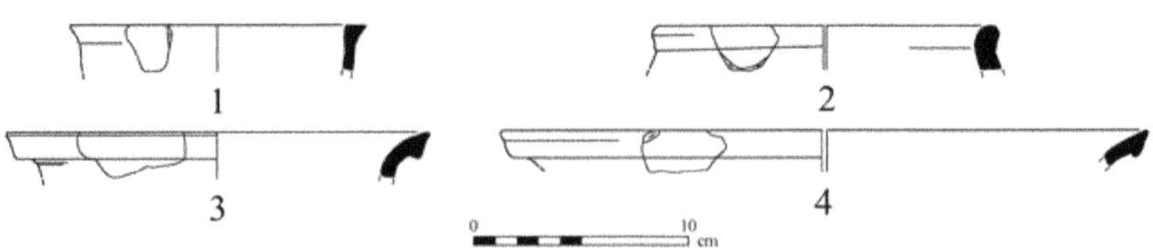

189. Pottery from **Wadi el-Baqar (3)**: 1. Bowl, lt br, LR; 2. Bowl, lt br, IA I; 3-4. CP A, br, IA I.

Site 75: 19-15/14/3

NETIV HAGDUD (1)

Israel grid: 1918/1542
UTM grid: 7307/5410
Elevation: 190 m b.s.l., 50 m b.s.a.
Name: nearest place
Site type: enclosures
Area: 10 dunams (1 ha)
Topography: plain at the foot of a slope
Rock type: Judea Group
Soil type: marl silt
Soil quality: 3
Cultivation: none
Cisterns: none
Water source: Nahal Yitav (182), 4 km distant
Road: Beit She'an–Jericho (B10), 1.3 km distant
Visit: January 2003; 146 sherds

An enclosure site in the western side of the Jordan Valley, 800 m south-south-west of Netiv Hagdud, and close to the south of the Netiv Hagdud (2) site (no. 172). The location is between the shallow flat channel of Wadi el-Baqar in the east and the bottom of the slope of the ridge in the west.

There are three parts to the site:

1. A square tower measuring 7×7 m, built of especially large, 1.5×0.8×0.7 m on average, conglomerated flint stones. The tower stands two to three courses high, built in the stretchers-headers pattern. The date and construction purpose are unknown.
2. About 70 m north of the tower is a square courtyard, measuring about 35×35 m, built as a double wall of two rows of medium-sized stones with

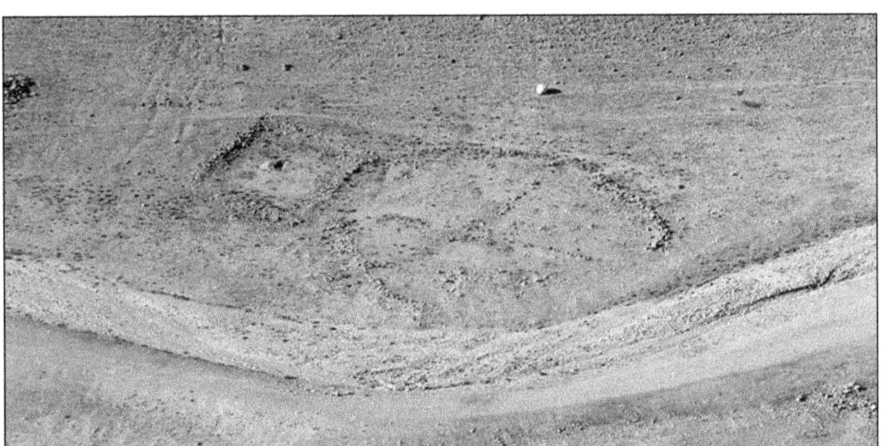

190. Aerial view south-west at **Netiv Hagdud (1)**, 2008. Note the ancient, Iron Age, round enclosure and the square Roman one. At left is seen the solitary tower (N. Eshed).

fill between them. The wall thickness is over 1 m and it is well built. The entrance was not traced. The courtyard is void of structures or walls, and there is a moderate sherd scatter in it.

3. North and adjacent to yard no. 2 were found remains of an oval enclosure, about 80 m across. Its northern and southern parts have been washed away by the wadi or displaced, but enough remains to allow layout reconstruction. The enclosure wall is built of a double row of medium-sized square stones well laid and matched. The pattern of construction is identical to that in Iron Age enclosures in the region between the Sartaba and Jericho. In the centre of the enclosure there are thin walls, one stone thick; apparently later than the enclosure itself: apart from these the enclosure is empty.

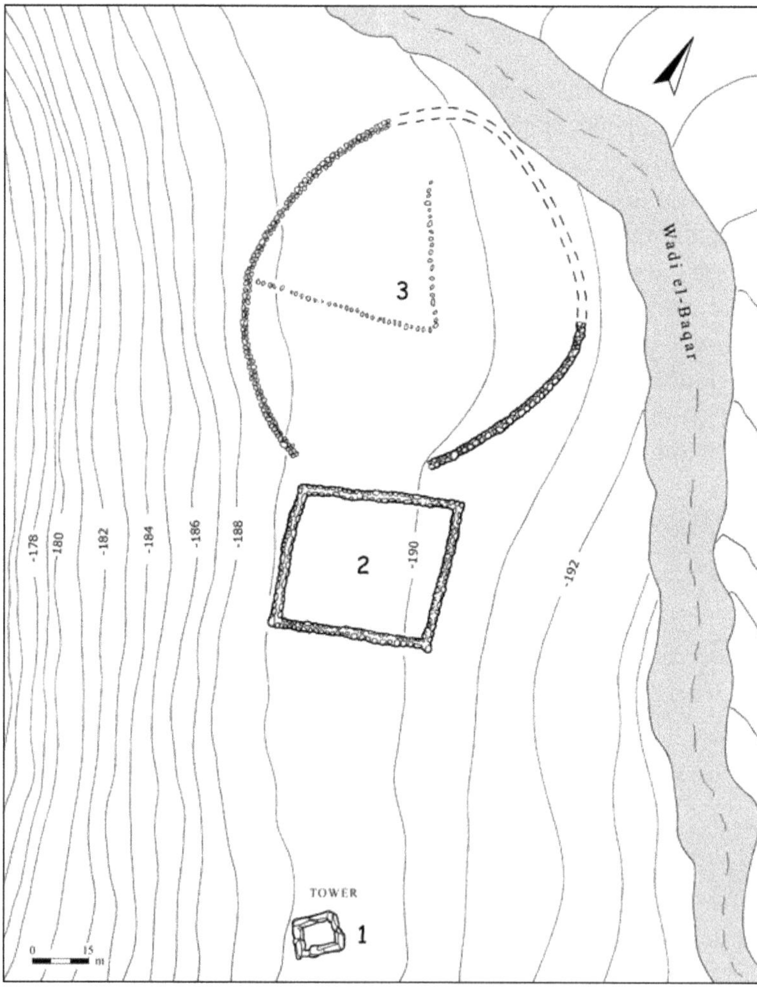

191. Plan of **Netiv Hagdud (1)**.

The square courtyard no. 2 was apparently built in Roman times, but the rounded enclosure belongs almost certainly to the Iron Age; the difference between the courtyards is obvious, based on the gaps in the eastern wall of the enclosure and the separation between the round enclosure and the square one. Apparently both served for livestock husbandry.

The linkage of the tower to the other parts of the site is not clear.

Pottery: Iron I – 22%; Iron II – 24%; Hellenistic – 7%; Late Roman – 27%; Byzantine – 20%.
Flint: 7 items, IA (see Appendix A).
Additional surveys: none.

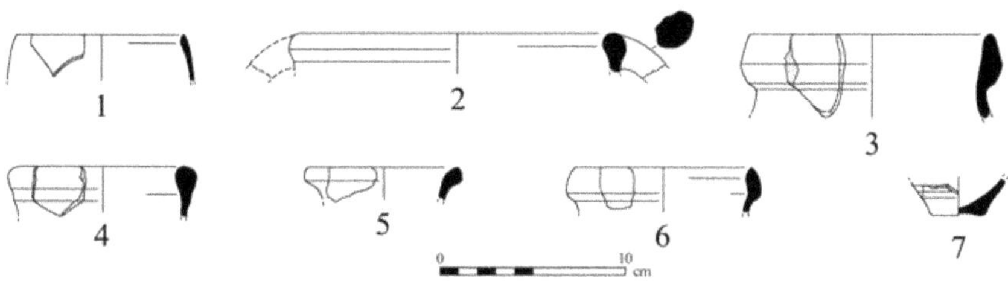

192. Pottery from **Netiv Hagdud (1)**: 1. Bowl, lt br, LR; 2. CP, br, IA II; 3. CP, br, IA I-II; 4. Jar, br, IA II; 5-6. Jugs, lt br, IA I-II; 7. Base, rd, LR.

♦ ♦ ♦

Site 76: 18-15/94/3

WADI EL-BAQAR (1)

Israel grid: 1893/1540
UTM grid: 7281/5408
Elevation: 40 m b.s.l., 40 m b.s.a.
Name: nearest place
Site type: enclosure
Area: 2 dunams (2000 sq. m)
Topography: shoulder above wadi
Rock type: Judea Group
Soil type: stony-desert
Soil quality: 2
Cultivation: none
Cisterns: none
Water source: Nahal Yitav (182), 3.3 km distant
Road: Beit She'an–Jericho (B10), 4.8 km distant
Visit: April 2007; 100 sherds

A site on a high shoulder, in the ridge area west of the Jordan Valley plain and above the deep riverbed of Wadi Naqb el-Baqar. It is close to the unpaved road junction from Wadi 'Aujah towards the village of Netiv Hagdud.

Above the steep slope descending to Wadi el-Baqar there are remains of a large enclosure, the maximum diameter of which is 60–70 m. The enclosing wall is of a single row of large stones, and its average thickness is 70 cm. The enclosure has been badly damaged by the wadi channel and other occurrences. The eastern and northern parts of it and a section of the western wall mostly survive: the linkage of the latter to the site is not certain. There is a built opening in the eastern side (marked by an arrow in the plan) made from two large standing jamb stones about 50 cm apart. The extension and end of the wall further south is not clear and apparently this section did not exist, or has been removed.

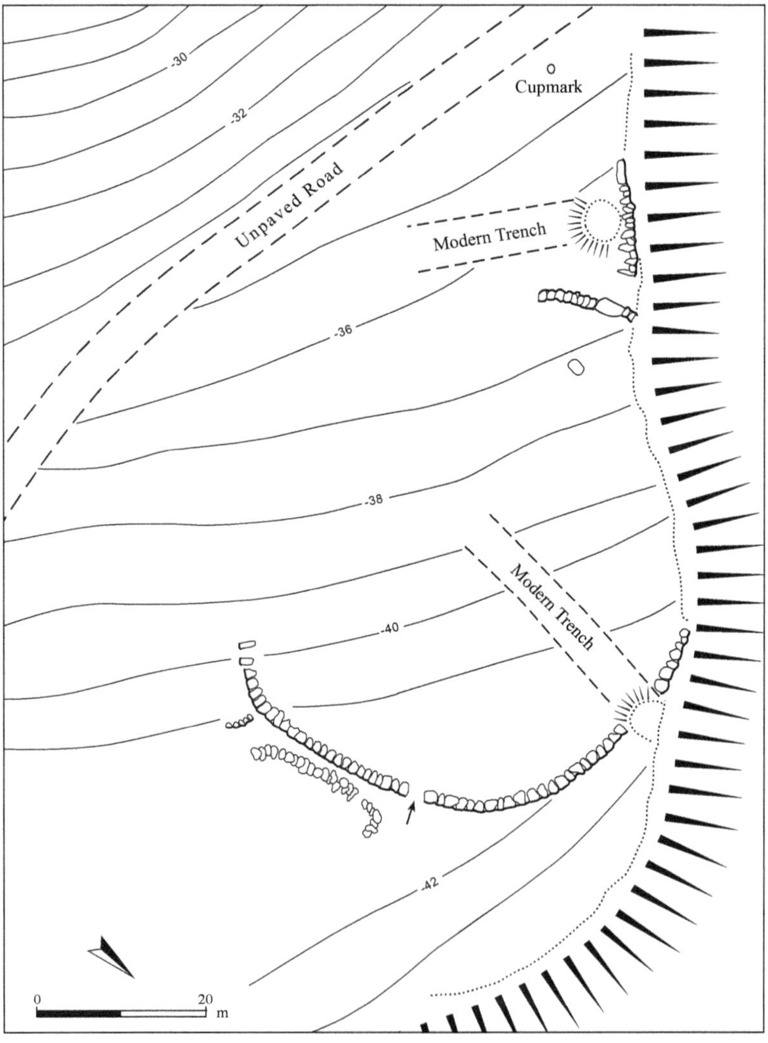

193. Plan of **Wadi el-Baqar (1)**.

In the western part of the site a wall is built crosswise to the enclosure with a stone about 2 m long embedded in it. The construction in this place is different, and it is doubtful whether the wall is part of the original construction.

East of the enclosure wall are stones arranged in line: apparently they come from that wall.

There is a relative abundance of sherds in the site. At least three phases have been identified: ancient (Chalcolithic and/or Middle Bronze); middle (Iron Age I and perhaps II); and late (Roman-Byzantine).

Despite the primitive architecture, it is obvious that the place was particularly active. In many sites of this kind advanced architecture has been found with meagre finds.

Pottery: Chalcolithic/Early Bronze I – 8%; Middle Bronze II – 9%; Iron I – 19%; Iron II (?) – 11%; Late Roman – 21%; Byzantine – 16%; Medieval-Ottoman – 16%.
Flint: 7 items, Pre-Pottery Neolithic B (?) (see Appendix A).
Additional surveys: possibly the site appears in Spanier's survey (1992: site 128; 1994: 68) who notes IA II, Roman, and Early Moslem sherds.
Bibliography: Bar 2014: site 104.

194. **Wadi el-Baqar (1)**: the enclosure, view west, 2012. Note deep Wadi el-Baqar (S. Bar).

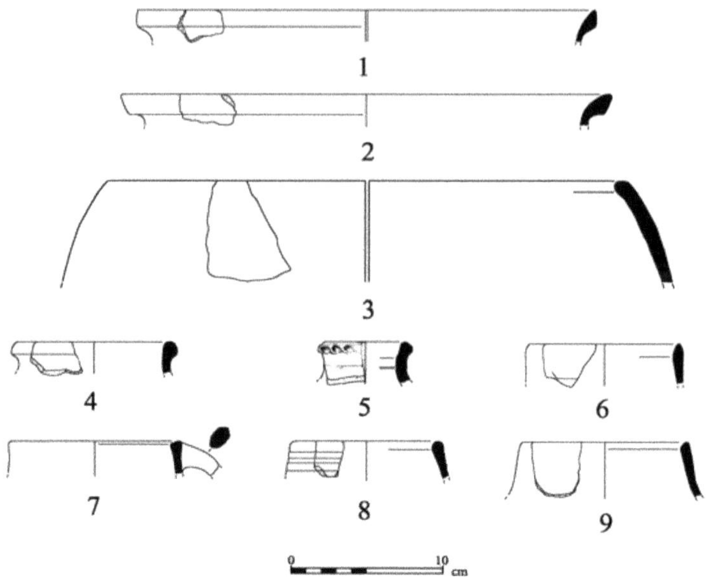

195. Pottery from **Wadi el-Baqar (1)**: 1-2. CP A, br, IA I; 3. HM jar, lt br, Chal-EB; 4. Jug/jar, lt br, IA I-II; 5. Jug/jar, br, thumbed dec, MA; 6. Jug, br, IA I-II; 7-8. Jugs, lt br, MA; 9. Jug, blk, MA.

◆ ◆ ◆

Site 77: 18-15/24/2

NETIV HAGDUD (5)

Israel grid: 1920/1540
UTM grid: 7309/5409
Elevation: 185 m b.s.l., 50 m b.s.a.
Name: nearest place
Site type: enclosures
Area: 5 dunams (5000 sq. m)
Topography: slope at valley edges
Rock type: Judea Group
Soil type: stony-desert
Soil quality: 2
Cultivation: none
Cisterns: none
Water source: Nahal Yitav (182), 4 km distant
Road: Beit She'an–Jericho (B10), 2 km distant
Visit: December 2006; 50 sherds

A well-built enclosure complex, on a slope overlooking the plains of Wadi Maqor edh-Dhib, and 1 km south of Netiv Hagdud. There is a fine lookout to Netiv Hagdud and Niran, the later being located 1.7 km to the south-east.

There are several parts and construction stages in the site:

1. There is a round enclosure about 35 m in diameter in the southern part. The perimeter wall was initially built from two rows of medium-sized stones, but in most of the wall sections only one row survives.
2. The lower quarter of the enclosure was divided by a straight wall that extends about 6 m outside the enclosure in a northward direction, and was apparently built at a later stage. From this wall another wall descends eastward. In the southern part of the enclosure there is another small enclosure.
3. A thick wall which forms a kind of backbone to the site descends eastward from the round enclosure.
4. Another small enclosure, 10 m in diameter, is on the east side of no. 3.
5. Another large enclosure, about 25 m in diameter is on the east side of no. 1.

In various places there are sections of walls, indicating the apparent existence of structures. The construction of local stones is fairly good. Apparently there were at least two stages in the site, which at present are difficult to relate to periods.

Pottery: Iron I (body sherds) – 20%; Iron II – 10%; Late Roman – 40%; Medieval – 5%; unidentified – 25%.
Additional surveys: none.

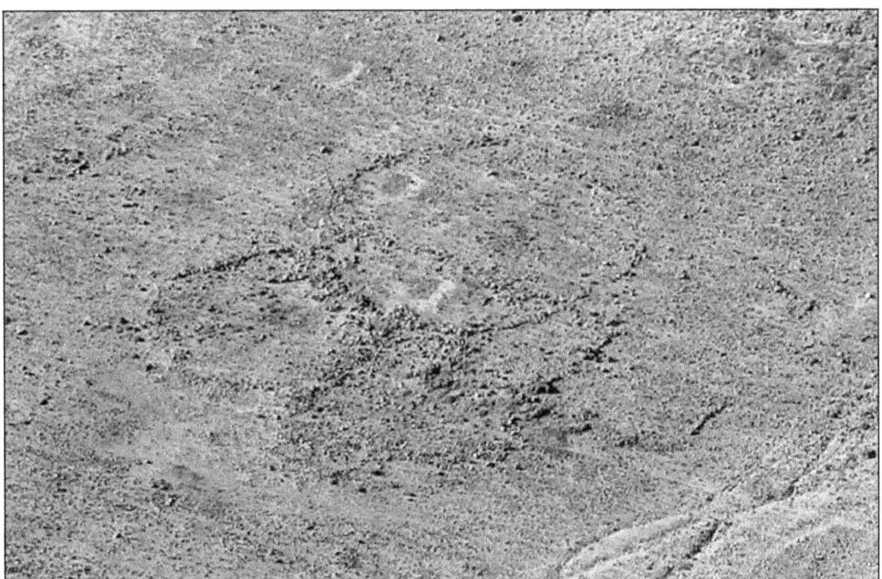

196. Aerial view south-west at **Netiv Hagdud (5)**, 2008 (N. Eshed).

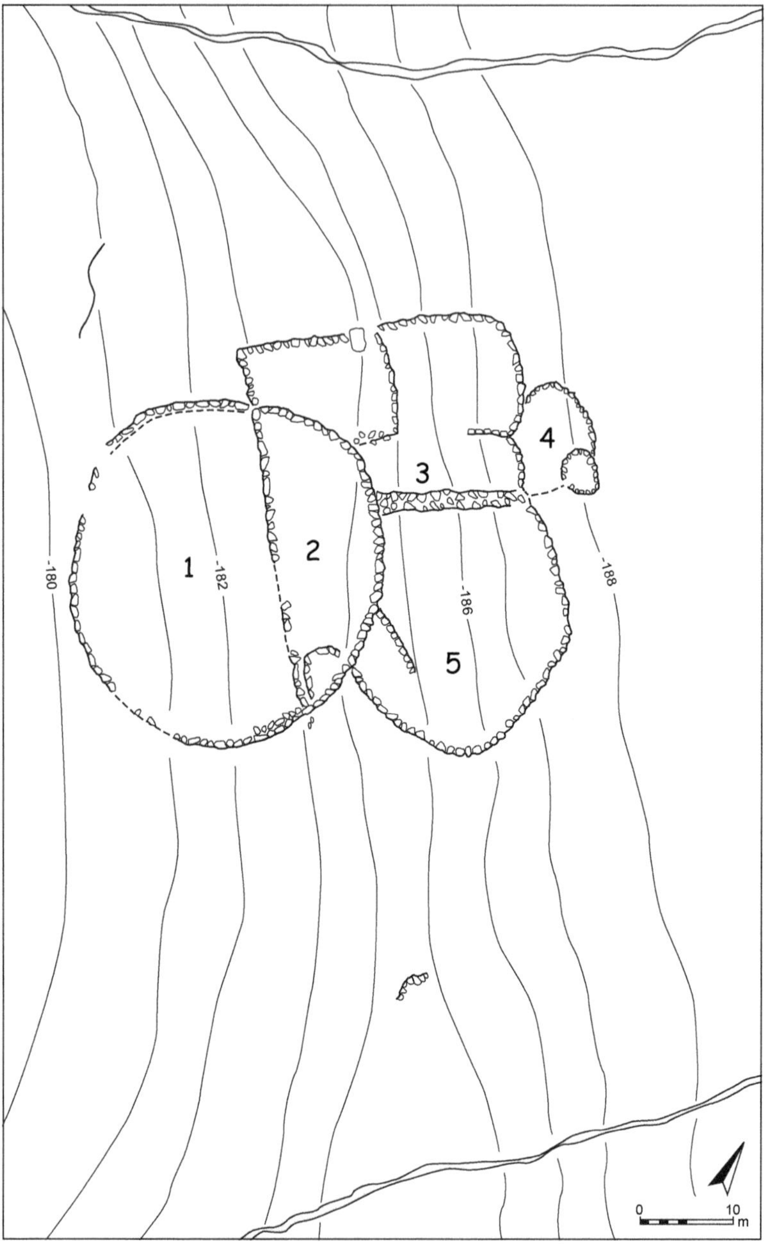

197. Plan of **Netiv Hagdud (5)**.

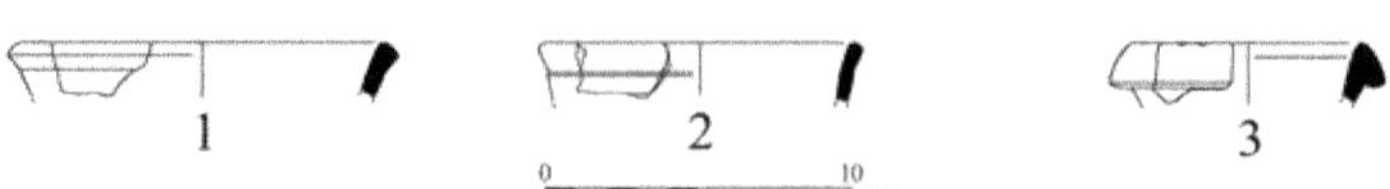

198. Pottery from **Netiv Hagdud (5)**: 1. Jug, lt br, MA; 2. Jug, br, LR; 3. Jug, br, IA II.

Site 78: 19-15/34/2

EL-MUSLABAH (3)

Israel grid: 1934/1540
UTM grid: 7322/5409
Elevation: 210 m b.s.l., 40 m b.s.a.
Name: nearest place
Site type: enclosure
Area: 2 dunams (2000 sq. m)
Topography: slope below ridge
Rock type: Judea Group
Soil type: stony-desert
Soil quality: 1
Cultivation: none
Cisterns: none
Water source: Nahal Yitav (182), 3.8 km distant
Road: Beit She'an–Jericho (B10), 500 m distant
Visit: December 2010; 46 sherds

A large enclosure at the bottom of the western slope of el-Muslabah ridge, 1.5 km south-east from the centre of Netiv Hagdud. North of it is a broad saddle with a lookout to the Jordan Valley road.

The enclosure is oval and is about 50 m long (west-east axis) and about 20 m wide. The enclosure perimeter wall is built from a single row of medium-sized non-uniform stones. Some stones were laid in contact and there are gaps between others.

In and around the enclosure various stages, annexes and small structures, perhaps tombs, are visible. North of it is a long segmented wall, possibly an ancient phase. In the east side there is probably an enclosure wall. The stages of construction and annexes testify to a relatively long time of usage.

The majority of sherds are Roman-Byzantine, and the few Iron Age ones hint at the establishment of the site during that period. Buckles and a glass bottle plug, apparently from World War I, were also found.

Pottery: Iron II – 6%; Late Roman-Byzantine – 92%; Modern – 2%.
Stone: a fragment of basalt grinding stone.
Miscellaneous find: an iron pin; iron buckle; glass plug of medicine bottle.
Additional surveys: none.

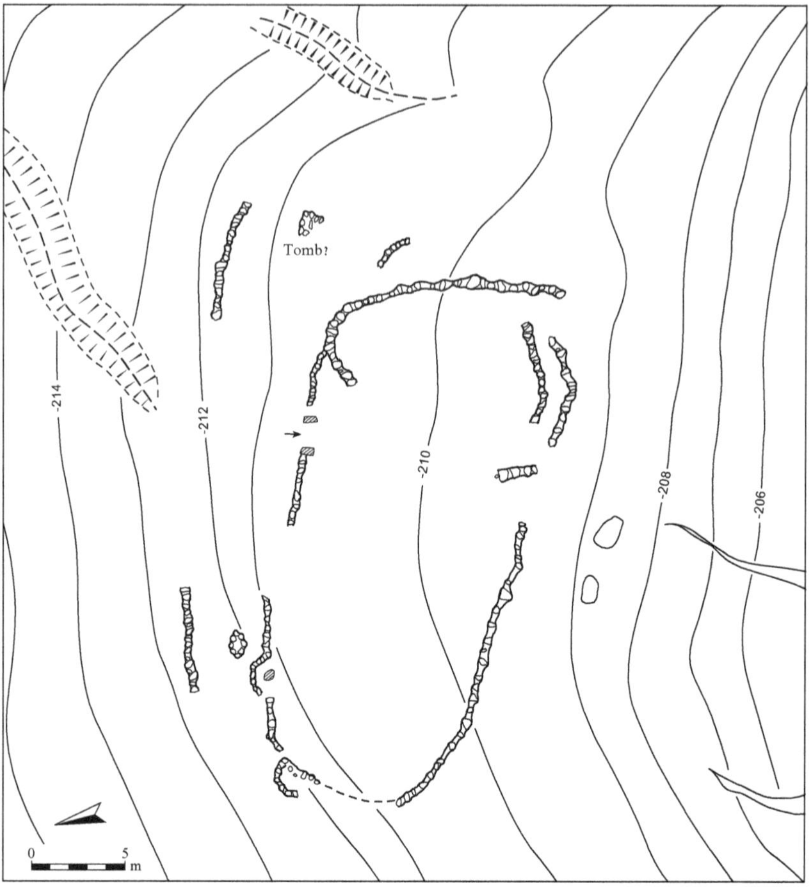

199. Plan of **El-Muslabah (3)**.

◆ ◆ ◆

Site 79: 19-15/34/3

EL-MUSLABAH (2)

Israel grid: 1939/1540
UTM grid: 7328/5409
Elevation: 235 m b.s.l., 50 m b.s.a.
Name: nearest place
Site type: enclosures
Area: 1 dunam (1000 sq. m)
Topography: slope below ridge
Rock type: Judea Group
Soil type: stony-desert
Soil quality: 1
Cultivation: none
Cisterns: none
Water source: Nahal Yitav (182), 3.6 km distant
Road: Beit She'an–Jericho (B10), next to the site
Visit: December 2010; 7 sherds

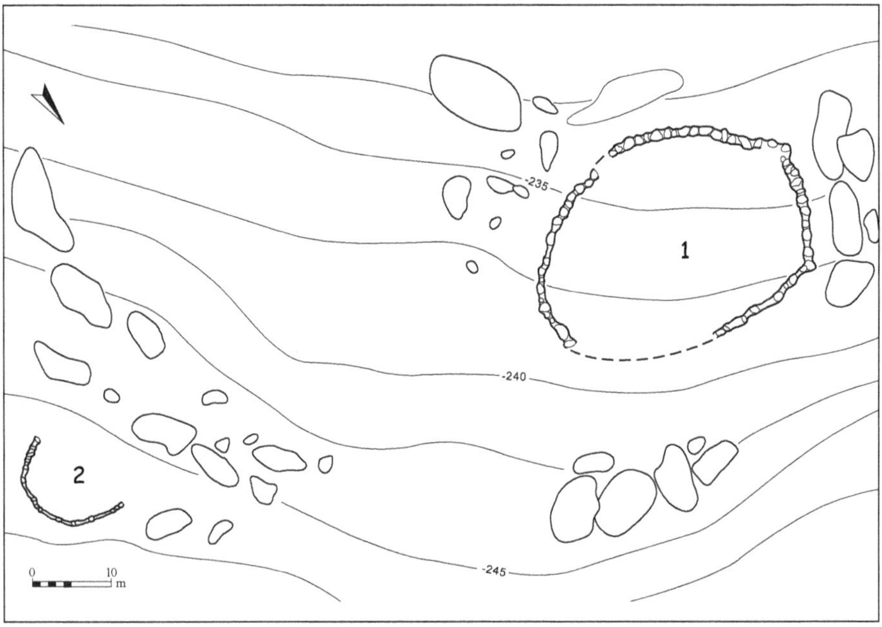

200. Plan of **el-Muslabah (2)**.

Two enclosures at the bottom of the eastern slope of el-Muslabah ridge, near the marl plain of the Jordan Valley, north of the entrance from the Jordan Valley to Kibbutz Niran. The ridge is about 80 m west of the Jordan Valley road, and the site is about 150 m north-west of el-Muslabah (1) (no. 83).

Both enclosures are built within a concentration of large rocks, which rolled down from the ridge above. They are now at the eastern foot of el-Musalabah ridge.

This is the description:

1. The large enclosure is 45 m in diameter, and is built on an elevated platform, supported all around by natural rocks. The perimeter wall is of especially large boulders. The enclosure inside is full of silt. No sherds have been found.
2. The small enclosure is about 90 m south-east of no. 1, and 10 m lower than the former. It is 15 m in diameter, enclosed by medium-sized stones. Only its eastern half has been preserved, the western one is silted.

Pottery: Late Roman-Byzantine – 75%; Modern – 25% (body sherds).
Additional surveys: none.

Site 80: 19-15/23/1

THE 'SILO SITE' (2)

Israel grid: 1927/1539
UTM grid: 7315/5407
Elevation: 220 m b.s.l., 0 m a.s.a.
Name: given by the survey
Site type: structures
Area: 0.5 dunam (500 sq. m)
Topography: slight slope
Rock type: Judea Group
Soil type: stony-desert
Soil quality: 1
Cultivation: none
Cisterns: none
Water source: Nahal Yitav (182), 3.4 km distant
Road: Beit She'an–Jericho (B10), 1.3 km distant
Visit: December 2010; 69 sherds

A cluster of quarried and built silos, 400 m west of the 'Silo Site' (1) (Site 81), at the end of a low spur descending to Wadi Maqor edh-Dhib.

Unlike in the other site, a large stone slab was found at the centre of a subgroup of silos, used perhaps for grinding or crushing. There is no doubt that both sites were parts of one site.

Pottery: Late Roman-Byzantine – 22%; Medieval – 11%; Modern – 11%; unidentified – 56%.
Additional surveys: none.

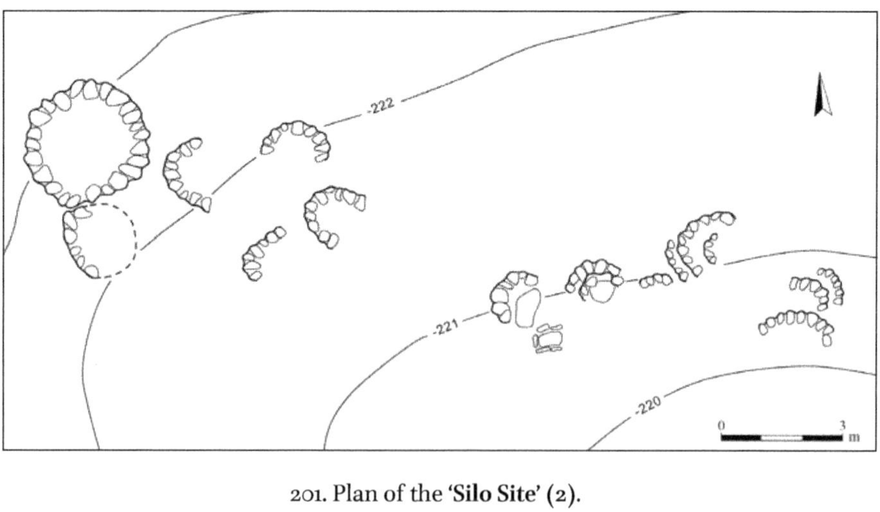

201. Plan of the '**Silo Site**' (2).

202. **The 'Silo Site'** (2): a stone-built silo, 2010 (M. Einav).

♦ ♦ ♦

Site 81: 19-15/33/1

THE 'SILO SITE' (1)

Israel grid: 1932/1539
UTM grid: 7320/5407
Elevation: 213 m b.s.l., 0 m a.s.a.
Name: given by the survey
Site type: structures
Area: 4 dunams (4000 sq. m)
Topography: slight slope
Rock type: Judea Group
Soil type: stony-desert
Soil quality: 1
Cultivation: none
Cisterns: none
Water source: Nahal Yitav (182), 3.4 km distant
Road: Beit She'an–Jericho (B10), 1 km distant
Visit: December 2010; no dateable finds

A cluster of quarried and built silos in the western plain west of el-Muslabah ridge, 1 km north of kibbutz Niran.

At least 40 quarried and built silos were found in a strip of land about 210 m long and 120 m wide, on a moderate slope descending from the south-west to north-east. They are arranged in two or three irregular rows, and a significant number of them have been only partially preserved.

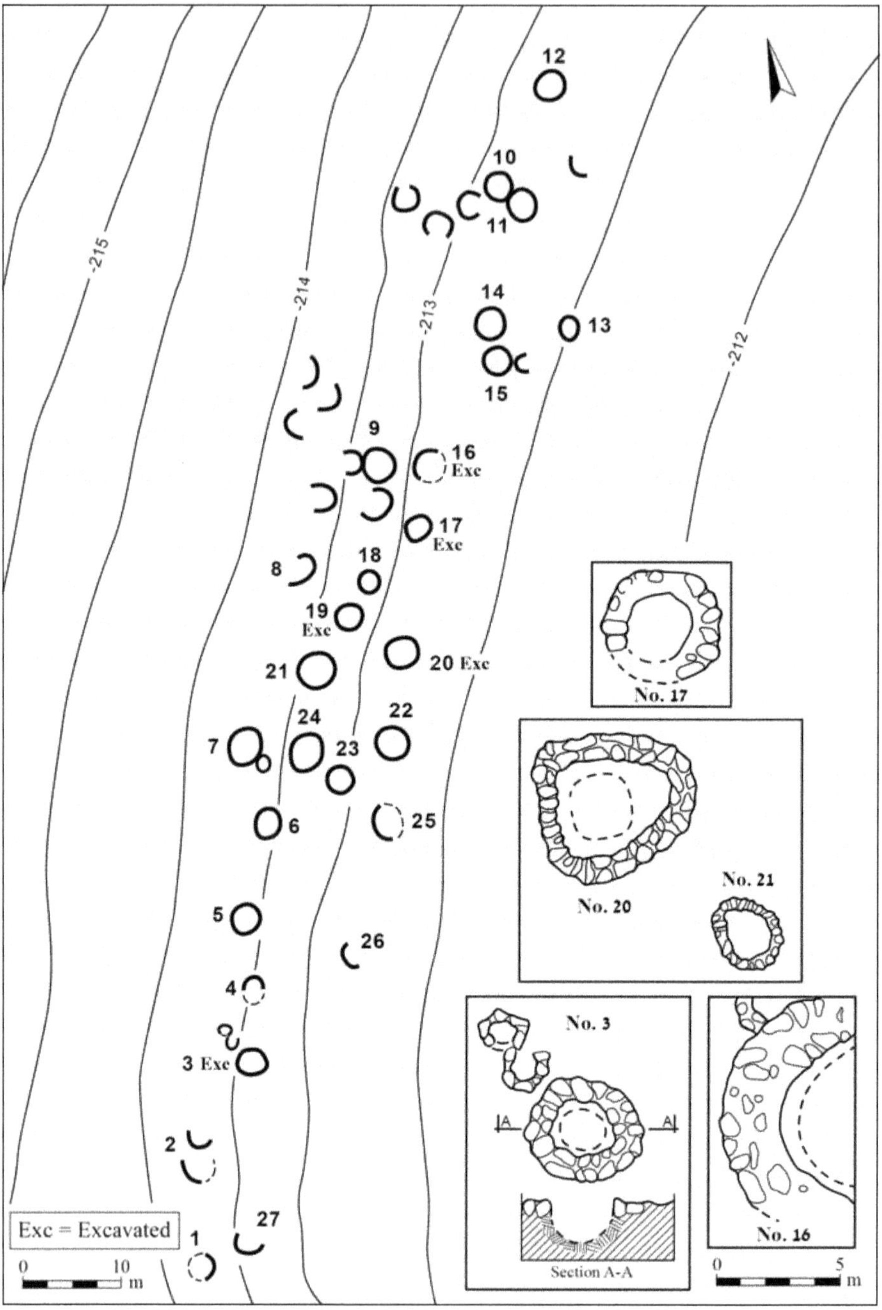

203. Plan of the **'Silo Site'** (1).

The round silos were quarried in the soft rock 60–70 cm deep, and between 1 and 2.5 m in diameter. Their mouths are encircled by round walls, built of two rows of local stones one course high. The silos are completely full of earth. Four of them were partially excavated in 2008 by Y. Peleg, but have not yet been published.

No datable sherds have been found.

Flint: 6 items (see Appendix A).
Additional surveys: none.

204. **The 'Silo Site' (1)**: view south-west, 2012. Each person is standing by a round dug silo. In the background are the valley of Netiv Hagdud and the Nabiris ridge (S. Bar).

Site 82: 19-15/33/3

PREHISTORIC SITES IN THE SOUTH-EASTERN SALIBIYAH BASIN

Israel grid: 1932/1539 (centre)
UTM grid: 7320/5408
Elevation: 230 m b.s.l., 0 m a.s.a.
Name: given by the survey
Site type: prehistoric
Area: irrelevant
Topography: plain
Rock type: Judea Group
Soil type: stony-desert
Soil quality: 1
Cultivation: none
Cisterns: none
Water source: Nahal Yitav (182), 5 km distant
Road: Beit She'an–Jericho (B10), 1 km distant
Visit: December 2010; hundreds of flint items

A group of prehistoric sites in the south-east of the Salibiya basin, west of el-Muslabah ridge, and south of the Wadi Abu Baqar tributaries.

The six newly discovered sites, not found in the surveys of the 1970s and 1980s (Appendix B), are additions to the prehistoric settlement in the region which existed from the Natufian period to the Pre-Pottery Neolithic period (see also Sites 75, 80, 81).

Following are references to the sites from north to south:

1. Site 82A, Israel grid 1928/1540

A find spot south of the wadi in the Salibiya basin. Flint items were gathered over an area of about 50 sq. m.

Flint: 112 items. Date: Natufian Epipalaeolithic (see Appendix A).

2. Site 82B, Israel grid 1931/1539

Two adjacent find spots south of the wadi.

Flint: the items from this site were lost before processing.

3. Site 82C, Israel grid 1932/1539

A find spot south of the wadi, about 70 m east of 82A above; it was scattered over an area of about 100 sq. m.

Flint: 55 items. Date: Natufian Epipalaeolithic (see Appendix A).

4. Site 82D, Israel grid 1931/1538

Find spot south of the wadi. Scatter as above.

Flint: 112 non-indicative items (see Appendix A).

5. Site 82E, Israel grid 1930/1538

Find spot south of the wadi. Scatter as above over an area of about 200 sq. m.

Flint: 182 items. Date: Natufian Epipalaeolithic (see Appendix A).

6. Site 82F, Israel grid 1930/1533

Find spot north of a tributary of Wadi Maqor edh-Dhib, 500 m north of sites 82A-E. A scatter of flint was found on the steep bank of the wadi, over an area of about 150 sq. m, similar to those mentioned above. It is likely that the site is larger, but the lichen cover renders it difficult to determine its area. The find was discovered when rainwater penetrated, removing the lichen layer.

Flint: 90 items. Date: Natufian Epipalaeolithic (see Appendix A).
Additional surveys: none.

♦ ♦ ♦

Site 83: 19-15/43/2

EL-MUSLABAH (1)

Israel grid: 1940/1538
UTM grid: 7328/5408
Elevation: 245 m b.s.l., 50 m b.s.a.
Name: nearest place
Site type: enclosures
Area: 1 dunam (1000 sq. m)
Topography: slope below ridge
Rock type: Judea Group
Soil type: stony-desert
Soil quality: 1
Cultivation: none
Cisterns: none
Water source: Nahal Yitav (182), 5 km distant
Road: Beit She'an–Jericho (B10), next to the site
Visits: December 2010, 2014; 20 sherds

A site at the bottom of the eastern slope of el-Muslabah ridge, close to the Jordan Valley marl plain and north of the entrance from the Jordan Valley road to Kibbutz Niran. The ridge is about 120 m west of the Jordan Valley road.

In the site are remains of an enclosure about 30 m in diameter, built from one row of medium-sized stones. About 80 m east of this is a tumulus 6 m in diameter rising slightly above its surroundings. It is built as a circle of small stones filled with small stones and earth.

Some 50 m north-west of the enclosure is a built wall about 70 m long; possibly a part of another enclosure.

Pottery: Late Roman-Byzantine – 30%; Modern – 50%; unidentified – 20%.
Additional surveys: none.

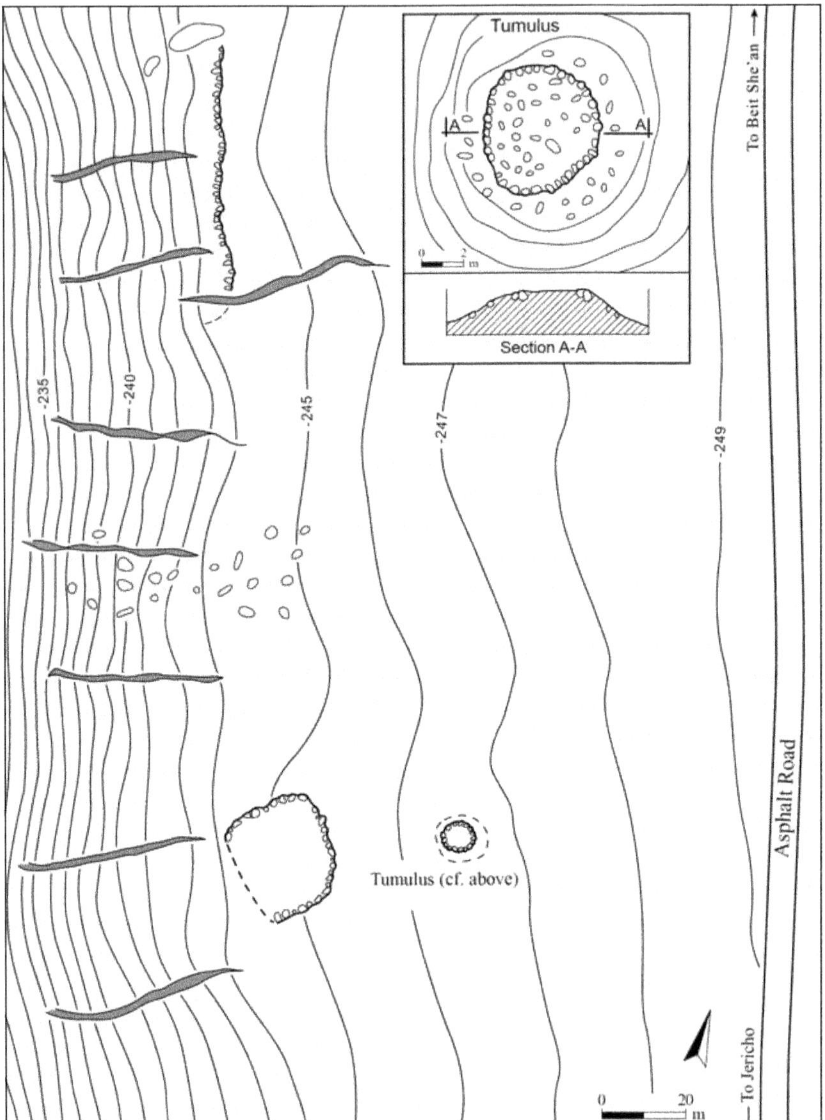

205. Plan of **el-Muslabah** (1).

Site 84: 18-15/93/1

WADI EL-BAQAR (2)

Israel grid: 1890/1539
UTM grid: 7279/5408
Elevation: 0 m a.s.l., 70 m b.s.a.
Name: nearest place
Site type: enclosure
Area: 1 dunam (1000 sq. m)
Topography: steep slope
Rock type: Judea Group
Soil type: stony-desert
Soil quality: 1
Cultivation: none
Cisterns: none
Water source: Nahal Yitav (182), 3.2 km distant
Road: 'Aujah Tahtah–'Ein 'Aujah (B48), 3 km distant
Visit: April 2007; 25 sherds

An enclosure on a high spur above the deep channel of Wadi Naqb el-Baqar, 3 km west-south-west from the centre of Netiv Hagdud. The site is surrounded by high ridges and a difficult unpaved road from Yitav to Netiv Hagdud passes at a short distance from its foot. The location, on a platform on a steep slope, is particularly prominent. The location of the site is unlike that of other sites of the same type, and seems to have been dictated by the topography.

The diameter of the incomplete irregular oval enclosure is about 35 m. The perimeter wall is well built of two rows of stones and is 1 m thick. Some parts of the site are covered by earth, but the wall outline remains clear thanks to the good construction.

A short wall projects westward from the enclosure wall; in other places there are heaps of stone which appear to be later.

A group of caves is located 50 m west and above the site. The largest one, with an entrance 10 m high, is 15 m deep and nearly 25 m in diameter. In front of the cave there is a courtyard supported by a wall on its lower side; its diameter is 15 m and it serves currently as a flock-pen. Mainly Roman-Byzantine body sherds were found in a litter spill on the slope in front of the cave. In this cave Peleg and Hameiri (2002) found a figurine, dated by them to the Chalcolithic period.

Pottery: Iron II – 12%, Late Roman – 36%; Byzantine – 30%; Early Moslem – 10%; Medieval – 8%; Ottoman – 4%.
Additional surveys: none.

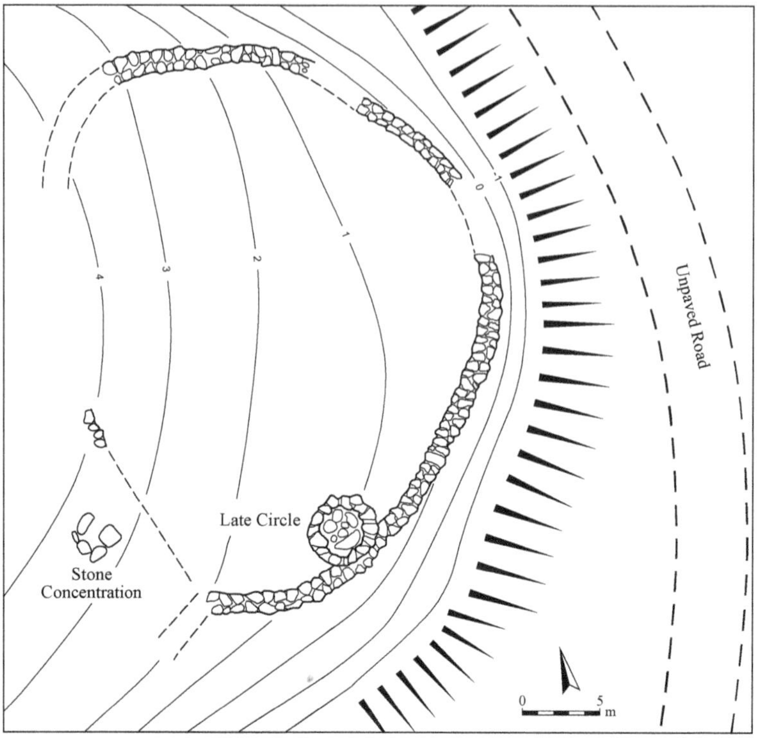

206. Plan of **Wadi el-Baqar (2)**.

207. Aerial view north-west of the enclosure in **Wadi el-Baqar (2)**, 2012 (A. Solomon).

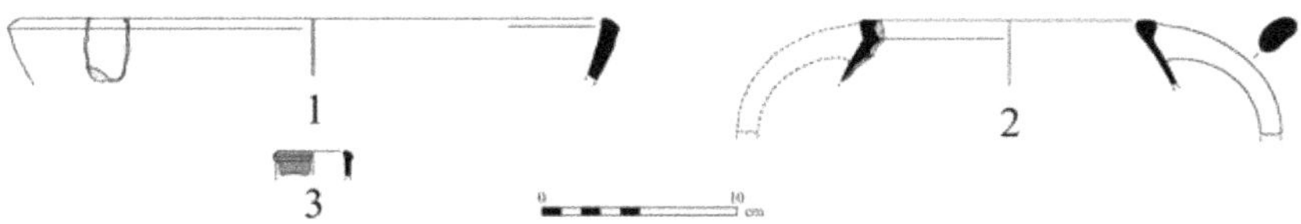

208. Pottery from **Wadi el-Baqar (2)**: 1. Bowl, gr, MA; 2. CP, blk, Byz-EM; 3. Pipe, rd, rd burnish, Ott.

♦ ♦ ♦

Site 85: 19-15/23/2

NIRAN (1)

Israel grid: 1925/1537
UTM grid: 7314/5406
Elevation: 208 m b.s.l., 0 m a.s.a.
Name: nearest place
Site type: enclosure and installations
Area: 3 dunams (3000 sq. m)
Topography: plain
Rock type: Judea Group
Soil type: silt
Soil quality: 2
Cultivation: none
Cisterns: none
Water source: Nahal Yitav (182), 3.3 km distant
Road: Beit She'an–Jericho (B10), 1.4 km distant
Visit: January 2003; 14 sherds

A small site in the alluvial plain of Wadi Naqb el-Baqar, 1 km north of Kibbutz Niran.

The site has two parts:

1. A round enclosure, 30 m in diameter. The perimeter wall is of a single row of medium-sized stones, with an entrance on the eastern side, from which a 6 m-long straight wall projects.
2. There are 24 clusters of rock quarried installations, in each one of which there are one to 20 cup-marks, mostly 10 cm in diameter and depth. Three oval basins with cup-marks in them were found and cleared out. Apparently, the cutters made a secondary use of the basins.

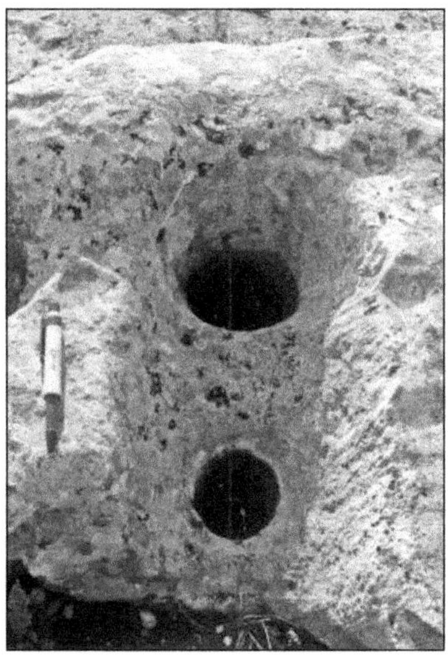

209. **Niran (1):** some of the quarried installations are basins and cup-marks (M. Einav).

This significant cluster of installations is unique in the alluvial plains of the Jordan Valley. The date of quarrying and the purpose of the installations, and the connection between them and the enclosure is not clear.

Pottery: Middle Bronze II – 21%; Iron II – 8%; Late Roman – 71%.
Flint: 10 items (see Appendix A).
Stone: two basalt grinding stones.
Additional surveys: Schuldenrein 1983: site Salibiya XII.

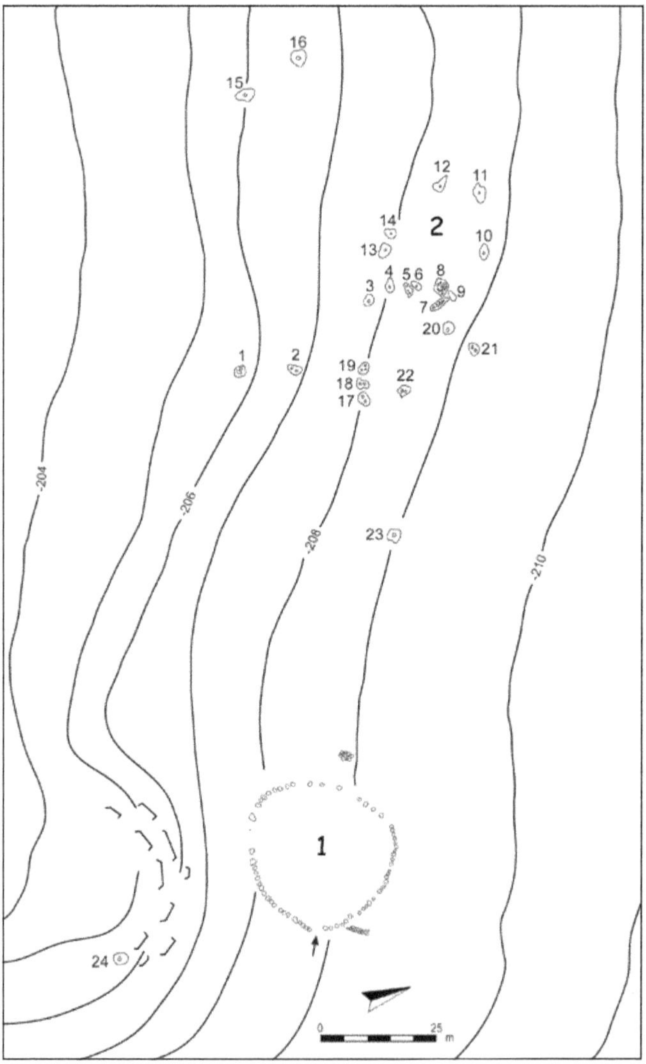

210. Plan of **Niran (1)**

Site 86: 19-15/33/2

ELEVATION POINT -200

Israel grid: 1930/1537
UTM grid: 7319/5406
Elevation: 200 m b.s.l., 0 m a.s.a.
Name: nearest place
Site type: structures
Area: 1 dunam (1000 sq. m)
Topography: moderate slope
Rock type: Judea Group
Soil type: stony-desert
Soil quality: 1
Cultivation: none
Cisterns: none
Water source: Nahal Yitav (182), 4 km distant
Road: Beit She'an–Jericho (B10), 1 km distant
Visit: December 2010; 50 sherds

Three adjacent structures, situated on a very slight slope east of the Netiv Hagdud valley, and west of el-Muslabah ridge. The location is 900 m north of kibbutz Niran, between two wadis – tributaries of Wadi Maqor edh-Dhib.

The structures are oval with a maximum diameter of 10 m. They are similar in shape and features, and all are encircled by a thin double wall, about 60 cm wide. The outer wall is built of medium-sized stones and the inner one of small stones. In each of the structures is a compartment, paved with medium-sized stones, whose area is about one third of the area of the structure.

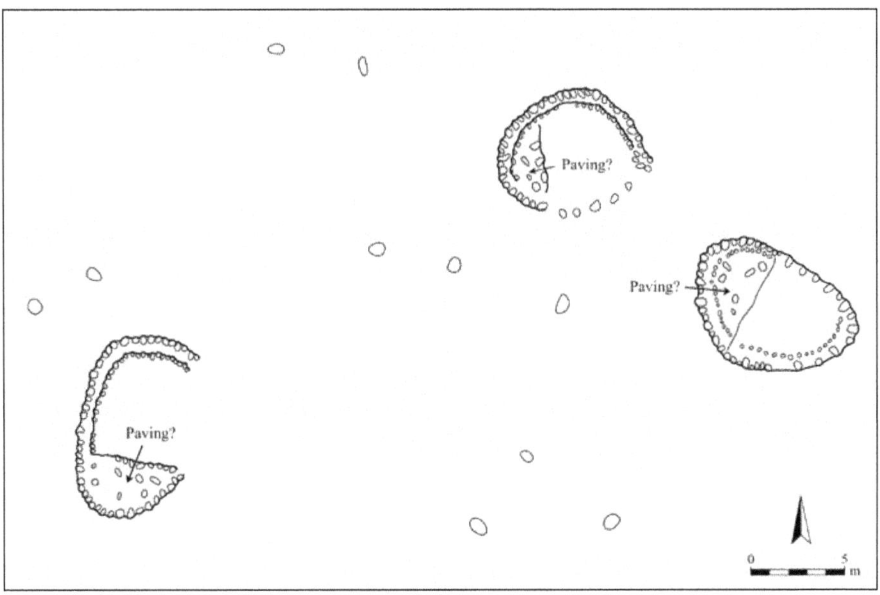

211. Plan of E.P. -200.

Around the structures are 20 small graves, apparently of children. Each of the graves is marked by a heap of small stones or a frame of larger stones (cyst grave).

The building stones were laid on the ground, without digging, meaning that these are tent encampments. At present the stones are sunk into the soil, testimony to the considerable time since they were laid.

Activity in the site began in the Iron Age, but the existing structures are later. The encampments probably originated some time between the Medieval and Ottoman periods, but there are numerous sherds from earlier periods.

Pottery: Iron II – 8%; Late Roman – 32%; Byzantine – 24%; Early Moslem – 12%; Medieval-Ottoman – 24%.
Additional surveys: none.

♦ ♦ ♦

Site 87: 18-15/93/2

ELEVATION POINT 58

Israel grid: 1890/1534
UTM grid: 7279/5402
Elevation: 40 m a.s.l., 50 m b.s.a.
Name: nearest place
Site type: enclosures
Area: 2.5 dunams (2500 sq. m)
Topography: slope
Rock type: Judea Group
Soil type: stony-desert
Soil quality: 1
Cultivation: none
Cisterns: none
Water source: Nahal Yitav (182), 2.8 km distant
Road: 'AujahTahtah–'Ein 'Aujah (C48), 2.7 km distant
Visit: March 2007; 50 sherds

A site of enclosures and structures on a steep slope descending eastward to Wadi el-Hamam, 3 km north-north-west of Yitav, and south-west of Elevation Point 58. The Netiv Hagdud–Yitav road passes the site, and the steep Samaria ridge rises in the west.

Two abutting enclosures are situated on a sloping spur between two deep tributaries of Wadi el-Hamam. Close by these enclosures are at least three structures, described below:

1. The western and top enclosure is a circular wall of a single row of large stones, 50 m in diameter, with a flat base . This enclosure and no. 2, which is below it, are separated by two parallel, straight and echeloned walls oriented north-south. These walls served as supporting walls for both enclosures. At the southern end of one of these walls is a triangular room.

212. Aerial view west at the enclosure in E.P. 58, 2012 (A. Solomon).

In the lower third of no. 1 there are remains of a room with a 2 m space between its walls. Another wall projects northward from it.

2. The eastern and lower enclosure is elliptical. Its major (north-south) axis is 45 m and the minor (east-west) one is 35 m. It is encircled by a double wall of large stones with fill between them, parts of which survive. The original wall was 1.5 m thick, but it is not clear if the entire wall was built in this format. Next to the north corner is a round structure, 7 m in diameter.
3. Nearby structures: South of no. 1 are remains of a rectangular structure, measuring 5×3 m, built of one row of medium-sized stones. South of no. 2 is another structure. Three of its walls survive, built of elongated slab-like stones whose construction differs from that of the rest of the site. In the open side of the structure is a small round structure.

The relative abundance of sherds is noteworthy. Apparently, there were other structures in the site whose format is unclear, and therefore were not included in the plan.

There is probably a connection between this site and the site Wadi el-Haiyat (4 [no. 103]), which is located 600 m south and in the same land type area.

Pottery: Iron I – 96%; Late Roman – 4%.
Flint: 10 items (see Appendix A).
Additional surveys: none.

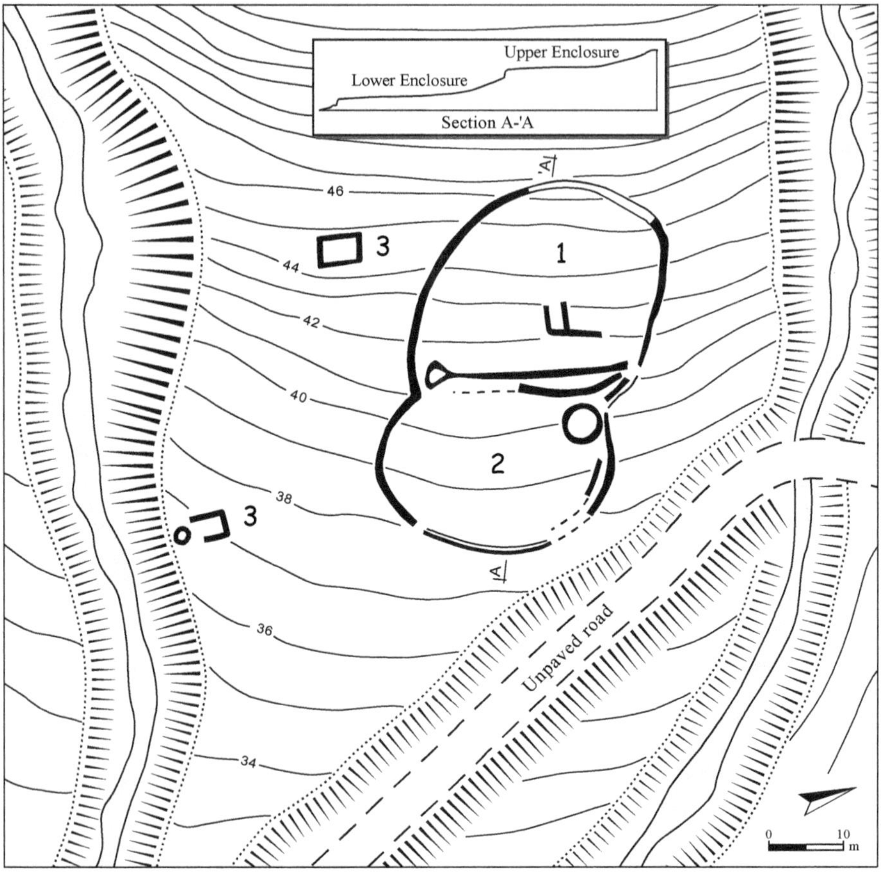

213. Plan of E.P 58.

◆ ◆ ◆

Site 88: 19-15/03/1

WADI MAQOR EDH-DHIB (1)

Israel grid: 1900/1535
UTM grid: 7289/5403
Elevation: 40 m b.s.l., 30 m b.s.a.
Name: nearest place
Site type: encampment
Area: 3 dunams (3000 sq. m)
Topography: slope
Rock type: Judea Group
Soil type: stony-desert
Soil quality: 2
Cultivation: none
Cisterns: none
Water source: Nahal Yitav (182), 3.3 km distant
Road: 'Aujah Tahtah–'Ein 'Aujah (C48), 3.3 km distant
Visit: May 2007; 30 sherds

A small multi-period encampment site, 2.5 km west-south-west of the centre of Netiv Hagdud. The location is in the lower part of Wadi Maqor edh-Dhib, over a shoulder facing east and descending to the wadi channel. There is a junction of small ravines in the place, descending to the main wadi.

There are the bases of a few modern tents and Bedouin graves. No architecture has been found.

The place served nomads as an encampment for long periods of time.

Pottery: Iron I-II – 14%; Late Roman – 67%; Byzantine – 6%; Medieval – 13%.
Additional surveys: none.

♦ ♦ ♦

Site 89: 19-15/03/2

WADI MAQOR EDH-DHIB (2)

Israel grid: 1902/1535
UTM grid: 7290/5403
Elevation: 40 m b.s.l., 30 m b.s.a.
Name: nearest place
Site type: encampment
Area: 1 dunam (1000 sq. m)
Topography: slope above wadi
Rock type: Judea Group
Soil type: stony-desert
Soil quality: 2
Cultivation: none
Cisterns: none
Water source: Nahal Yitav (182), 3.3 km distant
Road: 'Aujah Tahtah–'Ein 'Aujah (C48), 3.3 km distant
Visit: May 2007; 218 sherds

A small encampment site close to the confluence of two shallow channels of Wadi Maqor edh-Dhib, 2 km south-west from Netiv Hagdud.

The remains of 15 modern Bedouin tent bases were found over a wide area. Graves were also traced, but no remains of ancient structures.

An abundance of sherds from various periods were found; apparently the site served as an encampment for a long period of time.

Pottery: Middle Bronze II – 3%; Iron I – 6%; Hellenistic – 2%; Early Roman – 8%; Late Roman – 13%; Medieval – 51%; Ottoman-Modern – 17%.
Miscellaneous finds: glass bracelets, iron arrow, iron armour scale.
Additional surveys: none.

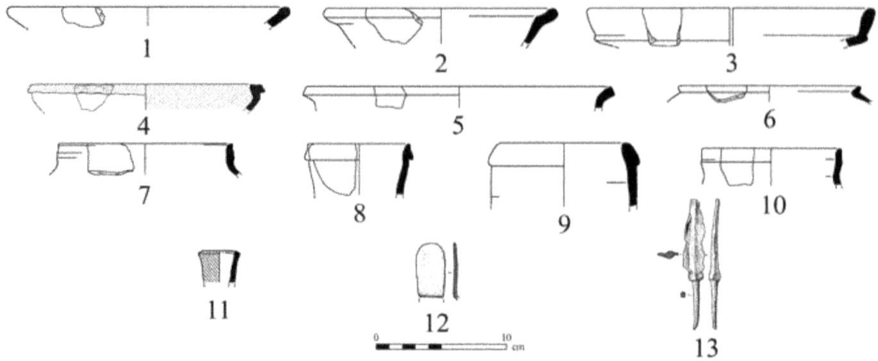

214. Finds from **Wadi Maqor edh-Dhib (2)**: 1. Bowl, br, MB II; 2. Bowl, br, LR; 3. Bowl, buff, Ott/Mod; 4. Bowl. Buff, yel glaze, MA; 5. CP A, br, IA I; 6. CP, rd, MA; 7. Jar, rd, Rom; 8. Jar, buff, Mod; 9. Jar, br, LR; 10. Jug, br, Rom; 11. Pipe, gr, rd slip, Ott; 12. Armour scale, iron; 13. Arrowhead, iron.

♦ ♦ ♦

Site 90: 19-15/02/2

NIRAN (3)

Israel grid: 1907/1523
UTM grid: 7296/5392
Elevation: 85 m b.s.l., 0 m a.s.a.
Name: nearest place
Site type: structures
Area: 0.5 dunam (500 sq. m)
Topography: broad ridge
Rock type: Judea Group
Soil type: stony-desert
Soil quality: 2
Cultivation: none
Cisterns: none
Water source: Nahal Yitav (182), 2.2 km distant
Road: 'Aujah Tahtah–'Ein 'Aujah (C48), 2.2 km distant
Visit: March 2007; 6 sherds

The site consists of two rounded structures close to each other, above the western slope of the ridge between Wadi Maqor edh-Dhib and Wadi el-Hamam, and near the Niran–Yitav road. The ridges in this region are notably broad with deep wadis between them.

Following is their description:

1. A structure, made of one layer of stones, measuring 6×4.5 m, with a frame of medium-sized stones and flooring of one layer of small and medium stones. In its central part is a gap or round hollow, encircled by a row of elongated stones arranged in a frame-like pattern. An entrance is in the western wall.

2. About 10 m eastward is another structure, destroyed to a greater extent than no. 1, built in the form of two stone circles, one inside the other.

The two structures are extraordinary in format and their purpose is not clear. They were not used for residence, but served as built bases, possibly the bottom part of tumuli, but there are no stone heaps of stones from dismantled tumuli in the area.

Pottery: Late Roman (body sherds) – 100%.
Additional surveys: none.

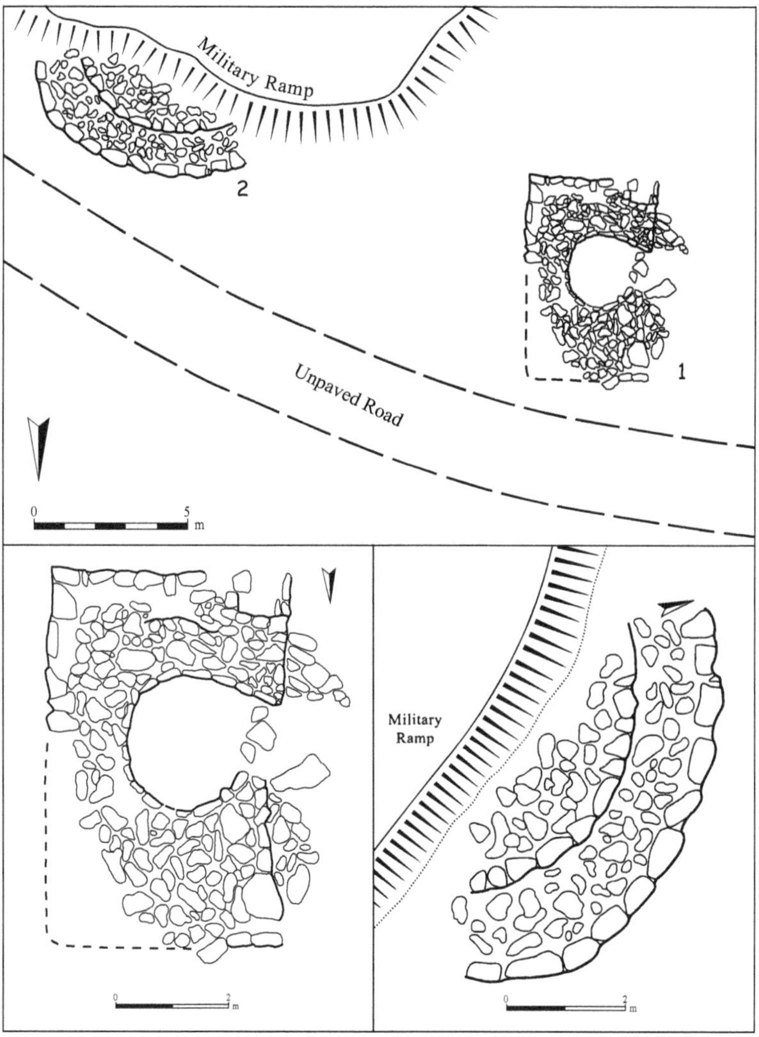

215. Plan of **Niran (3)**.

Site 91: 19-15/43/1

ARCHELAIS – CEMETERY

Israel grid: 1943/1534
UTM grid: 7332/5403
Elevation: 250 m b.s.l., 0 m a.s.a.
Name: nearest place
Site type: cemetery
Area: 20 dunams (2 ha)
Topography: plain with channels
Rock type: Judea Group
Soil type: Lisan marl
Soil quality: 2
Cultivation: none
Cisterns: none
Water source: Nahal Yitav (182), 3 km distant
Road: Beit She'an–Jericho (B10), next to the site
Visits: January 2005 and more; 40 sherds

A large necropolis in low hills and area with channels, 1.3 km north-east of Niran. It is near the exit of the approach road to Niran from the Jordan Valley road.

At least 20 built graves have been located over the site's surface. The length of a typical grave is 1 m; and it is built as a frame of stones. Some of the graves had been plundered. Heaps of stones are scattered over the entire area, apparently belonging to the plundered graves, The cemetery was once much larger than its present area.

There are large accumulations of homogeneous Roman pottery over the entire area.

This was probably one of the cemeteries of the nearby Roman town of Archelais.

Pottery: Roman – 100%.
Additional surveys: none.

Site 92: 19-15/13/1

NIRAN (4)

Israel grid: 1915/1533
UTM grid: 7303/5402
Elevation: 160 m b.s.l., 40 m b.s.a.
Name: nearest place
Site type: enclosure
Area: 1 dunam (1000 sq. m)
Topography: shoulder above wadi
Rock type: Judea Group
Soil type: stony-desert
Soil quality: 1
Cultivation: none
Cisterns: none
Water source: Nahal Yitav (182), 3 km distant
Road: Beit She'an–Jericho (B10), 2.7 km distant
Visit: March 2007; 29 sherds

An enclosure on a low shoulder, north of a nameless wadi between Netiv Hagdud and Niran. The site is located above the channel of the wadi, northwest of Elevation Point 111, and 800 m east of the Jordan Valley plain.

The enclosure is built of large dark flint stones originating in the vicinity. Parts of the perimeter wall and the inner courtyard survive, apparently part of the enclosure; the estimated diameter of which was 30-40 m.

The stone scatter suggests that there were other structures in the site: some were dismantled, and others washed away by the wadi. Remains of walls were found in the neighbouring shoulder east of the site, but no other finds.

216. **Niran (4)** is on a spur above the wadi. The structure's foundations are visible. Looking west, 2011 (S. Bar).

Pottery: Middle Bronze II (?) – 7%; Iron I – 17%; Iron II (?) – 7%; Late Roman – 60%; Medieval – 9%.
Flint: 10 items (see Appendix A).
Additional surveys: none.

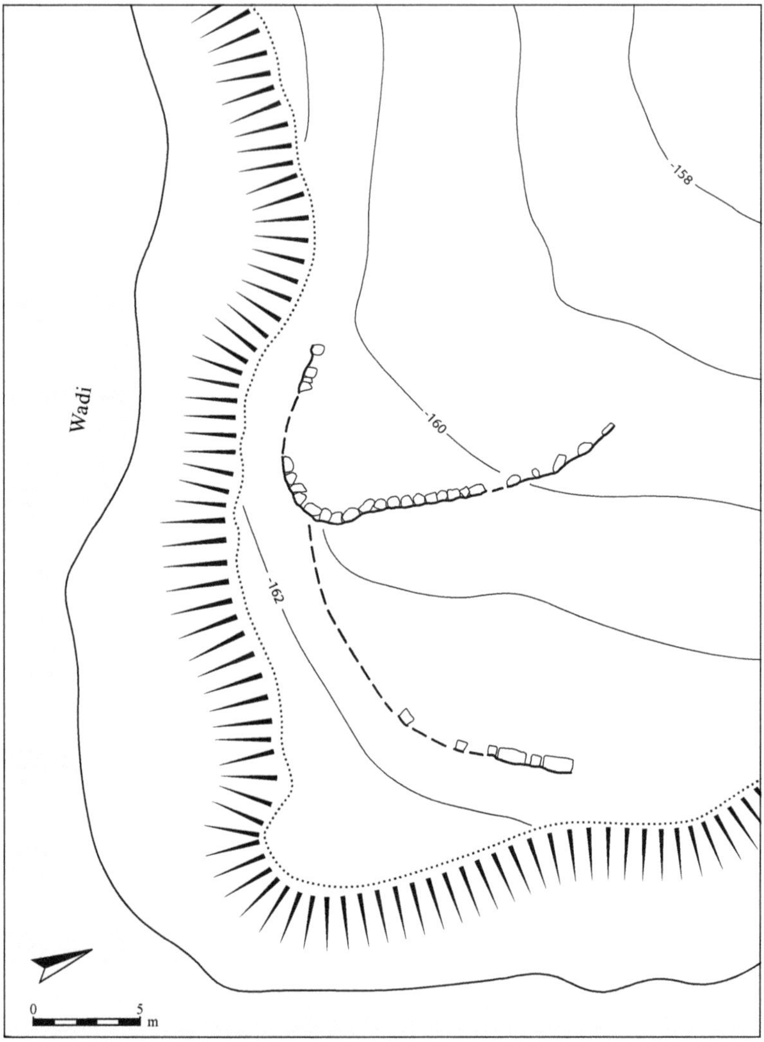

217. Plan of **Niran (4)**.

218. Pottery from **Niran (4)**: 1. CP, rd, MA; 2. Jug, lt br, IA II (?).

Site 93: 19-15/23/3

NIRAN (9)

Israel grid: 1922/1534
UTM grid: 7311/5403
Elevation: 190 m b.s.l., 30 m b.s.a.
Name: nearest place
Site type: enclosures
Area: 2 dunams (2000 sq. m)
Topography: plain and valley edge
Rock type: Judea Group
Soil type: stony-desert
Soil quality: 3
Cultivation: none
Cisterns: none
Water source: Nahal Yitav (182), 3.3 km distant
Road: Beit She'an–Jericho (B10), 2 km distant
Visit: February 2007; 11 sherds

An enclosure site in the west of the valley which descends southward to Wadi Maqor edh-Dhib, between Netiv Hagdud and Niran. The location is 1.5 km south of the centre of Netiv Hagdud, and 800 m north-west of Niran. The unpaved Netiv Hagdud–Niran East road passes close by the site, and 60 m north of it is the channel of a wadi.

Parts of a large oval enclosure, measuring about 40×30 m, survive. The wall around it, which was originally continuous, but of which now only sections are standing, is built of large fieldstones.

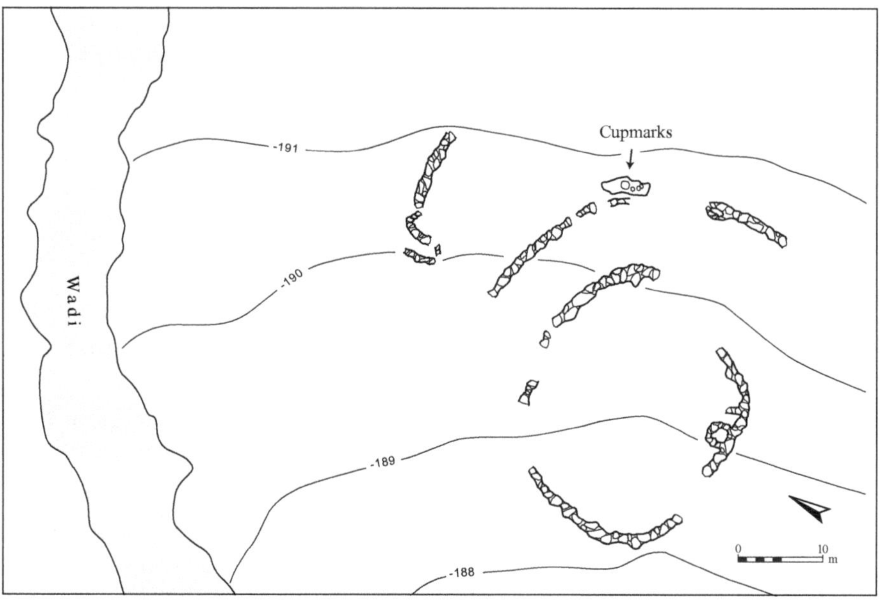

219. plan of **Niran (9)**.

East of the enclosure are remains of another larger one, only the eastern wall of which survives. This is probably an ancient phase of the original enclosure.

To the North, in the direction of the wadi, is another wall, perhaps the remnains of another enclosure. East of the complex are sections of several walls.

Next to the outmost wall were found four rock-cut circular cupmarks, about 30 cm in diameter and depth.

Pottery: Middle Bronze II – 10%; Late Roman – 90%.
Additional surveys: none.

♦ ♦ ♦

Site 94: 19-15/23/4

NIRAN (2)

Israel grid: 1923/1533
UTM grid: 7312/5401
Elevation: 190 m b.s.l., 50 m b.s.a.
Name: nearest place
Site type: enclosures
Area: 4 dunams (4000 sq. m)
Topography: plain and valley edge
Rock type: Judea Group
Soil type: stony-desert
Soil quality: 4
Cultivation: none
Cisterns: none
Water source: Nahal Yitav (182), 3.1 km distant
Road: Beit She'an–Jericho (B10), 2 km distant
Visit: February 2007; 55 sherds

An enclosure site in the western side of a valley, 800 m north-west of Niran. The unpaved Netiv Hagdud–Niran road passes nearby.

The site includes two enclosures with annexes and other parts:

1. The eastern one is east of the road, oval and about 40 m across. The construction is simple: a single row of medium-sized uncut stones, mostly flint from the vicinity. The western side was bulldozed off during the construction of the road. There are very few sherds.
2. In the western enclosure, about 70 m west of the road, there are at least three parts:
   A. A circular enclosure 25 m in diameter, built similarly to enclosure no. 1. Sections of the perimeter wall are built of two rows of stones: this is probably the original construction. Outside the north-western wall and attached to it is a circular wall 6 m in diameter, partially preserved.

B. East of the enclosure and parallel to it is a large rounded wall; remains of a more ancient enclosure or a support wall.
C. North of part B is another wall on the slope, with a round cell next to it.

Close to no. 2, at varying distances, are six quarried installations: four deep cup-marks with concave bottoms and two oval basins. A similar installation is found in no. 1. Some of the installations are cut into detached rocks, and others into rock surfaces. They are all marked in the plan by small numbered squares. **Pottery:** Early Bronze – 4%; Middle Bronze II – 4%; Iron I (?) – 9%; Late Roman

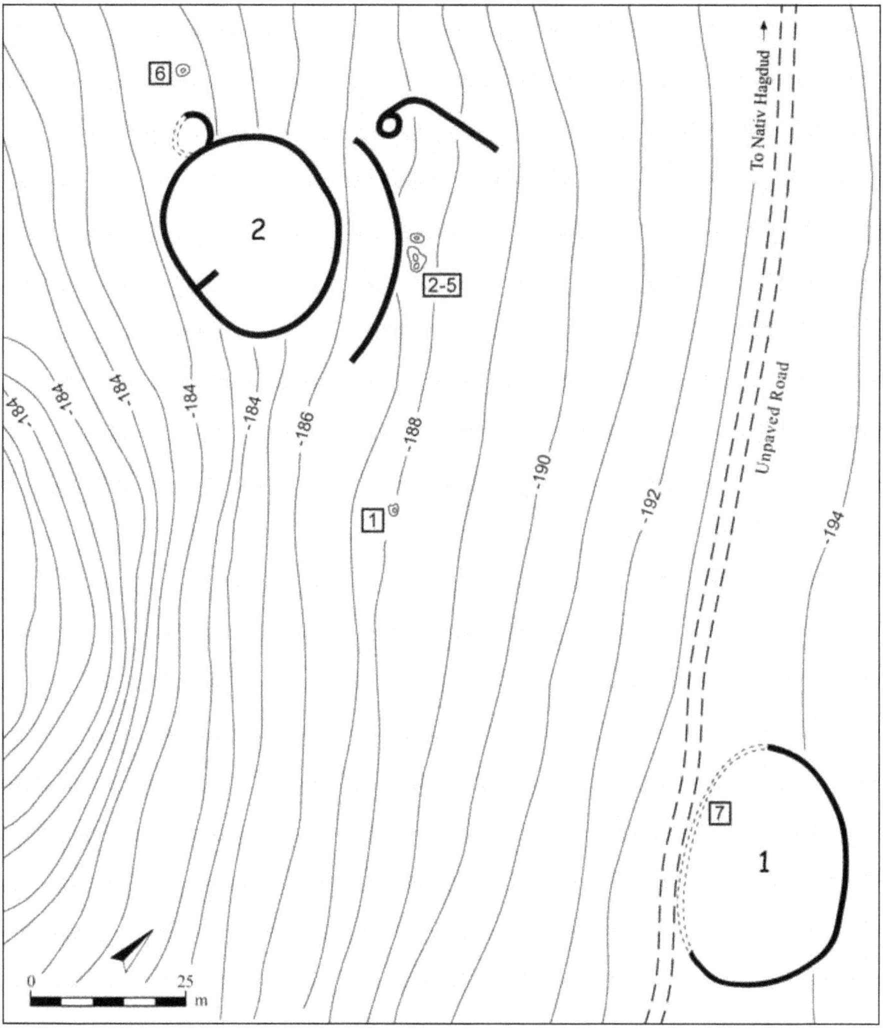

220. Plan of **Niran (2)**.

– 61%; Byzantine – 18%; Medieval – 4%.
Flint: 2 items (see Appendix A).
Additional surveys: none.

221. **Niran (2)**: Aerial view south west at the enclosure site, 2008 (N. Eshed).

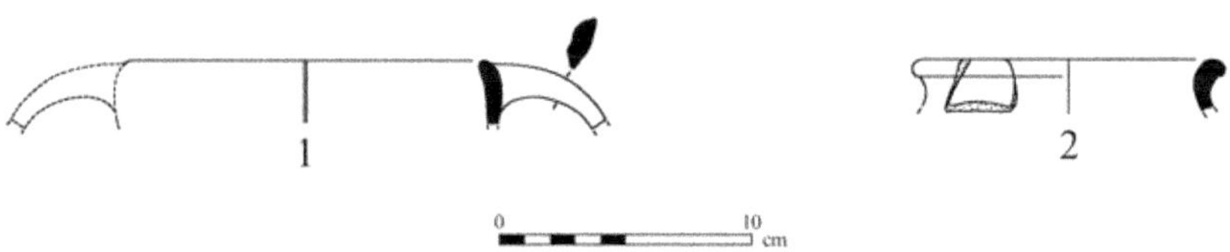

222. Pottery from **Niran (2)**: 1. CP, rd, Rom-Byz; 2. Jar, gr, EB.

Site 95: 19-15/23/5

NIRAN (6)

Israel grid: 1924/1533
UTM grid: 7313/5402
Elevation: 205 m b.s.l., 30 m b.s.a.
Name: nearest place
Site type: enclosure, structure and graves
Area: 5 dunams (5000 sq. m)
Topography: plain and valley edge
Rock type: Judea Group
Soil type: stony-desert
Soil quality: 2
Cultivation: none
Cisterns: none
Water source: Nahal Yitav (182), 3.2 km distant
Road: Beit She'an–Jericho (B10), 1.7 km distant
Visit: December 2006; 100 sherds

A site of encampments in the flat western border of the Jordan Valley, between Netiv Hagdud and Niran, on a platform between two wadis, 1 km north-west of Niran. The unpaved Netiv Hagdud–Niran road passes close by.

There are two main parts in the site:

1. Remains of an enclosure about 25 m in diameter, built of small stones: only its western side survives.
2. An apse-like structure. The principal wall is 8 m long and is oriented north-south. The northern end is a semicircular arch. Byzantine sherds were found here.

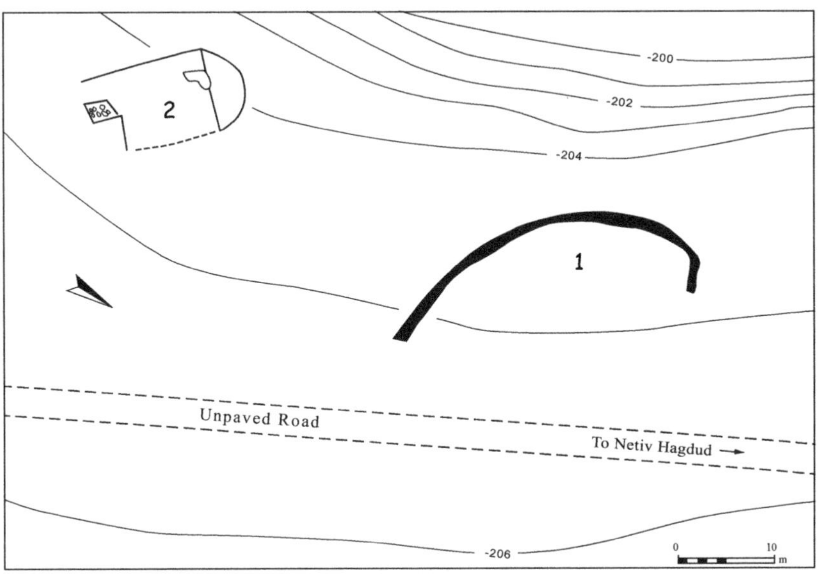

223. Plan of **Niran (6)**.

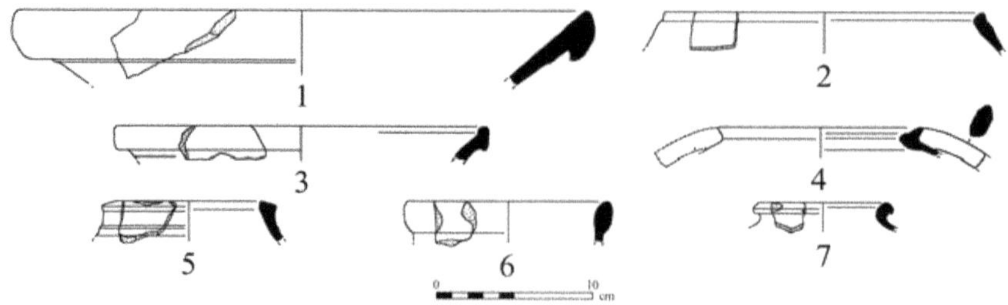

224. Pottery from **Niran (6)**: 1. Mortaria, rd, Pers; 2. CP, rd, LR; 3. CP A, br, IA I; 4. CP, blk, Byz-EM; 5. Jar, blk, IA II; 6. Jar, rd, IA I-II; 7. Jug, blk, LR.

Nearby are four tombs made from large stones of 2 m maximum diameter. The construction is exceptionally good. One of the tombs was found opened and plundered. Near these tombs are numerous Bedouin graves.

There are plenty of varied sherds in the site, untypical to the region, indicating intensive habitation over long periods.

Pottery: Iron I – 20%; Iron II – 5%; Persian – 6%; Late Roman – 25%; Byzantine – 14%; Early Moslem – 5%; Medieval – 15%; Unidentified – 10%.
Additional surveys: none.

♦ ♦ ♦

Site 96: 19-15/23/8

NIRAN (8)

Israel grid: 1925/1531
UTM grid: 7314/5399
Elevation: 205 m b.s.l., 0 m a.s.a.
Name: nearest place
Site type: structures
Area: 1 dunam (1000 sq. m)
Topography: plain
Rock type: Judea Group
Soil type: stony-desert

Soil quality: 3
Cultivation: none
Cisterns: none
Water source: Nahal Yitav (182), 3 km distant
Road: Beit She'an–Jericho (B10), 1.7 km distant
Visit: February 2007; 28 sherds

A site of structures in the western edge of the valley between Netiv Hagdud and Niran, close to Wadi Maqor edh-Dhib, located close east of the site of Niran (7 [no. 99]) and to the unpaved road from Netiv Hagdud to Yitav, which crosses the edge of the valley.

Three structures have been found in the plain; the connection between them is unknown:

1. A structure measuring 10×7 m with a rounded room at the centre, surrounded by walls pointing in various directions. The construction is of large fieldstones. Because of the collapse of the structure it is difficult to reconstruct all the walls.
2. A structure built of two rows of medium-sized stones in the form of the letter **m**, open to the east.

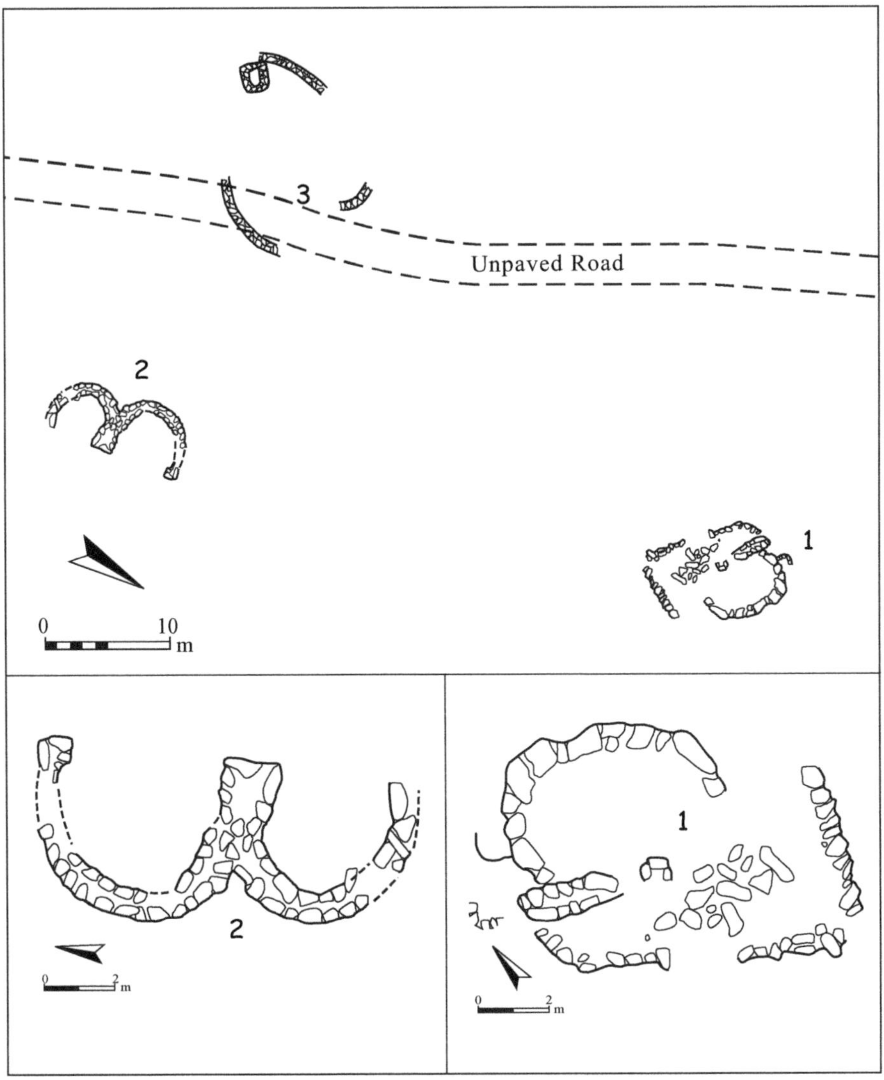

225. Plan of **Niran** (8).

3. Remains of an enclosure, crossed by the road, with structures by it.
The site is probably connected to nearby Niran (7), but there is no explanation for the unique construction.

Pottery: Structure no. 1 (22 sherds): Iron I-II – 73%; Late Roman – 27%; Structure no. 2 (2 sherds): Iron II – 100%; Structure no. 3 (4 sherds): Iron II – 50%; Late Roman – 50%.
Additional surveys: none.

226. Pottery from **Niran (8)**: 1. CP, lt br, IA II; 2. CP, rd, LR.

♦ ♦ ♦

Site 97: 19-15/23/6

NIRAN (10)

Israel grid: 1924/1530
UTM grid: 7313/5399
Elevation: 160 m b.s.l., 30 m b.s.a.
Name: nearest place
Site type: enclosure
Area: 1.5 dunam (1500 sq. m)
Topography: plain
Rock type: Judea Group
Soil type: stony-desert
Soil quality: 3
Cultivation: none
Cisterns: none
Water source: Nahal Yitav (182), 2.7 km distant
Road: Beit She'an–Jericho (B10), 1.7 km distant
Visit: March 2007; 40 sherds

An enclosure in the plain gradually descending southward to Wadi Maqor edh-Dhib, between Netiv Hagdud and Niran, 500 m north-west from the centre of Niran.

The oval enclosure, measuring 40×24 m, is encircled by a wall 50 cm thick, built from a single row of medium-sized fieldstones with large flint stones inserted in it; these are mostly the opening jambs. In the north side there is 1 m-wide opening, and the southern part is partitioned by an inner wall, different from the original construction; with thin walls attached to it, probably forming rooms.

227. The enclosure site at **Niran (10)**, view to the east, 2010. In the background is the tortuous channel of Wadi Maqor edh-Dhib (S. Bar).

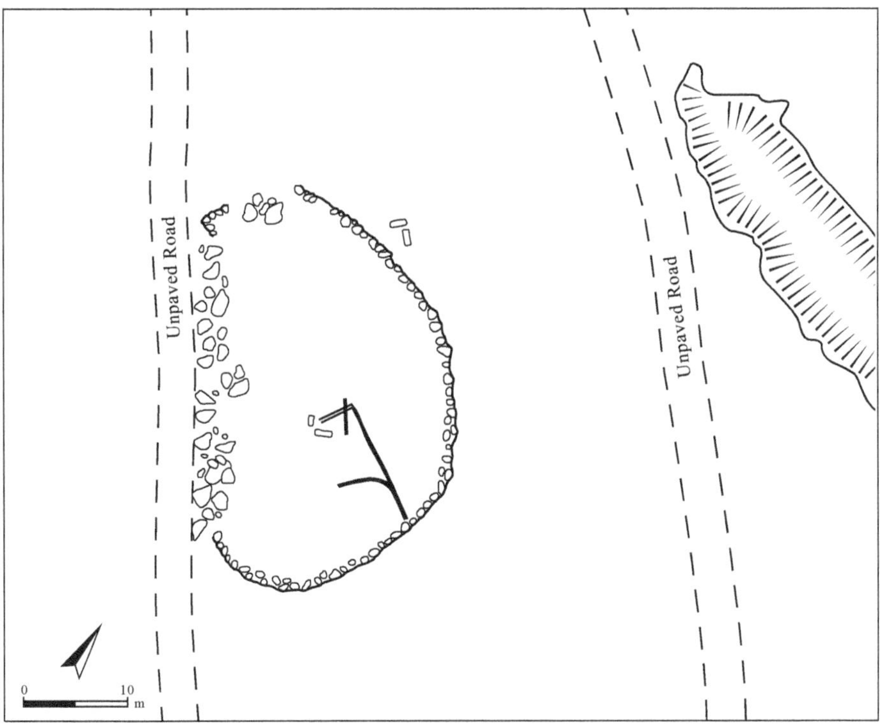

228. Plan of **Niran (10)**.

The western side of the site was demolished during the construction of the unpaved Netiv Hagdud–Niran road.

Nearby is the site of Niran (7 [no. 99]).

Pottery: Iron I-II – 25%; Late Roman – 75%.
Additional surveys: none.

229. Pottery from **Niran (10)**: 1. CP, rd, IA II; 2. CP, rd, Rom.

◆ ◆ ◆

Site 98: 19-15/22/1

NIRAN (11)

Israel grid: 1925/1528
UTM grid: 7314/5397
Elevation: 190 m b.s.l., 30 m b.s.a.
Name: nearest place
Site type: enclosure
Area: 1 dunam (1000 sq. m)
Topography: slope and valley edge
Rock type: Judea Group
Soil type: stony-desert
Soil quality: 2
Cultivation: none
Cisterns: none
Water source: Nahal Yitav (182), 3 km distant
Road: Beit She'an–Jericho (B10), 1 km distant
Visit: April 2011; 20 sherds

An oval enclosure 500 m from the centre of Niran, at the bottom of the Niran spur, and between it and Wadi Maqor edh-Dhib. There is a line of low cliffs above the site.

The enclosure, about 40 m across, is partly built as a double wall 1 m thick; the inner wall of large stones, and the outer one of smaller stones.

The number of sherds is particularly small.

Pottery: Iron II – 20%; Late Roman – 60%; Ottoman-Modern – 20%.
Other find: Close to the enclosure a round copper pendant with a *tughra* (Ottoman Imperial emblem) impression was found.
Additional surveys: none.

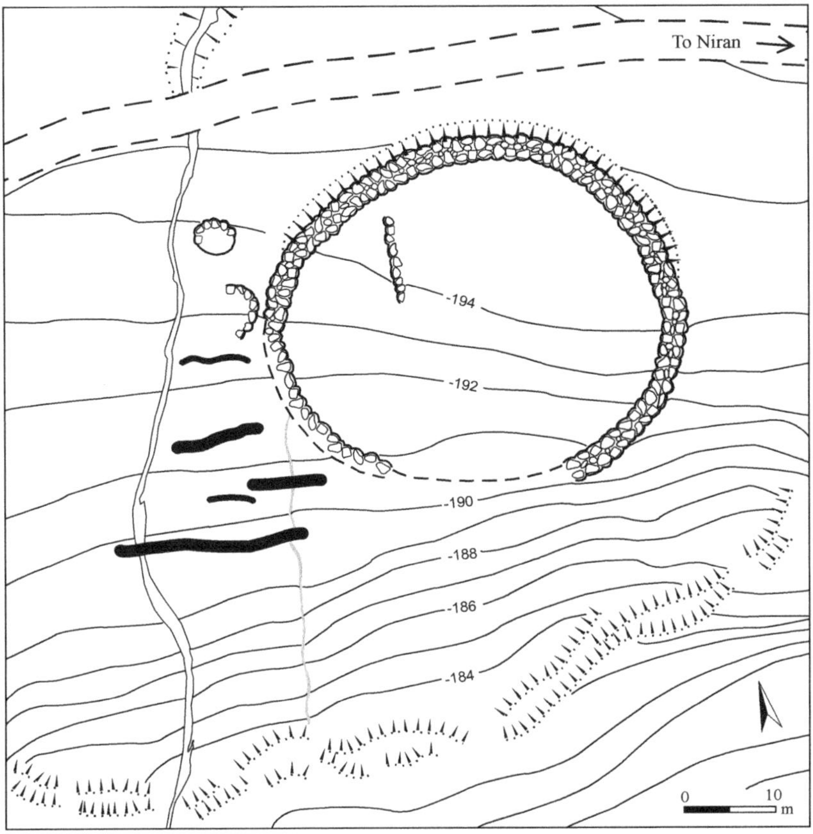

230. Plan of **Niran (11)**.

◆ ◆ ◆

Site 99: 19-15/23/7

NIRAN (7)

Israel grid: 1924/1530
UTM grid: 7313/5398
Elevation: 200 m b.s.l., 0 m a.s.a.
Name: nearest place
Site type: enclosures
Area: 1.5 dunam (1500 sq. m)
Topography: valley edge
Rock type: Judea Group
Soil type: stony-desert
Soil quality: 2
Cultivation: none
Cisterns: none
Water source: Nahal Yitav (182), 2.7 km distant
Road: Beit She'an–Jericho (B10), 1.7 km distant
Visit: December 2006; 10 sherds

Partially preserved enclosures, in the western edge of the Jordan Valley plain, north of Wadi Maqor edh-Dhib, and 800 m north-west of Niran. Nearby are Niran (10) [no. 97]) and the unpaved road from Netiv Hagdud southward to Niran.

There are several enclosures in the site close to and inside each other, which demonstrate phases in the evolution of the site. The largest, only the eastern part of which has survived and has been reconstructed, is about 50 m in diameter, and is built of one row of large stones. Its higher western part was washed away or covered. Within this enclosure are three others, one inside the other. The inner enclosures are built similarly to the large one.

Very few sherds were found.

Pottery: Iron I-II (?) – 30%; Late Roman – 70%.
Additional surveys: none.

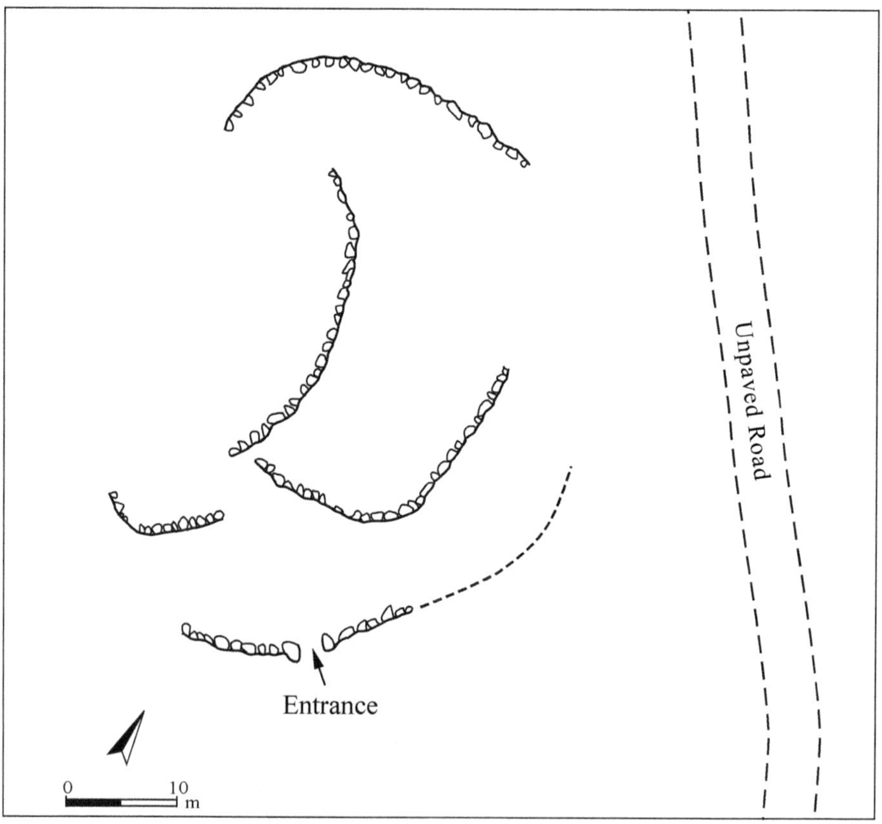

231. Plan of **Niran** (7).

Site 100: 19-15/23/9

'THE TUMULI SITE'

Israel grid: 1925/1530
UTM grid: 7314/5398
Elevation: 202 m b.s.l., 0 m a.s.a.
Name: given by the survey
Site type: tumuli graves
Area: 0.5 dunam (500 sq. m)
Topography: shoulder above wadi
Rock type: Judea Group
Soil type: stony-desert
Soil quality: 2
Cultivation: none
Cisterns: none
Water source: Nahal Yitav (182), 2.7 km distant
Road: Beit She'an–Jericho (B10), 1.7 km distant
Visit: March 2011; 32 sherds

Two built tumuli, one well preserved and the other only partially, in the Jordan Valley plain, 800 m north-west of Niran, and above Wadi Maqor edh-Dhib tributaries.

Tumulus no. 1 is about 6.5 m in diameter, built as a circle of a single row of medium-sized well laid stones. In the centre is a burial cyst, 2 m long, 1 m wide and 1 m deep, built of large stone slabs. Between the built circle and the cyst is a dense stone filling; more stones are scattered around. The tumulus rises 1 m above the plain.

232. **'The Tumuli Site'**, view to the west, 2011. In the photo is A. Halevi (S. Bar).

Tumulus no. 2 is about 10 m east of no. 1. Its stones have been removed and its form has been totally distorted.

Both graves were apparently plundered in earlier times.

Pottery: Iron II – 15%; Late Roman – 78%; Byzantine – 7%.
Additional surveys: none.

233. Pottery from '**The Tumuli Site**': 1. Bowl, dk br, LR-Byz; 2. Jar, dk br, LR-Byz.

◆ ◆ ◆

Site 101: 18-15/82/6

WADI EL-HAIYAT (7)

Israel grid: 1884/1529
UTM grid: 7274/5397
Elevation: 100 m a.s.l., 100 m b.s.a.
Name: nearest place
Site type: enclosures and a flint scatter
Area: 0.5 dunam (500 sq. m)
Topography: spur and slope
Rock type: Judea Group
Soil type: stony-desert
Soil quality: 3
Cultivation: none
Cisterns: none
Water source: Nahal Yitav (182), 2 km distant
Road: 'Aujah Tahtah–'Ein 'Aujah (C48), 2 km distant
Visits: May 2011 and more; 20 sherds

A small site on a slope, 500 m west of the Netiv Hagdud–Yitav road, and at the edge of the high ridge of east Samaria, the source of the tributaries of Wadi el-Haiyat.

Two enclosures were discovered, upper and lower. In the upper enclosure is a circle about 0.5 m in diameter of small stones, perhaps remains of a hearth.

Pottery: (body sherds): Iron I-II – 15%; Late Roman – 65%; Medieval – 20%.
Flint: 100 items, Pre-Pottery Neolithic B-C and Iron Age (see Appendix A).
Additional surveys: none.

Site 102: 18-15/82/5

WADI EL-HAIYAT (8)

Israel grid: 1889/1529
UTM grid: 7278/5396
Elevation: 0 m b.s.l., 100 m b.s.a.
Name: nearest place
Site type: flint scatter
Area: 0.5 dunam (500 sq. m)
Topography: spur and moderate slope
Rock type: Judea Group
Soil type: stony-desert
Soil quality: 3
Cultivation: none
Cisterns: none
Water source: Nahal Yitav (182), 2 km distant
Road: 'Aujah Tahtah–'Ein 'Aujah (C48), 2 km distant
Visit: May 2011

A site on a spur descending east to Wadi el-Haiyat tributaries, 300 m from Wadi el-Haiyat (4 [no. 103]), and 200 m west of the Netiv Hagdud–Yitav unpaved road.

There is no architecture, and over the surface there is a scatter of flint implements.

Flint: 107 items (see Appendix A).
Additional surveys: none.

♦ ♦ ♦

Site 103: 18-15/92/1

WADI EL-HAIYAT (4)

Israel grid: 1890/1529
UTM grid: 7279/5397
Elevation: 10 m b.s.l., 0 m a.s.a.
Name: nearest place
Site type: enclosure
Area: 1.5 dunam (1500 sq. m)
Topography: spur and moderate slope
Rock type: Judea Group
Soil type: stony-desert
Soil quality: 3
Cultivation: none
Cisterns: none
Water source: Nahal Yitav (182), 2 km distant
Road: 'Aujah Tahtah–'Ein 'Aujah (C48), 2 km distant
Visits: April 2004 and more; 95 sherds

A site on a moderate slope of a narrow spur descending eastward from Elevation Point 273, 2.8 km west-north-west from Yitav, and near an unpaved road

234. View west to the enclosure in **Wadi el-Haiyat (4)**, 2012 (S. Bar).

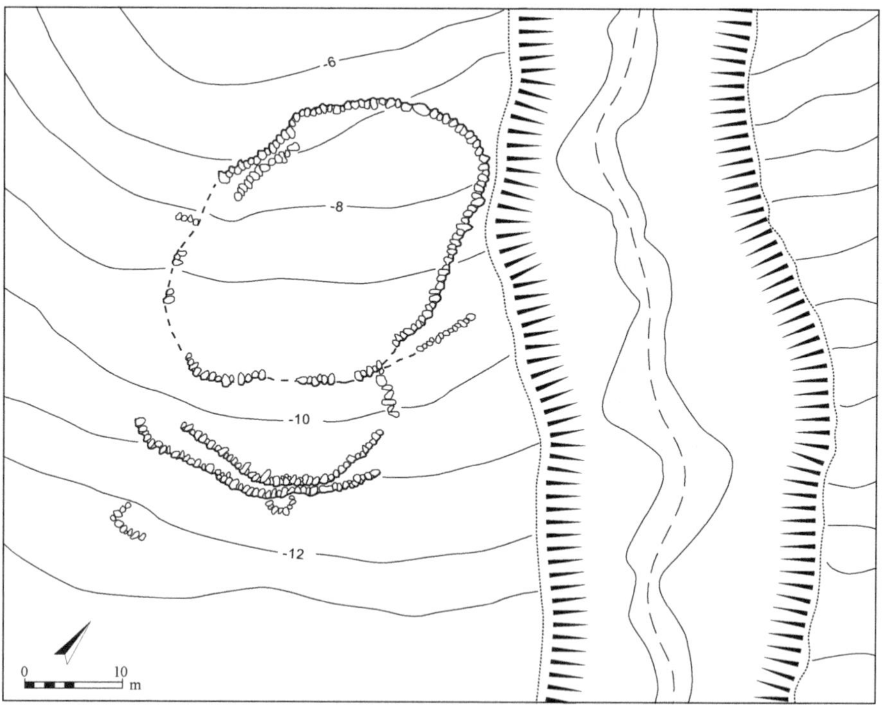

235. Plan of **Wadi el-Haiyat (4)**.

from Yitav to Netiv Hagdud. East of it is the deep channel of one of Wadi el-Haiyat tributaries.

The dimensions of the oval enclosure are 45 m (north-south axis) and 25 m (east-west axis). To the southern part of it are attached presumably various structures and parts of former enclosures.

Part of the main enclosure is built of two rows of stones protruding above their surroundings. Other ones are lying down, thus the long dimension faces the wall. In the north the wall reaches the edge of the gully. North of the enclosure there are several Bedouin graves.

The many building stones scattered at the site indicate that houses once stood there. The considerable number of sherds in the area greatly surpasses the typical find in an enclosure site, and suggests the existence of a demolished or covered small village, inhabited repeatedly in various periods.

The site is part of dense habitation in the outlet areas of Wadis el-Haiyat and Nabiris.

Pottery: Chalcolithic/Early Bronze (?) – 10%; Iron I – 50%; Iron II – 20%; Late Roman – 20%.
Flint: 48 items (see Appendix A).
Stone: three basalt items.
Additional surveys: none.

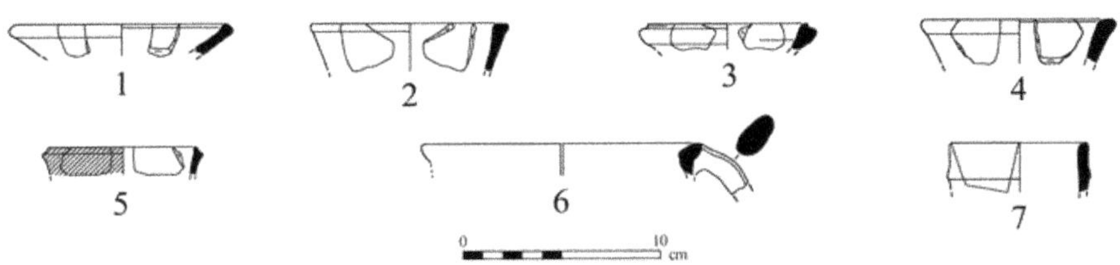

236. Pottery from **Wadi el-Haiyat (4)**: 1. Bowl, lt br, IA II; 2. Bowl, br, LR; 3-4. Jugs, dk br, IA I-II; 5. Jug, br, rd slip, LR; 6-7. Jugs, lt br, LR.

Site 104: 19-15/23/10

NIRAN (5)

Israel grid: 1922/1530
UTM grid: 7311/5399
Elevation: 180 m b.s.l., 0 m a.s.a.
Name: nearest place
Site type: enclosures
Area: 2 dunams (2000 sq. m)
Topography: shoulder above wadi
Rock type: Judea Group
Soil type: alluvium
Soil quality: 2
Cultivation: none
Cisterns: none
Water source: Nahal Yitav (182), 3 km distant
Road: Beit She'an–Jericho (B10), 2.3 km distant
Visit: December 2006

Two enclosures situated on high shoulders on both sides of a deep wadi, 1.8 km south-west of Netiv Hagdud. There is a broad lookout of the Jordan Valley from the site to the region of Niran and Wadi Maqor edh-Dhib.

The enclosures are built of one row of large undressed local stones. Following are the enclosure descriptions:

1. Eastern enclosure: is elliptical, about 22 m across. In the west is attached a room.
2. Western enclosure: diameter 40 m. Most of the encircling wall has been preserved while the eastern part has been silted up. At the centre of the eastern part there is a round room, well-built of upright standing walls. A wall projects towards the centre.

No sherds were found in these enclosures.

Additional surveys: none.

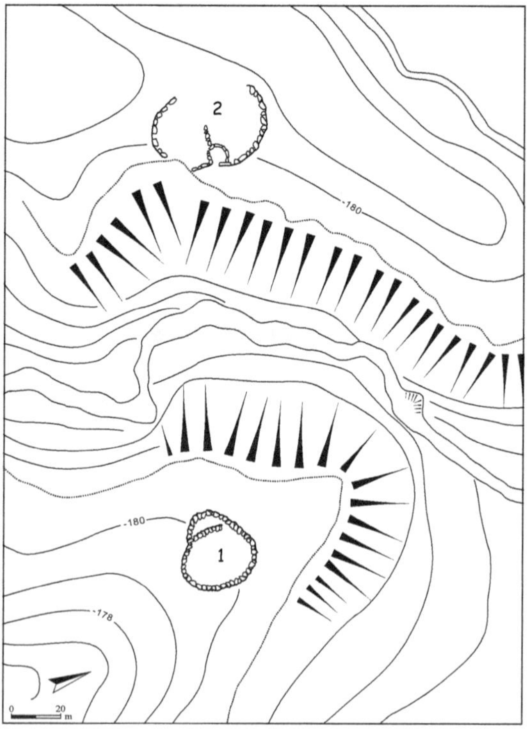

237. Plan of **Niran** (5).

Site 105: 18-15/92/5

WADI EL-HAIYAT (6)

Israel grid: 1890/1528
UTM grid: 7279/5396
Elevation: 0 m a.s.l., 100 m b.s.a.
Name: nearest place
Site type: walls and flint scatter
Area: 0.5 dunam (500 sq. m)
Topography: spur and moderate slope
Rock type: Judea Group
Soil type: stony-desert
Soil quality: 3
Cultivation: none
Cisterns: none
Water source: Nahal Yitav (182), 2 km distant
Road: 'Aujah Tahtah–'Ein 'Aujah (C48), 2 km distant
Visits: May 2011 and more; 40 sherds

A small site near the tributaries of Wadi el-Haiyat, on a moderate spur descending eastward to the unpaved Netiv Hagdud–Yitav road.

The remnants of structures do not add up to a full picture. They indicate the existence of several houses, connected perhaps to the site of Wadi el-Haiyat (4 [no. 103]) above it. The place has been separated from the larger site by the surveyors because it is a Pre-Pottery Neolithic flint scatter, differentiating it from the other nearby sites.

Pottery: (body sherds): Iron I-II – 75%; Byzantine – 12.5%; unidentified – 12.5%.
Flint: 122 items, Pre-Pottery Neolithic B-C (see Appendix A).
Additional surveys: none.

♦ ♦ ♦

Site 106: 18-15/92/8

WADI EL-HAIYAT (5)

Israel grid: 1891/1528
UTM grid: 7279/5396
Elevation: 25 m b.s.l., 100 m b.s.a.
Name: nearest place
Site type: structures and flint scatter
Area: 2 dunams (2000 sq. m)
Topography: spur and moderate slope
Rock type: Judea Group
Soil type: stony-desert
Soil quality: 3
Cultivation: none
Cisterns: none
Water source: Nahal Yitav (182), 2 km distant
Road: 'Aujah Tahtah–'Ein 'Aujah (C48), 2 km distant
Visit: May 2011; 50 sherds

A site close to Wadi el-Haiyat on a spur sloping eastward to the unpaved Netiv Hagdud–Yitav road.

There are several small enclosures, built of large stones, on the spur and structure remains with a moderate sherd scatter. There is also a Pre-Pottery Neolithic flint scatter.

Pottery: Middle Bronze II – 20%; Iron I – 16%; Iron II – 40%; Late Roman – 24%.
Flint: 145 items, Pre-Pottery Neolithic C (see Appendix A).
Additional surveys: none.

238. Pottery from **Wadi el-Haiyat** (5): 1. CP A, dk br, IA I; 2. Perforated cp, dk br, MB II.

♦ ♦ ♦

Site 107: 18-15/92/6

WADI EL-HAIYAT (10)

Israel grid: 1891/1527
UTM grid: 7280/5396
Elevation: 0 m a.s.l., 100 m b.s.a.
Name: nearest place
Site type: enclosure and encampment
Area: 1.5 dunam (1500 sq. m)
Topography: spur and moderate slope
Rock type: Judea Group
Soil type: stony-desert
Soil quality: 3
Cultivation: none
Cisterns: none
Water source: Nahal Yitav (182), 2 km distant
Road: 'Aujah Tahtah–'Ein 'Aujah (C48), 2 km distant
Visits: May 2011 and more; 100 sherds

A site on the southern bank of one of the Wadi el-Haiyat tributaries, west of the unpaved Netiv Hagdud–Yitav road.

The site consist of a large enclosure about 50 m in diameter whose southern part has not survived. The wall is built of one row of medium-sized stones. Between the enclosure and the bank of the wadi are remains of walls and a large stone with a cupmark.

A small tumulus was found within the enclosure. Additional walls, probably terraces, were found in the vicinity.

The site is outstanding, with particularly numerous sherds, testifying to the presence of tent encampments for many generations.

Pottery: Iron I – 10%; Iron II – 15%; Persian – 5%; Hellenistic – 5%; Late Roman – 40%; Byzantine – 5%; Medieval – 15%; Ottoman – 5%.
Additional surveys: none.

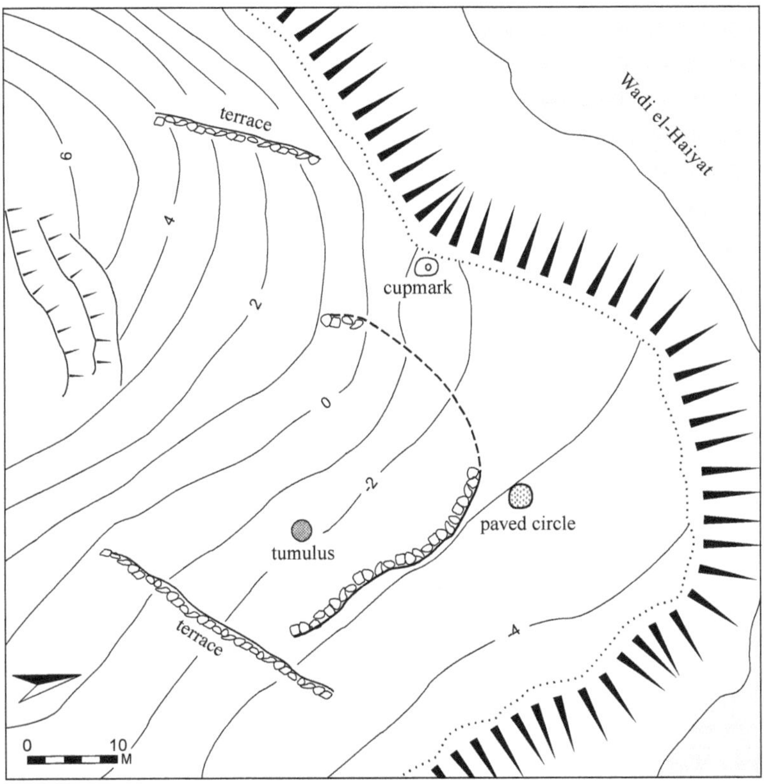

239. Plan of **Wadi el-Haiyat** (10).

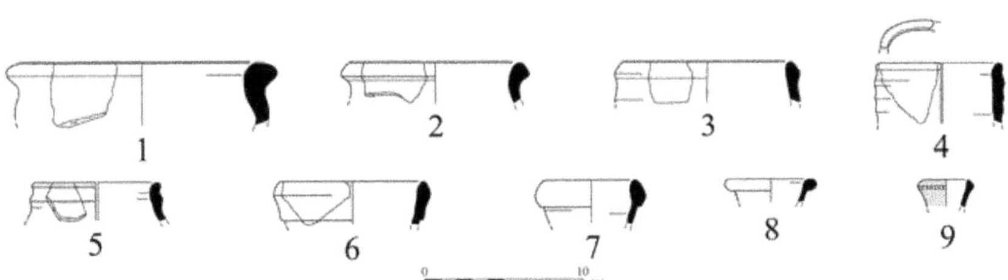

240. Pottery from **Wadi el-Haiyat** (10): 1. CP, lt br, IA (?); 2. Jar, lt br, Hel (?); 3. Jar, lt br, LR-Byz; 4. Jar, lt br, MA (?); 5. Jar, dk br, LR-Byz; 6. Jug, lt br, LR-Byz; 7. Jug, dk br, LR-Byz; 8. Jug, lt gr, LR-Byz; 9. Pipe, lt br, br slip, Ott.

Site 108: 19-15/42/4

ARCHELAIS NORTH-WEST

Israel grid: 1943/1527
UTM grid: 7332/5396
Elevation: 240 m b.s.l., 0 m a.s.a.
Name: nearest place
Site type: courtyard and structures
Area: 2 dunams (2000 sq. m)
Topography: slope
Rock type: Judea Group
Soil type: Lisan marl
Soil quality: 2
Cultivation: none
Cisterns: none
Water source: Nahal Yitav (182), 2 km distant
Road: Beit She'an–Jericho (B10), next to the site
Visits: November 2010 and more; 40 sherds

A site on a slope in the north of the ridge west of Archelais (its local name is et-Tulul), 200 m west of the Beit She'an–Jericho road, and 1 km east of Niran. The unpaved Niran–Yitav road passes to the north-west of the site.

In the northern part, below the low cliffs, is a square courtyard, measuring 40×40 m, built on a high slope overlooking the plain of the city of Archelais (Kh. Beiyudhat [Site 111]). The construction of the 1 m-thick perimeter wall is good, of two rows of large stones. There is a square room, measuring 4×4 m in the south-eastern corner of the courtyard. No other structures were found

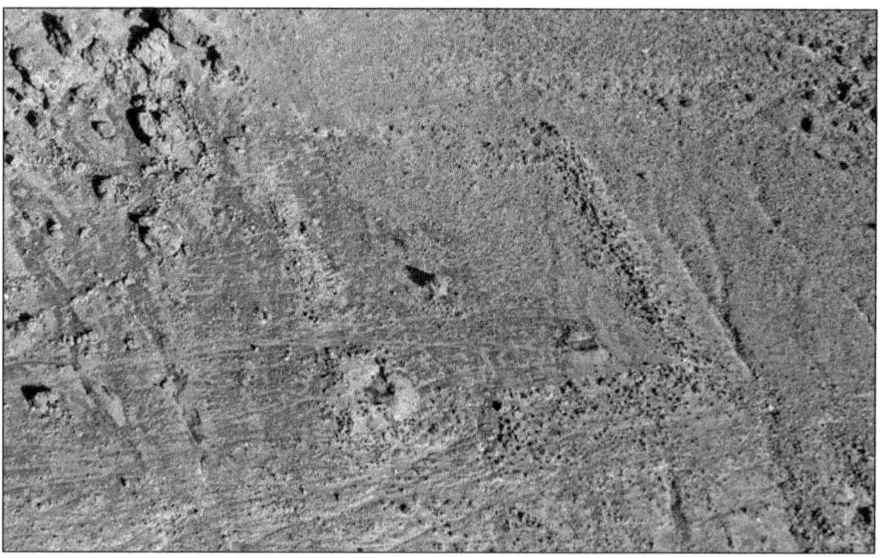

241. **Archelais North-West:** Aerial view north-west at the courtyard, 2012. At left is the et-Tulul cliff (A. Solomon).

in the yard, except an especially large boulder. The courtyard rests on a thick support wall, built of small stones across the slope in the east.

In the slope below and east of the site are several remains of structures, with no obvious format. It seems that the area, which is mostly built up, was part of the city of Archelais. The walls, which are about 0.6 m, are built from two rows of pebbles and local stones. Remains of an enclosure built of small stones was found south of the courtyard and below the cliffs.

The principal aqueduct to Archelais passed from north to south, about 120 m east and below the courtyard, a linkage between this upper courtyard and the aqueduct is probable, but is not certain.

Pottery: Late Roman – 80%; Byzantine – 20%.
Additional surveys: none.

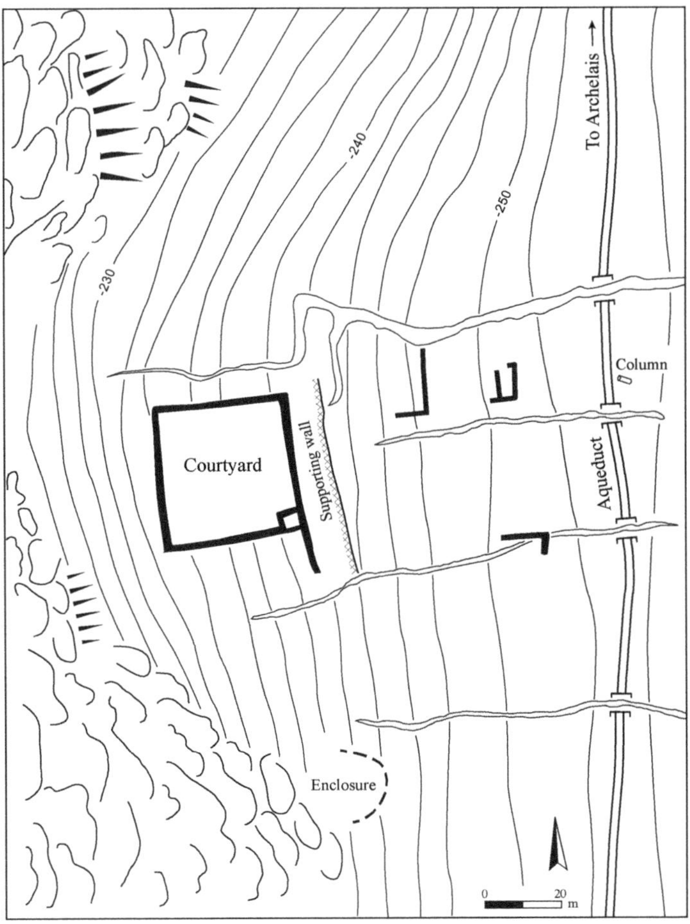

242. Plan of **Archelais North-West.**

Site 109: 18-15/92/7

WADI EL-HAIYAT (9)

Israel grid: 1893/1527
UTM grid: 7282/5395
Elevation: 30 m b.s.l., 100 m b.s.a.
Name: nearest place
Site type: enclosure
Area: 1.5 dunam (1500 sq. m)
Topography: spur edge
Rock type: Judea Group
Soil type: stony dessert
Soil quality: 3
Cultivation: none
Cisterns: none
Water source: Nahal Yitav (182), 2 km distant
Road: 'Aujah Tahtah–'Ein 'Aujah (C48), 2 km distant
Visit: May 2011; 66 sherds (main site), 25 sherds (western house)

A site close to the west side of the unpaved Netiv Hagdud–Yitav road, between the tributaries of Wadi el-Haiyat and Wadi Nabiris.

The site is on an artificial mound formed by supporting walls, located above the high eastern bank of the wadi. The site has been badly damaged by the construction of the road.

There are three parts at least in the site:

1. In the centre and by the road are remains of damaged walls, and on the northern side is a small structure.
2. The 'western house' is about 70 m north-west of the main site, and contains late medieval pottery. To the north-west is a 4 m diameter tumulus.

243. **Wadi el-Haiyat (9)**: remains of structures (no. 1 in the plan), view east, 2011 (S. Bar).

3. East of the 'western house' are two courtyards, and stones cleared to the side of the road. The date of the stone clearance is uncertain.
   Additional wall remains are also found to the west of the wadi channel.

Pottery: in the site: Iron I-II – 30%; Late Roman – 45%; Byzantine – 10%; Medieval – 15%; In the western house: Late Roman – 40%; Medieval – 60%.
Miscellaneous find: A copper Mamluk coin; glass bracelets.
Additional surveys: none.

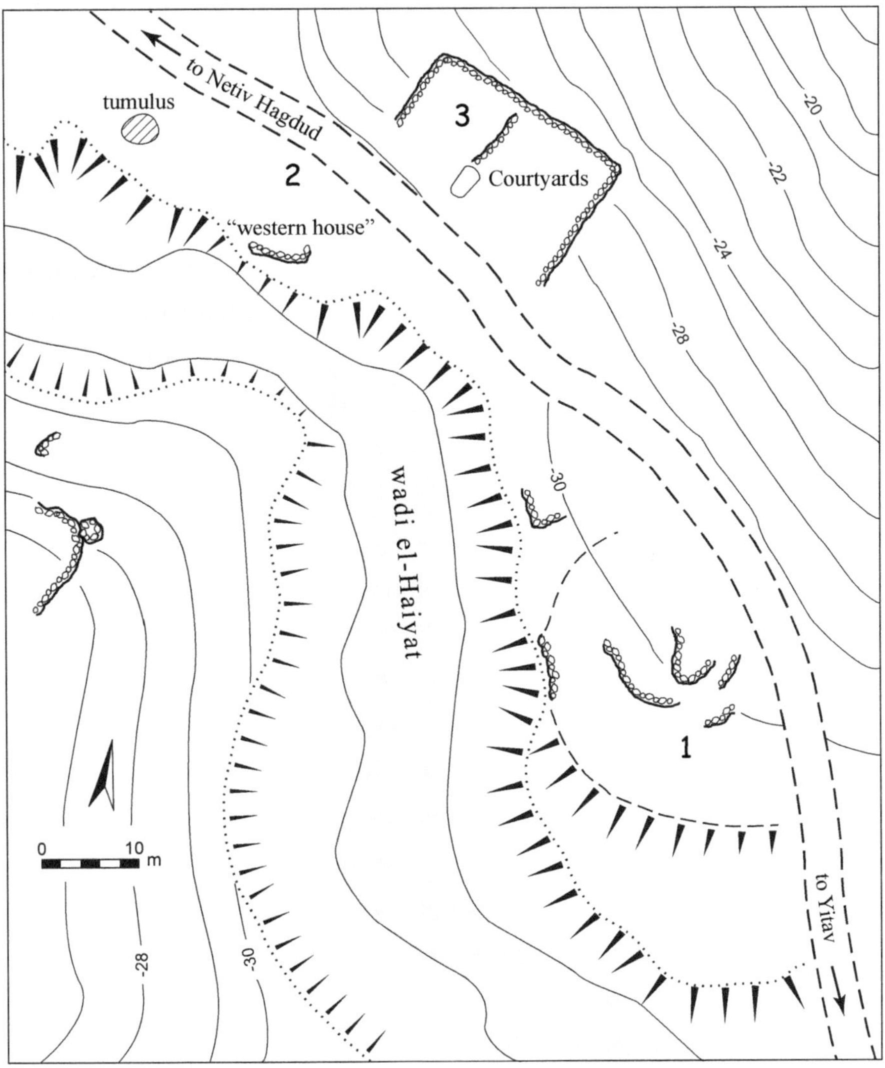

244. Plan of **Wadi el-Haiyat (9)**.

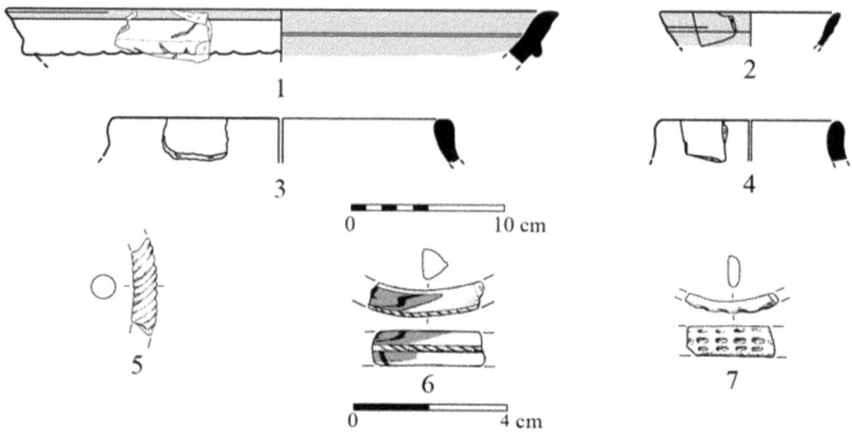

245. Finds from the **western house in Wadi el-Haiyat (9)**: 1. Basin, wh, amber slip, rope dec, MA; 2. Bowl (?), rd, Rom; 3. Jar, dk br; 4. Jar, rd; 5. Bracelet, green glass; 6. Bracelet, variegated green glass; 7. Bracelet, blue glass.

♦ ♦ ♦

Site 110: 18-15/82/1

WADI NABIRIS (2)

Israel grid: 1889/1526
UTM grid: 7278/5394
Elevation: 0 m a.s.l., 40 m b.s.a.
Name: nearest place
Site type: village (?)
Area: 15 dunams (1.5 ha)
Topography: slope, spur and narrow gully
Rock type: Judea Group

Soil type: stony dessert
Soil quality: 2
Cultivation: none
Cisterns: none
Water source: Nahal Yitav (182), 1.9 km distant
Road: 'Aujah Tahtah–'Ein 'Aujah (C48), 1.8 km distant
Visit: March 2004; 47 sherds

A large site spread over narrow spurs at the foot of the eastern ridge of the Samaria Mountains, 2.5 km north-west of Yitav. A high ridge rises to the west of the site. The site is located on both sides of a rocky ravine in a large rockfall. There is a fine view of the Wadi el-Haiyat valley.

The main part of the site is on a broad spur, about 70 m wide, between two deep channels, tributaries of Wadi Nabiris. The other part is on a spur south of the main channel.

In the centre of the northern spur is a round tower (no. 1) about 10 m in diameter built as three concentric stone circles. The tower is built from large stones, and around it a collapse of large stones indicates that the structure was once several metres high.

About 25 m south and west of this tower were located three round or oval courtyards, built of large stones (no. 3). A two-room broadroom structure is attached to the north-westernmost one. About 30 m east of the tower is a 13 m diameter enclosure (no. 2). Two rectangular rooms abut it from the south. Walls surrounding this structure suggest additional earlier and/or dismantled enclosures at the spot.

On a narrow spur between a junction of wadis and south-west of the main part is a 5×5 m structure and three squares with stones cleared around them, the purpose of which is not known (no. 4).

In another part of the site, on a spur south of the main part, is another unit (no. 5), with a two-room structure and a built courtyard, 10×10 m. Further

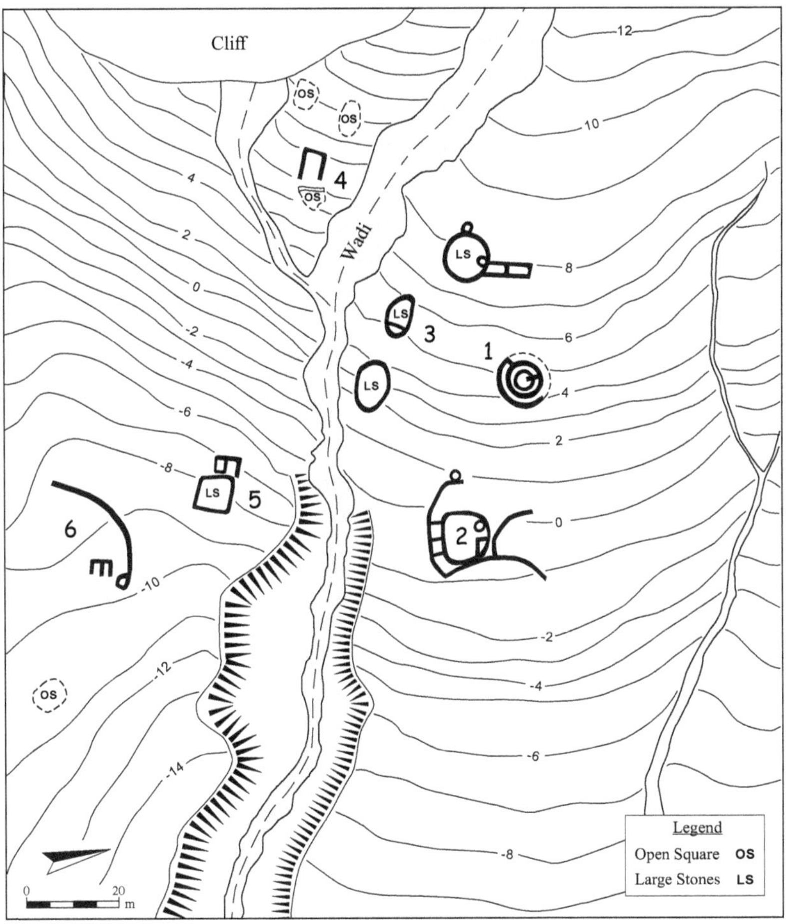

246. Plan of **Wadi Nabiris (2)**.

south are remains of another enclosure (no. 6) with a two-roomed structure at its end.

The location is outstanding, in an area covered by large stones, giving the place very good defense qualities.

Few sherds were found.

Pottery: Iron I-II (body sherds) – 53%; Early Roman – 21%; Late Roman – 15%; Modern – 11%.
Flint: 110 items, Iron Age (see Appendix A).
Additional surveys: none.

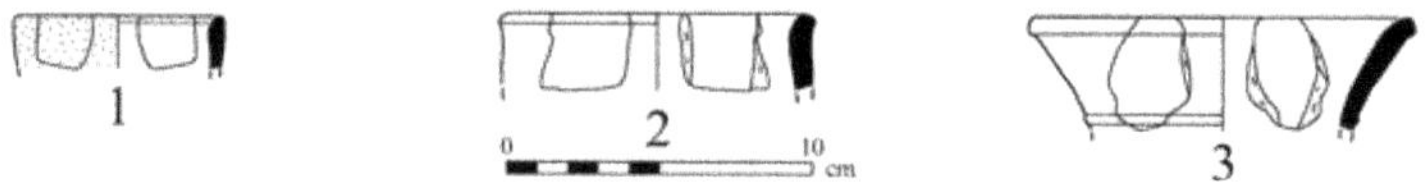

247. Pottery from **Wadi Nabiris (2)** – all Rom: 1. Bowl, buff, wh slip; 2. Bowl, lt br; 3. Jug, lt br.

♦ ♦ ♦

Site 111: 19-15/42/1

KHIRBET BEIYUDHAT (ARCHELAIS)

Israel grid: 1945/1526 (centre)
UTM grid: 7334/5396
Elevation: 270 m b.s.l., 0 m a.s.a.
Name: ancient and in the map
Site type: city
Area: 355 dunams (35.5 ha)
Topography: intersected plain
Rock type: Judea Group
Soil type: Lisan marl
Soil quality: 2
Cultivation: none
Cisterns: at least two
Water source: Nahal Yitav (182), 2 km distant
Road: Beit She'an–Jericho (B10), next to the site
Visits: March 2003 and many more; 250 sherds

A city in the Jordan Valley plain, north of the modern village of 'Aujah et-Tahtah, and 1.5 km east of Niran. The site is crossed by the modern Beit She'an–Jericho road.

The site was partially excavated from 1986 to 1991 by H. Hizmi (1993; 2008a; 2008b). In the winter of 2003-2004 we dealt with measuring, mapping and a fresh investigation of Kh. Beiyudhat. The results of the published excavation were also used for the following description, which is based mainly on our new mapping of the city.

A. Location, geographical data and the research history

Kh. el-Beiyudhat is situated in the southern part of the Jordan Valley, 11 km north of Jericho. The city is on a broad plain sloping gently eastward from the ridge (et-Tulul) bordering the ancient Beit She'an–Jericho road in the west, and about 2 km north of the Wadi 'Aujah riverbed. The plain is a spacious area of Lisan marl, descending eastward to the River Jordan.

The area of the city is roughly 355 dunams (35.5 ha) – 810 m from north to south by 430 m from east to west. In the west it borders a relatively high ridge, and in the north a steep ridge on which a fortress is located (el-Maskarah). The city probably extended further south, over an area which is now beneath the houses of the modern village of el-'Aujah.

The site was described for the first time by Guèrin (1874: 227-228), who visited it in April 1870 on his way from the south, relating as follows: "At 9:15 we rode by another site of ruins named Kh. el-Maskarah. I discovered here at ground level traces of ancient aqueduct, ruined and dry: in the past it carried water from 'Ein el-'Aujah. This section seems to me to be part of the aqueduct mentioned by Josephus and attributed to King Archelaus. Currently there is not a single palm growing in the once-watered plain, yet the name Maskarah, given to this site, seemingly testifies to it having been surrounded by date palms in the past."

248. **Archelais:** Aerial view northward of the city, 2012. At bottom left is the church complex and at top right are the remains of the tower (A. Solomon).

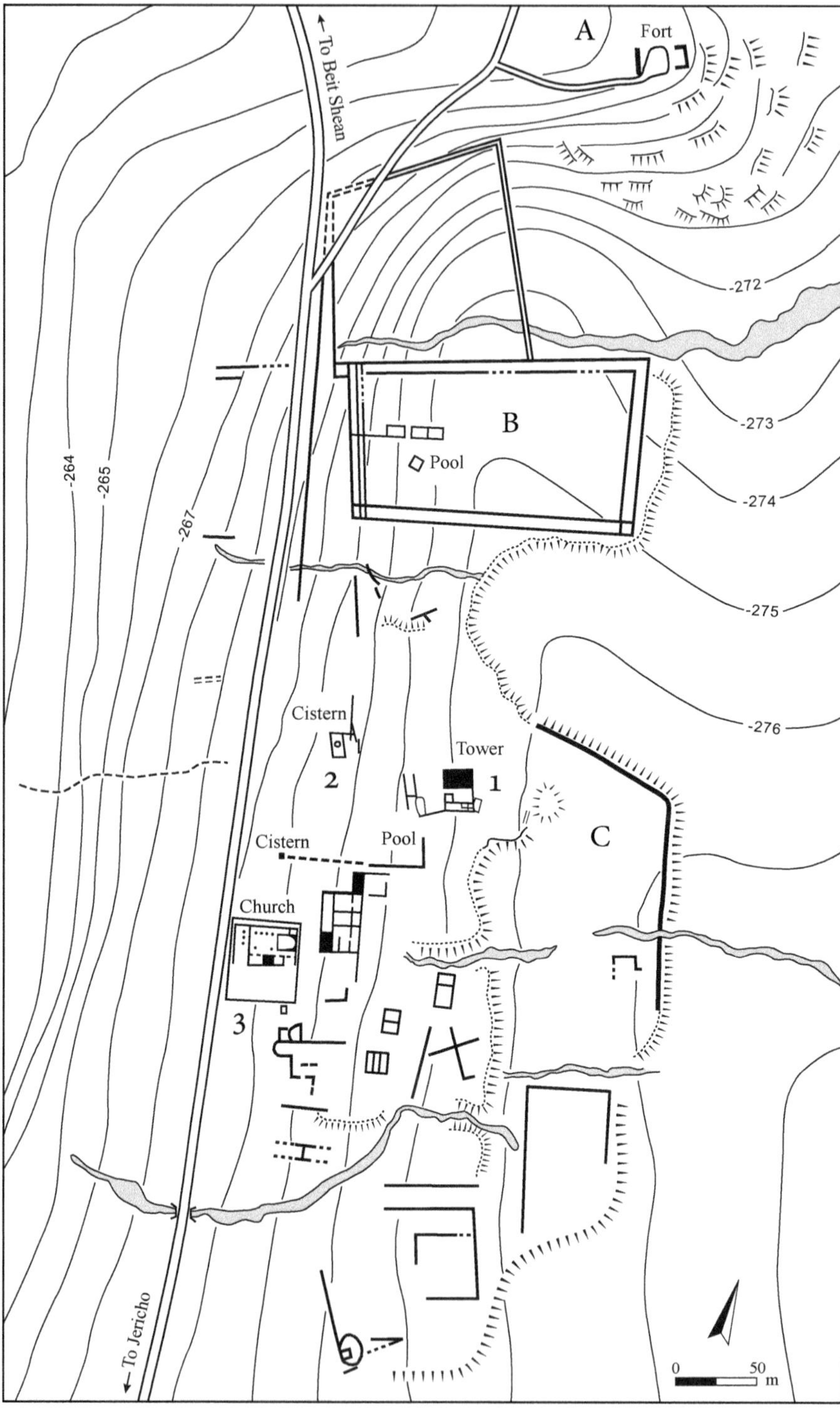

249. Plan of **Kh. el-Beiyudhat (Archelais).**

The British surveyors (Conder and Kitchener 1882: 391-392) did not note the site's dimensions, and only remarked: "Khurbet el Beiyudat (P r). – A watch-tower, with a moat beside the road, perhaps a military post; north of it is another little watch-tower."

Glueck visited it in 1943, describing it as: "It consists today of the remains of a large *birkeh* or reservoir. This *birkeh*, however, is so full of dirt now...On its east side are the remains of a stone wall, 1.5 m thick... It seems likely that water for the *birkeh* was led into it from one of the canals which diverted the water of the Wadi el-'Auja." (Glueck 1951: 413). Glueck proposed to identify the place as Magdalsenna, from the books of Nehemiah, Ezra and The Antiquities of the Jews (Book 17).

Bar-Adon's team surveyed the site in 1967, as part of the Emergency Survey, describing it as follows (Bar-Adon 1972: site 22): "A ruin measuring 600×250 m. Definite house remains, with rooms. Around some are stone walls enclosing courtyards. In the middle of the ruin rises a mound, on which there are construction remains of dressed stones and mosaic stone flooring [the tower, A. Z.]. Pottery find: from the Roman I, Roman II, Byzantine and Arab periods ". (translation from the Hebrew).

The Madaba Map shows a tower east of Archelais. Avi-Yonah assumed that this was Magdalsenna. Based on the excavations, Hizmi (2008a; 2008b) proposed identifying the site with the city of Archelais: this identification has been accepted.

B. History

Josephus Flavius tells of the foundation of the city by Archelaus, Herod's son, as follows: "He (Archelaus son of Herod) also rebuilt the royal palace in Jericho in splendid fashion, and diverted half the water that served to irrigate the village of Neara, leading it into a plain that had been planted by him with palm trees. He also created a village and gave it the name of Archelais" (Ant. XVII, xiii: 1).

After the banishment of Archelaus by Augustus Caesar the city was transferred to Salome, Herod's sister. In her will she bequeathed the city to Julia, Augustus' wife, and Josephus describes it thus: "...Marcus Ambivulus, during whose administration Salome, the sister of King Herod, died. To Julia she bequeathed Jamnia and its territory, together with Phasaelis, which lay in the plain, and Archelais, where palms are planted in very great numbers and the dates are of highest quality" (Ant. XVIII, ii: 2).

Pliny the Elder (1st century CE) notes that Archelais is situated between Jericho and Phasaelis, and the place is famous for the quality of its fruit (Natural History XIII, ix: 44 [Rackham 1962]).

When Julia died Archelais became Caesar's property. Agrippa I received it in 41 CE, and after his death the place was transferred to the possession of the Roman governor in Caesarea. In the Ptolemy's Canon (VII, xvi: 5 [Nobbe 1966]) from the 2nd century CE, the place is mentioned as a settlement north of Jericho and Phasaelis. The Peutinger map (2nd century CE), recorded a distance of 12 miles between Jericho and Archelais (Miller 1962: Segmentum X:1-2), and such is its relative location also in the Madaba map (6th century CE [Avi-Yonah 1953: 140 and pl. 5]).

A document from the beginning of the Byzantine era (Russell 1980: 50) states that the place was affected, with several other settlements, by the 363 CE earthquakes.

C. Description

1. The city plan

Hizmi (2008b: 1601) drew the general plan of the city, differing in some details from ours.

Archelais is the largest Roman-Byzantine site in the Jordan Valley, except perhaps for Roman Jericho. Other cities in this category are Kh. es-Sakut (Zertal and Bar 2017: site 32), Corae (Tell es-Simadi and Qarawet et-Tahta in Zertal and Bar 2017: sites 84, 85) and Phasaelis (Kh. Fusayil, Site 34), all of which are smaller than Kh. Beiyudhat.

The city is built as a north-south strip. There are three reasons for this arrangement:

A. The cliffs, which rise 15 m above the plain, limit the city in the north. The fortress of el-Maskarah in the eastern part of the cliffs overlooks the city.

B. A long north-south ridge, et-Tulul, runs parallel to the city, preventing expansion of the city to the west. At the bottom of the ridge are located most of the aqueducts from Wadi 'Aujah. The difference in elevation between the ridge and the city enabled the supply of water to the city and its agricultural areas.

C. The city is built on an artificial step, 2–3 m above the plain east of it. A thick stone wall, about 2 m high, nearly 200 m long runs along the step. It supported the podium and/or served as a defence wall for the city in the east. The irregular form of the step is the result of the considerable silting and the ravines intersecting the city area.

2. The main parts of the city

A. The citadel (el-Maskarah):

On the northern ridge, enclosed by cliffs descending eastward, are remains of a large stone structure, perhaps a fortress. The structure has been badly damaged by modern activities. It is reached by a modern asphalt road, and there is a fine lookout from it to the Jordan Valley plains.

B. The northern quarter:

Below and south of the northern cliffs are two large square enclosures, in different orientations. The more prominent southern one is 150×100 m, built with two parallel walls, 5 m apart. Along the inner wall are columns, pedestals and other structures. In the western part of the enclosure are a pool and other structures.

The nature of the northern enclosure is not clear. It appears to be a part of an aqueduct descending from the northern cliffs, but other explanations are possible.

Another enclosure was excavated by Hizmi, and was identified to have been a 'road station' 40 dunams (4 ha) in area. According to the excavation, the walls are built of two rows of stones with a fill of earth and small stones. In the inner part, parallel to the southern and eastern walls and 3 m from them, is a row of stone columns. Two parallel rows of stone columns were exposed along the northern and western walls. The entrance, opening on a wide courtyard, is at the centre of the eastern wall. In the south-western part of the enclosure there is ritual bath (*miqveh*) with two pools linked to each other by a shallow duct (this is most probably the pool drawn in our survey map, Fig. 249:B). Outside the enclosure, near its north-western corner, is another pool entered by stairs. All the pools were plastered. West and south-east of the *miqve* were structures which were apparently used for supply and drainage of the water. In the south-western corner of the enclosure is a cluster of rooms, including semi-rounded installations and water reservoirs. The excavation report notes that the find of sherds and stone artefacts is typical of the Herodian period. Among the finds was a trimmed multi-nozzle oil lamp and a 6th year Agrippa I coin (41/2 CE).

C. The centre of the site:

This part includes the tower, the residential structure and the church, exposed in the excavation. Many other structures, some of them revealed during the excavation, still protrude above the surface. The walls are two stones thick. At the south part of the site are additional enclosures and structures, the nature of which is not clear. Following is a description of the remains exposed and published from Hizmi's excavations:

1. **The tower:** this is a square tower 17×14.3 m, preserved 9 m high. The walls are built of ashlars in the alternating stretchers and headers method and are 1.2 m thick. The core of the walls is of soft limestone reinforced by clay and plaster. The inside of the tower is divided into square rooms, two of which (measuring 3.5×3 m and 3×2.5 m) have been fully exposed. Their wall thickness is 1.1 m with a fill of stones 3 m high, the ashlar facing of which did not survive. The entrance to the tower was not found, and the excavator

proposed an entry in the upper part, maybe by ladder. Bowls decorated with vegetal motives, trimmed oil lamps, stone artefacts and architectonic elements were found in the tower. Among the noteworthy coins are those of the Roman procurators Valerius Gratus, Pontius Pilatus, and Antonius Felix, and an Agrippa I coin.

2. **The residential structure:** Remains of a residential structure about 360 sq. m in area were exposed north-west of the tower. The walls are of two rows of stones with a fill of small stones and earth. The walls and floors are plastered. A portico with two column pedestals leads to a courtyard nearly 100 sq. m in area, divided into two by a row of columns, and roofed in its eastern part. The eastern wing, comprising two rooms, is entered through the roofed courtyard. East and south of the courtyard are dwelling and storage rooms. In the south wing are rooms arranged in two rows. No entrance from the courtyard to the rooms has been discovered; however, openings lead from room to room. A *miqveh* with two pools connected by a channel was found in the north-western part of the structure.
3. **The church:** 100 m south-west of the tower were exposed remains of a Byzantine church, built as a basilica with an apse, the outer dimensions of which are 23.6 m by 15.5 m. The structure has three spaces: the nave with aisles on both sides, separated from the nave by two colonnades. The narthex and atrium at the front of the church have been exposed. The ashlar

250. **Archelais**, view eastward to the remains of the tower at the city centre, 2012 (S. Bar).

stones of the walls, which are 80 cm thick, were almost certainly taken from the remains of the tower. The other walls are brick-built. The floors of the church are covered by mosaics with geometric patterns. Some of have Greek inscriptions (and see below).

The narthex is 6.2 m wide, divided into two by a colonnade of four columns. The grave of a woman from a later period of the church was found here. An opening, 1.2 m wide, led from the narthex to the central prayer hall. There is an inscription in Greek in the mosaic floor of the apse. The northern aisle is 3.3 m wide and in eastern wall an opening leads to a square paved with stone slabs. Another Greek inscription was found in the mosaic of the southern aisle. At the end of the aisle an opening leads to an outside room attached to the church.

The altar and the apse are one unit elevated above the floor by about 60 cm. This stage (8×5.2 m) is enclosed by grille slabs supported by pillars 1 m apart. On three sides of the stage are entrances about 60 cm wide, ascended by two steps. North-west of the altar stage is a pulpit, the ambo. Signs of a fire indicate that the upper part of the stage was made of wood. Beside the stage is a stone bowl, apparently a baptismal font. The apse (8×3.2 m) has been preserved to a height of three courses, and on its plastered walls there are red paint and drawn crosses. The apse is paved with a geometric mosaic laid in two phases. In the second phase the floor was decorated with

251. **Archelais:** Aerial view eastward of the church, 2012 (A. Solomon).

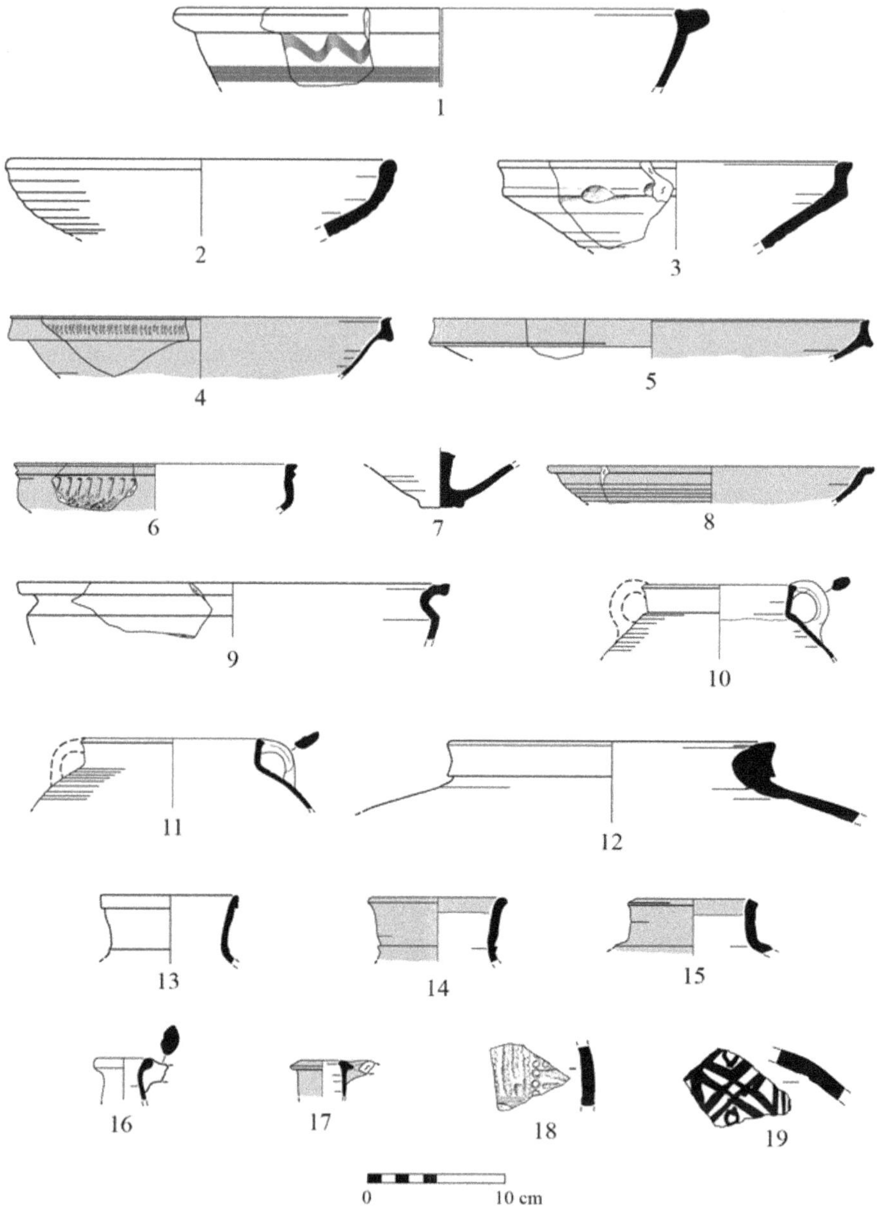

252. Pottery from **Kh. el-Beiyudhat (Archelais)**: 1. Basin, lt br, incised dec, Byz-EM; 2-3, 7. Bowls, wh, EM; 4. Bowl, rd, rd slip, roulette dec, Rom-Byz; 5. Bowl, rd, rd slip, Rom-Byz; 6. Bowl, lt br, rd slip, roulett dec, Rom-Byz; 8. Frying pan, lt br, rd slip, Rom-Byz; 9. CP, lt br, ER; 10. CP, blk, Rom-Byz; 11. CP, rd, Rom-Byz; 12. Dolium, lt br, Rom-Byz; 13. Jar, blk, Rom-Byz; 14. Jar, dk br, blk slip, Rom; 15. Jar, lt br, blk slip, Rom; 16. Jug, dk br, rd slip (?), Rom-Byz; 18. Sherd, lt br, roulette dec, Rom-Byz; 19. Sherd, lt br, violet dec, MA.

two amphoras, out of one of which sprout boughs of a vine with bunches of grapes, and a medallion with a cross in it. At the centre of the mosaic is another inscription in Greek bearing a date. Remains of a stone reliquary decorated with a cross were found on the stage. A marble chest, with a carved cross was found near the south aisle.

The Greek inscriptions in the mosaic floors (except no. 4, below) are set in a *tabula ansata*.

Translations of the inscriptions:

1. In the southern aisle: "Lord, help (Thy) servants Aphleos and Lukas the priests, and Stephanus and Sama(ios?) and Eliseos and Lypon."
2. In the room adjoining the church in the south-east: "Lord, remember Lukas the priest, because (this room) was paved at his expenses."
3. At the foot of the stage: "In the time of our most holy and pious bishop Porphyrius, this church was paved, owing to the zeal of the priest Eglon and for the salvation of the benefactors." This Prophyrius probably officiated during the second half of the 6th century CE.
4. "Under the pious reign of our master Flavius Iustinus, [this inscription] was written, in the month of November 12, of the 4th indiction, and the mosaic was made thanks to the God-loving priest Abbossoubbos and to Eliseos son of Saoras son of Salamanes, and to Stephanus and to Georgius." In the apse: apparently, the reference is to Justinian II (565–578 CE); hence the year of the inscription is 570/1 CE.
5. In the room adjacent to the church in the south: "O Lord Jesus Christ, receive the offering of thy servants, John the priest and Abbosobbos, for they erected this room by their exertions." (Di Segni 1993).

There was a limited assortment of types of pottery vessels in the church, mostly bowls, cooking pots and jars. The architectonic elements were built of sandstone, limestone and blackish bituminous limestone (Nebi Mussa stone). Among them there are grille pillars, grille slabs, table feet (altars), a reliquary and an architrave decorated with an egg-and-dart pattern. A sundial on a column drum, 43 cm in diameter and 47.5 cm high, made of Nubian sandstone was also found. On its upper part were engraved the lines of the time scale, and in the centre was an effigy, perhaps Hercules, reclining on his left side. At the bottom was a Greek inscription (not yet deciphered). The sundial was apparently made in the 2nd century CE, and was in use for a long time.

According to the excavator the church was built in the second half of the 5th century CE, and was in service with several alterations during the Persian conquest in 614 CE.

D. The water supply system

Water was supplied to the city by aqueduct from 'Ein 'Aujah, which is about 8.5 km away (see Appendix D). During the excavations the branches of the aqueduct were followed for a distance of 1.2 km. The western section of the aqueduct is rock-cut and the eastern is stone-built: in several places it was supported to prevent collapse. The aqueduct is 1.5 m wide and the duct is 60 cm deep, with several layers of plaster. The water carried by the aqueduct was collected and channelled to the cultivated fields.

During our survey at least five aqueducts at different levels were recorded in the low part of the western cliff. Apparently all of them came from 'Ein 'Aujah and fed the city and its fields by connecting channels. In the northern part of the cliff, above the slope, was a square enclosure, 20×20 m, perhaps connected to the aqueducts (Site 108). The aqueducts crossed the city eastward, and one of the branches passed along and at the bottom of the eastern cliff. The aqueduct branches for irrigating the fields, have been identified and recorded up to 2 km east of the city and south of the northern cliff.

The aqueduct of Archelais is one of the most significant of its type in the Jordan Valley.

E. Archaeological history

The site was established during Iron Age II, apparently as a small settlement. It also existed during the Hellenistic period, and the transition to a city format began in the Herodian period. According to the sherds, the settlement reached its peak in the Late Roman and Byzantine periods, and continued to exist in the Early Moslem and Mamluk periods.

In a return visit in 2017 we noticed that the site had been looted and its south-eastern part was completely destroyed.

Pottery (in our survey): Iron II – 3%; Hellenistic – 4%; Early Roman – 10%; Late Roman – 48%; Byzantine – 21%; Early Moslem – 10%; Medieval (Mamluk) – 4%.
Additional surveys: Glueck 1951: 413; Bar-Adon 1972: site 22.

Site 112: 19-15/02/1

WADI MAQOR EDH-DHIB (3)

Israel grid: 1907/1526
UTM grid: 7297/5393
Elevation: 80 m b.s.l., 30 m b.s.a.
Name: nearest place
Site type: encampment
Area: 1 dunam (1000 sq. m)
Topography: spur above wadi
Rock type: Judea Group
Soil type: stony desert
Soil quality: 2
Cultivation: none
Cisterns: none
Water source: Nahal Yitav (182), 2.5 km distant
Road: 'Aujah Tahtah–'Ein 'Aujah (C48), 2.5 km distant
Visit: May 2007; 10 sherds

A small multi-period encampment site on a hilltop, above the deep channel of Wadi Maqor edh-Dhib, 2.3 km west of Niran.

There are remains of recent walls, Bedouin burials and a small sherd scatter. No significant architecture was found.

Pottery: Iron I–II – 50%; Late Roman – 50%.
Flint: 4 items (see Appendix A).
Additional surveys: none.

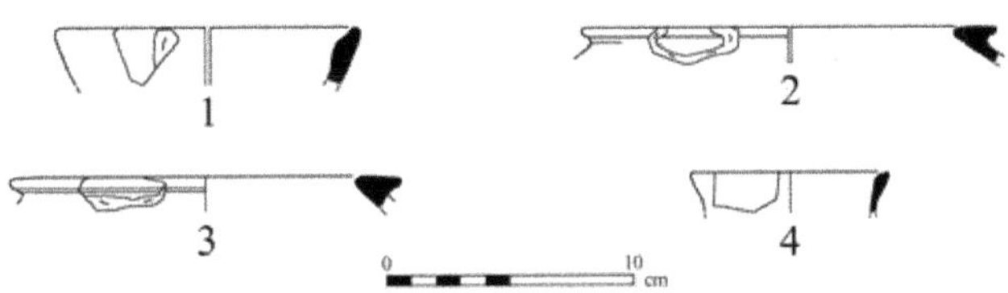

253. Pottery from **Wadi Maqor edh-Dhib (3)**, all LR: 1. Bowl, br; 2-3. CP, rd; 4. Jug, lt br.

Site 113: 18-15/82/2

EL-MASTARAH (1)

Israel grid: 1888/1520
UTM grid: 7276/5388
Elevation: 15 m b.s.l., 50 m b.s.a.
Name: nearest place
Site type: village
Area: 5 dunams (5000 sq. m)
Topography: spur between wadis
Rock type: Judea Group
Soil type: stony desert
Soil quality: 3
Cultivation: none
Cisterns: none
Water source: Nahal Yitav (182), 2 km distant
Road: 'Aujah Tahtah–'Ein 'Aujah (C48), 1.7 km distant
Visits: April 2004 and more; excavation 2017; 180 sherds

A settlement on a narrow spur, in a valley enclosed by mountainous ridges and between merging tributaries of Wadi Nabiris, 2.2 km north-west of Yitav. There is a limited field of view, and south of it are a summit (E.P. 44) and a high saddle. The approach is particularly difficult, and the site is concealed from the open valleys of Wadi el-Haiyat and Wadi Nabiris. This is perhaps the origin of the site's Arabic name, translated as "The hidden one".

The site is a narrow elongated triangle, the apex of which is in the north-east above the confluence of the wadis. It is about 70 m long and the average width

254. **el-Mastarah (1)**, an aerial view northward at the settlement, 2008 (N. Eshed).

is 40 m. There is a dense cluster of structures over an area of 5 dunams (5000 sq. m), built of large and medium-sized fieldstones. Enclosures and courtyards are common, connected to the residential structures. The settlement is protected by the earth cliffs descending to the surrounding wadis.

Below is an account of the parts of the site:

1. In the north-eastern narrow side there are at least two enclosures with walls built of large stones. The eastern one is about 25 m in diameter, and the

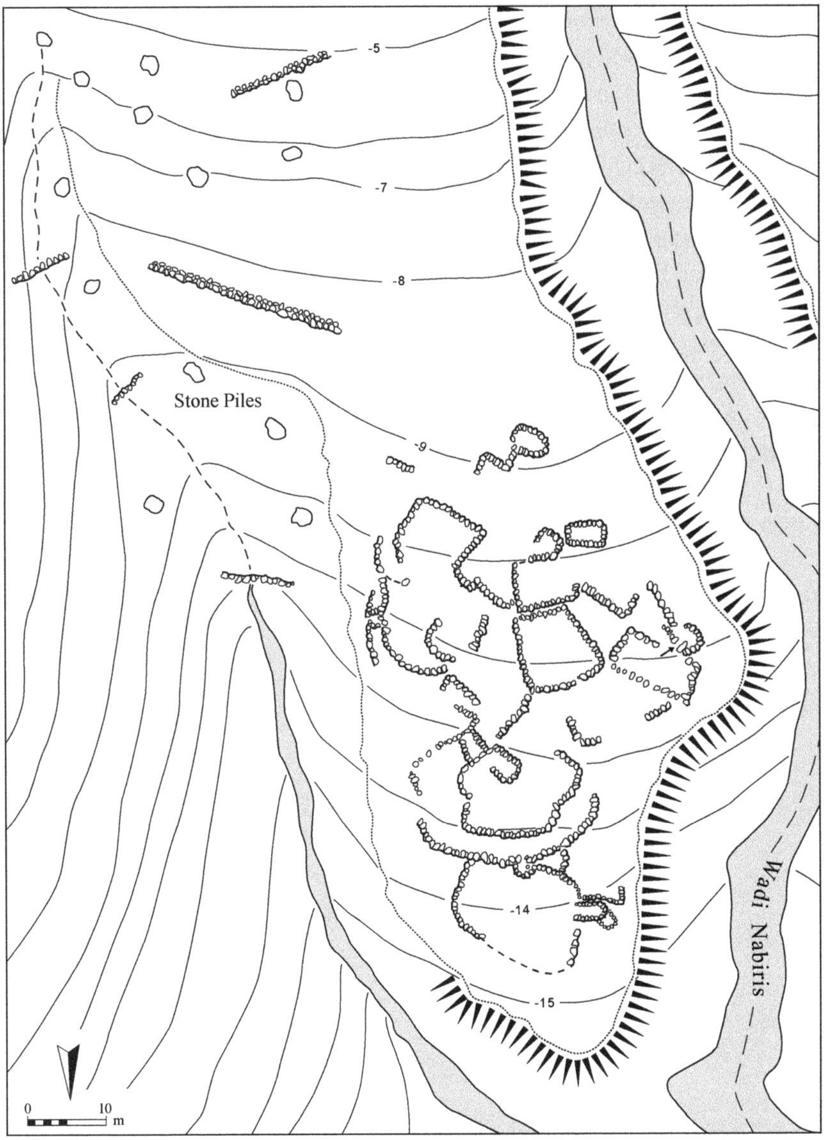

255. Plan of **El-Mastarah** (1).

adjacent western one is about 40 m in diameter. Inside the latter is a courtyard with two attached rooms, each measuring 5×3 m. There is a passage between the enclosures.

2. There are about 10 higher structures in the centre and at the west of the site, built with large stones or boulders, apparently dwellings. Around them are remains of other structures and courtyards which are not well preserved. The densely built area and the numerous collapses make it difficult to identify the structures with certainty.

A permanent settlement whose main livelihood was based on flock husbandry once stood here.

Stretching for 100 m west of the settlement are cultivated fields with terraces and stone clearance heaps. Remains of walls and numerous sherds cover an area of 15 dunams (1.5 ha). Additional structures which probably stood in these areas and their walls were dismantled and the stones used in other structures.

There are a great number of sherds. Apparently the settlement was founded in the MBII and functioned mostly during the Iron Age, with reuse during later periods. The architecture is fairly impressive and is well preserved. It would be worth checking its linkage to the Iron Age settlements situated close to 'Aujah el-Foqa (Site 143).

An excavation project at the site was begun in June 2017 headed by R. Hawkins and D. Ben-Shlomo (Ben-Shlomo and Hawkins 2017). The results of this new project should shed light on this intriguing site and its connection to the Iron Age habitation of the Jordan Valley.

Pottery: Middle Bronze II – 3%; Iron I – 14%; Iron II – 26%; Hellenistic – 9%; Roman – 38%; Byzantine – 5%; Medieval – 5%.
Flint: 15 items, Iron Age (see Appendix A).
Additional surveys: none.

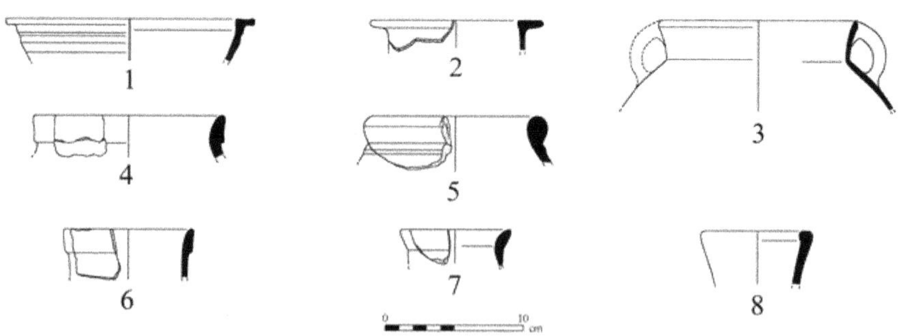

256. Pottery from **el-Mastarah (1)**; 1. Bowl, lt gr, Rom; 2. Bowl, blk, MA; 3. CP, rd, Rom; 4-6. Jars, lt gr, Hel-ER; 7. Jar, rd, Hel-ER; 8. Jug, rd, Byz.

Site 114: 19-15/22/2

WADI MAQOR EDH-DHIB (4)

Israel grid: 1923/1524
UTM grid: 7312/5392
Elevation: 170 m b.s.l., 40 m b.s.a.
Name: nearest place
Site type: enclosures and encampment
Area: 10 dunams (1 ha)
Topography: broad wadi
Rock type: Judea Group
Soil type: stony desert
Soil quality: 1
Cultivation: none
Cisterns: none
Water source: Nahal Yitav (182), 2.2 km distant
Road: 'Aujah Tahtah–'Ein 'Aujah (C48), 2 km distant
Visits: May 2007 and more; 55 sherds

This is a multi-period site south of the wide river bed of Wadi Maqor edh-Dhib and 500 m south-west of Niran.

The site contains two partially preserved circular enclosures, about 20 m in diameter, built of small stones. The enclosures are located on the southern shoulders of the fairly wide valley of the wadi. The construction date is not certain.

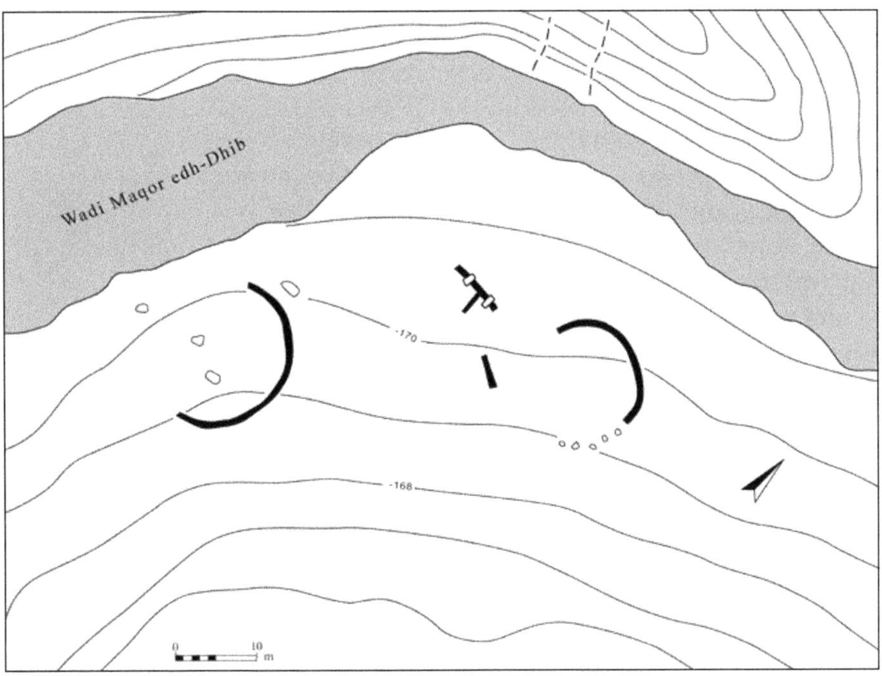

257. Plan of **Wadi Maqor edh-Dhib** (4).

Small paved surfaces were found in and around the enclosures. The construction differs from that in the other ancient enclosures in the vicinity, which are built of large stones. The remains of the numerous walls do not add up to a clear plan.

Pottery: Middle Bronze II – 3%; Iron I – 10%; Iron II – 24%; Hellenistic – 7%; Early Roman – 14%; Late Roman – 24%; Medieval-Ottoman – 18%.
Additional surveys: none.

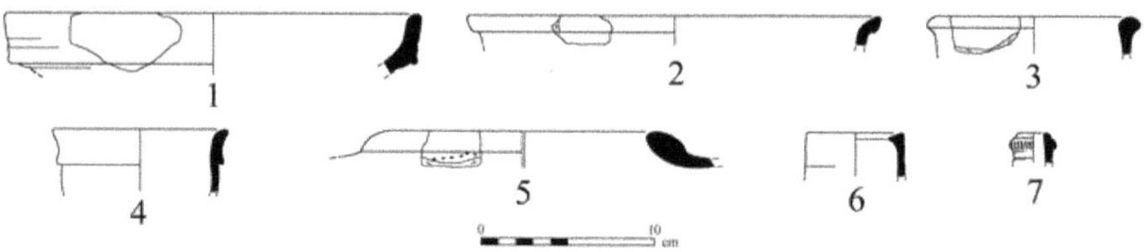

258. Pottery from **Wadi Maqor edh-Dhib (4)**: 1. Bowl, br, MA (?); 2. CP A, br, IA I; 3. Jar, br, LR; 4. Jar, br, Hel-ER; 5. Jar, lt br, dotted dec, MA (?); 6. Jug, rd, Rom; 7. Pipe, gr, Ott.

♦ ♦ ♦

Site 115: 19-15/42/2

ARCHELAIS-WEST

Israel grid: 1942/1523 (centre)
UTM grid: 7331/5392
Elevation: 250 m b.s.l., 30 m b.s.a.
Name: nearest place
Site type: courtyards, structures and aqueducts
Area: 100 dunams (10 ha)
Topography: slope
Rock type: Judea Group
Soil type: stony desert
Soil quality: 2
Cultivation: none
Cisterns: none
Water source: Nahal Yitav (182), 1.5 km distant
Road: Beit She'an–Jericho (B10), next to the site
Visits: February 2008 and more; 50 sherds

A large site on a slope, west of the remains of the city of Archelais, and east of the ridge (et-Tulul) overlooking the ruins of the city. South of the site are a valley and a plain (Sahel 'Aujah), reaching the houses of the nearby village of 'Aujah.

Several structures have been found, presumably in use at the same time:

1. A south-western courtyard, measuring about 40×50 m. The surrounding

wall, built of two rows of stones, is 1 m thick. Inside, 4 m from the western wall is a parallel wall. In the north-eastern corner is a room measuring 6×3 m, which was built together with the courtyard walls.

2. A north-eastern courtyard, measuring about 55×80 m. It is built similarly to no. 1, including the inner wall parallel to the eastern outer wall. From the courtyard walls stretch down the slope eastward, perhaps remains of another structure. In the north-eastern corner is a rectangular room, measuring 7×3 m, built to a similar pattern to no. 1. This is probably the 'southern camp' mentioned by Hizmi (below).

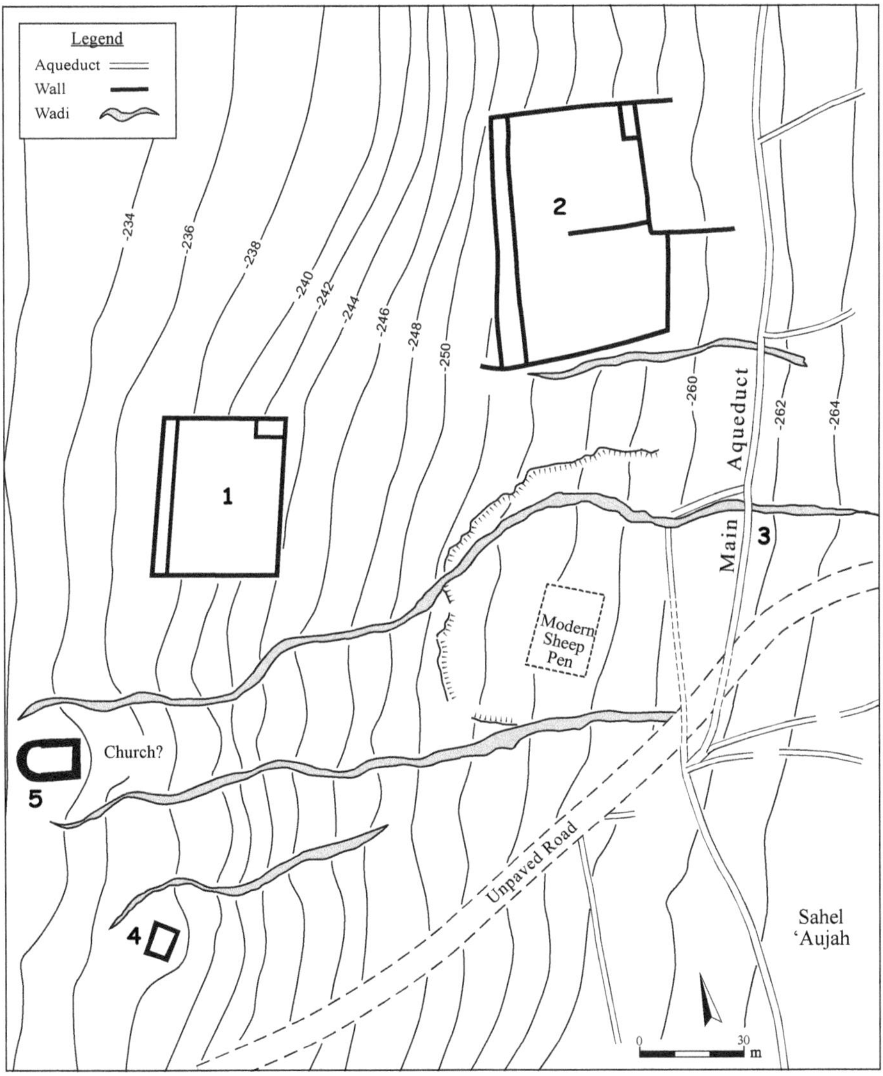

259. Plan of **Archelais-West.**

3. Aqueducts: parallel and east of the north-eastern courtyard no. 2 were found two adjacent plastered aqueducts: upper (1 m wide) and lower (2 m wide). The latter is the main one, from which branch out several aqueducts supplying the city.

   All the aqueducts are built with deep plastered ducts 0.8–1 m wide. The top one stretches about 35 m and then disappears. Most of the aqueducts branch off the intersection with the modern unpaved road.
4. A dugout structure: south of courtyard no. 1 and the church (no. 5), there is a solitary structure measuring 5×4 m on a scarp in the upper part of the slope. The wall thickness, built of two rows of stones, is 0.7 m.
5. An apsidal structure, perhaps a church, has been found on a scarp between courtyard no. 1 and structure no. 4. The construction is good. The wall is 1 m thick and is built of dressed stones with a thick layer of plaster on the outside. This is probably a tall apsidal church, the eastern part of which has been almost totally destroyed.

A thick wall was found on the slope, possibly serving an aqueduct flowing from south to north (not on plan). Some 40 m west of the apsidal structure are remains of a round enclosure, 20 m in diameter, built of medium-sized stones (not on plan).

Bar-Adon (1972: 108) describes it in the Emergency Survey as follows: "Two Roman camps 200 m apart. One, measuring 42×40 m with inner towers in the corners… A structure, measuring 18×12 m, with a curved western wall. One can

260. **Archelais-West:** Aerial view west, 2012. The small courtyard at left and the large one at right. In the background above the ridge is Niran (A. Solomon).

see remains of two storeys with plaster on the walls and a plastered floor... Three aqueducts...the upper aqueduct feeds a pool measuring 80×25 m." (translation from Hebrew).

All the sherds are dated to the Roman-Byzantine periods.

It is noteworthy that the distance between the camps is much shorter than stated above (50 m instead of 200 m) and there is only a single corner tower.

Hizmi, who excavated in nearby Kh. Beiyudhat-Archelais (Site 111), found a Roman camp on the ridge west of the city: "The Roman Army Camp: Opposite the way station, high up in the upper third of the mountain range on the west side, two camps were erected: a square camp and a larger one to its south. In the former, which covered an area of 780 sq. m, a room was uncovered in the southeastern corner that was used as a lookout post. On the east side, a doorway 1.2 m wide served as an entrance into the camp. Due to its elevated position, the camp could protect the settlement, the aqueduct, the way station, and the main road running east of the settlement." (Hizmi 2008b: 1600-1602).

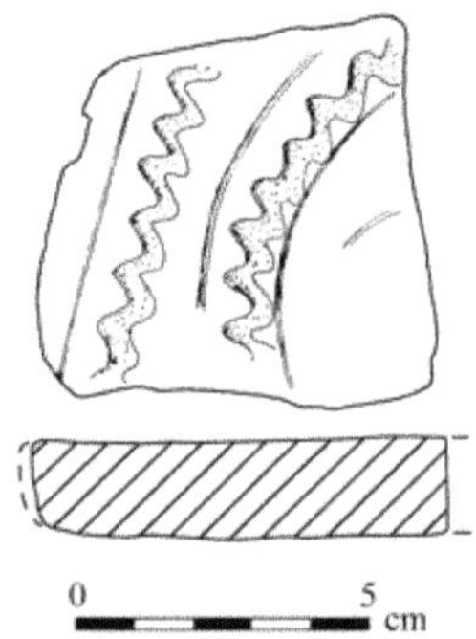

261. **Archelais-West**, fragment of typically ornamented stone ossuary.

Pottery: Roman-Byzantine – 100%.
Additional surveys: Bar-Adon 1972: site 23.

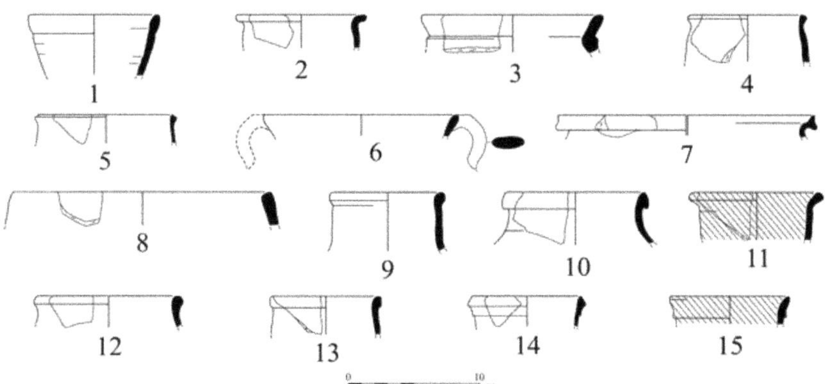

262. Pottery from **Archelais-West**, all Rom-Byz: 1. Bowl, lt br; 2. Bowl, gr; 3. Bowl, buff; 4-5. Bowls, rd; 6. CP, br; 7. CP, lt br; 8, 10. Jars, br; 9. Jar, wh; 11. Jug, gr, blk slip; 12-13, 15. Jugs, br; 14. Jug, lt br.

Site 116: 18-15/82/3

EL-MASTARAH (3)

Israel grid: 1888/1521
UTM grid: 7277/5389
Elevation: 20 m b.s.l., 50 m b.s.a.
Name: nearest place
Site type: enclosure and structures
Area: 5 dunams (5000 sq. m)
Topography: wadi bank
Rock type: Judea Group
Soil type: stony desert
Soil quality: 3
Cultivation: none
Cisterns: none
Water source: Nahal Yitav (182), 2 km distant
Road: 'Aujah et-Tahtah-'Ein 'Aujah (C48), 1.7 km distant
Visit: November 2006; 48 sherds

A site on the north bank of Wadi Nabiris, near el-Mastarah (1) (Site 113) and el-Mastarah (2) (Site 118). The location is at the foot of the east Samaria high ridge, 2.2 km north-west from Niran and 2 km north of Wadi 'Aujah.

The site is in two parts:

1. Enclosure remains from various stages, measuring about 50×40 m. The southern part is a wall, about 20 m long, built of particularly large boulders. In the north-eastern part are wall remains, perhaps enclosure remains of a later period.
2. About 70 m east of the enclosure are remains of a small settlement; of which at least two structures survive, built of especially large square stones. In the western structure is a built opening, 80 cm wide. Next to it is another intact structure of large stones, measuring 6×3 m, with an adjacent courtyard. The pottery in this area is scarce.

It is possible that el-Mastarah (3) was a part of el-Mastarah (1).

Pottery: Iron II – 42%; Persian-Hellenistic – 10%; Late Roman - 17%; Byzantine – 8%; Medieval – 4%; Ottoman – 4%; unidentified – 15%.
Flint: 6 items, Iron II (see Appendix A).
Additional surveys: Spanier 1992: site 141.

263. Aerial view north-east at the **el-Mastarah** site complex, 2008. At top right, on the spur, is **el-Mastarah (1)**; bottom left is **el-Mastarah (2)**; at top left is **el-Mastarah (3)** (N. Eshed).

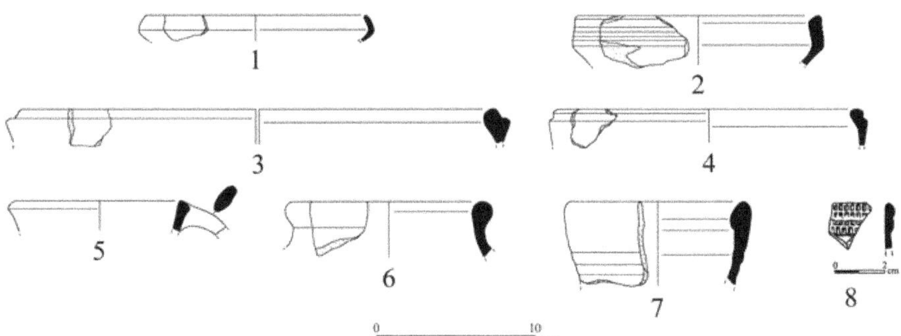

264. Pottery from **el-Mastarah (3)**: 1. Bowl, lt br, LR; 2. Bowl, blk, Ott/Mod; 3-4. CP D, br, IA II; 5. Cooking jug, br, IA II; 6. Jar, wh, MA; 7. Jar, br, MA; 8. Pipe, purple, Ott.

Site 117: 18-15/92/2

TOMB WITH INSCRIPTION

Israel grid: 1895/1522
UTM grid: 7284/5390
Elevation: 50 m b.s.l., 0 m a.s.a.
Name: given by the survey
Site type: tomb
Area: 0.25 dunam (250 sq. m)
Topography: spur tip
Rock type: Judea Group
Soil type: stony desert
Soil quality: 1
Cultivation: none
Cisterns: none
Water source: Nahal Yitav (182), 2 km distant
Road: 'Aujah et-Tahtah-'Ein 'Aujah (C48), 1.8 km distant
Visit: November 2004; 4 sherds

A built tomb at the western tip of a rocky spur between the ravines of Wadi Nabiris. The spur, running from east to west, is 1.5 km north of Yitav.

The original dimensions of the dismantled cyst-like grave were 2×1 m. It was built of square stones next to a circle of small stones. A tombstone 40 cm high and about 70 cm wide was found near the tomb. A nine letter inscription engraved on its flat surface in an old South-Arabian script reads: 'a tombstone to Mazrat'. This person, perhaps a merchant, was buried in the Roman period, and the tombstone was mounted on his grave (for a detailed account and decipherment of the inscription, see Appendix C).

Pottery: Roman (body sherds) – 100%.
Additional surveys: none.

265. The South-Arabian inscription from the tomb near Wadi el-Haiyat (see Appendix C).

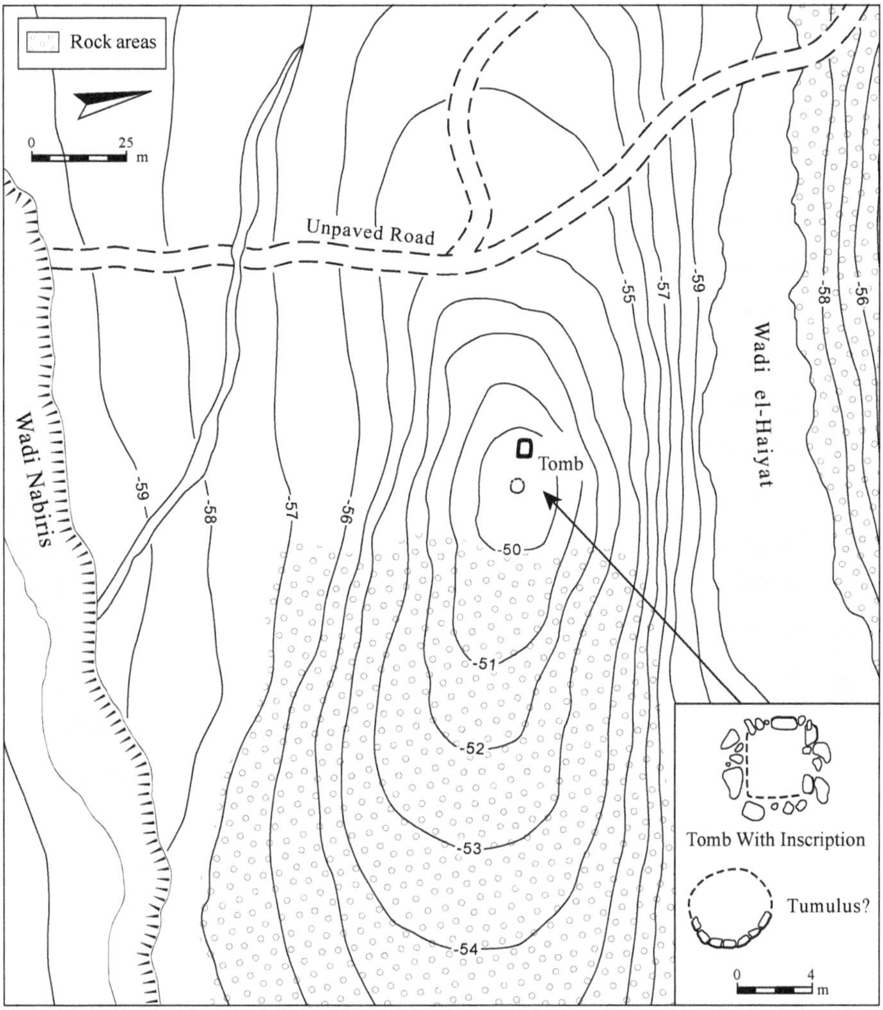

266. Tomb plan and map of vicinity.

Site 118: 18-15/82/4

EL-MASTARAH (2)

Israel grid: 1887/1522
UTM grid: 7276/5390
Elevation: 20 m b.s.l., 100 m b.s.a.
Name: nearest place
Site type: village
Area: 6 dunams (6000 sq. m).
Topography: broad spur between wadis
Rock type: Judea Group
Soil type: stony desert
Soil quality: 3
Cultivation: none
Cisterns: none
Water source: Nahal Yitav (182), 1.5 km distant
Road: 'Aujah et-Tahtah–'Ein 'Aujah (C48), 1.3 km distant
Visits: April 2004 and more; 80 sherds

A medium-sized village on a broad spur between Wadi Nabiris and Wadi el-Haiyat, east and below the high ridge of East Samaria, and 2.2 km north-west of Yitav. There is a fine lookout from the site to the Wadi el-Haiyat plain, around which there is a concentration of sites.

Four built complexes built of partially dressed large stones survive. The walls are built of one row of stones, and most of the entrances are made of two dressed erect jamb stones with a threshold stone between them. The preservation is particularly good, as there was no plunder of stones.

Following is a description of the structures in south to north order:

1. A partially ruined rectangular structure built of large stones, in the south-western part of the site on the slope facing Wadi Nabiris. Nearby is a lime pit.
2. A partially ruined rectangular structure built of large stones with a paved cell attached to it in the west with an inner access to the structure.
3. This is the largest complex in the site. In the centre is an enclosure, about 30 m across, and in its eastern part a row of well-built structures containing rectangular rooms measuring approximately 6×4 m.
4. North of no. 3 are three well preserved structures. The eastern one has an apsidal plan with the entrance through a rounded arch. West of it is another, 5×5 m, structure of especially large stones, perhaps a tower. The principal structure in this complex has three or four rooms and remains of a court-yard.

There are numerous in-situ jamb stones and remains of walls, suggesting that the built-up area was nearly double that now visible. The other structures were washed away or buried as a result of the considerable erosion on the high westerly slope.

Pottery: Chalcolithic/Early Bronze (?) – 10%; Intermediate Bronze – 12%; Middle Bronze II – 13%; Iron II – 44%; Late Roman – 21%.
Flint: 39 items (see Appendix A).
Additional surveys: none.

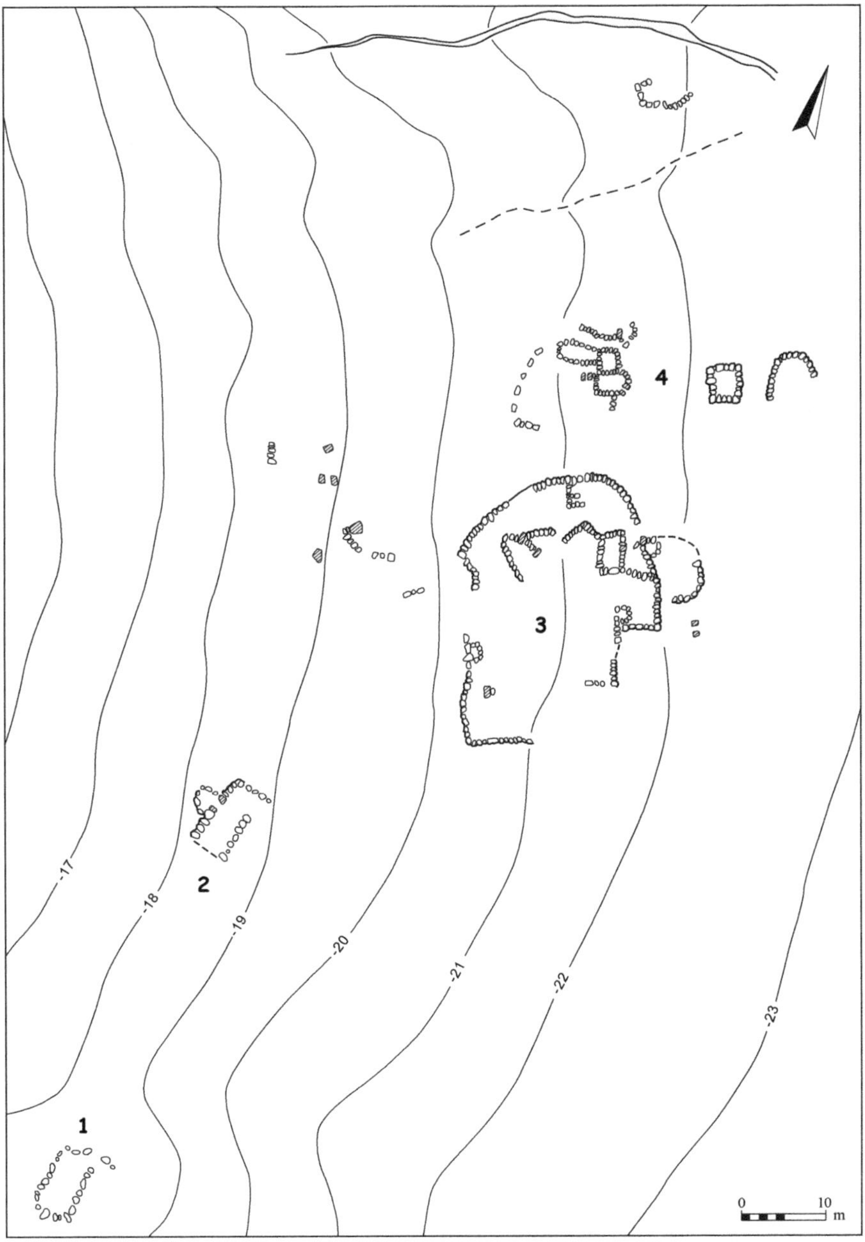

267. Plan of **el-Mastarah** (2).

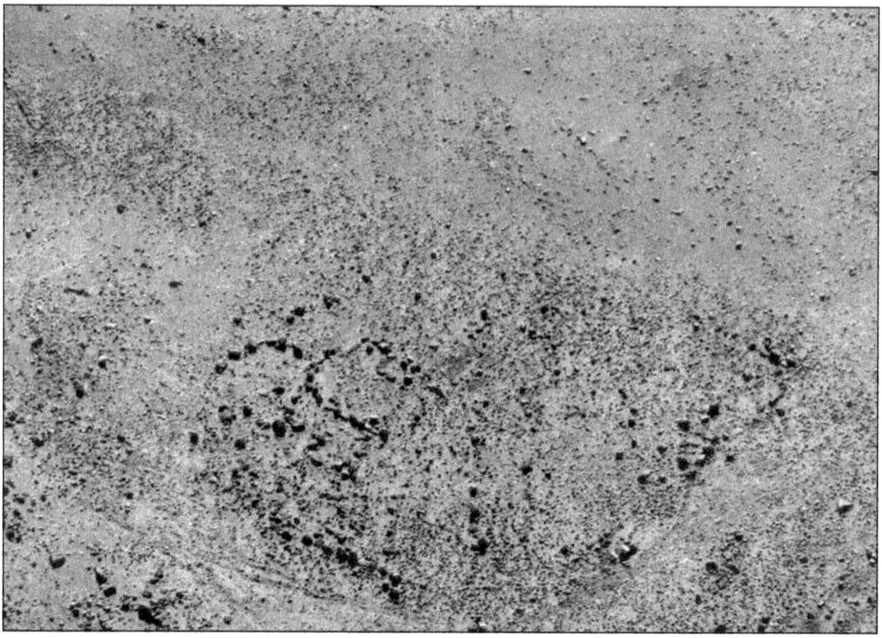

268. **el-Mastarah (2)**, an aerial view east at the Bronze and Iron Ages settlement, 2008. The remains of Complex 3 are visible (N. Eshed).

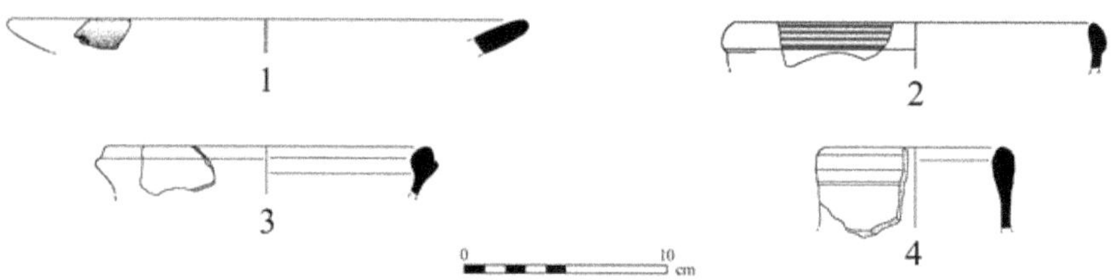

269. Pottery from **el-Mastarah (2)**: 1. Bowl, br, MB II; 2. Bowl, rd, rd slip, IA II; 3. CP D, br, IA II; 4. Jar, gr, Rom.

Site 119: 19-15/22/3

NIRAN POOL

Israel grid: 1929/1523
UTM grid: 7318/5392
Elevation: 180 m b.s.l., 20 m b.s.a.
Name: given by the survey
Site type: enclosure
Area: 1 dunam (1000 sq. m).
Topography: shoulder at slope bottom
Rock type: Judea Group
Soil type: stony desert
Soil quality: 1
Cultivation: none
Cisterns: none
Water source: Nahal Yitav (182), 1.7 km distant
Road: Beit She'an–Jericho (B10), 1.3 km distant
Visit: March 2007; 60 sherds

A large enclosure on the bank of a small ravine, 700 m south of Niran. It is located at the western edge of the valley of the wadi which empties to the Jordan Valley, and 400 m west of Niran quarry.

The major axis of the elliptical enclosure is about 60 m. At its north and south ends well-built walls of two to three rows of stones survive. The northern wall is built as a glacis and its overall thickness is about 4 m. The southern wall is partially ruined, and appears to have been similar to the northern one. The eastern part of the enclosure was washed away by the wadi channel, and the taller western wall partially survives. The steep slope with the small cliffs which rises above the enclosure is the cause of the erosion and the partial ruin.

A north-south wall divides the enclosure lengthwise. The wall is not continuous, and survives as scattered stones.

At the centre of the wall there is a small round stone paved stage, 2.5 m in diameter, built of one row of medium-sized stones, most of them standing upright. The function and date of the stage, are not clear. South of the dividing wall is an elevated and rounded area, apparently covering a structure of some sort. Possible remains of built entrances were found in the north and south walls.

This enclosure is similar to numerous enclosures, which according to pottery finds, were built during Iron Age I. The uniqueness of this site lies in the fact that there is no continuation into Iron Age II, which is typical of the majority of the sites of this type.

Pottery: Iron I – 25%; Persian-Hellenistic – 19%; Late Roman – 56%.
Additional surveys: none.

270. The enclosure at **Niran Pool** view north, 2012. On top of the hill is the water pool (S. Bar).

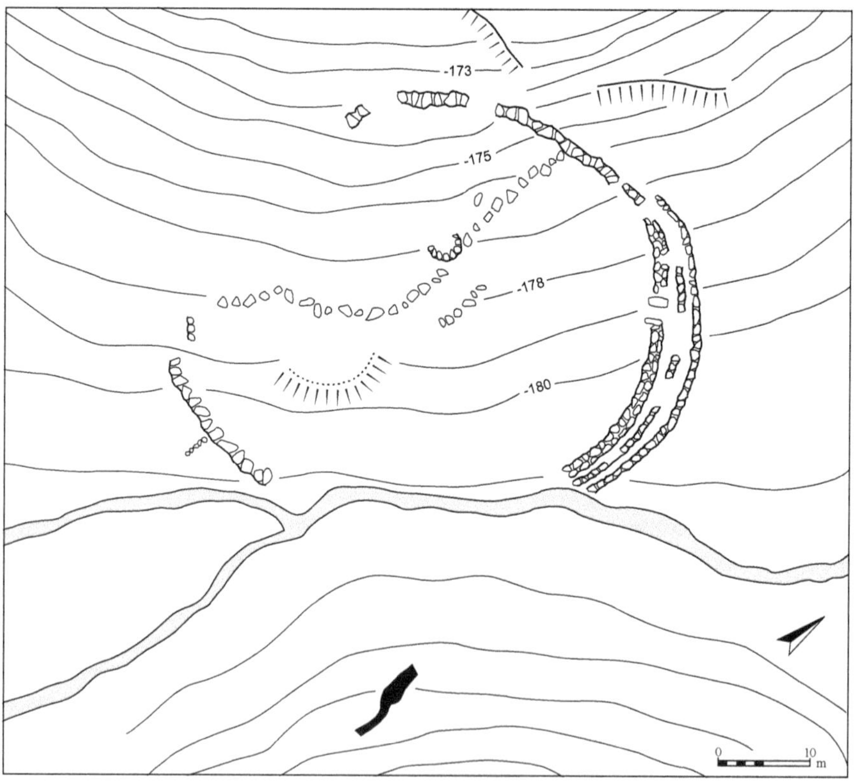

271. Plan of **Niran Pool**.

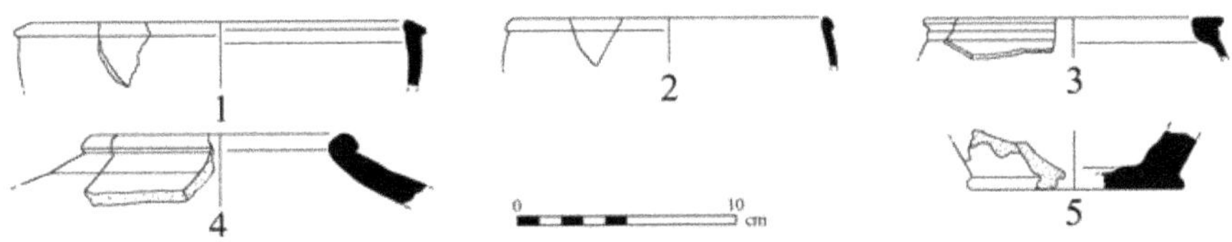

272. Pottery from **Niran Pool**: 1. Bowl, rd, Hel; 2. Bowl, rd, LR; 3. Bowl, gr, LR; 4. Jar, lt br, Pers; 5. Base, lt br, Pers-Hel.

♦ ♦ ♦

Site 120: 18-15/92/3

WADI NABIRIS (1)

Israel grid: 1892/1521
UTM grid: 7281/5389
Elevation: 60 m b.s.l., 0 m a.s.a.
Name: nearest place
Site type: enclosure
Area: 1.5 dunam (1500 sq. m).
Topography: alluvial plain
Rock type: Judea Group
Soil type: stony desert
Soil quality: 2
Cultivation: none
Cisterns: none
Water source: Nahal Yitav (182), 1.7 km distant
Road: 'Aujah et-Tahtah (C48), 1.6 km distant
Visit: March 2004; 1 sherd

An enclosure in the alluvial plain of Wadi Nabiris, near its exit from the western ridge, 1.8 km north-west of Yitav.

The dimensions of the elliptical enclosure are east-west axis 40 m and 30 m north-south. The encircling wall is built of one row of stones and is 60–70 cm thick. A room measuring 4×3 m is attached to the outside of the southern side. Inside the enclosure close to the eastern and western outer walls are two segments of partially preserved walls, and the supposed entrance was between two jamb stones in the south-west.

The central part of the site has been bulldozed away.

In the absence of sherds it is impossible to date the structures.

Pottery: a single unidentified sherd.
Flint: 79 items (see Appendix A).
Additional surveys: none.

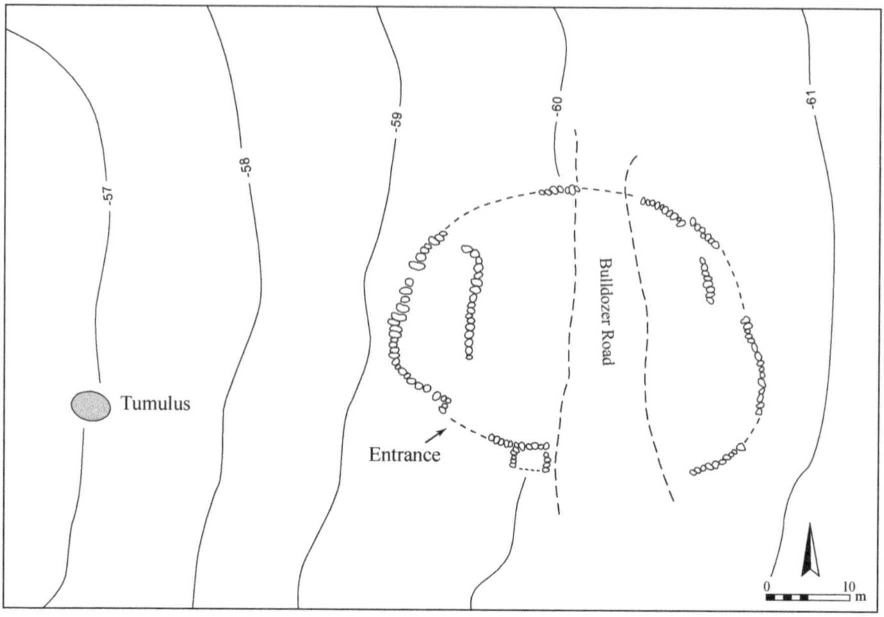

273. Plan of **Wadi Nabiris** (1).

♦ ♦ ♦

Site 121: 18-15/92/4

WADI NABIRIS (3)

Israel grid: 1892/1521
UTM grid: 7280/5389
Elevation: 50 m b.s.l., 0 m a.s.a.
Name: nearest place
Site type: enclosure
Area: 2 dunams (2000 sq. m).
Topography: alluvial plain
Rock type: Judea Group
Soil type: stony desert
Soil quality: 2
Cultivation: none
Cisterns: none
Water source: Nahal Yitav (182), 1.7 km distant
Road: 'Aujah et-Tahtah (C48), 1.5 km distant
Visit: November 2010; 1 sherd

An enclosure in the alluvial plains south of Wadi Nabiris riverbed, 2 km north of Wadi 'Aujah, and 1.8 km north-west from Yitav.

This is a round enclosure, about 40 m in diameter, built of one row of medium-sized stones. A dividing north-south wall creates a separate half-moon shaped area.

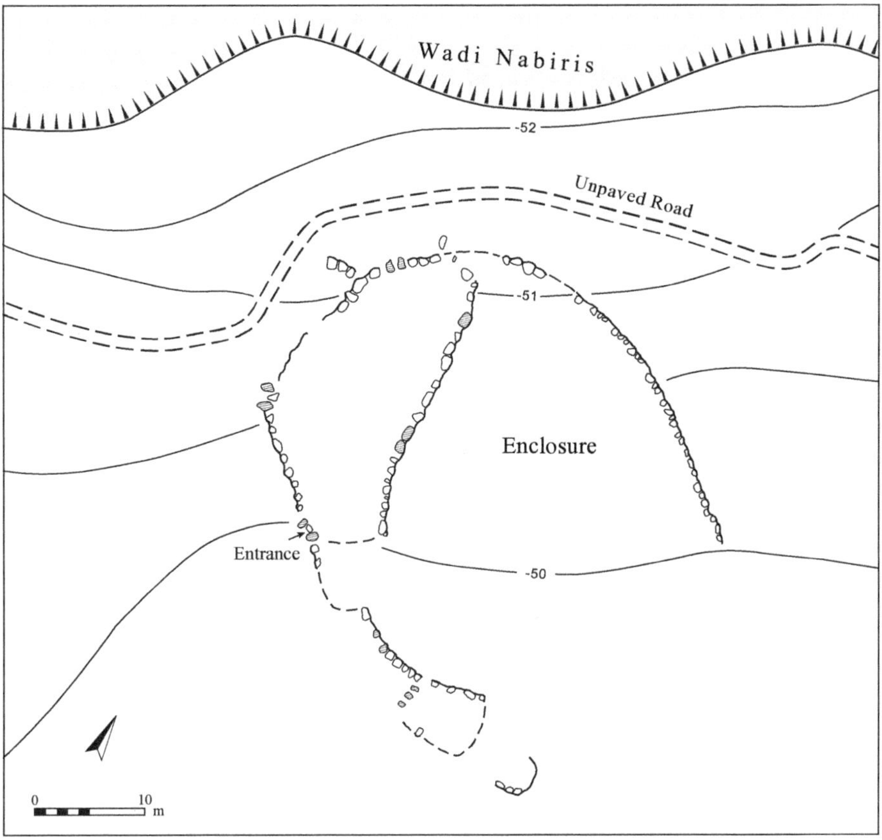

274. Plan of **Wadi Nabiris (3)**.

The wall is built of large stones (about 70 cm in diameter on average), along which there are pairs of erect monoliths 60 to 100 cm apart; apparently serving as entrances. Flat threshold slabs survive in some of the gaps. This was possibly a residential area, being part of the larger enclosure. A wall projects from the southern part, connecting to a structure measuring 4×3 m.

A single non-indicative sherd was found.

Pottery: one non-indicative sherd.
Flint: 95 items, Chalcolithic? (see Appendix A).
Additional surveys: none.

Site 122: 19-15/32/1

ELEVATION POINT -140

Israel grid: 1933/1520
UTM grid: 7322/5389
Elevation: 150 m b.s.l., 0 m a.s.a.
Name: nearest place
Site type: structures
Area: 6 dunams (6000 sq. m).
Topography: flat plateau
Rock type: Judea Group
Soil type: stony desert
Soil quality: 2
Cultivation: none
Cisterns: none
Water source: Nahal Yitav (182), 1.6 km distant
Road: Beit She'an–Jericho (B10), 1 km distant
Visit: January 2005; 40 sherds

A site on a high flat plateau, 1 km north-west from the outskirts of the village of 'Aujah.

There are several remains of disconnected walls of medium-sized stones, which apparently functioned as enclosures and/or structures. The area over which the structures are scattered stretches 200 m north from the centre of the site.

A small settlement existed in the place; most of its stones have been plundered or disappeared.

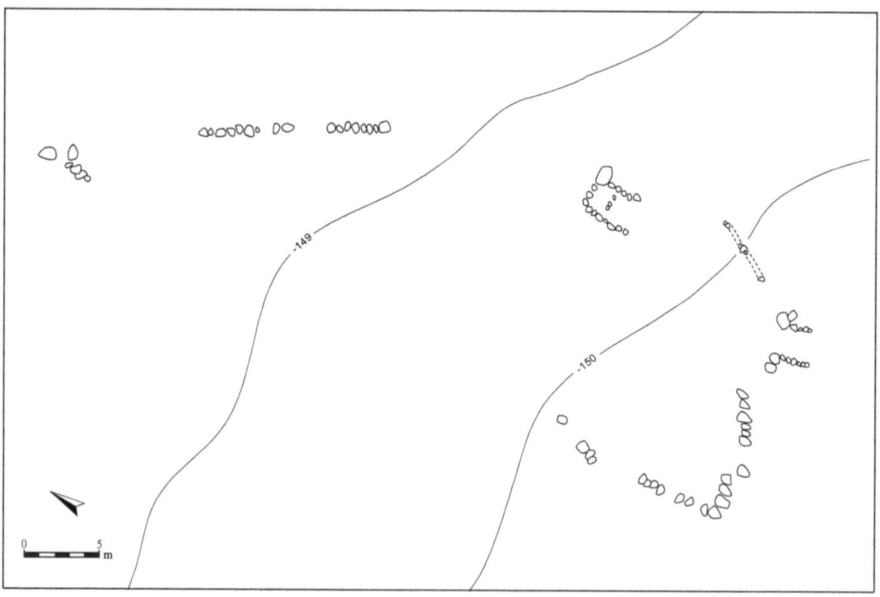

275. Plan of E.P. -140.

Pottery: Iron I – 37%; Iron II – 37%; Late Roman – 20%; Medieval – 6%.
Flint: 18 items, Iron Age (see Appendix A).
Additional surveys: none.

♦ ♦ ♦

Site 123: 19-15/42/3

SAHEL 'AUJAH (2)

Israel grid: 1943/1521
UTM grid: 7332/5390
Elevation: 250 m b.s.l., 30 m b.s.a.
Name: nearest place
Site type: enclosures
Area: 3 dunams (3000 sq. m)
Topography: slope and riverbed
Rock type: Judea Group
Soil type: stony desert
Soil quality: 2
Cultivation: none
Cisterns: none
Water source: Nahal Yitav (182), 1.6 km distant
Road: Beit She'an–Jericho (B10), 200 m distant
Visit: April 2003; 25 sherds

An enclosure site south and north of the Wadi 'Aujah riverbed, draining the Sahel 'Aujah (et-Tulul) plateau eastward. They are located 1.3 km south-east of Niran, at the outskirts of the village of 'Aujah. Near to the north passes a new unpaved road leading in the direction of Yitav.

Two enclosures are north of the riverbed and one is south of it:

1. The enclosures north of the riverbed: the diameter of the eastern and larger one, which is built of one row of medium-sized stones, is 35 m, and it is bisected by two branches of the unpaved road. West and close to it is a smaller enclosure, 25 m in diameter, only half of which survives.
2. South of the riverbed, about 100 m from no. 1 and on a relatively steep slope, is another enclosure, 30 m in diameter, the form of which has been disturbed by stone-falls. The construction stones are particularly large and some stand upright. No sherds were found in this enclosure.

These Iron Age enclosures are part of a dense complex of sites of this type in the area between the Sartaba and Jericho.

Pottery: Iron I-II – 80%; Late Roman – 20%.
Additional surveys: none.

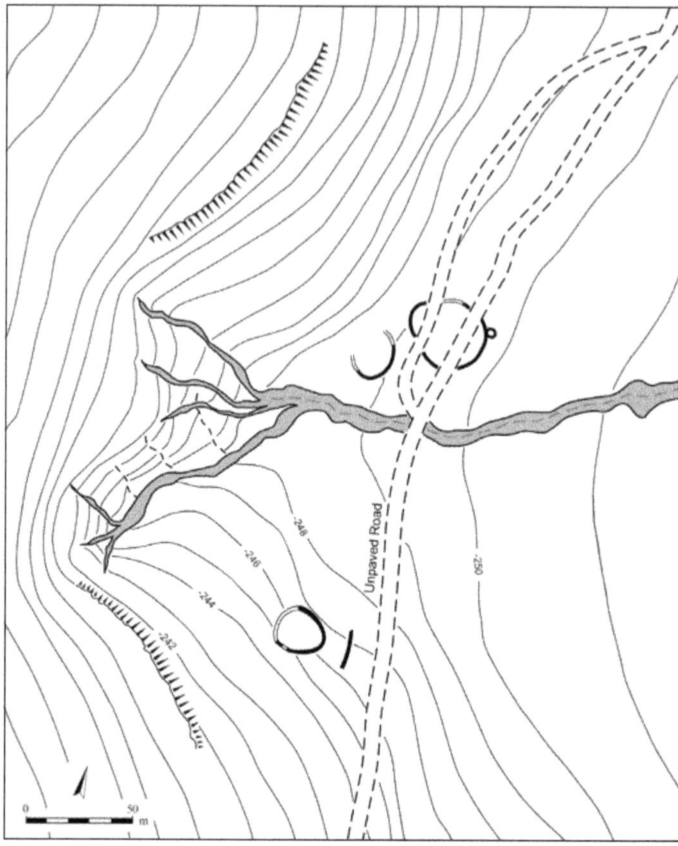

276. Plan of **Sahel 'Aujah (2)**.

♦ ♦ ♦

Site 124: 19-15/31/1

SAHEL 'AUJAH (1)

Israel grid: 1937/1519
UTM grid: 7326/5388
Elevation: 190 m b.s.l., 30 m b.s.a.
Name: nearest place
Site type: enclosures
Area: 2 dunams (2000 sq. m)
Topography: slope
Rock type: Judea Group
Soil type: stony desert
Soil quality: 2
Cultivation: none
Cisterns: none
Water source: Nahal Yitav (182), 1.7 km distant
Road: Beit She'an–Jericho (B10), 500 m distant
Visit: April 2003; 40 sherds

Two partially preserved enclosures, on a western slope bordering Sahel 'Aujah (et-Tulul), 1 km south-east from Niran, and 500 m north-west of the village of 'Aujah et-Tahtah. The unpaved Niran–Yitav road passes between the enclosures.

The enclosure details are:

1. This is an especially large round enclosure, more than 120 m in diameter, encircled by a double wall of medium-sized flat stones. The inner western part is presently covered by silt and fallen stones, rendering it difficult to trace the precise circumference. However, the general layout is clear. In the bottom part a homogeneous sherd scatter has been found, dated to the Iron Age I-II.
2. About 150 m south-south-east of no. 1, east of the unpaved road, is another

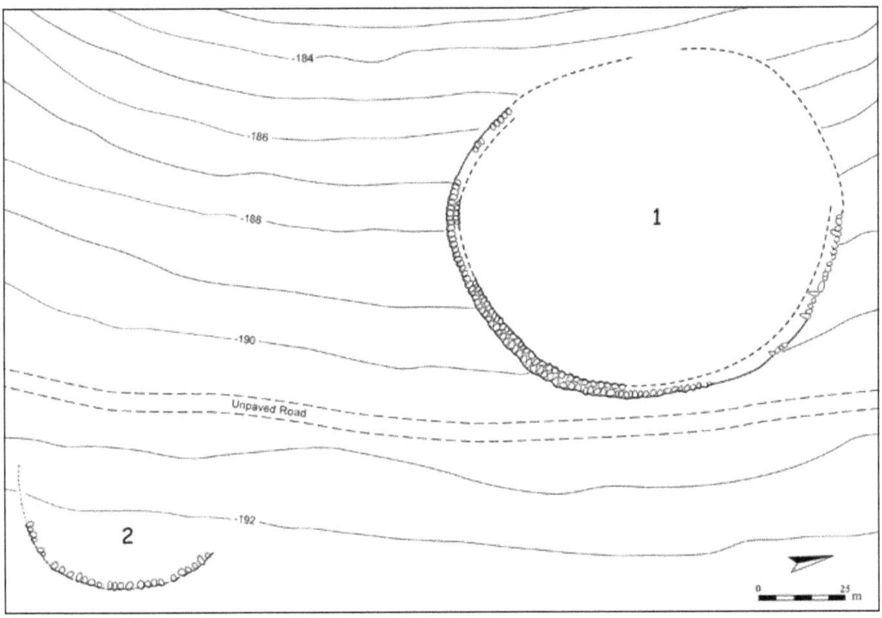

277. Plan of **Sahel 'Aujah (1)**.

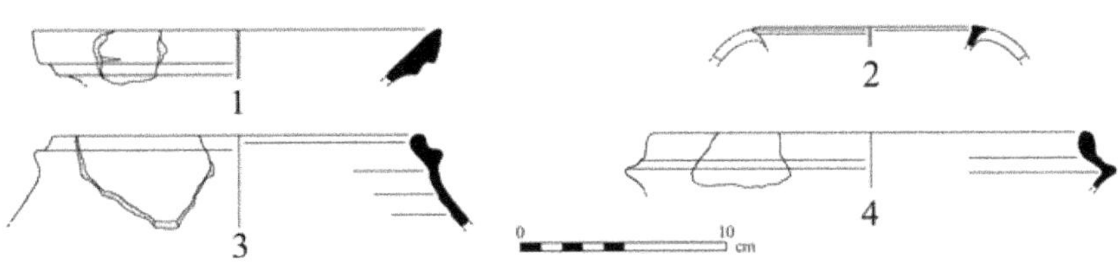

278. Pottery from **Sahel 'Aujah (1)**: 1. Bowl (?), dk-br, IA I-II; 2. CP, rd, Rom; 3-4. CP, br, IA I-II.

partially preserved enclosure, the diameter of which is about 55 m, built of one row of medium-sized stones.

Both enclosures are built similarly to numerous other sites of the same type between the Sartaba and Jericho.

Pottery: Iron I-II – 95%; Roman – 5%.
Additional surveys: none.

◆ ◆ ◆

Site 125: 18-15/81/1

ELEVATION POINT 44

Israel grid: 1887/1518
UTM grid: 7276/5386
Elevation: 40 m a.s.l., 30 m a.s.a.
Name: nearest place
Site type: structures
Area: 2 dunams (2000 sq. m)
Topography: spur and shoulder
Rock type: Judea Group
Soil type: stony desert
Soil quality: 3
Cultivation: none
Cisterns: none
Water source: Nahal Yitav (182), 1.2 km distant
Road: 'Aujah et-Tahtah–'Ein 'Aujah (C48), 1 km distant
Visit: December 2004; 30 sherds

A site on a spur and hilltop in the western part of Sahel 'Aujah, 2 km north-west of Yitav. There is a view over the valley and to the sites of 'Aujah el-Foqa and 'Aujah et-Tahtah (Sites 143 and 146).

There are two parts to the site:

1. On the lower part of a broad shoulder are two small structures, 5×5 m each, built of large stones. To the southern one is linked a large courtyard, measuring some 20×15 m. About 100 m south-west of the compound is a single support wall on the slope (not on plan).
2. In the upper part there is a structure built of large stones. Only one room survives, but it is certain that there were additional rooms. The top structure was apparently used for observation.

The site is apparently linked to the array of Iron Age sites around 'Aujah el-Foqa, 'Aujah Fortress (Site 140), el-Mastarah settlements (nos. 113, 116, 118), Wadi el-Haiyat (nos. 107, 109), Wadi Nabiris (nos. 110, 120, 121) and others.

Pottery: Iron II – 100%.
Flint: 2 items (see Appendix A).
Additional surveys: none.

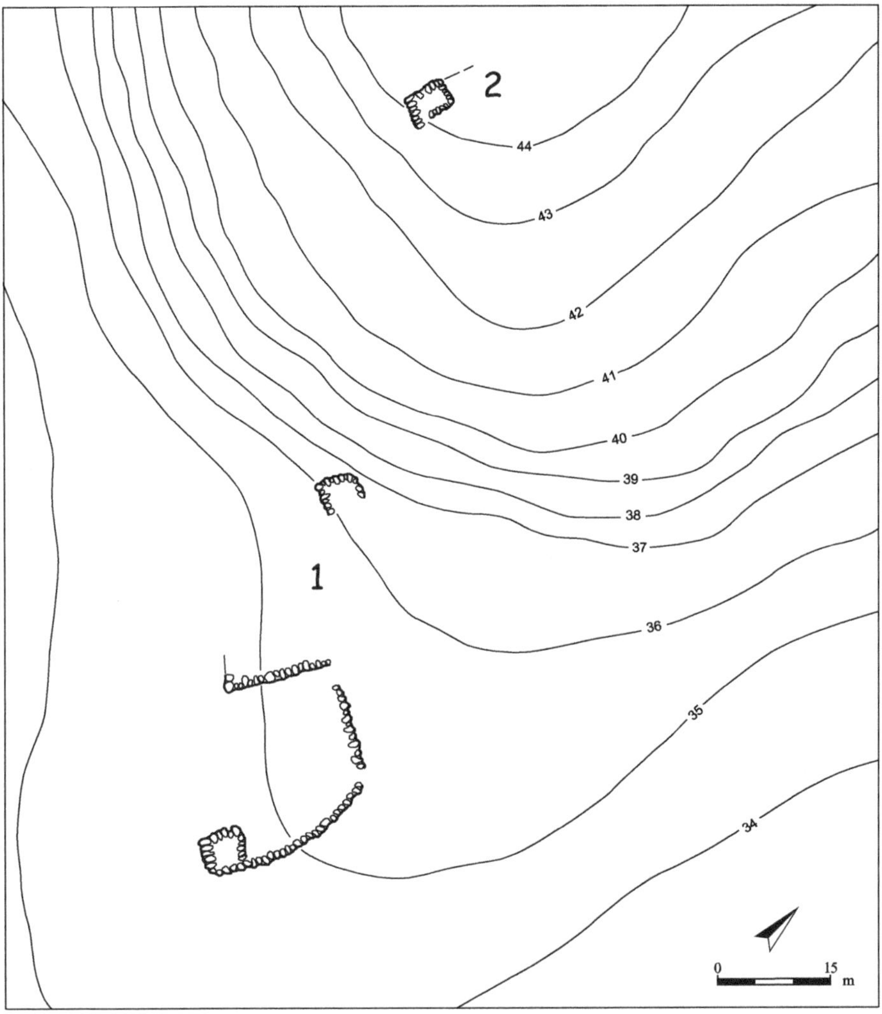

279. Plan of **E.P. 44**.

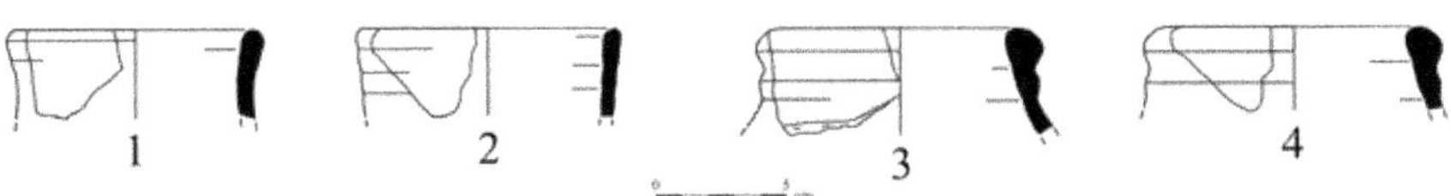

280. Pottery from **E.P 44**, all IA II: 1. Jar, br; 2. Jar/jug, dk br; 3-4. Jars, dk br.

Site 126: 19-15/01/1

WADI EL-HAIYAT (2)

Israel grid: 1902/1517
UTM grid: 7291/5385
Elevation: 110 m b.s.l., 30 m b.s.a.
Name: nearest place
Site type: enclosures
Area: 5 dunams (5000 sq. m)
Topography: silt terrace in an enclosed glen
Rock type: Judea Group
Soil type: stony desert
Soil quality: 2
Cultivation: none
Cisterns: none
Water source: Nahal Yitav (182), 2 km distant
Road: 'Aujah et-Tahtah–'Ein 'Aujah (C48), 1.8 km distant
Visits: March 2004 and more; 137 sherds

An elaborate enclosure on the north bank of one of the tributaries of Wadi el-Haiyat, 1.2 km north of Yitav. It is located in a narrow wadi surrounded by hills, between a low cliff in the north and the wadi channel in the south.

There are two clear phases in the site:

1. The ancient enclosure, a wall of small stones, 1 m thick at least. The flows in the wadi eroded the wadi's northern bank, thus the enclosure wall is presently tied to the earth cliff of the channel. In other places the ancient enclosure is elevated some 50 cm over the nearby area. Apparently, several structures existed in it.
2. Later enclosures: These were built over the ancient site, presumably during the Byzantine period. The walls are of one row of stones, one course high. The walls form a large enclosure in the west, measuring 30×20 m and another, smaller enclosure, 20×10 m, north of no.1. Enclosure no. 2 ends in the east with a small round structure, measuring 2×2 m. The enclosure walls meet the cliff in the north, in which there is also a small cave.

West of the site are remains of a modern Bedouin tent encampment.

Pottery: Iron I – 3%; Early Roman – 18%; Late Roman – 50%; Byzantine – 18%; Early Moslem and Medieval – 9%; Ottoman – 2%.
Additional surveys: none.

281. The site at **Wadi el-Haiyat (2)**, view northward, 2012. Note the various courtyards (S. Bar).

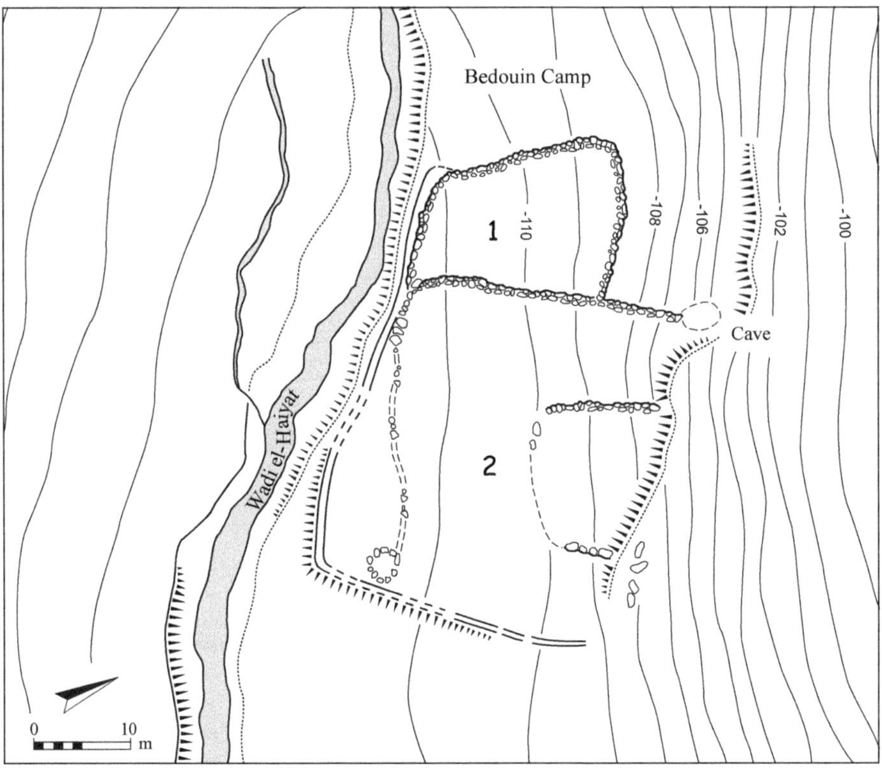

282. Plan of **Wadi el-Haiyat (2)**.

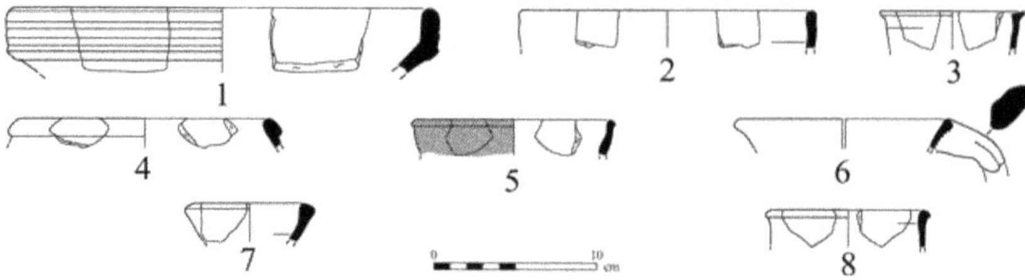

283. Pottery from **Wadi el-Haiyat (2)**: 1. Bowl, blk, Ott/Mod; 2-3. Bowls, lt br, Rom; 4. Bowl, dk br, IA I (?); 5. Jar, br, rd slip, Rom-Byz; 6. Jug, rd, Rom; 7. Jug, br, Rom-Byz; 8. Jug, lt br, Rom.

♦ ♦ ♦

Site 127: 19-15/01/2

WADI EL-HAIYAT (3)

Israel grid: 1905/1517
UTM grid: 7294/5385
Elevation: 115 m b.s.l., 0 m a.s.a.
Name: nearest place
Site type: small
Area: 1 dunam (1000 sq. m)
Topography: wadi bank
Rock type: Judea Group
Soil type: Mediterranean forest
Soil quality: 3

Cultivation: none
Cisterns: none
Water source: Nahal Yitav (182), 1.8 km distant
Road: 'Aujah et-Tahtah–'Ein 'Aujah (C48), 1.7 km distant
Visits: December 2004 and more; 15 sherds

A small ruined site at the junction of unpaved roads crossing Wadi el-Haiyat, 1.2 km north of Yitav. The location is on a small island between two channels in the plains of Wadi el-Haiyat and Wadi Nabiris.

There are remains of walls built of medium-sized stones, which do not add up to a real plan. The original site has been bulldozed by modern construction works.

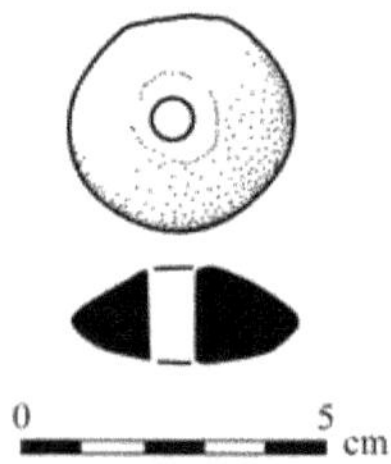

284. A find from **Wadi el-Haiyat (3)**: Ceramic loom weight, gr, Chal (?).

Pottery: Chalcolithic (?) – 100% (body sherds).
Miscellaneous find: a convex ceramic loom weight with a hole drilled at the centre.
Additional surveys: none.
Bibliography: Bar 2014: site 106.

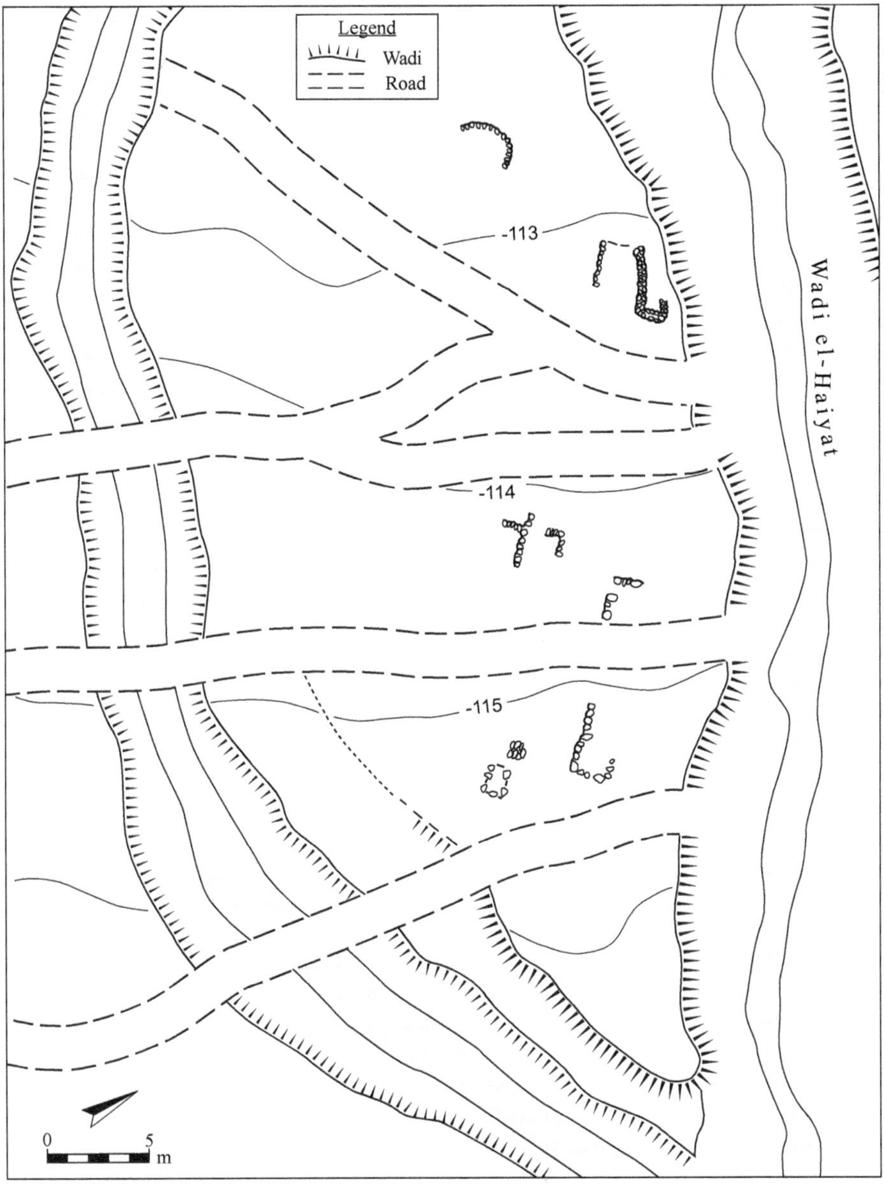

285. Plan of **Wadi el-Haiyat (3)**.

Site 128: 18-15/90/1

YITAV

Israel grid: 1897/1508
UTM grid: 7286/5377
Elevation: 110 m b.s.l., 20 m a.s.a.
Name: nearest place
Site type: structure
Area: 1 dunam (1000 sq. m)
Topography: slope
Rock type: Judea Group

Soil type: stony-desert
Soil quality: 2
Cultivation: none
Cisterns: none
Water source: Nahal Yitav (182), 700 m distant
Road: 'Aujah et-Tahtah–'Ein 'Aujah (C48), 600 m distant

A salvage excavation was made in 1998, headed by H. Hizmi (2003), of a structure: 500 sq. m in area, with a trapezoidal courtyard and two adjacent rooms west of it. The walls of the structure are 80 cm thick, built from two rows of medium-sized fieldstones with earth fill. They survive to at least one course high. Most of the sherds were found in the smaller room of the two (L101).

About 30 m west of the structure is a round installation, 3.5 m in diameter, built of especially large stones laid on their narrow side.

All sherds in both the structure and in the installation are Chalcolithic.

Additional Bibliography: Bar 2014: site 110.

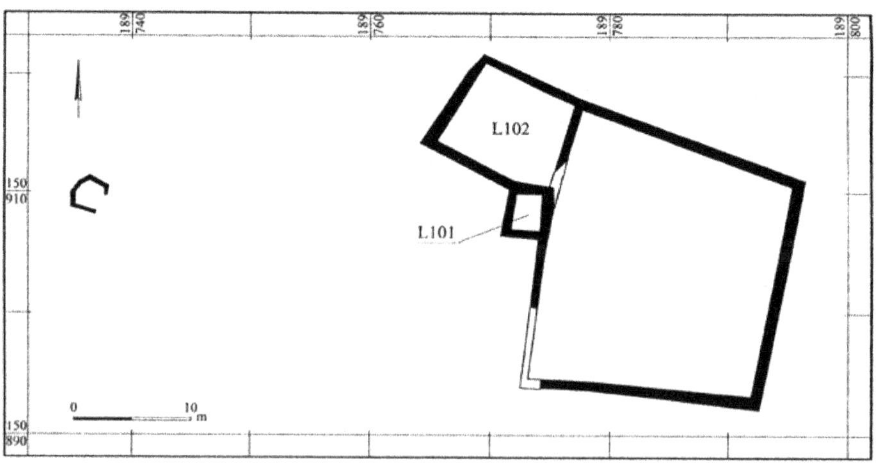

286. Plan of **Yitav** (Hizmi 2003: illustration 76).

287. **Yitav**, view north-eastward at the Chalcolithic site, 2011 (S. Bar).

♦ ♦ ♦

Site 129: 18-15/71/2

'EIN 'AUJAH (2)

Israel grid: 1872/1514
UTM grid: 7261/5382
Elevation: 54 m a.s.l., 100 m b.s.a.
Name: nearest place
Site type: caves and courtyards
Area: 2 dunams (2000 sq. m)
Topography: slope
Rock type: Judea Group
Soil type: stony-desert
Soil quality: 2
Cultivation: none
Cisterns: none
Water source: Nahal Yitav (182), at the site
Road: 'Aujah et-Tahtah–'Ein 'Aujah (C48), next to the site
Visits: May 2008, 2010; 30 sherds

Caves and courtyards on a steep slope descending south to Wadi 'Aujah riverbed. The site of 'Ein 'Aujah (1 [no. 133]) is at the bottom of the slope to the south.

In the site there are three built courtyards, descending from north to south along the river channel and close to the rocky low cliff to their west. At least three dwelling caves have been found in the rocky cliff.

Below are the details:

1. The upper courtyard: is located on the slope, bounded by terrace walls built of large stones. In the cliff to the west is a small cave.

2. The middle courtyard: this links both the main courtyards (upper and lower), and west of it there is a fairly large cave in the cliff, measuring about 6×4 m. The cave is blocked by a front wall.
3. The lower courtyard: this, measuring approximately 35×15 m, served as the principal dwelling unit. West, close to it, is a particularly large cave, about

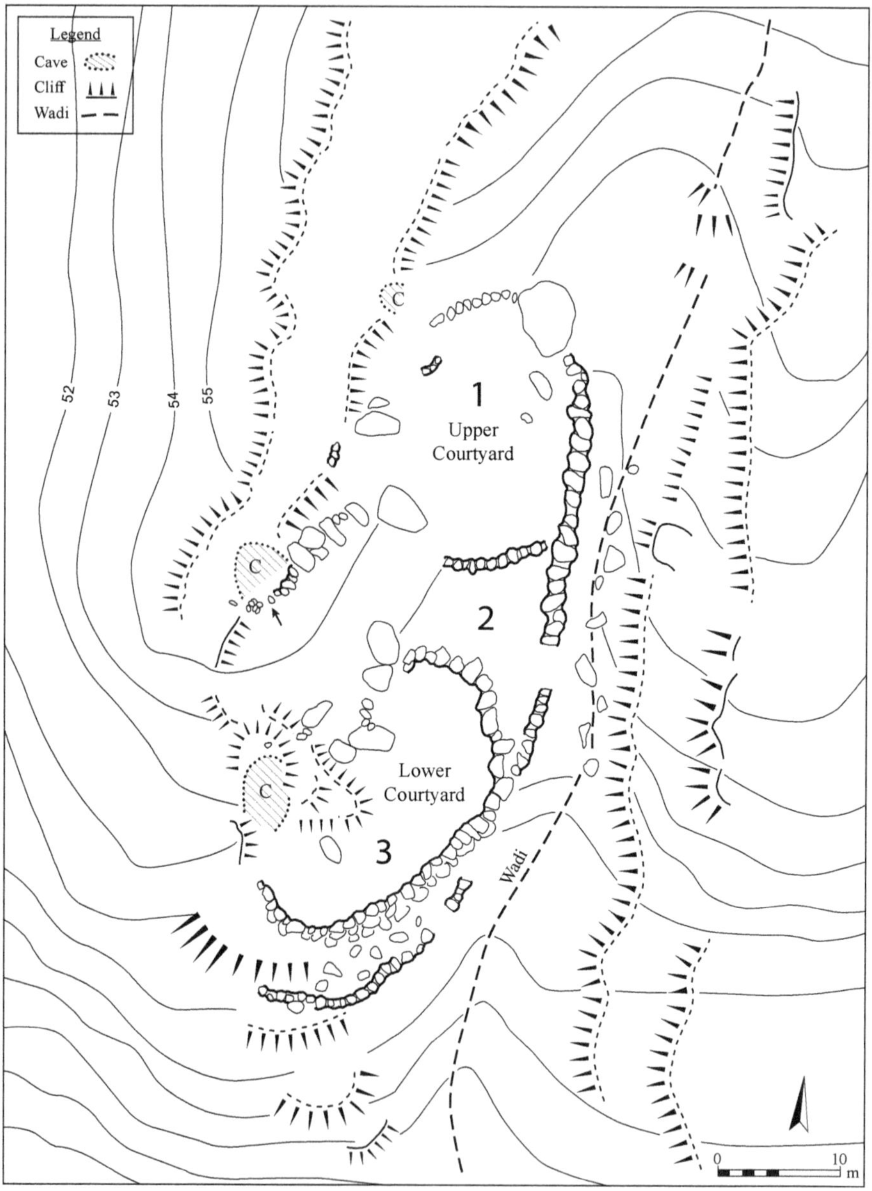

288. Plan of 'Ein 'Aujah (2).

8 m deep, with an entrance about 4 m wide. The courtyard is enclosed by a rounded terrace wall of four or five courses, built on the wadi bank. This courtyard was filled and levelled to form a living surface.

Another terrace wall was built on the slope, south of the lower courtyard, for strengthening the whole complex.

Pottery: Byzantine – 26%; Early Moslem – 26%; Medieval – 32%; Ottoman – 16%.
Stone: basalt grinding stone fragment.
Additional surveys: none.

289. **'Ein 'Aujah (2)** at the heights of the cliff above Wadi 'Aujah, 2011. There is a combination of caves and enclosures, conforming to the mountainous topography (M. Einav).

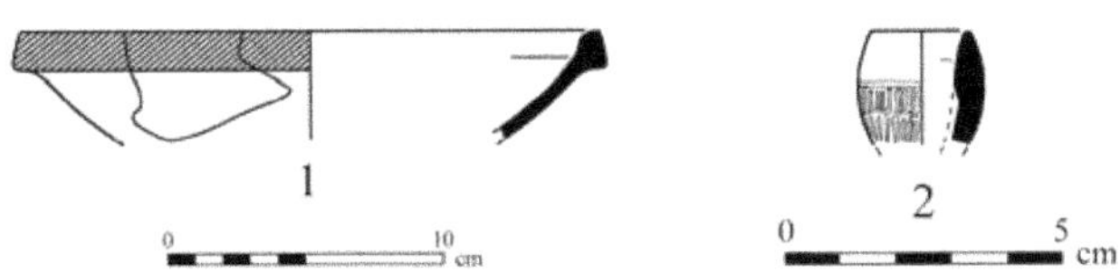

290. Pottery from **'Ein 'Aujah (2)**: 1. Bowl, rd, Byz; 2. Pipe, violet, Ott.

Site 130: 19-15/01/3

WADI EL-HAIYAT (1)

Israel grid: 1907/1515
UTM grid: 7297/5383
Elevation: 145 m b.s.l., 0 m a.s.a.
Name: nearest place
Site type: enclosures
Area: 2 dunams (2000 sq. m)
Topography: a wadi valley
Rock type: Judea Group
Soil type: stony-desert
Soil quality: 2
Cultivation: none
Cisterns: none
Water source: Nahal Yitav (182), 1.8 km distant
Road: 'Aujah et-Tahtah–'Ein 'Aujah (C48), 1.6 km distant
Visits: March 2004 and more; 6 sherds

A small site of enclosures in the wide part of Wadi el-Haiyat, 1 km north-north-west of Yitav. South and north of the wadi valley rise ridges of medium height, and around the riverbed is a large plain. The area has been badly interfered with by modern constructions.

The site contains remains of an enclosure, about 45 m in diameter, with an encircling wall built of one or two rows of medium-sized stones. Parts of the wall have been washed away by the wadi, and only its eastern part survives. This enclosure, about 2 m above the wadi channel, is divided by a straight wall. Part of another round enclosure survive 50 m to the west.

Pottery: Chalcolithic – one sherd; Iron I – four sherds; Late Roman – one sherd.
Flint: 9 items (see Appendix A).
Additional surveys: none.

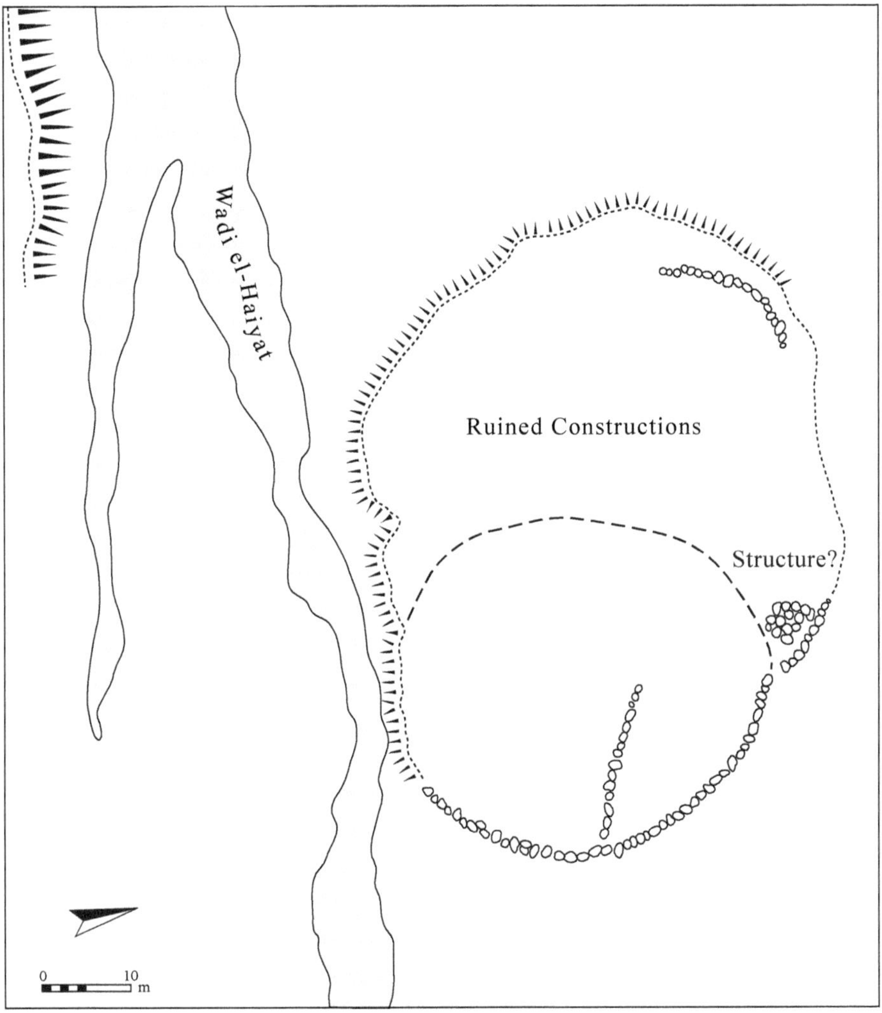

291. Plan of **Wadi el-Haiyat (1)**.

CHAPTER FIVE

NAHAL YITAV (WADI 'AUJAH) AND ITS TRIBUTARIES

LANDSCAPE UNIT 33

292. **River Jordan landscape**, engraving by P. Lortet (in Schiller 1977).

Site 131: 18-15/61/1

'EIN 'AUJAH (3)

Israel grid: 1866/1514
UTM grid: 7255/5381
Elevation: 30 m b.s.l., 0 m a.s.a.
Name: nearest place
Site type: enclosures
Area: 2 dunams (2000 sq. m)
Topography: wadi plain
Rock type: Judea Group
Soil type: stony-desert
Soil quality: 2
Cultivation: none
Cisterns: none
Water source: 'Ein 'Aujah (184), at the site
Road: 'Aujah et-Tahtah–'Ein 'Aujah (C48), next to the site
Visits: November 2010 and more; 20 sherds

An enclosure site in the narrow channel north of Wadi 'Aujah, 3 km west of Yitav. The spring of 'Ein 'Aujah flows nearby.

The site contains a large rectangular enclosure; 30 m north-south, and about 70 m east-west. The enclosure was originally built of two rows of medium-sized stones. It is north and above the channel of Wadi 'Aujah, and adjoins a high rock cliff to the north; one of the cliffs on both sides of the stream. Above it are two other enclosures, one rectangular and one nearly square. These are probably part of the large enclosure, but the quality of their construction is by far inferior to that of the large one.

293. The built enclosure **'Ein 'Aujah (3)** in the channel of Wadi 'Aujah and close to the spring, view to south-west. In the centre is a modern lime pit, 2010 (S. Bar).

In the eastern part, near a meander of the wadi, is 'Ein 'Aujah, which was practically dry in November 2010. A lime pit, apparently modern, is situated in the centre of the site.

The location of the enclosure-corral in the wadi channel is unusual; it is reasonable that it was built in relation to the spring of 'Ein 'Aujah.

Pottery: Middle Bronze II (?) – 10%; Iron II – 10%; Persian-Hellenistic – 15%; Roman – 50%; Medieval – 10%; Ottoman – 5%.
Additional surveys: none.

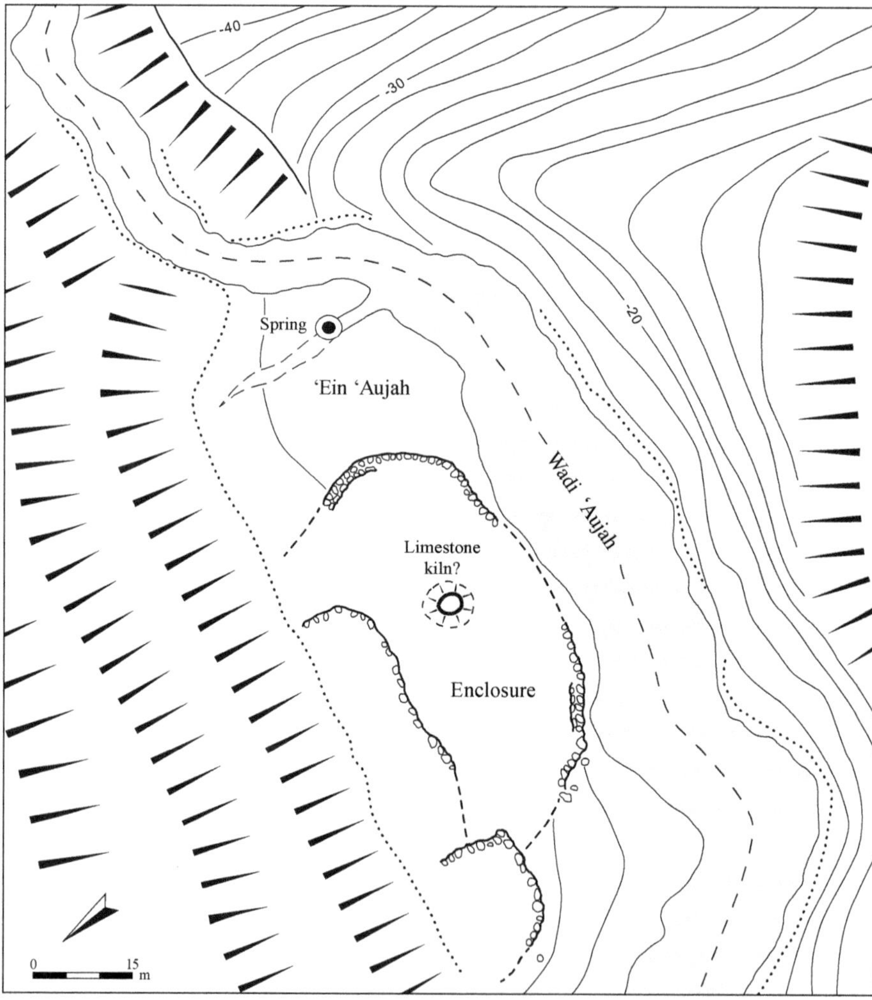

294. Plan of **'Ein 'Aujah (3)**.

Site 132: 18-15/61/2

'EIN 'AUJAH (4)

Israel grid: 1868/1514
UTM grid: 7258/5382
Elevation: 20 m b.s.l., 20 m a.s.a.
Name: nearest place
Site type: enclosure
Area: 1 dunam (1000 sq. m)
Topography: wadi channel
Rock type: Judea Group
Soil type: stony-desert
Soil quality: 1
Cultivation: none
Cisterns: none
Water source: Nahal Yitav (182), at the site
Road: 'Aujah Tahtah–'Ein 'Aujah (C48), next to the site
Visit: November 2010; 20 sherds

An enclosure on a raised stage on the high north bank of Wadi 'Aujah in the narrow part of the riverbed, 3 km west of Yitav.

On the north cliff above the wadi is a curved enclosure (major axis 25 m, minor axis about 13 m), built of large stones. Inside its east side is a smaller enclosure, measuring 6×6 m, apparently part of the larger one. In the cliff nearby is a rock shelter, and along the cliff south of the wadi are the remains of the aqueduct which carried water from nearby 'Ein 'Aujah (see Appendix D). East of the enclosure and close to it is a deep channel descending to Wadi 'Aujah.

295. The enclosure at **'Ein 'Aujah (4)** (arrowed), looking north-west, 2011 (S. Bar).

The site was mainly in use in the Roman and Byzantine periods.

Pottery: Roman – 70%; Byzantine – 25%; Early Moslem – 5%.
Additional surveys: none.

296. Plan of **'Ein 'Aujah (4)**.

297. Pottery from **'Ein 'Aujah (4)**: 1-2. Bowls, lt br, Rom-Byz.

Site 133: 18-15/71/3

'EIN 'AUJAH (1)

Israel grid: 1871/1513
UTM grid: 7260/5381
Elevation: 0 m a.s.l., 60 m b.s.a.
Name: nearest place
Site type: large
Area: 10 dunams (1 ha)
Topography: shoulder
Rock type: Judea Group
Soil type: stony-desert
Soil quality: 2
Cultivation: none
Cisterns: none
Water source: Nahal Yitav (182), at the site
Road: 'Aujah et-Tahtah–'Ein 'Aujah (C48), next to the site
Visits: May 2008 and more; 135 sherds

A large site on a rocky flat shoulder in the narrow section of Wadi 'Aujah, above and north of an asphalted parking area (where pumps had been installed) and

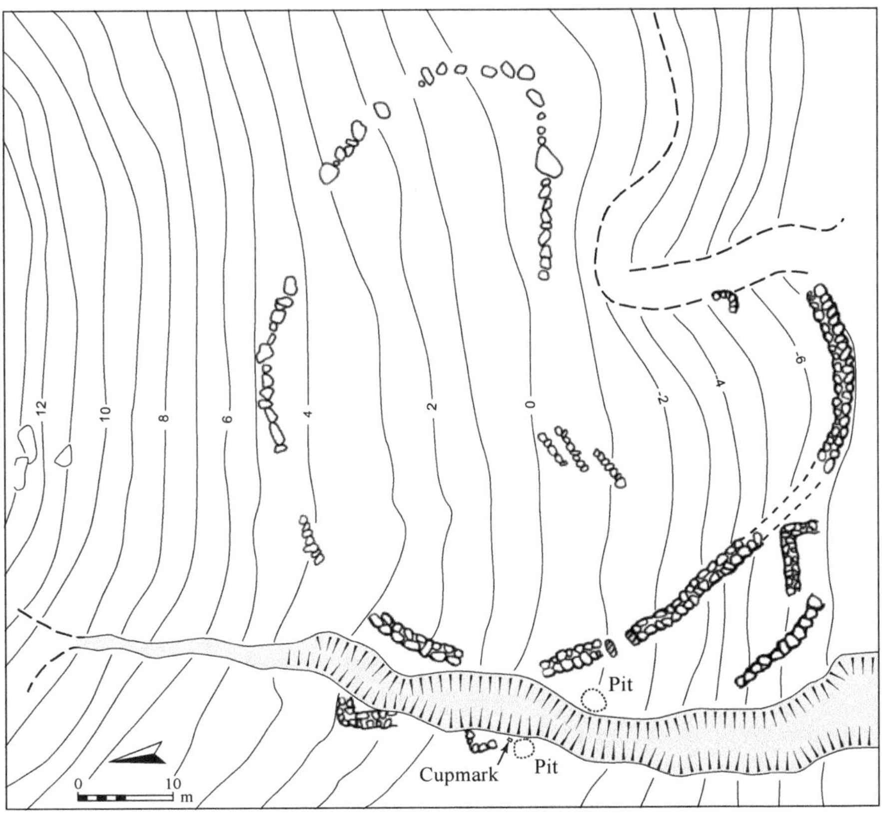

298. Plan of **'Ein 'Aujah (1)**.

500 m east of the spring. Steep slopes rise northward and westward about 8 m above the parking lot. Wadi 'Aujah flows eastward below and south of the parking lot.

The site contains a large elliptical enclosure (east-west axis 65 m, north-south 60 m). In the north and east it is enclosed by a wall of one row of large stones. The wall does not close the enclosure in the south, and is built of one straight row of stones reaching a particularly large rock. In the western part, next to the deep riverbed, the wall has two rows of medium-sized stones 1 m thick. In the south-western part of the wall is an opening 1 m wide with two upright standing jamb stones.

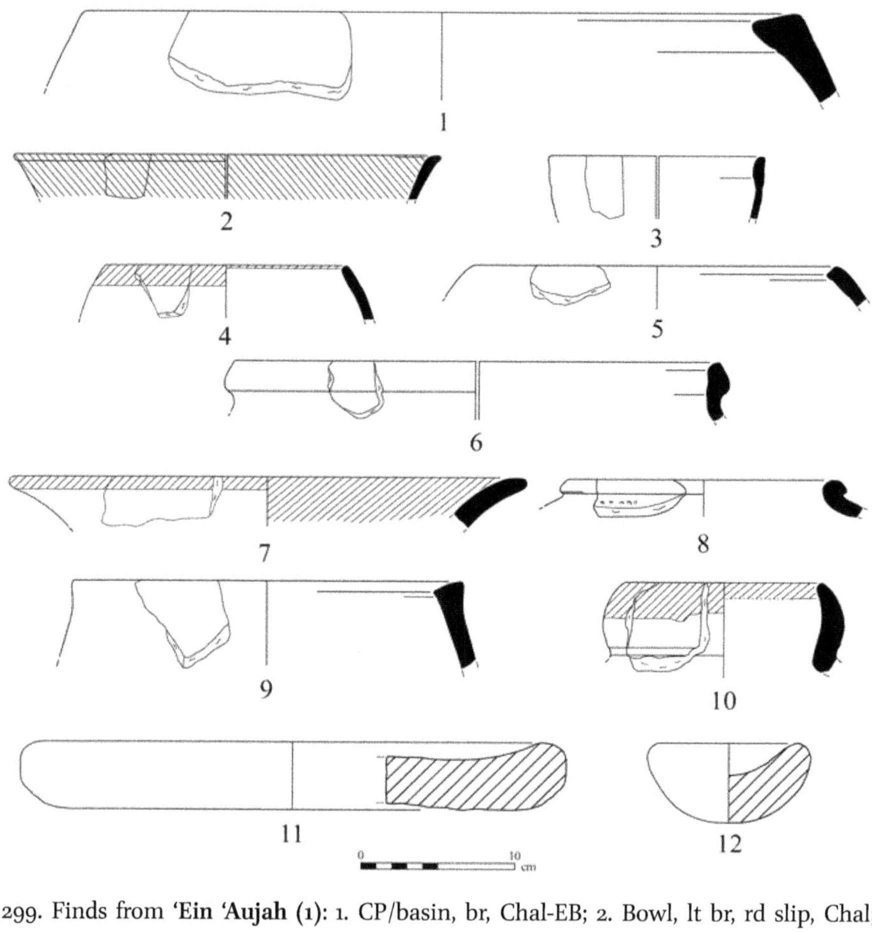

299. Finds from **'Ein 'Aujah (1)**: 1. CP/basin, br, Chal-EB; 2. Bowl, lt br, rd slip, Chal; 3. Bowl, br, LR; 4. Bowl, buff, rd slip, Chal-EB; 5. HM jar, buff, Chal-EB; 6. CP, br, IA I-II; 7. Bowl, buff, rd slip, EB; 8. Jar, buff, dotted dec, EB; 9. Jar, lt br, Chal; 10. Bow-rim jar, lt br, rd dec, Neo-Chal; 11-12. Bowls, basalt.

Outside and to the west of the enclosure wall, by the 5 m-deep channel, are remains of other structures. The channel disrupted the structures; so it must have been built after the EBA. There are two deep pits in the vicinity of the disruption, each about 2 m in diameter. In the channel section there is a fine stratification which includes from top to bottom: a top silt layer about 35 cm deep; a living level (EBA I) about 80 cm deep, within which were revealed remains of a wall running parallel to the enclosure wall; a fill layer, 35 cm deep; a living level (Wadi Rabah culture), 35 cm deep with a visible floor and mudbrick remains; and a burnt level without remains, 30 cm deep. The total depth of these layers is more than 2 m.

There is a moderate sherd scatter on the surface. Numerous sherds were found in the section cut by the stream channel.

Pottery: Late Neolithic/Early Chalcolithic (Wadi Rabah Culture) – 40%; Early Bronze I – 35%; Iron I-II – 5%; Late Roman – 20%.
Flint: 19 items, Pottery Neolithic/Early Chalcolithic (Wadi Rabah culture, see Appendix A).
Stone: 5 basalt bowls, limestone bowl, basalt grinding tool.
Additional surveys: Spanier 1992: site 151; 1994: 68 (He did not identify the protohistoric material, describing it as an Iron II, Hellenistic, Byzantine and Early Moslem site – none of these were found in our survey, which suggests a wrong identification of the site).
Bibliography: Bar 2014: site 108.

♦ ♦ ♦

Site 134: 18-15/81/2

'IRAQ EL-GHAWARNEH (1)

Israel grid: 1880/1512 (centre)
UTM grid: 7270/5380
Elevation: 0 m a.s.l., 0 m a.s.a.
Name: local
Site type: enclosures
Area: 20 dunams (2 ha)
Topography: slope
Rock type: Judea Group
Soil type: stony-desert
Soil quality: 2
Cultivation: none
Cisterns: none
Water source: Nahal Yitav (182), 300 m distant
Road: 'Aujah et-Tahtah–'Ein 'Aujah (C48), next to the site
Visits: April 2005 and more; 60 sherds

A site of enclosures on a slope descending southward in the direction of Wadi 'Aujah and the nearby road, 2 km west-north-west of Yitav. The slope is cut by numerous ravines and entirely covered by fallen stones. There is a fine lookout to the narrow section of Wadi 'Aujah and to the sites of 'Aujah Fortress, Kh. 'Aujah el-Foqa and the Ottoman flour water mill (Sites 140, 143, 142 respectively).

All enclosures are close by and architectonically similar:

Enclosure no. 1 is an irregular oval in form (east-west axis 37 m, 25 m north-south). It is encircled by a particularly thick 3–5 m wall, built of parallel rows of medium-sized stones. Part of the wall is step-built longitudinally, with the outer side higher than the inner. Each of the two entrances in the east side is marked by two upstanding monoliths with a gap between them. In the northern part is a semicircular stage paved with large stones, projecting into the enclosure. There are various other projections into and out of the enclosure. Long walls intersect the enclosure from west to east and near them there are remains of structures. In the north part are stone circular installations, 1 m in diameter; with walls projecting from them reaching to the structures in the past.

300. **'Iraq el-Ghawarneh (1)**, view to north-east at the slope with its sites, 2012. Four enclosures over the slope and parts of the settlement are visible (A. Solomon).

Enclosure no. 2 is a circle 28 m in diameter. The wall is particularly thick – 4 m, built of four rows of step-laid stones. In the inside there are a number of constructed circles, which may be installations.

Only a corner and an entrance of a large stones structure survive in the area between the enclosures.

Southward down the spur, in the direction of the modern concrete aqueduct are the following enclosures:

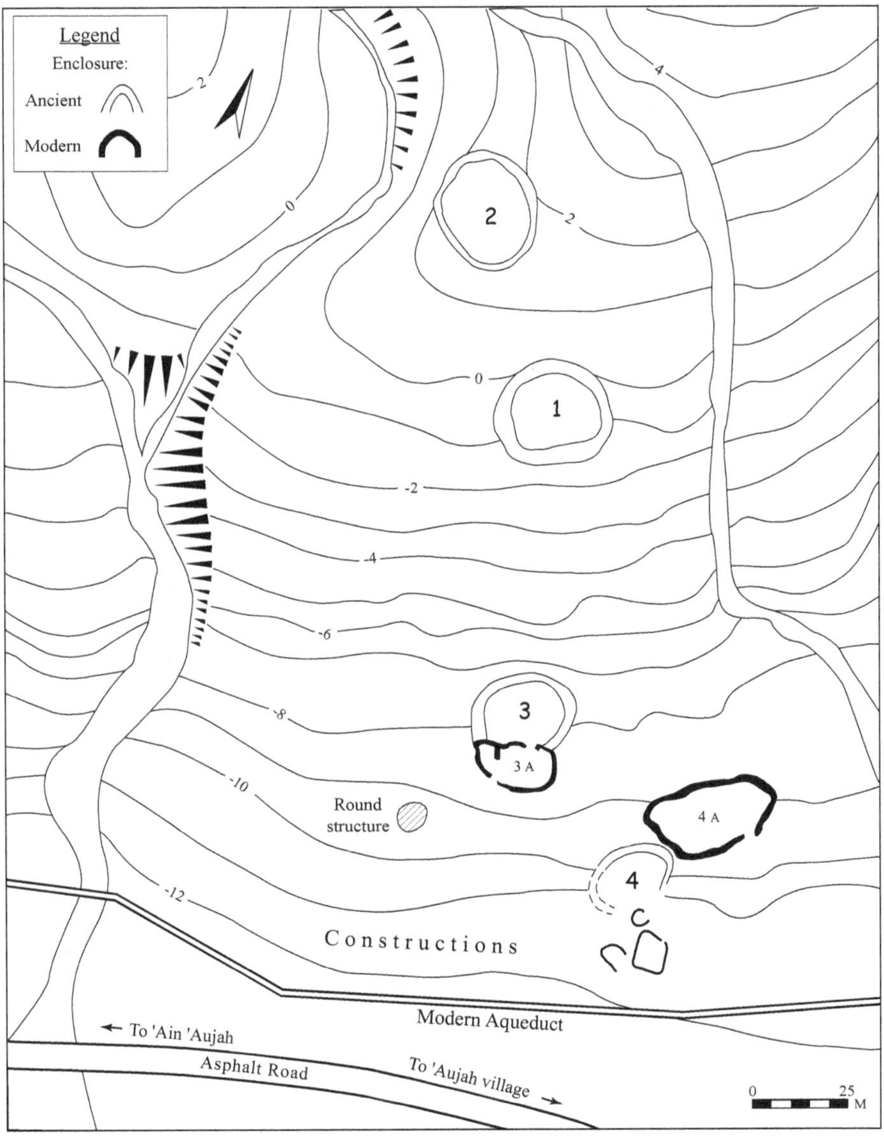

301. Plan of **'Iraq el-Ghawarneh (1).**

Enclosure no. 3 is similar to no. 2, and is about 22 m in diameter, built of one row of stones. This enclosure is less well preserved than enclosures 1 and 2. A corral (marked 3A on the plan) is built on its southern part. This corral is a modern sheepfold, measuring about 20 m long by 8 m wide. Around it is an 80 cm-thick wall 1 m high. It has entrances and subdivisions.

Enclosure no. 4 is located 35 m south-east of no. 3. It is partially preserved, and its construction is similar to that of the other enclosures. It is certain that it was one in the series of enclosures on the spur.

East of enclosure no. 4 is corral no. 4A. This is a large modern flock pen, measuring 32 m by 15 m, built like no. 3A, with the entrance in the south-eastern part.

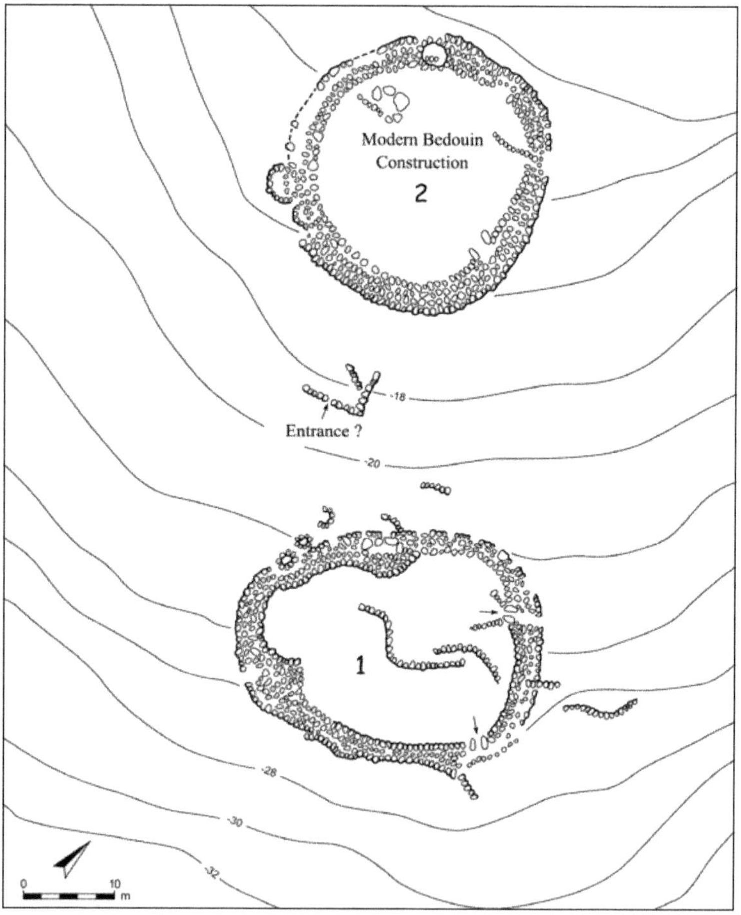

302. **'Iraq el-Ghawarneh (1)**: a detailed plan of enclosures 1 and 2.

There are several structures south of enclosure no. 4, the nature of which is not clear. The whole area between enclosure no. 3 and the aqueduct, standing prominently above the plain, is covered with building stones, testifying to past construction. A round structure, perhaps a tower, is conspicuous south-west of enclosure no. 3.

All the ancient enclosures in the site are outstanding in their shape and the great thickness of the encircling walls.

Pottery: Chalcolithic – 10%; Intermediate Bronze (?) – 2%; Middle Bronze II – 30%; Iron II – 36%; Late Roman – 20%; Early Moslem – 2%.
Flint: 95 items (see Appendix A).
Bibliography: Bar 2014: site 109
Additional surveys: none.

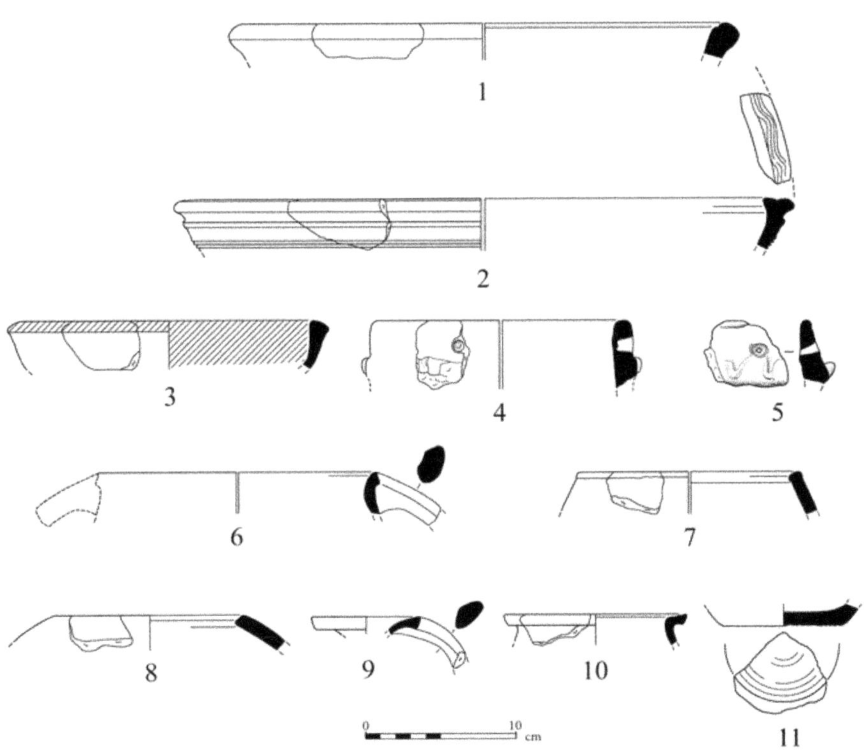

303. Pottery from **'Iraq el-Ghawarneh (1)**: 1. CP (?), lt br, MB II; 2. CP, buff, incised dec, EM; 3. Bowl, lt br, rd slip, IA II; 4-5. CP, br, MB II; 6. CP, rd, LR; 7-8. HM jars, lt br, Chal; 9. Jug, rd, LR; 10. Jug, lt br, LR; 11. Base with mat impression, buff, Chal.

Site 135: 18-15/71/1

'EIN 'AUJAH (5)

Israel grid: 1872/1512
UTM grid: 7261/5380
Elevation: 0 m b.s.l., 25 m b.s.a.
Name: nearest place
Site type: structure and sherd scatter
Area: 2 dunams (2000 sq. m)
Topography: platform above wadi bank
Rock type: Judea Group
Soil type: stony-desert
Soil quality: 1
Cultivation: none
Cisterns: none
Water source: Nahal Yitav (182), at the site
Road: 'Aujah et-Tahtah–'Ein 'Aujah (C48), next to the site
Visit: November 2010; 108 sherds

A site on the south bank of Wadi 'Aujah, 100 m south-east of the parking lot at the end of the road to 'Ein 'Aujah, and about 2.7 km west of Yitav.

There are three parts in the site:

1. A well-built structure, measuring 11×6 m, disrupted in its north part by the wadi. The walls of the structure, consisting of two elongated rooms with several exits east cut by the wadi, are built of two rows of dressed stones. It was probably related to the maintenance of the aqueduct.
2. Part of an ancient aqueduct (Qanat el-Far'un) preserved between the wadi and the cliff. It is 1 m wide and construction and plaster remains survive. The

304. View west at part of **'Ein 'Aujah (5)**, which is south and above Wadi 'Aujah, 2011. Shay Bar is standing. In the background, marked by an arrow, is the site of **'Ein 'Aujah (1)**.

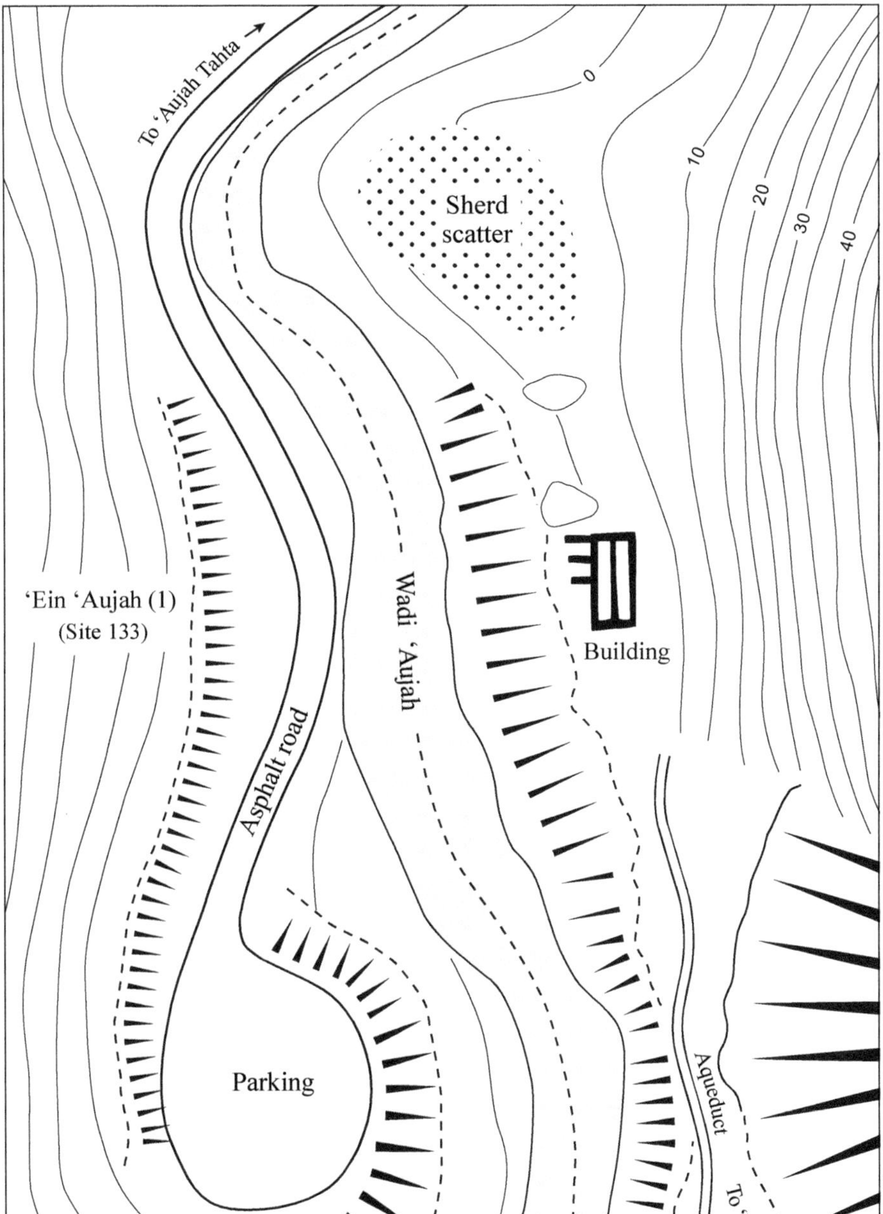

305. Plan of **'Ein 'Aujah (5)**.

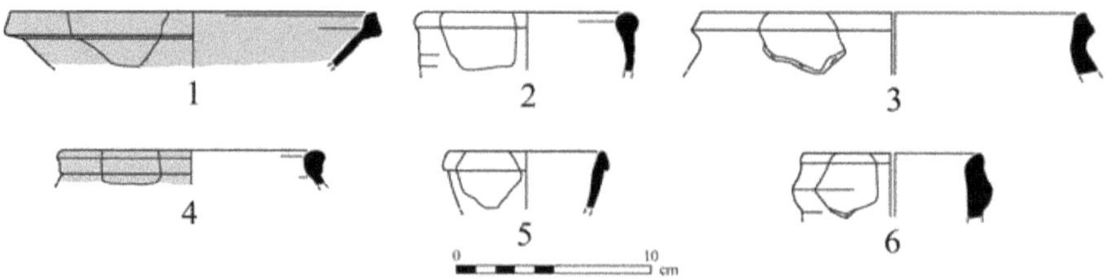

306. Pottery from **'Ein 'Aujah (5)**: 1. Bowl (Terra Sigillata), rd, rd slip, Rom-Byz; 2. Bowl, lt br, Rom-Byz; 3. CP, dk br, IA I-II; 4. Jar, lt br, rd slip, Rom-Byz; 5. Jug, rd, Rom-Byz; 6. Jug, dk br, IA I-II.

continuation of the aqueduct disappears in the vicinity of the structure; so the linkage between them is not clear.

3. There is a sherd scatter of various periods about 30 m east of the structure on a spur descending towards the wadi. The relation between the sherd scatter and the structure and the aqueduct is not clear.

Pottery: Chalcolithic/Early Bronze (?) – 4% (body sherds); Middle Bronze II (?) – 3% (body sherds); Iron I-II – 9%; Roman-Byzantine – 34%; Medieval – 4% (body sherds); undefined – 46%.
Flint: 6 items (see Appendix A).
Additional surveys: none.

♦ ♦ ♦

Site 136: 18-15/71/4

'IRAQ EL-GHAWARNEH (2)

Israel grid: 1878/1512
UTM grid: 7267/5380
Elevation: 5 m b.s.l., 0 m a.s.a.
Name: local
Site type: large
Area: 15 dunams (1.5 ha)
Topography: slope
Rock type: Judea Group
Soil type: stony-desert
Soil quality: 2
Cultivation: none
Cisterns: none
Water source: Nahal Yitav (182) , at the site
Road: 'Aujah et-Tahtah–'Ein 'Aujah (C48), next to the site
Visits: May 2005 and more; 200 sherds

A large site on a moderate slope, descending south towards Wadi 'Aujah and the road passing it, 2.3 km west of Yitav. The site is enclosed by a deep channel in the east and a cliff in the west. In the upper north-western part of the site is the so-called 'pool' and in the south and east are the rest of the remains:

1. The 'pool': this is a large rectangular structure measuring 40×30 m, enclosed by a well-built wall of two rows of large stones, some of which are dressed,

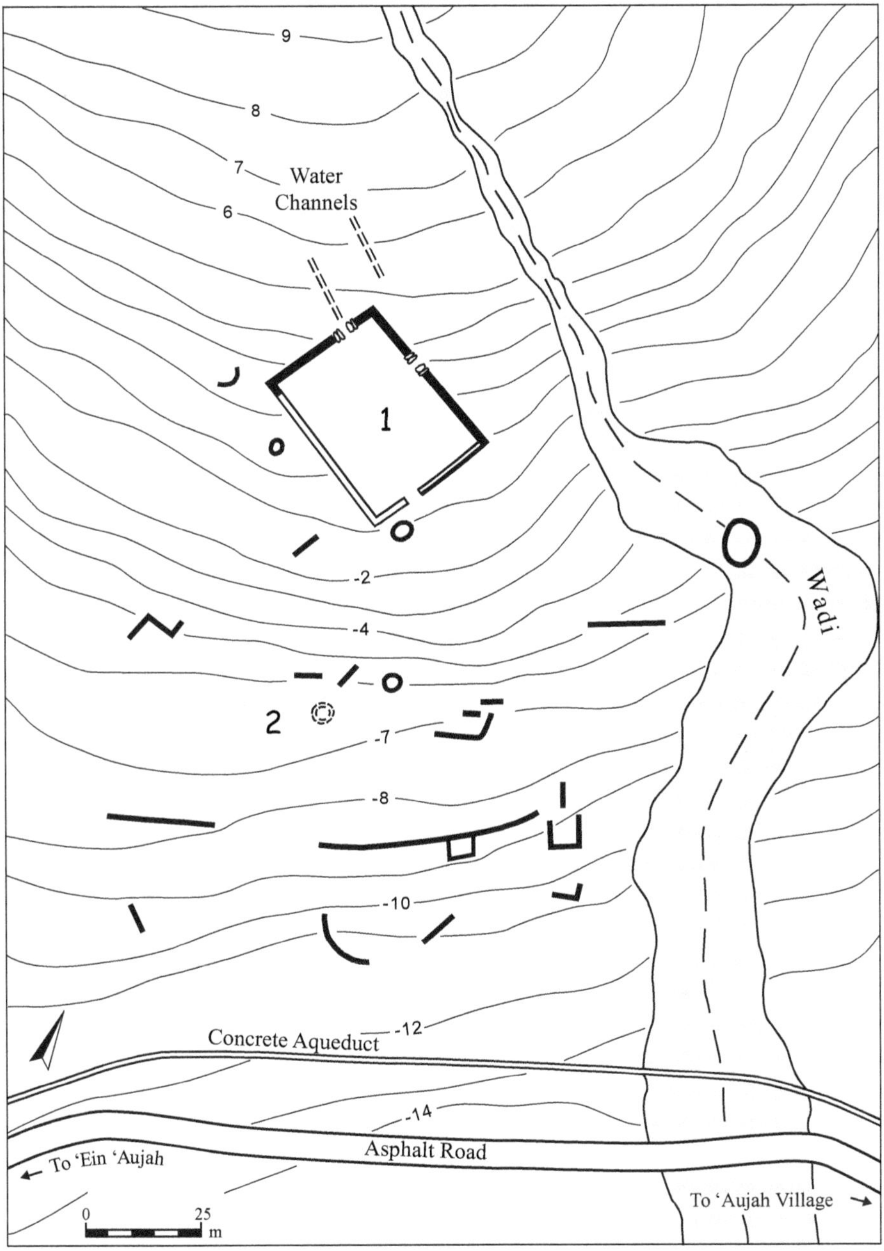

307. Plan of **'Iraq el-Ghawarneh (2)**.

with a fill of small stones between them. The thickness of the wall is 1.2 m. Inside the structure is a long recess, indicating a possible function as a water reservoir. Near the north-western corner is a built entrance, an entry of a duct between two large stones with a stone cover. This entrance is approached by the remains of a duct. In the middle of the northern wall is another entrance, and it is likely that water flowed into the facility through these openings.

The quality of construction and the openings support the suggestion that this is a water reservoir; but the source of the water, as well as the reason for the elevated position are not known.

2. The structures: there are remains of numerous structures between the pool and the concrete aqueduct over an area 150 m long, mostly covered by silt and fallen stones, and only partly projecting above the surface. Along the slope have been preserved sections of walls and well-built structures of medium-sized stones, long supporting walls and a series of circular structures, 4–5 m in diameter. Those point to the existence of a settlement on the alluvial fan, and that parts of it were already built in the Late Neolithic/Chalcolithic period. Other structures were added later.

The site is close to the west of 'Iraq el-Ghawarneh (1 [Site no. 134]).

Pottery: Late Neolithic/Chalcolithic (Wadi Raba Culture) – 11%; Middle Bronze II – 11%; Iron I – 16%; Iron II – 7%; Late Roman – 18%; Byzantine – 26%; Medieval – 11%.
Additional surveys: Spanier (1992: site 152) identified the rectangular enclosure and noted Byzantine pottery only.
Bibliography: Bar 2014: site 109.

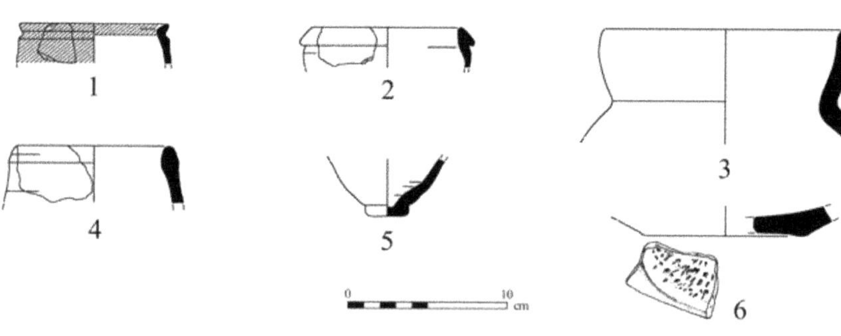

308. Pottery from **'Iraq el-Ghawarneh (2)**: 1. Bowl, rd, rd slip, LR; 2. Bowl, rd, LR; 3. Bow-rim jar, dk br, Neo-Chal; 4. Jar, dk br, IA II; 5. Base, rd, LR; 6. Base, amber, mat-impression, Neo-Chal.

Site 137: 18-15/91/1

ELEVATION POINT -66

Israel grid: 1894/1513
UTM grid: 7283/5381
Elevation: 60 m b.s.l., 20 m a.s.a.
Name: nearest place
Site type: small
Area: 1 dunam (1000 sq. m)
Topography: hilltop
Rock type: Judea Group
Soil type: stony-desert
Soil quality: 2
Cultivation: none
Cisterns: none
Water source: Nahal Yitav (182), 1.2 km distant
Road: 'Aujah et-Tahtah–'Ein 'Aujah (C48), 1 km distant
Visits: May 2005, 2007; 100 sherds

A small site on a hilltop west of Elevation Point -66, 1 km north-west from Yitav, and east of the unpaved road from the 'Aujah road to Wadi Maqor edh-Dhib and Wadi el-Hamam.

There are very few remains of structures – sections of walls and a single corner. Also round structures were found that are probably installations or tombs.

The poor degree of preservation did not allow measurements or drawing a plan.

Pottery: Early Bronze I – 66%; Intermediate Bronze – 4%; Middle Bronze II (?) – 4%; Iron – 4%; Hellenistic (?) – 4%; Late Roman – 23%.
Flint: 91 items, Early Bronze I Age (see Appendix A).
Additional surveys: none.
Bibliography: Bar 2014: site 107.

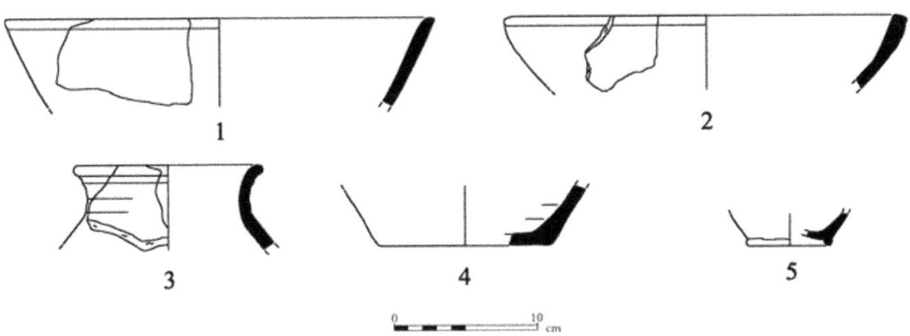

309. Pottery from **E.P. -66** (all EB I but no. 5): 1-2. Bowls, lt br; 3. Jar, br; 4. Base, lt br; 5. Base, blk, Mod.

Site 138: 19-15/51/1

ELEVATION POINT -249

This site (Israel grid 1951/1513; UTM grid: 7340/5382) was surveyed in the Emergency Survey (1968) and described as follows: "Structures north of Kh. el-'Aujah et-Tahtah. Enclosure built of flint stones measuring 23×19 m, and a 50 m long wall coming out from its north-east corner. To north-east there are remains of rectangular structures and a round structure with most of its stones removed. **Pottery:** from the Roman, Byzantine and Arabic periods..."

Our attempts to find the site failed. It was apparently destroyed during the enlargement of the village of 'Aujah et-Tahtah.

Bibliography: Bar-Adon 1972: site 24.

♦ ♦ ♦

Site 139: 18-15/71/5

VILLA 'AUJAH

Israel grid: 1876/1510
UTM grid: 7265/5378
Elevation: 35 m b.s.l., 0 m a.s.a.
Name: given by the survey
Site type: structure
Area: 1 dunam (1000 sq. m)
Topography: valley and wadi bank
Rock type: Judea Group
Soil type: stony-desert
Soil quality: 4
Cultivation: none
Cisterns: none
Water source: Nahal Yitav (182), at the site
Road: 'Aujah Tahtah–'Ein 'Aujah (C48), next to the site
Visits: January 2005 and more; 50 sherds

A structure on the northern high bank of Wadi 'Aujah, near and south of the approach road to 'Ein 'Aujah.

The measurements of the large structure are 20×18 m, with three longitudinal spaces from north to south. The enclosing western wall has been eroded away by the wadi. The structure is on a slope descending south in steps. The construction is good, and some of the walls are of dressed stones combined with boulders. The bottom wall (the southern one) of the structure, built of large stones, stretches eastward as a support wall.

The room description:

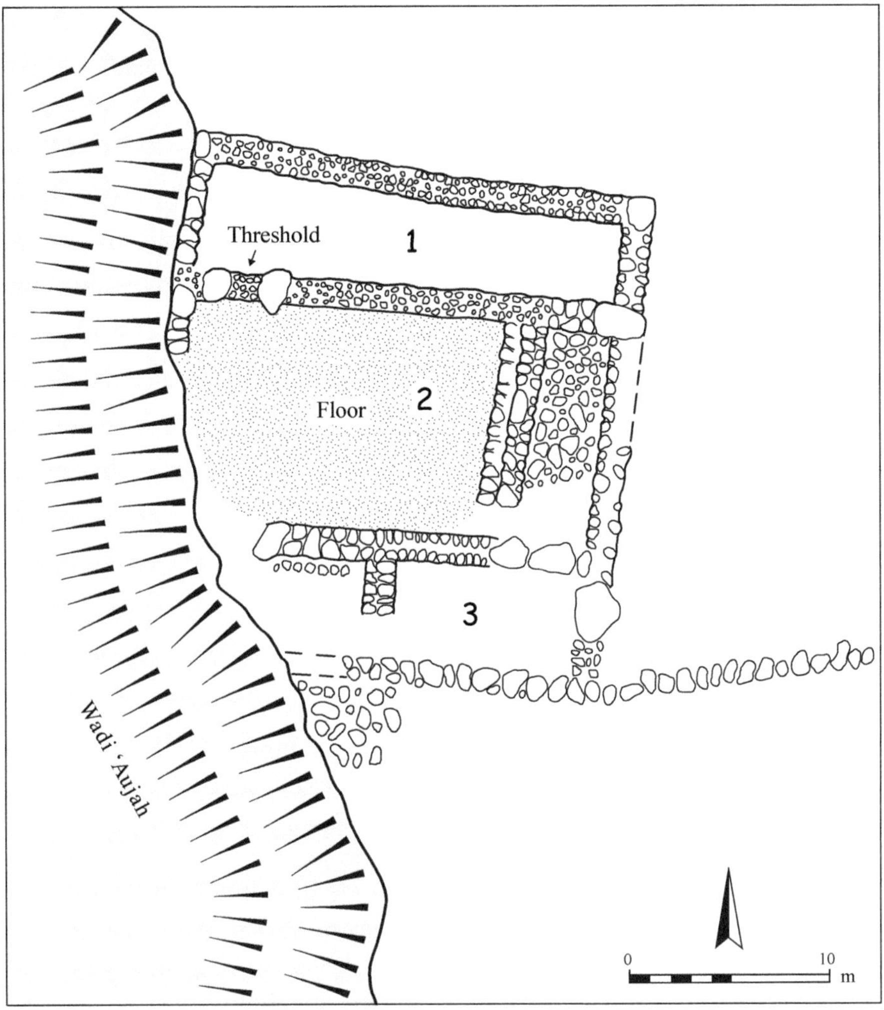

310. Plan of **Villa 'Aujah**.

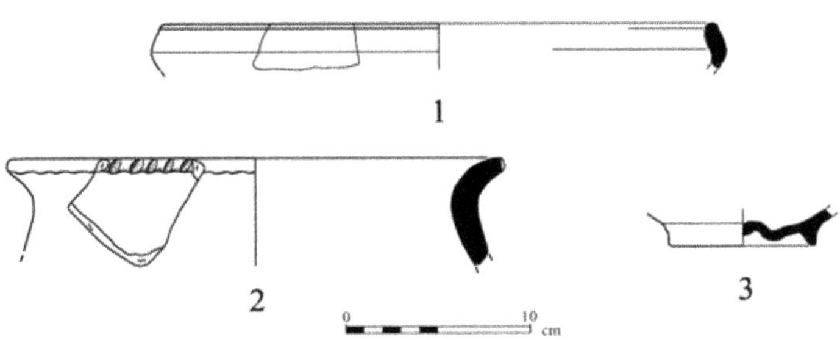

311. Pottery from **Villa 'Aujah**: 1. Bowl, dk br, IA II; 2. Jar, lt br, thumbed dec, EB; 3. Jug base, lt br, ER.

1. The northern room (measuring 18×3.5 m) has large stones in the corners and in the western wall. In the rest of the room only infrastructure made of small stones survives.
2. In the centre of the structure is a large hall (12×10 m) with a wall east of it. The hall is paved with a thick layer of white plaster appearing on the surface. There is stone paving adjacent to and outside the eastern wall.
3. The southern room (12×3.5 m) is divided into two by a pilaster.

The structure is dated to the Early Roman period, built over an Iron Age site.

Pottery: Early Bronze – 2%; Iron II – 48%; Early Roman – 50%.
Flint: 8 items (see Appendix A).
Additional surveys: none.

♦ ♦ ♦

Site 140: 18-15/80/1

'AUJAH FORTRESS

Israel grid: 1883/1506
UTM grid: 7272/5374
Elevation: 60 m b.s.l., 0 m a.s.a.
Name: given by the survey
Site type: fortress and monastery
Area: 4 dunams (4000 sq. m)
Topography: wadi bank
Rock type: Judea Group
Soil type: Mediterranean forest
Soil quality: 3
Cultivation: none
Cisterns: one (by the site)
Water source: Nahal Yitav (182), at the site
Road: 'Aujah et-Tahtah–'Ein 'Aujah (C48), next to the site
Visits: December 2004 and many more; 400 sherds

A large fortress and a Byzantine monastery on the north bank of Wadi 'Aujah, 400 m east of Kh. 'Aujah el-Foqa (Site 143) and well below it. The road to 'Ein 'Aujah passes nearby to the north.

The site is triangular; its south-western leg is slightly curved, about 75 m long, and follows the high bank of Wadi 'Aujah. The south-western casement wall is parallel to it.

The northern, straight, leg is about 50 m long, with a casement wall about 6 m wide running along it.

The eastern leg was originally about 40 m long, also with a casement wall, of which only a few remnants survive. The enclosing outer wall is about 1.2 m thick.

A large pit, about 24 m in diameter with a maximum depth of 6 m, was dug at the eastern wall (no. 2 on plan). The pit damaged the original walls of the site. Its function and date of digging are unknown.

In the centre there is a rectangular structure (no. 4), measuring 14×8 m, with a stone-built double wall, connecting to the eastern leg.

At the upper side of the site there are 50-60 graves (no. 5), apparently a Moslem cemetery from the 19-20th centuries.

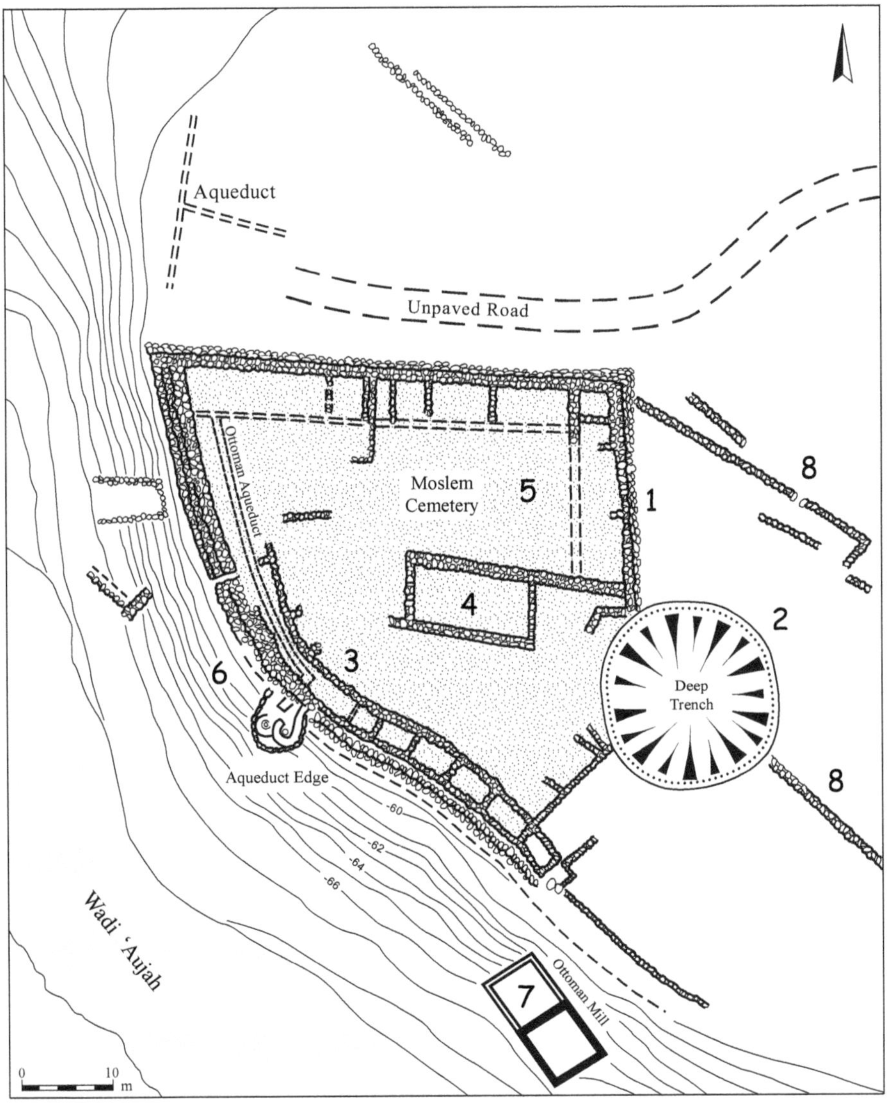

312. **'Aujah Fortress**, plan before the recent unpublished excavation.

The south-western slope descending steeply to the wadi was strengthened by thick support walls (no. 6), which have been partly washed away. These walls reinforce the superstructure against floods and serve as a podium.

In the centre of the south-western leg is a water shaft with two openings (near no. 6). The water was supplied through an aqueduct crossing the south-western part of the fortress. Further along this leg, at the bottom of the slope, is a structure, measuring 14×9 m, now standing about 3 m high, including its stone roof. The structure was utilized as a flourmill during the Ottoman period (no. 7).

On all sides of the site are walls, some connected to the fortress/monastery, and others to the aqueduct.

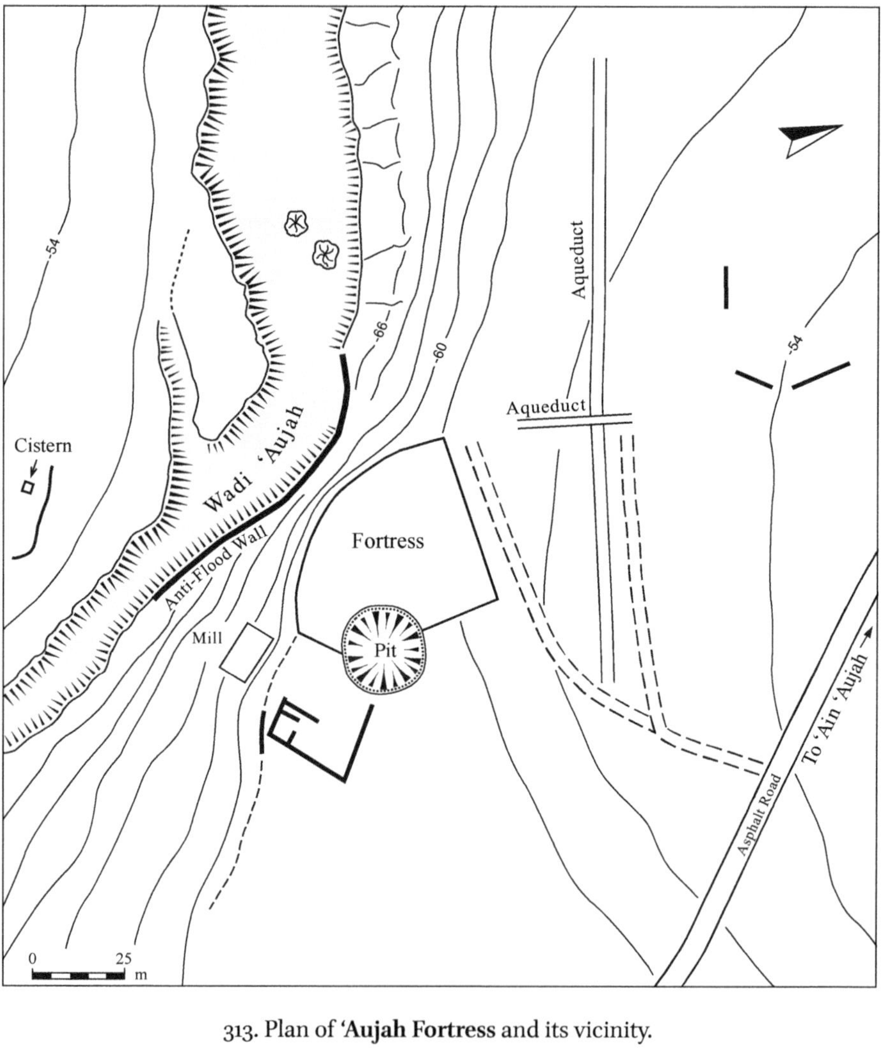

313. Plan of **'Aujah Fortress** and its vicinity.

314. **'Aujah Fortress**, view south at the new excavation by the Archaeology Staff Officer for Judea and Samaria, 2012. The site is an Iron Age II fortress, over which a Byzantine monastery has been built (A. Solomon).

315. **'Aujah Fortress**: an elongated room dug in the Byzantine monastery, 2012. Standing: Shoshi Lotan (S. Bar).

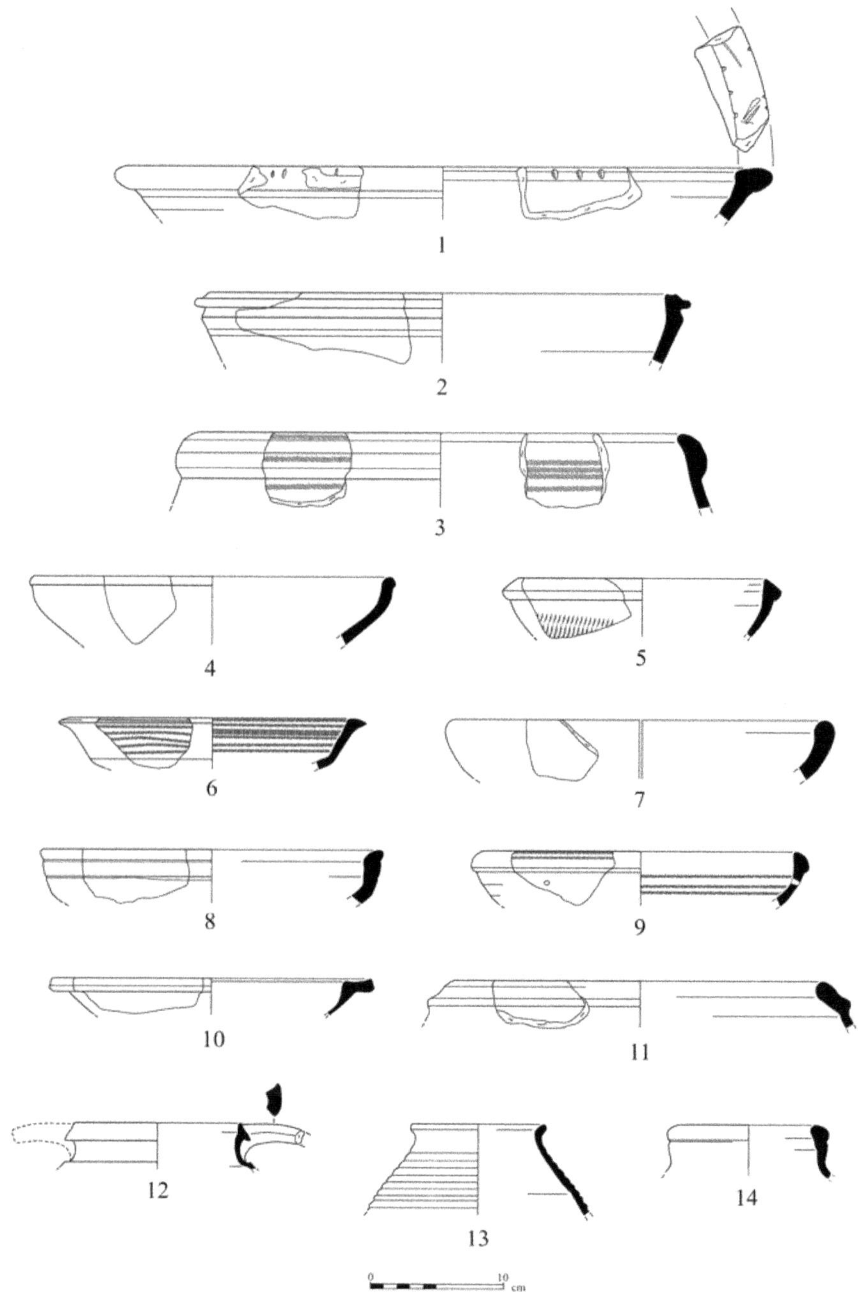

316. Finds from **'Aujah Fortress**: 1. CP, buff, incised dec, Byz-ER; 2. CP, rd, Rom-Byz; 3. CP, lt br, rd slip, IA II; 4. Bowl, dk br, IA I-II; 5. Bowl, rd, LR-Byz; 6, 9. Bowls, lt br, rd slip, IA II; 7. Manasseh type bowl (?), dk br, IA I; 8. Bowl, br, IA II; 10. Bowl, rd, Rom; 11. CP, dk br, IA I-II; 12. CP, rd, Rom; 13. Jar, br, Byz; 14. Jar, br, IA I-II.

The site was apparently originally linked to the city in 'Aujah el-Foqa; situated above and south of it. Both were established at the same period – Iron Age II – and belonged to the same complex. Apparently, the fortress by the wadi protected the water and the road, while the city was the hub for the whole region.

During the Byzantine period the site was converted to a monastery. Some of its remains were revealed in 2010, during an excavation by the Archaeology Staff Officer, not yet published. Several rooms of a church including, a plastered pool and a mosaic paved room were exposed.

An inscription was found in the mosaic floor in the entrance to the prayer hall in the church. It is not yet published, but is already on display in the "Good Samaritan Museum" on the main road between Jerusalem and Jericho. It reads:

"My saint Anastasius, bless this spring and give endurance to Eli".

The spring mentioned is the near-by 'Ein 'Aujah spring.

Pottery: Iron I – 12%; Iron II – 25%; Persian-Hellenistic – 5%; Roman – 12%; Byzantine/Early Moslem – 25%; Medieval – 12%; Ottoman – 9%.
Flint: 20 items, Iron Age (see Appendix A).
Additional surveys: Spanier 1992: site 168.

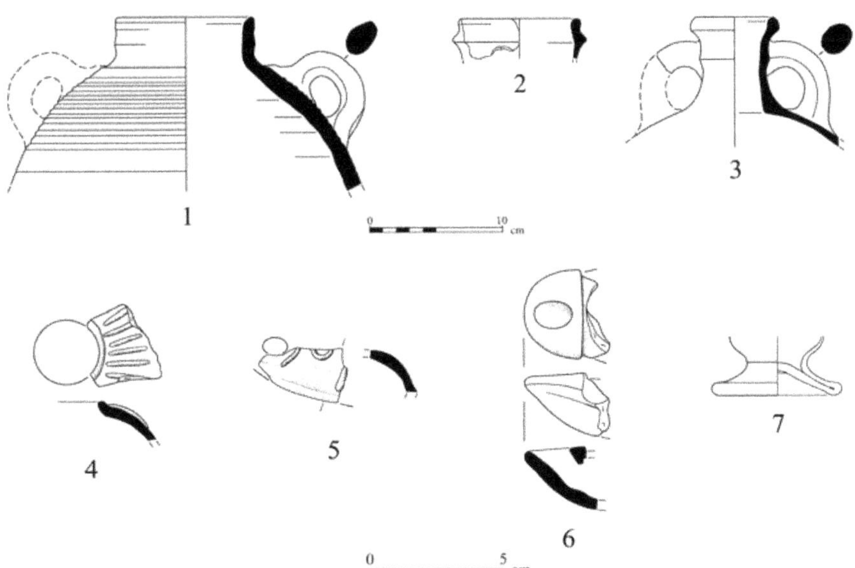

317. Finds from '**Aujah Fortress** (continuation): 1. Jar, br, Byz; 2. Jug, lt br, IA I-II; 3. Pilgrim flask, lt br, Rom-Byz; 4-5. Lamps, lt br, Byz; 6. Lamp, lt br, ER; 7. Jug, green glass, Rom-Byz.

Site 141:

THE AQUEDUCTS OF WADI ‘AUJAH

This is a sophisticated system of aqueducts, bridges and passages, originating at ‘Ein ‘Aujah and going north-east (to Archelais) and south-east (to Jericho). For details see Appendix D.

♦ ♦ ♦

Site 142: 18-15/80/2

‘AUJAH FLOURMILL

Israel grid: 1881/1504
UTM grid: 7270/5372
Elevation: 60 m b.s.l., 0 m a.s.a.
Name: given by the survey
Site type: small
Area: 1 dunam (1000 sq. m)
Topography: valley edge
Rock type: Judea Group
Soil type: alluvium
Soil quality: 6
Cultivation: none
Cisterns: none
Water source: Nahal Yitav (182), at the site
Road: ‘Aujah Tahtah–’Ein ‘Aujah (C48), 400 m distant
Visits: December 2004, 2005 and more; 20 sherds

A flour mill at the edge of the narrow valley of Wadi ‘Aujah, at the northern low end of the ‘Aujah el-Foqa hill.

The six parts of the mill are:

1. A plastered stone aqueduct with a built outlet to the mill, on a support wall built of medium-sized stones, which crosses the upper slope.
2. A conduit, 8 m long with a 1 m circular cross-section, built of small stones and well plastered, starts from the aqueduct and empties into the mill water supply cistern. The conduit is mounted on a large stone bridge-like building with two arches.
3. The conduit bridge, built on the slope descending to the valley, is about 10 m long, the maximum height near the water supply cistern is about 4.5 m, and it is about 3 m wide, narrower at the top.
4. The water contains a base on which there is a tall narrow tower with a plastered stone pipe, through which the water falls to the grinding area.
5. The grinding area: a structure on the slope 18×5 m with a grinding hall and three other rooms of the same dimensions (about 5×4.5 m). In the centre of

the milling room there are a water conduit and the millstone area with the overflow duct to the valley.

6. A long narrow structure 33×4 m, and 1.5 m high, runs down the slope west of the mill. On one side is a support wall and on the other is an earth rampart. It appears that the structure was dug into the slope. The structure (now in disrepair) is built of medium-sized stones. A small room with an entrance is attached to it in the north-east.

Two millstones were found outside the milling hall, not in situ. They are made of special concrete with reinforcement of iron bars. The stones are engraved: "Fabrique generale Moulin" (general millstone factory).

The flour mill was perhaps noted by the British Survey (Conder and Kitchener 1882: 391), which did not give details. It is also mentioned, accompanied with a photograph, by Ilan (1973: 262), again without details. The dating by the British Survey of "Medieval" is not substantiated.

The source of the Iron Age pottery appears to have been the site of 'Aujah el-Foqa (no. 143) which is located above the mill. The rest of the finds indicate construction of some sections of the site (the courtyards?), during the Byzantine or Early Moslem period. The mill was probably built in the Ottoman

318. The Ottoman period (?) **'Aujah flourmill**, an aerial view south-east, 2008. The conduit structure and the mill remains are visible (N. Eshed).

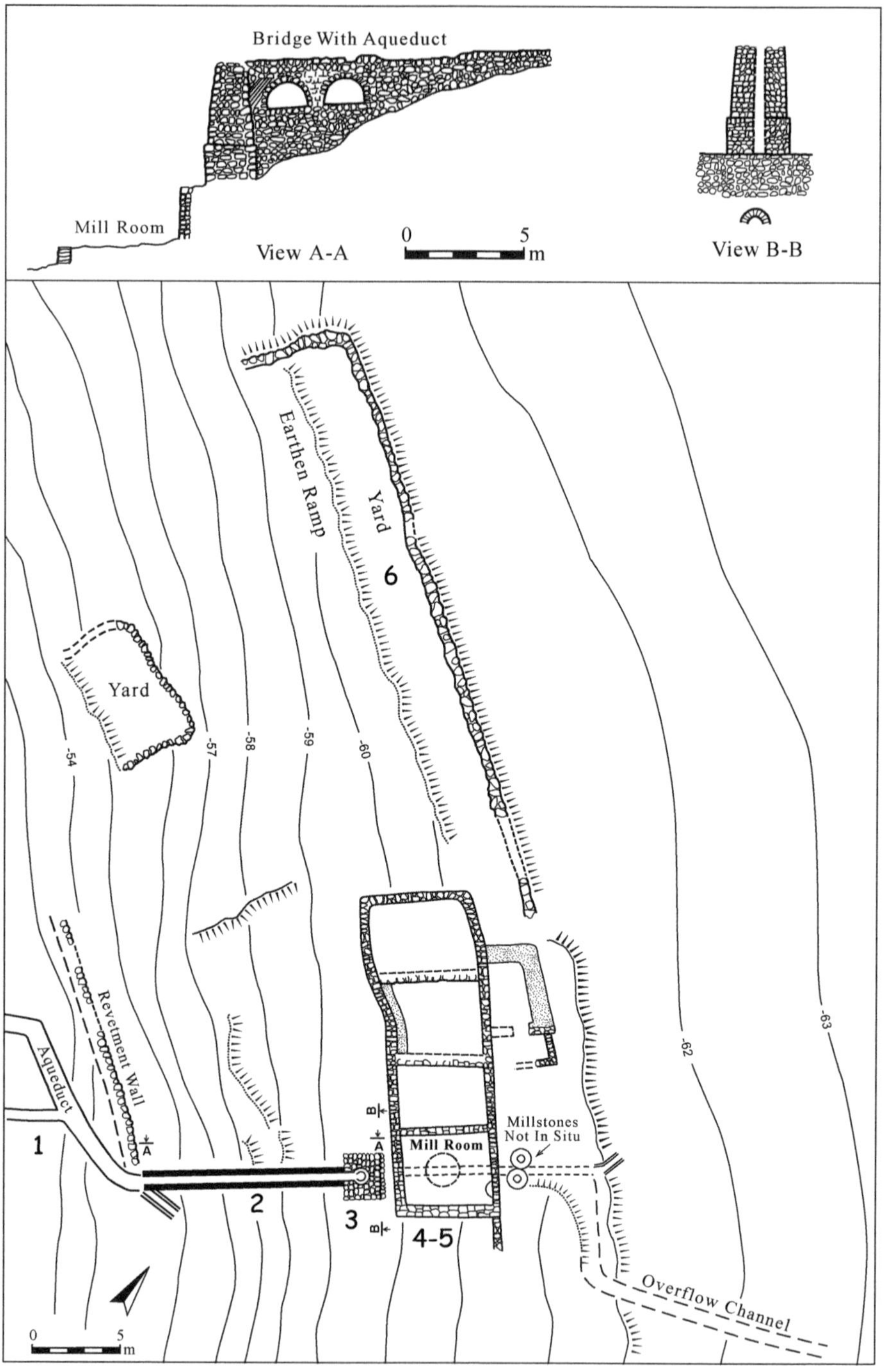

319. **'Aujah flourmill**, plan and views.

period, and it was in use into the 19th century, according to the French millstones.

See a detailed discussion in Appendix D.

Pottery: Iron II – 20%; Byzantine-Early Moslem – 10%; Medieval-Ottoman – 70%.
Additional surveys: none.

320. **'Aujah flourmill**, perspective view east (O. Gadir).

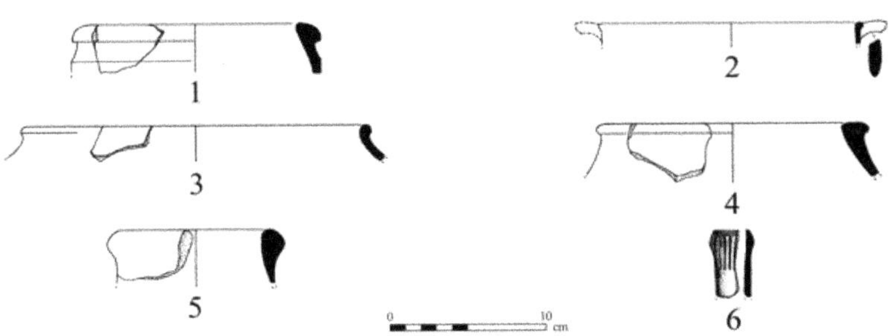

321. Pottery from **'Aujah flourmill**: 1. Bowl, lt br, IA II; 2. Jug, rd, Byz-EM; 3. Jar/CP, rd, MA (?); 4. Jar/CP, lt br, MA (?); 5. Jar, lt br, IA II; 6. Pipe, rd, Ott.

Site 143: 18-15/70/1

KHIRBET 'AUJAH EL-FOQA

Israel grid: 1879/1504
UTM grid: 7268/5372
Elevation: 27 m a.s.l., 100 m a.s.a.
Name: on map
Site type: fortified town
Area: 15 dunams (1.5 ha)
Topography: high hilltop
Rock type: Judea Group
Soil type: stony-desert
Soil quality: 4
Cultivation: none
Cisterns: 5
Water source: Nahal Yitav (182), 400 m distant
Road: 'Aujah Tahtah–'Ein 'Aujah (C48), 400 m distant
Visits: December 2003 and many more; 400 sherds

A well-preserved fortified city on a hill summit to the south, and above Wadi 'Aujah, 2 km west of Yitav.

The Iron Age II city was first discovered and investigated in the framework of our survey and the results were published in 2009 (Zertal et al. 2009).

This is a summary of the published data:

The site is situated on a high stony hill isolated by steep slopes, and can be approached only over a narrow saddle to the north-west. The site is almost circular (110 m north–south, and 85 m east–west), with a projection on its south eastern edge. The overall area, including the parts outside and around the Iron Age walls, is 15 dunams (1.5 ha). The city was defended around most of its perimeter (east, south and west), by a casemate wall. A tall tower is located at the centre of the site. The location of the site is uncomfortable ecologically: it is very hard to climb, not easily accessible from the nearest water source, and far from the main roads of the period. However, its position on a hilltop, with an excellent view, hints at its military qualities. Therefore, we suggest defining this site as a fortified town.

The site was visited by the British Survey in 1874 (Conder and Kitchener 1882: 391), who described it as 'A ruined village on a mound, apparently modern'. This description, obviously deduced from its good state of preservation, especially concerning the Medieval hamlet's remains, dissuaded other scholars from studying or even visiting the place.

The site has the following main parts:

1. The central tower (no. 1 on the plan, Squares I/17–18) is located in the western part of the site, with a good view of its surroundings. It is 5 m high, measuring 7.5×7.5 m. The walls, built of smoothed stones, are well plastered inside. It is entered through an opening in the western wall. The tower, partially looted by robbers, stands inside a court measuring 15×15 m.

2. The western casemate wall (CW1, Squares E–L/13–19): The western and south-western sides of the summit were fortified by a casemate wall 90 m long and 5 m wide on average. Both the walls (outer and inner) are regularly built of a double row of stones, although the western one sometimes contains an extra row. The dividing walls, built one stone thick, create more than 20 rooms. Several small constructions, 1 m high, the purpose of which is unknown, are attached to the inside of the wall . A wall connects CW1 to the tower.
3. The north-western buildings (nos. 3–8, F–H/18–21). Close to the northern end of the casemate wall (E/18) are six adjoining structures. The complex consists of a cluster of three structures (nos. 3–5) irregular in shape, with common walls, and a courtyard. The next cluster comprises two attached structures (nos. 6–7) and one separated (no. 8). The walls, like those of all the houses at the site, are 1 m wide and built of two spaced rows of medium-sized stones with a fill between them. The walls twisted overtime, and it is difficult to reconstruct their original shape. Between the clusters of buildings (nos. 3–5 and 6–7) is a 5-m gap. It is assumed that the entrance to the site was located here.
4. Tower no. 9 (D–E/19–21). This is a large (15×12 m) square structure protruding westward from the line of the wall. This building might have been a

322. Aerial view south-east at the fortified site of **Kh. 'Aujah el-Foqa**, 2008. Note the remains of the casemate wall, the tower, various structures and 'chains' of rooms (N. Eshed).

part of the entrance complex. An additional isolated small tower (no. 10, C–D/22) is located in the north-western saddle, about 12 m from the wall. Its function is unknown.

5. The northern complex (nos. 11–14. G–L/21–23). The northern complex, covering an area of 2.5 dunams (2500 sq. m), differs from the other parts of the site, since its terrain is flat and it is densely built. In this area, the walls are buried under a massive collapse of stones. This area contains several large units (nos. 11–14). Some parts of these protrude from the line of the wall. No. 11 could have been a high tower (judging by the quantity of fallen stones); no. 12 refers to three courtyards, and no. 13 seems to be a typical four-room house with a courtyard to its south. No. 14 is a long narrow building along the wall line. The general nature of the northern part is not yet clear. It seems to contain public buildings, including fortified towers.
6. The north-eastern casemate wall (CW2, Squares O–M/18–23). The 45-m long section of this wall is composed of twin parallel walls, each 1 m wide, 4–5 m apart. More than 10 casemate rooms were seen between these walls, but it seems that there were more. Like CW1, the walls stand to the height of only one course of stones. Higher than this casemate wall and west of it is another parallel wall, creating an additional space, partly divided by partition walls.
7. The central group of buildings (nos. 15–29, 30–32, J–N/15–20). This central group is located in the geometric centre of the oval site, and east of tower no.1. It consists of several sub-groups of structures. A. This is a chain of four rooms (nos. 15–18), aligned north–south, all of similar dimensions (4×6 m on average) and of the same standard of construction, as described above (no. 3). The four buildings have common walls, and all have 1 m-wide entrances with monoliths on either side of the door. This group was preserved to a height of 1–1.5 m. We assume that it is an original Iron Age construction. Two courtyards (nos. 20–21) are attached to this chain of rooms. B. The next four constructions, nos. 22–25, are similar to group A in their technical details. C. The four eastern structures, nos. 26–29, are located east of group A with a wide gap separating them, presumably a courtyard.
8. The southern casemate wall (CW3, Squares L–N/9–15). This is also a chain of rooms defined again as casemate wall, despite its difference from CW1–2. There are two rows of buildings similar to those described above (nos. 3 and 7) along the 65-m stretch. The northern row contains seven buildings (nos. 31–37). Its width is 5–6 m and the length of each unit is 4–5 m. Almost all of the short walls are coupled to the inner and outer walls, and the whole chain may be regarded as one single construction. The southern part consists of five units (nos. 38–42), three of which form a chain (nos. 38–40) with two

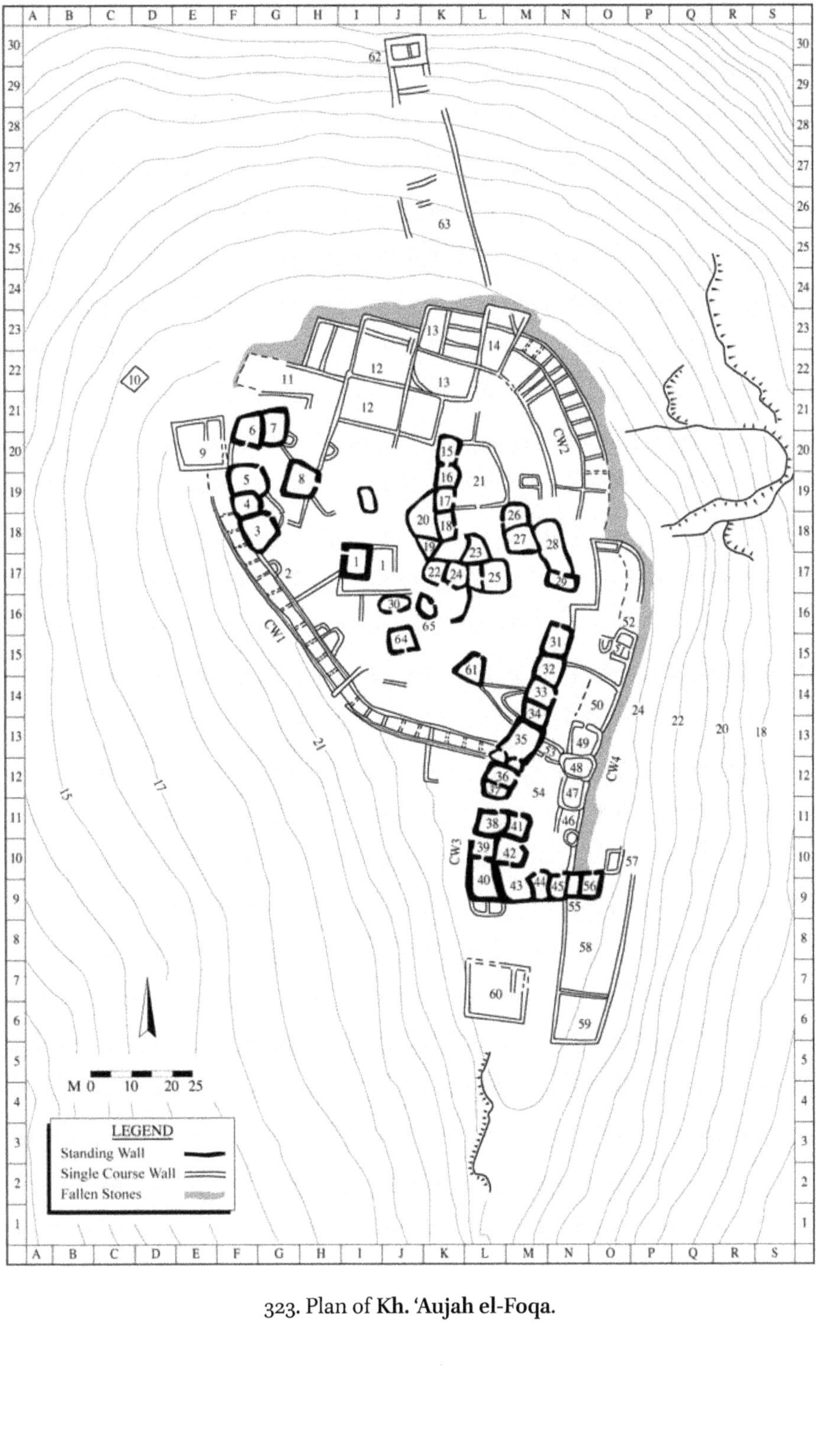

323. Plan of **Kh. 'Aujah el-Foqa.**

attached units (nos. 41–42). Between the northern and the southern chains there is an opening 3–4 m wide. All the units of this group are preserved to a height of 1–1.5 m.

9. The south-eastern casemate wall (CW 4, squares N–P/9–15). The narrow southern side of the site is blocked by a chain of four rooms (nos. 40, 43–45). These rooms, built similarly to the other units, connect CW3 and CW4. CW4 is similar in character to CW3, but not as well preserved. There are eight units along the south-eastern perimeter, (nos. 45–52). This line is parallel to CW3 with a 6–10 m distance between them.
10. Inner square no. 54. Between CW3 and CW4 there is an inner square 150 sq. m in area. It is entered through the opening between rooms nos. 37 and 38. The connection northwards, presumably originally open, was blocked by room no. 53.
11. Rooms east of the defensive wall (nos. 55–57, N–O/9–10). These three rooms were built outside the south-eastern corner of the site, on a steep slope. Their function is unknown.
12. Supporting walls on the slope (nos. 58–59). South of the south-eastern corner 40 m-long supporting walls form a podium and support the upper part and the casemate walls.
13. Southern square building (no. 60, squares L–M/6–8). The foundations of a square building measuring about 15×15 m isolated from the site, were found south of the town's defensive wall.
14. The outer tower (no. 62, squares J–K/29–30) stands about 50 m north of the site on a steep slope. It consists of two rooms or units built of very large

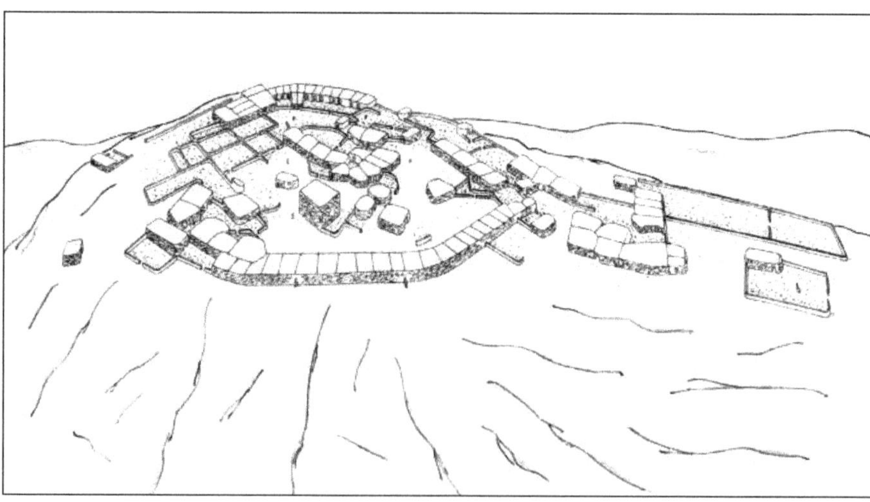

324. Reconstruction proposal of **Kh. 'Aujah el-Foqa**, looking eastward (O. Gadir).

boulders. The northern one (6×10 m), is divided into two rooms; the southern, upper, one is slightly larger (7×10 m). Tower 62 is attached to the site by two long walls on the slope, with several wide connecting walls in between. These may have been used as a support preventing erosion, or a base for a presumed path from the town to the tower. The northern tower was built to keep watch northwards, where a large depression in the slope provided a concealed approach to the site.

The long life-span of the site hints at the existence of several architectural stages. This assumption is supported by the difference in the state of preservation and the inconsistency of the plan.

About 400 randomly picked sherds were collected for classification over the course of seven visits to the site. Of these, 90% belong to the Iron Age. The rest are attributed to other periods (see below). The small number of shards attributed to the other periods suggests that except for the Iron Age there was only sporadic activity at the site (for a detailed discussion of the assemblage retrieved at the site see Zertal et al. 2009: 110-117).

Identification of the site:

The Manasseh–Ephraim boundary description in Josh 16. 6–7 presents a concentration of places between Shechem and Jericho: "And the border went out toward the sea to Michmetath on the north side; and the border went about eastward unto Taanath-Shiloh and passed by it on the east to Janohah; And it went down from Janohah to 'Ataroth and to Naarath, and came to Jericho, and went out at Jordan".

The first site after Shechem, Taanath-Shiloh, has justly been identified at one of the two neighbouring sites — Kh. Tana el-Foqa or Tahta (see Bar and Zertal 2016: site 47). Janohah is presumably to be located in one of the Iron Age sites of Kh. Yanun north of Aqrabeh (Israel grid 1842/1739) or its neighbouring Neby Nun (Israel grid 1844/1721). 'Ataroth raised difficulties. Kallay (1971: 168) and Franklyn (1992) suggested that the name originates from the Hebrew 'atr'"עטר" . This may indicate a circular site which crowns a hilltop. The name 'Ataroth relates to six places in the Bible, and the relation between them is not quite clear: 'Ataroth in Gad (Numb 32: 34), 'Atroth Shopan (Numb 32: 35), 'Ataroth of the Archites (Josh 16: 2), 'Atroth Adar (Josh 18: 13), and 'Atroth Beth Joab (I Chron 2: 54). In addition, Eusebius, in his Onomasticon (Notley and Safrai 2005: 28, 29, 90, 91, 94) mentions five different sites with this name. From this list, only 'Ataroth Shopan in Trans-Jordan has been identified with some certainty, at Kh. Atruz (Dearman 1989: 177–178). 'Ataroth, a site and a region, is mentioned as an important place in the Mesha stela (Nicacci 1994; Rosener 1997; Na'aman 1997; Routledge 2000). Our 'Ataroth, that of Josh 16, should be located between Kh. Yanun and Jericho. Its identification depends on the boundary between Manasseh and Ephraim, and on the relationship between the tribal allotments. Alt (1926: 33) suggested locating 'Ataroth in Kh. 'Aujah et-Tahta, 1 km east of Kh. 'Aujah el-Foqa. This view seems reasonable, yet the place itself (Site 146) is a very small tell with few sherds. The next scholars, Elliger (1930: 279), later Alt (1927: 32), followed by Kallay (1971: 165–166) 'bent' the boundary eastwards, to Wadi Far'ah and the River Jordan. With this, the Ephraimite territory was extended, and either Tel Simadi or Tell Sheikh Dhiyab was suggested for 'Ataroth. However, this notion created a boundary line which is geographically and topographically illogical. The boundary runs for 10 km, from Shechem to Kh. Yanun, southeast in a straight line, following Wadi Tal'ah and Wadi Ahmar. If 'Ataroth is identified in the Jordan Valley, then the boundary 'breaks', changes direction, and crosses the high range of Jebel Kebir. Such a line can hardly be justified. What could have been the reasons for such a theory? All this relates to Jokmeam. This place appears once as a Levite city in Ephraim (1 Chron 6: 43), and then as a city in the Solomonic 5th district (1 Kgs 4: 12). Mazar (1960: 199), who dated the Levite cities to the time of the United Monarchy, placed Jokmeam at Tel Simadi. Jokmeam was in the territory of Ephraim, yet the family was of a southern (Hebronite–Judahite) origin; the territory of the 5th district, which generally belonged to Manasseh, was then extended by him southward along the Jordan Valley to Wadi Far'ah, just including Jokmeam. This compromise created a double identification of Tel Simadi: Jokmeam as Ephraimite Levite city and 'Ataroth on the Manasseh — Ephraim border. Apart from other inconsistencies, this by itself cannot stand logically: a double identification of the same tell at one time. In another place (Zertal 1984: 20–49), it was suggested that the Solomonic districts spread between the extreme points described in the text. According to 1 Kgs 4: 12, the 5th district should have ended in the Jordan Valley near Beit She'an. It seems that Jokmeam in Manasseh should be located in Tell Qa'un (Zertal and Bar 2017: site 3) or its vicinity. Then 'Ataroth can return to its normal location on the Ephraim–Manasseh boundary. The identification of the site with 'Ataroth seems to conform not only to both the Israel–Judah and the tribal borders mentioned above, but also to suit its name and importance as a first-rate fortress near Jericho.

Pottery: Early Bronze – 1%; Middle Bronze II/Late Bronze – 1%; Iron I-II – 90%; Early Roman – 1%; Late Roman-Byzantine – 4%; Medieval – 2%; Ottoman – 1%.
Flint: 23 items (see Appendix A).
Stone: see Eitam 2007.

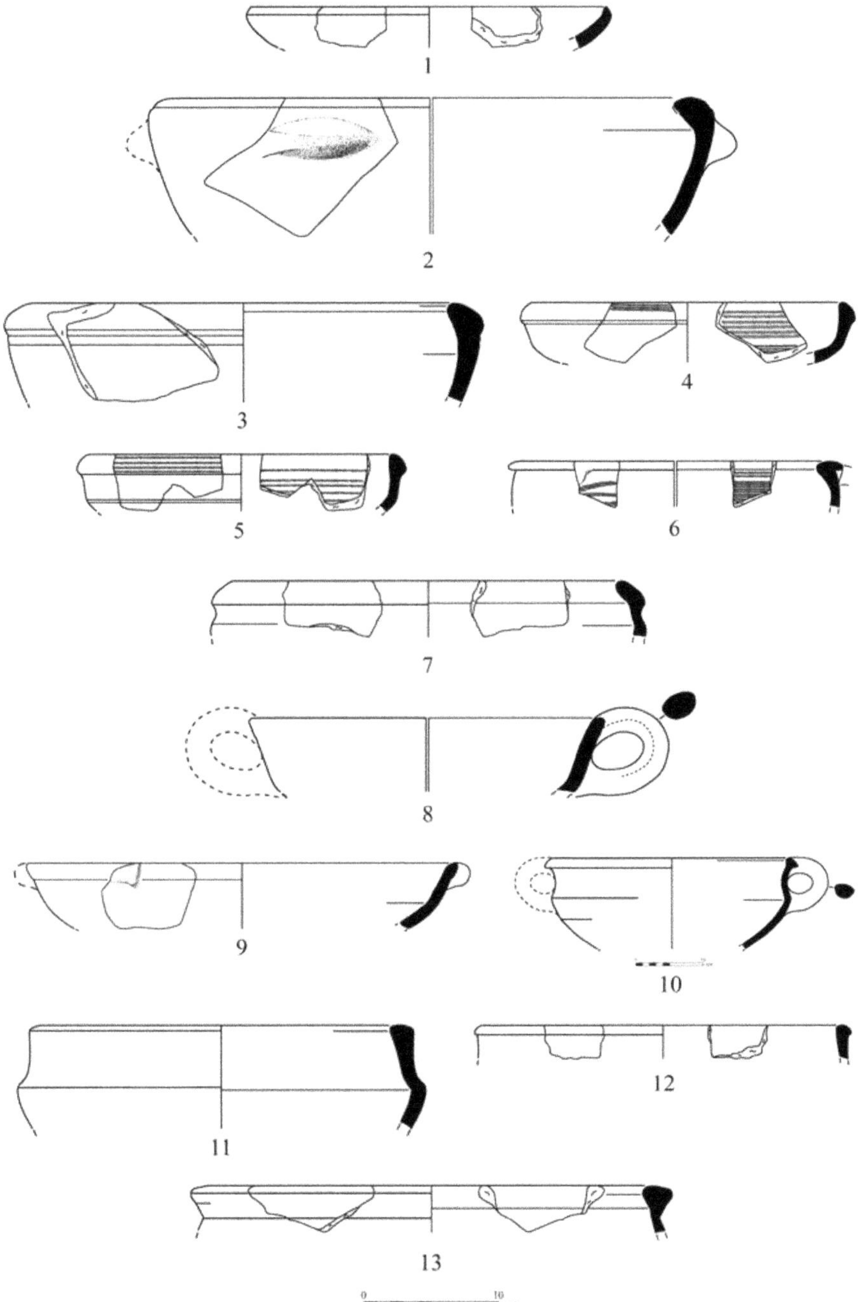

325. Iron Age II bowls and kraters from **Kh. 'Aujah el-Foqa**.

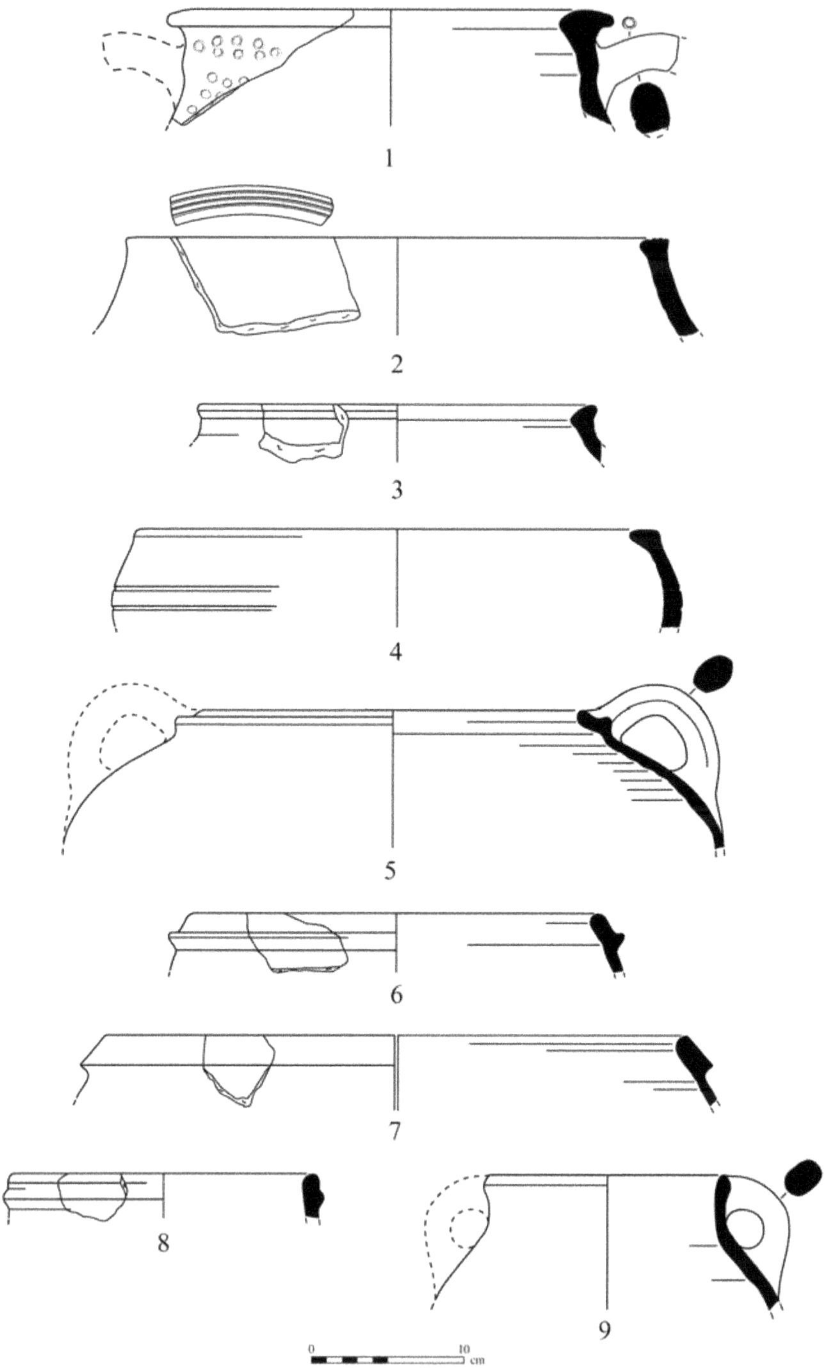

326. Iron Age II cooking pots and kraters from **Kh. 'Aujah el-Foqa.**

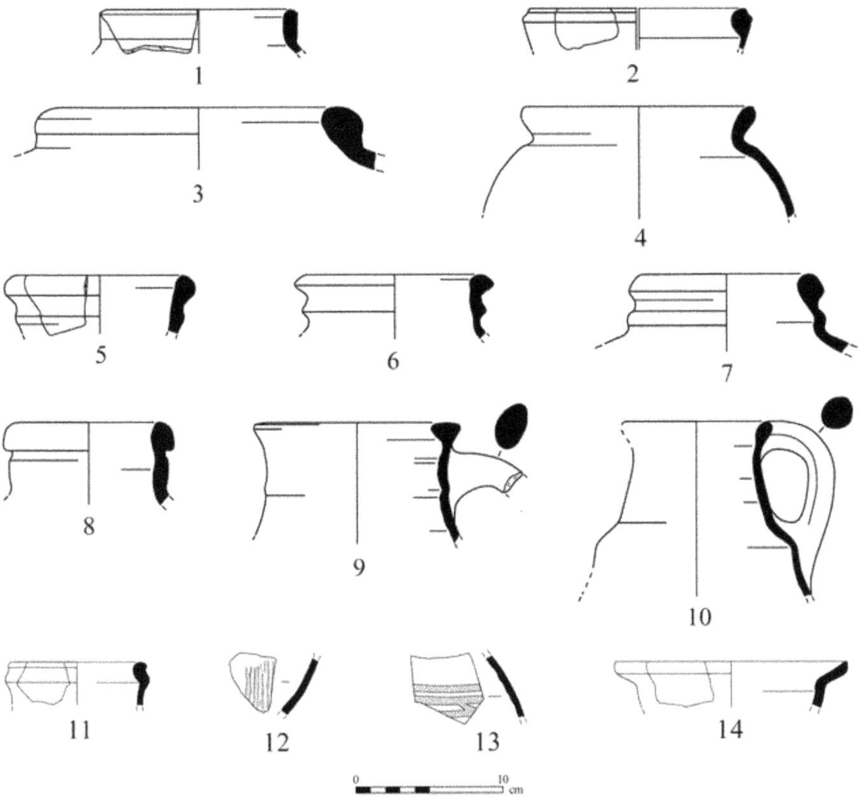

327. Iron Age II cooking vessels, pithoi, jars and varia from **Kh. 'Aujah el-Foqa**.

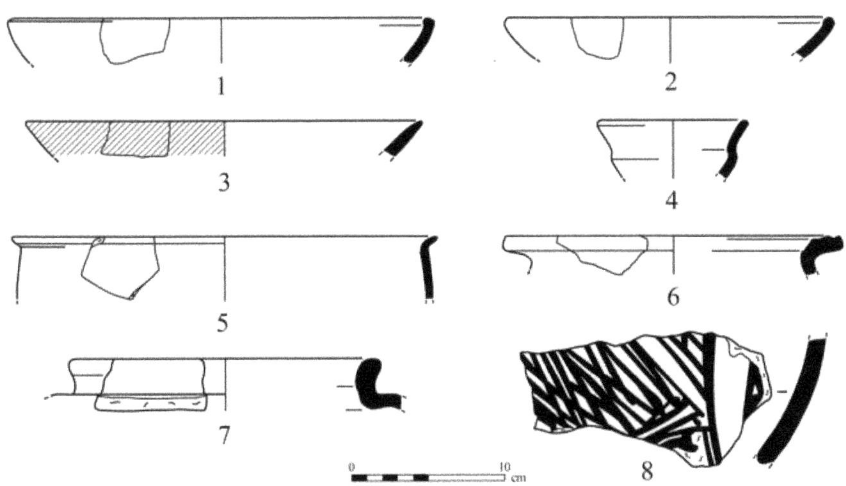

328. Pottery from **Kh. 'Aujah el-Foqa:** 1. Bowl, lt br, MB II; 2. Bowl, br, MB II; 3. Bowl, lt br, rd slip, MB II; 4. Bowl, lt br, MB II/LB (?); 5. Bowl, buff, EB (?); 6. CP, rd, Byz-EM; 7. Jar, lt br, EB; 8. Sherd, buff, violet dec, MA.

Site 143 (1): 18-15/80/3

KHIRBET 'AUJAH EL-FOQA NORTHERN VILLAGE

Israel grid: 1880/1506
UTM grid: 7270/5374
Elevation: 50 m b.s.l., 100 m b.s.a.
Name: given by the survey
Site type: small
Area: 2 dunams (2000 sq. m)
Topography: slope
Rock type: Judea Group
Soil type: stony-desert
Soil quality: 4
Cultivation: none
Cisterns: none
Water source: Nahal Yitav (182), 200 m distant
Road: 'Aujah Tahtah–'Ein 'Aujah (C48), 300 m distant
Visits: December 2014; 40 sherds

An excavated Iron Age II village, to the north, probably an extension of the fortified city of Kh. 'Aujah el-Foqa, 1.8 km west of Yitav.

The Staff Officer of Archaeology of Samaria excavated the site and the results have not yet been published.

The traces of the excavation squares are still visible (in 2014) and the remains of poorly preserved stone walls are scattered along the slope.

This was probably an extension, or a suburb, of the nearby Iron Age II city at Kh. 'Aujah el-Foqa.

Pottery: Iron II – 100%.
Additional surveys: none.

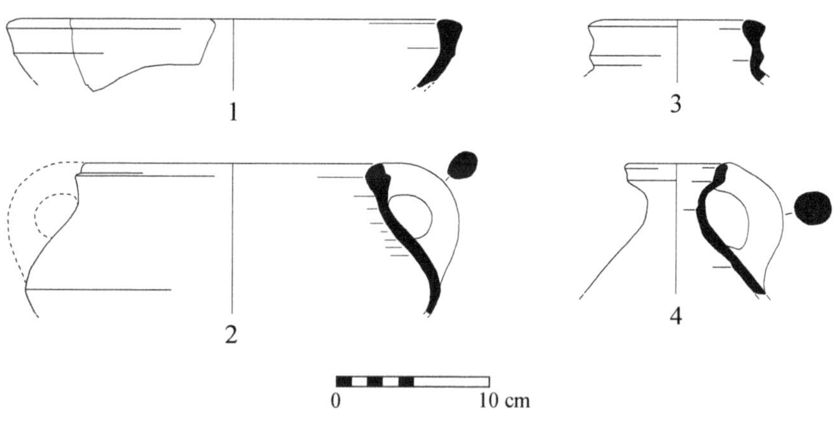

329. Pottery from **Kh. 'Aujah el-Foqa northern village** (all IA II): 1. Bowl, lt-br; 2. CP, br; 3. Jar, lt-br; 4. Jug, lt-br.

Site 144: 19-15/40/1

KHIRBET EL-'AUJAH ET-TAHTAH (VILLAGE)

This is a group of sites around the centre of the village of 'Aujah et-Tahtah (Israel grid: 1946/1504; UTM grid: 7335/5373), surveyed by Nelson Glueck and by the Emergency Survey (1968).

The sites are:

1. Sheikh 'Ibrahim. This was investigated by Glueck, who called it "Kh. el-'Aujah et-Tahtah", and found remains of structures from the Roman and Medieval periods, and apparently up to modern times. Glueck mentions the remains of a mosque with a mosaic floor at its centre in the south of the site. In an adjacent courtyard was a large water reservoir, and traces of reservoirs were found in remains of structures around the area. Glueck, who also notes irrigation ditches running from Wadi 'Aujah to the fields of the village, identified the site with Archelais. Archelais is now identified with Kh. el-Beiyudhat (no. 111). In the Israel Map 1:50,000 (2004) the site is marked as a Moslem structure.
2. A low mound (Kh. el-Ayash) in the Wadi 'Aujah floodplain. Irrigation ditches from the wadi to the fields passed nearby. Remains of structures were not found; only numerous Iron Age I-II, Roman, Byzantine and medieval sherds. Glueck proposed identifying the site with the settlement of Naarath (Josh 16: 7).

In our survey, the above cooordinates were checked, but no archaeological remains were found. They were apparently destroyed when the village was expanded.

Bibliography: Glueck 1951: 412-413; Bar-Adon 1972: site 27.

Site 145: 18-15/80/5

WADI 'AUJAH (1)

Israel grid: 1886/1504 (centre)
UTM grid: 7276/5372
Elevation: 70 m b.s.l., 0 m a.s.a.
Name: nearest place
Site type: enclosures and prehistoric
Area: 12 dunams (1.2 ha)
Topography: plain
Rock type: Judea Group
Soil type: stony-desert
Soil quality: 2
Cultivation: none
Cisterns: none
Water source: Nahal Yitav (182), at the site
Road: 'Aujah et-Tahtah–'Ein 'Aujah (C48), next to the site
Visit: November 2003; 52 sherds

A site of enclosures and courtyards on the north bank of Wadi 'Aujah, between the channel of the wadi in the south and the road to 'Ein 'Aujah in the north and the asphalted road to 'Aujah et-Tahtah in the east. The area is a plain, covered by stones washed in by the floods.

Four enclosures and courtyards have been discovered over an area about 400×400 m:

1. A large well preserved rectangular courtyard, measuring 75×45 m. The encircling wall is built of large stones, on average 80×40 cm, most standing upright. The walls rise slightly above the plain. There are no structures inside the courtyard, and there are gaps along the wall.
2. A round enclosure about 17 m in diameter 120 m north of the courtyard, only its western part partially surviving. The perimeter wall is built of two rows of medium-sized stones.
3. An irregular-oval enclosure, about 30 m in diameter, slightly elevated above its surroundings, about 50 m east of the courtyard. The encircling wall is built of particularly large stones, some up to 1 m long. Inside, and parallel to the wall is another wall built of medium-sized stones. The entrance is constructed in the north side. Similarly to courtyard no. 1 this enclosure also overlooks the channel of Wadi 'Aujah.
4. About 85 m north-east of no. 3 is a structure measuring 20×7 m, and attached to it on the west is a structure, 6×4 m, built of large stones. There are two straight walls, perhaps remains of ruined structures, to the north, and a small round enclosure 6 m in diameter, 5 m to the south-east.

Along Wadi 'Aujah and on its banks are other enclosures of this type. It appears likely that the entire region was settled during the Iron Age.

Hovers and Bar Yosef (1987: 79) describe a 4 sq. m area of exposed Upper

Palaeolithic artefacts that might represent a site. It was in a section cut by one of the tributaries of Wadi 'Aujah.

Pottery: Iron I – 12%; Iron II – 56%; Late Roman-Byzantine – 26%; Unidentified – 6%.
Flint: 5 items (see Appendix A).
Stone: round basalt millstones and a square basalt tablet.
Additional surveys: Spanier (1992: site 170), identified enclosures no. 1 and no. 3.

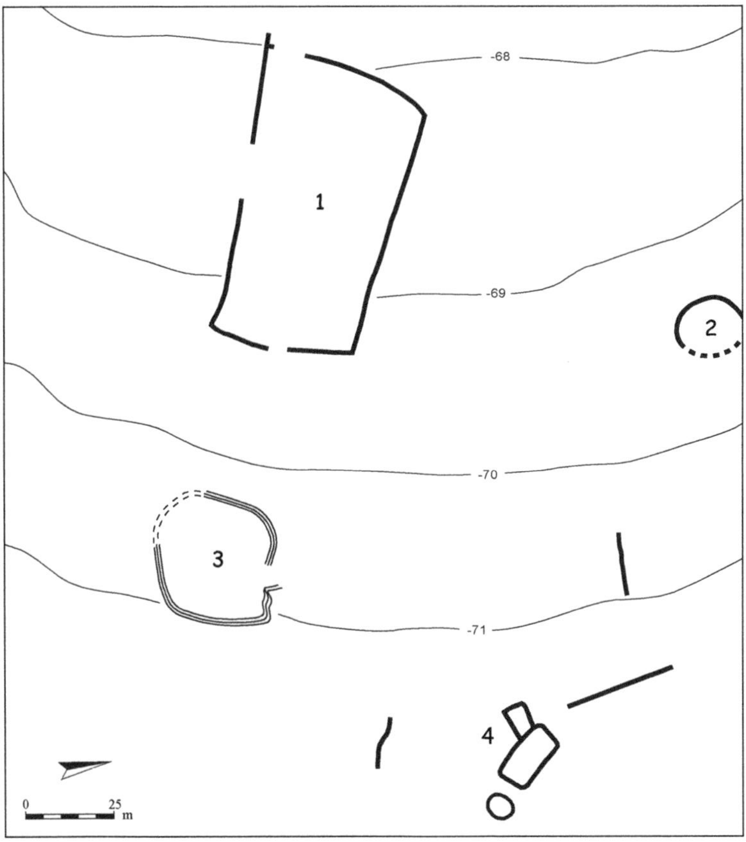

330. Plan of **Wadi 'Aujah (1)**.

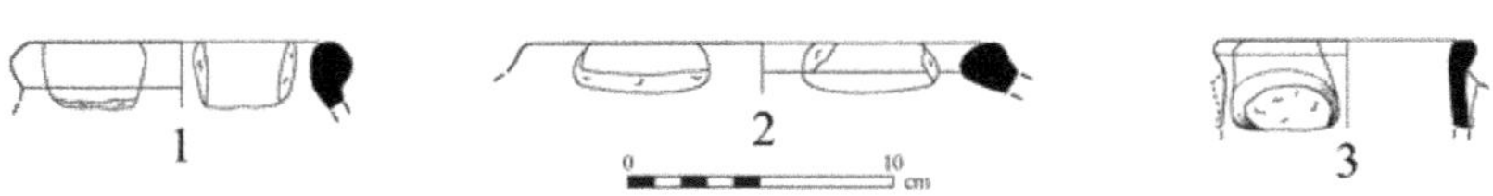

331. Pottery from **Wadi 'Aujah (1)** (all IA I-II): 1-2. Jars, dk br; 3. Jug, br.

Site 146: 18-15/80/4

KHIRBET 'AUJAH ET-TAHTAH (TELL ET-TRUNI)

Israel grid: 1888/1501
UTM grid: 7277/5369
Elevation: 81 m b.s.l., 10 m a.s.a.
Name: historical and in the map
Site type: tell
Area: 4 dunams (4000 sq. m)
Topography: hillock
Rock type: Judea Group
Soil type: stony-desert
Soil quality: 3
Cultivation: none
Cisterns: none
Water source: Nahal Yitav (182), at the site
Road: 'Aujah Tahtah–'Ein 'Aujah (C48), next to the site
Visits: November 2003, 2008; 160 sherds

A small tell south of Wadi 'Aujah and the road leading to 'Ein 'Aujah. The tell is currently surrounded by Bedouin dwellings and flock pens.

The tell rises about 10 m above the plain, and has a view over Wadi 'Aujah and the aqueducts around it. In the tell's south-eastern part are remains of walls which do not add up to form structures: several of them could be parts of a perimeter wall.

The summit has been severely damaged by bulldozers. In the north-eastern part is a Bedouin cemetery, and the Roman aqueduct starting at 'Ein 'Aujah passes the north side of the tell (not on plan). A modern concrete aqueduct also follows this route. It appears that there were only few structures in the site.

332. **Kh. 'Aujah et-Tahtah (Tell et-Truni)**, view north at the tell (M. Einav).

Alt (1926; 1927) and Elliger (1930) propose identifying the site with Ataroth (Josh 16: 7). Today, after the survey at the site resulted in a very limited Iron Age presence, and the proposed identification of Ataroth with Kh. 'Aujah el-Foqa (Site 143), this is no longer acceptable.

On October 1946 Glueck visited the site, writing: "Tell el-Truni (249a)…The small tell is almost completely covered with modern graves and fallen building

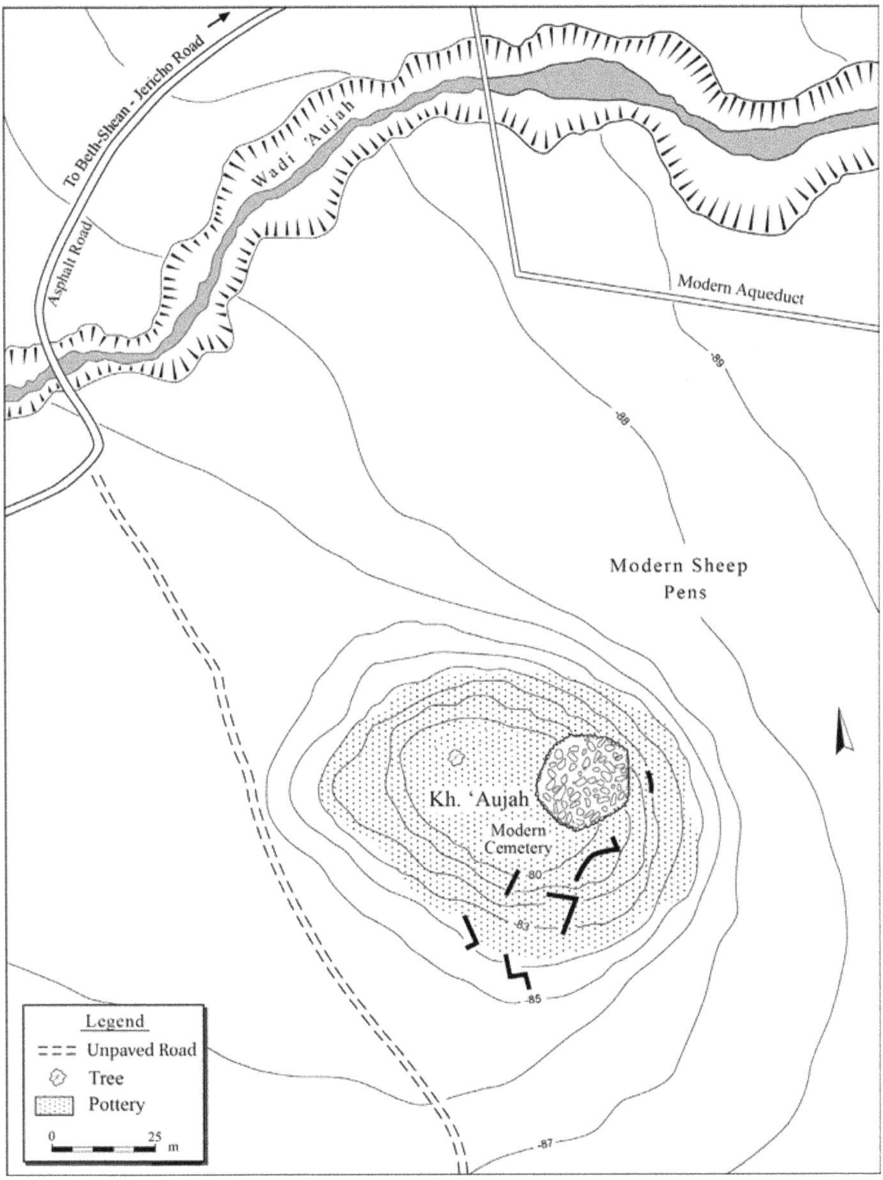

333. Plan of **Kh. 'Aujah et-Tahtah (Tell et-Truni).**

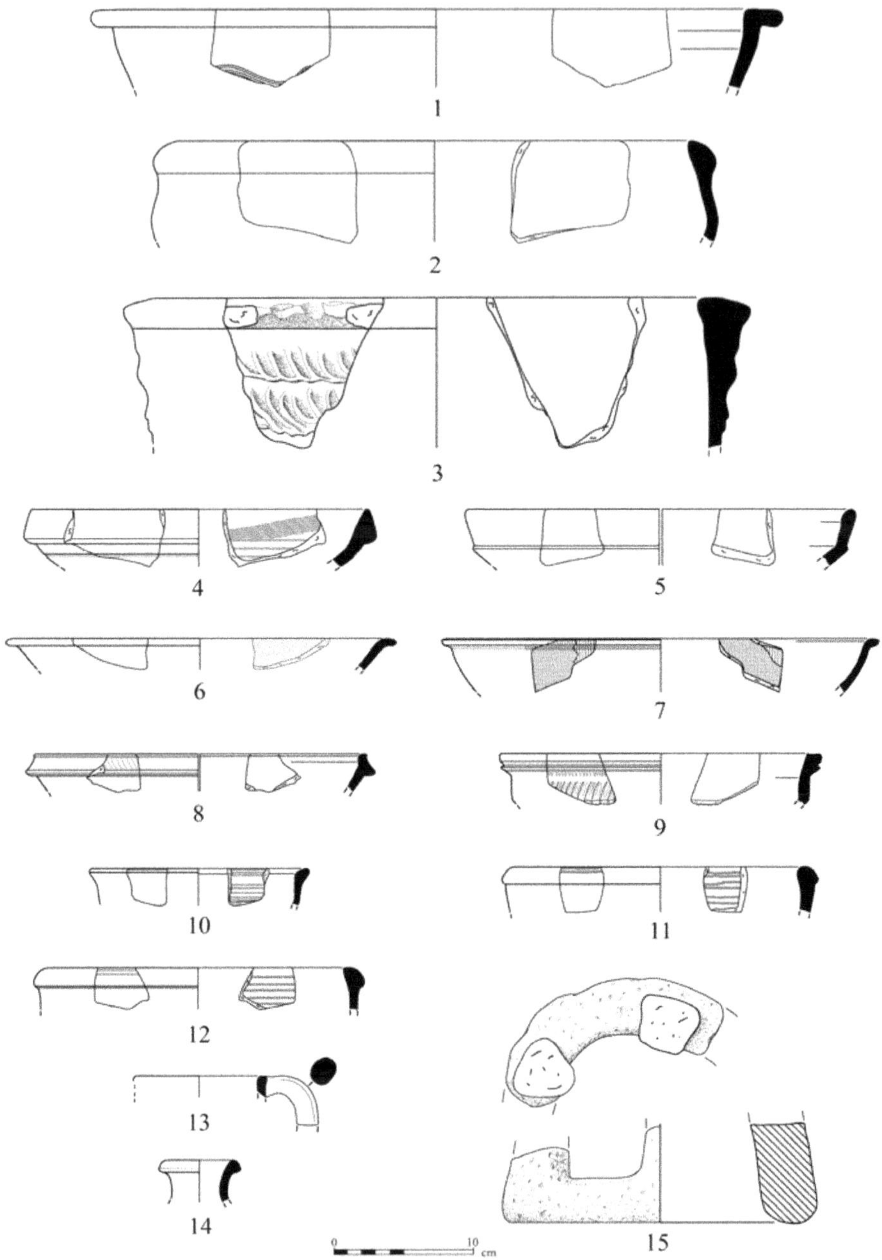

334. Finds from **Kh. 'Aujah et-Tahtah (Tell et-Truni)**: 1. CP, buff, incised décor, EM; 2. CP, buff, IA II; 3. CP, buff, EM; 4, 10. Bowls, lt br, rd burnish, IA II; 5. Bowl, blk, Ott/Mod; 6. Bowl, rd, wh glazing, MA; 7. Bowl, rd, yel-green glazed, MA; 8, 9. Bowls, rd, Rom-Byz; 11-12. Bowls, lt br, rd slip, IA II; 13-14. Jugs, rd, Rom; 15. Chalice, basalt, Chal.

stones of all kinds. Numerous Iron Age I-II sherds were found, most of which, however, belonged to Iron Age II. In addition, there were large numbers of Roman to Mediaeval Arabic sherds." (Glueck 1951: 408, 411).

In the Emergency Survey (1968) it is described as: "A small tell, area about 3 dunams. Construction remains and a circling wall. Modern cemetery. North of the foot of the tell – an aqueduct. **Pottery:** Chalcolithic, Israelite II, Roman, Byzantine and Arabic periods" (Bar-Adon 1972: site 26).

Pottery: Chalcolithic – 2%; Iron II – 7%; Early Roman – 9%; Late Roman – 28%; Byzantine – 28%; Early Moslem – 15%; Medieval – 9%; Ottoman – 2%.
Stone: 10 basalt items, including a Chalcolithic fenestrated chalice.
Additional surveys: Bar-Adon 1972: site 26; Spanier 1992: site 172.
Additional Bibliography: Bar 2014: site 111.

♦ ♦ ♦

Site 147: 18-14/89/1

QANAT EL-MUSA

Israel grid: 1880/1499
UTM grid: 7270/5368
Elevation: 60 m b.s.l., 0 m a.s.a.
Name: ancient and on map
Site type: aqueduct
Area: 1 dunam (1000 sq. m)
Topography: valley
Rock type: Judea Group
Soil type: brown forest
Soil quality: 4
Cultivation: none
Cisterns: none
Water source: Nahal Yitav (182), 1 km distant
Road: 'Aujah et-Tahtah–'Ein 'Aujah (C48), 1 km distant
Visits: March 2005 and more; 40 sherds

A constructed aqueduct with culverts, starting at 'Ein 'Aujah ('Aujah Springs), bypassing 'Aujah el-Foqa hill and leading south-east towards Jericho.

The culvert, built across Wadi el-Mubra, was measured and documented. It served in the past as essential bridging for the aqueduct across the wadi. The central part of the culvert over the wadi is ruined, only the sections north and east of the riverbed surviving.

The total length of the culvert was 35 m, only about 22 m now remain. The maximum height at the riverbed is some 5.5 m, the base is about 2.5 m wide, and the upper part containing the duct is about 2 m wide. The duct is about 1 m wide and about 30 cm deep. The duct is well sealed with a bright 3 cm-thick plaster. The construction of medium-sized stones is good. A section of the lower part is constructed from smaller stones. There are various building phases and repairs of uncertain dating.

The aqueduct comes from the north-east, and its route is visible along the slope, running south-west towards another smaller culvert.

Qanat el-Musa is described in several sources under the name of Kanat el Manil:

The British Survey members visited the site in 1874, describing it as: "Kanat el-Manil – A ruined aqueduct which leads down the water from 'Ein el 'Aujah to the *Ghor*, running east some 5 miles to the neighbourhood of Khurbet el 'Aujeh et Tahtani. Here it turns north and runs for about a mile, having five branches of various length…" (Conder and Kitchener 1882: 390).

In the Emergency Survey states: "Kanat el Manil: aqueducts supported by culverts, carrying water from 'Ein el-'Aujah towards Jericho, parallel and higher to Qanat Faraun. There are two culverts over Wadi el-Mubra and its tributaries. A principal aqueduct from which branch out ducts covered by stone slabs, leading to the fields in the slope." (Bar-Adon 1972: site 29).

For additional data and discussion see Appendix D.

Pottery: Late Roman (by the culvert).
Additional Bibliography: Porath 1985b: 49-50.

335. **Qanat el-Musa**, view north at the culvert carrying the aqueduct, 2011 (M. Einav).

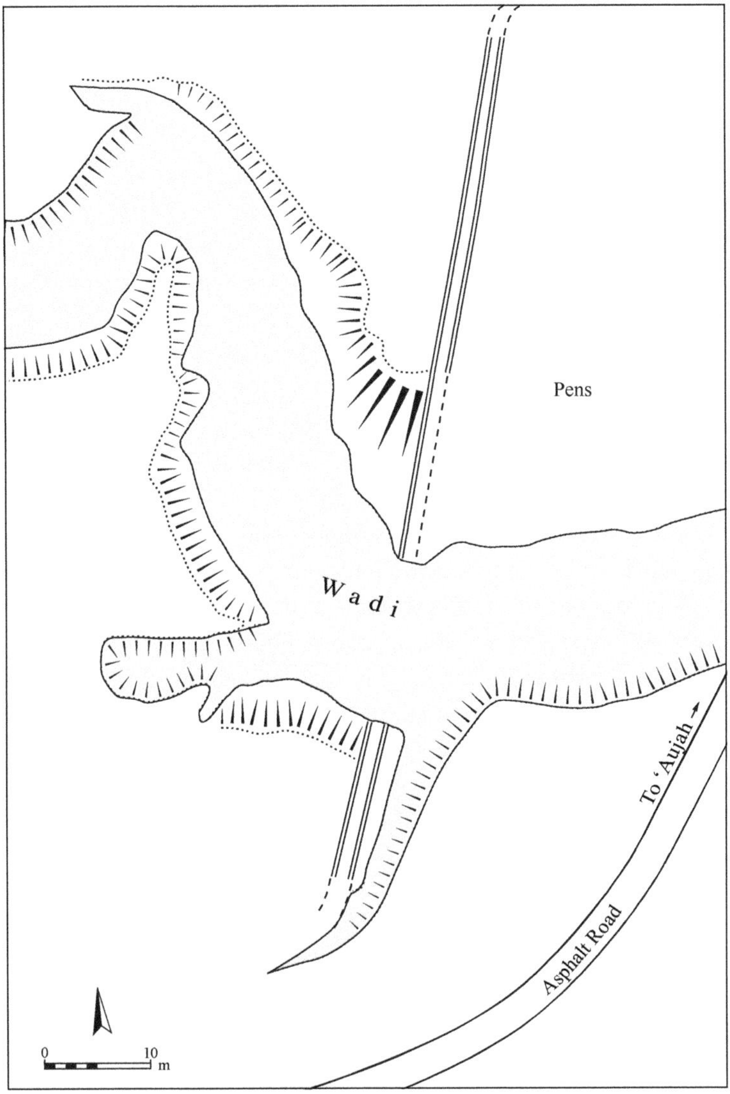

336. Plan of **Qanat el-Musa.**

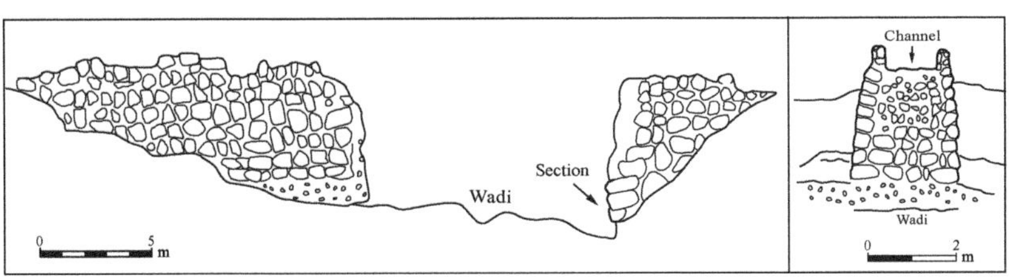

337. **Qanat el-Musa** culvert (drawn by Osnat Gadir).

Site 148: 19-14/19/1

ELEVATION POINT -156

Israel grid: 1911/1497
UTM grid: 7300/5366
Elevation: 156 m b.s.l., 0 m a.s.a.
Name: nearest place
Site type: tower and courtyard
Area: 1.5 dunam (1500 sq. m)
Topography: low knoll
Rock type: silt cover
Soil type: alluvium
Soil quality: 7
Cultivation: field crops
Cisterns: none
Water source: Nahal Yitav (182), 300 m distant
Road: 'Aujah et-Tahtah–'Ein 'Aujah (C48), 300 m distant
Visits: January 2007 and more; 105 sherds

A small site in the centre of the wide valley of Wadi 'Aujah, situated on a knoll slightly elevated above the plain, and between two deep branches of the wadi. The site is 300 m south of the 'Aujah-Yitav road, and 1 km south-east of Yitav.

There are three parts to the site, apparently built during different periods:

1. In the north is a round tower, 10 m in diameter, showing slightly above the surface. It is built of one row of large stones paired by another row of smaller stones inside.
2. North-east of the tower are remains of an enclosure wall, built of a single row of large stones. East and south of it are discontinuous sections of inclined constructions.

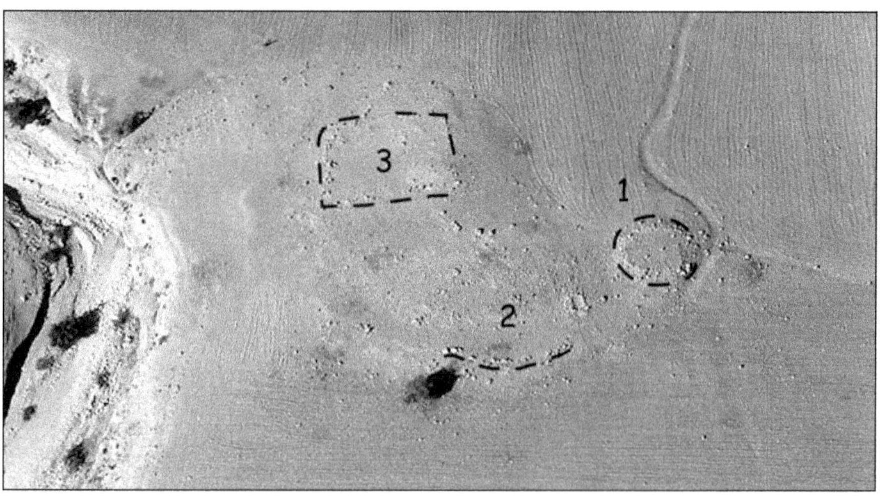

338. **E.P. -156**: Aerial view west at the site, 2008. The outline of the site with one of Wadi 'Aujah tributaries to its left is visible (N. Eshed).

3. About 40 m south-west of the tower is a square courtyard, measuring 21×21 m, with a perimeter wall of two kinds of construction: a section built of one row of large stones, and another of two rows of medium-sized stones. In the north-eastern part of the courtyard is a squarish room, measuring 6×5 m.

In this site, at the centre of Wadi 'Aujah, are outstanding unusual features in both architecture and ceramic continuity. The ancient part was probably already established during the Chalcolithic (?) or Iron Age. Afterwards the existence of the site continued with long intervals. The tower was perhaps built to guard the settlements in the wadi.

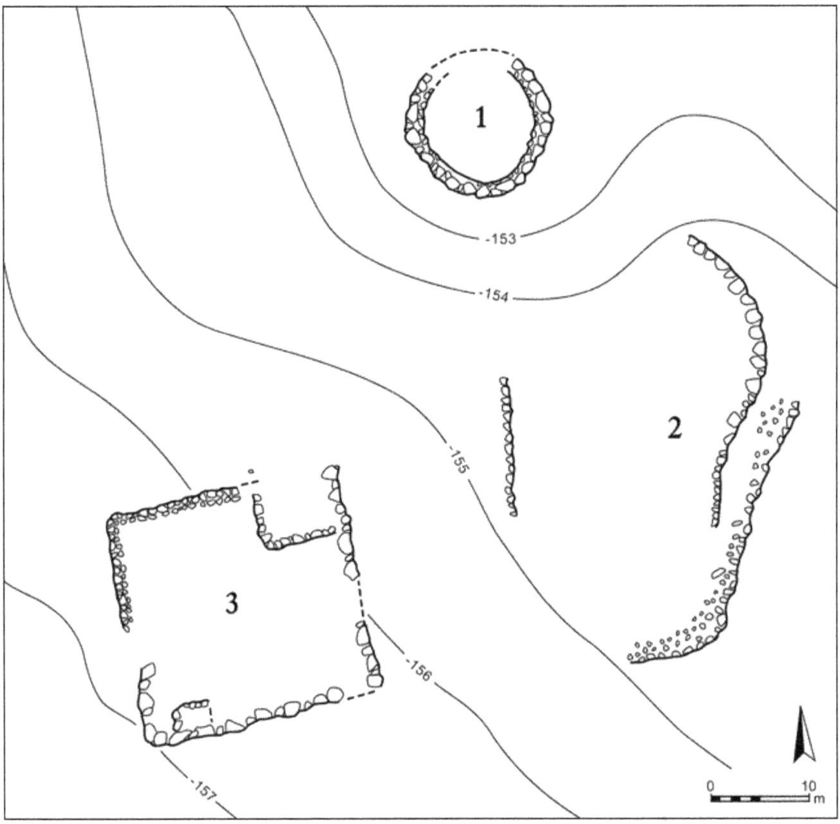

339. Plan of **E.P. -156.**

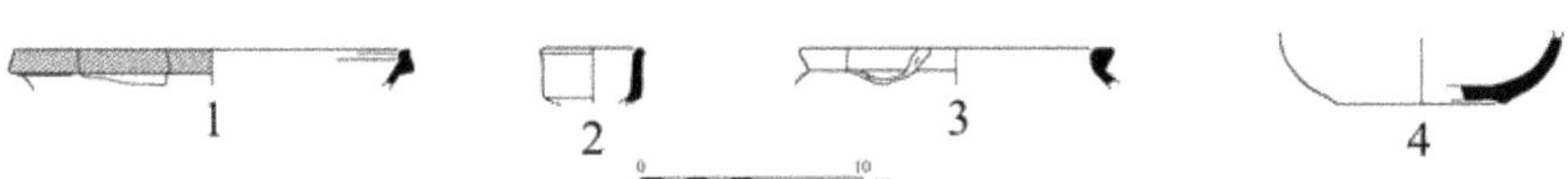

340. Pottery from **E.P. -156**: 1. Bowl, rd, LR; 2. Bowl, lt br, Rom; 3. CP, blk, Rom-Byz; 4. Base, lt gr, Rom.

The ancient pottery was collected only in the southern part of the courtyard (no. 3 above).

Pottery: Chalcolithic (?) – 9%; Iron II – 5%; Late Hellenistic-Early Roman – 33%; Late Roman – 29%; Byzantine – 19%; Early Moslem – 5%.
Flint: 24 items (see Appendix A).
Additional surveys: none.

♦ ♦ ♦

Site 149: 19-14/49/2

KHIRBET UMM 'AZEBEH

A site surveyed in the Emergency Survey (Israel grid: 1940/1497; UTM grid: 7329/5355).

This site is a ruin in a rocky area on the ridge west of the Jordan Valley road. According to the Emergency Survey (Bar-Adon 1972: site 32), there were a few construction remains and caves in the site . The pottery find is from the Roman and Ottoman periods.

No archaeological remains were found in our visit to the site.

Additional surveys: Bar-Adon 1972: site 32.

♦ ♦ ♦

Site 150: 19-14/49/1

KHIRBET UMM ZAQUMEH

Israel grid: 1944/1497
UTM grid: 7334/5367
Elevation: 235 m b.s.l., 0 m a.s.a.
Name: ancient, not on map
Site type: large structure
Area: 1.5 dunam (1500 sq. m)
Topography: low hill above wadi
Rock type: marl
Soil type: marl
Soil quality: 2
Cultivation: none
Cisterns: 1 (?)
Water source: Nahal Yitav (182), at the site
Road: Beit She'an–Jericho (B10), next to the site
Visits: January 2009, 2016; 200 sherds

A small site on a low hill, north and above the wide riverbed of Wadi 'Aujah, and by the southern boundary of the village of 'Aujah et-Tahtah. The location is 100 m west of the Jordan Valley road and close to the Wadi 'Aujah bridge.

The large structure, measuring nearly 30×20 m, is located mostly on the southern part of the hill. The northern part was recently demolished by a tractor. Inside the structure was a courtyard measuring 12×12 m, the eastern part of which consists of a pool 6×6 m in size. The pool has a double wall. The inner wall is 30 cm thick, built of small stones and lined with pebbles and plaster remains. Outside the pool is a thicker (40 cm thick) wall, built of dressed stones. The pool is a component of the inner part of the structure. Intermediate walls link the various sections of the structure.

In the northern part is a well (?), 1.5 m in diameter, lined with stones, and nearby are remnants of a pebble floor with remains of plaster.

The pottery is abundant and the lumps of clay for the manufacture of pottery indicate the possibility of a pottery workshop.

In the Emergency Survey the description is as follows: "A structure inside enclosure next to the Kh. el-'Aujah et-Tahtah–Jericho road. Enclosure which measures 51×35 m, its wall thickness is 80 cm. To south-east are remains of steps. Plaster remnants and mosaic stones are present, and also a structure on a knoll, the walls of which have been preserved up to 1.5 m high. In the

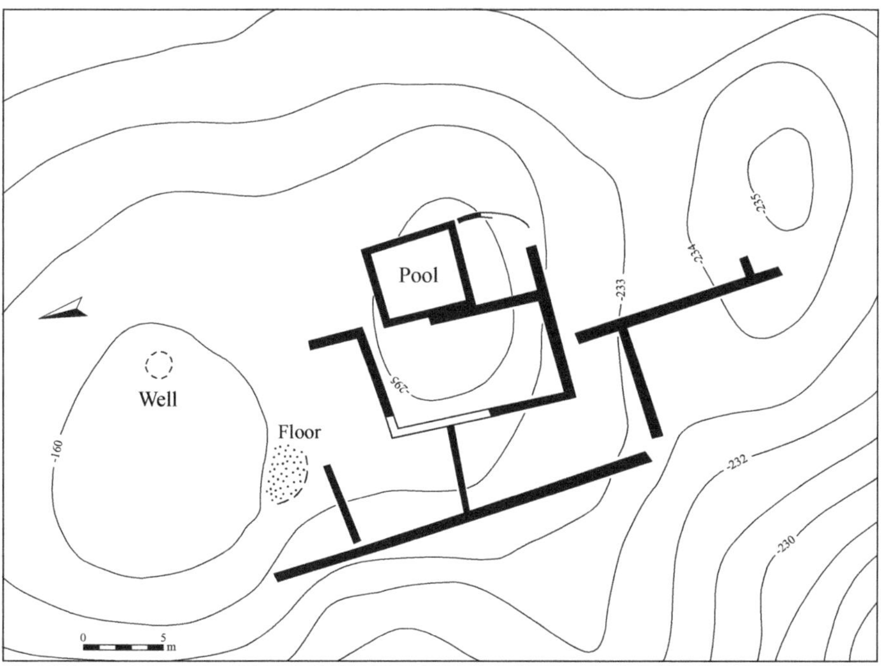

342. Plan of **Kh. Umm Zaqumeh.**

341. **Kh. Umm Zaqumeh** close to 'Aujah et-Tahtah village: part of the Byzantine ruined structure. Oren Cohen is standing on the remains of the pool (?). In the background (south) is Wadi 'Aujah, 2012 (S. Bar).

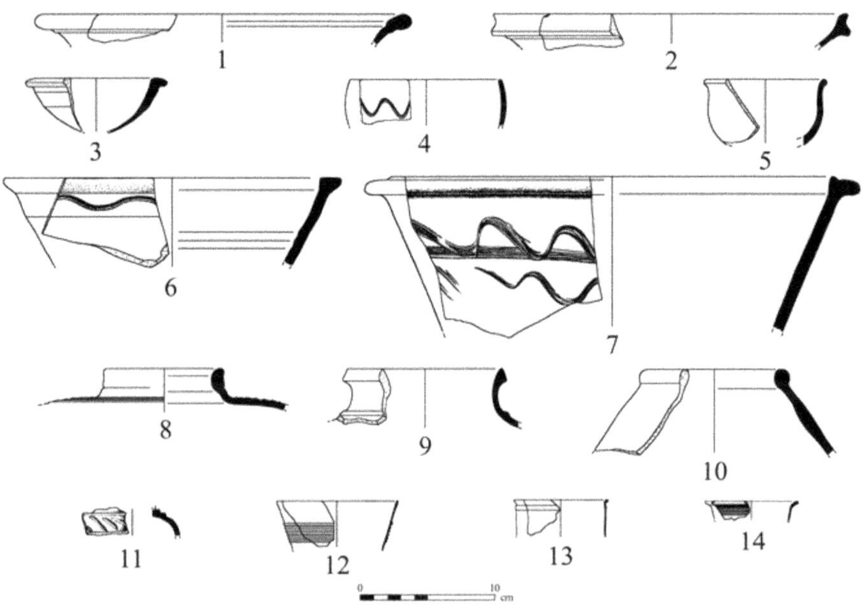

343. Finds from **Kh. Umm Zaqumeh**: 1-2. Bowls, rd, Byz; 3, 5. Bowls, wh, EM; 4. Bowl, rd, incised décor, Byz; 6. CP, wh, EM; 7. CP/basin, lt br, incised décor, EM; 8. Jar, br, Byz-EM; 9. Jar, wh, EM; 10. Jar, lt br, Byz; 11. Lamp, lt br, Byz; 12. Bowl, green glass, Byz-EM; 13. Jug (?), green glass, Byz-EM; 14. Tube (?), green glass, Byz-EM.

structure are integrated a plastered pool and a ceramic pipe. In the courtyard north of the structure is a plastered cistern the ceiling of which is vaulted. The pottery find is from the Byzantine and Arabic periods." (Bar-Adon 1972: site 31).

Unpublished excavation took place in the site by the Archaeology Staff Officer for Judea and Samaria.

In a return visit to the site in 2016 it was found that most of the site had been destroyed by the local inhabitants.

Pottery: Byzantine – 30%; Early Moslem (Umayyad, 7-8th centuries CE) – 70%.
Ceramic notes: at least 20 Eastern Terra Sigillata sherds; Umayyad oil-lamp and top part of Byzantine sandal lamp; Byzantine pan handle (7th century CE).
Additional surveys: Bar-Adon 1972: site 31.

♦ ♦ ♦

Site 151: 19-14/79/1

ELEVATION POINT -289

Israel grid: 1975/1497
UTM grid: 7364/5367
Elevation: 285 m b.s.l., 0 m a.s.a.
Name: nearest place
Site type: enclosure/pool
Area: 2 dunams (2000 sq. m)
Topography: plain and wadi bank
Rock type: Judea Group
Soil type: Lisan marl
Soil quality: 2
Cultivation: none
Cisterns: 1
Water source: Nahal Yitav (182), at the site
Road: Beit She'an–Jericho (B10), 3 km distant
Visit: January 2004; 35 sherds

The site consists of an enclosure or pool on the north bank of Wadi 'Aujah, and in the alluvial plain of the Jordan Valley, 2.5 km east of the 'Aujah road junction.

The enclosure is a large square 80×80 m. The perimeter wall is built of small pebbles and is 80 cm thick, appearing to have been plastered. The wall survived in sections, and can easily be fully reproduced.

The northern part is crossed by a new irrigation canal. In the south-eastern part there are a number of simple graves built as a stone frame with headstone.

The structure apparently served as an irrigation reservoir during the Roman-Byzantine period. A similar enclosure has been found next to the monastery at Malhaqa el-Wadian (no. 157). It is similar to a present-day irrigation system: ditches, dams and pools.

Bar-Adon (1972: site 33) found in the place: "An enclosure, measuring 80×75 m... in the centre of the east wall is an entrance, the jambs of which are built of dressed stones. Square rooms or towers next to the walls outside. Pottery find from the Israelite IIC (?) period, Byzantine II and Arabic."

The entrance and towers were not found in our survey.

Pottery: Iron II – 6%; Late Roman – 47%; Byzantine/Early Moslem – 47%.
Additional surveys: Bar-Adon 1972: site 33.

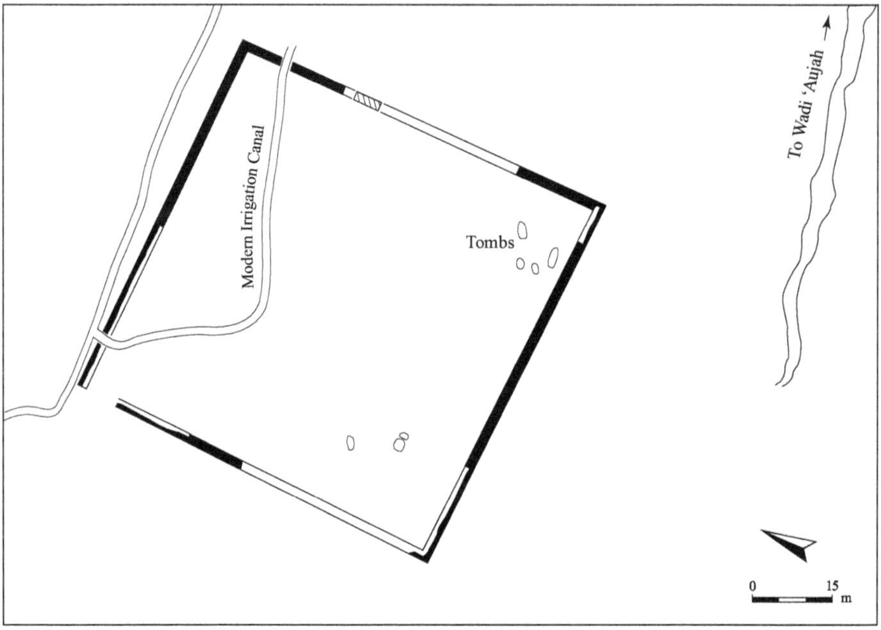

344. Plan of E.P. -289.

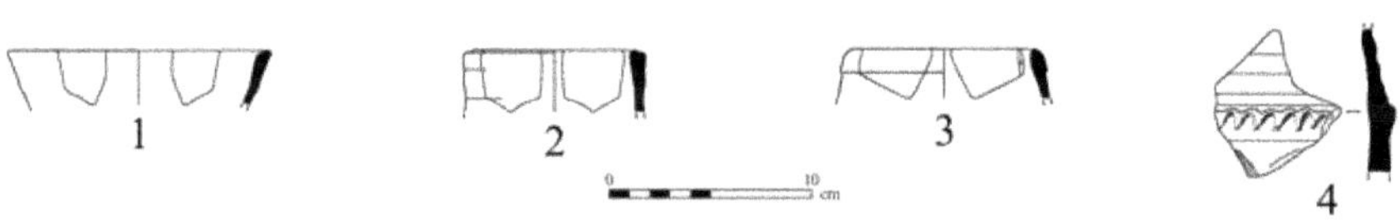

345. Pottery from E.P. -289: 1. Bowl, br, IA II; 2. Jar, rd, Rom; 3. Jar, rd, Rom-Byz; 4. Sherd, buff, EM.

Site 152: 19-14/49/3

SHEIKH IBRAHIM

Israel grid: 1946/1496
UTM grid: 7336/5365
Elevation: 260 m b.s.l., 0 m a.s.a.
Name: nearest place
Site type: medium-size
Area: 5 dunams (5000 sq. m)
Topography: carved wadi bank
Rock type: Lisan marl
Soil type: Lisan marl
Soil quality: 2
Cultivation: none
Cisterns: none
Water source: Nahal Yitav (182), at the site
Road: Beit She'an–Jericho (B10), next to the site
Visits: December 2007 and more; 150 sherds

A site spread over the north bank of Wadi 'Aujah, 300 m east of the Beit She'an–Jericho road, and 700 m south of the centre of 'Aujah et-Tahtah village.

The site is located on the marl badlands, part of the wadi bank. Scatters of building stones and sherds are the result of erosion by floods and the earth collapses into the channel. The remains, scattered in the past over the plain, have been washed down, and only some remained between the ditches. Presumably, the site was larger in the past.

The site was apparently discovered by Glueck, and surveyed by Bar-Adon's party during the Emergency Survey (1968).

The pottery is typical of the Late Neolithic/Early Chalcolithic Wadi Rabah culture.

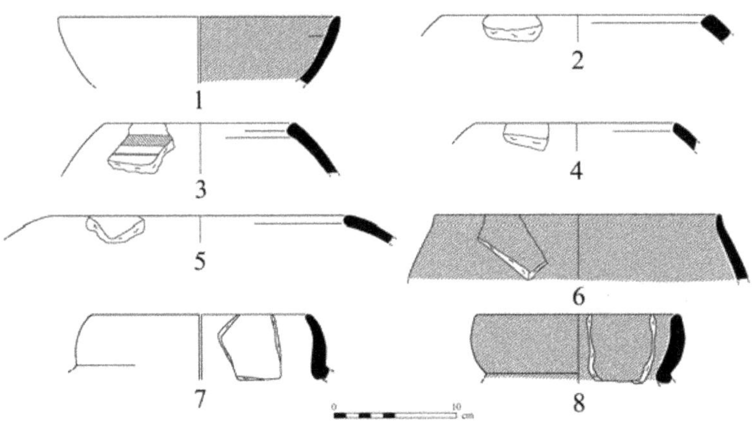

346. Pottery from **Sheikh Ibrahim**, all Late Neolitic-Early Chal; 1. Bowl, lt br, rd slip; 2. HM jar, gr; 3. HM jar, lt br, rope dec; 4-5. HM jars, lt br; 6. Jar, lt br, rd slip; 7. Bow-rim jar, lt br, rd slip and burnish.

Pottery: Late Neolithic/Early Chalcolithic – 100%.
Flint: 29 items, Neolithic-Early Chalcolithic (Wadi Rabah culture) (see Appendix A).
Additional surveys: Glueck 1951: site 249 (?); Bar-Adon 1972: site 27.
Bibliography: Bar 2014: site 113.

♦ ♦ ♦

Site 153: 19-14/49/4

KHIRBET UMM ZAQUM

Israel grid: 1949/1496
UTM grid: 7339/5366
Elevation: 260 m b.s.l., 15 m a.s.a.
Name: given by the survey
Site type: monastery
Area: 1 dunam (1000 sq. m)
Topography: shoulder above wadi
Rock: Lisan marl
Soil: Lisan marl
Soil quality: 3
Cultivation: none
Cisterns: 2
Water source: Nahal Yitav (182), 300 m distant
Road: Beit She'an–Jericho (B10), 500 m distant
Visits: December 2007, 2011; 20 sherds

An excavated site with remains of a large structure, probably a monastery, in the arable land south of 'Aujah et-Tahtah village. Apparently, this is the site of Kh. Umm Zaqum, reported in *Hadashot Arkhaeologiot* 39 and *'Atiqot* 17.

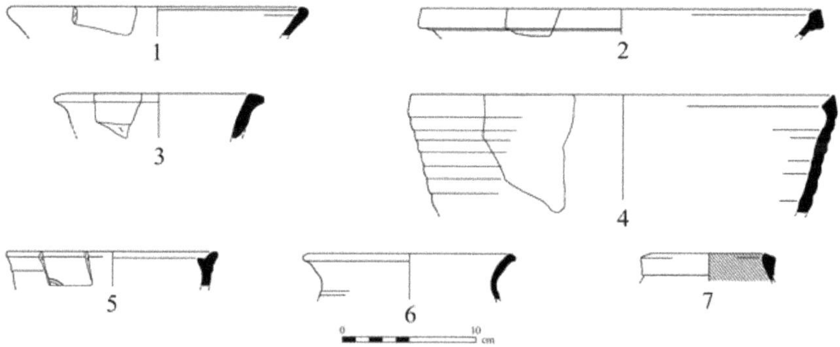

347. Pottery from **Khirbet Umm Zaqum**, all LR-Byz: 1. Bowl, lt br; 2. Bowl, dk br; 3. Bowl, rd; 4. Bowl, br; 5. Bowl, wh, incised déc; 6. Cooking jug, br; 7. Jug, br.

There are remains of a chapel paved with a mosaic with geometric decorations, a water supply system built of ducts and several rock-hewn cisterns.

The sherds found have been dated to the 5th–6th centuries CE.

Pottery: Late Roman-Byzantine – 100%.
Bibliography: Hadashot Arkhaeologiot 39 (1971): 23; Reich 1985.

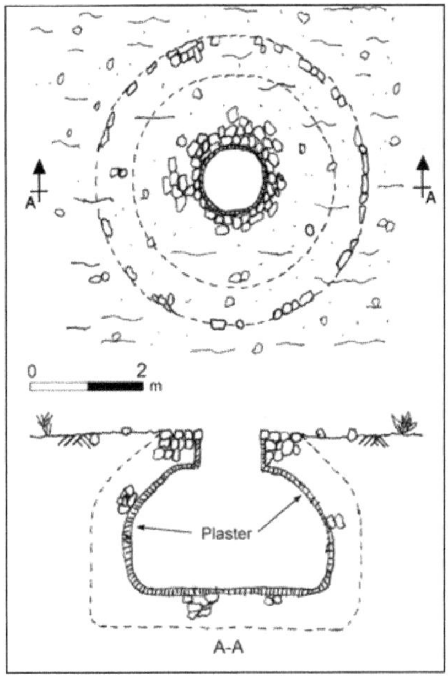

348. **Khirbet Umm Zaqum**, cistern plan.

349. **Khirbet Umm Zaqum**, remains of installations - part of the large structure, apparently a Byzantine monastery, east of the current village of 'Aujah et-Tahtah, 2012 (M. Einav).

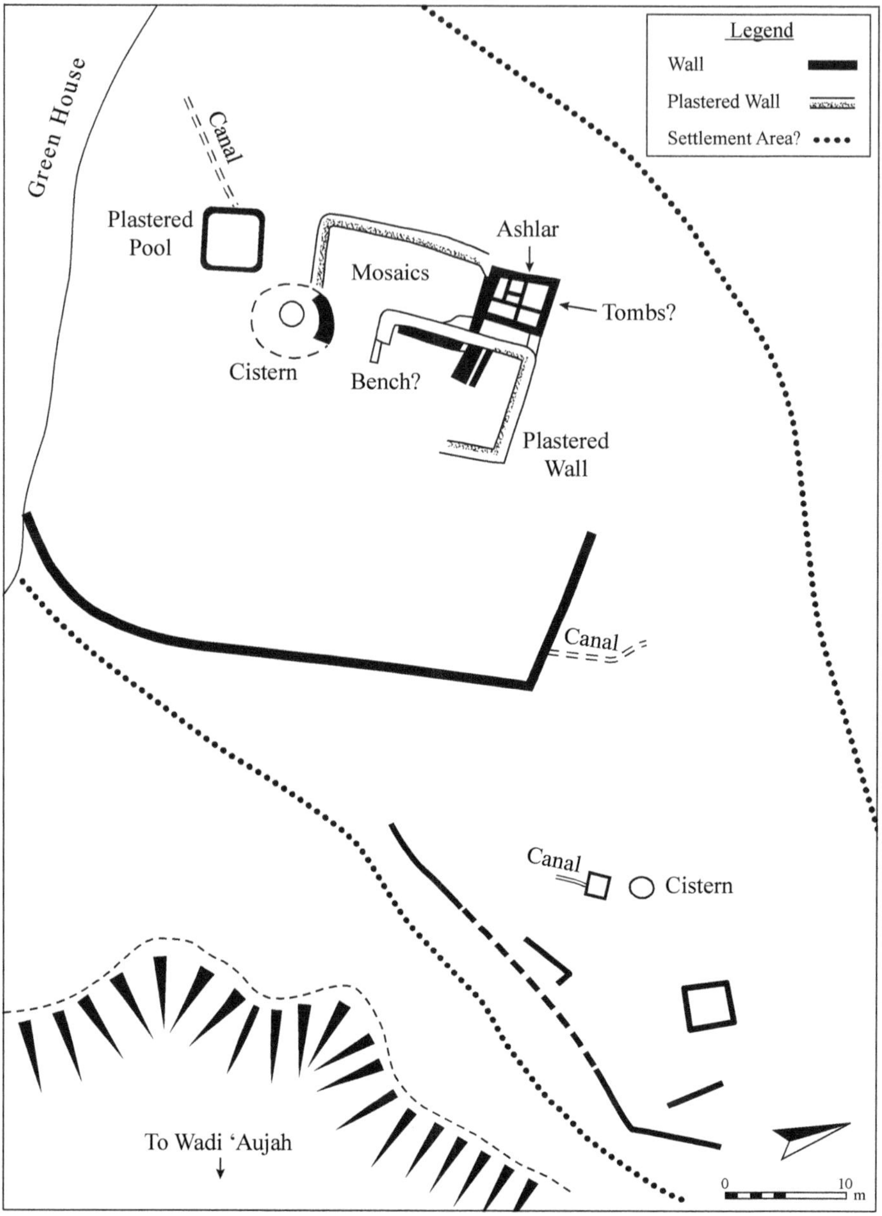

350. Plan of **Khirbet Umm Zaqum**.

Site 154: 19-14/69/1

ELEVATION POINT -261

Israel grid: 1960/1495
UTM grid: 7349/5365
Elevation: 270 m b.s.l., 15 m a.s.a.
Name: nearest place
Site type: large
Area: 15 dunams (1.5 ha)
Topography: shoulder above wadi
Rock: alluvium covered
Soil: marl
Soil quality: 2
Cultivation: vegetables
Cisterns: none
Water source: Nahal Yitav (182), 300 m distant
Road: Beit She'an–Jericho (B10), 1.5 km distant
Visit: December 2007; 230 sherds

A large dispersed site in the northern ravine-cut area of Wadi 'Aujah, 1 km south-east from the centre of the village of 'Aujah, and 1.5 km east of the Beit She'an–Jericho road. The site is at the end of a large vegetable-growing greenhouse on the bank of the wadi.

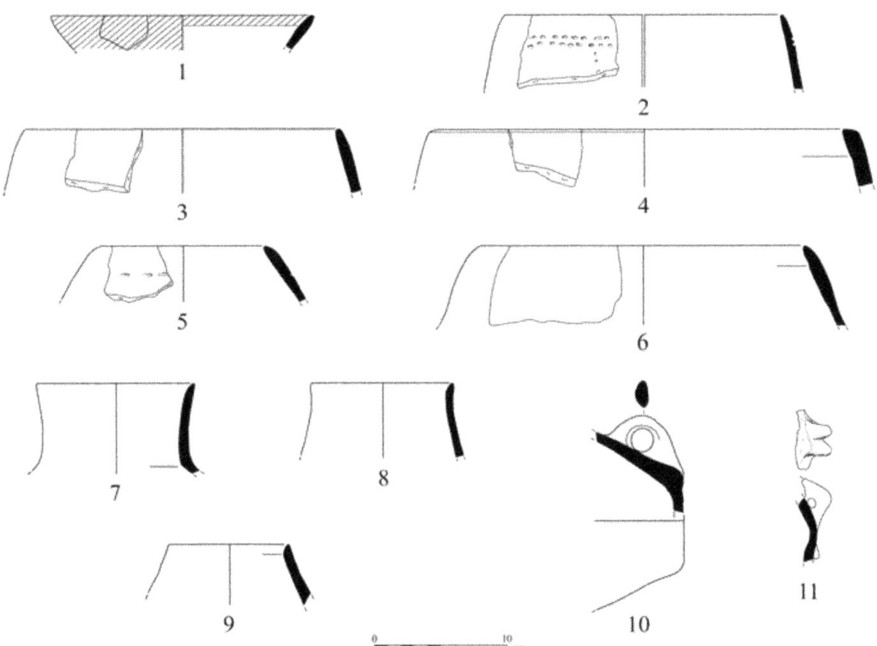

351. Pottery from **E.P. -261**, all Chal: 1. Bowl, br, rd slip; 2. HM, gr, dotted dec; 3. HM, buff; 4. HM, gr; 5. HM, gr, rope dec; 6-8. Jars, gr; 9. Jar, lt br; 10-11. Churns, lt gr.

The site is dispersed over several separate spurs, resulting from erosion by the small tributaries emptying to Wadi 'Aujah in the north. No construction remains have been found over the surface, except a particularly large sherd scatter, stone artefacts and a few flint items gathered in the ravines.

The settlement was spread over a fairly large area, and apparently has been washed away.

Pottery: Chalcolithic – 100%.
Flint: 22 items, Chalcolithic (see Appendix A).
Stone: three basalt grinding stones and a limestone mortar.
Additional surveys: none.
Bibliography: Bar 2014: site 114.

♦ ♦ ♦

Site 155: 18-14/99/1

WADI 'AUJAH (2)

Israel grid: 1896/1494
UTM grid: 7286/5363
Elevation: 125 m b.s.l., 0 m a.s.a.
Name: nearest place
Site type: scattered structures
Area: 50 dunams (5 ha)
Topography: valley
Rock: Judea Group
Soil: alluvium
Soil quality: 3
Cultivation: none
Cisterns: none
Water source: Nahal Yitav (182), 400 m distant
Road: 'Aujah et-Tahtah–'Ein 'Aujah (C48), 600 m distant
Visit: December 2003; 39 sherds

A large spread-out site in the centre of Wadi 'Aujah, next to two of its tributaries, 1.5 km south-south-west from Yitav. The remains are located on long narrow spurs, part of the wadi plain and between its ravines.

The remains of seven structures built from medium-sized stones were found on the spurs, but it appears that their original number was much greater, and they were partially or completely ruined by flood water. There are two rounded enclosures, broad rooms and three tumuli. There are also flood-protection walls. There are few sherds. It appears that the initial construction was in the Chalcolithic period, with secondary usage during subsequent periods.

There are sites of this type throughout Wadi 'Aujah, suggesting that the valley was a hub of Chalcolithic settlement.

Little remains of most of these sites, they are eroded and there are few finds.

Pottery: Chalcolithic (?) – 15%; Iron II – 10%; Late Roman – 22%; Byzantine – 13%; Medieval – 5%; Modern – 35%.
Flint: 6 items (see Appendix A).
Additional surveys: none.
Bibliography: Bar 2014: site 112.

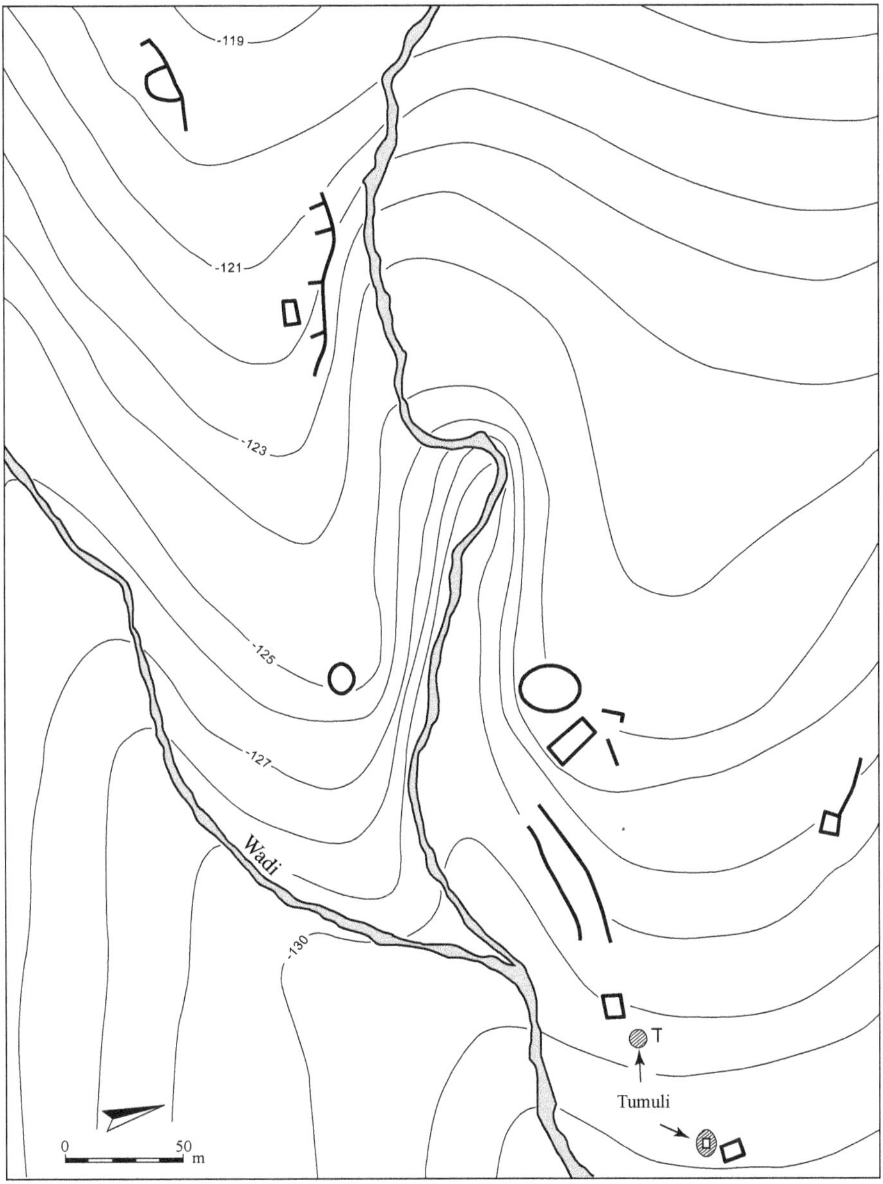

352. Plan of **Wadi 'Aujah (2)**.

Site 156: 18-14/89/2

WADI 'AUJAH (3)

Israel grid: 1887/1492 UTM grid: 7277/5360

This is a site of remains of structures on knolls. It was surveyed in the Emergency Survey (Bar-Adon 1972: sites 30B-C). A few flint artefacts and ancient sherds were found in the site in the archaeological survey of the Benjamin region (Goldfus and Golani 2013: sites 418-419), but not enough to allow dating. Their account describes walls, some straight and some curved, built of medium-sized and large fieldstones. Remains of another round structure containing Byzantine and Ottoman period sherds, were found 100 m east of the former walls.

Additional surveys: Bar-Adon 1972: sites 30B-C; Goldfus and Golani 2013: sites 418-19.

♦ ♦ ♦

Site 157: 19-14/79/2

MALHAQA EL-WADIAN

Israel grid: 1979/1491 (centre)
UTM grid: 7368/5361
Elevation: 295 m b.s.l., 4 m a.s.a.
Name: nearest place
Site type: monastery and enclosure
Area: 12 dunams (1.2 ha)
Topography: plain and wadi bank
Rock: Judea Group
Soil: Lisan marl

Soil quality: 2
Cultivation: none
Cisterns: 1
Water source: Nahal Yitav (182), by the site
Road: Beit She'an–Jericho (B10), 3.5 km distant
Visits: January 2004, 2008; 78 sherds (monastery) and 92 (enclosure)

A site with a monastery and an enclosure nearby, in the flood plains on the northern bank of Wadi 'Aujah. The site has been partially cut by the deep wadi.

There are two parts to the site:

1-2. The monastery and the cistern: spread over 2000 sq. m. The remains of walls and an entrance built of plastered ashlars survive. The construction is of good quality. About 15 m west is a constructed bell-shaped cistern,

4.8 m diameter at the bottom and 3.3 m high, lined with stones and red-painted plaster (no. 2 in the plan). Two clay pipes enter the cistern, and next to it there is a constructed and plastered water pool.

Plundering digs at the site have revealed many sections of a mosaic floor made of stones of at least four different colours. Apparently, this is one of the Byzantine monasteries of the area of Jericho.

3. A large enclosure or pool, measuring 70×70 m, situated 100 m north-east of the monastery. The perimeter wall is 1 m thick, built of small stones. Inside the pool were various construction remains. In the south-eastern opening is a gutter, suggesting that this is water reservoir with a built aqueduct. Other explanations are also possible.

The site is crossed by an unpaved road running along the wadi to the village of 'Aujah et-Tahtah.

Bar-Adon (1972: site 34) found: "A ruin with many of its structures washed away... remains of walls and parts of structures, cisterns and pools. A round cistern, the ceiling of which is vaulted...numerous multicoloured mosaic stones scattered in the area. Pottery find: by the enclosure is from the Chalc, Byz and EM periods." (translation from Hebrew).

353. **Malhaqa el-Wadian**, the built cistern at the monastery, view west, 2012. In the background is the broad and deep Wadi 'Aujah (S. Bar).

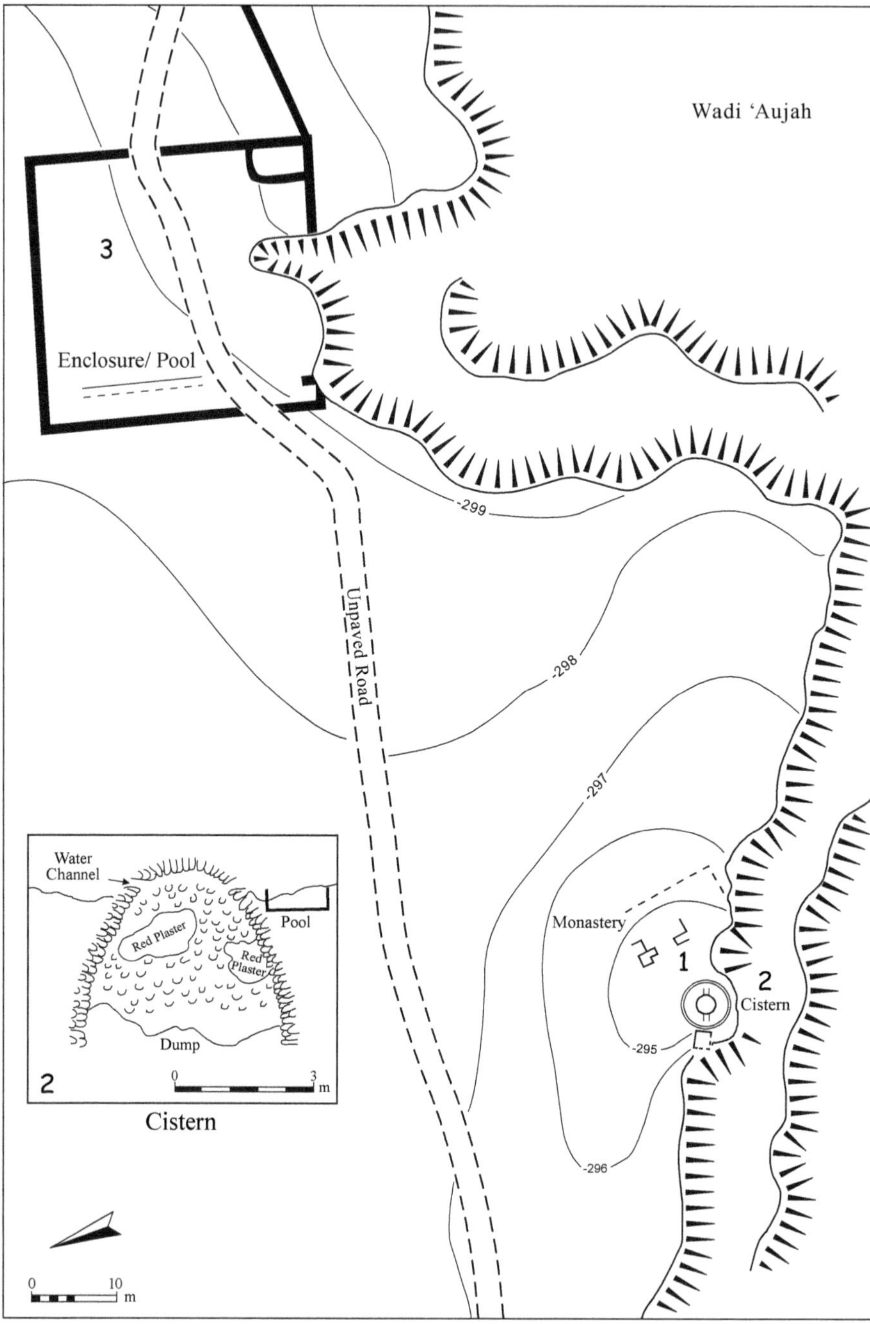

354. Plan of **Malhaqa el-Wadian**.

Hirschfeld (1990: 39) visited the site in 1987, identifying it as "A Byzantine coenobium". He notes also: "that because of natural erosion half the site hill has been ruined; numerous remains which are scattered over an area of one dunam (0.25 acre), are typical of the finds of monasteries in the Judean desert: coloured mosaic stones, roof tile fragments, parts of marble and considerable quantities of Byzantine ceramics. At the top of the mound an intact cistern (3.9 m in diameter and more than 3.5 m deep) survived. In comparison to other monasteries, one can assume that the cistern was in the centre of the monastery courtyard. The cistern was fed by clay pipes 16 cm in diameter, sections of which have been preserved in situ." (translation from Hebrew). For some reason the site has been located by Hirshfeld at elevation point -289, northwest of its actual location.

Pottery (in our survey): In the monastery: Chalcolithic (?) – 2%; Iron II – 8%; Late Roman – 45%; Byzantine – 32%; Early Moslem – 13%. In the enclosure: Iron II – 9%; Late Roman – 41%; Byzantine – 33%; Early Moslem – 13%; Ottoman – 3%.
Flint: 5 items, Iron Age (see Appendix A).
Additional surveys: Bar-Adon 1972: site 34; Hirschfeld 1990: 39.
Additional Bibliography: Bar 2014: site 115.

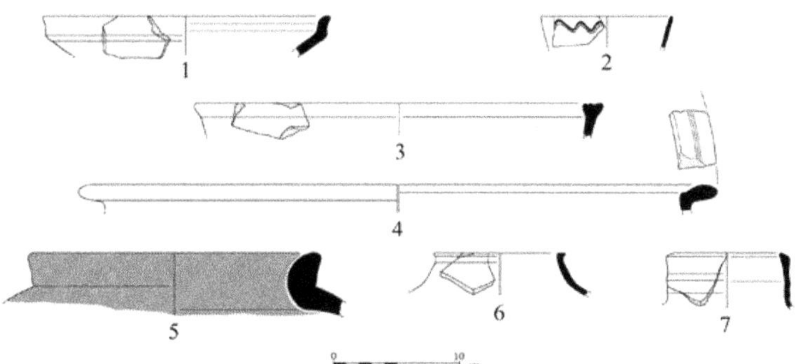

355. Pottery from **Malhaqa el-Wadian:** 1. Bowl, buff, Ott; 2. Bowl, br, Byz; 3. CP, buff, EM; 4. Basin, buff, EM; 5. Jar, buff, rd slip, EM; 6. Jar, gr, LR-Byz; 7. Jar, blk, Byz-EM.

GENERAL BIBLIOGRAPHY

ABBREVIATIONS

AASOR = *The Annual of the American Schools of Oriental Research.*
ABD = Friedman, D.N., (ed.), 1992. *Anchor Bible Dictionary*, vols. 1-6, New York.
Ant. = *Josephus, Jewish Antiquities*, with an English Translation by Thackeray, H.St.J., and Marcus, R., (The Loeb Classical Library), London 1966-1969.
BAR = *Biblical Archaeology Review.*
BASOR = *The Bulletin of the American Schools of Oriental Research.*
CHANE = *Culture and History of the Ancient Near East* (Series).
EB = *Encyclopaedia Biblica*, vols. I-VIII, Jerusalem 1950-1982 (Hebrew).
EI = *Eretz Israel.*
ESI = *Excavations and Surveys in Israel.*
HA = *Hadashot Arkheologiyot* (Hebrew).
IAA = Israel Antiquities Authority.
IEJ = *Israel Exploration Journal.*
JIPS = *Journal of the Israel Prehistoric Society.*
JSP = *Judea and Samaria Publications.*
JSRS = *Judea and Samaria Research Studies.*
NEAEHL = Stern, E. (ed.), 1993-2008. *The New Encyclopedia of Archaeological Excavations in the Holy Land,* 5 vols, Jerusalem and Washington.
PEQ = *Palestine Exploration Quarterly.*
PJB = *Palaestina Jahrbuch des Deutschen Evangelischen Institut Fuer Altertum-wissenschaft des Heiligen Landes zu Jerusalem.*
RB = *Revue Biblique.*
TA = Tel Aviv.
War = *Josephus, The Jewish War*, with an English Translation by Thackeray, H.St.J., (The Loeb Classical Library), London 1967-1968.
ZDPV = *Zeitschrift des Deutschen Palastina – Vereins.*

LITERATURE

Abel, F.-M., 1913. "Melanges: Exploration de la valée du Jordain (1)", *RB* 10, 218-245.
Abel, F.-M., 1935. *Géographie de la Palestine*, I-II, Paris.
Aharoni, Y., 1979. *The Land of the Bible, A Historical Geography*, Philadelphia.
Alon, G., 1976. *Researches in the History of Israel* 2, Tel Aviv (Hebrew).
Alt, A., 1926. "Ataroth", *PJB* 22, 33.
Alt, A., 1927. "'en fasail", *PJB* 23, 31-32.

Ammar, Z., 1992. "Notes on Flora and Agriculture in Mamluk Palestine", in Drory, J. (ed.), *Palestine in the Mamluk Period*, Jerusalem, 220-236 (Hebrew).

Avi-Yonah, M., 1953. "The Madaba Mosaic Map – Translation and Commentary", *EI* 2, 129-156 (Hebrew).

Avi-Yonah, M., 1970. *In the Days of Rome and Byzantium*, Jerusalem (Hebrew).

Avi-Yonah, M., 1976. *Gazeteer of Roman Palestine* (*Qedem* 5), Jerusalem.

Baedeker, K. (ed.), 1876. *Palestine and Syria, Handbook for Travellers*, Leipsic and London.

Bar, S., 2008. *The Pattern of Settlement in the Lower Jordan Valley and the Desert Fringes of Samaria during the Late Chalcolithic Period and Early Bronze Age 1* (Ph.D. Dissertation), University of Haifa, Haifa (Hebrew with English summary).

Bar, S., 2010. "Early Bronze Age I 'Um Hammad Ware' – A Study in Regionalism", *PEQ* 142/2, 82-94.

Bar, S., 2013a. "Shifting Settlement Patterns in the Southern Jordan Valley and the Desert Fringes of Samaria during the Early Bronze Age I Period", *PEQ* 145/2, 90-107.

Bar, S., 2013b. *'Al Yogvim Ve-Noqdim I*, Haifa (Hebrew).

Bar, S., 2014. *The Dawn of the Bronze Age, the Pattern of Settlement in the Lower Jordan Valley and the Desert Fringes of Samaria during the Chalcolithic Period and Early Bronze Age* I (*CHANE* 72), Leiden and Boston.

Bar, S., 2017a. "Excavations at Elevation Point -167 (Site 192): 2007 Season", in Zertal, A., and Bar, S. *The Manasseh Hill Country Survey, vol. 4: From Nahal Bezeq to the Sartaba* (*CHANE* 21.4), Leiden and Boston, 719-739.

Bar, S. 2017b. "A new suggestion for the identification of Thena of Eusebius", *In the Highland's Depth* 7, 207-217 (Hebrew).

Bar, S., Bar-Oz, G., Ben-Yosef, D., Boaretto, E., Raban-Gerstel, N., and Winter, H., 2013a. "Fazael 2: One of the Latest Chalcolithic Sites in the Jordan Valley? Report of the 2007-2008 Excavation Seasons", *JIPS* 43, 148-185.

Bar, S., Bar-Oz, G., Cohen-Klonymus, H., and Pinsky, S., 2014. "Fazael I, a Chalcolithic Site in the Jordan Valley: Report of the 2013-2014 Excavation Seasons", *JIPS* 44, 180-201.

Bar, S., Bar-Oz, G., Ben-Yosef, D., Raban-Gerstel, N., and Winter, H., 2011. "Sheikh Diab 2: An Early Bronze Age I Hamlet in the Jordan Valley", *JIPS* 41, 95-154.

Bar, S., Cohen, O., and Zertal, A., 2013b. "New Aspects of the Intermediate Bronze Age (IB/MBI/EBIV): Khirbet el-Meiyiteh – A Fortified Site on the Eastern Fringe of Samaria", *RB* 120/2, 161-181.

Bar, S., Cohen, O., Zuckerman, R., and Winter, H., 2012. "The Archaeological Excavations at the Early Bronze Age I Site Fazael 4, Jordan Valley, Israel", *JIPS* 42, 1-34.

Bar, S., Cohen-Klonymus, H., Pinsky, S., Bar-Oz, G., and Shalvi, G., 2015. "Fasael 5: Soundings in a Chalcolithic Site in the Jordan Valley," *JIPS* 45, 193-216.

Bar, S., Cohen-Klonymus, H., Pinsky, S., Bar-Oz, G., Zuckerman, R., Shalvi, G., and Davidovich, U., 2017. "Fasael 7: A Large Chalcolithic Architectural Complex in the Jordan Valley, the 2009-2016 Excavations", *JIPS* 47, 208-247.

Bar, S., and Winter, H., 2010. "Canaanean Flint Blades in Chalcolithic Context and the Possible Onset of the Transition to the Early Bronze Age: A Case Study from Fazael 2", *TA* 37, 33-47.

Bar, S., and Zertal, A., 2016. *The Manasseh Hill Country Survey, vol. 6: The Eastern Samaria Shoulder: From Wadi Far'ah to Maale Ephraim Junction*, Haifa (Hebrew).

Bar-Adon, P., 1972. "The Judaean Desert and Plain of Jericho", in Kochavi, M. (ed.), *Judaea, Samaria and the Golan, Archaeological Survey 1967-1968*, Jerusalem, 91-149 (Hebrew).

Bar-Yosef, O., and Gopher, A., 1997. *An Early Neolithic Village in the Jordan Valley, vol. 1: The Archaeology of Netiv Hagdud*, Cambridge.

Be'eri, R., and Cohen, O., 2008. "Burial Remains at Huzuk Musa", *RB* 115/3, 421-439.

Belitzky, S., 1999. "Recent Faulting and Folding in the Jordan Valley", *JSRS* 9, 439-450 (Hebrew).

Ben-Nun, Y., 1993. "'He has come to Aiath ...', a New Solution to The Identification of the 'Ai", *JSRS* 2, 43-67 (Hebrew).

Ben-Shlomo, D., and Hawkins, R.K., 2017. "Excavations at Khirbet el Mastarah, the Jordan Valley, 2017", *JSRS* 26/2, 49*-82*.

Ben-Yosef, D., 2007. *The Jordan Valley during Iron Age I, Aspects of its History and the Archaeological Evidence for its Settlement* (Ph.D. Dissertation), University of Haifa, Haifa (Hebrew with English summary).

Ben-Yosef, D., 2017a. "Excavations at Bedhat esh-Sha'ab, an Early Iron Age Enclosure in the Jordan Valley: 2002-2003 Excavation Seasons", in Zertal, A., and Bar, S. *The Manasseh Hill Country Survey, vol. 4: From Nahal Bezeq to the Sartaba* (*CHANE* 21.4), Leiden and Boston, 667-702.

Ben-Yosef, D., 2017b. "Excavations at Yafit (3), an Iron Age Sandal-Shaped Enclosure in the Jordan Valley", in Zertal, A., and Bar, S. *The Manasseh Hill Country Survey, vol. 4: From Nahal Bezeq to the Sartaba* (*CHANE* 21.4), Leiden and Boston, 703-718.

Bergdall, C.R., 1992. "Senaah", *ABD* 5, 1086.

Beyer, G., 1940. "Neapolis (Nablus) und sein Gebiet in der Kreuzfahrzeit", *ZDPV* 63, 155-209.

Braun, E., 1997. *Yiftah'el: Salvage and Rescue Excavations at a Prehistoric Village in Lower Galilee, Israel* (*IAA Reports* 2), Jerusalem.

Cohen-Klonymus, H., and Bar, S., 2016. "Ground Stone Tool Assemblages at the End of the Chalcolithic Period: A Preliminary Analysis of the Late Chalcolithic Sites in the Fazael Valley", *Journal of Lithic Studies* (2016) vol. 3, nr. 3 (http://journals.ed.ac.uk/lithicstudies/article/viewFile/1676/2199).

Conder, C.H., and Kitchener, H.H., 1879. *The Palestine Exploration Fund Map, Sheet XV*, London.

Conder, C.H., and Kitchener, H.H., 1882. *The Survey of Western Palestine II: Samaria,* London.

Dalman, G., 1913 (1939). *Arbeit und Sitte in Palaestina* VI, Bertelsman.

Dearman, A., 1989. "Historical Reconstruction and the Mesha Inscription", Dearman, A. (ed.), *Studies in the Mesha Inscription and Moab,* Atlanta, 155-210.

Di Segni, L., 1993. "The Inscriptions at Khirbet el-Beiyudat", Tsafrir, Y. (ed.), *Ancient Churches Revealed,* Jerusalem, 164-169.

Drory, J., 1981. "Eretz Israel in the Mamluk State", in Shavit, Y. (series ed.), *The History of Eretz Israel, VII: The Mamluk and Ottoman Rule (1260-1804)*, Jerusalem, 9-91 (Hebrew).

Eitam, D., 2007. "The Stone tools from Khirbet Aujah el-Foqa", Crawford, S.W. (ed.), *"Up th the Gates of Ekron" – Studies on the Archaeology and History of the Eastern Mediterranean in Honor of Seymour Gitin,* Jerusalem, 93-106.

Elliger, K., 1930. "Die Grenze zwischen Ephraim und Manasseh", *ZDPV* 53, 265-309.

Erlich, B.Z., 1987. *Samaria during the First World War,* Jerusalem (Hebrew).

Felix, Y., 1957. *The Biblical Faunal World,* Tel Aviv (Hebrew).

Franklyn, P.N., 1992. "Ataroth (I)", *ABD,* 510.

Garbrecht, G., and Netzer, E., 1991. *Die Wasserversorgung des geschichtlichen Jericho und seiner Koeniglichen Anlagen* (*Gut. Winterpalaeste*), Mitteilungen Heft 115/1991, Leichtweiss-Institut Fuer Wasserbau der Technischen Universitaet Braunschweig, Braunschweig-Jerusalem.

Glueck, N., 1939. *Explorations in Eastern Palestine* III (*AASOR* 18-19), New-Haven.

Glueck, N., 1951. *Explorations in Eastern Palestine* IV, Part I: Text (*AASOR* 25-28), New- Haven.

Goldfus, H., and Golani, A., 2013. "Wadi el-Makokh – Benjamin archaeological survey – 83/12" (http://survey.antiquities.org.il/index_Eng.html#/MapSurvey/73).

Gopher, A., 1993. "Netiv Ha-Gedud", *NEAEHL* 3, 1150-1152.

Goring-Morris, A.N., 1980. *Lare Quaternary Sites in Wadi Fazael, Lower Jordan Valley* (MA Dissertation), The Hebrew University, Jerusalem.

Grabois, A., 1983. "Jericho under the Byzantine and the Crusade Rules", in Schiller, E. (ed.), *Jericho and its Vicinity,* Jerusalem, 51-54 (Hebrew).

Grintz, Y., 1969. "The Ai which is with Beit-Aven", *Motzaei Dorot*, Jerusalem, 278-289 (Hebrew).

Guérin, V., 1874. *Description géographique, historique et archéologique de la Palestine*, Seconde partie, samarie, tôme premier, Paris.

Gutmann, J., 1940. "Alexander the Great in Palestine", *Tarbiz* 12/3-4, 271-294 (Hebrew).

Hamilton, R.W., 1959. *Khirbet al-Mafjer, An Arabian Mansion in the Jordan Valley*, Oxford.

Hamilton, R.W., 1993. "Mafjar, Khirbet el-", *NEAEHL* 3, 922-929.

Hirschfeld, Y., 1990. "Monasteries in the Judean Desert and in Samaria – 1987 (B)", *HA* 94: 39-43 (Hebrew).

Hirschfeld, Y., 1992. *The Judean Desert Monasteries in the Byzantine Period*, New Haven and London.

Hizmi, H., 1993. "Beiyudat, Khirbet el", *NEAEHL* 1, 181-182.

Hizmi, H., 2003. "Yitav", *ESI* 115, 41*-42*.

Hizmi, H., 2008a. "Archelaus Built Archelais", *BAR* 34/4, 49-59.

Hizmi, H., 2008b. "Beiyudhat, Khirbet el- (Archelais) ", *NEAEHL* 5, 1600-1602.

Hizmi, H., 2012. "Phasaelis – The Last Building Project of King Herod: Summary of the First Excavation Season (2011) ", *In the Highland's Depth* 2, 153-172 (Hebrew with English summary).

Horowitz, A., 2001. *The Jordan Rift Valley*, Abingdon-Tokyo.

Horowitz, A., and Zak, I., 1968. "Preliminary Pelynological Analysis of an Evaporitic Sequence from Mount Sedom, Israel", *Review for Palaeobotanical Palynology* 7, 25-30.

Horowitz, Y.S. 1923. *The Land of Israel and its Neighbors*, Vienna (Hebrew).

Hovers, E., and Bar-Yosef, O., 1987. "A Prehistoric Survey of Eastern Samaria: Preliminary Report", *IEJ* 37/2-3, 77-87.

Hütteroth, W.D., and Abdulfattah, K., 1977. *Historical Geography of Palestine, Transjordan and Southern Syria in the Late 16th Century*, Erlangen.

Ilan, Z. 1973. *The Jordan Valley and the Desert of Samaria*, Tel Aviv (Hebrew).

Ilan, Z., and Damati, E., 1975. "Ancient Roads in the Samarian Desert", *Museum Haaretz, Tel Aviv*, Yearbook 17-18, 43-52 (Hebrew with English Abstract).

Itach, G., 2015. "The Wedge-Incised Bowl and the Assyrian Deportation – A Reexamination", *In the Highland's Depth, Ephraim Range and Binyamin Research Studies*, vol. 5, 71-92 (Hebrew with English Summary).

Kagan, E.D., 2009. "Remains of Pens and Seasonal Residential Structures at Tomer", *Excavations and Discoveries in Samaria*, Jerusalem, 243-245 (Hebrew with English summary).

Kallay, Z., 1968. "Senaah", *EB* V, 1056-1057.

Kallay, Z., 1971. "Ataroth (1)", *EB* VI, 165-166.

Kenyon, K.M., 1993. "Jericho, Tell es-Sultan", *NEAEHL* 2, 674-681.

Kochavi, M., 1972 (ed.). *Judaea, Samaria and the Golan, Archaelogical Survey 1967-1968*, Jerusalem (Hebrew).
Koifman, Y., 1970. *The Book of Joshua*, Jerusalem (Hebrew).
Lapp, N.L., 1993. "Daliyeh, Wadi ed-", *NEAEHL* 1, 320-323.
Lemaire, A., 1994. "Histoire et administration de la Palestine a l'époque perse", in Laperrousaz, E.-M. (ed.), *La Palestine a l'époque perse*, Paris, 11-55.
Le Strange, G., 1890. *Palestine under the Moslems*, Paris.
London, A., 2003. *Date Plantations in the Land of Israel during the Second Temple, the Mishnah and the Talmud Periods* (M.A. Dissertation), Bar-Ilan University, Ramat-Gan (Hebrew).
London, A., 2005. "Growing Palm Trees in the Land of Israel during the Second Temple, Mishnah and Talmud Periods", *JSRS* 14, 77-88 (Hebrew with English Summary).
Lynch, W.F., 1849. *Narrative of the United States' Expedition to the River Jordan and the Dead Sea*, Philadelphia.
Magen, Y., 2004. "Two Tumuli in the Jordan Valley (Yafit)", in: Hizmi, H., and De-Groot, A., (eds.), *Burial Caves and Sites in Judea and Samaria from the Bronze and Iron Ages* (*JSP* 4), Jerusalem, 285-299.
Markus, M., (ed.), 1992. *The Jordan Valley and Eastern Samaria*, Tel Aviv (Hebrew).
Mazar, B., 1960. "The Cities of the Priests and the Levites", *Vetus Testamentum Supplement* 7, 193-205.
Mazar, B., 1970. "Migdal", *EB* IV, 633-636.
Mazar, B., 1980. "The Campaign of Shishaq to Canaan", *Canaan and Israel, Historical Essays*, Jerusalem, 234-244 (Hebrew).
Miller, K., 1962. *Die Peutingersche Tafel*, Stuttgart.
Möller, C., and Schmitt, G., 1976. *Siedlungen Palästinas nach Flavius Josephus*, Wiesbaden.
Na'aman, N., 1997. "King Mesha and the Foundation of the Moabite Monarchy", *IEJ* 47, 83-92.
Netzar, E., 2006. "The Contribution of the Hasmoneans and Herod to the Development of Jericho", *JSRS* 15, 73-84 (Hebrew with English Summary).
Neusner, J. (tr.), 1992. *The Talmud of Babylonia, an American Translation, vol. II.A: Shabbat, Chapters 1-2*, Atlanta.
Niccacci, A., 1994. "The Stela of Mesha and the Bible: Verbal System and Narrativity", *Orientalia* 63, 226-248.
Nir, D., and Ben-Arieh, Y., 1965. "Relics of an Intrermediate Terrace between the Ghor and the Zor in the Central Jordan Valley, Lake Tiberias Kfar Rupin (Israel) ", *Israel Journal for Earth Sciences* 14/1, 1-8.
Nobbe, C.F.A. (ed.), 1966. *Claudii Ptolemaei, Geographia*, Hildesheim.

Notley, R.S., and Safrai, Z., 2005. *Eusebius, Onomasticon, The Place Names of Divine Scripture,* Boston, Leiden.

Noy, T., 1993. "Gilgal", *NEAEHL* 2, 517-518.

Patrich, J., and Cohen, R., 1993. "Monasteries", *NEAEHL* 3, 1063-1070.

Peled, A., 2009. *Sugar in the Kingdom of Jerusalem: Crusade Technology between East and West,* Jerusalem (Hebrew).

Peleg, Y., 2000a. "Peza'el (East)", *ESI* 112, 53*.

Peleg, Y., 2000b. "Peza'el (North)", *ESI* 112, 53*-54*.

Peleg, Y., 2006. "A *Menorah* Relief from H. Dasha in the Jordan Valley", *Qadmoniot* 132, 121-122 (Hebrew).

Peleg, Y., 2009. "Early Roman Period Aqueducts and Early Muslim Structures at Kh. Fusail", *Excavations and Discoveries in Samaris,* Jerusalem, 156-169 (Hebrew with English summary).

Peleg, Y., and Hameiri, N., 2002. "Region I: Survey and Excavations of Caves along Wadi el-Makkuk and Wadi ed-Daliya", *'Atiqot* XLI, part 2, 1-4.

Porath, Y., 1968. *The Samaria Survey* (*B*), Unpublished Text (Hebrew).

Porath, Y., 1973. "Fasael Region", *HA* 46, 9-13.

Porath, Y., 1985a. "A Chalcolithic Building at Fasa'el", *'Atiqot* 17, 1-19.

Porath, Y., 1985b. *Ancient Irrigation Agriculture in the Arid Zones of Eretz Israel* (Ph.D. Dissertation), Tel Aviv University, Tel Aviv.

Raba, J., 1992. "Palestine in the Late Mamluk Period as Reflected in Russian Travellers' Descriptions", in Drory, J. (ed.), *Palestine in the Mamluk Period,* Jerusalem, 157-171 (Hebrew).

Rackham, H. (trs.), 1962. *Pliny, Natural History* (The Loeb Classical Library), London.

Reich, R., 1985. "Some Byzantine Remains", *'Atiqot* 17, 205-213.

Rosener, D., 1997. *The Moabites and their Military, Political and Cultural Relationship with the Kingdoms of Israel and Judah,* Jerusalem (Hebrew).

Rosenson, Y., 1987. "Date Growing in the Past in the Land of Israel According to the Literature", in Ayalon, E. (ed.), *The Date – Tree of Life,* Tel Aviv, 94-104 (Hebrew).

Routledge, B., 2000. "The Politics of Mesha: Segmented Identities and State Formation in Iron Age Moab", *Journal of the Economic and Social History of the Orient* 43/3, 221-256.

Russell, K.W., 1980. "The Earthquake of May 19, AD 363", *BASOR* 238, 47-64.

Sabah, A., 1992. "The Vegetation of the Jordan Valley and Eastern Samaria", in: Markus, M., (ed.), *The Jordan Valley and Eastern Samaria,* Tel Aviv, 48-55 (Hebrew).

Schiller, E., 1976. *The Palace of Hisham* (*Kh. El-Mafjar*), Jerusalem (Hebrew).

Schiller, E., (ed.), 1977. *The Holy Land in Old Engravings and Illustrations,* Jerusalem.

Schiller, E., 1983. "Jericho from the Middle Age to Our Time", in Schiller, E. (ed.), *Jericho and its Vicinity*, Jerusalem, 55-56 (Hebrew).

Schuldenrein, J., 1983. *Late Quaternary Paleo-Enviroment and Prehistoric Site Distribution in the Lower Jordan Valley* (Ph.D Dissertation), University of Chicago, Chicago.

Sion, O., 1996. "The Monasteries of the 'Desert of the Jordan'", *Liber Annus* 46, 245-264.

Spanier, Y., 1992. *Eastern Samaria in the Hellenistic Roman and Byzantine Periods* (M.A. Dissertation), Bar-Ilan University, Ramant-Gan (Hebrew).

Spanier, Y., 1994. "Map of el-Mughayir Survey", *HA*, 68-69.

Spanier, Y., 1997. "The Eastern Desert of Israel – A Place of Refuge during the Hellenistic and Roman Periods", *JSRS* 6, 97-109 (Hebrew with English Summary).

Stern, M., 1968. "The Description of Palestine by Pliny the Elder and the Administrative Division of Judea at the End of the Period of the Second Temple", *Tarbiz* 37, 215-229 (Hebrew with English Summary).

Stewart, A., 1896. *Burchard of Mount Sion* (Palestine Pilgrim Text Society XII), London.

Tchernov, E., 1994. *An Early Neolithic Village in the Jordan Valley, vol. 2: The Fauna of Netiv Hagdud*, Cambridge.

Thomson, W.M., 1880. *The Land and the Book – The Holy Land*, London.

Tristram, H.B., 1865. *The Land of Israel, a Journal of Travels in Palestine*, London.

van de Velde, C.W.M., 1854. *Narrative of a Journey through Syria and Palestina in 1851 and 1852*, vol. II, Edinburgh and London.

Wavell, A.P., 1941 (first published 1928). *The Palestine Campaigns*, London.

Yeivin, Z., 1974. "Israelite Towers at Khirbet Mahrouq", *Qadmoniot* 27/28, 102-104 (Hebrew).

Yeivin, Z., 1992. "Two Watchtowers in the Jordan Valley", *EI* 23, 155-174 (Hebrew with English Abstract).

Yekutieli, U., 1971. "Samaria during the Moslem Period", in: Dar, S., and Ruth, Y., (eds.), *Shomron, a Collection of Articles and Sources*, Tel Aviv, 204-218 (Hebrew).

Yelin, D., 1972. *Jerusalem of Yesterday*, Jerusalem (Hebrew).

Younker, R.W., 1992. "Cherit, Brook of", *ABD* 1, 899.

Zertal, A., 1984. *Hepher, Arubboth and the Third Solomonic District*, Tel Aviv (Hebrew).

Zertal, A., 1988. "'From Watchtowers to Fortified Cities' - on the History of Highway Forts in the Israelite Kingdom", *Qadmoniot* 83-84, 82-86 (Hebrew).

Zertal, A., 1989. "The Wedge-Decorated Bowl and the Origin of the Cuthaeans", *EI* 20, 181-187 (Hebrew with English Summary).

Zertal, A., 1991. "Two Roman Castellae in the Jordan Valley, and the Location of Coabis", *Cathedra* 62, 3-17 (Hebrew with English Abstract).

Zertal, A., 1994. "'To the Land of the Perizzites and the Giants': On the Israelite Settlement in the Hill-Country of Manasseh", in Finkelstein, I., and Na'aman, N. (eds.), *From Nomadism to Monarchy*, Jerusalem, 47-69.

Zertal, A., 1995. "Three Iron Age Fortresses in the Jordan Valley and the Origin of the Ammonite Circular Towers", *IEJ* 45/4, 253-273.

Zertal, A., 2000. *A Nation Born, the Altar on Mt. Ebal and the Birth of Israel*, Tel Aviv (Hebrew).

Zertal A., 2001. "The Heart of the Monarchy: Pattern of Settlement and Historical Considerations of the Israelite Kingdom of Samaria", in: Mazar, A., (ed.), *Studies in the Archaeology of the Iron Age in Israel and Jordan*, London, 38-64.

Zertal, A., 2004. *The Manasseh Hill Country Survey, vol.1: The Shechem Syncline* (*CHANE* 21.1), Leiden and Boston.

Zertal, A., 2008. *The Manasseh Hill Country Survey, vol.2: The Eastern Valleys and the Fringes of the Desert* (*CHANE* 21.2), Leiden and Boston.

Zertal, A., 2012. *The Manasseh Hill Country Survey, vol.5: The Middle Jordan Valley* (*From Wadi Fasael to Wadi 'Aujah*), Haifa (Hebrew).

Zertal, A., and Bar, S., 2017. *The Manasseh Hill Country Survey, vol. 4: From Nahal Bezeq to the Sartaba* (*CHANE* 21.4), Leiden and Boston.

Zertal, A., Bar, S., and Cohen, O., 2012. "The Excavations at Tell esh-Sheikh Diyab", in Zertal, A., *The Manasseh Hill Country Survey, vol. 5: The Middle Jordan Valley* (*From Wadi Fasael to Wadi 'Aujah*), Haifa, 608-631 (Hebrew).

Zertal, A., and Ben-Yosef, D., 2009. "Bedhat esh-Sha'ab - An Iron Age I Enclosure in the Jordan Valley", in: Schloen, J.D., (ed.), *Exploring the Longue Durée: Essays in Honour of Lawrence E. Stager*, Winona Lake, 517-529.

Zertal, A., Ben-Yosef, D., Cohen, O., and Be'eri, R., 2009. "Kh. 'Aujah el-Foqa (Ataroth) - an Iron Age Fortified City in the Jordan Valley", *PEQ* 141/2, 104-123.

Zertal, A., and Mirkam, N., 2016. *The Manasseh Hill Country Survey, vol. 3: From Nahal 'Iron to Nahal Shechem* (*CHANE* 21.3), Leiden and Boston.

Zutovski, K., and Bar, S., 2017. "Canaanean Blade Knapping Waste Pit from Fazael 4, Israel", *Lithic Technology* 42/2-3, 109-125.

PART THREE

APPENDICES AND INDICES

APPENDIX A

THE FLINT ASSEMBLAGES

Haim Winter

During the years of field-work since the publication of the Manasseh Hill Country Survey, Volume 4 (in Hebrew) in 2005, the area between Wadi Ras el-Ahmar and Nahal Yitav was surveyed, and much new data have been accumulated. The main problem was, and still is, the dating of flint artefacts collected at random from the surface in the course of a general survey. The considerations and alternatives for a possible solution of this problem are discussed in detail in Volumes 2 and 4 of the survey (Winter 2008; 2017).

The late Prof. Adam Zertal provided the artefacts and gave me the opportunity to study and analyze the assemblages, and my son Yuval read the initial draft. He added important remarks which contributed to the accuracy of details and the expansion of the geological part. I am grateful to both of them.

The sketches of the flint artefacts were prepared by me, and drawn by Ron Shimelmitz. The responsibility for any mistakes is entirely mine.

INTRODUCTION

Seventy-one flint assemblages were discovered in the course of the current survey, in 44% of the sites described in this volume. The difference between the quantities of flint finds in the sites was significant, from a few artefacts to hundreds per site. The number of diagnostic artefacts, compared to previous volumes, was low. The composition of the finds and the small number of diagnostic artefacts made it difficult to date many of the sites, and did not allow a distinction between sub-periods – such as in the IA or EP phases. Although it was not a specific survey of flint artefacts, it should be noted that the awareness of the participants in flint gathering had grown considerably, even though they were not trained especially for this subject. The facts that the finds were collected at random, as well as post-depositional processes, such as erosion, tectonic changes and human activity, added to the difficulty of analyzing the finds. All the sites in which flint was found, even if only a few artefacts, have been included in this study. Small flint assemblages in nearby sites contribute to insights about the area. Furthermore, the presence of even a few flint tools attests to the way of life of a community, particularly in early historical periods. The conclusions were suggested with great caution, and we tried to indicate trends and directions which arise from the problematic material collected at random. Our approach to the finds was similar to that in Volumes 2 and 4 (Winter 2008; 2017), with changes resulting from the nature of the region, the material, and the emphasis on some of the conclusions in the analysis. Hence, the adherence of the author to the principles set out below (in a short version for the convenience of the reader: for full information see Winter 2008; 2017).

METHODOLOGY

Due to the fact that the assemblages were collected at random from the surface, we refrained from drawing definitive conclusions about specific sites, and determined four levels of probability for identifying the period:

1) highly reasonable, 2) reasonable, 3) possible, 4) not identified.

Due to the complexity of the above classification, the following guidelines were introduced:

- The presence of diagnostic flint artefacts, or an identifiable composition of the assemblage, dates the flint finds at the level of **highly reasonable.**
- Finds of diagnostic sherds from periods in which flint tools were still used, and no evidence for other periods was found, dates the flint finds at the level of **reasonable.**
- In the absence of diagnostic flint artefacts, but with finds of sherds which could be affiliated according to their morphology to a single period, and finds of sherds from several periods in which flint tools were still in use, the flint finds were dated according to all periods present at the level of **possible.**
- In the absence of diagnostic sherds or diagnostic flint artefacts, or an identifiable composition of the assemblage, the flint finds were defined as **not identified.**

Categorization of the finds

Usually the bulk of flint finds (from surveys or excavations) are products knapped from flint chunks or pebbles, and divided into categories according to the morphology of the artefacts.

In Volume 2 (Winter 2008), three categories were introduced:

1. Waste: artefacts unusable due to their shape or size;
2. Debitage: knapped artefacts (mainly flakes, blades and bladelets) suitable for secondary processing in order to shape specific tools.

3. Tools: artefacts, mainly from the Debitage group, shaped for a specific purpose by flaking, retouching or polishing. Occasionally, an artefact with partial cortex cover (such as a primary flake) was also chosen for secondary processing in order to shape a tool.

In Volume 4 (Winter 2017) we divided the finds into two categories - unretouched artefacts and retouched artefacts. This division turned out to be too simple, because even at the low magnification inspection of the artefacts which we carried out (Vol. 5) on many of the artefacts attributed to the Debitage group, use-wear signs were found, meaning that some artefacts without secondary processing (such as retouch) could also be used as working tools (bearing use-wear signs). These tools were thus actually incorrectly counted together with waste. Thus, the definition of a tool should not necessarily depend on secondary processing. Therefore we decided to introduce the category of Debitage for all items without retouch, but suitable for secondary processing (mainly flakes, blades and bladelets), which were not included in other categories. The French term *débitage* was introduced by Bordes in the mid-20th century, and included unretouched artefacts according to their morphology, but disregarded the fact that morphologically similar artefacts could actually belong to different categories – those with use-wear signs to the tool group, and those without to the Debitage category proper. According to this morphological division the Debitage category included both pieces to be discarded later as waste, and artefacts which could be shaped into tools by secondary processing. Some of the latter were used as tools (without secondary processing, but bearing use-wear signs): according to their function: they are similar to retouched tools, the end-products. Actually, the assemblages should be divided to four groups, but we refrained from doing so because an analysis of use-wear was beyond the scope of this study. As a matter of fact, the flint tool production process is similar to a modern industrial process, which includes raw material, waste to be discarded, semi-finished products, and finally end-products.

Considering the above, we decided to divide the categories as follows:

1. **Waste:** artefacts unusable due to their shape or size;
2. **Debitage:** knapped artefacts (mainly flakes, blades and bladelets) suitable for secondary processing in order to shape a certain tool. Some of these could have been used as tools without being modified by retouch.
3. **Tools**: artefacts, mainly from the Debitage group, shaped for a specific purpose by flaking, retouching or polishing. Occasionally, artefacts with partial cortex cover (such as primary flakes) were also chosen for secondary processing in order to shape a tool.

The absence of Lower Palaeolithic and Middle Palaeolithic sites in the area of this volume (see Table 1.1) will not be discussed here, as this subject has been dealt with in Volume 4 (Winter 2017).

Publications and general characteristics for the identification of the periods

1. For typological identifications we used the following publications: Hours 1974; Bordes 1961; Bar-Yosef 1970; Lee 1973; and for specific tools, such as arrowheads Gopher 1985; for sickle blades: Burian and Friedman 1979; Gopher 1989; and Rosen 1997.
   The dating by typological identification has several shortcomings:
   a. In various typological lists identical artefacts were attributed to different periods;
   b. Some artefacts are difficult to define according to the existing lists, because they are exceptional in some of their characteristics;
   c. Some of the tools were in use during several successive periods, and thus their value as chronological markers is limited;
   d. Local or regional phenomena might deviate from a general list;
   e. Sometimes there is no correlation between typological and radiometric dating (Hovers and Marder 1991: 51-53).

   Hence, whenever possible, dating by more than one method is preferable.
2. The morphology of cores and waste, the use of the micro-burin method, transverse blows, pressure retouch and the Canaanean blade technique also served for identification of periods.
3. In absence of diagnostic flint artefacts, sherds whose cultural affinity was known according to their morphology helped to date the flint assemblage of the site. Some examples: Canaanean sickle blades could not be considered as diagnostic markers for a single period, as they were produced and used from the CH (Bar and Winter 2010) to the EBA and IBA (Bar and Winter 2010), and Geometric sickle blades, which were used from MBA II to the IA. The cross-checking of flint and sherd finds is very important, especially for periods in which improvised 'ad hoc' flint tools without prominent characteristics were produced, mainly for casual tasks (Rosen 1997: 34, 158-159).
4. The compositions of the tool group, the Debitage and the industrial waste may help to date assemblages. In the absence of period-defining artefacts, the relative quantities of types in the assemblage and the composition of the industrial waste were checked. Examples are the percentages of blades, end-scrapers and burins which are general markers of the Upper Palaeolithic (without discussing the details of its different cultures), and the shares of geometric microliths (markers of the Geometric Kebaran).
5. Diagnostic artefacts, unique to a period, are important for identification, but we usually refrained from relying on a single artefact. Supporting evidence is needed for dating. In many cases these were dated sherds.

Assemblages of similar or approximately the same composition, differing from each other due to the presence of a unique artefact in one of them, might lead to a different dating. For example – the Kebara Point, which is missing in the Geometric Kebaran, helps to distinguish it from Kebaran assemblages.

Specific characteristics of the different periods:

Upper Palaeolithic period (*UP*)
- Relative abundance of blades, tools on blades, and bladelets.
- Relatively large numbers of end-scrapers and burins, and presence of carinated end-scrapers.

Epipalaeolithic period (*EP*)
- Morphology of cores and industrial waste.
- The number of microliths and their shapes, which also enable identification of the different phases.
- Morphology of end-scrapers and burins.
- Presence of sickle blades.

Neolithic period (*NE*)
- Presence of a certain component of microliths in the assemblage.
- Bifacial tools and their distinctive shape (axe, adze, and chisel).
- Naviform (boat-shaped) cores.
- Arrowheads of all kinds.
- Sickle blades and reaping knives (all with sickle gloss).

Wadi Raba phase
- Typical sickle blades.
- Morphology of bifacial tools.

Chalcolithic period (*CH*)
- Bifacial tools and their typical shape.
- Sickle blades and their shape.
- Perforated discs.
- Fan-scrapers (tabular scrapers).

Early and Intermediate Bronze Ages
- Canaanean blades and Canaanean sickle blades.
- Fan-scrapers (tabular scrapers).

Middle Bronze II, Late Bronze and Iron Ages
- Geometric sickle blades (Large Geometric, Rosen 1997).

In sites with few artefacts, special attention was paid to the preparation of the striking platforms and the bulbs of percussion. These indicate a regular production, even if other elements indicating intentional flaking were missing.

Flint industries generally ceased to exist after the Iron Ages.

Some other definitions used in this study

- The flint artefacts have been classified according to the common typological lists mentioned above. Artefacts which could not be classified according to these lists have been defined as 'Varia', with occasional explanations in the text.
- A roughout is an unfinished tool in preparation: axe, adze or pick, generally NE or CH.
- A backed knife is an artefact with a natural or retouched back, while on the opposite side there is a sharp cutting edge, with or without retouch. The tool is intended to be hand-held during use.
- An *ad hoc* tool is usually prepared for casual tasks, with minimal work invested in its preparation.

CATALOGUE OF SITES CONTAINING FLINT ARTEFACTS AND THEIR PROPOSED DATING

Site 1: E.P. -290

Israel Grid 1974/1640, Elevation 290 m b.s.l; 111 flint artefacts (Fig.1.1).

Waste: Core 2; Primary element 14; Chunk 9; Chip 3; Total 28.
Debitage: Flake 42; Blade 25; Bladelet 4; Total 71.
Tools: End-scraper 2; Transverse scraper 2; Side-scraper 1; Burin 1; Awl 2; Retouched blade 1; Notch 2; Axe (fragment) 1; Total 12.

This site, close to the River Jordan, is the topographically lowest within the survey boundaries in which flint artefacts were found. The light brown raw flint is of high quality, and the artefacts are large and abundant. The number of finds indicates the existence of a regular industry. Apart from the axe, no diagnostic pieces were found. The artefacts are sharp and without patina (only a few have undergone rolling or scorching), testifying to a relatively late date and being *in situ*. The axe has a lentoid cross-section and a transverse blow at the cutting edge – typical of the PPNB period. Arrowheads and sickle blades were missing, but the other finds match the period and enable a highly reasonable dating. Most sherds were from late periods, with few from CH or EBA; thus

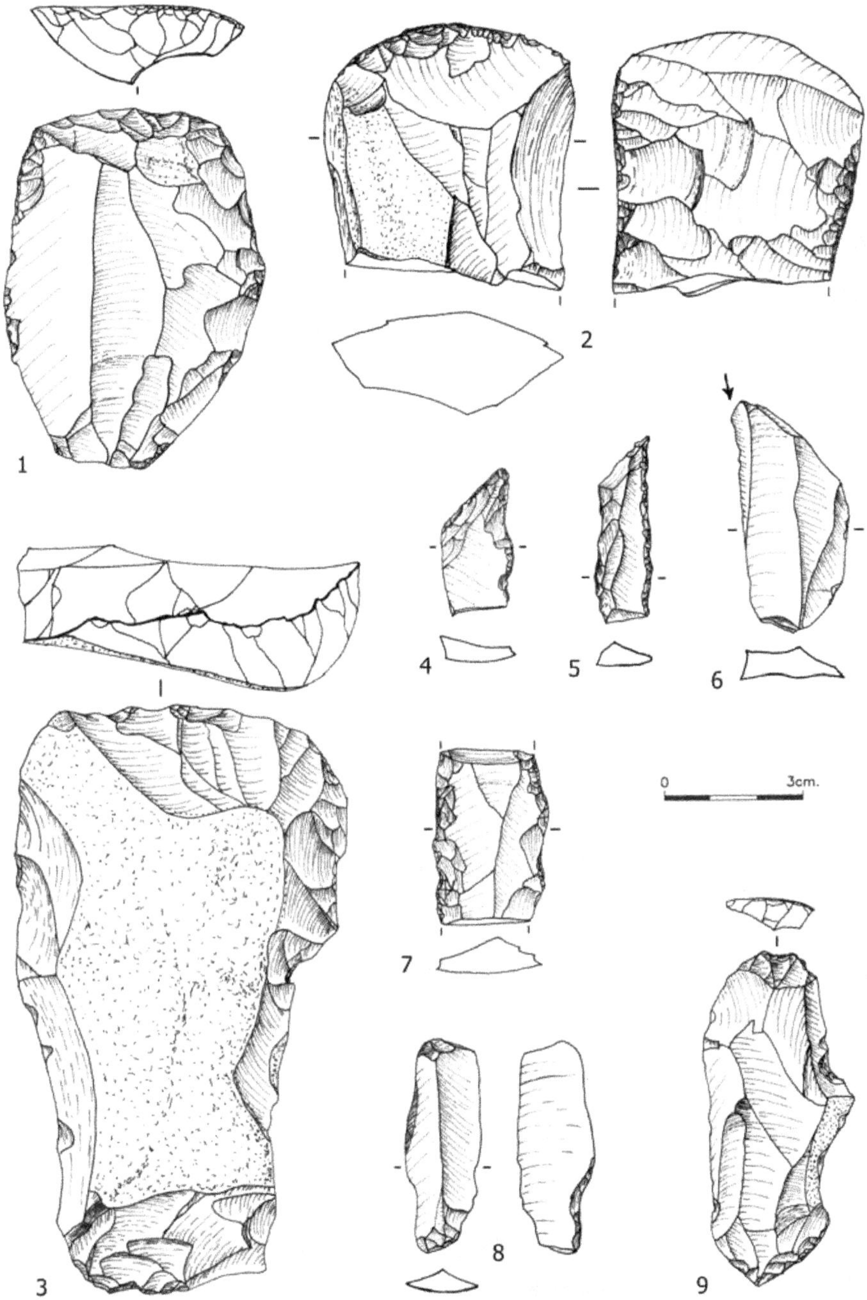

Fig. 1.1. E.P. -290: 1-End-scraper on flake; 2-Axe with transverse blow (fragment); 3-Transverse scraper on exhausted core; 4-5-Awls; 6-Burin; 7-Retouched blade; 8-Notch on blade; 9-End-scraper.

some flint artefacts could originate from these periods, and they were dated at the level of possible.
Periods: PPNB (bulk of the assemblage) – highly reasonable.
EBA – possible.
CH – possible.

Site 3: E.P. 111

Israel Grid 1888/1630, Elevation 111 m a.s.l.; 3 flint artefacts.

Waste: Chunk 1.
Debitage: Flake 1.
Tools: Retouched flake 1.
The small number of artefacts does not allow dating.
Period: ND.

Site 4: Mughur el Hableh

Israel Grid 1885/1627, Elevation 40 m b.s.l.; 148 flint artefacts (Fig. 1.2).

Waste: Core 4; Primary element 10; Chunk 8; Chip 18; Total 40.
Debitage: Flake 27; Blade 30; Bladelet 21; Total 78.
Tools: End-scraper 8; Side-scraper 2 (1 fan scraper?); Burin 2; Borer 1; Retouched flake 2; Retouched blade 1; Retouched bladelet 1; Backed knife 2 (1 natural back); Sickle blade (not typical) 1; Notch 3; Truncation 2; bifacial (fragment) 1; Varia 4; Total 30.

Most of the sherd find at the site is attributed to the EBA, but only two flint artefacts might be from this period. One of these can be defined as a side scraper / fan scraper, and the other is a sickle blade on a thick bladelet with obvious sickle gloss. However, its shape is not characteristic of the period; it is more like a Chalcolithic sickle blade. Apparently, the bulk of the flint find is from another period. Although diagnostic artefacts were not found, the composition of the find allows us to draw conclusions. In the waste category, at least half of the cores are blade and bladelet cores. In the Debitage category the number of blades and bladelets (some are broken) constitute an absolute majority. In the tool group there was an abundance of end-scrapers (nearly 27%) and a few burins, which are generally missing in later periods. There is no doubt that in the flint assemblage blades and tools on blades are dominant. On the other hand almost no retouched microliths typical of the EP were found. All these point to an UP assemblage. The site is at an elevation of about 40 m above the highest level of Lake Lisan (about 164 m b.s.l. – see Fig. 1.17), similarly to other sites of this period which were never flooded by Lake Lisan, and were

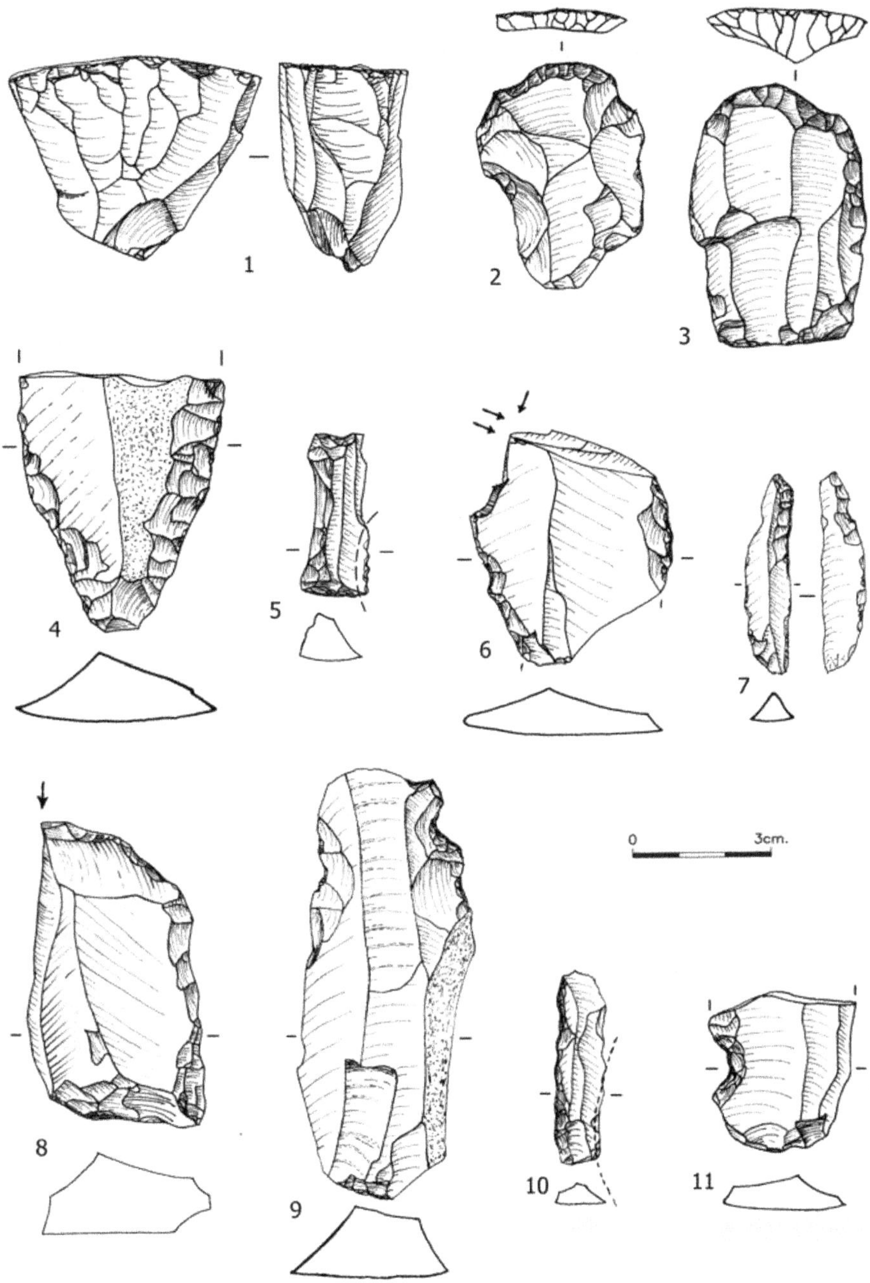

Fig. 1.2. **Mughur el-Hableh**: 1-Core; 2-3-End-scrapers; 4-Side-scraper/Fan-scraper; 5-Untypical sickle blade; 6, 8-Burins; 7-Borer; 11-Notch. **E.P. 55**: 9-Unfinished bifacial; 10-Sickle blade with retouched back, truncation and sickle gloss.

not covered by lake sediments. Most of the find is Upper Palaeolithic, and the conclusions in this case are highly reasonable, even without diagnostic artefacts.

Periods: UP – highly reasonable.
EBA – possible.

Site 6: E.P. 55

Israel Grid 1885/1624, Elevation 50 m a.s.l.; 50 flint artefacts (Fig. 1.2).

Waste: Primary flake 2; Chunk 3; Chip 3; Total 8.
Debitage: Flake 27; Blade 4; Bladelet 5; Total 36.
Tools: Retouched flake 1; Retouched blade 1; Sickle blade 2; Roughout 2; Total 6.

The sickle blades have a truncation and a retouched back (one on a primary blade), the two roughouts (intended for the preparation of bifacials), and the composition of the assemblage indicate a flint industry which should be attributed to the CH, as do the sherds.

Period: CH – highly reasonable.

Site 14: Fasael (1)

Israel Grid 1909/1620, Elevation 200 m b.s.l.; 37 flint artefacts (Fig. 1.3).

Waste: Core 4; Total 4.
Debitage: Flake 2; Blade 7; Bladelet 5; Total 14.
Hammerstone: 1.
Tools: Awl 1; Retouched flake 2; Retouched blade 1; Sickle blade 5; Notch 3; Truncation 2; Axe 1; Adze 1; Bifacial (broken) 2; Total 18.

The sickle blades with a retouched back – three with one truncation and one snap and two with double truncations, particularly characterize the CH, as do the axe, adze and other fragmented bifacial tools. The cores are small and exhausted, and the bladelet core is also typical of the period. The flint find indicates an industry which should be attributed to the CH, similarly to the sherd collection.

Period: CH - highly reasonable.

Site 15: Thahunet el-Fusayil

Israel Grid 1891/1620, Elevation 130 m b.s.l.

Three waste and Debitage, non-indicative flint artefacts.
Period: ND.

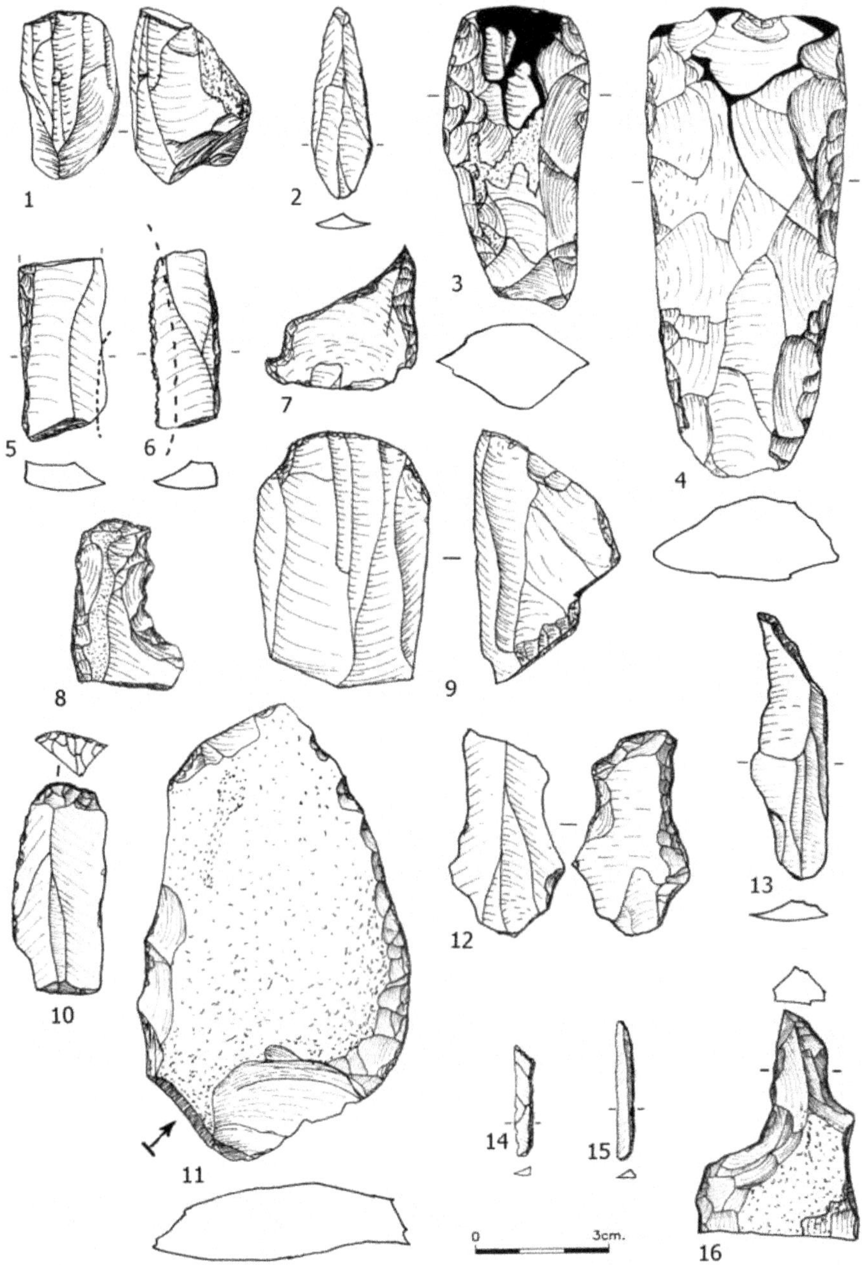

Fig. 1.3. **Fasael (1)**: 1-Bladelet core; 2-Bladelet; 3-Polished axe; 4-Adze (partial polishing); 5-6-Sickle blades with retouched back, truncation and sickle gloss; 7-Awl; 8-Notch. **Fasael (4)**: 9-Core; 10-End-scraper; 11-Fan-scraper; 12-Double notch (ventral); 13-14-Bladelets with oblique truncation; 15-Backed bladelet; 16-Borer.

Site 16: Fasael (3)

Israel Grid 1913/1620, Elevation 180 m b.s.l.; 11 flint artefacts.

Debitage: Flake 2; Blade 4; Bladelet 2; Total 8.
Tools: End-notch 1; Varia 2; Total 3.

The small assemblages of flint and sherds do not allow conclusions.
Period: ND.

Site 17: Fasael (6)

Israel Grid 1905/1618, Elevation 160 m b.s.l.; 17 flint artefacts.

Waste: Core 1; Primary element 2; Chip 1; Total 4.
Debitage: Flake 4; Blade 5; Bladelet 2; Total 11.
Tools: Naturally backed knife 1; Truncation 1; Total 2.

The single bladelet core prepared from a tabular flint and the Canaanean blade fragment do not allow dating.
Period: ND.

Site 18: 19-16/01/6, Fasael (4)

Israel Grid 1907/1617, Elevation 175 m b.s.l.; 105 flint artefacts (Fig. 1.3).

Waste: Core 1; Primary flake 2; Total 3.
Debitage: Flake 18; Blade 13; Bladelet 33; Blade/bladelet fragments 12; Total 76.
Tools: End-scraper 3; Rounded scraper 2; Fan-scraper 1; Borer 2; Retouched flake 6; Retouched blade 1; Notch 2; Denticulate 1; Retouched microlith 4; Bladelet with retouched back 2; Blade with oblique truncation 1; Bladelet with oblique truncation 1; Total 26.

The bladelets, the microliths and the blade/bladelet core indicate a microlithic industry. The two obliquely truncated blade / bladelets with a retouched back, the other non-geometric microliths and the narrow end scraper belong to the Kebaran Culture. The fan scraper, and perhaps the coarse borer, tend to be CH or EBA. The absence of celt tools is typical of the EBA, thus some of the flint artefacts should be attributed to this period.
Period: EP – Kebaran Culture (most of the artefacts) – highly reasonable;
EBA (fewer artefacts) – highly reasonable.

Site 21: Tell esh-Sheikh Diyab (2)

Israel Grid 1905/1615, Elevation 170 m b.s.l.; 240 flint artefacts (Fig. 1.4).

Waste: Core 4; Primary element 37; Chunk 42; Chip 61; Total 144.
Debitage: Flake 47; Blade 9; Canaanean blade 2; Bladelet 5; Total 63.

Tools: End-scraper 2; Transverse (oblique) scraper 1; Fan-scraper 1; Side-scraper 1; Burin 1; Awl 2; Retouched flake 1; Retouched blade 4; Retouched bladelet 1; Backed knife 3; Sickle blade 1; Notch 12; Denticulate 1; Truncation 1; Varia 1; Total 33.

The site is located on a slope with architectonic features and sherds attributed to the EBA I. The fan-scraper, the Canaanean blades and the retouched Canaanean blade match this period. The many rolled artefacts with blunt edges present at the site were swept down-slope by erosion, and the variety of qualities and colours indicate that these flint artefacts originated from various cultures. The sole sickle blade (retouched back, truncated and snapped), is typical CH; and the abundance of end scrapers, the burin and the retouched bladelet point to the EP, or even UP. It is obvious that that part of the mixed assemblage belongs to the EBA, while another part is not defined.

Periods: EBA (part of the find) – highly reasonable.
Part of the find – ND.

Site 22: Fasael (5)

Israel Grid 1912/1615, Elevation 205 m b.s.l.; 32 flint artefacts (Fig. 1.5).

Waste: Core 1; Primary element 2; Chunk 2; Total 5.
Debitage: Flake 10; Blade 9; Bladelet 1; Total 20.
Tools: End-scraper 1; Retouched flake 1; Retouched blade 1; Sickle blade 2; Notch 1; Fragment of bifacial artefact 1; Total 7.

Few diagnostic artefacts were found. The backed sickle blade and the bifacial tool fragment (axe or adze) tend to be CH; the Canaanean sickle blade, and two sherds as well, could be EBA. The backed sickle blade and the Canaanean sickle blade were found together. Previously the latter were attributed to the EBA and MBA, and this is another site where Cananean blades were found in a CH context (see Bar and Winter 2010).

Period: CH – reasonable.

Site 25: Fasael (12)

Israel Grid 1915/1615, Elevation 205 m b.s.l.; 350 flint artefacts (Fig. 1.5).

Waste: Core 2; Primary element 38; Chunk 41; Chip 97; Total 178.
Debitage: Flake 89; Blade 33; Bladelet 23; Total 145.
Tools: End-scraper 6; Awl 3; Retouched flake 4; Retouched blade 1; Notch 6; Denticulate 3; Truncation 3; Varia 1; Total 27.

There were no diagnostic artefacts in this large assemblage. The grey-beige flint was difficult to knap and the flakes and blades are irregular. The tools and bladelets are coarse, many of them broken, and it is difficult to reconstruct

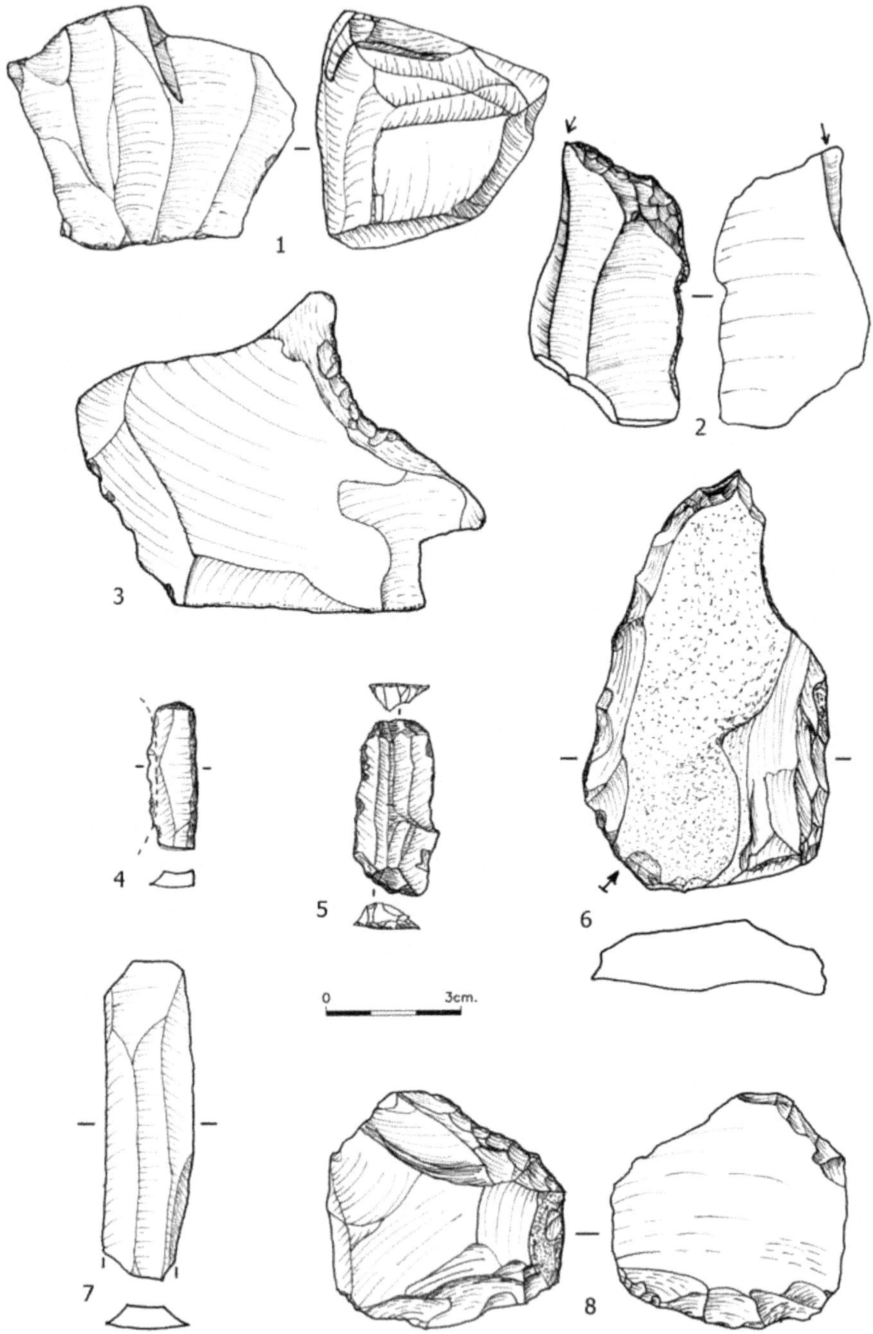

Fig.1.4. **Tell esh-Sheikh Diyab (2)**: 1-Core; 2-Burin; 3-Notch; 4-Sickle blade with retouched back, truncation and sickle gloss; 5-End-scraper; 6-Fan-scraper; 7-Canaanean blade; 8-Déjeté (oblique) scraper, its striking platform removed.

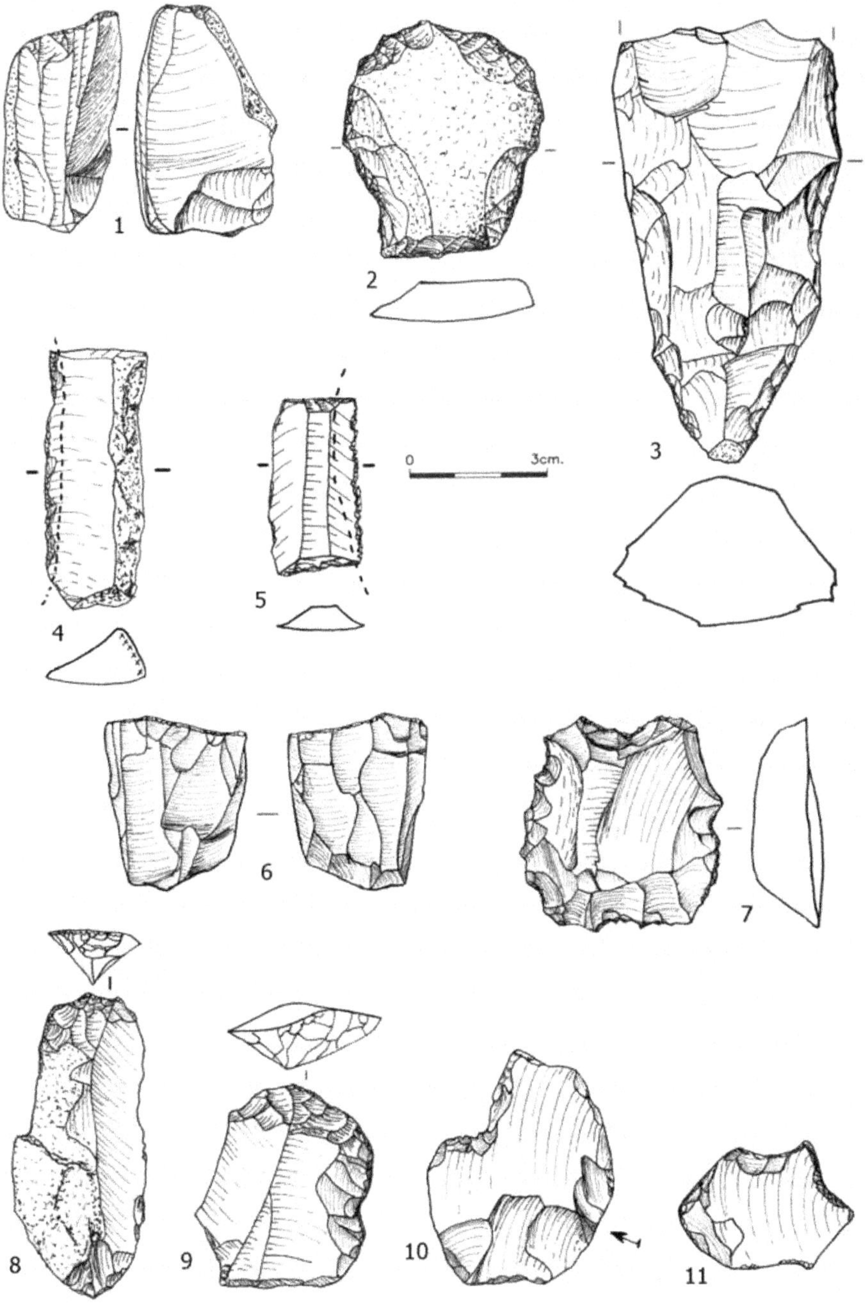

Fig. 1.5. **Fasael (5)**: 1-Bladelet core; 2-Fan-scraper; 3-Broken adze or axe; 4-Sickle blade with natural back and sickle gloss; 5-Canaanean sickle blade with truncation and sickle gloss. **Fasael (12)**: 6-Pyramidal bladelet core; 7-Denticulate; 8-9-End-scrapers; 10-Notch; 11-Awl.

their original shape. Some of them have a thin whitish patina. The two small pyramidal cores tend to be EP, but there is no verification of this notion in the assemblage. 63 of the 145 artefacts in the Debitage category (43%) are fragments, and nine fragmented tools (33%) point to the existence of a workshop. The altitude of the site, 205 m b.s.l., is higher than the level of Lake Lisan 22,000 years BCE (see Lake Lisan sea level - Fig. 1.17), hence the lake sediments have never covered the site. The assemblage, containing blades, bladelets and end-scrapers, should be attributed to the Late UP in transition to the EP.
Period: Late UP – highly reasonable.

Site 26: el-Hisha

Israel Grid 1909/1613, Elevation 200 m b.s.l.; 3 flint artefacts.

Debitage: Flake 3.

The sherds and the few flint artefacts do not allow any conclusions.
Period: ND.

Site 29: Umm Suwei'ad

Israel Grid 1907/1610, Elevation 190 m b.s.l.; 20 flint artefacts (Fig. 1.6).

Waste: Core 1; Primary element 3; Total 4.
Debitage: Flake 4; Blade 2; Total 6.
Tools: Awl 1; Retouched blade 2; Backed knife 1; Denticulate 2; Truncation 1; Roughout 1; Varia 2; Total 10.

The small assemblage without diagnostic artefacts makes the dating difficult. The roughout with bifacial preparation could indicate the NE or CH, of which few sherds were found. The thick artefact with flat retouch on its ventral face and perhaps also a burin blow does not fit any type list, perhaps because it is a re-used core. Because of its workmanship it does not fit the IA, and has been included as Varia. About half of the sherds are from the IA, and the rest to later periods.
Periods: IA – reasonable.
CH – possible.

Site 31: Wadi ez-Zimrah

Israel Grid 1906/1606, Elevation 150 m b.s.l.; 33 flint artefacts (Fig. 1.6).

Waste: Primary element 7; Chunk 1; Chip 6; Total 14.
Debitage: Flake 6; Blade 6; Bladelet 1; Total 13.
Tools: Awl 3; Naturally backed knife 1; Sickle blade 1; Notch 1; Total 6.

Only the sickle blade, with retouched back and truncation, is diagnostic.

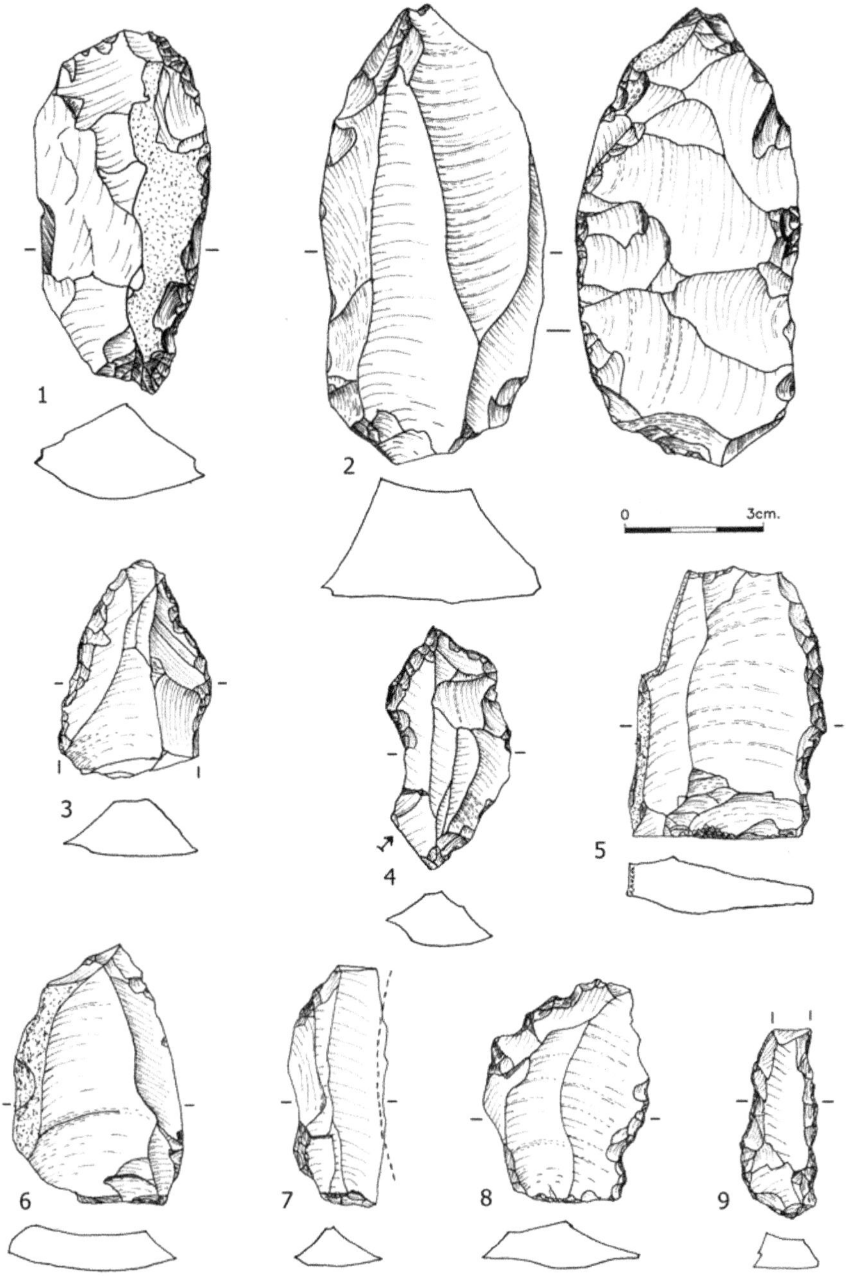

Fig. 1.6. **Umm Suwei'ad:** 1-Roughout with lentoid cross-section; 2-Undefined, core in secondary use (?); 3-Retouched flake; 4-Awl; 5-Naturally backed knife. **Wadi ez-Zimrah**: 6-Naturally backed knife; 7-Sickle blade with retouched back, truncation and faint sickle gloss. **Tomer (1)**: 8-Retouched flake; 9-Retouched blade (fragment, possibly a broken borer).

Half the sherds are CH, and the rest are from IA I. The sickle blade indicates the CH, but both periods are possible.
Periods: CH – reasonable.
IA I – possible.

Site 34: Khirbet Fusayil (Phasaelis)

Israel Grid 1918/1597, Elevation 220 m b.s.l.; 22 flint artefacts.

Waste: Primary element 2; Chunk 2; Chip 1; Total 5.
Debitage: Flake 9; Blade 1; Bladelet 5; Total 15.
Tools: Retouched flake 2; Total 2.

The small artefacts were made from fine grained, light-brown flint. In the absence of diagnostic artefacts the period has not been defined.
Period: ND.

Site 35: Tomer (1)

Israel Grid 1913/1588, Elevation 180 m b.s.l.; 23 flint artefacts (Fig. 1.6).

Waste: Primary element 3; Chunk 2; Chip 2; Total 7.
Debitage: Flake 8; Blade 2; Total 10.
Tools: Retouched flake 3; Retouched blade (possibly a fragment of a massive borer) 1; Truncation 1; Varia (an artefact with lentoid cross-section) 1; Total 6.

The bifacial artefact with the lentoid cross-section cannot be classified. The lack of diagnostic artefacts does not allow the determination of the period.
Period: ND.

Site 37: Tomer (7)

Israel Grid 1906/1586, Elevation 140 m b.s.l.; 7 flint artefacts.

Waste: Chunk 1.
Debitage: Flake 4.
Tools: Varia 2.

The sherd collection originates from the CH and EBA periods. The sparse flint assemblage just indicates the continuous use of flint during these periods.
Period: ND.

Site 40: Tomer (5)

Israel Grid 1908/1582,Elevation 180 m b.s.l.;10 flint artefacts (Fig. 1.7).

Waste: Chunk 2.
Debitage: Flake 7.

Tools: Naturally backed knife 1.

40% of the sherd collection originates from IA II, and the rest are LR. The sparse flint assemblage just indicates the continuous use of flint during IA II.
Period: IA II - reasonable.

Site 41: Tomer (2)

Israel Grid 1908/1580, Elevation 163 m b.s.l.; 5 flint artefacts.

Waste: Primary element 1.
Debitage: Flake 3; Blade 1; Total 4.

53% of the sherds are from IA II, the rest are from later periods; thus the flint is attributed to IA II.
Period: IA II – reasonable.

Site 44: Tomer (4)

***Israel Grid 1907/1579, Elevation 200 m b.s.l.; 7 flint artefacts* (*Fig. 1.7*).**

Waste: Chip 2;
Debitage: Flake 3; Blade 1; Total 4.
Tools: Denticulate 1.

63% of the sherds are from IA II, the rest are from later periods, and it seems reasonable to attribute the small flint collection to IA II. The denticulate, a rolled and worn typical *ad hoc* artefact, was prepared from a large primary flake. The flint is similar to that of Tomer (5) – Site 40.
Period: IA II – reasonable.

Site 45: Tomer (6)

Israel Grid 1906/1580, Elevation 110 m b.s.l.; 12 flint artefacts.

Waste: Primary element 2; Chunk 2; Chip 3; Total 7.
Debitage: Flake 2.
Tools: Awl 1, Retouched flake 1; Denticulate (?) 1; Total 3.

The small assemblage and the lack of sherds do not allow conclusions.
Period: ND.

Site 48: Wadi Sa'ad (2)

Israel Grid 1901/1579, Elevation 120 m b.s.l.; 3 flint artefacts.

Debitage: Flake 2; Bladelet 1; Total 3.

The few flint artefacts and the lack of diagnostic items do not allow dating. Half of the sherds were from IA I, and the flint artefacts apparently attest to the

continuous use of flint during this period. As few sherds from periods preceding IA I were found, the period was defined as possible.
Period: IA I – possible.

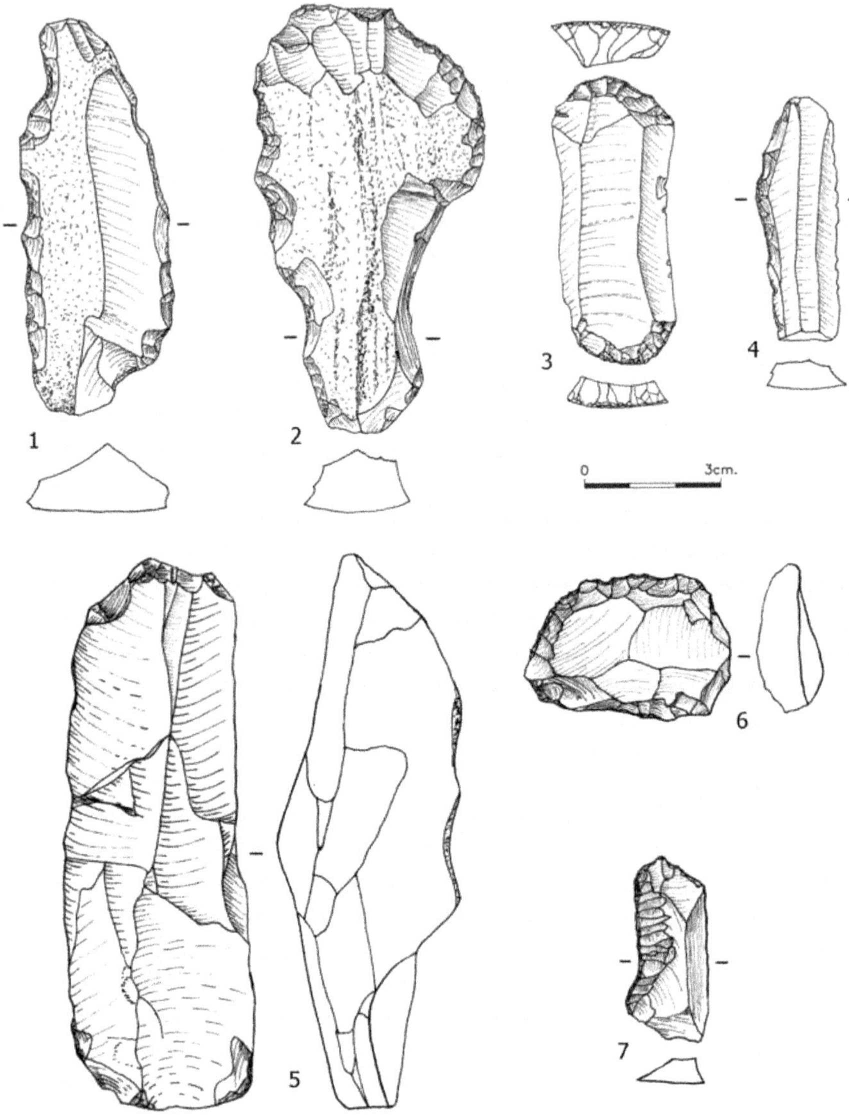

Fig. 1.7. **Tomer (5)**: 1-Backed knife on primary blade. **Tomer (4)**: 2-Denticulate on primary flake. **'Well Site'**: 3-Double end-scraper; 4-Backed Canaanean blade. **Gilgal (5)**: 5-Naviform core. **Wadi el-Baqar (1)**: 6-Rounded scraper; 7-Pressure retouched blade.

Site 49: Wadi Sa'ad (3)

Israel Grid 1895/1577, Elevation 20 m b.s.l.; 3 flint artefacts.

Waste: Chip 1.
Debitage: Flake 2.

The few flint artefacts and the multi-period sherd collection do not allow identification, but indicate the use of flint during the MBA and the IA, to which most of the sherds belong.

Periods: IA – possible.
MBA II – possible.

Site 50: Jebel Fasil

Israel Grid 1893/1577, Elevation 0 m a.s.l; 4 flint artefacts.

Four waste and Debitage non-indicative artefacts do not allow dating.
Period: ND.

Site 51: Thor el-Walad

Israel Grid 1896/1573, Elevation 60 m b.s.l.; 4 flint artefacts.

The sherds are from the Bronze and Iron Ages, but the few waste and Debitage, non-indicative flint artefacts do not allow dating.
Period: ND.

Site 54: The 'Well Site'

Israel Grid 1893/1567, Elevation 50 m b.s.l.; 9 flint artefacts (Fig. 1.7).

Waste: Primary element 1; Chip 1; Total 2.
Debitage: Blade 3; Total 3.
Tools: End-scraper 2; Backed Canaanean blade (unused sickle?) 1; Notch 1; Total 4.

The small assemblage, lack of diagnostic artefacts and the diversity of the ceramics makes the dating difficult. 40% of the sherds are from the IA and 6% from the Bronze Age. The end-scrapers are well-made from good-quality, light-coloured flint, and one of them has an active edge at both ends. These are present in earlier periods and uncommon in the Iron and Bronze Ages. The Canaanean blade, perhaps an unused sickle blade, matches the Bronze Ages.

Period: Bronze Age – reasonable.

Site 58: Gilgal (4)

Israel Grid 1909/1564, Elevation 210 m b.s.l.; 6 flint artefacts.

Waste: Chunk 1.
Debitage: Flake 2; Blade 2; Total 4.
Tools: Notch 1.

The flint find is small, without diagnostic artefacts. 46% of the sherds are from the IA, and the rest from later periods. The flint find is attributed to the IA.

Period: IA – reasonable.

Site 60: Gilgal (5)

Israel Grid 1913/1563, Elevation 215 m b.s.l.;57 flint artefacts (Fig. 1.7).

Waste: Core 1; Primary element 6; Chunk 10; Chip 8; Total 25.
Debitage: Flake 20; Blade 6; Total 26.
Tools: Retouched flake 1; Notch 3; Truncation 1; Varia 1; Total 6.

The flint of the assemblage is of dark grey, medium quality, uniform composition. Except for the naviform core of the same flint, usually attributed to the PPNB, no diagnostic artefacts were found. The rest of the finds do not contradict or confirm this dating. The identity of the raw material of the core and some of the other artefacts allows their attribution to the NE. Half of the sherds were from the IA, and the rest from later periods. It makes sense, therefore, that at least some of the artefacts are from the IA.

Periods: PPNB (part of the find) – highly reasonable.
IA (part of the find) – reasonable.

Site 64: Wadi Tal'at Zagharah (1)

Israel Grid 1914/1555, Elevation 205 m b.s.l.; 2 flint artefacts (Debitage)

The few flint pieces and the diversity of the sherds do not allow dating.
Period: ND.

Site 75: Netiv Hagdud (1)

Israel Grid 1918/1542, Elevation 190 m b.s.l.; 7 flint artefacts.

Waste: Chunk 2.
Debitage: Flake 3; Bladelet 2; Total 5.

The few flint artefacts should be attributed to the IA, as are 46% of the sherds; the rest of which are from late periods.

Period: IA – reasonable.

Site 76: Wadi el-Baqar (1)

Israel Grid 1893/1540, Elevation 40 m b.s.l.; 7 flint artefacts (Fig. 1.7).

Debitage: Flake 2; Blade 2; Total 4.
Tools: Rounded scraper 1; Retouched flake 1; Retouched blade 1; Total 3.

The blade, of dark, brown-grey, high quality flint, shaped by pressure retouch, is typical of the PPNB. The artefact might be intrusive, but the rounded scraper may also match this period.
Period: PPNB – possible.

Site 81: The 'Silo Site' (1)

Israel Grid 1932/1539, Elevation 223 m b.s.l.; 6 flint artefacts.

No indicative artefacts were found.
Period: ND.

A cluster of prehistoric sites at south-east Salibiyeh Basin - Sites 82 A-F:

Israel Grid 1932/1539 (the centre of the cluster), Elevation 230 m b.s.l.

These six newly discovered sites were not found in the surveys of the 1970s and 1980s. Their location is west of el-Muslabah ridge and south of Wadi Abu Baqar tributaries, and they have been added to the prehistoric find spots in the region (see Appendix 2).

Site 82 A

Israel Grid 1928/1540, Elevation 230 m b.s.l.; 112 flint artefacts (Fig. 1.8).

Waste: Core 2; Primary element 6; Chunk 7; Chip 10; Total 25.
Debitage: Flake 48; Blade 11; Bladelet 15; Total 74.
Tools: End-scraper 1; Thumbnail scraper 1; Burin 1; Retouched flake 2; Retouched blade 2; Retouched bladelet 1; Sickle blade 1; Borer 1; Denticulate 2; Truncation 1; Total 13.

All the components of the find are indicative of a microlithic industry from the EP period (a distinct bladelet core, bladelets and retouched bladelets), but in the absence of diagnostic microliths it is impossible to define the phase to which the assemblage should be attributed. The sickle blade – a backed bladelet with sickle gloss – is similar in material and morphology to sickle blades from the nearby Sites 82 C and 82 F. The borer on the bladelet, with abrupt retouch on both sides, is similar to those from Huzuq Musa (Winter 2017: 585-591) and Nahal 'Ein Gev 2 (Bar-Yosef and Belfer-Cohen

2000: 67-68). Both sites are characterized by sickle blades and borers, and are attributed to the end of the EP, the late phase of the Natufian Culture.
Period: Natufian Culture – highly reasonable.

Site 82 B
Israel Grid 1931/1539, Elevation 230 m b.s.l.

The collected artefacts were not found.

Site 82 C
Israel Grid 1932/1539, Elevation 230 m b.s.l.; 55 flint artefacts (Fig. 1.8).

Waste: Primary element 5; Chunk 11; Chip 10; Total 26.
Debitage: Flake 17; Blade 3; Bladelet 7; Total 27.
Tools: Sickle blade 1; Truncation 1; Total 2.

The assemblage included most components of a flint industry. The sickle blade on a retouched backed bladelet with sickle gloss is similar in material and morphology to those from nearby Sites 82 A and 82 F, and it can be assumed that it indicates the Natufian culture.
Period: Natufian Culture – reasonable.

Site 82 D
Israel Grid 1931/1538, Elevation 230 m b.s.l.; 102 Flint artefacts.

Waste: Core 1; Primary element 15; Chunk 22; Chip 20; Total 58.
Debitage: Flake 32; Blade 5; Bladelet 5; Total 42.
Tools: Notch 2.

The number of finds is considerable, but no diagnostic artefacts were found. The raw flint, as at the nearby sites, is of low quality. The knapping yielded mostly small artefacts with irregular surfaces. The core had been abandoned, and its scars indicated that the products were useless hinge fractured flakes. The site apparently belonged to one of the EP sites in the region, but no decisive evidence was found.
Period: ND.

Site 82 E
Israel Grid 1930/1538, Elevation 230 m b.s.l.; 182 flint artefacts (Fig. 1.9).

Waste: Primary element 17; Chunk 19; Chip 33; Total 69.
Debitage: Flake 72; Blade 8; Canaanean blade 1; Bladelet 23; Total 104.

Tools: End-scraper 1; Thumbnail scraper 1; Déjeté (oblique) scraper 1; Burin 1; Retouched flake 2; Retouched blade 1; Retouched bladelet (with oblique truncation?) 1; Sickle blade 1; Total 9.

The relatively high number of bladelets (13%) and the composition of the assemblage (the end-scrapers and the burin), indicate an EP industry. The single fragment of a blade with a trapezoidal cross-section, resembling a Canaanean blade, seems to belong to the EBA, although it could be intrusive.

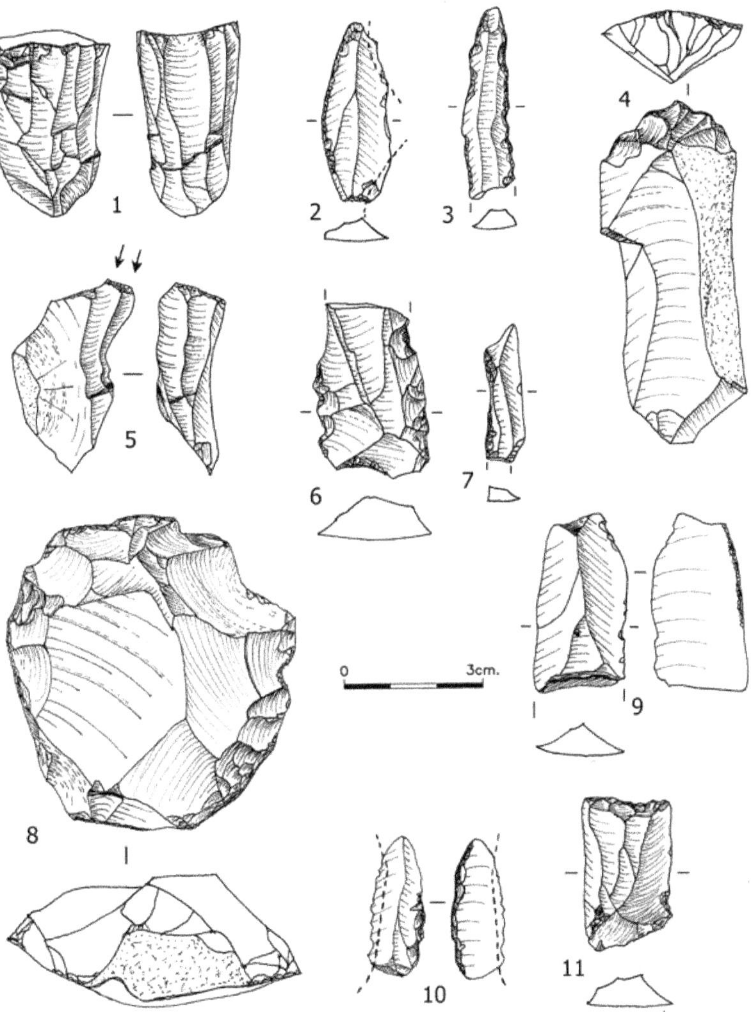

Fig. 1.8. **Site 82 A**: 1-Core; 2-Sickle blade; 3-Borer; 4-End-scraper; 5-Burin; 6-Retouched flake; 7-Retouched bladelet; 8-Denticulate; 9-Retouched blade (ventral). **Site 82 C**: 10-Sickle blade; 11-Truncation.

There were no diagnostic EP artefacts present, but the numerous bladelets and the sickle blade on an unretouched flake with sickle gloss indicate the Natufian Culture.
Period: Natufian Culture – reasonable.

Site 82 F
***Israel Grid 1930/1533, Elevation 230 m b.s.l.; 90 flint artefacts* (*Fig. 1.9*).**

Waste: Primary element 5; Chunk 19; Chip 30; Total 54.
Debitage: Flake 20; Blade 4; Bladelet 8; Total 32.

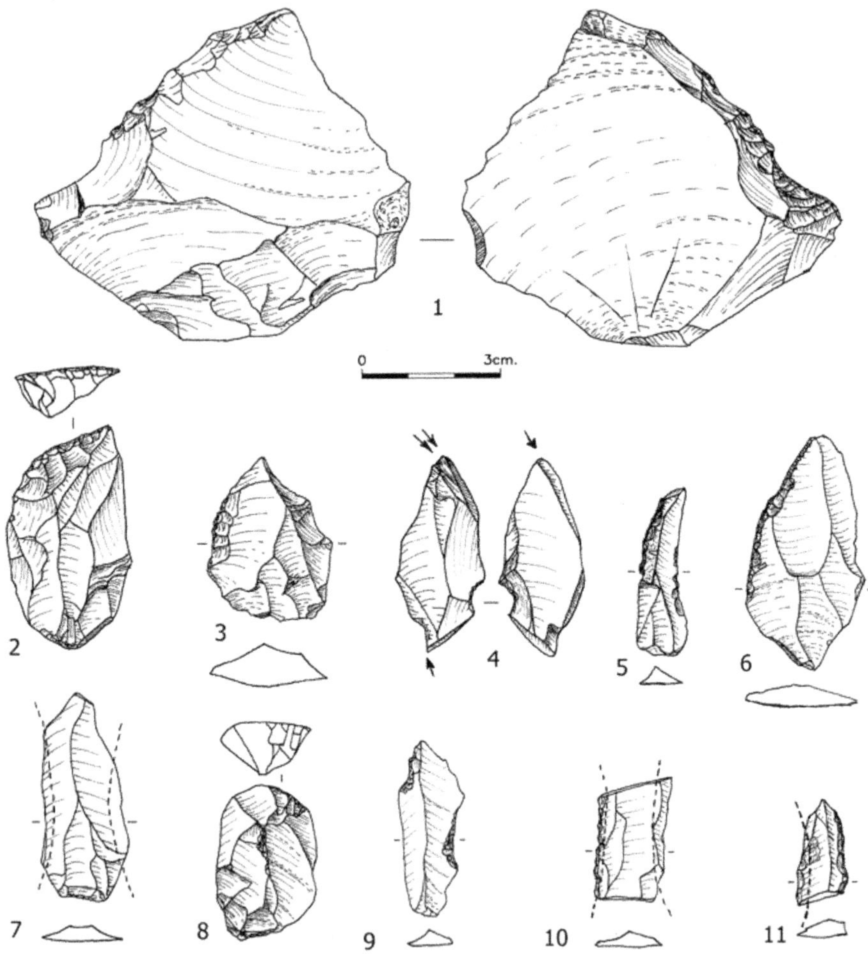

Fig. 1.9. **Site 82 E**: 1-*Déjeté* (oblique) scraper; 2-End-scraper; 3-Thumbnail scraper; 4-Burin; 5-Retouched bladlet; 6-Retouched flake; 7-Sickle blade. **Site 82 F**: 8-End-scraper; 9-Retouched bladelet; 10-11-Sickle blades.

Tools: End-scraper 1; Retouched bladelet 1; Sickle blade (fragments) 2; Total 4.

The bladelets, the end-scraper and the sickle blades originate from an EP industry. The fragment of a backed sickle blade prepared from a bladelet is similar to those from the nearby Sites 82A and 82C. There were no diagnostic artefacts of the EP, but the end-scraper, the bladelets and the fragment of the sickle blade with sickle gloss indicate the Natufian Culture.

Period: Natufian Culture – reasonable.

Site 85: Niran (1)

Israel Grid 1925/1537, Elevation 208 m b.s.l.; 10 flint artefacts.

Waste: Core 1; Primary element 1; Chunk 1; CTE 1; Total 4.

Debitage: Flake 1; Blade 5; Total 6.

Few flint artefacts were found, but the lack of diagnostic tools and the multi-period ceramics make dating difficult. Since 21% of the sherds are from MBA and 8% from IA II, it is reasonable to assume that the flint is from these periods.

Periods: IA II – possible.
MBA – reasonable.

Site 87: E.P. 58

Israel Grid 1890/1534, Elevation 40 m a.s.l.; 10 flint artefacts (*Fig. 1.10*).

Waste: Core 1; Primary element 3; Total 4.

Debitage: Flake 2; Bladelet 1; Total 3.

Tools: End-scraper (on bladelet) 1; Retouched flake 2; Total 3.

96% of the sherds originate from IA I, and most of the flint find should be attributed to this period. The bladelet and the end-scraper on a bladelet are apparently from earlier periods.

Period: IA I - highly reasonable.

Site 92: Niran (4)

Israel Grid 1915/1533, Elevation 160 m b.s.l.; 10 flint artefacts (*Fig. 1.10*).

Waste: Chunk 1; Chip 2; Total 3.

Debitage: Flake 5; Blade 1; Total 6.

Tools: Denticulate (on a large primary blade with a truncation) 1.

The lack of diagnostic artefacts and the multi-period ceramics make dating difficult. 24% of the sherds are from IA II, 7% from MBA and the rest from later periods.

Periods: IA II – reasonable.
MBA – possible.

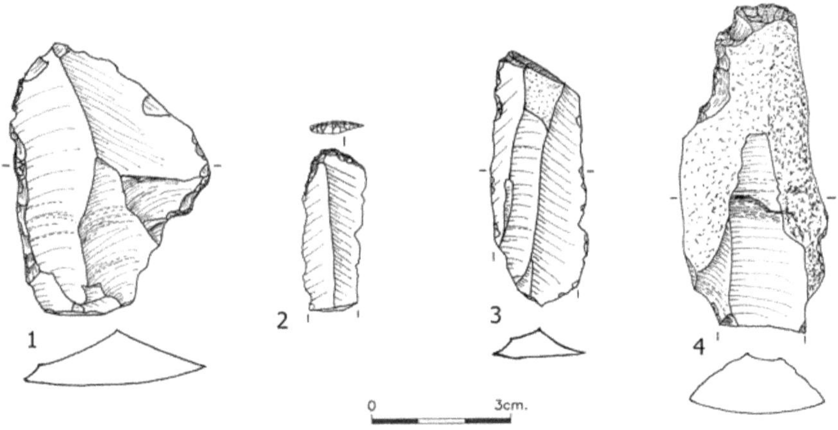

Fig. 1.10. **E.P. 58**: 1-Retouched flake; 2-End-scraper on bladelet. **Niran (4)**: 3-Blade; 4-Denticulate (on a large primary blade with truncation).

Site 94: Niran (2)

Israel Grid 1923/1533, Elevation 190 m b.s.l.; 2 flakes.

Period: ND.

Site 101: Wadi el-Haiyat (7)

Israel Grid 1884/1529, Elevation 100 m a.s.l.; 100 flint artefacts (Fig. 1.11).

Waste: Primary element 6; Chunk 11; Chip 45; Total 62.
Debitage: Flake 28; Blade 4; Bladelet 4; Total 36.
Tools: Borer 1; Retouched flake 1; Total 2.

The relatively large number of flint artefacts indicates the existence of a local industry. The abundance of flakes and the scarcity of retouched artefacts apparently indicate an *ad hoc* flint production, common in the IA. The period is difficult to determine, but 15% of the sherds originate from the IA, similarly to the nearby sites 103, 105 and 106. The well made, flat retouch on one flake is unusual for these periods, and it should be attributed to an earlier period, apparently the PPNB/C, similar to nearby Sites 105 and 106.

Periods: PPNB/C – possible.
IA – possible.

Site 102: Wadi el-Haiyat (8)

Israel Grid 1889/1529, Elevation 0 m b.s.l.; 107 flint artefacts (Fig. 1.11).

Waste: CTE 2; Primary element 11; Chunk 21; Chip 38; Total 72.

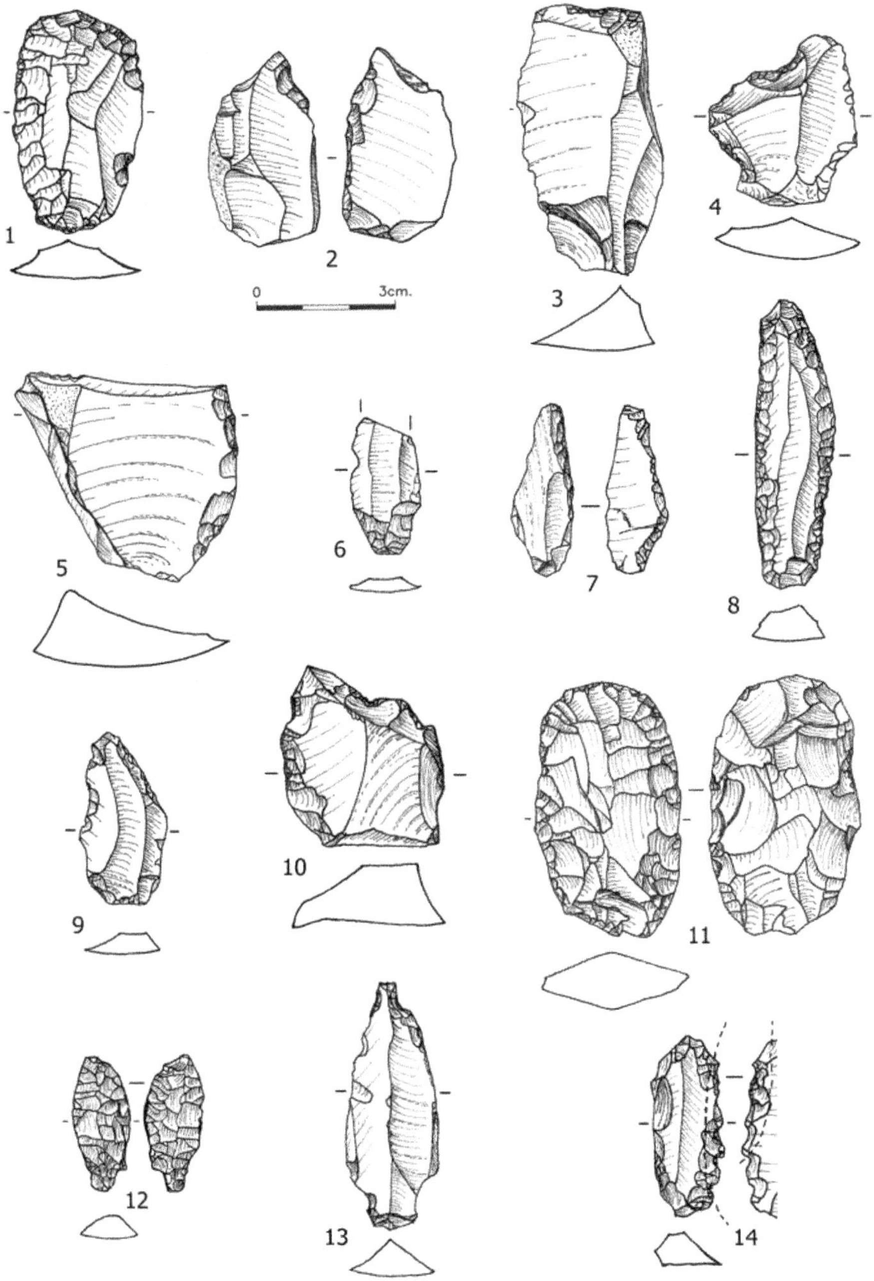

Fig. 1.11. **Wadi el-Haiyat (7)**: 1-Retouched flake. **Wadi el-Haiyat (8)**: 2-Awl. **Wadi el-Haiyat (4)**: 3-Backed knife; 4-Notch. **Wadi el-Haiyat (6)**: 5-Backed knife; 6-Arrowhead; 7-8-Borers. **Wadi el-Haiyat (5)**: 9-Oblique truncation; 10-Retouched flake; 11-Axe; 12-13-Arrowheads; 14-Sickle blade.

Debitage: Flake 24; Blade 4; Bladelet 2; Total 30.
Tools: Awl 1; Varia (various small flakes with marginal retouch) 4; Total 5.

The abundance of Waste and Debitage and the scarcity of retouched artefacts indicate a flint industry of the later periods. Lacking diagnostic artefacts – both flint and sherds – the period cannot be determined (see also Sites 101, 103, 105 and 106).
Period: ND.

Site 103: Wadi el-Haiyat (4)

Israel Grid: 1890/1529, Elevation 10 m b.s.l.; 48 flint artefacts (Fig. 1.11).

Waste: Core 1; Primary element 11; Chip 3; Total 15.
Debitage: Flake 24; Blade 4; Bladelet 1; Total 29.
Tools: Backed knife 1; Notch 3; Total 4.

The composition of this relatively small assemblage indicates a local flint industry. The raw flint is light brown or grey, of medium quality, which did not allow the knapping of long artefacts. The marginal secondary processing confirms the poor quality of the industry. The backed knife bears clear use-wear signs. In the absence of diagnostic artefacts from other periods, the flint find must be attributed to the IA (70% of the sherds). The poor quality of the artefacts supports this supposition.
Period: IA – reasonable.

Site 105: Wadi el-Haiyat (6)

Israel Grid 1890/1528, Elevation 0 m a.s.l.; 122 flint artefacts (Fig. 1.11).

Waste: Core 2; Primary element 11; Chunk 14; Chip 44; Total 71.
Debitage: Flake 26; Blade 5; Bladelet 9; Total 40.
Tools: Borer 2; Retouched flake 3; Backed knife 2; Notch 3; Arrowhead 1; Total 11.

The majority of the sherds are from the IA, and a part of the flint – mainly waste and Debitage – perhaps belongs to this period. The few indicative artefacts point to the PPNB/C. The arrowhead with a tang formed by pressure retouch, and the long borer with a trapezoidal cross-section and abrupt retouch on both sides belong to this period, and are not found in the IA (see also Sites 101-103 and 106).
Periods: IA (part of the find) – possible.
PPNB/C (part of the find) – highly reasonable.

Site 106: Wadi el-Haiyat (5)

Israel Grid 1891/1528, Elevation 25 m b.s.l.;145 flint artefacts (Fig. 1.11).

Waste: Core 1; Primary element 10; Chunk 13; Chip 60; Total 84.
Debitage: Flake 31; Blade 7; Bladelet 4; Total 42.
Tools: End-scraper 1; Retouched flake 4; Retouched blade 2; Sickle blade 1; Notch 1; Denticulate 2; Truncation 1; Oblique truncation 2; Axe 1; Arrowhead 2; Bifacial roughout 1; Retouched bladelet 1; Total 19.

At this site, in contrast to most sites in the area, a few artefacts could be identified at the level of 'highly reasonable'. The small axe with the lentoid cross-section, flat bifacial retouch without a transverse blow, the denticulated sickle blade, and the arrowheads, especially the smaller one of the Herzliya type, are apparently from the PPN (the Yarmukian Culture). This culture was first discovered in the Jordan Valley, about 70 km north of this site, and other sites have been discovered in the Jordan Valley since then. However, the complete lack of NE pottery contradicts this notion and indicates the PPNC, and the rest of the find does not contradict this. Some of the flint artefacts may also belong to the IA, to which 56% of the sherds were attributed, or even to the MBA (20%). The rest of the sherds are LR.

There are other flint concentrations in Wadi el-Haiyat (see Sites 101-103 and 105), with many non-indicative flint artefacts. In some of these, many IA sherds were found; apparently these are multi-period sites. The composition of the assemblages, the raw flint, the sharpness and the nearly complete lack of patina on the artefacts suggest a possible link between the sites. Further research could clarify the problem.

Periods: IA – possible.
PPNC – highly reasonable.

Site 110: Wadi Nabiris (2)

Israel Grid 1889/1526, Elevation 0 m a.s.l.; 6 flint artefacts.

Waste: Chunk 4; Chip 1; Total 5.
Debitage: Blade 1.

53% of the sherds are from the IA, to which the flint apparently belongs.

Period: IA – reasonable.

Site 112: Wadi Maqor edh-Dhib (3)

Israel Grid 1907/1526, Elevation 80 m b.s.l.; 4 flint artefacts.

Debitage: Flake 2.
Tools: End-scraper 2.

About half of the sherds are from the IA, and the rest are LR. No diagnostic flint artefacts were found at the site. The End-scrapers are not specifically typical of the IA, but nevertheless, it is possible that some of the few flint artefacts are from that period.
Period: IA – possible.

Site 113: el-Mastarah (1)

Israel Grid 1888/1520, Elevation 0 m b.s.l.; 15 flint artefacts.

Waste: Primary element 1; Chunk 3; Total 4.
Debitage: Flake 4; Blade 4; Total 8.
Tools: Retouched blade 1; Notch 1; Denticulate 1; Total 3.

50% of the sherds originated from the IA, 3% from MBA, and the rest are from late periods. Without any diagnostic artefacts it is reasonable to attribute the small flint assemblage to the IA: there are too few MBA sherds to give an indication.
Period: IA – reasonable.

Site 116: el-Mastarah (3)

Israel Grid: 1888/1521, Elevation 20 m b.s.l.; 6 flint artefacts.

Waste: CTE 3.
Debitage: Flake 3.

42% of the sherds originate from IA II and the rest from late periods. In the absence of diagnostic artefacts, it is reasonable to attribute the flint to IA II.
Period: IA II – reasonable.

Site 118: el-Mastarah (2)

Israel Grid 1887/1522, Elevation 20 m b.s.l.; 39 flint artefacts (Fig. 1.12).

Waste: Primary element 8; Chunk 1; Chip 5; Total 14.
Debitage: Flake 15; Blade 2; Bladelet 1; Total 18.
Tools: End-scraper 1; Borer 1; Retouched flake 1; Retouched blade 2; Retouched bladelet 1; Notch 1; Total 7.

44% of the pottery is from IA II and 35% from the Bronze Ages. The lack of diagnostic artefacts and the multi-periodical pottery make it difficult to attribute the flint assemblage to a specific period, but it confirms the continuous use of flint during early historical periods. Possibly the flint originates from these periods.

Periods: IA II (part of the find) – possible.
Bronze Ages (part of the find) – possible.

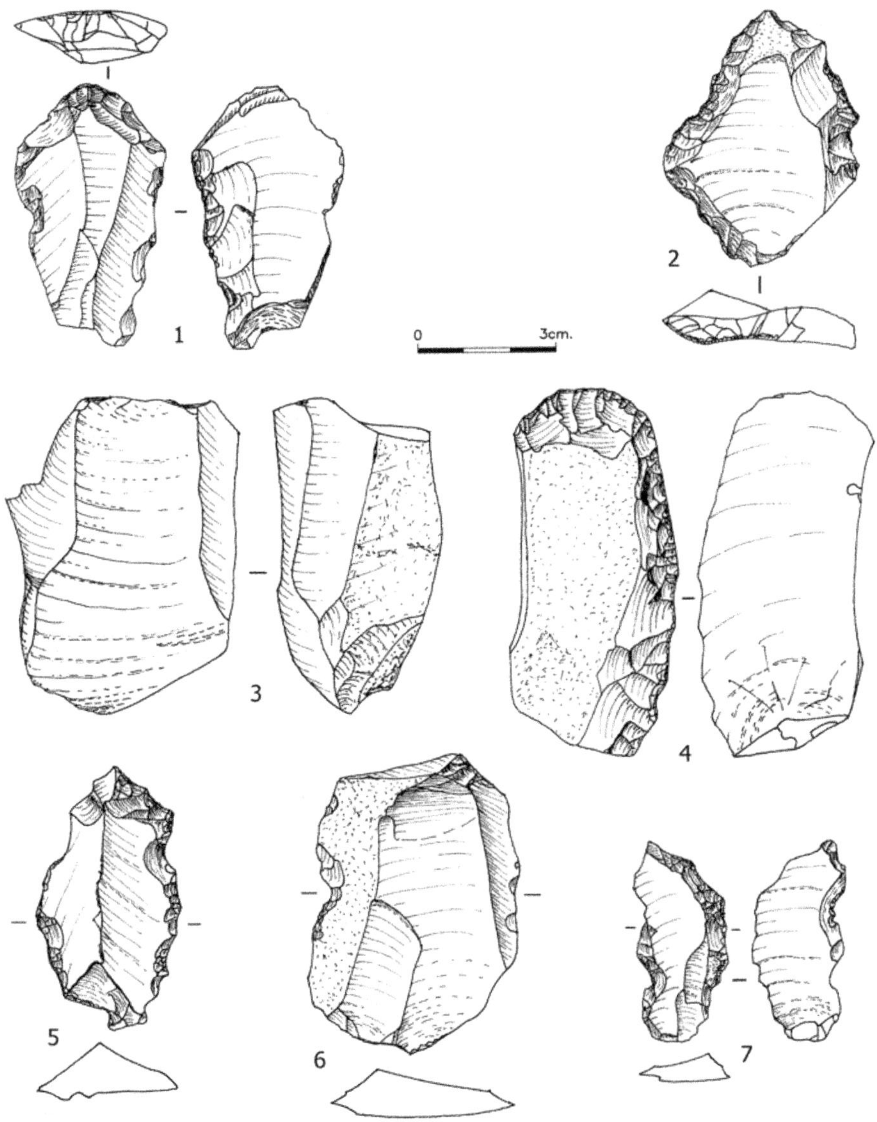

Fig. 1.12. **el-Mastara (2)**: 1-End-scraper; 2-Notch. **Wadi Nabiris (3)**: 3-Core; 4-Fan scraper on primary blade. **E.P. -140**: 5-Retouched flake; 6-Flake; 7-Double notch.

Site 120: Wadi Nabiris (1)

Israel Grid 1892/1521, Elevation 60 m b.s.l.; 79 flint artefacts.

Waste: Core 2; Primary element 5; Chunk 22; Chip 21; Total 50.
Debitage: Flake 27; Total 27.
Tools: End-scraper 1; Notch 1; Total 2.

No sherds were found at the site. Many of the flint artefacts show signs of scorching, and the site seems to be a workshop. In the absence of sherds and diagnostic flint artefacts the assemblage cannot be dated. An excavation or a flint-oriented survey could clarify the matter.
Period: ND.

Site 121: Wadi Nabiris (3)

Israel Grid 1892/1521, Elevation 50 m b.s.l.; 95 flint artefacts (Fig. 1.12).

Waste: Core 1; Primary element 5; CTE 1; Chunk 19; Chip 18; Total 44.
Debitage: Flake 36; Blade 6; Bladelet 1; Total 43.
Tools: Fan scraper on blade 1; Borer 1; Retouched flake 3; Retouched blade 1; Sickle blade 1; Notch 1; Total 8.

No indicative sherds and only few diagnostic flint artefacts were found. The large, thin primary blade, with flat retouch along one side and the distal end, is a fan/tabular scraper associated with both the CH or EBA, and the small sickle blade with retouched back, truncation, snap and sickle gloss is characteristic of the CH. These tools show high quality workmanship of expert craftsmen.
Period: CH – reasonable.

Site 122: E.P. -140

Israel Grid 1933/1520, Elevation 150 m b.s.l.; 18 flint artefacts (Fig. 1.12).

Waste: CTE 1; Primary element 1; Chunk 1; Chip 6; Total 9.
Debitage: Flake 5; Bladelet 1; Total 6.
Tools: Retouched flake 1; Notch 1; Varia 1; Total 3.

Most of the sherds (74%) are from the IA, and it is reasonable that the flint originates from this period.
Period: IA - reasonable.

Site 125: E.P. 44

Israel Grid 1887/1518, Elevation 40 m a.s.l.; 2 flint artefacts.

The sherds are from Iron Age II, but no conclusions can be drawn from two artefacts.
Period: ND.

Site 130: Wadi el-Haiyat (1)

Israel Grid 1907/1515, Elevation 145 m b.s.l.; 9 flint artefacts.

Waste: Core 1; Primary element 1; Chunk 3; Total 5.
Debitage: Flake 2; Blade 2; Total 4.

The few flint artefacts and sherds and the absence of diagnostic artefacts do not allow conclusions to be drawn.
Period: ND.

Site 133: 'Ein 'Aujah (1)

Israel Grid 1871/1513, Elevation 0 m a.s.l.; 19 flint artefacts (Fig. 1.13).

Waste: Chip 2.
Debitage: Flake 4; Blade 1; Bladelet 1; Total 6.
Tools: Carinated scraper 1; End-scraper 2; Awl 3; Borer on bladelet 1; Backed knife 2; Roughout for the preparation of a bifacial tool 1; Varia (double notched artefact) 1; total 11.

The majority of the sherds belong to the Wadi Raba culture and the EBA. Diagnostic flint tools – the delicate awls – appear in the NE (Hatula – Ronen, Winter and Chinn 1994) and the EBA (Camel Site – Rosen 1994/5). The borer on a bladelet is identical to those from the EP in the Jordan Valley (Nahal 'Ein Gev 2, Huzuq Musa). The roughout with a square cross-section, for the preparation of an adze or bifacial axe, is related mainly to the end of the PN (Wadi Raba phase) and to the CH. The single artefact with double notches, similar to the el-Khiam Point from the PPNA, is too wide to have been an arrowhead. The retouch at the distal end suggests that it may have been a scraper. Attributing a part of the flint to the EBA, due to the presence of the delicate awls, seems unreasonable. Affiliation of most of the assemblage to the Wadi Raba phase seems reasonable.
Period: PN (Wadi Raba phase) – reasonable.

Site 134: 'Iraq el-Ghawarneh (1)

Israel Grid 1880/1512, Elevation 0 m a.s.l.; 95 flint artefacts.

Waste: Core 3; Primary element 8; Chunk 14; Chip 9; Total 34.
Debitage: Flake 30; Blade 9; Bladelet 1; Total 40.
Tools: End-scraper 2; Side-scraper 4; Transverse scraper 1; Awl 4; Retouched flake 3; Retouched blade 1; Notch 4; Adze (roughout) 1; Varia 1;
Total 21.

The composition of the assemblage and the quantity of artefacts indicate a flint industry with all its components. The dark-brown raw flint is of medium quality, unsuitable for the manufacture of long artefacts. The roughout of an adze is of light grey flint with a trapezoidal cross-section, typically CH. No other diagnostic artefacts were found. Even though only 9% of the sherds are CH, according to the composition of the assemblage, apparently a part of it

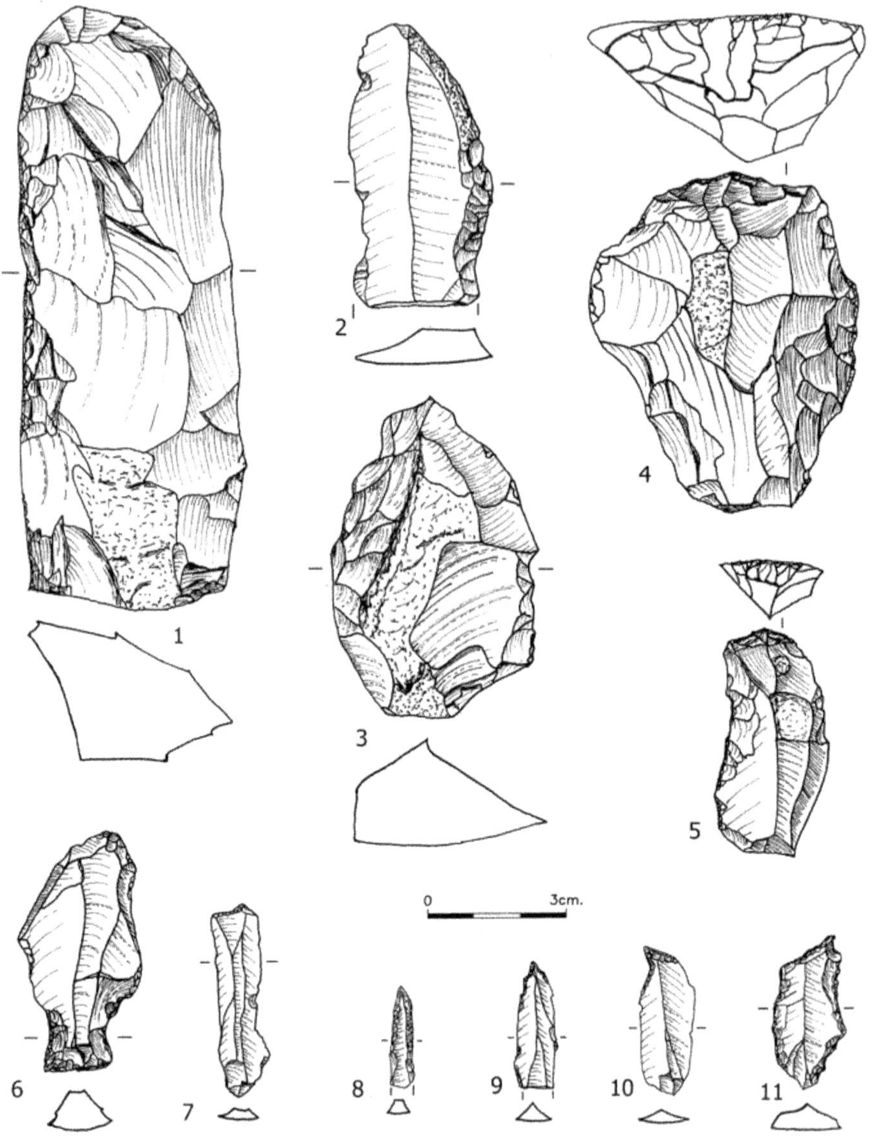

Fig. 1.13. 'Ein 'Aujah (1): 1-Roughout for the preparation of a bifacial tool; 2-3-Backed knives; 4-Carinated scraper; 5-End-scraper; 6-Varia (artefact with double notches); 7-Bladelet; 8-Borer on bladelet; 9-11-Awls.

belongs to this period. Other parts originate perhaps from the MBA and IA, of which high proportions of pottery were present.
Periods: CH (part of the assemblage) – reasonable.
MBA (part of the assemblage) – possible.
IA (part of the assemblage) – possible.

Site 135: 'Ein 'Aujah (5)

Israel Grid 1872/1512, Elevation 20 m b.s.l.; 6 Flint artifacts.

6 non-indicative waste and debitage artefacts were found.
Period: ND.

Site 137: E.P. -66

Israel Grid 1894/1513, Elevation 60 m b.s.l.; 91 flint artefacts (Fig. 1.14).

Waste: Core 1; Primary element 12; Chunk 16; Chip 21; Total 50.
Debitage: Flake 31; Blade 3; Bladelet 3; Total 37.
Tools: Awl 1; Sickle blade 2; Truncation 1; Total 4.

Most components of a local flint industry were present in the assemblage. The coarse-grained flint, grey or beige in colour, is of poor quality, and many of the artefacts are fragments. Both sickle blades, on tiny backed bladelets, with truncations and sickle gloss, were prepared from grey, fine-grained, good quality flint. They match the CH, but no sherds from this period were found. 61% of the sherds are from the EBA I, and only a few are from the later Bronze and Iron Ages. The sickle blades might indicate the sporadic continuation of CH technology in the EBA. A similar phenomenon happens in CH sites where Canaanean technology, attributed to the EBA, was present, as in Fazael 2 (Bar and Winter 2010). It seems reasonable that the flint is mainly from the EBA I. An excavation or a repeated survey could shed further light on this problem.
Periods: EBA I (the bulk of the assemblage) – reasonable.
MBA (part of the assemblage) – possible.
IBA (part of the assemblage) – possible.
IA (part of the assemblage) – possible.

Site 139: Villa 'Aujah

Israel Grid 1876/1510, Elevation 35 m b.s.l.; 8 flint artefacts.

Waste: Primary element 2; Chunk 1; Total 3.
Debitage: Flake 2; Bladelet 2; Total 4.
Tools: Retouched flake 1.

About half the pottery is from IA II, and the rest is Roman. In the absence of any diagnostic artefacts the flint is attributed to the first period.
Period: IA II – reasonable.

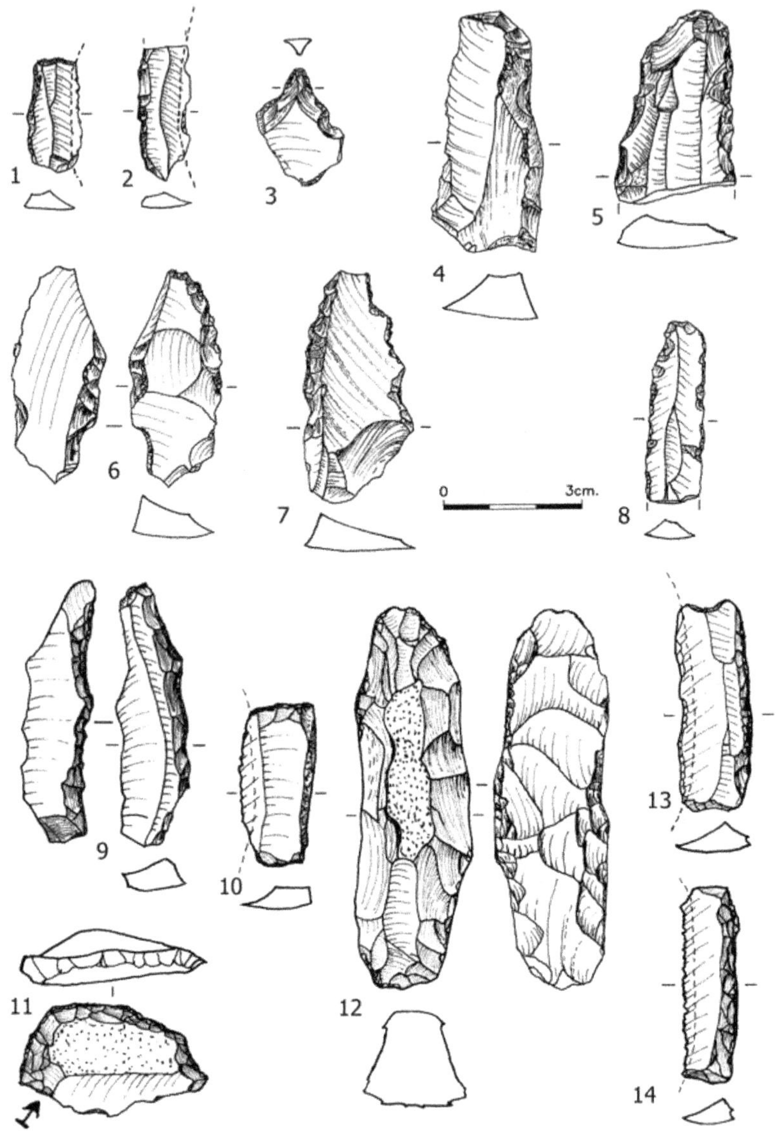

Fig. 1.14. **E.P. -66**: 1-2-Sickle blades; 3-Awl. **'Aujah fortress'**: 4-Backed knife; 5-Retouched blade. **Khirbet 'Aujah el-Foqa**: 6-Retouched flake with notches; 7-Denticulate. **Sheikh Ibrahim**: 8-Retouched bladelet; 9-Borer; 10-Sickle blade; 11-Rounded scraper. **E.P. -261**: 12-Chisel; 13-14-Sickle blades.

Site 140: Aujah Fortress

Israel Grid 1883/1506, Elevation 60 m b.s.l.; 20 flint artefacts (Fig. 1.14).

Waste: Primary element 3; Chunk 5; Chip 7; Total 15.
Debitage: Bladelet 1.
Tools: Retouched blade 1; Retouched and backed bladelet 1; Backed knife 2; Total 4.

As 37% of the pottery originates from the IA, and in the absence of diagnostic artefacts, the flint is dated to these periods.
Period: IA – reasonable.

Site 143: Khirbet 'Aujah el-Foqa

Israel Grid 1879/1504, Elevation 27 m a.s.l.; 23 flint artefacts (Fig. 1.14).

Waste: Core 1; Chunk 5; Total 6.
Debitage: Flake 10; Blade 3; Total 13.
Hammerstone 1.
Tools: Notch on retouched flake 1; Notch 1; Denticulate 1; Total 3.

90% of the pottery originates from the IA, and no diagnostic flint artefacts were found. Hence, the flint is attributed to this period.
Period: IA – reasonable.

Site 145: Wadi 'Aujah (1)[1]

Israel Grid 1886/1504, Elevation 70 m b.s.l.; 5 flint artefacts.

Debitage: Flake 1; Blade 1; Bladelet 2; Total 4.
Tools: Retouched flake 1.

The number of artefacts is small, and no diagnostic pieces were found. 70% of the sherds were from the IA and it makes sense to attribute the flint also to these periods.
Period: IA – reasonable.

Site 148: E.P. -156

Israel Grid 1911/1497, Elevation 156 m b.s.l.; 24 flint artefacts.

Waste: Primary element 2; Chunk 1; Chip 2; Total 5.
Debitage: Flake 10; Blade 3; Bladelet 3; Total 16.
Tools: Retouched flake 1; Truncation 1; Multipurpose 1; Total 3.

The lack of diagnostic artefacts, and the attribution of the sherds to late

1 At a nearby location, map reference *1889/1503 Auja II*, a UP find spot was discovered by the "Prehistoric Survey of Easrtern Samaria" (Hovers and Bar-Yosef 1987: 79).

periods, precludes the drawing of conclusions.
Period: ND.

Site 152: Sheikh Ibrahim

Israel Grid 1946/1496, Elevation 260 m b.s.l.; 29 flint artefacts (Fig. 1.14).

Waste: Primary element 2; Chunk 1; Total 3.
Debitage: Flake 7; Blade 9; Bladelet 2; Total 18.
Tools: Borer 2; Retouched flake 2; Retouched bladelet 1; Rounded scraper 1; Sickle blade 1; Truncation 1; Total 8.

The few diagnostic artefacts, such as the sickle blade with retouched back and two truncations, and perhaps also the borers, indicate the CH.
Period: CH – reasonable.

Site 154: E.P. -261

Israel Grid 1960/1495, Elevation 270 m b.s.l.; 22 flint artefacts (Fig. 1.14).

Waste: Primary element 2; Chunk 1; Total 3.
Debitage: Flake 6; Blade 6; Bladelet 3; Total 15.
Tools: Sickle blade 3; Chisel 1; Total 4.

The sickle blades with retouched back and truncations and the chisel with a trapezoidal cross-section, date the small assemblage to the CH, similar to the sherd collection.
Period: CH – highly reasonable.

Site 155: Wadi 'Aujah (2)

Israel Grid 1896/1494, Elevation 125 m b.s.l.; 6 flint artefacts.

Waste: Primary element 1; Chunk 1; Total 2
Debitage: Flake 2; Bladelet 1; Total 3
Tools: Notch 1.

No conclusions can be drawn from this small collection.
Period: ND.

Site 157: Malhaqa el-Wadian

Israel Grid 1979/1491 (centre), Elevation 295 m b.s.l.; 5 flint artefacts.

Waste: Chip 1.
Debitage: Flake 4.

Except for a few IA II sherds, the rest of the sherds originate from later periods.
Period: IA II – reasonable.

DISCUSSION AND EVALUATIONS

An important difficulty in dating the finds was due to the absence of large assemblages (hundreds or even thousands of items per site, including diagnostic artefacts) such as those published in previous volumes: Khirbet el-Meiyiteh (Winter 2008: 681-684), Khirbet el-Malih (C), (Winter 2008: 684-688), es-Suweiseh (Winter 2016), and Huzuq Musa (Winter 2017: 585-591). We shall therefore concentrate on the spatial distribution and its influences on the nature of the societies. In future, a discussion about a larger area would be preferable, including all sites without flint in this volume, and sites which were not included in the current survey. Such a discussion is beyond the scope of this study.

Summary of the results of the finds by the survey (*Table 1.1*)

A total of 3,078 flint artifacts from 71 assemblages, were examined. The variations in the numbers of artefacts from site to site have several possible reasons:

– The number of artefacts at the site;

Level of Identification Period	Number of sites	Highly reasonable identification	Reasonable identification	Possible identification
Lower Palaeolithic	0	-	-	-
Middle Palaeolithic	0	-	-	-
Upper Palaeolithic (general)	2	2	-	-
Epipalaeolithic (general)	5	2	3	-
Neolithic (general)	7	4	1	2
Chalcolithic	10	3	5	2
Early/Middle Bronze	10	2	3	5
Late Bronze	0	-	-	-
Iron Age I-II	30	-	18	12
Assemblages whose periods has been defined (including multi-period assemblages)	66	13	29	24
Undefined period assemblages	24	-	-	-
Total	90			

Table 1.1. Assemblages, according to periods and identification levels.
Note: The sum of identified and unidentified periods exceeds the number of assemblages examined, as some assemblages are multi-period.

- Artefacts which were not found due to their small size or being covered by natural soil;
- Terrain features: topography, vegetation, structures, etc.
- Skill and awareness of the surveyors.

The sites with few artefacts will serve as background information for the spatial discussion. Further studies and excavations could confirm, expand, or contradict our conclusions.

The level of Lake Lisan and the elevation of the sites discovered by the survey

Many sites discovered during the survey were from comparatively late and short periods, compared to prehistoric sites from hundreds of thousands of years ago. Human beings existed along the Syrian-African Great Rift Valley, and particularly in the Jordan Valley, from the earliest periods. This is evident from surveys and excavations, such as the sites at Gesher (Central Jordan Valley), Gesher Benot Ya'aqov, Ma'ayan Baruch and 'Ubeidiya – the age of which is 1.4 million years, and maybe even more (Bar-Yosef and Goren-Inbar 1993: 19-21): all these are in the Great Rift Valley. The absence of such sites in the area of the survey has to be explained. The issue has been discussed in Volume 4 (Winter 2017), but we will return to it, based on further studies.

During the Late Pleistocene the Jordan Valley was flooded for long periods by lakes which formed its unique landscape. Lake Samara, after still more ancient lakes, existed from approximately 135,000 to 75,000 years BP. From approximately 70,000 to 15,000 years BP, Lake Lisan covered the Valley. At its maximum level Lake Lisan extended from the north of the Sea of Galilee south to Hatzeva, about 230 km (Fig. 1.15). The sediments of the lake had already been discovered in the 19th century, and investigated by Picard in 1943 and others in the 20th century.

Bartov et al. (2002), who studied Lake Lisan with modern radiometric methods, based their research on the shoreline sediments at different elevations. These were traced within the Lisan formation in the floodplain of Nahal Ze'elim and Nahal Pratzim. Lisker et al. (2009) relied on sediments of fossilized algal mats (stromatolites), preserved in caves in the western fault escarpment of the Dead Sea. These often became sediment traps for deposits and fossils, which were not preserved on the surface due to later erosion processes. The level of Lake Lisan reached its maximum of 164 m b.s.l. (Bartov et al. 2002: fig. 7), or alternatively, 180 m b.s.l. (Lisker et al. 2009: fig. 9) 35,000 to 25,000 years BP. Lisker et al. suggested the possibility of a higher level (question mark in Fig. 1.17). These methods (both radiometric) and their different results leave some unanswered questions, which are irrelevant to this study. However, the overall results prove that the Jordan Valley was flooded by the water of the lake for tens of thousands of years. Fig. 1.17 shows that possible prehistoric sites, whose elevations were lower than 164 m b.s.l., and whose age was more than 20,000 years BP, were flooded for long periods of time, and covered by aquatic sediments. Later remnants of such sites can be discovered only above the maximum level of the lake, or on its shore. The sediments contained carbonates (Aragonite), Foramenifera (calcareous skeletons of microscopic organisms) and gypsum horizons which were deposited during times when the water of the lake was brackish. These sediments were mixed with clays transported to the alluvial basin by wind or water. The mixture of calcareous Aragonite and clays is known as Lisan marl. Whenever the level of the lake rose the periods of flooding grew longer and the lake sediments became thicker. There were intervals of exposure to the atmosphere, erosion, removal and compaction between the sedimentation periods of the lake, and times of accumulation of terrestrial silt. All these occurrences influenced the thickness of the lake sediments, making it difficult to calculate the annual accumulation rate. However, it is possible to calculate the accumulation rate between two dated points within the same sedimentary sequence. A generalized figure of the average accumulation has been calculated. The Lisan marl layers, which reach a thickness of up to 40 m (Fig. 1.16), accumulated during the time of the main flooding event with high water levels for over 40,000 years (from 55,000 to 15,000 years BP – Bartov et al. 2002: 9), show an average sediment accumulation of 1 mm per year – 1 m in the relatively short period of 1000 years. Artefacts deposited at elevations below 164 m b.s.l. will therefore not be found on the present-day surface, as they were submerged and buried under the lake deposits for up to tens of thousands of years, and covered by

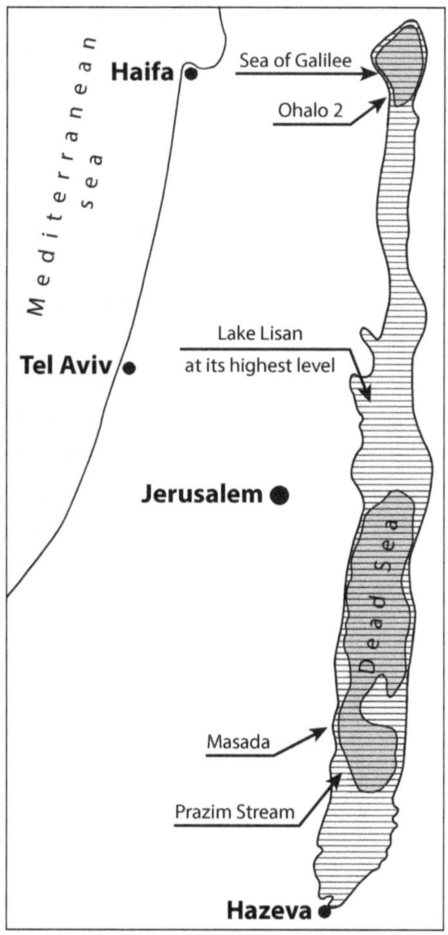

Fig. 1.15. The area of Lake Lisan.

Fig. 1.16. The layers of the Lisan marl and the tectonic cracking.

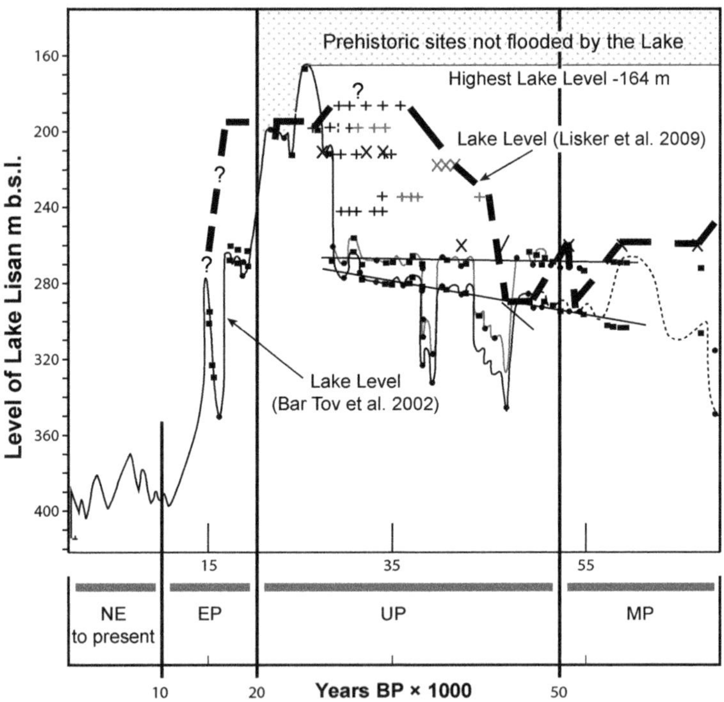

Fig. 1.17. The periods (approximately) from the Middle Palaeolithic to present time compared to the level of Lake Lisan (combined after Lisker et al. 2009, fig. 10 and Bartov et al. 2002).

sediments. Sites of this type could be found only at an elevation higher than 164 m b.s.l., the maximum elevation of the lake surface according to Bartov et al. (2002). As a matter of fact the elevations of all Middle Palaeolithic sites reported in Volumes 2 and 4 (Winter 2008; 2017) are above 164 m b.s.l., thus confirming the proposed thesis. There are also some exceptions – evidence of the fluctuations in the fall of the lake level – sites from the end of the Upper Palaeolithic at the transition to the EP, later than 22,000 years BP, whose elevation is as low as 200 m b.s.l. (see Fig. 1.17). At locations exposed by human activities or natural forces (e.g. at stream channels) ancient layers were discovered beneath the layers of marl from the Lisan formation.

Lake Lisan began to recede about 22,000 years BP. The process started at the dawn of the EP and continued in the NE, CH and Bronze Ages. Flint from these periods begins to appear in the lower regions according to the declining lake level. Over time the number of sites increased and reached its peak in the IA, evidence of a relatively high habitation density. The finds from the IA – mostly Debitage and *ad hoc* tools for casual tasks – mark the continued use of flint up to this period as an effective, accessible and cheap material.

The elevation of sites and their distribution in the area (Table 1.2)

The geopolitical, geomorphological and climatological aspects and their influence on the location of the sites deserve a more extensive discussion, which is beyond the scope of this study. However, an analysis of the distribution of the sites, according to periods and elevations, might point to preferences concerning the way of life of a specific society. The results (Table 1.2) are inconclusive, and the small number of sites makes it difficult to draw conclusions. Only four sites were lower than 250 m b.s.l.: Site 1 (290 m b.s.l., NE, CH, EBA); Site 152 (260 m b.s.l., CH); Site 154 (270 m b.s.l., CH) and Site 157 (295m b.s.l., IA II). The location of the latter three is along Nahal Yitav (Wadi 'Aujah), which was a relatively steady flowing water source. The rest of the sites were located higher (Table 1.2) at the bottom of hills, and some of them were close to streams. The few Upper Palaeolithic, EP and NE sites do not allow an analysis, but the majority of these societies were hunter-gatherers, who preferred a location close to the lake. The model of settlement in the CH changed: only a few were higher than 200 m b.s.l., but most of them were located lower, close to the Fazael and Yitav streams. Also during the EBA and MBA the bottoms of the hills were preferred, and from the LBA not a single site was found. During the IA the high area at the foot of the mountains was preferred, and the location of many of the sites was at the bottom of hills, west of the modern settlements in the plain – Fasael, Tomer, Gilgal, Netiv Hagdud and Yitav. Some were organized in clusters, and some of the single ones were west of and close to the sites of modern settlements (Fig. 1.20). Only Site 122 (E.P. -140), a small site in the plain, and Site 157 (Malhaqa el-Wadian), located close to Nahal Yitav, are exceptions.

The current elevations of the River Jordan in the boundaries of the survey area are 258 m b.s.l. in the north and 323 m b.s.l. in the south. The still marshy lowlands close to the river were probably not suitable for habitation because of malaria which prevented the establishment of permanent sites. A modern example is the Valley of Yezreel, which was almost devoid of habitation, with villages only located at the edges of the valley, until the swamps were drained early in the 20th century.

The UP and EP sites at an elevation of about 200 m b.s.l. are of special interest. Excavations or thorough investigations could enable the comparison of the finds of these sites to those of Ohalo 2 (Bar-Yosef and Nadel 1988; Nadel 1990; 1991). This site, located on the shore of the Sea of Galilee at an elevation of 212 m b.s.l., was close to the ancient shoreline of the lake. It was discovered in the 1980s, when the water level of the lake was low, and excavated in the 1990s (Nadel et al. 1995). It is dated to the end of the UP at the transition to the EP (17500-21050 years BP according to 25 radiometric tests; Nadel et al. 1995: 811). The outstanding state of preservation provided rich data on the lifestyle at the site. The presence of fish bones in the survey sites, similar to those found

Elevation m / period	-251 to -300	-201 to -250	-151 to -200	-101 to -150	-51 to -100	-1 to -50	+50 to 0	+100 to +51	+101 and higher	Total
Lower Palaeolithic										
Middle Palaeolithic										
Upper Palaeolithic		1				1				2
Epipalaeolithic		4	1							5
Neolithic	1	1				2	2	1		7
Chalcolithic	3	1	2	1		1	2			10
Early/Middle Bronze	1	1	3		1	3	1			10
Late Bronze										
Iron Age	1	3	6	3	4	6	6	1		30
Sites with defined period	6	11	12	4	7	14	10	2		66
Sites with undefined period		5	6	6	2	1	3		1	24
Total	6	16	18	10	9	15	13	2	1	90

Table 1.2. Number of sites with flint finds according to period and elevation.
Note: Some of the assemblages are multi-period, thus the number of identified periods exceeds the number of assemblages examined.

in abundance at Ohalo 2 (Nadel 1991: 159), could testify that the subsistence of these societies was also based on fishing, and not only on hunting and gathering. This could explain the location of these sites at similar elevations, close to the ancient shoreline.

The current elevations of the sites were possibly affected in the past by possible tectonic events, sedimentation and erosion, hence the data here are approximate. Furthermore, it should be noted that this discussion is not complete, as it refers only to sites with flint finds, thus providing only indications and tendencies. A wider discussion has to consider the data from all sites discovered in the surveyed area and larger samples of all possible diagnostic items, and not only sporadic finds of flint artefacts from a surface survey.

Average quantity of artefacts per site according to periods (*Table 1.3*)

Only single-period sites from the EP, CH and IA are included in Table 1.3. From the UP, NE and Bronze Age only two single-period sites of each period were found, and are therefore not included in the comparison.

According to Table 1.3 it is obvious that the number of flint artefacts per site decreases gradually from the EP to the IA, when the use of flint terminated. In the majority of the IA sites the number of flint artefacts is small, the number of retouched artefacts still smaller, and the function of most of them is unknown. This matches the decline in the importance of flint, and its gradual substitution by bronze, and later by iron.

Diagnostic artefacts - remarks and possible implications

Epipalaeolithic

Site 18 – Fasael (4) – EP, Kebaran Culture, two bladelets with oblique truncations.

Sites 82 A, B, E and F – EP, the Natufian period. The affiliation was determined mainly according to the composition of the assemblages, containing end-scrapers, burins, sickle blades and an assortment of bladelets. Apparently, typical microliths escaped the attention of the surveyors.

Neolithic

Site 1 – E.P. -290 – PPNB, one axe with transverse blows.
Site 60 – Gilgal (5) – PPNB, one naviform core.
Site 76 – Wadi el-Baqar (1) – PPN, one blade with pressure retouch.
Site 105 – Wadi el-Haiyat (6) – PPNB/C, one arrowhead.
Site 106 – Wadi el-Haiyat (5) – PPNC/PN, two arrowheads, one denticulated sickle blade.

Chalcolithic

Site 14 – Fasael (1) CH – one polished axe; one adze (partially polished); two backed and truncated sickle blades.
Site 22 – Fasael (5) CH – one fan scraper; one broken bifacial tool (adze or axe); one sickle blade with natural back; one truncated Canaanean sickle blade.
Site 31 – Wadi ez-Zimrah CH – one backed and truncated sickle blade.
Site 121 – Wadi Nabiris (3) CH – one fan scraper; one backed sickle blade.
Site 152 – Sheikh Ibrahim CH – one backed and truncated sickle blade.
Site 154 – E.P. -261 CH – one chisel; three backed and truncated sickle blades.

Early Bronze

Site 4 – Mughur el-Hableh – EBA (according to sherds), one sickle blade and one fan scraper.
Site 18 – Fasael (4) – EBA (according to sherds), one fan scraper.
Site 21 – Tell esh-Sheik Diyab (2) – EBA, two Canaanean blades, one retouched Canaanean blade, one fan scraper.

The relatively small number of sites with just a few diagnostic artefacts makes the discussion difficult, although a summary of the data could contribute to a wider discussion including the sites without flint. Furthermore, some of the data could also contribute some insights concerning the way of life and economy of the communities.

Site no.	EP	CH	IA
6		50	
14		37	
22		32	
40			10
41			5
44			7
48			3
58			6
75			7
82a	112		
82c	55		
82e	182		
82f	90		
87			10
103			48
110			6
112			4
113			15
116			6
121		95	
122			18
139			8
140			20
143			24
145			5
152		28	
154		22	
157			5
Total	439	264	207
Average quantity per site	110	44	12

Table 1.3. Number of artefacts per site by period.

Whenever a single diagnostic item was found and no other indications were present, the period was usually classified as possible. The axe (or adze - Site 22 above), an integral part of the CH toolkit, is completely missing in the Bronze Ages.

In sites attributed to the CH, backed and truncated sickle blades, typical of the period, were found together with Canaanean blades and Canaanean sickle blades, considered typical of the EBA/MBA (Site 22). Furthermore, in EBA sites, in addition to Canaanean blades, sickle blades of the CH type (backed and truncated, Sites 21, 137 above) were present. The application of Canaanean technology in CH sites has already been published (Bar and Winter 2010; Bar et al. 2011). The indications here are meagre, and there is no room for generalization; but this phenomenon in the Jordan Valley indicates a gradual transition of the new Canaanean technology from the CH to the EBA, and the simultaneous continuation of the CH tradition in the EBA.

Despite the small sample, the new innovation – the sickle blade (Table 1.4) has a significant importance, as it marks changes in the ways of life and economy. Table 1.4 shows that no sickle blades were found from the UP. From the EP

Site	UP	EP	NE	CH	EBA / MBA	LBA	IA
4					1		
6				2			
14				5			
21					1		
22				2			
31				1			
82 A		1					
82 C		1					
82 E		1					
82 F		2					
106			1				
121				1			
137					2		
152				1			
154				3			
Sickle blades Total	0	5	1	15	4	0	0
Number of identified sites	2	5	7	10	10	0	30

Table 1.4. Sickle blades by period

to the end of the MBA (except for the NE) sickle blades were found, evidence of the exploitation of wild cereals by hunter-gatherers, or later, growing of cereals by farming communities, reaching its peak during the CH.

At the end of the last Ice Age and the onset of the Holocene, about 10,000 years BCE, climatic changes fluctuating between warmer and cooler periods occurred, resulting generally in higher temperatures, decreased precipitation and expansion of deserts. This phenomenon was caused by both cosmic and geological factors (Fig. 1.18). An example of this process is the well known gradual expansion of the Sahara desert since the onset of the Holocene. With the onset of the LBA, about 1500 BCE, another cycle of global warming started, continuing until IA I, and reaching its peak about 1100 BCE (as above), and a habitation crisis occurred in the surveyed area. The population in the area of the survey dwindled during the MBA (also for geopolitical reasons - Zertal and Bar 2017: 56-58), and in the LBA the region was actually abandoned by its inhabitants, neither sites nor sickle blades being found (Table 1.4). Then a dramatic change occurred – from the IA 30 sites (18 reasonable and 12 possible identification – Table 1.1), with even a few flint artefacts in each, were identified, but not a single sickle blade was found (see a detailed discussion of this phenomenon in Winter 2017: 655). The gradual warming cycle, the abandonment of the area by its population and the gradual disappearance of sickle

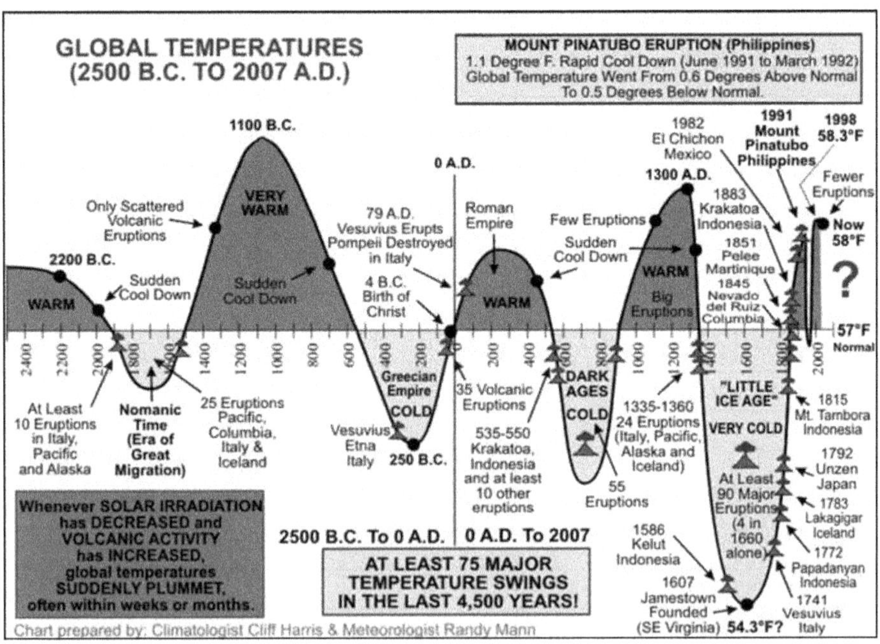

Fig. 1.18 Global climate changes during the past 4500 years (Source: Harris-Mann Climatology & Long Range Weather - http://www.longerangeweather.com/).

blades coincide; thus it seems reasonable to consider the hypothesis that the warming climate was one of the reasons for the disappearance of the population in the LBA. The agricultural way of life, common during the CH and the EBA, was no longer possible, and in the LBA the area was practically deserted. In the following IA, the presence of 30 sites with flint assemblages not including sickle blades, may indicate the arrival of a new population with a different subsistence strategy – an economy based on herding and grazing. Despite the small sample the indications are clear. This thesis is supported also in the section 'The settlement by periods' (Chapter 1 of this Volume).

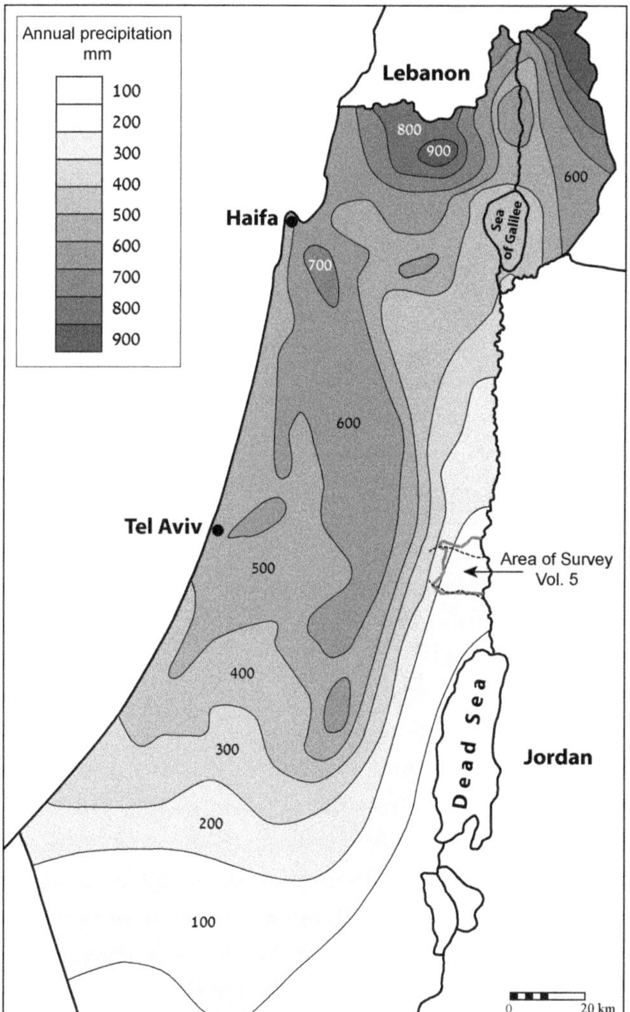

Fig. 1.19. Current average yearly precipitation, including the survey area in the rain shadow of the Samaria Mountains.

A possible example of a similar process is the abandonment of cities resulting in the destruction of the Maya civilization of Central America, after climatic changes which brought prolonged periods of drought and famine. The analysis of human bones found there confirms a period of starvation.

The surveyed area of Volume 5, in Eastern Samaria, located in the rain shadow of the Samaria mountain range, has currently a minimal amount of precipitation (see Introduction of this volume and Fig. 1.19). During the IA the region was even warmer than today (Fig. 1.18), and apparently arid, and grazing was possible only for a limited part of the year; thus the survival of herds was at risk. Regional nomadism of populations seeking pasture is a well known phenomenon from ethnographic records. It includes ascending in summer to higher altitudes, where rainfall is higher. And indeed, in the upper part of the area, at the higher altitudes of the eastern slopes of the Samaria mountain range (Zertal and Bar 2017), IA sites with sickle blades were found. The most

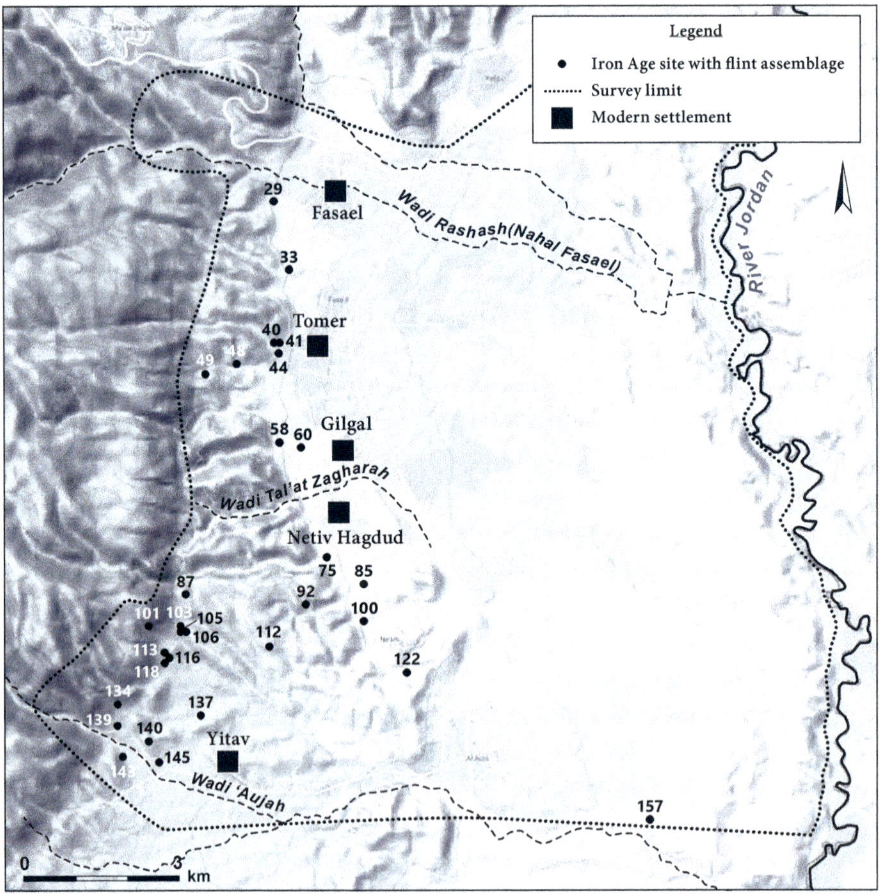

Fig. 1.20. Iron Age sites in which flint assemblages were found.

dominant of these were 55 sickle blades, mostly of the Large Geometric type, excavated on Mount Ebal (Winter, unpublished). This type of sickle blade was used from the MBA until the end of the IA (for a detailed discussion with sources see Winter 2017: 658-659).

To conclude, this hypothetical model describes nomad tribes of herders, coming from the east, crossing the Jordan in order to find grazing land for their flocks. A possible scenario and reasons for this process is:

- The gradual abandoning of the lowlands on the west bank of the Jordan by the agricultural population during the EBA/MBA periods due to geopolitical events (see Chapter 1 above) and a drying climate (Fig. 1.18). During the LBA the area was actually uninhabited.
- The settled farmers in the rainier parts, on the western slopes of the Trans-Jordan mountains, were in a permanent struggle with nomad (or regional nomad) herder tribes who arrived in the area in search of grazing land and damaged crops. Actually the latter were forced to cross the Jordan into the arid area, which was at that time unpopulated. In populated areas this penetration would encounter resistance, and would not be feasible. The struggle between farmers and nomads, or regional nomads, the Semitic tribes from Sinai and Canaan, who repeatedly penetrated the green Delta of the Nile in order to graze their herds in years of drought, is a well-known example of this phenomenon.

After the penetration to the west bank of the Jordan the search for better pastures continued, especially during the dry seasons. Such pastures were located higher in the mountains of Samaria, where sickle blades are evidence of their gradual settlement as farmers.

REFERENCES

Bar, S., Bar-Oz, G., Ben-Yosef, D., Raban-Gerstel, N., and Winter H., 2011. "Sheikh Diyab 2: An Early Bronze Age I Hamlet in the Jordan Valley", *Mitekufat Haeven: Journal of the Israel Prehistoric Society* 41, 95-154.

Bar, S., and Winter, H., 2010. "Canaanean Flint Blades in Chalcolithic Context and the Possible Onset of the Transition to the Early Bronze Age: A Case Study from Fazael 2", *Tel Aviv* 37, 33-47.

Bartov, Y., Stein, M., Enzel, Y., Agnon, A., and Reches, Z., 2002. "Lake Levels and Sequence Stratigraphy of Lake Lisan, the Late Pleistocene Precursor of the Dead Sea", *Quaternary Research* 57, 9-21.

Bar-Yosef, O., 1970. *The Epi-Palaeolithic Cultures of Palestine* (Unpublished Ph.D. Dissertation), The Hebrew University, Jerusalem.

Bar-Yosef, O., and Belfer-Cohen, A., 2000. "Nahal Ein Gev II, A Late Epi-Paleolithic Site in the Jordan Valley", *Mitekufat Haeven: Journal of the Israel Prehistoric Society* 30, 49-71.

Bar-Yosef, O., and Goren-Inbar, N., 1993. *The Lithic Assemblages of 'Ubeidiya: A Lower Palaeolithic Site in the Jordan Valley* (*Qedem* 34), Jerusalem.

Bar-Yosef, O., and Nadel, D., 1988. "Ohalo – A Prehistoric Site in the Sea of Galilee", *Mitekufat Haeven: Journal of the Israel Prehistoric Society* 21, 87-94.

Bordes, F., 1961. *Typologie du Paléolitique, ancien et moyen* (*Memoire No. 1 de l'Institut de préhistoire de l'Université de Bordeaux*), Bordeaux.

Burian, F., and Friedman, E., 1979. "A Typology of Arrowheads and Sickle Blades and Its Chronological Implication", *Mitekufat Haeven: Journal of the Israel Prehistoric Society* 16, 1-11 (Hebrew).

Gopher, A., 1985. *Flint Tool Industries of the Neolithic Period in Israel* (Unpublished Ph.D. Dissertation), The Hebrew University, Jerusalem.

Gopher, A., 1989. *The Flint Assemblage of Munhata, Final Report* (*Les Cahiers du Centre de Recherche Française de Jerusalem* 4), Paris.

Hours, F., 1974. "Remarques sur l'utilisation de listes-types pour l'étude du paléolithique supérieure et de l'epipaléolithique du levant", *Paléorient* 2/1, 3-18.

Hovers, E., and Bar-Yosef, O., 1987. "A Prehistoric Survey of Eastern Samaria: Preliminary Report", *Israel Exploration Journal* 37/2-3, 77-87.

Hovers, E., Horwitz, I. K., Bar-Yosef, D. E. and Cope-Miyashiro, C., 1988. "The Site of Urkan er-Rub IIa: A Case Study of Subsistence and Mobility Patterns in the Kebaran Period in the Lower Jordan Valley", *Mitekufat Haeven: Journal of the Israel Prehistoric Society* 21, 14-28.

Hovers, E. and Marder, O., 1991. "Typo-Chronology and Absolute Dating of the Kebaran Complex: Implications from the Second Season of Excavations at Urkan er-Rub IIa", *Mitekufat Haeven: Journal of the Israel Prehistoric Society* 24, 34-58.

Lee, J. R., 1973. *Chalcolithic Ghassul: New Aspects and Master Typology* (Unpublished Ph.D. Dissertation), The Hebrew University, Jerusalem.

Lisker, S., Vaks, A., Bar-Matthews, M., Porat, R., and Frumkin, A., 2009. "Stromatolites in Caves of the Dead Sea Fault Escarpment: Implications to Latest Pleistocene Lake Levels and Tectonic Subsidence", *Quaternary Science Reviews* 28, 80-92.

Nadel, D., 1990. "Ohalo II – Preliminary Report", *Mitekufat Haeven: Journal of the Israel Prehistoric Society* 23, 48-59.

Nadel, D., 1991. "Ohalo II – The Third Season (1991)", *Mitekufat Haeven: Journal of the Israel Prehistoric Society* 24, 158-163.

Nadel, D., Carmi, I., and Segal, D., 1995. "Radiocarbon Dating of Ohalo II: Archaeological and Methodological Implications", *Journal of Archaeological Science* 22, 6, 811-822.

Ronen, A., Winter, H., and Chinn, D., 1994. "The Hatoula Borers and their Possible Role in the Neolithic", in Lechevallier, M., and Ronen, A. (eds.), *Le gisement de Hatoula en Judée occidentale, Israel* (Association Paléorient), Paris, 181-192.

Rosen, S. A., 1994/5. "Microlithic Drills from the Camel Site, Mitzpeh Ramon", *Mitekufat Haeven: Journal of the Israel Prehistoric Society* 26, 149-158.

Rosen, S. A., 1997. *Lithics after the Stone Age*, Walnut Creek.

Winter, H., 2008 (Hebrew 1996). "Flint Findings in East Manasseh", in Zertal, A., *The Manasseh Hill Country Survey, vol. 2: The Eastern Valleys and the Fringes of the Desert*, Leiden and Boston, 659-737.

Winter, H., 2016 (Hebrew 2000). "Es-Suweisseh (Site 194) – A Neolithic-Chalcolithic Site at the Foot of the Samaria Hills", in Zertal, A., and Mirkam, N., *The Manasseh Hill Country Survey, vol. 3: From Nahal 'Iron to Nahal Shechem*, Leiden and Boston, 479-505.

Winter, H., 2017 (Hebrew 2005). "The Flint Assemblages", in Zertal, A. and Bar, S., *The Manasseh Hill Country Survey, vol. 4: From Nahal Bezeq to the Sartaba*, Leiden and Boston, 571-665.

Winter, H., unpublished. "Mount Ebal – The Flint Assemblage".

Zertal, A, and Bar, S., 2017. *The Manasseh Hill Country Survey, vol. 4: From Nahal Bezeq to the Sartaba*, Leiden and Boston.

APPENDIX B

PREHISTORIC SURVEYS IN THE MIDDLE JORDAN VALLEY

Shay Bar

INTRODUCTION

During the 1970s and 1980s two prehistoric surveys were performed and published in the Middle Jordan Valley (Goring-Morris 1980; Schuldenrein 1983). The area between Wadi Ahmar and the southern outskirts of Netiv Hagdud was surveyed and many prehistoric sites were discovered, some of them excavated (Gilgal and Netiv Hagdud, Sites 70 and 72). The main concentration of sites was in Wadi Fasael and the Salibiya Basin. Nadel (2008) analyzed the pattern of settlement from the Natufian to the Pottery Neolithic periods. He found discontinues settlement activity that he suggested was caused by competition for limited available resources and social complexity.

This appendix reviews the above-mentioned works as a supplement and addition to the data published in the current Volume. The sites are described from north to south (Fig. 2.1) with a short summary on each period.

A "find spot" in this appendix refers to a scatter of flint tools on a limited area that was not registered as a site.

Additional bibliography: Hovers 1988; Nadel 2008 (with additional bibliography therein).

The names of the sites derive from the original publications (thus name inconsistencies might occur: e.g. Fazael versus Fasael).

THE SITES

1-2. Israel grid: 1883/1622

Fazael VII-VIII – Two Epipalaeolithic assemblages, Kebaran and Geometric Kebaran A, found in a section of the riverbed of Wadi Hableh (ez-Zananir) south of the Fasael springs. The most common find is the microlith (Goring-Morris 1980: sites VII-VIII).

3. Israel grid 1894/1621

Fazael IV – A Late Epipalaeolithic (Late Natufian) assemblage on a terrace on the northern bank of Wadi Fasael. In the limited finds a high percentage of sickle blades and tools made with the micro-burin technology (Goring-Morris 1980: site IV; Grosman et al. 1999).

4. Israel grid: 1885/1621

Fazael VI – An Epipalaeolithic (Early Natufian) site ca. 0.5 dunam (500 sq. m) in size, on a terrace above and north-west of the Fasael springs. A small probe exposed a rich assemblage of faunal remains and basalt stone tools. The lithic assemblage includes many Helwan blades (Goring-Morris 1980: site VI).

5. Israel grid: 1886/1621

Fazael IX – Two Upper Palaeolithic strata were excavated in a small probe west of the Fasael springs. The lithic assemblage is characterized by the flake technology, and especially common are various scraper types on flakes and blades. Three limestone hammerstones with pecking signs on all sides were also found. The faunal remains include *Gazella gazella* and *Gazella subgeterrosa*. Also found are *Sus scrofa*, *Capra aegagrus* and *Felis silvestris*. Some bone tools, mainly burins, were made from *deer* bones (Goring-Morris 1980: site IX).

6. Israel grid: 1898/1618

Fazael II – A small Pre-Pottery Neolithic find spot on the southern bank of Wadi Fasael. Axes, scrapers and burins were common in the lithic assemblage (Goring-Morris 1980: site II).

7. Israel grid: 1894/1621

Fazael V – A very small, possibly Kebaran, occurrence on the northern bank of Wadi Fasael. This find spot is located near Fazael IV (Goring-Morris 1980: site V).

8. Israel grid: 1912/1620

Fazael I – A small Middle Palaeolithic Mousterian find spot on an alluvial fan east of the Fasael springs (Goring-Morris 1980: site I).

9. Israel grid: 1900/1619

Fazael XII – An Epipalaeolithic, probably Kebaran, site on the northern bank of Wadi Fasael (Goring-Morris 1980: site XII).

10. Israel grid: 1907/1618

Fazael III – An Epipalaeolithic site on the northern bank of Wadi Fasael, in the exit of the stream from its narrow gorge to the alluvial fan. It is situated in the same location as the site Fasael (4) appearing in this volume (Site 18). In a small excavation in four different parts of the site, three Kebaran strata and one Geometric Kebaran stratum were identified (Goring-Morris 1980: site III). The lithic assemblage mainly includes blade and bladelet technology. The dominant faunal species is the *Gazella gazella*. The latest occupation at the site was mistakenly attributed to the Chalcolithic period, and only in a recent excavation at the site (Bar et al. 2012) was corrected to the Early Bronze Age I.

11-12. Israel grid: 1905/1618

Fazael X-XI – Two very close Upper Palaeolithic sites on the noerthern bank of Wadi Fasael, near the exit of the stream from its narrow gorge to the alluvial fan. They are only 25 m apart, and were probably one site in antiquity. The lithic assemblage is also homogeneous in both sites. In a small probe Goring-Morris (1980: sites X-XI) noted that the sites are characterized by the blade and bladelet technology, and especially common are various microliths. The common stone tools were limestone hammerstones and basalt grinding tools. The faunal remains mainly include *Gazella gazella* alongside molluscs of various types. Some bone tools were also found, mainly points and burins made from deer bones.

13. Israel grid: 1911/1607

Hisha – A find spot dated to the Middle Palaeolithic, south-west of Fasael (Schuldenrein 1983: table A2).

14. Israel grid: 1907/1607

Asmara I – A find spot dated to the Middle Palaeolithic, on a ridge south of Wadi ez-Zamra and 1 km south-west of Fasael (Schuldenrein 1983: table A2).

15. Israel grid: 1905/1607

Asmara II – Another find spot dated to the Middle Palaeolithic, on a ridge south of Wadi ez-Zamra and 1 km south-west of Fasael (Schuldenrein 1983: table A2).

16. Israel grid: 1905/1605

E-Main – Another find spot dated to the Middle Palaeolithic, on a ridge south of Wadi ez-Zamra and 1 km south-west of Fasael (Schuldenrein 1983: table A2).

17. Israel grid: 1913/1596

El-Amri I – A lithic assemblage dated to the Epipalaeolithic, on the banks of a Wadi bearing the same name south-west of Fasael (Schuldenrein 1983: table A2).

18. Israel grid: 1913/1596

El-Amri II – An undated lithic assemblage very close to El-Amri I (Schuldenrein 1983: table A2).

19. Israel grid: 1912/1596

El-Amri III – A lithic assemblage dated to the Middle Palaeolithic adjacent to sites El-Amri I and II (Schuldenrein 1983: table A2).

20. Israel grid: 1907/1586

El-Butum I – An undated lithic assemblage on the banks of Wadi Butem west of Tomer (Schuldenrein 1983: table A2).

21. Israel grid: 1912/1583

El-Butum II – An undated lithic assemblage on the banks of Wadi Butem west of Tomer (Schuldenrein 1983: table A2).

22. Israel grid: 1911/1583

El-Butum III – A lithic assemblage possibly dated to the Middle Palaeolithic on the banks of Wadi Butem (Schuldenrein 1983: table A2).

23. Israel grid: 1915/1575

Bif I – A lithic assemblage dated to the Middle Palaeolithic on the banks of a small stream between Wadis Sa'ad and Abu Mahmud west of Tomer and Netiv Hagdud (Schuldenrein 1983: table A2).

24. Israel grid: 1907/1575

Bif II – A lithic assemblage dated to the Upper Palaeolithic on the banks of a small stream between Wadis Sa'ad and Abu Mahmud (Schuldenrein 1983: table A2).

25. Israel grid: 1912/1555

Tal'at Za'arah I – A small Epipalaeolithic site, less then 75 sq. m, 2 km north-west of Netiv Hagdud. It seems that this was a seasonal encampment site. Notable in the assemblage are Kebaran microliths (Schuldenrein 1983: table A2).

26. Israel grid: 1912/1555

Tal'at Za'arah II – A small Geometric Kebaran site, close to Tal'at Za'arah I. It is very similar to the Tal'at Za'arah I site, both in size and in possible function.

Notable in the assemblage are Geometric microliths (Schuldenrein 1983: table A2).

27. Israel grid: 1925/1548

Salibiya X – A Natufian find spot on the banks of Wadi Salibiya south-west of Netiv Hagdud (Schuldenrein 1983: table A1).

28. Israel grid: 1929/1546

Salibiya VI – An undated find spot on the banks of Wadi Salibiya south-west of Netiv Hagdud (Schuldenrein 1983: table A1).

29. Israel grid: 1929/1545

Salibiya II – A Late Natufian find spot on the banks of Wadi Salibiya south-west of Netiv Hagdud. In the assemblage are many microliths, backed bladelets, awls and cores (Schuldenrein 1983: table A1).

30. Israel grid: 1932/1545

Salibiya IV – A Late Natufian find spot on the banks of Wadi Salibiya (Schuldenrein 1983: table A1).

31. Israel grid: 1929/1545

Salibiya V – A possible Natufian site with meagre finds on the banks of Wadi Salibiya south-west of Netiv Hagdud (Schuldenrein 1983: table A1).

32. Israel grid: 1926/1545

Salibiya VII – A find spot on the banks of Wadi Salibiya. In the meagre assemblage are a few backed bladelets, drills and cores (Schuldenrein 1983: table A1).

33. Israel grid: 1929/1545

Salibiya VIII – An undated find spot on the banks of Wadi Salibiya (Schuldenrein 1983: table A1).

34. Israel grid: 1931/1543

Salibiya III – An Epipalaeolithic site on the banks of Wadi Salibiya. In the assemblage are many microliths, backed bladelets, cores and picks (Schuldenrein 1983: table A1).

35. Israel grid: 1929/1542

Salibiya I – A large Late Natufian site on the banks of Wadi Salibiya. Its size is estimated to be more than 500 sq. m, with two strata. In the assemblage are many microliths. In the possible early stratum are many sickle blades and tiny picks (Schuldenrein 1983: table A1).

36. Israel grid: 1925/1548

Salibiya XI – An undated find spot on the banks of Wadi Salibiya (Schuldenrein 1983: table A1).

37. Israel grid: 1925/1541

Salibiya XII – An Early Natufian site, more than 150 sq. m in size, on the banks of Wadi Salibiya 2 km south of Netiv Hagdud. The remains of quarried cupmarks

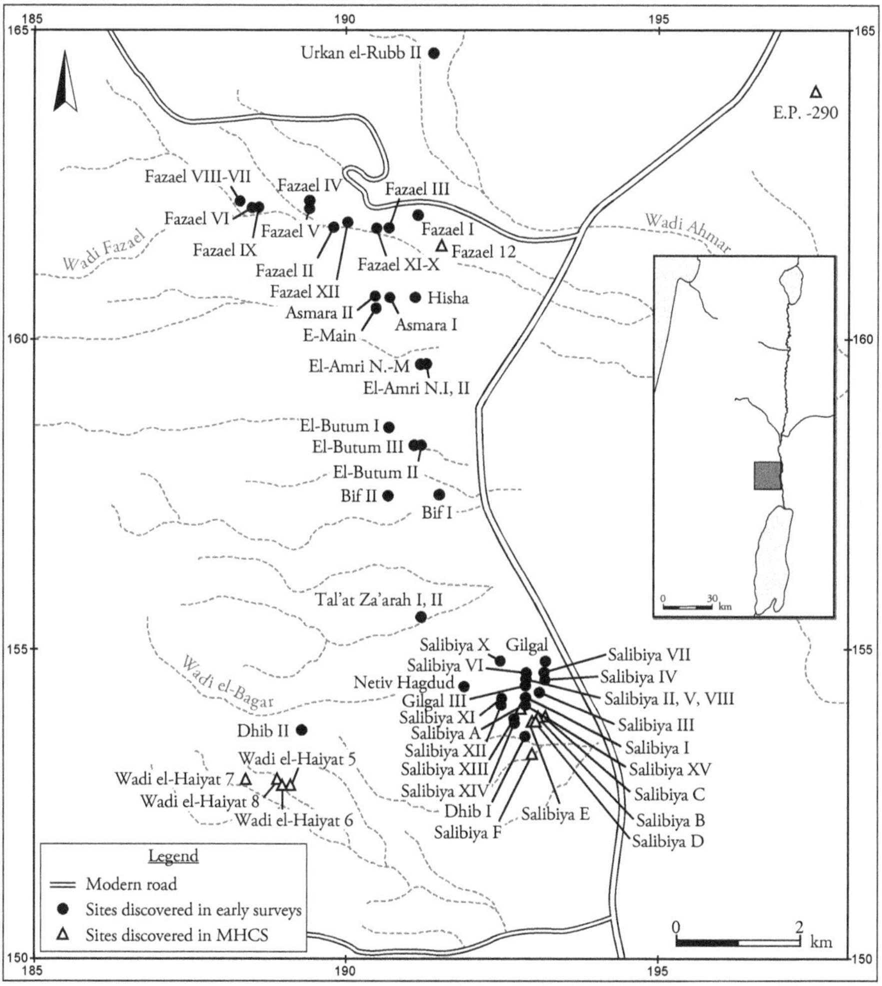

Fig. 2.1. Prehistoric sites in the Middle Jordan Valley.

were found. Notable in the assemblage are the Helwan lunates (Schuldenrein 1983: table A1). For additional data see Niran (1) site (Site 85).

38. Israel grid: 1929/1541

Salibiya XV – A Late Natufian site on the banks of Wadi Salibiya. In the meagre assemblage are backed bladelets, drills and cores (Schuldenrein 1983: table A1).

39. Israel grid: 1927/1539

Salibiya XIII – A Late Natufian find spot on the banks of Wadi Salibiya. In the assemblage are backed bladelets, drills and cores (Schuldenrein 1983: table A1).

40. Israel grid: 1927/1538

Salibiya XIV – A Late Natufian find spot on the banks of Wadi Salibiya near Salibiya XIII. In the assemblage are backed bladelets, drills and cores (Schuldenrein 1983: table A1).

41. Israel grid: 1929/1536

Dhib I – A Neolithic find spot on the northern banks of Wadi Maqor edh-Dhib. (Schuldenrein 1983: table A1).

42. Israel grid: 1893/1537

Dhib II – A Middle Palaeolithic find spot on a ridge between wadis el-Baqar and el-Hamam 3 km south-west of Netiv Hagdud (Schuldenrein 1983: table A1). This is the western site found in the prehistoric surveys: its connection to the sites in the Jordan Valley plain is not yet clear.

THE PATTERN OF SETTLEMENT IN THE DIFFERENT PREHISTORIC PERIODS

In the previous section a detailed description of the different prehistoric sites and find spots, discovered prior to the work of the Manasseh Hill Country Survey, is presented. The time span ranges between the Middle Palaeolithic and the Pre-Pottery Neolithic. It is interesting to note that in the earlier surveys the Pottery Neolithic and the Early Chalcolithic/Wadi Rabah phase were not discovered. This changed when Bar and Rosenberg (2011) published several sites from these periods based on re-evaluating published and working on unpublished materials from the Manasseh Hill Country Survey collection. The intensively settled Chalcolithic period is well represented in the current Volume (see Chapter 1, section D, and Bar 2014) and will not be further discussed here.

Middle Palaeolithic

Eight small sites and find spots were discovered, between the Jordan Valley plain and the eastern Samaria mountain slopes. The lowest altitude, 220 m b.s.l., might suggest the highest level of Lake Lisan at that period. These sites can be annexed to the cluster of sites, mainly in the slopes of the Sartaba, previously published in Volume 4 of the Survey (Winter 2017). Toghether they represent a moderate human activity in the Jordan Valley in the period.

Upper Palaeolithic

Two of the four small sites were found in Wadi Fasael, and the others were found in the area between the Jordan Valley plain and lower sections of the slopes of the eastern Samaria Mountains. The human activity in this period was very limited. Another site (Fasael 12 – Site 25; and see Appendix A) was not discovered in earlier surveys, and is now annexed to the four known sites.

Epipalaeolithic period

The 23 sites and find spots, mainly located in Wadi Fasael and the Salibiya basin, represent the increase in activity in the Middle Jordan Valley.

In the Early Natufian the settlement spread into the Jordan Valley plain, mainly to the Salibiya basin that became the centre of human presenvce in the region.

The five small Kebaran settlements were mainly located in the Fasael region, the largest being a Geometric Kebaran site - Fazael III. Hovers (1988: 91) suggested that at the end of the period there was a dry era and Lake Lisan shrank. It is possible that the first Epipalaeolithic sites in the Fasael region were coastal encampments. Later in the period, with the retreat of the lake shore, the sites in the region became more dependent on the streams (Fasael and Ahmar). Hovers (1988: 122) suggested that one or a few groups of people settled the area on a seasonal basis. They were probably interconnected with each other and returned to the region.

Only two large sites were discovered dating to the Early Natufian – Fazael VI and Salibiya XII. It seems that Salibiya XII was the earlier site in the somewhat crowded Salibiya basin.

During the Late Natufian the Salibiya basin had a flourishing settlement wave, while the Fasael region remained unsettled. All 13 sites and find spots are located within the Salibiya basin. The main site was probably Salibiya I with an estimated size of over 500 sq m. Hovers (1988: 116) suggested that the

Natufian settlement here was not seasonal, but rather one of the first examples of a permanent site. During this period a gradual shift from hunting-gathering societies to an agricultural oriented economy began. The Salibiya basin, rich in water and possible agricultural flat lands (because of the retreat of Lake Lisan), had all the economic benefits to support all-year-round settlement in the area.

To these sites are annexed four other sites near the Salibiya basin that were not discovered by the previous surveys in the region. These sites (82a, 82c, 82e-f) were dated by Winter to the Natufian (see Appendix A).

Pre-Pottery Neolithic

The settlement in the Salibiya basin and its vicinity continued (five of the six sites). Most prominent are the excavated sites at Netiv Hagdud and Gilgal I and III (see Sites 70 and 72 for additional data). In Wadi Fasael only one find spot was discovered – Fazael II.

To these sites are annexed four more sites discovered by the Manasseh Hill Country Survey: one in the Jordan Valley plain north of Wadi Ahmar (E.P. -290, Site 1), that was dated to the Pre-Pottery Neolithic B (Appendix A) and the others in Wadi el-Haiyat (Wadi el-Haiyat 5-7, Sites 101, 105-106), that were dated to the Pre-Pottery Neolithic B-C (Appendix A).

SUMMARY

In the early prehistoric periods (Middle Palaeolithic to the Early Natufian) the settlement in the Middle Jordan Valley was sparse. Only after the Late Natufian, and especially during the the Pre-Pottery Neolithic, a larger settlement emerged. The settlement map shows a major concentration in the Salibiya basin, and the other areas are almost deserted. Especially noticeable is the emptiness of settlement in Wadi Fasael at the end of the Epipalaeolithic. The settlement in this wadi was restored only during the Chalcolithic period, when the place became the hub of settlement in the region (Bar 2014).

A note of caution: reliability of the data presented here has two main constraints: major prehistoric surveys were only conducted in the Fasael and Salibiya areas and not elsewhere in the region; and the Manasseh Hill Country Survey is not a prehistoric survey and some sites might have not been recognized. This situation results in a possibly inaccurate map of settlements during the different periods (as often happens in archaeological research). Therefore, the conclusions derived from this appendix should be regarded as preliminary until further, large scale, prehistoric surveys are made in the region.

REFERENCES

Bar, S., 2014. *The Dawn of the Bronze Age*, Leiden and Boston.

Bar, S., Cohen, O., Zuckerman, R., and Winter, H., 2012. "The Archaeological Excavation at the Early Bronze Age I Site Fazael 4, Jordan Valley, Israel", *Journal of the Israel Prehistoric Society* 42, 1-34.

Bar, S., and Rosenberg, D., 2011. "Newly Discovered Yarmukian and Wadi Rabah Sites in the Southern Jordan Valley and the Desert Fringes of Samaria during the 7th and 6th Millennia BC: Preliminary Report", *Archaeology Ethnology and Anthropology of Eurasia* 39/3, 32–39.

Goring-Morris, A.N., 1980. *Late Quaternary Sites in Wadi Fazael, Lower Jordan Valley* (M.A. Dissertation), the Hebrew University, Jerusalem.

Grosman, L., Belfer-Cohen, A., and Bar-Yosef. O., 1999. "A final Natufian site – Fazael IV", *Journal of the Israel Prehistoric Society* 29, 17-40.

Hovers, E., 1988. *Subsistence and Settlement Patterns in the Lower Jordan Valley during Epipalaeolithic to Neolithic Times* (M.A. Thesis), the Hebrew University, Jerusalem (Hebrew).

Nadel, D., 2008. "Pre-Pottery Neolithic Settlement Patterns in the Jordan Valley (Between the Sea of Galilee and the Dead Sea)", in: Bar, S. (ed.), *In The Hill Country, and in the Shephelah and in the Arabah (Josh 12: 8)*, Jerusalem, 41-52 (Hebrew).

Schuldenrein, J., 1983. *Late Quaternary Paleo-Enviroments and Prehistoric Site Distribution in the Lower Jordan Valley* (Ph.D dissertation), University of Chicago, Chicago.

Winter, H., 2017. "The Flint Assemblages", in Zertal, A., and Bar, S., *The Manasseh Hill Country Survey Volume 4: From Nohal Bezeq to the Sartaba*, Leiden and Boston, 571-665.

APPENDIX C

A SOUTH-ARABIAN TOMB INSCRIPTION FROM THE VICINITY OF JERICHO

Adam Zertal and Yaakov Gruntfest

INTRODUCTION

During the Survey a plundered tomb was discovered on a spur in the vicinity of Jericho. The spur is located between Wadis Nabiris and el-Haiyat, which descend from the mountain escarpment of east Samaria and converge in the floodplain of the Jordan Valley, north of Yitav, nearly 2 km north of Wadi 'Aujah, at an elevation of 50 m below sea level. The tomb is located at the western end of the spur.

A stone with an inscription (Figs. 3.1-3.2) was found next to the tomb (Fig. 3.3). The inscription is recorded as Site 117; Israel grid 1895/1522.

It appears that the area has always been used for grazing; but the Survey also discovered habitation remains: Middle Bronze Age, Iron Age and Roman sites at the foot of the mountains have been investigated.

DESCRIPTION

The tomb is a stone square frame, each side 2 m long, nearly 0.8 m deep. It was built of two courses of two rows of stones. Only the outer form has been preserved. The tomb was plundered, apparently in ancient times, and its stones

Fig. 3.1: The South-Arabian inscription.

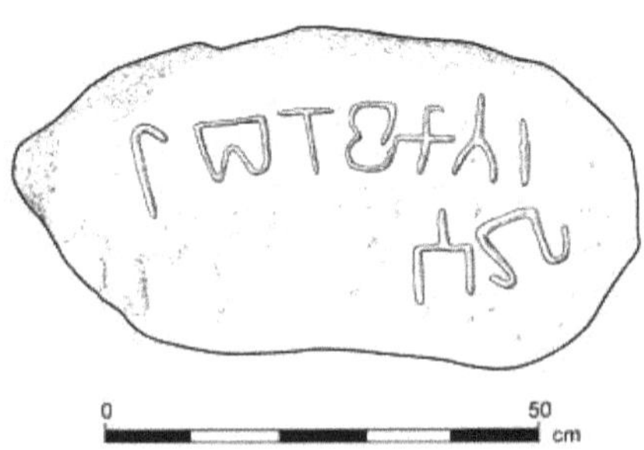

Fig. 3.2: Drawing of the inscription.

were scattered. Next to it is a circle of small stones, remains of a tumulus or another burial mound. A few sherds near the tomb are Roman.

An irregular oval stone measuring about 70×30×40 cm was discovered next to the tomb in a horizontal position. The stone was almost unworked; its flat side was slightly worked and smoothed, and on it was engraved an inscription containing nine letters in South-Arabian script.

THE INSCRIPTION

The nine letters are arranged in two rows, in the *boustrophedon* mode; i.e. the upper row of seven letters is inscribed from left to right, and the lower one of two letters from right to left. The letters are large and clear, about 10–11 cm high, and about the same width. The upper row is nearly 47 cm long, and the lower one is nearly 8 cm long. The top row of letters is slightly arched, parallel to the top edge of the stone. The engraving is 1–2 mm deep, and obviously considerable effort was invested in it.

The transliteration of the inscription is:

Upper row: *l m z r t h n*

Lower row: *s f*

translated as: "to *Mzrt* (is dedicated) the tombstone".

The script is Thamudic with slight variations. Seven signs distinctly belong to the Thamudic B script, a branch of the Thamudic script which occurs, according to MacDonald (2000: 72, note 117) throughout western Arabia, from Yemen to southern Syria. The last two letters of the name *mzrt* differ from the standard script. The top of the vertical stroke of the *t* bends at right angles; and the *r* is a figure-of-eight shaped ring, which clearly differs from the rest of the letters. The lengthening and curvature of the *r* is typical of the Safaitic script, in order to differentiate between the *r* and the *b* (Littman 1940: 21). In the tomb inscription the issue can be explained in two ways: Safaitic influence on the writer, or penetration of cursive style into the Thamudic script. The second alternative is supported by the fact that the *r* and *t* are joined – the horizontal line of the *t* touches the middle of the *r*, and also by the unique shape of the last letter.

The name *mzrt* is, according to all the indications, the feminine form of the name *mzr*. No parallels to this name are known to us, either in its masculine or feminine form, in the archive of Pre-Islamic Arabic inscriptions. A man named "Mazīr b. Gulmūd" from the Rabi'ah tribe is mentioned in the genealogical research of Hisham el-Kalbi (Caskel 1966: 107). Therefore we have proposed reading the name as *mzyrt* or *mzrt*.

The term *nfs*(*t*), meaning "tombstone" or "stela", is well known in Nabataean, Lahianic, Safaitic, and Hasaitic and other ancient South-Arabian inscriptions (Sabaic, Minaean, Qatabanic) throughout the Arabian peninsula. This form of the word *nfs* appears in this tomb inscription for the first time in Thamudic inscriptions.

The grammatical form specifying possession (belongs to…) was widely used both in Thamudic and Safaitic. In these, largely as graffiti, it appears as: *lbn ld' hnfst*, meaning "The gravestone belongs to *bn ld*" This emphasizes the name of the deceased.

In contrast to the above, in Lihyanite, Hasaitic and the ancient South-Arabian inscriptions, including those from en-Namrah, another form of

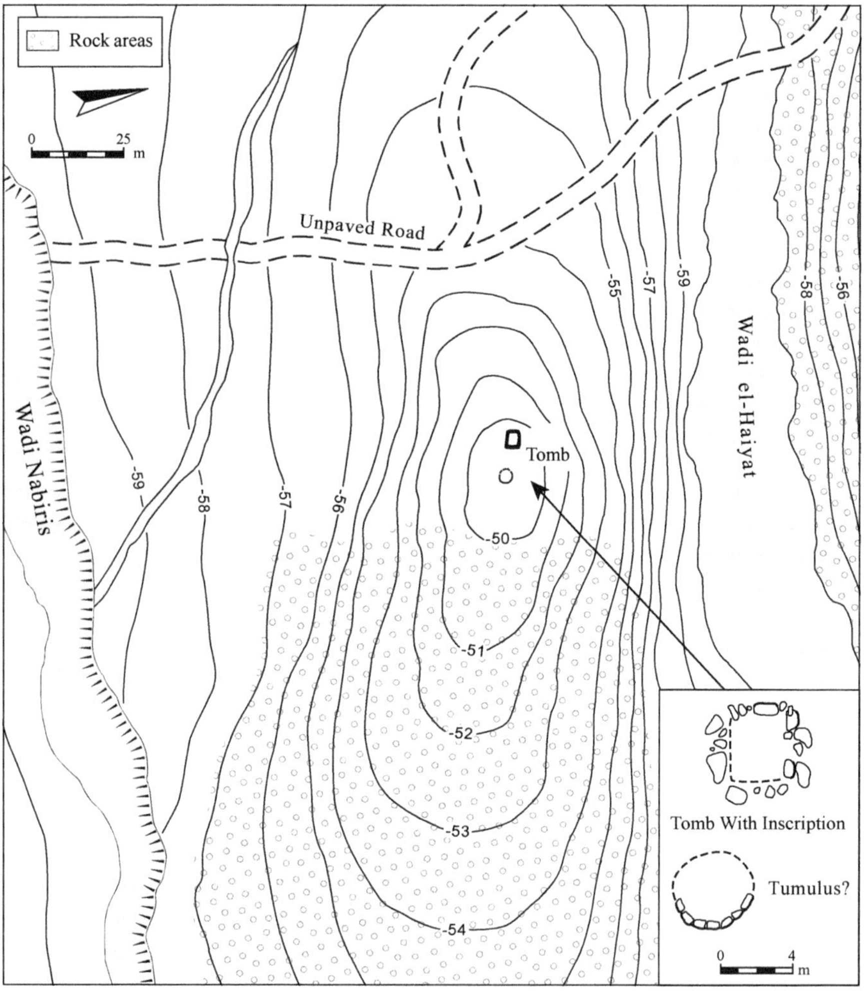

Fig. 3.3: Tomb plan and map of vicinity, see 266, p.337.

possession (genitive) is preferred, such as: *nfs hyo bt hyo* (*hyo* daughter of *hyo*'s gravestone), where the emphasis is on the gravestone itself, and not on the deceased.

In his review of the South-Arabian inscriptions, MacDonald (1992) introduces Thamudic script under the title "Safaitic inscriptions". This case and other texts cause considerable confusion in the names of the tribes and the various scripts.

WHO WERE THE THAMUDIS/SAFAITS?[1]

Members of the Thamudi tribe have appeared in historical sources over a long period. They are already mentioned in the 8th century BCE in an Assyrian source as one of the tribes surrendering to Sargon II; and in the 5th century CE Thamudi soldiers fought against the Byzantine army. Apparently their origin was in Yemen, and they migrated to the vicinity of Mecca. Their centre at this phase was in the mountains of the Hejaz. Later, according to their inscriptions, the Thamudi tribes expanded into northern Arabia.

The inscriptions provide limited information on these tribes. Concentrations of inscriptions were discovered in the places where the tribes wandered, or settled into permanent domicile. One of the drawings, for example, next to text no. 690 (*Repertoire* 1938), shows a field cultivation; and another drawing shows a village (*Repertoire* 1938: 772B) dedicated to the deity Nahi. There are no lists of ancestors in the Thamudic inscriptions, whereas they exist with the Safaits, and to a certain degree with the Lihyanites. The latter were still closer to nomadism, despite the transition to permanent domicile.

Sources indicate that the Thamudis were farmers and hunters: they hunted deer, wild camels, rabbits and even lions. In the desert, water supply was the focal issue. Springs and wells were possessed, as now, by clans and tribes (see Zertal 2007: 334-336). Guarding and maintaining water sources was essential, and there is evidence of more than one conflict over water sources. In times of emergency it was customary to conceal and block the springs to prevent their falling into the hands of the enemy (cf. Gen 26: 18-24).

There is little mention of food and its supply in the texts. Like all the tribes, the Thamudis subsisted on agriculture, raising camels and flocks, supplemented by hunting. One of the inscriptions refers to honey – a valued and popular food, and in another inscription is a man named *'asal* – Honey. The camel, the most important beast, enjoyed numerous names. Horses, cattle and donkeys were also mentioned: these few excerpts are the sole sources of

1 This review is an abstract from Van den Branden's articles, 1950: 28-54 and 1960: 6-15.

information on economic conditions.

Engravings and inscriptions almost always give only the first names of the individual, his father and grandfather. There are also blessings and requests, and many of the inscriptions bear a religious character.

Inscriptions also provide some rare knowledge of the Thamudic deities to whom the requests and prayers are directed. There are few details about the power of the gods, their magnitude, their compassion and their attributes, which are common to a great extent to the entire Semitic world. Some of the deities mentioned are: Athirat (Astarte?) – Qatabanic sun deity; Wadd – moon-god of Middle Arabian peoples and the Lihyanites; Sahar – Sheba's star deity, identified with Atar, known also by the Thamudis; Sin – moon-god from Hadramaut (Sin – the Mesopotamian moon-god); and Amm – Qatabanic moon-god. The important deities of the Thamudis are Nahi and Ruda. The cult of the goddess Ruda is also known in Safa and Tadmor-Palmyra. Nahi, "wise", appears as the god of wisdom, joy and happiness, famous for the help, support and protection granted to his followers.

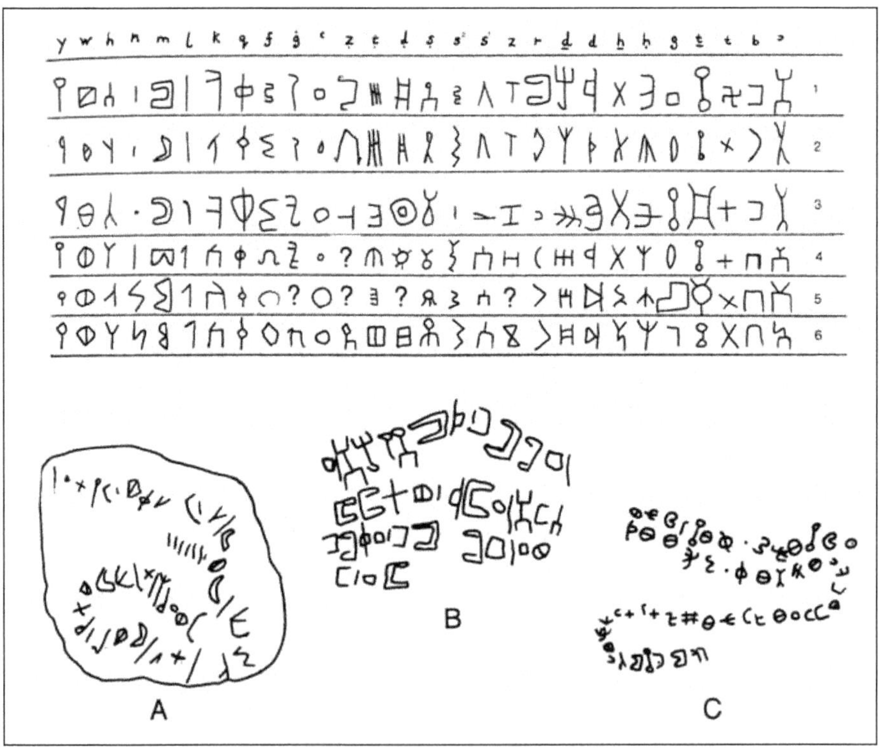

Fig. 3.4: Examples of Thamudic script (after MacDonald 1992: 419).

The Thamudic language – 'Thamudic' – was not a dialect or script, but the name of the group of languages to which all the ancient inscriptions of North-Arabian belonged. However, this was not the language of the oases, the Safaitic or the Hisami, which differed from it. Taymanitic (previously Thamudic A) and Hismaic (previously Thamudic F) were once included within the Thamudic category, until the progress of research distinguished between these languages and scripts (see MacDonald 1992: 418 ff). The previous classes, such as Thamudic B, C and D and South Thamudic, were a preliminary sub-division of the category. Most of the inscriptions are not dateable, and the time range between those that can be dated is wide: an inscription in Thamudic B mentions the King of Babylon (i.e. pre-539 BCE), while another inscription in Thamudic D is dated to 267 CE. Few South Thamudic inscriptions have been published.

THE INSCRIPTION AND ITS CONTEXT

The publication of Thamudic inscriptions from the Negev and the Arabah began in 1952. Zori (1952) published an inscription which was erroneously considered to be Hebrew; Anati (1956) published Thamudic engravings from Mount Karkom, and Nave (1975) published an engraving of identical script from Har (Mount) Sagi. Nave, (1975: 129-131) discussed a significant number of inscriptions, and suggested that they were only first names. There is some resemblance between the letters in the inscriptions from the Negev and Arabah and the tomb inscription, but geographically they belong to different areas.

As far as we know, inscriptions of this type have not been found in Israel west of the River Jordan or north of the Dead Sea, although they are very abundant in the south of Transjordan. In his review of the South-Arabian cultures and texts MacDonald (1992: 418) defines their spread as: "The inscriptions have since been found over a wide area of S. Syria, Jordan, and N. Saudi Arabia, with isolated examples as far afield as Palmyra, Ha'il, Wadi Hauran in W. Iraq, and the Lebanon. However, the largest concentration appears to be in the *harra*, or basalt desert, stretching S and E from the Jebel Druze."

Such an inscription west of the River Jordan is not a complete surprise. It appears to be a tombstone erected over the grave of a merchant or shepherd who died while visiting the place.

Several facts should be noted: a), the geographical location of the inscription; b), the existence of a separate tombstone, while the rest of the inscriptions are rock-engraved; c), the isolated grave, when grave inscriptions are generally part of a cemetery; and d), as far as is known to us, this is the first grave inscription in the area which is not a person's first name.

Nomads were accustomed to bury their dead in central cemeteries. The very burial in this location perhaps indicates the relationship between the inhabitants east and west of the River Jordan: trade, pasture, and perhaps even family relations.

REFERENCES

Anati, E., 1956. "Rock Engravings from Jebel Ibeid (Southern Negev)", *PEQ* 88, 5-13.

Caskel, W., 1966. *Gamharat an-Nasab. Das genealogische Werk des Hisam ibn Muhamad al-Kalbi*, Bd. I, E.J., Leiden.

Littman, E., 1940. *Thamud und Safa*, Leipzig.

MacDonald, M.C.A., 1992. "Inscriptions, Safaitic", *ABD* 3, 418-423.

MacDonald, M.C.A., 2000. "Reflections on the Linguistic Map of Pre-Islamic Arabia", *Arabian Archaeology and Epigraphy* 11, 28-79.

Nave, Y., 1975. "Thamudic Inscriptions from the Negev", *EI* 12, 129-131 (Hebrew).

Repertoire d'épigraphie Semitique, Tome VII, Paris 1938.

Van den Branden, A., 1950. *Les inscriptions thamoudéens*, Louvain-Heverle.

Van den Branden, A., 1960. *Histoire de Thamoud*, Beyrouth.

Zertal, A., 2007. *A Nation Born. The Altar on Mt. Ebal and the Birth of Israel, Tel Aviv* (Hebrew).

Zori, N., 1952. "A Hebrew Inscription from the Arabah", *Bulletin of the Israel Exploration Society* 17, 67-68 (Hebrew).

APPENDIX D

THE IRRIGATION SYSTEMS AND THE AQUEDUCTS IN NAHAL FASAEL AND WADI 'AUJAH (NAHAL YITAV)

Adam Zertal

PREFACE AND HISTORY OF RESEARCH

The irrigation systems and aqueducts of the two streams flowing in the middle Jordan Valley, namely Nahal Fasael (Wadi Rashash) and Nahal Yitav (Wadi 'Aujah), have attracted researchers since the beginning of travels from Europe to the Holy Land in the 19th century. In the introduction to the current volume and elsewhere, travellers and researchers who described both systems have been cited.

This appendix presents these systems, about 30 years after being described by Porath (1985: 29-57). His work was done when the majority of the systems were fairly intact. The system of Nahal Yitav (Wadi 'Aujah) was re-examined during the 1980s by a German expedition from Braunschweig University (Garbrecht and Netzer 1991).

The destruction suffered by the irrigation systems since then, together with the wish to deepen our knowledge, were the motivations for surveying and analyzing them afresh. Both systems were mapped in detail in the winters from 2010 to 2012. On the basis of the topography the two aqueducts and the Fasael reservoir were measured and photographed, and cross-sections of several sites have been produced. In the winter of 2011-2012 the section between Qanat el-Musa (2) up to Wadi Abiyad Bridge (Qanat el-Musa (4)) was surveyed.

The mapping was done by the Survey team. The graphics were sketched by Sapir Haad and Osnat Gadir. The cross-sections and reproductions are also by Osnat Gadir.

Nearly 25 years ago Spanier published an article dealing with the mills in Wadi 'Aujah and Wadi Fasael (Spanier 1993). In Wadi 'Aujah he discovered remains of a northern mill, which we have not found (Spanier 1993: 247). It should be noted that in the book *The Aqueducts of Ancient Palestine* (Amit et al. 1989) these aqueducts are not mentioned, despite the fact that Porath's publication was published several years earlier. General data concerning watermills, their history and mode of operation are found in Avitsur, 1976: 80-86; and 1986: 209-222.

1. THE WATER SYSTEM OF NAHAL FASAEL

This includes the outlet of the aqueducts from the Fasael Springs (Rashash Springs), an array of aqueducts built on the south bank of Nahal Fasael, the Fasael Mill (Tahunath Fusayil), a large water reservoir near Tell esh-Sheikh Diyab (the Fasael Pool), the aqueducts leading to Khirbet Fusaiyl (Fasaelis, Site 34) and its ancient fields.

Almost none of the irrigation systems in the Fasael Valley survive, apart from some of walls around fields and about ten partially preserved *qanats*: their description follows, with Porath's previous description.

The Fasael Springs ('Uyun Rashash) are located in a small valley, where the valley of Nahal Fasael and the confluence of Wadis Rashash and Zananir widens. This has been published as a separate site (Site 12) in the current volume, containing an updated description and a detailed plan.

1.1. Springs and a dam (*see Site 12 and Fig. 4.1*)

Two aqueducts run eastwards from the springs in the valley. The more recent of the two is a concrete aqueduct from Jordanian or British times, after which the aqueducts fell into disuse. In the vicinity are scattered sherds from various periods, but in the absence of permanent settlement it is difficult to date the commencement of activity in the valley.

The modern dam in Nahal Fasael is built of stones and concrete over an ancient foundation. The remains are about 30 m long and 1.5 m wide, with a large breach at its centre, allowing a little flow eastwards. Perpendicular to and west from the dam is another stone wall, perhaps an ancient dam.

There are at least two large flowing springs in the valley, about 110 m below sea level, with a total discharge ranging from 30 to 150 cbm/hour (Spanier 1993: 244). Porath (1985: 29) writes that the average hourly discharge of the springs is 65 cbm/hour and the minimum is 7 cbm/hour. He also could not find the primary collection place ("consolidation" in his words) of the water from the aqueducts. In the eastern part of the valley, only a small section of an ancient stone aqueduct has been located, and the water collection and transportation system to the ancient aqueducts near the springs disappeared during the erection of the concrete duct. For the sake of orientation, the coordinates of the new pump house (Israel old grid 18860/16188), the starting point of the narrow asphalt road to Fasael, were taken (Fig. 4.1).

1.2. The modern aqueduct which conducts the water from the springs ("The concrete aqueduct" – Figs. 4.1-4.5; and see also Site 10)

The date of the construction of the duct is unknown, but it was probably during Jordanian rule in the region (1948-1967). Indirect evidence of this date exists in the concrete Jordanian irrigation ducts south of the Damia Crossing in the northern part of the Nahal Tirzah flood plain. The entire area is crossed by similar ducts which carried water from the river for flood-irrigating the

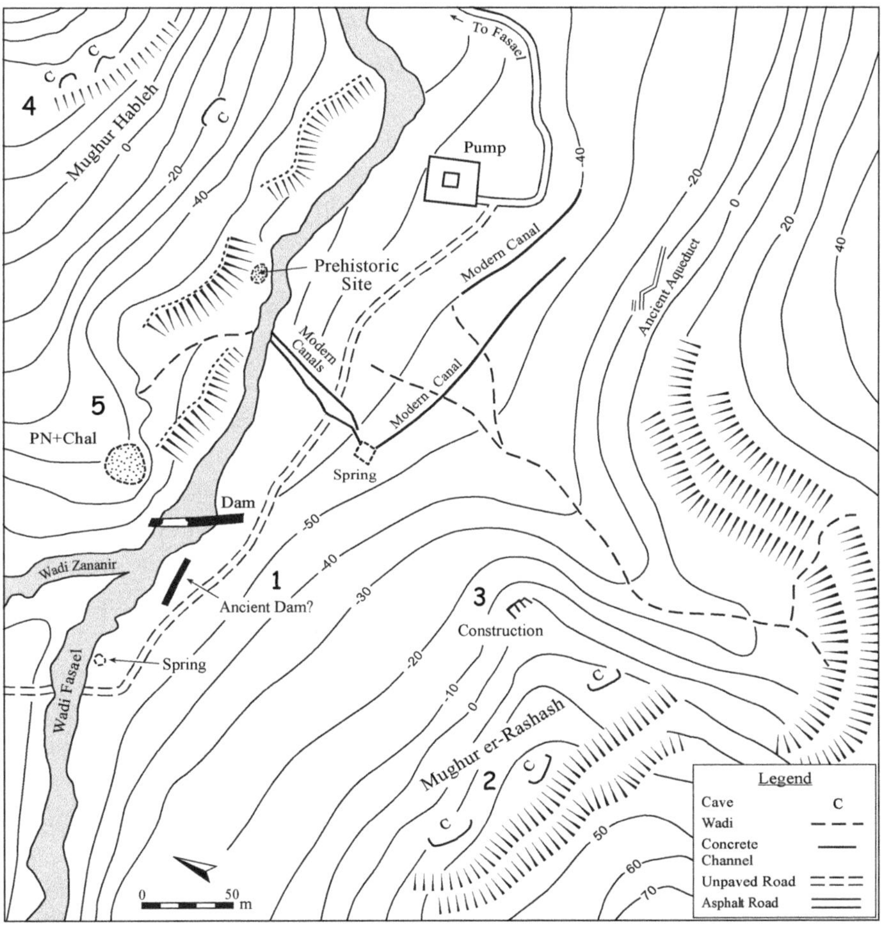

Fig. 4.1: The Fasael Aqueducts – a general plan of Fasael Springs and the inlet of the two aqueducts, the first section from the west.

fields. This aqueduct is a moulded concrete duct 60 cm wide and 40 cm high. The duct walls are of reinforced concrete about 6 cm thick – relatively thin. The aqueduct is marked in Fig. 4.1 from its start close to the springs. From the pump house area (marked I in Fig. 4.2) the duct sets out as two separate ducts across the valley in an east-south-east direction. The modern asphalt road crosses over the northern end of both ducts. The aqueducts were built on the ground in zigzagging sections of 4-6 m, in order to control the flow of the water and thus avoid possible damage to the ducts. Such a design does not exist in ancient aqueducts, perhaps thanks to their much stronger foundations and their relatively greater capacity than those of the concrete conduit (see below).

The concrete aqueducts join in a spot between contours -100 and -110, about 60 m west of the start of the ancient aqueduct, and from there continue as a single duct where it meets the ancient one (Fig. 4.2, marked II, coordinates 18900/161945). From this point the concrete aqueduct runs parallel to the ancient one, enabling checking its route.

Elevations: as the Fasael Springs emerge at an elevation of about -110 m below sea level, and the reservoir near Tell esh-Sheikh Diyab is at about -150 below sea level, the water descends about 40 m along a 2.5 km stretch, an incline of 1.6%. Such an elevation change allows convenient water flow rate.

1.3. The ancient aqueduct (the stone aqueduct – Figs. 4.2 and onwards; Site 10)

There is a general sketch in Porath's report (1985: drawing 5), from which it is difficult to comprehend the course of the aqueduct. This ancient one is constructed as fairly wide stone substructure on the steep slope. The foundation is built of medium-sized stones, and varies in width from 1.5 to 3 m, and bears the conduit on top. At least two adjacent stone aqueducts were built along the entire course, but it is not clear if they functioned simultaneously, and what was the order of their construction.

From the vicinity of the pump house (Fig. 4.2) the two aqueducts (ancient and modern) run parallel for about 100 m along the slope in an east-north-easterly direction. The length of the concrete aqueducts from the pump house to their join is about 260 m, and the total length of the aqueducts illustrated in Fig. 4.2 is about 360 m. From this point we shall follow the course the aqueducts by the maps.

Fig. 4.3: The aqueducts run next to each other, with the modern one is always above the ancient one and resting generally on the stone foundation of the former. The height of the foundation here varies from 1.5 to 2 m, and the duct of the ancient aqueduct is only partially exposed. At coordinates 18906/16196 sections of the modern aqueduct are missing, while the ancient one is almost intact. Both aqueducts are 60-70 m from the south bank of Nahal Fasael and are about 20 m above it.

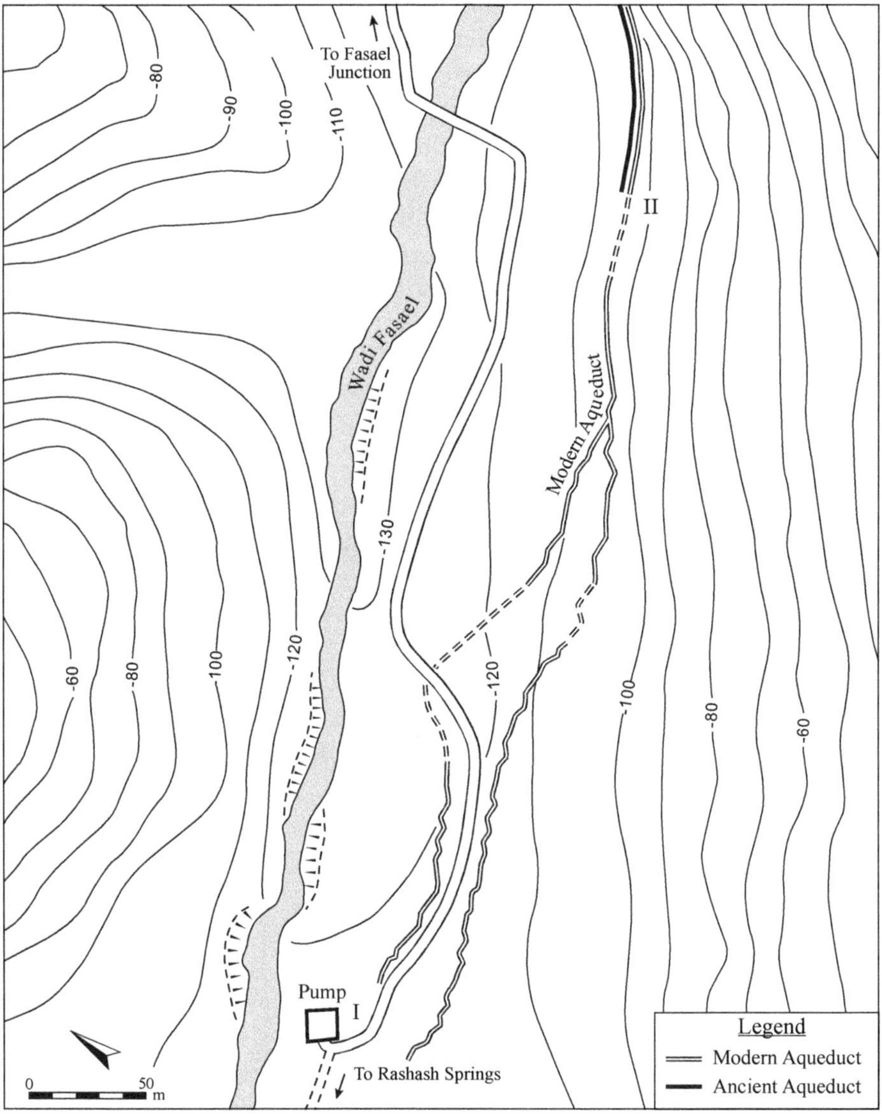

Fig. 4.2: Fasael Aqueducts – the second section from the west.

1.4. Tahunet el-Fusail (Figs. 4.3-4.8; Site 15)

The mill location is at coordinates 18916/16299, which is the start of the mill's feeding duct from the aqueduct, and its upper end is about 30 m south of the south bank of the wadi.

1.4.1. The history of research and the dating: the mill is mentioned in the British Survey (Conder and Kitchener 1882: 392), and Porath (1985: 32) advises that a stone with an unpublished Arabic inscription was found in it. According to him Prof. M. Sharon dated the inscription to the Umayyad period, to the learned caliph Abed al-Malik (685-705), son of Marwan I. If so, it is likely that the mill was built in the 7th-8th centuries. It is interesting that the traveller Burchard of Mount Zion who visited Nahal Fasael in the Crusader period (at the end of the 13th century) does not mention the mill.

According to Porath (1985: 39), a flour mill with a flume of the type studied by him in Wadi Qelt was erected first. The foundation date is not certain,

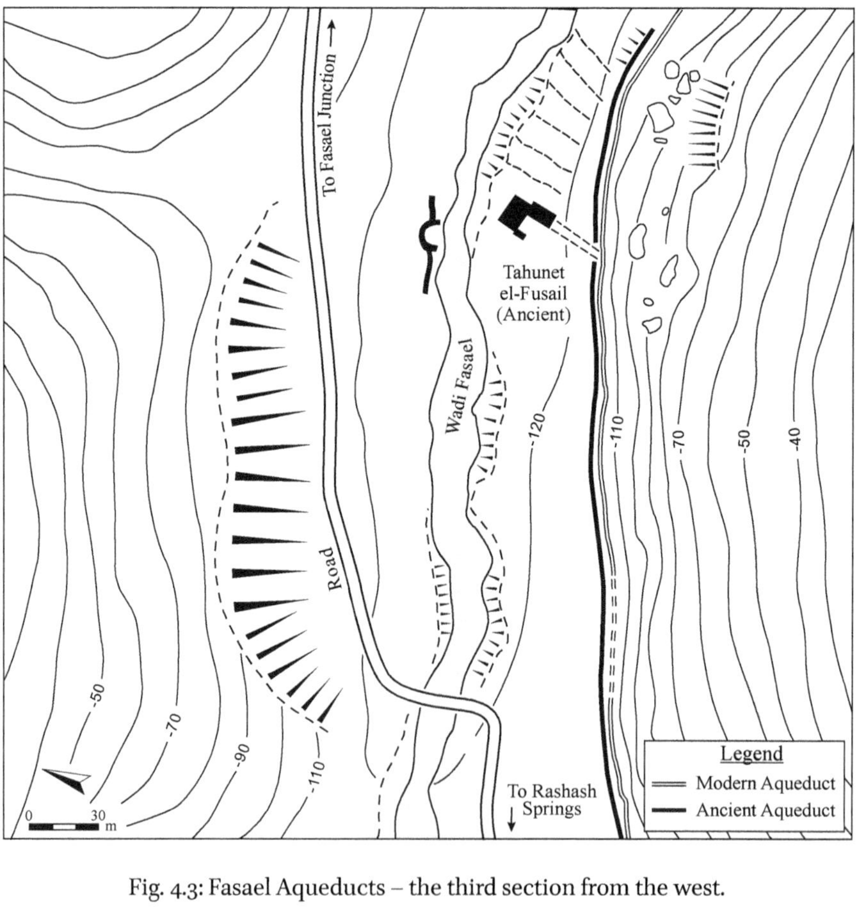

Fig. 4.3: Fasael Aqueducts – the third section from the west.

perhaps during the Umayyad period according to Porath. In the second phase, the date of which is also unknown, a mill with a chute was built for the same purpose.

Porath (1985: 184) also claims that all the flour mills in the Jordan Valley were integrated into Early Moslem era systems. This suggests that Herod, who founded the agricultural network in the Valley, definitely did not apply water power for milling. Porath offers three reasons for this: lack of awareness and need, low discharge of the systems and non-recognition of this innovation. However, it seems that this conclusion deserves reconsideration, and that the dates suggested do not rest on obvious proofs.

1.4.2. Survey in the vicinity of the mill: in April 2010 a sherd collection took place in the mill area:

Ancient (EB/MB/IA)	7
Early Bronze	1
Roman-Byzantine (all stages)	45 (75% of the total)
Medieval	5
Ottoman-Modern	2
Total number of sherds collected	**60**

This means that the original site preceded the Roman period. This information helps in dating the aqueducts. No sherds from the Early Moslem period, during which, as Porath states, the aqueducts and the mill were built, were found, and very few from Medieval times and after. With all reservations from the survey for the sake of precise dating, it is apparent that the establishment and use of the site preceded Umayyad times.

1.4.3. Description of the mill: The primary description is available at Porath (1985: 39-40): "To the mill structure led an aqueduct mounted on a constructed wall along the section before the mill. The mill was integrated with the aqueduct without a bypass duct. In the section leading to the mill the duct narrowed (30 cm), and before the wall an opening was installed to divert the flow during maintenance. In the section of the aqueduct near the mill the duct was renovated by applying fresh plaster over the original one. During the renovation the opening was blocked with stones and the fresh plaster covered the blockage. Close to the mill a stone-link built section of duct was exposed, the connection of which to the mill was destroyed ...hence, it is impossible to determine its phase and period. Two stages were found in the mill structure: of the first one the lower part of a square structure (2.8×1.7 m) with a wall 1.2 m high survived. The walls and floor were covered with plaster identical to that of the duct. In the second phase a chute mill was built, of which only the bottom

part of the chute and the paddlewheel house remain, built in a vault which was built within a structure of the first phase. In the mill floor above the vault a fieldstone circle was exposed, which held the lower grindstone. The lower stone diameter was 1.8 m, and the waterfall height was 4.3 m.
No elements of the ancient structure survived to indicate its function ...but its location hints that this was a flourmill..." (translated from Hebrew).

Only partial data can be drawn from the sketches enclosed by Porath. In our fresh survey the mill was measured and sketched in a perspective south-westerly view. In the discussion below we rely on the fresh material, with the phases noted earlier.

1.4.4. The structure and plan of the mill (Figs. 4.4-4.8): The mill is built on a rather steep slope. The chute rests on the slope and the halls are built on an artificial level surface on the southern bank of the wadi (Fig. 4.5). The building contains two halls, a chute and an aqueduct.

The building and halls (plan – Fig. 4.4, views and cross-sections – Figs. 4.6-4.8): the length of the lower structure is 11.5 m and its original width is 5.4 m; the walls are about 80 cm thick, built of medium-sized cut stones, plastered outside with thick mortar. From the outer, northern, wall of the structure three pilasters, each 1 m wide, protrude about 40 cm from the surface of the structure. Two pilasters or bulges are also attached to the eastern wall. There is a repair stage on the south wall and an additional reinforcing pilaster in the south-western corner. Constructed repair stages are present also at the bottoms of the pilasters.

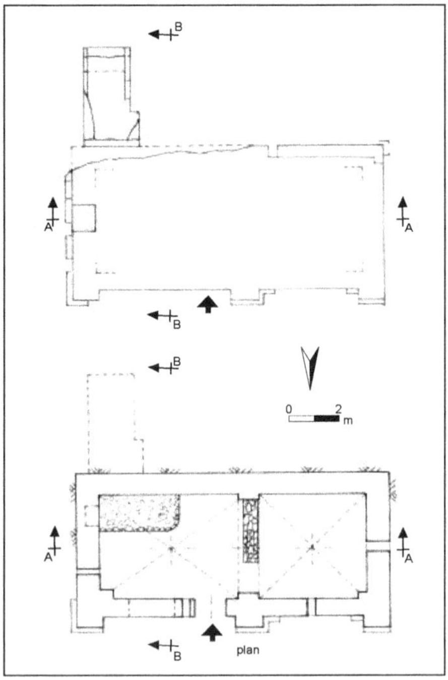

Fig. 4.4: Fusail watermill – plan.

The structure has two entrances, one of which is blocked. Both are in the northern part of the eastern hall and are vault roofed: The vault of the blocked entrance is pointed and that of the open one is rounded. The eastern, blocked, entrance is 1.5 m wide and 2 m high; the functioning, western entrance is 1.1 m wide and 2.2 m high (Figs. 4.5, 4.6).

The structure has two halls; a) the eastern one, where the millstones were installed, measuring 5×4.2 m, fed by water via the chute pipe; and b) the western hall, measuring 4.5×4 m. Both halls have vaulted roofs (Fig. 4.8), with ceilings 3.5 m high, and were illuminated through small openings in the northern and western walls. The passage between the two halls is also vaulted.

In the south-eastern corner of the eastern hall is a low stone dais (about 30 cm high), apparently for supporting the millstones: above this is a stone structure which received the water flow from the chute.

The function of the chute structure, erected over the steep slope, was to divert the water by a duct from the high stone aqueduct bringing it to the mill. The chute structure, built of medium-sized cut stones, was originally 3.8 m long and averaged 1.2 m wide; at its northern part it widens a little. The original height of the chute structure was 6.6 m from the roof of the lower structure

Fig. 4.5: Fusail watermill – south-westerly view.

Fig. 4.5A: Fusail watermill, south-westerly view (S. Bar).

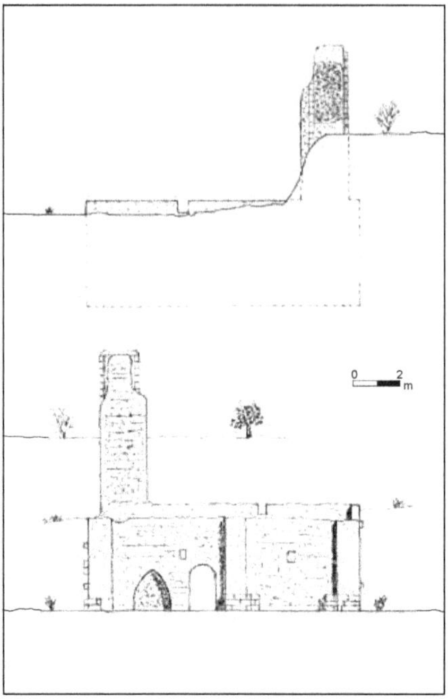

Fig. 4.6: Fusail watermill – views north (top) and south (bottom).

up to the level of the aqueduct. The chute structure is now completely detached from the slope and the aqueducts, and stands as a separate tower. In its lower part the chute structure is joined to the eastern hall of the mill. At the time of our survey there was no trace of the connections from the aqueducts mentioned by Porath.

The remains of an ancient stone structure were found on the north bank of Nahal Fasael, the width of which is about 15 m. This stone enclosure (Fig. 4.3) is a circle about 6 m in diameter built of large stones, with two walls projecting west and east. The date is unknown, but it is probable that it was linked to the ancient site in the vicinity of the mill.

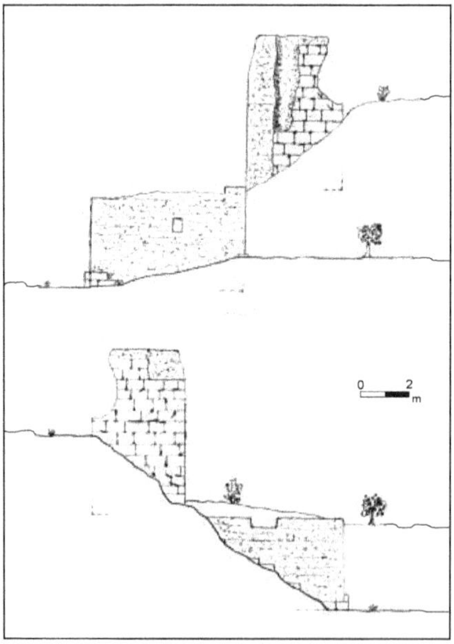

Fig. 4.7: Fusail watermill – views east (top) and west (bottom).

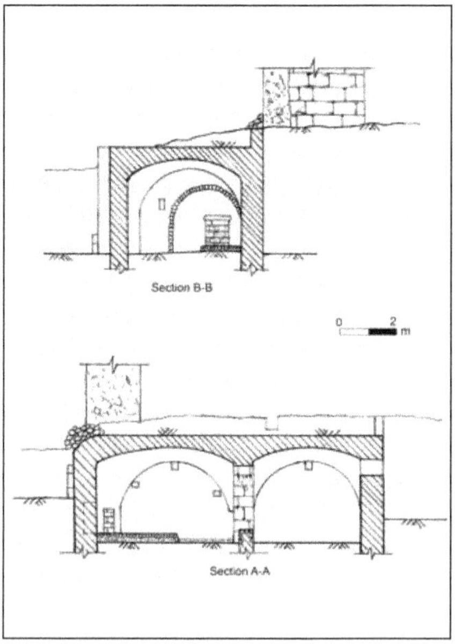

Fig. 4.8: Fusail watermill – cross-sections (for their locations see Fig. 4.4).

1.5. The aqueducts from Tahunet Fusail eastwards (Figs. 4.9-4.11)

From Tahunet Fusail the two aqueducts run in an easterly direction to Tell esh-Sheikh Diyab. From their outlet from the mill they pass below a big rockslide (coordinates 18931/16199), and extend over an earthen step, above steep earth cliffs, descending northward to the wadi. At coordinates 169251/16200 the

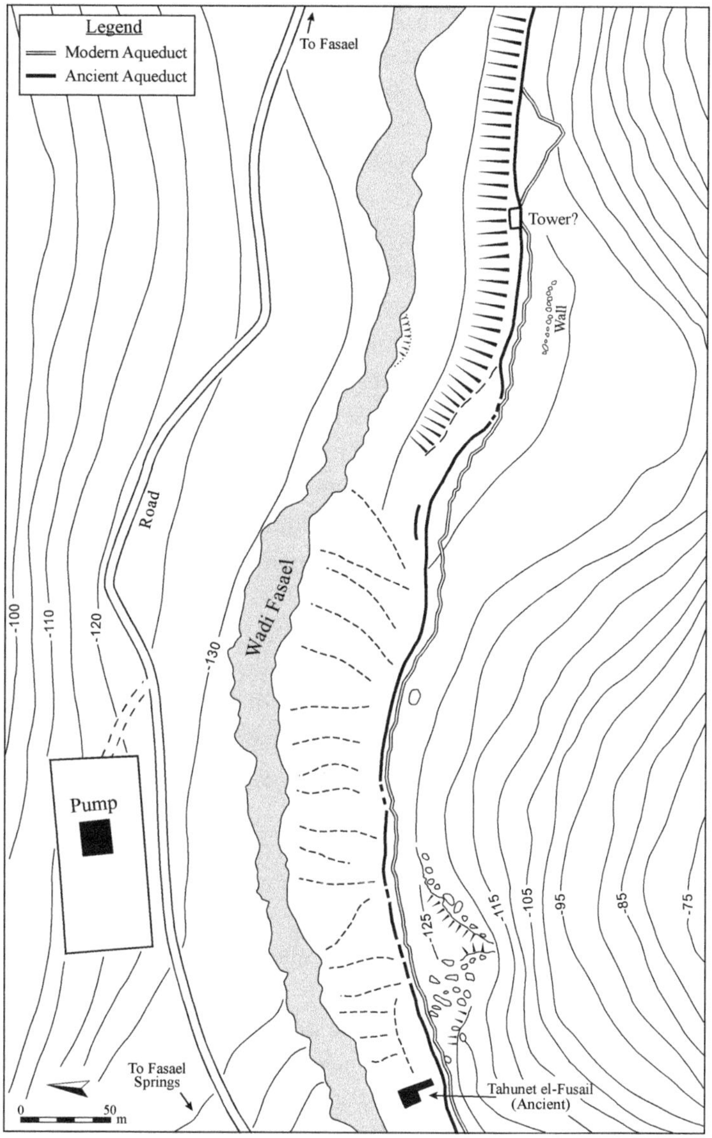

Fig. 4.9: Fasael Aqueduct – the fourth section from the west (from Fusail watermill eastward).

ancient aqueduct reappears after a gap, and then disappears again at coordinates 189400/16195. About 360 m east of the mill (coordinates 18941/16191) the ancient double aqueduct appears. Both aqueducts, the double ancient one and the modern one, pass into small valley between the southern ridges above the wadi. The route of the aqueducts crosses the low part of the valley at this point, maintaining its contour. The modern aqueduct is routed above the ancient one, maintaining a distance of 2–5 m from it. Remains of another stone aqueduct, 4 m from the former and 1 m below it, were found in the western part of the valley. The ancient aqueduct has been completely preserved in almost all places, apart from two short sections.

A little further east from the additional aqueduct, the route of the aqueducts continues over a fairly steep stone cliff (Fig. 4.10). In this area there is a wall of especially large boulders, built above the aqueducts about 15 m south of them. It seems that the wall was intended to protect the aqueducts from floods and erosion which are common almost every winter in the area.

Further along the route of the aqueducts, at coordinates 18963/16182, is a stone built, bridge-like wall, 6.5 m long, 2.3 m wide and 2 m high, apparently meant to carry the aqueduct, remains of which were found on it. The function of the bridge is unclear, in the absence of an obvious need to elevate the aqueduct, an issue requiring additional investigation.

The new concrete aqueduct reaches and touches the so-called bridge and from there it turns rather sharply eastward and then back north. The reason for the turn is not clear. The length of the aqueducts from Tahunet Fusail to the eastern end of Fig. 4.10 is 652 m.

Just where the concrete aqueduct rejoins the ancient one, the ancient aqueduct reaches a cliff. In this section it is well preserved, with the original double aqueduct visible in some places and only one of the aqueducts in others. The ancient aqueducts join at this point (coordinates 19013/16177). The height of the wall is 1.7 m, and the upper plastered duct is 0.4 m wide, and the lower one, which is also plastered, is 0.33 m wide.

All along the section appearing in the map, about 500 m and more, the two aqueducts – ancient and modern – are almost on the same line, while the concrete duct is always above the other. At coordinates 19015/16175 a concrete pool, measuring 3×2 m, is built on the course of the modern aqueduct, and extends eastward.

Further along the route south of the aqueducts is a medium-sized cave in the cliff, and then the aqueduct passes through a large tunnel in the rock (coordinates 19026/16173), like a rock shelter open at both ends. The tunnel is made of two caves linked together. Their combined total length is about 15 m and their ceiling, about 2 m high, is charred – evidence of residence or shelter. The ancient aqueduct is supported here, east and west by built foundations.

The narrow asphalt road to Fasael Springs is routed along and north of the aqueducts, its average distance from them varying from 30 to 40 m. 100 m to the east the cliffs are closer to the road, forming a relatively narrow space through which the aqueducts cling to the cliff.

Fig. 4.11 is the fifth in the sequence, illustrating the route of the aqueducts from west to east to the Fusail reservoir. Both the ancient and modern aqueducts reach a narrow passage, from where the small valley of Sheikh Diyab

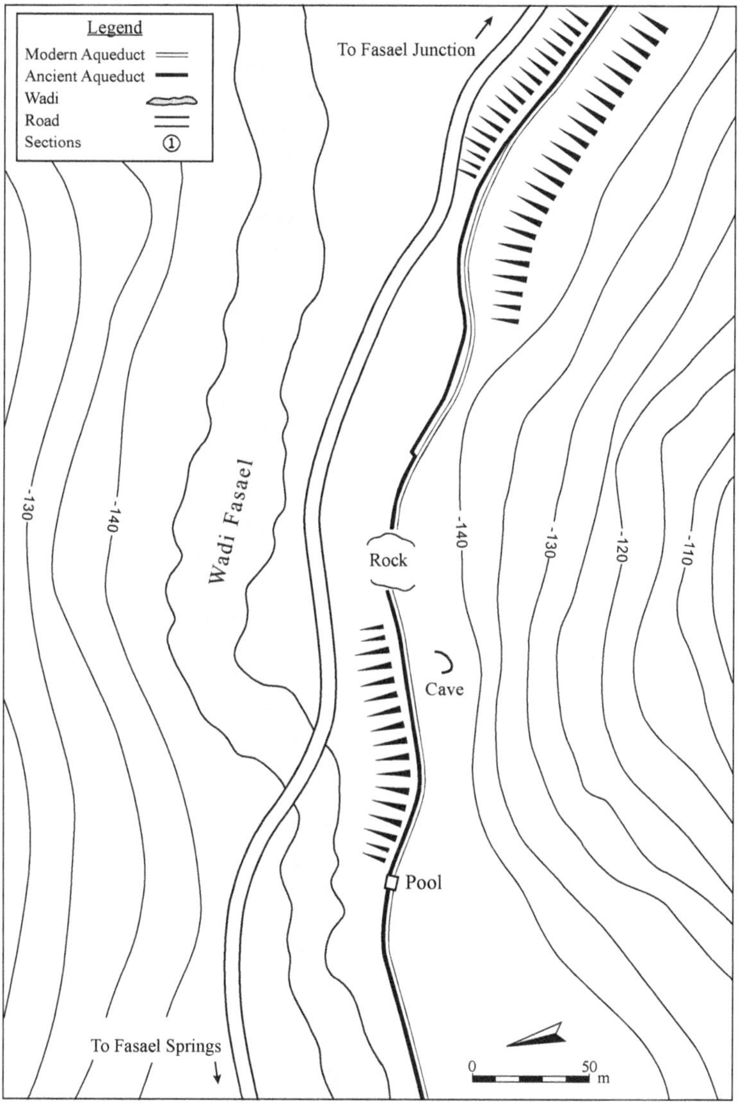

Fig. 4.10: Fasael Aqueduct – the fifth section from the west (at the centre is the narrow canyon of Nahal Fasael).

expands, and turn south-south-east. Here they pass at the foot and north-east of the spur on which is the site of Tell esh-Sheikh Diyab (2). At coordinates 19048/16163 the ancient aqueducts merge, with a common wall between them. Here the built wall carrying the ancient aqueducts is about 1 m high.

The location of the cross-section in Fig. 4.12 is at coordinates 19052/16159, below the site of Tell esh-Sheikh Diyab (2) – Site 21. Below are the details from top to bottom:

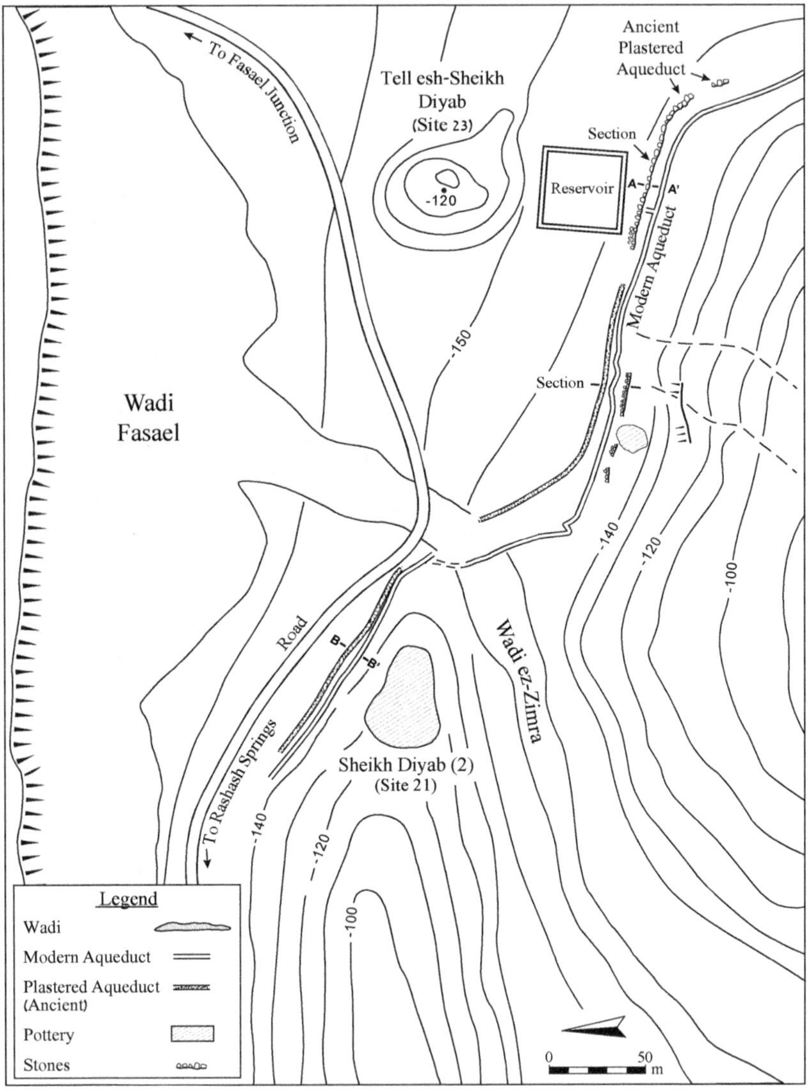

Fig. 4.11: Fasael Aqueduct – the sixth section from the west (the access to Nahal Fasael floodplain).

A. Plan. The supporting wall is about 1 m high. Both ancient aqueducts appear: the lower aqueduct below, above is the support wall of the upper aqueduct. Further to the left is the concrete aqueduct.
B. A cross-section of both aqueducts. The upper one (the concrete one) is about 3 m further to the south of the ancient aqueduct, and runs more or less over the same contour. It is about 50 cm wide, and built over a low stone foundation. The two ancient aqueducts are joined, and are built to the same design: upper and lower support walls with a duct with a plastered bottom and sides.
C. View of the ancient aqueduct from above.

Continuation of description of Fig. 4.11: The ancient and modern (concrete) aqueducts separate at coordinates 19052/16159, at the meeting point of the aqueducts and the roadway with Wadi ez-Zimrah. The concrete one turns

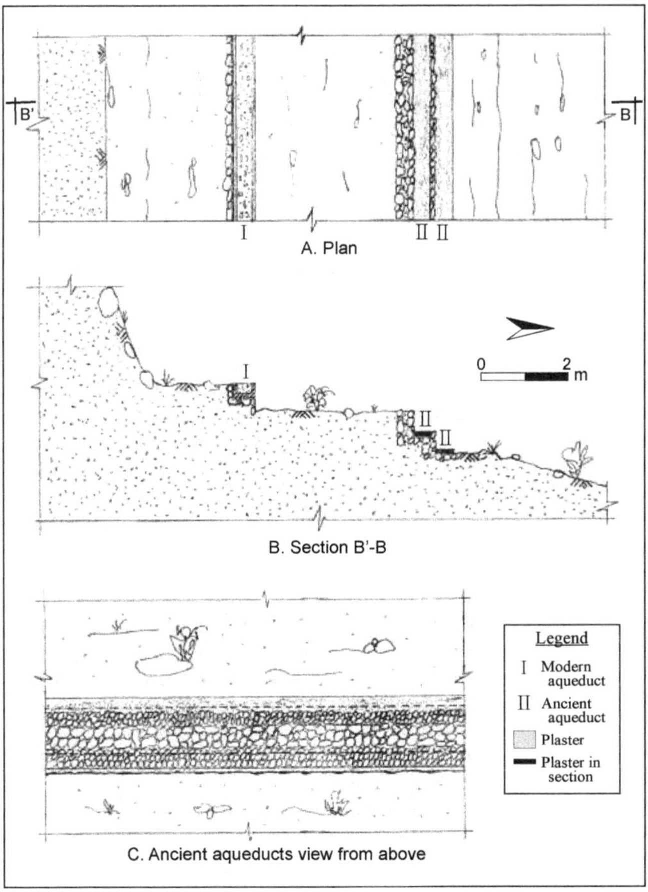

Fig. 4.12: cross-section BB (see location in Fig. 4.11).

south and crosses the valley almost in a straight line towards the ridge (zigzagging sharply about halfway). The ancient aqueduct crosses the valley slightly further down. At coordinates 19055/16148 it passes below a small site – remains of a structure and an Early Bronze I sherd accumulation over the slope. This structure is apparently connected to Tell esh-Sheikh Diyab (2). A wall of boulders was located here, belonging to an upper unpreserved aqueduct, and apparently also to protect the aqueducts from floods.

Near the large reservoir (see below), all four ancient aqueducts mentioned by Porath are visible. From the modern aqueduct there is a constructed outlet to enable filling the reservoir (coordinates 19073/16139). This is also the location of cross-section AA (Fig. 4. 13).

Description of Fig. 4:13: at the top is a plan of both aqueducts and the ancient one has two support walls, upper and lower. The inside of the duct

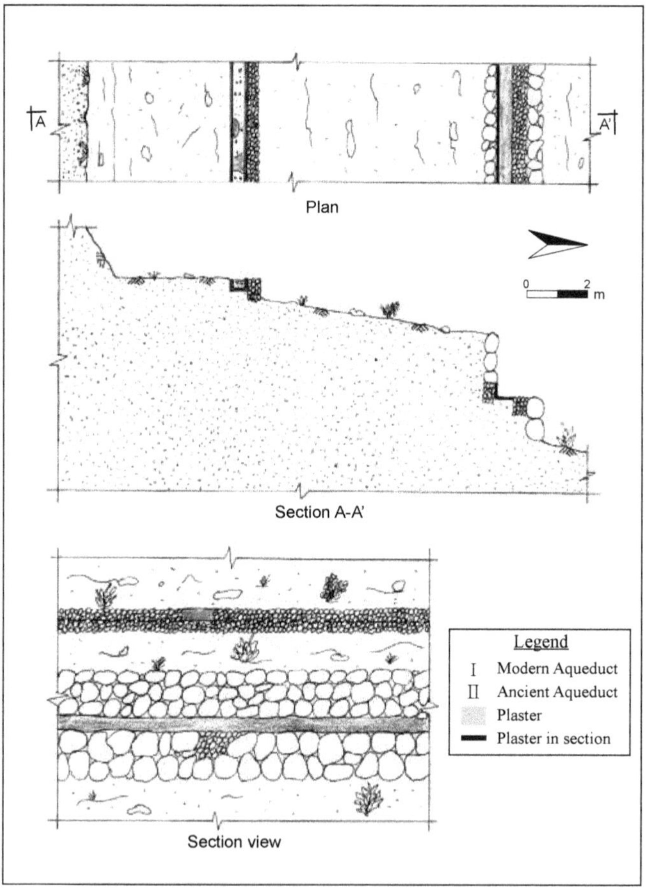

Fig. 4.13: cross-section AA (see location in Fig. 4.11), top – plan; centre – cross-section; bottom – upper view south of the ancient aqueducts.

itself is about 50 cm wide and plastered. In the centre of the illustration is a cross-section through both aqueducts, resting on relatively tall walls; their function is to adjust the level of the aqueduct to control the flow of water from the outlet at the springs. The two stages of the ancient aqueduct (at right) are seen in the drawing. The bottom drawing presents a southward look at the two support walls, lower and upper, of the ancient aqueduct, and between them is the course of the plastered duct. Also visible is a repair of small stones. The concrete aqueduct passes 7.5 m above the upper support wall, based on a foundation of small stones.

1.6. The reservoir near Tell esh-Sheikh Diyab ('The Fusail Reservoir', 'The Samsam Reservoir'; Figs. 4.14-4.16)

1.6.1. General: The reservoir is described in some of the sources (see the general introduction for this volume and the preface for this Appendix), with data about its dimensions, and assumptions regarding the dating. During our work at the site it was freshly measured, thoroughly investigated, and the walls have been drawn, including the existing plastering phases. The excavations in Tell esh-Sheikh Diyab (Site 23) provided data concerning likely dating of the reservoir.

The reservoir is almost square and the measurements are (Fig. 4.14): Inside – south, north and west sides: 37.5 m each; east side 36.25 m. Outside – south side and north side: 43.75 m each, west side 41.75 m, east side 42 m. The average thickness of the outside wall of the reservoir is 2.5 m. In places where its construction has been exposed (Fig. 4.14, east wall) a line of large stones is seen on the eastern side (the outside) and the western one (inside) alike, with a smaller stone filling in the middle.

In a perspective view to the north-west (Fig. 4.15) are seen the various layers of the wall coatings: a core of large stones with layers of plaster over them. At the bottom of the western side, 7.5 m north of the south-western corner, is the lower part of a staircase which descends into the reservoir. The staircase extends about 1.2 m from the wall. Between the staircase and the south-west corner on the floor there are remains of a small plastered pool. Along the walls of the reservoir there are collapses of building materials which slid down into it. The largest of the collapses is next to the north-west corner, while other ones are scattered along the walls.

The reservoir walls from the inside (Fig. 4.16):

The average depth of the reservoir is 5 m. Originally it was deeper. On the floor there is a layer of silt of unknown depth. The water capacity, based on 5 m depth, is about 6,800 cbm. According to Porath, who based it on 7.5 m depth, the full capacity was 10,550 cu. m (not 15,000 cu. m as published by him).

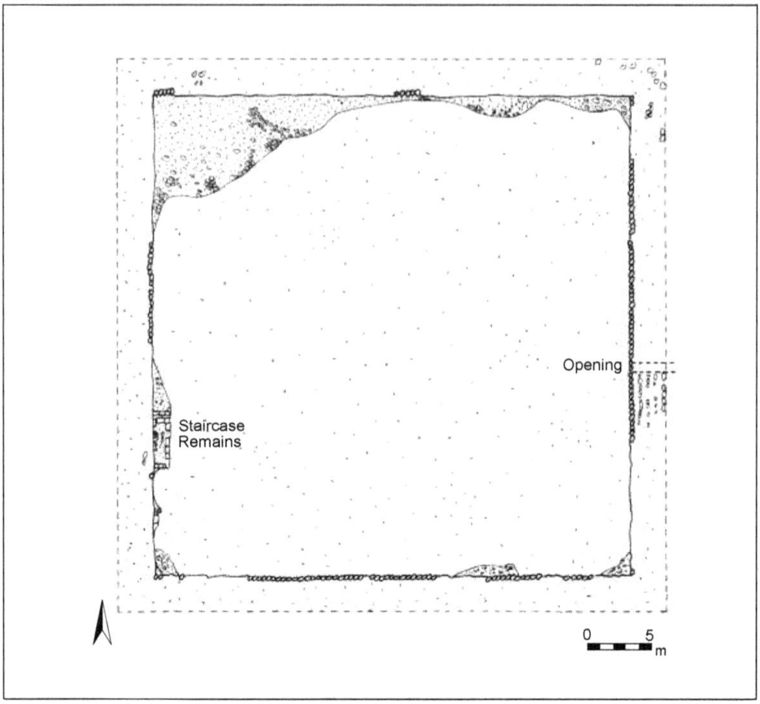

Fig. 4.14: Fasael reservoir – plan (for location see Fig. 4.11).

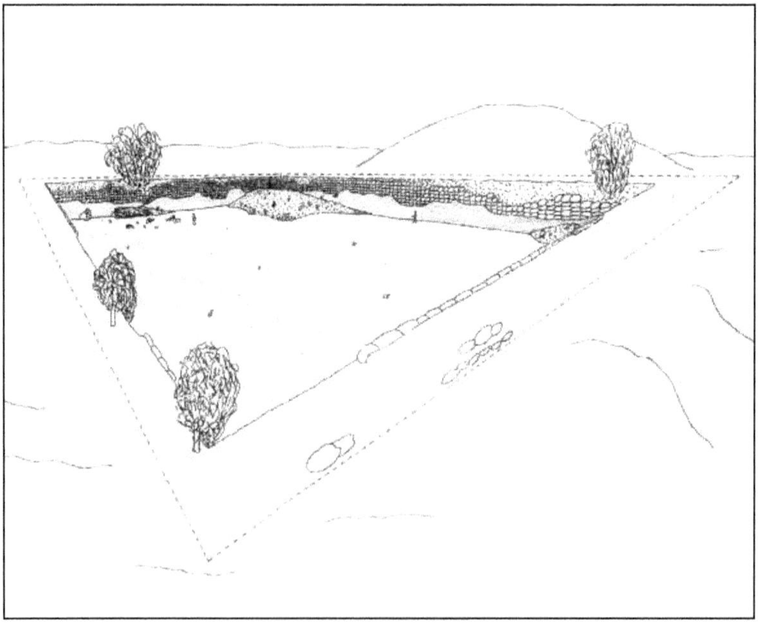

Fig. 4.15: Fasael reservoir – perspective view to north-west.

Fig. 4.15A: Fasael reservoir – view north. At top above it, is Tell esh-Sheikh Diyab (S. Bar).

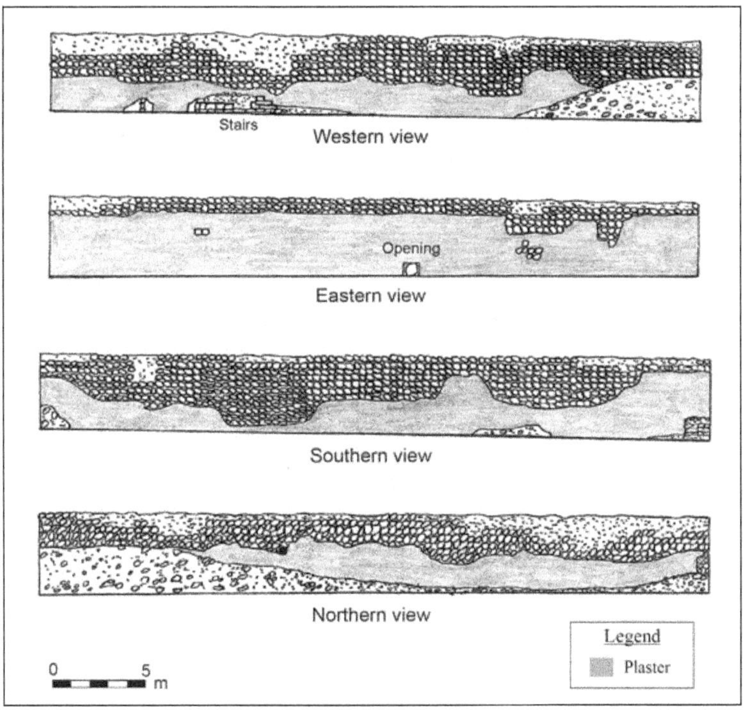

Fig. 4.16: Fasael reservoir – The walls from the inside, from top to bottom: views west, east, south and north.

Explanation of Fig. 4.16: on the West side are the remains of a staircase with the small pool next to and south of it, and the large collapse heap by the right end. The reservoir wall includes a core of large stones, measuring 40×40 cm, slightly cut for the sake of fitting and laid in well-arranged courses. Over the core of large stones there are at least two layers of plaster.

East side. Over the eastern wall the plaster has been preserved relatively intact. The only small exit, about 80×80 cm, is not in the centre of the wall, but about 27.5 m south of the north corner, and 16.2 m north of the southern one. The plaster over the Southern and Northern walls is in various stages of deterioration and detaching.

1.6.2. The reservoir date and location: the dates and construction phases have not been investigated, and therefore are unknown. Researchers' proposals, determining the date as "Roman Herodian", "Early Moslem" and likewise, are not founded on fact. The dating requires excavations and approach to the walls, not yet carried out, although indirect considerations could assist in this matter.

The reservoir is well set between the foot of the southern spur on which the aqueducts are located and Tell esh-Sheikh Diyab (Fig. 4.11). This setting is not random. Secondly, the excavation in the tell indicates its date. A date for the construction of the reservoir can be indirectly hypothesized from the above information.

Tell esh-Sheikh Diyab was founded as a pyramid-like foundation (podium) during Iron Age II, at the end of the 8th century BCE or a little earlier. The earth pyramid was undoubtedly designed to bear a robust structure, perhaps a fortress, to guard the waters of Fasael Springs. Only foundations survive from the structure, and any superstructure was dismantled at an unknown time.

The pyramid was built with surrounding stone walls, laid across and around the structure. Layers of earth were deposited over them, narrowing from bottom to top, thus forming the unique structure. A southern cross-section of the tell to examine its foundations and date the reservoir was partly excavated. In the foundations of the 'pyramid'-podium Iron Age II pottery was found, with no later period sherds (Roman or Moslem).

The topographical connection between the tell and the reservoir brings to mind the possibility that they were constructed as a single project in the Iron Age. Otherwise the reservoir would have been included artificially within the tell. The order of construction from south to north, which includes in sequence: aqueduct, reservoir, tell and Nahal Fasael, without gaps between them, is self-explanatory (Fig. 4.11). Iron Age II reservoirs or pools and other water projects are well known, and one cannot reject the assumption – until a thorough study is done – that the basic subject system is from the Iron Age, the days of the kingdom of Israel.

Fig. 4.16A: Fasael reservoir – inside view of the west wall. The staircase is to the left of the human figure at the left (S. Bar).

Fig. 4.16B: Fasael reservoir – inside view at the staircase in the west wall (S. Bar).

1.6.3. Porath's opinion about the reservoir and its date: Porath (1985: 24-25) examined the reservoir during the early 1970s, describing it as follows:

"A reservoir and operational pool in which were accumulated surpluses of water seasonal or daily and night time flow, peak water flows, rain, etc. measuring 46.5 by 45 m and about 7.5 m deep...built in a recess, maybe a secondary channel of Nahal Fasael, between Tell esh-Sheikh Diyab in the north and the foot of the mountain in the south. The recess was deepened and the soil was used for a rampart for the diversion of the floods into the river channel. The walls are coated on the inside by three layers: A. stone construction coated with a thick layer of clay of formula 2. The clay surface was incised in a fishbone pattern in order to create a good bond with the layer over it. B. A layer of thin stone slabs was stuck to the one beneath with clay of formula 2. Many sherds are embedded among the stones. The stones and sherds were laid with their surfaces facing the wall. C. Plaster of type...about 7 cm thick also coats the reservoir floor. The total thickness of the reservoir walls is more than 2 m. There is a 15 cm diameter hole at the bottom and centre of the eastern wall through which the water drained... the hole was blocked by a wooden peg or stone wrapped with cloth...The water reached through the south-western side...the connecting duct did not survive, but there was a thick accumulation of travertine on the reservoir wall ... The staircase erected in the south-western corner allowed entry to the reservoir for cleaning and maintenance. The stairs were completed together with the reservoir and the plaster coating them. The top part of the staircase rests on two arches, which collapsed, leaving only the pillar between them; the bottom of which was built of solid stone... The capacity of the reservoir was about 15,000 cu. m, equivalent to the average discharge of the spring over 230 hours. The quality of construction and the type of plaster testify that the construction of the reservoir was part of a major development project during which duct C and the distribution system in the eastern part were built ..." (translated from Hebrew).

1.7. The aqueducts from Fusail to the Fasael plain and Phasaelis (Fig. 4.17)

The third section of the aqueducts started at the reservoir and irrigated the plain of Fasael Valley and supplied water to the city of Phasaelis. The course of the aqueducts was east-south-east down to the reservoir, and close to the bulge of the rocky slope both aqueducts – ancient and modern – turn to the south-east. The plain here descends very gently eastward. The aqueducts were routed in an almost straight line along a stretch of about 1125 m to the centre of the ancient city of Phasaelis (Fig. 4.17). In this section two new concrete aqueducts were recorded, and at least two ancient ones, whose state of preservation varies. The construction of two adjacent ancient aqueducts enabled diversion of the water from one to the other in case of repair or maintenance, and to regulate the flow in times of reduced summer flow or winter overflow.

Both the ancient and modern aqueducts turn north-west near the spur of el-Hisha (Site 26, coordinates 1909/1613) and a small duct (coordinates 190852/161327) convey water to Site 26. The two aqueducts follow the foot of

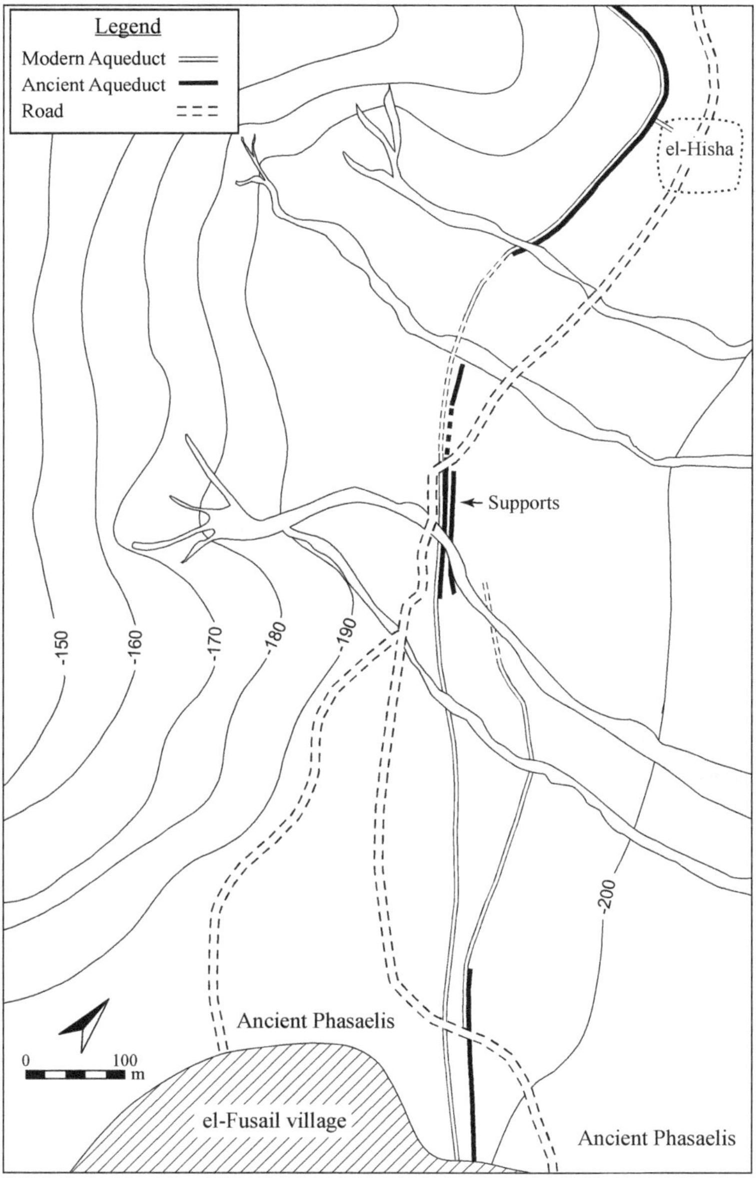

Fig. 4.17: The western section of the aqueducts from Fasael reservoir to the city of Phasaelis.

the ridge on the east. At coordinates 190794/161327 both aqueducts reach the riverbed descending from the west. After crossing several shallow wadis the concrete aqueduct splits into two branches. Here the two ancient aqueducts, one of which has been dug out, are clearly visible, 2–3 m apart. The ancient brick-built aqueduct, 0.8 m wide and about 0.3 m deep, is also exposed, including the layers of plaster inside. The multiple layers show the length of use of the aqueduct. Here the ancient aqueduct is elevated on an earth platform in order to control the water flow. Further on the two concrete aqueducts approach each other, and the ancient aqueduct reappears, continuing into the city of Phasaelis, where it was discovered by the public building (Site 34).

For the purpose of dating a designated survey and sherd gathering was conducted in a 1000 m^2 sample area in the plain, east and west of the place where the two ancient aqueducts are linked. The results are:

Ancient unidentified sherds (Bronze Age?)	9
Iron Age I (including cooking pots)	29
Iron Age II	35
Roman-Byzantine	80
Early Moslem and Medieval	10
unidentified	22
Total number of sherds gathered	**185**

From Iron Age material collected, it appears that there was already activity in the plain at that period. The source of the ceramics was not in Tell esh-Sheikh Diyab, which is not in the same location, and one can assume that the area was cultivated in this period, and may have been irrigated by means of aqueducts. In the meantime this conclusion remains only an assumption.

1.8. The aqueduct east of Phasaelis (Fig. 4.18)

The last measured section of the Fasael aqueducts is in a cultivated field, east of the modern village of Khirbet Fusayil and the Roman city of Phasaelis (Site 34). This section borders in the east both the asphalt road, marking the boundaries of the modern village, and the enclosure wall, perhaps marking the boundaries of the city at some past period (Early Moslem? - Fig. 4.18). The wall, built of medium-sized stones, is about 1.2 m thick, and stands on a rampart slightly elevated above the plain. North of it is a large area of archaeological plunder (checked in April 2011), the activities of which intruded into the Roman period structures. The robber digs exposed many

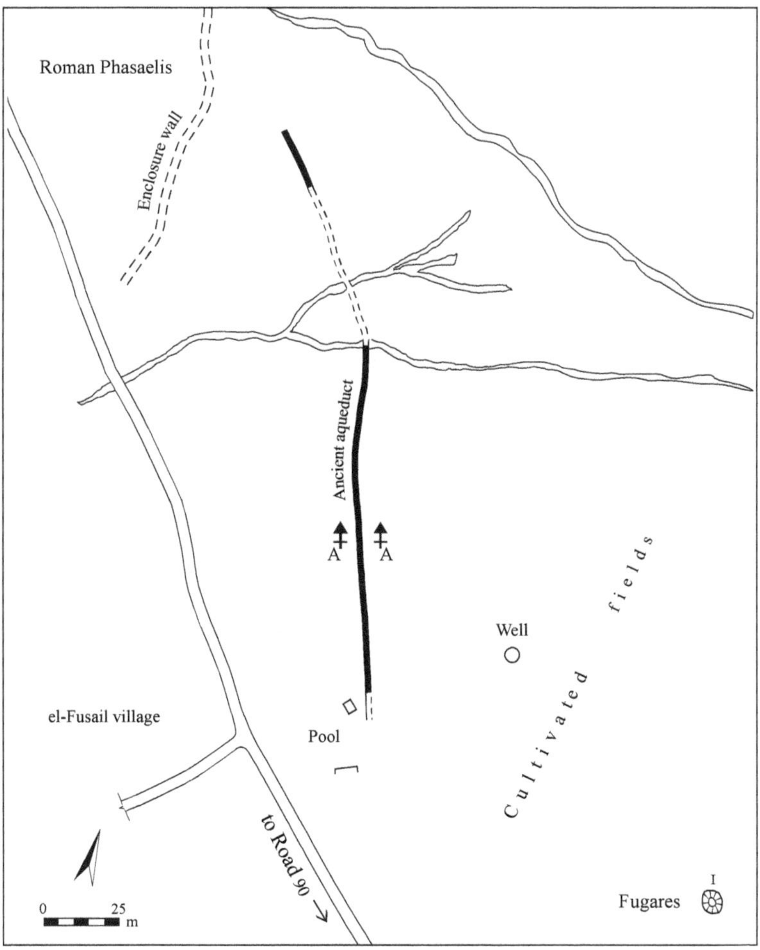

Fig. 4.18: The aqueduct east of Phasaelis.

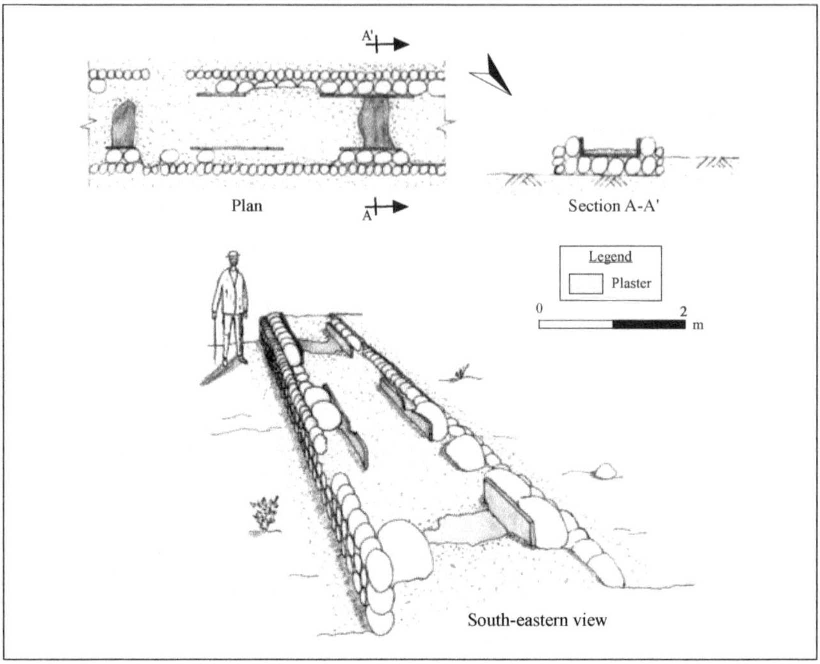

Fig. 4.19: Phasaelis – the eastern aqueduct (for the location of cross-section AA see Fig. 4.18): top – plan; centre – cross-section; bottom – perspective view south-east.

Fig. 4.19A: Phasaelis – eastern aqueduct (S. Bar).

structures with an abundance of ceramics, stone artifacts, etc. The many Herodian lamps together with *terra sigillata* artifacts, date the activity in the vicinity to the Herodian city (1st century BCE–1st century CE).

There are three distinct features in this area:

1.8.1. The eastern aqueduct: the length appearing on the maps is about 200 m, generally orientated from north to south. The aqueduct, mainly the southern section, where it includes a well-built foundation wall, is well preserved. Its overall thickness is about 1.5 m, and the duct, which is built of small stones cemented by calciferous plaster, is above it (Fig. 4.19). The duct is about 70 cm wide in the centre, and its walls rise about 30 cm above the floor, with several layers of plaster, indicating a long period of use. The aqueduct starts in the north at coordinates 1902/15981, where it is intact. At coordinates 19214/15963 it crosses two riverbeds and parts of it are covered currently by silt. At coordinates 19215/15997, where preservation is good, a cross-section and a perspective view (Fig. 4.19) have been drawn. In the south it terminates in a pool or a square structure, measuring about 8×8 m (coordinates 19215/15942). The link between the aqueduct and the pool is fairly clear, although the aqueduct does not reach the pool directly. South of the pool there are remains of another structure, and north of it is a small structure, which is not orientated with the large structure.

1.8.2. A constructed well (Fig. 4.20: for the location see Fig. 4.18): at coordinates 19224/15945, within the presently cultivated field, is a constructed circular well, about 4 m in diameter and about 4 m deep at present. The well's surrounding wall is built of small worked stones; the date of construction is unknown. The well is full of rubbish and the original depth is unknown; apparently the diggers reached a high level water table.

1.8.3. A plastered cistern by the aqueduct (Fig. 4.21): a square plastered cistern which was apparently connected to the eastern aqueduct was found nearby. It is about 2×2 m, and about 1 m deep. It is built of worked stones plastered with calciferous mortar, the function of which is unknown.

1.8.4. Qanats (chain wells - Fig. 4.22): a line of 20 *qanats*, orientated from west to east, was found to begin at coordinates 192275/159358 in the west. The *qanats* are circular pits – blocked nowadays, dug in the plain, and the diameter of the earth circle around them is 6–7 m. The row of *qanats* crosses the modern Beit Shean–Jericho road and continues with additional six more *qanats* east of the road; the last one in the line in the east at coordinates 19272/15921. Regarding the *qanats* see paragraph 1.11 (below) – Porath's description.

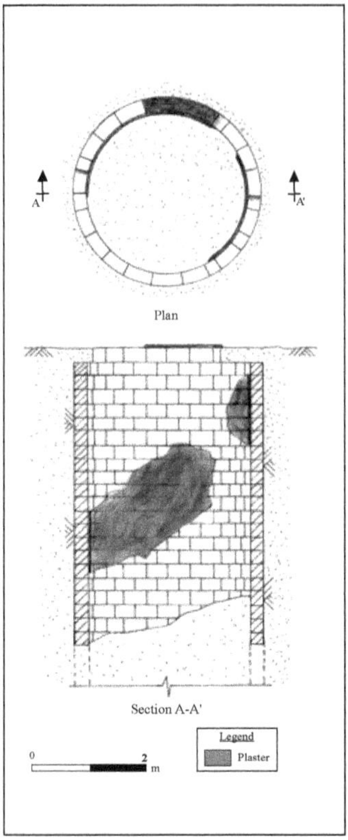

Fig. 4.20: Phasaelis east, a built water well. At top is a plan, at bottom is a cross-section.

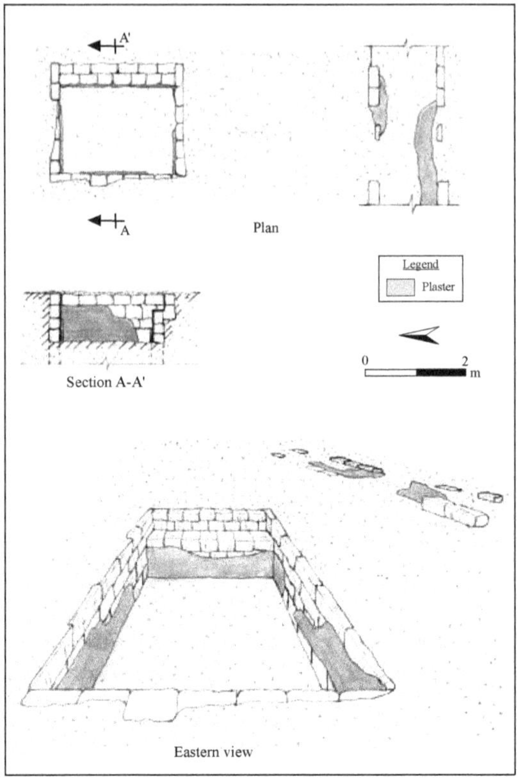

Fig. 4.21: Phasaelis East – a plastered cistern by the aqueduct. Plan and cross-section are at top and easterly view at bottom.

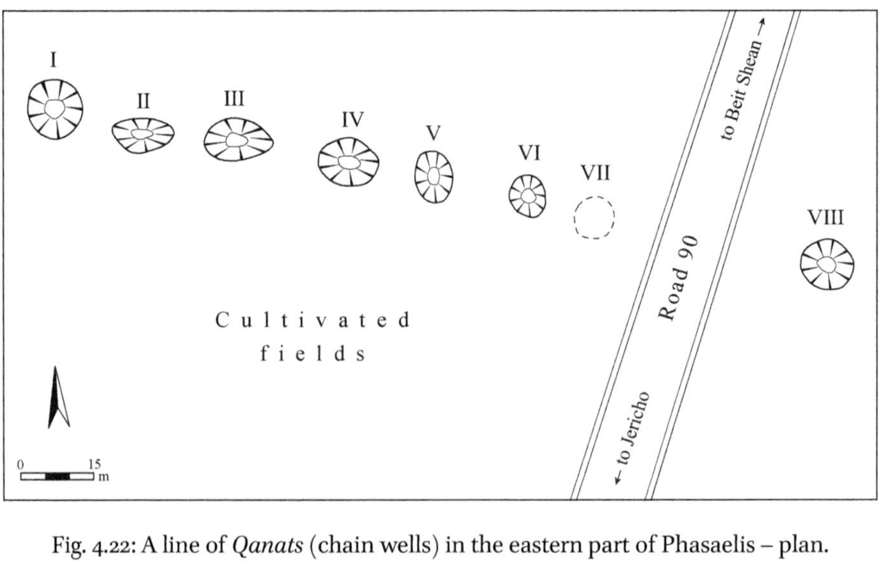

Fig. 4.22: A line of *Qanats* (chain wells) in the eastern part of Phasaelis – plan.

1.9. The settlement layout in the region

Preplanned Iron Age irrigation projects are hypothesized, since there are 14 sites along the stream in Fasael Valley with ceramics of the period (see Chapter 5). There are also two two-period forts, Rujm Abu Mukheir (Site 5) and Tell esh-Sheikh Diyab (Site 23), apparently established as a part of a royal system for the protection of the roads and water. The construction of a water reservoir, in that respect, is not surprising, but perhaps not in the dimensions of the large existing reservoir.

In any case it is probable that the large reservoir was essential for the Herodian irrigation projects and for the supply of water to the Roman city of Phasaelis. Therefore Porath's observation, claiming that the system was established only during the Early Moslem period, is odd.

1.10. Porath's description and opinion concerning the aqueducts and their dating

Porath (1985: 32ff) observes four ducts within the aqueducts. Below is the quotation, omitting the passages dealing with the irrigation systems in the Jordan Valley:

"The ancient duct A was built of fieldstones and plastered with calciferous mortar, it is 40 cm wide and 45 cm deep. It was refurbished once (B), when its walls were raised and another layer of plaster was added. A 'basin installation' (A plus B) was connected to it. Short sections of this aqueduct have been preserved in Nahal Fasael and a long section in the valley. On the walls of Duct B is an accumulated deposit of up to 32 cm thick... Ducts A and B were replaced by Duct C which is built of fieldstones and plastered. The route has been rebuilt anew along its entire length in the stream valley, and in the Jordan Valley there were rebuilt sections and sections in which the use of the old aqueduct continued...typical of Duct C is a gradual narrowing eastward – from 60 cm in the vicinity of the spring to 35 cm in the east. Inside Duct C was a new duct built of stone links...the duct is full of travertine up to its top in the section going through the stream...Duct C was refurbished by elevating its sides in the well preserved sections, or by replacing with a new duct, Duct D, of similar dimensions. This duct was restored later, when the sides were refurbished and plastered anew over the travertine layers. To Duct D are connected the flourmills... from the study of the settlement remains in the oasis of Fasael it turned out that only Ducts A, B and C were built and functioned during the periods dealt in the research..." (translation from Hebrew).

A detailed description of the aqueduct system is missing from the above text. However, there are relative dating attempts, and descriptions of the many installations which no longer exist. The difficulty in understanding the issues results from the awkwardness of the description and the lack of clarity of the linkage between the verbal description and the drawn plans. For extra details see Porath 1985.

1.11. Porath's description of the qanats (*the chain wells*)

"Chain wells are a sophisticated method of raising ground water by gravitation, by means of a tunnel dug with minimal gradient." (Porath 1985: 20). This method utilizes the flood water absorbed in the alluvial fans of streams. Chain wells were introduced from Persia by the Arabs and are found in Israel (in Fasael, 'Ein Yahav and Yotvata), Trans-Jordan, North Africa and Spain (Porath 1985: 21, 24).

As to the system in Fasael, Porath (1985: 35ff) found three branching systems. The main branch, system A1, starts in Wadi Ahmar, and runs north-south for 2200 m. A2 was straight, 750 m long, meeting A1 in the east. A3 ran in a curve 550 m long, joining A1 close to the junction with A2. The whole system received the water coming from the west beneath the channels of Wadi ez-Zimra and Nahal Fasael. System B consisted of two branches: B1 runs west-east and is the most noticeable one (this is the section we found). Twenty-two shafts have been found, spaced at an average of 22 m. B1 was noticed and described in 1873 by the British Survey (Conder and Kitchener 1882: 392); B2, about 1000 m long, runs north-south, and joins row B1. System C1, the southernmost one, was totally destroyed during preparation of the land for the settlement of Netiv Hagdud.

2. THE WATER SYSTEMS OF NAHAL YITAV (WADI 'AUJAH)

2.1 A. General and history of research

The first information about the water systems of 'Aujah was noted by Conder and Kitchener in the British Survey, and is as follows:

"Kanat el-Manil – A ruined aqueduct which leads down the water from 'Ain el 'Aujeh to the Ghor, running east some 5 miles to the neighbourhood of Khurbet el 'Aujeh et Tahtani [the present day village of 'Aujah, A. Z.]. Here it turns north and runs for about a mile, having five branches of various length, leading from the channel eastwards, probably for irrigation. There is another well called el Maskarah, connected apparently with the aqueduct, probably to control the irrigation. The date of this aqueduct would probably be the same with the Kanat Musa, which branches off from it, and which seems to be not earlier than medieval times, or repaired at least at that period. [See Sheet XVIII] The Crusaders cultivated the Ghor in many places (as for instance, in Wady Far'ah, where they cultivated the sugar-cane, and near Jericho and Beisan), and these aqueducts are probably connected with their irrigation of the valley." (Conder and Kitchener 1882: 390-391).

Porath (1985: 45-57), dedicated part of his work to these aqueducts. During the 1980s members of the German Braunschweig expedition probed here within the framework of the Jericho excavations (Garbrecht and Netzer 1991). We shall make use of all this information for comparison.

Unlike the Fasael Springs, which sustained a single system, two water systems originated from the 'Aujah Springs, one leading north-east to the city of Archelais and the other south-east to Jericho. The relatively large distance to the two Roman cities, between 10 and 20 km, necessitated the utilization of branching systems of which only parts remain. Discussions of both systems follow separately.

Close and parallel to the ancient aqueducts are modern concrete aqueducts from the British and Jordanian periods. Particularly notable is the concrete aqueduct south of the stream, although parts of a similar aqueduct were also found on the north side ('The Archelais Aqueducts', below). A third modern concrete aqueduct was built north of the stream, and was refurbished in 2010. It includes a chute and a new covered concrete duct, running eastward towards the village of 'Aujah et-Tahtah.

2.2. The water system to Archelais (The Archelais Aqueduct – north-east)

General: the British Survey (above) does not mention these aqueducts, claiming that Kanat el Manil runs directly eastward to the *Ghor* alongside Wadi 'Aujah. It is very difficult to explain the puzzling omission of the aqueduct from the British Survey.

It is possible to follow only the western and eastern parts – the start and finish – of the Archelais aqueduct. The other sections, which connected the 'Aujah area and the city of Archelais (Khirbet Beiyudhat, Site 111) – if they existed at all – have not been found, and the end of the aqueduct was found only close to the city itself (see below).

2.2.1. **The section from the springs to the area of the 'Aujah Fortress** (Site 140, coordinates 1884/1507 – Figs. 4.23, 4.24): The ancient aqueduct passes here north of and adjacent to the asphalt road (Fig. 4.23). East of the two sites of 'Iraq el-Ghawarneh (1) and (2), (Sites 134 and 136, respectively) the part of the area north of the wadi widens, and slopes fairly moderately to the south. About 30 m north of the road is the modern aqueduct descending to the relatively

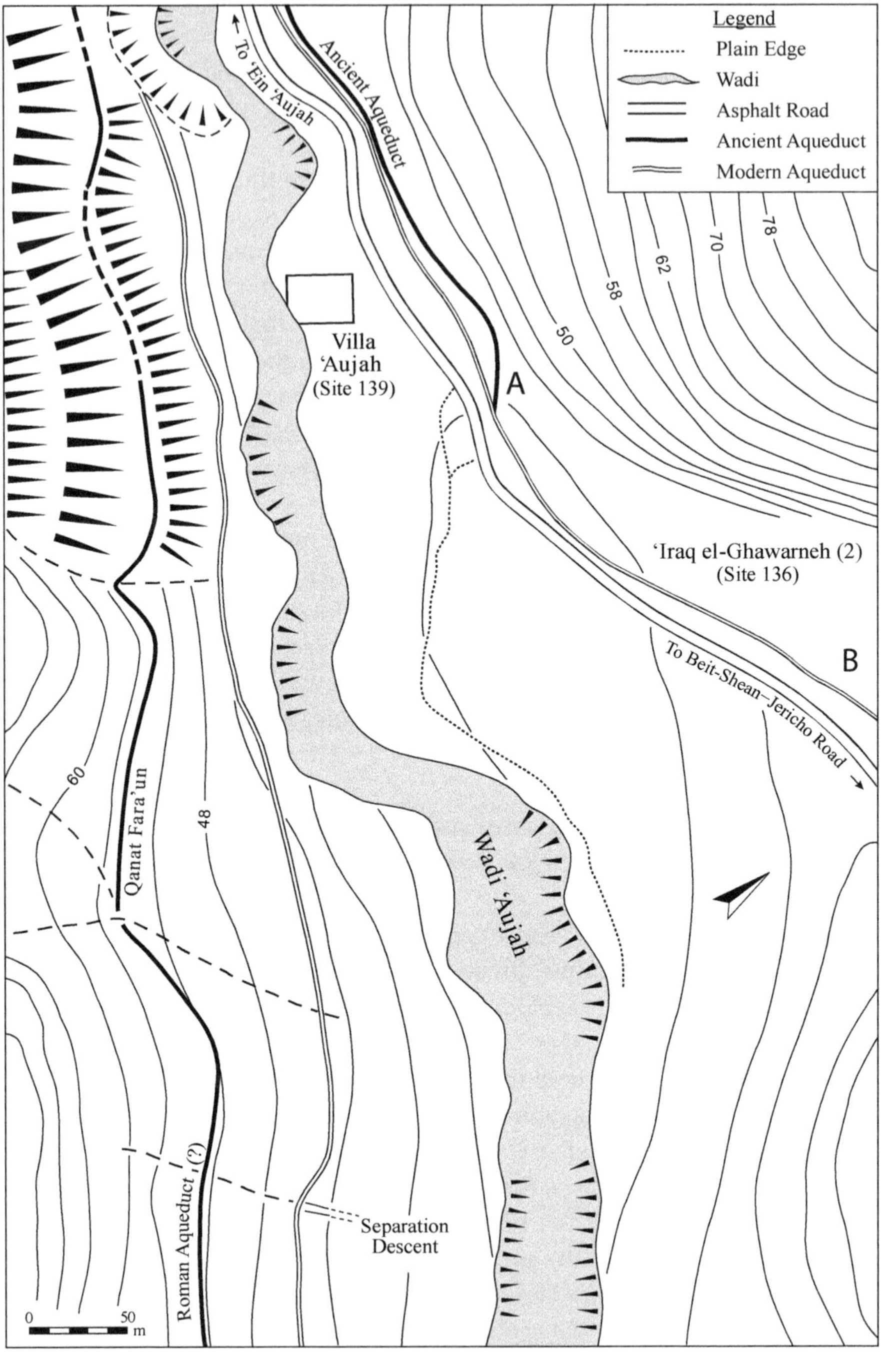

Fig. 4.23: 'Aujah aqueducts – the southern and northern aqueducts, the western section.

flat ridge, to the commencement of the new concrete chute. This one is built at an angle of about 25°, and the water accordingly flows rapidly. It is about 60 m long, and is about 1 m wide and deep. The reason for its construction is not clear.

2.2.2. The course of both aqueducts onward from 'Aujah Fortress (Fig. 4. 24): From coordinates 18837/15103 the remains of the two stone-built ancient aqueducts appear on the slope north of the asphalt road, marked in Fig. 4.24 by the letters A and B.

Aqueduct A – is the upper and northernmost one of the two. It is about 220 m long and a substantial section of its western part is speculative, based on the recess in the ground which contained the original aqueduct. It commences at coordinates 18837/15103, running 105 m to a pool-like built circle at coordinates 18849/15086. In this section the preservation is complete. About 20 m further on it crosses a ravine and thanks to erosion in the place, the aqueduct, including the foundations, is clearly visible. From coordinates 18891/15084 it continues 60 m to a pool (?) at coordinates 18850/15074. From here the aqueduct continues generally eastwards, and at coordinates 18861/15073 it turns with the spur to the north-east. Along the entire last section the aqueduct clearly survives.

This aqueduct continues northwards along the spur slope. After an unclear section it reappears at coordinates 18915/15090 and runs about 150 m to a saddle (the end of the aqueduct) at coordinates 18915/15110, where it turns sharply to the north-east to the next spur (Fig. 4.25). After crossing the saddle the aqueduct reappears, running about 50 m to coordinates 18924/15114. Here the ancient stone aqueduct is supplemented and reinforced by concrete of unknown date. From this last point, the original ditch of the aqueduct survives for more than 100 m, terminating at coordinates 18935/15122.

Aqueduct B – the lower (southern) aqueduct is considerably less well preserved than the other. It runs over the slope, about 30 m north of the roadway. Along its greater part only the silted up ditch has survived.

Aqueduct B starts at coordinates 18839/15092, and from that point is well preserved for about 50 m to coordinates 18842/15086. From here it extends east about 40 m in the form of a ditch indicating its course to coordinates 18844/15084. After a gap the aqueduct ditch reappears at coordinates 18857/15068, and then after about 30 m it terminates at coordinates 18857/15069.

In summary, the western section of Archelais aqueducts introduces a double problem:

1. The absence of the aqueducts from the maps and books of the British Survey.
2. The fact is that the aqueducts have no extension further east towards Archelais (or it was not found). The members of the British Survey clearly noticed that the water supply to the city was from an aqueduct running eastward

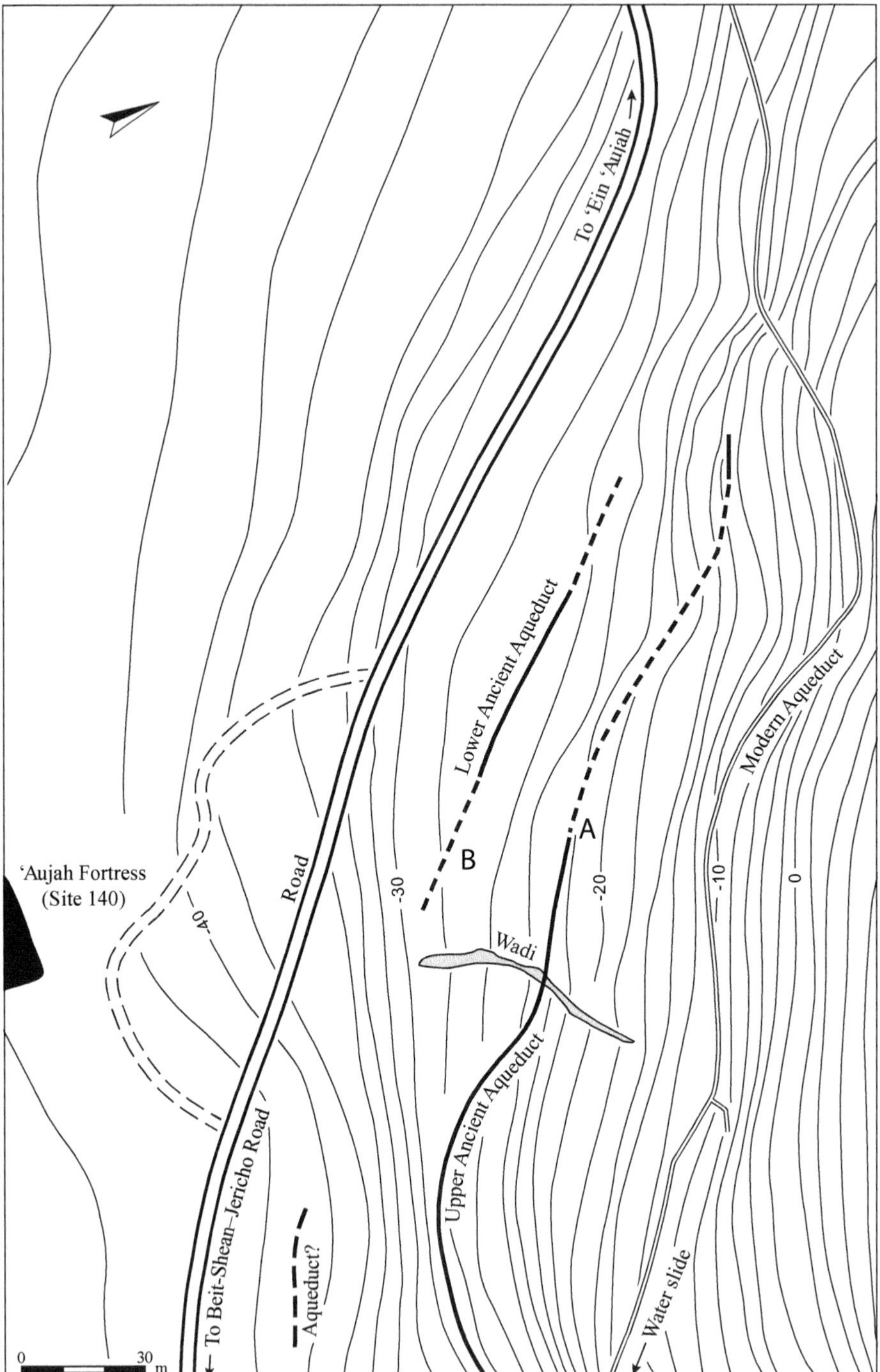

Fig. 4.24: 'Aujah aqueducts – the aqueduct to Archelais, second section from the west.

along the road to the village of 'Aujah. This issue requires further investigation.

2.2.3. The aqueduct layout around the city of Archelais (Figs. 4.26, 4.27): The aqueduct system around Archelais was measured and divided into two subsystems:

A. The western system (the aqueducts along the et-Tulul ridge);

B. The eastern system (the aqueducts for the irrigation of the fields east of the city). All these aqueducts, as in other places, are artificial ducts, of total width 1–1.2 m and net width of the water duct about 70 cm. The depth of the cleared duct, generally covered with several layers of plaster, is 50-60 cm.

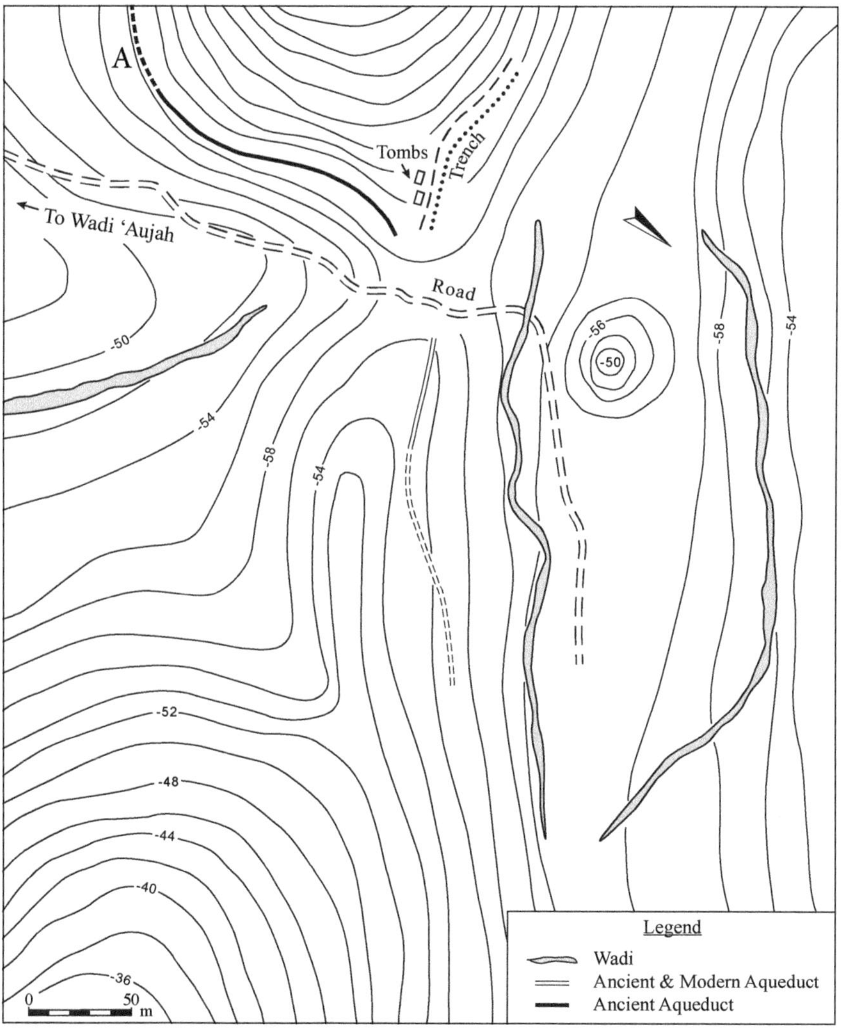

Fig. 4.25: 'Aujah aqueducts – the aqueduct to Archelais, third section from the west.

A. The western system (Fig. 4.26): is about 400 m long, located at the foot of et-Tulul cliffs. There are at least four aqueducts in the western system, followed by us along the eastern slope of the ridge, and are west of the Beit Shean-Jericho road. The four aqueducts, from top to bottom, are: upper (no. 1); middle a. (no. 2); middle b. (no. 3); and lower (no. 4).

1 – Upper aqueduct: is about 400 m long, located below and east of the et-Tulul cliffs. Its extension to the north was not found, and one can presume that became disused relatively early, and the other aqueducts, the middle and lower ones, replaced it. The southern part of the upper aqueduct is missing, but its route remains clear, and there is no doubt that it joined the aqueduct carrying water from 'Ein 'Aujah. The switch to the lower aqueducts was apparently executed when the upper aqueduct could not cope with the needs of the city, but these suppositions should be verified by excavations.

2-3 – Middle aqueducts: these are built as a parallel pair of aqueducts along the slope, one above the other, with an average distance between them of about 30 m. They are about 600 m long and are joined together in the north, about 50 m before the joint meeting point of all the aqueducts descending eastward to the city and the fields. The two aqueducts, nos. 2 and 3, are joined together in at least three places, a feature testifying to interoperability and directing water from one to the other in order to allow

Fig. 4.25A: The 'Aujah aqueducts – The concrete aqueduct to Archelais (S. Bar).

repairs and enhancing the flow in certain circumstances. Middle aqueduct no. 2 was also linked to the upper one in two sections, and in its southern part it zigzags in order to enable the crossing of a deep ravine. The two branches of the middle aqueduct join (opposite the junction where the road

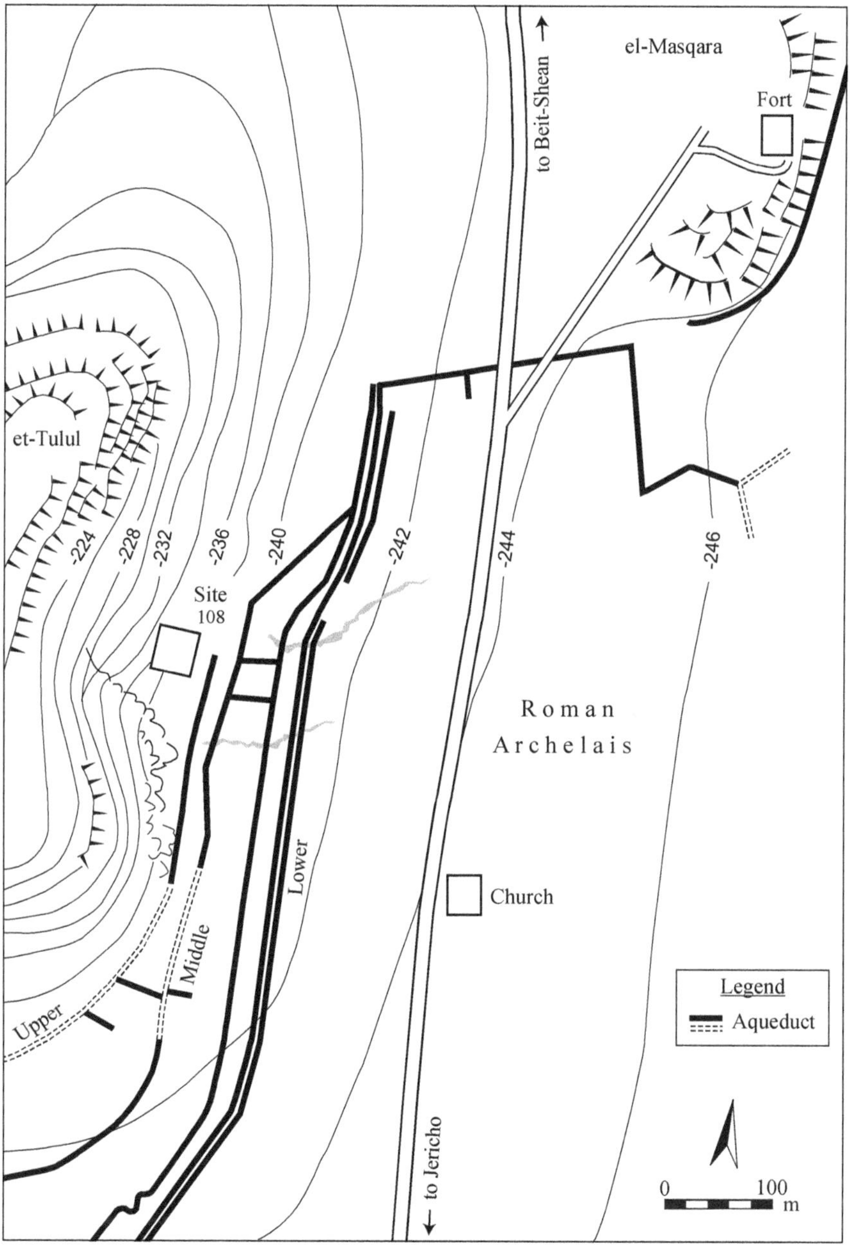

Fig. 4.26: Archelais Aqueducts – western section.

to el-Masqara starts from road 90), and the water flows via a single duct to the final join with the lower aqueduct.

4 – Lower aqueduct: this is built along its whole length (about 650 m) with two ducts. This fact proves that this aqueduct served as the principal aqueduct, at least in the late phase. Starting at the join mentioned above, the middle coupled aqueduct (2+3) merges with both paired lower ducts, and the water flowed to the city and fields via a single particularly wide duct. At the joining point there is a sharp turn eastward and the unified aqueduct reached the northern part of the city, close to el-Masqara. The reason for this is obvious: the northern part is higher than the plain in which the city was built, thus enabling easy flow of the water from north to south. However, it appears that there were additional connections leading eastward to the city, not found so far, as they have silted up. From the unified lower duct, the sole exit south to the city was traced, but this could be because the system is concealed as the surface over it is silted up.

B. The eastern system (Fig. 4.27): this starts from the cliff of el-Masqara, north of the city of Archelais, and extends more than 1000 m into the Jordan Valley plain. The 'unified' aqueducts (aqueducts 1-4, above), reach to the north of the city. Apparently, its main part watered the city, and the other part was assigned for irrigating the fields.

The irrigation system: A branch from the 'unified' aqueduct extended north, adjacent to and below the cliffs of el-Masqara. Where the aqueduct turns sharply east is a constructed pool, measuring about 7×6 m, apparently to release water pressure. From here the aqueduct turns east to the plain for about 500 m, until it turns sharply south. The reason for this turn is not clear, possibly additional

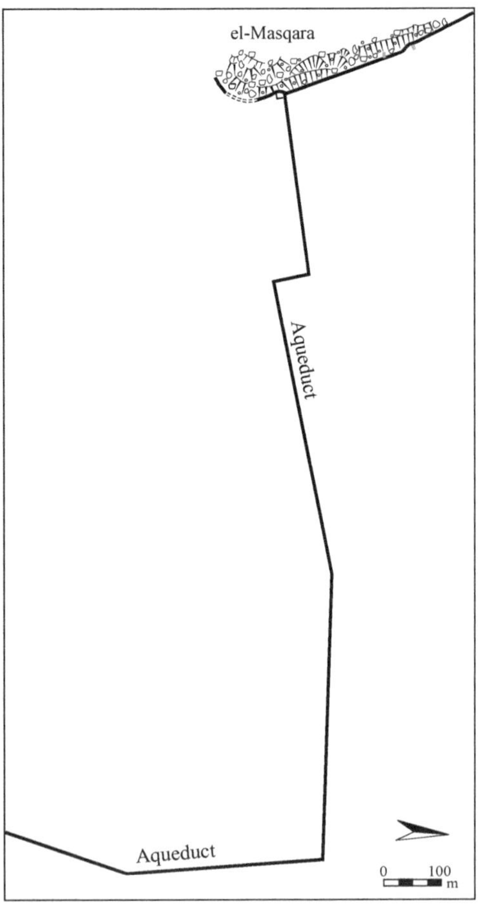

Fig. 4.27: Archelais Aqueducts – eastern section.

ducts branched here off to irrigate the fields. After the last turn the aqueduct turns sharply eastward for nearly 1000 m. Several exits were found along the aqueduct, but the branch ducts have not survived. All this amounts to a total course of about 1500 m, at the end of which the preserved aqueduct turns south and extends for nearly another 600 m, where it vanishes in the plain.

Due to the lack of additional data, one can propose, taking into account the length of the aqueducts, that an area of land of at least 100 ha (1000 dunams) was irrigated. The data from the Bar-Kokhba Roman archives (1st century CE) (Yadin 1971: 235) tell of an orderly irrigation regime of ducts and the granting of water rights to Shimon Avi (father of) Babatha. He (Shimon) is entitled to receive "one hour every Sunday, every year, forever" (Yadin 1971: 235), and: "Water – together with the heirs of Yehoseph son of Dormenes – one hour and half of three hours;" (Yadin 1971: 236-237).

2.3 The water system to 'Aujah Valley and Jericho

General and history of research: in this section are included the principal aqueduct (Qanat Fara'un) south of Nahal Yitav, the 'Aujah water flourmill, the division structure of the aqueducts east of the mill, the extension of the aqueduct eastward and the branch running from the division structure southward (Qanat el-Musa) to Wadi Abiyad. All these are relatively well preserved, close to the outlet from the springs and along the ridge south of the wadi. Eastward, in the direction of the open areas, the extension of the aqueducts vanishes after several hundred metres. The area has been recorded and mapped by the British Survey (Porath and the Braunschweig expedition).

2.3.1. The aqueduct originating from the spring running down to the 'Aujah mill (Figs. 4.23, 4.28): The start of the aqueduct, named in the sources and map as Qanat Fara'un, is not far from where the spring of 'Aujah originates at coordinates 1867/1514. Two sites ('Ein 'Aujah [3] and [4], Sites 131 and 132) have been discovered west and east of it in the wadi close to the spring. The preserved parts of the aqueduct are built in this section on a relatively high rocky step, orientated west-east. About 200 m further, south of the modern parking lot and next to 'Ein 'Aujah (1), Site 133, it extends into the wider valley south of the wadi. The two aqueducts – the ancient stone-built one and the modern concrete one – can be seen running parallel and at an average 30 m distance apart (Fig. 4.23). The ancient aqueduct in this place is 20–30 m higher than the modern one.

The section of the aqueduct over the cliff at coordinates 18757/15018 is well preserved; it is 6 m long and nearly 1.5 m high. The location is opposite the site of Villa 'Aujah (Site 139), across and south of the wadi. The length of the aqueducts along the cliff is roughly 80 m, up to the sharp curve (coordinates

18772/15092) forced by the deep wadi. From this point both aqueducts extend eastward, the ancient one above and the modern one below.

The width of this section of the ancient aqueduct is 1.05 m; it is well built and well plastered. At coordinates 18781/15078 the aqueducts cross another wadi coming from the south. A paved road covered by small pebbles runs beside the modern (lower) aqueduct. This is apparently the old Ottoman road along the wadi.

At coordinates 18795/15071, an excavation of the Judea and Samaria Archaeology Staff Officer touching the ancient aqueduct, was observed in March 2011. Over the slope, north and south of the aqueduct, remains of a small Iron Age II settlement are being exposed (Site 143 (1)), appearing to have been a 'suburb' of the city of 'Aujah el-Foqa. The site was dug down the slope, about 40 m below the 'lower fortress' of the city. The two aqueducts extend eastward from the excavation (coordinates 18800/15068), at the place marked as 'division chute', reaching (Tahunat) el-'Aujah water mill (Fig. 4.28).

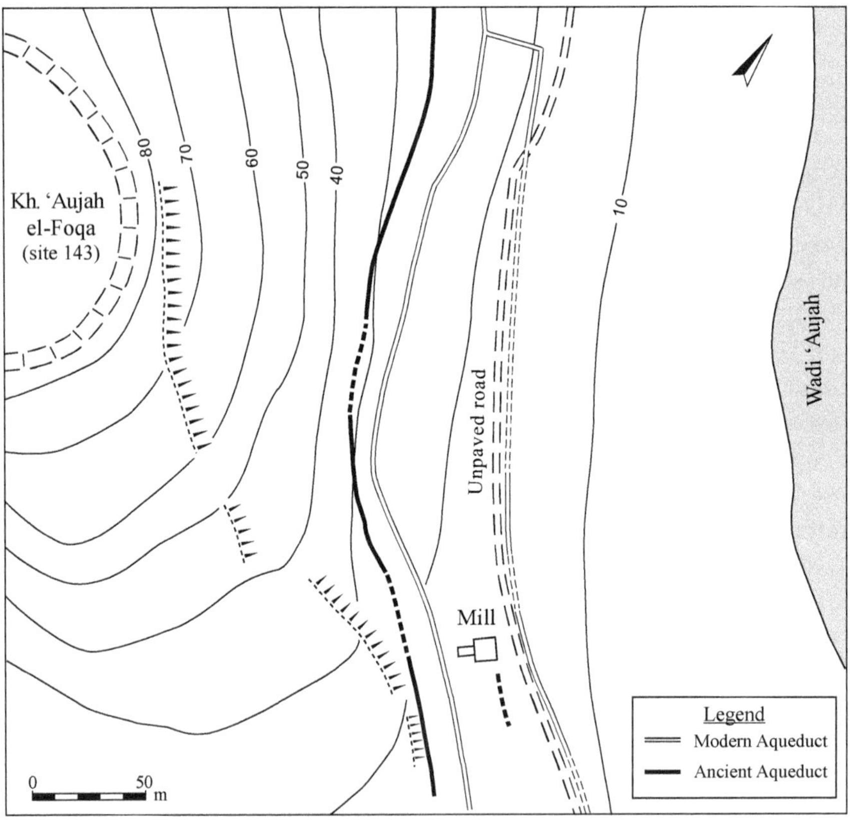

Fig. 4.28: 'Aujah aqueducts – the aqueduct to Jericho, second section from the west (see also Fig. 4.23).

2.3.2. 'Aujah water mill (Figs. 4.29-4.32 and Site 142): Presumably an Ottoman flour mill in the southern edge of Wadi 'Aujah Valley and close to the northern margins of the 'Aujah el-Foqa hill. There are six parts to the mill (Fig. 4.29), fed by the lower (modern) aqueduct:

2.3.2.1. an aqueduct over the upper slope, stone-built and plastered; from this there is a constructed outlet to the mill (coordinates 18815/150464). The aqueduct is supported by a wall across the slope built of medium-sized stones.

2.3.2.2. supply duct, about 8 m long and 1 m wide, built of small stones and well plastered with a rounded cross-section. It branches out from the aqueduct and leads to the mill water chute. It is based on a supporting long tall stone-built support structure with two large arches.

2.3.2.3. the length of the structure carrying the aqueduct is about 10 m; and its maximum height (by the water chute) is about 4.5 m. Its width is nearly 3 m, and narrows towards the top. The structure is built on the slope descending to the valley of Wadi 'Aujah (Fig. 4.32).

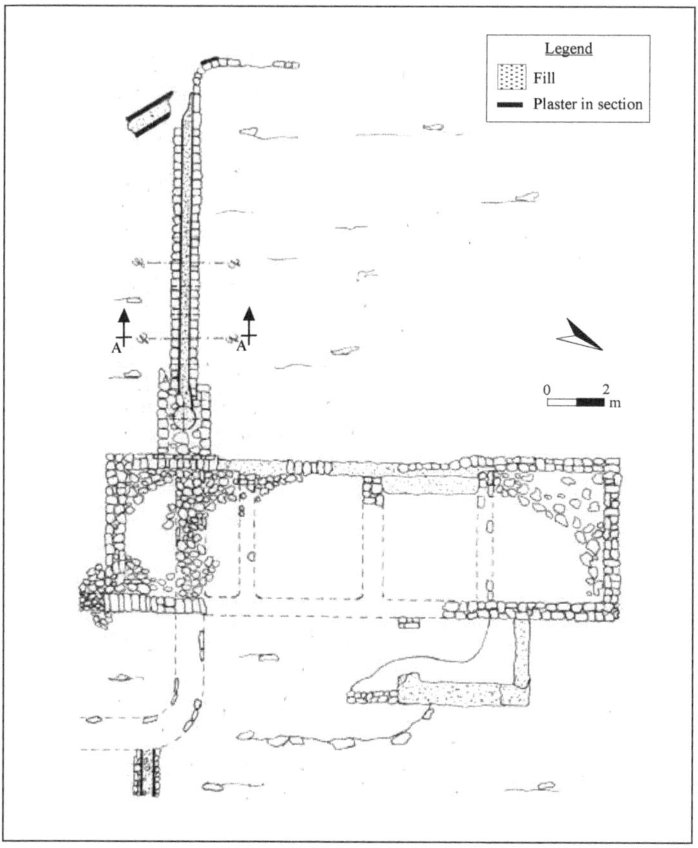

Fig. 4.29: 'Aujah watermill – detailed plan.

2.3.2.4. the waterfall room (the chute): above the base is built as a tall narrow tower. At its centre is a plastered stone pipe through which the water flows to the milling room (Fig. 4.30).

2.3.2.5. a structure containing the milling room: a longitudinal (18×5 m) structure on the slope in which are the milling room and three rooms of equal dimensions (5×4.5 m). At the centre of the milling room is the water duct and the space for the millstones. The water channel from the milling room runs to the valley. The structure (now disintegrating) is built of medium-sized stones, and the present height of the walls is 1.5 m. Attached to it on the north-east is a small room – a hallway(?) (Fig. 4.29). Two millstones were found out of context, outside the milling room. They are made of special cement and strengthened with iron straps. They bear the inscription in French: 'Fabrique generale Moulins'.

2.3.2.6. on the slope west of the mill is a long courtyard (33×4 m). On one of its sides is a support wall and on the other is an earth rampart. The courtyard was dug into the slope.

The mill is apparently mentioned in the British Survey (Conder and Kitchener 1882: 390-391), without details. It is dated without explanation, to be "Medieval". The mill is presented, with a blurred photograph in Ilan (1973: 262), also without details. The site was apparently built during the Ottoman period, but it is not clear in which century. The construction or renovation of the structure is ascribed to the 19th century CE, as substantiated by the millstones. The pottery find suggests a presence in the place from Byzantine times until now, but even this information is scanty.

Fig. 4.29A: 'Aujah watermill, view south-east – aerial photo (N. Eshed).

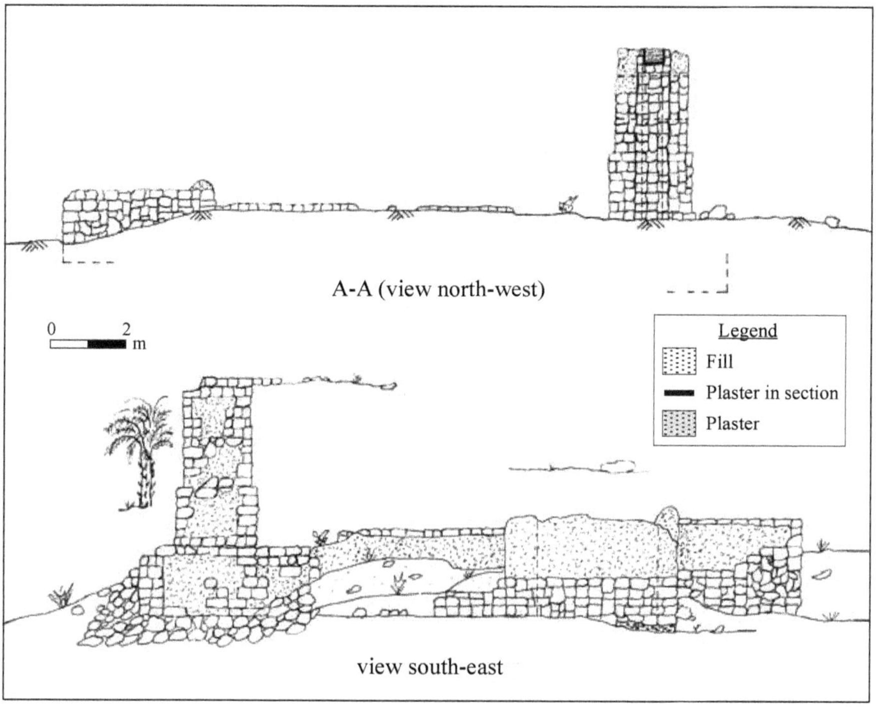

Fig. 4.30: 'Aujah watermill, views north-west (top) and south-east (bottom).

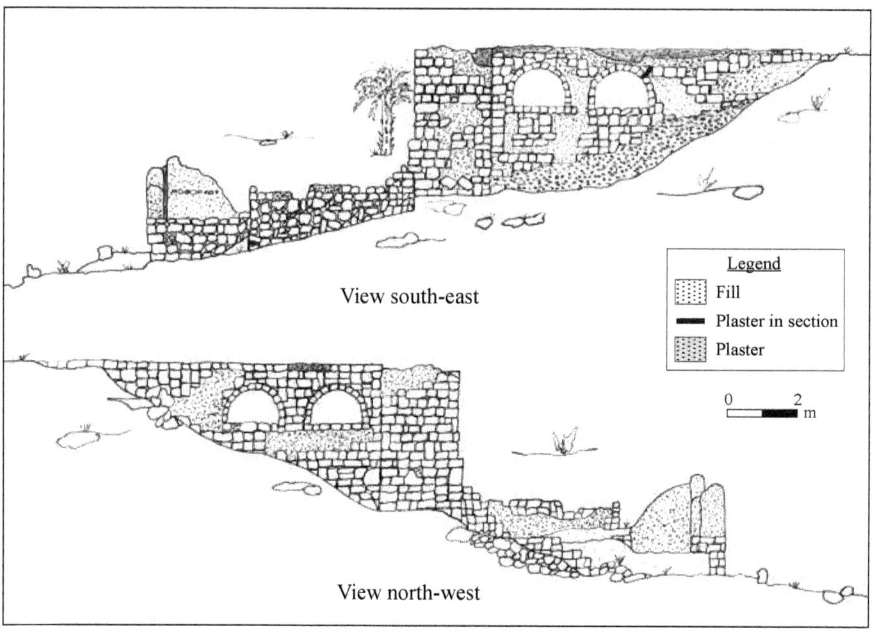

Fig. 4.31: 'Aujah watermill, view south-east (top) and north-west (bottom).

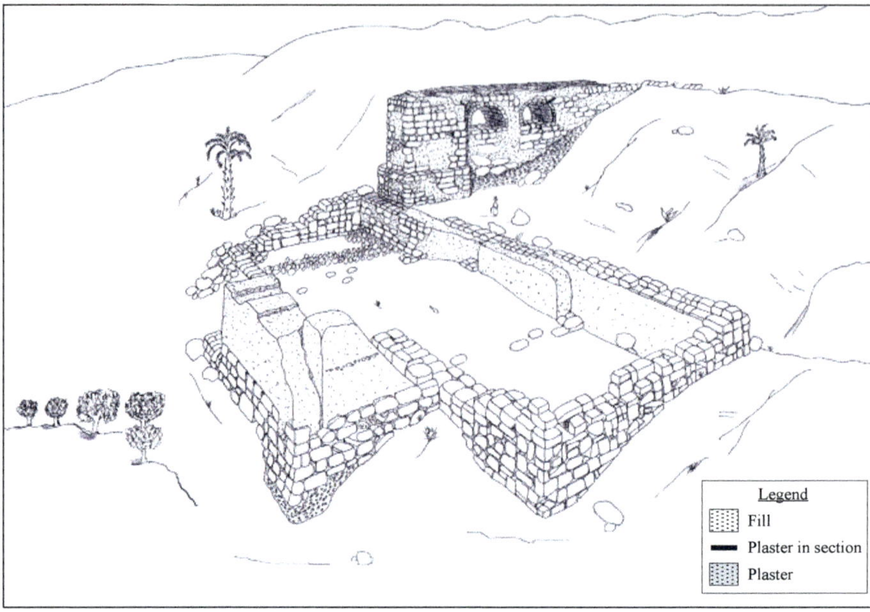

Fig. 4.32: 'Aujah watermill – perspective view east.

Fig. 4.32A: 'Aujah watermill – view south-west (S. Bar).

2.3.3. The aqueduct from the 'Aujah mill down to Qanat Musa (Fig. 4.33): From 'Aujah watermill (opposite the mill at coordinates 18815/15046) the ancient aqueduct extends about 60 m east-south-east on the upper northern slope of the spur to coordinates 18819/15040. Nearby on the spur is a rectangular structure (coordinates 18818/15039, marked in the plan), which served as a branching facility of the ancient aqueduct. The structure measures about 10×10 m. It was excavated twice by the Braunschweig expedition, and apparently in 2011 by the Judea and Samaria Archaeology Staff Officer. The new concrete aqueduct runs from the bottom of the spur in the north, along a paved road. This is probably the Ottoman road preceding the construction of the asphalt road to 'Ein 'Aujah.

In the rectangular structure the aqueduct branches into two. One branch extends eastwards over the spur for about 220 m to another rectangular structure (coordinates 18836/15031), the function of which is not clear. From this structure the aqueduct extends eastward and down until it vanishes in the nearby fields. Apparently this section served for irrigating the fields, supplying water to the settlements along the valley of Wadi 'Aujah (Kh. 'Aujah et-Tahtah – Site 146, and/or the settlement in the modern village of 'Aujah – Site 144), and to Archelais.

The other aqueduct (Qanat Musa in all sources) starts at the split, turns relatively sharply southward, and continues along the spur slope (coordinates 18818/15032), while crossing the curving stream channels descending eastwards (coordinates 18817/15023 – Fig. 4.33). The total length of this section is about 500 m, curving slightly west at coordinates 18810/15004, in order to reach the valley of Wadi Mubarah. This section is a little west of the modern road starting at 'Aujah et-Tahtah (Site 146) and leads to a well (coordinates 1873/1497). At coordinates 18817/15004 the aqueduct crosses a new unpaved road to the Bedouin houses in Wadi Mubarah. After a fairly sharp turn south this aqueduct reaches the bridge of Qanat Musa 1.

2.3.4. Qanat Musa:

2.3.4.1. History of research: the course of the aqueduct appears in the British Survey map, Sheet 15, where it is named Qanat Musa. In the Emergency Survey (Bar-Adon 1972: 109 and Site 29) the original name has been changed as follows: "Qanat el-Manil: aqueducts supported by bridges, carrying water from 'Ein el-'Aujah in the direction of Jericho, parallel to and higher than Qanat el-Fara'un. Two bridges pass over Wadi el-Mubarah and its tributaries. A principal aqueduct, from which branch out conduits covered by stone slabs, leading to the fields on the slope. Sherds find: Late Roman (by the bridge)." (translation from Hebrew)

In the Wadi el-Makukh map (Goldfus and Golani 1993: site 420) is a note: "The principal aqueduct continues south and it is possible to follow it most of the way. It is built of medium-sized and large field stones cemented together with clay. The aqueduct is plastered inside and out, the width is nearly 1.05 m, it is about 60 cm deep and the thickness of its walls is about 50 cm. The

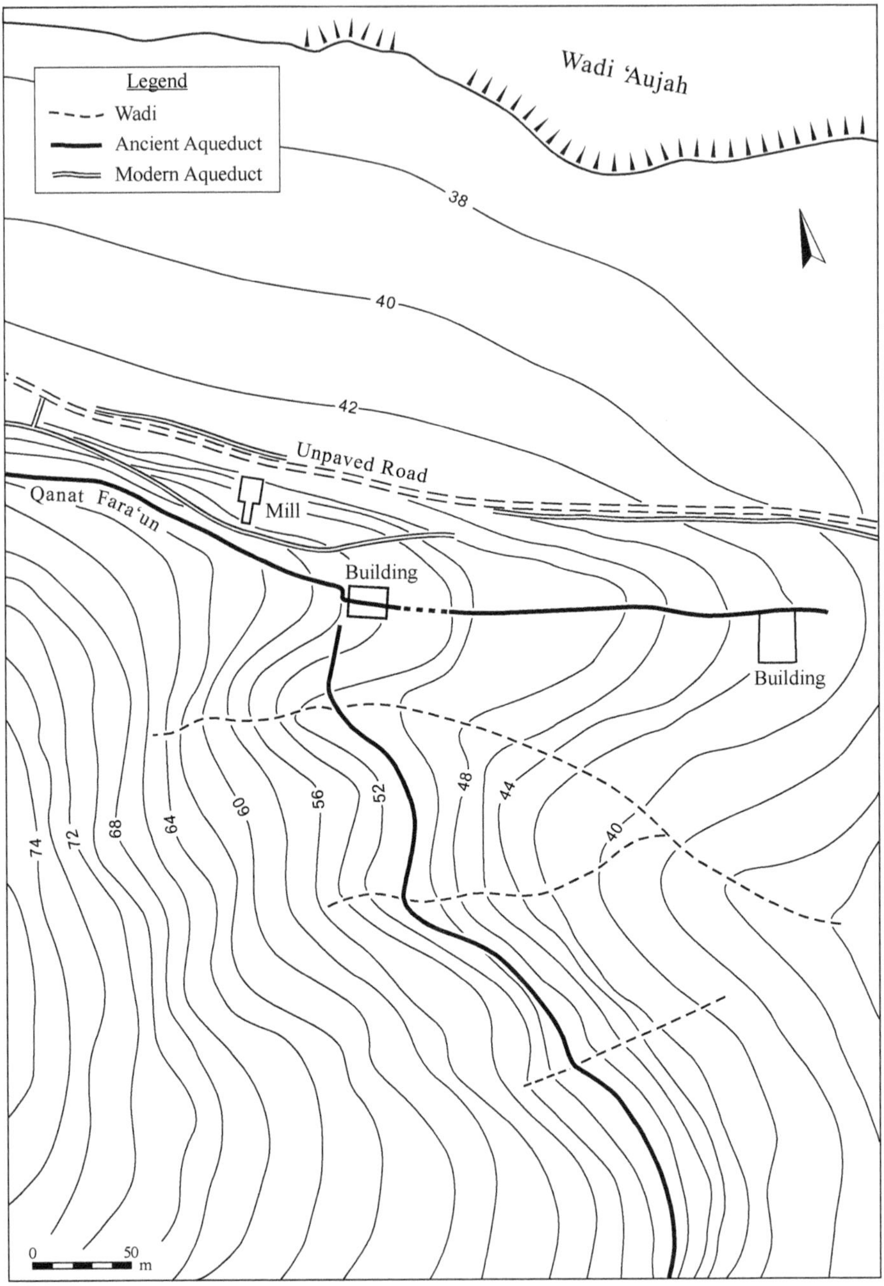

Fig. 4.33: 'Aujah aqueducts – Qanat Far'un and Musa, third section from the west.

total length of the aqueduct is about 10 km, although as the crow flies, the distance is only 5 km. Only in one case a quarried conduit crosses the spur…in two places tunnels are visible…" (translation from Hebrew).

2.3.4.2. Qanat Musa 1 Bridge – description: this is a built bridge carrying an aqueduct coming from 'Aujah Springs, bypassing the hill of 'Aujah el-Foqa to the east, and continuing to the south-east (Jericho) (Figs. 4.34, 4.36).

The bridge, built across Wadi el-Mubarah was measured, recorded and drawn (Figs. 4.35-36). Its central part over the wadi is now ruined, and only the parts north and south of the stream channel remain. The original length of the bridge was 35 m. About 22 m now survive at both ends (the northern one starts at coordinates 18805/15000 and the southern one ends at coordinates 18803/14991). The maximum height of the bridge, next to the stream channel, is nearly 5.5 m. The width at the base is about 2.5 m, and the upper part where the duct is, approximately 2 m. The inner width of the duct is about 1 m, and it is about 30 cm deep. The duct is well plastered with bright plaster approximately 3 cm thick. It is well constructed with medium-sized stones. In the lower part is a section built of smaller stones. Stages of raising and repair are visible, although of unclear date. The course of the aqueduct from the north-east is clearly visible along the slope, where it continues south-west towards another smaller bridge (Qanat Musa Bridge 2).

2.3.5. **The aqueduct from Qanat Musa Bridge 1 to Qanat Musa Bridge 2** (Fig. 4.37): The distance from the south end of Qanat Musa Bridge 1 to Qanat Musa Bridge 2 is about 250 m. In this vicinity the remains of the aqueduct meander along the lower part of the spur, following the topography. From the southern end of the bridge at Qanat el-Manil the aqueduct extends down to coordinates 18799/14983 in a clear line, while its structure is concealed from the outside. From this place the preserved route reaches coordinates 18795/14982. In this spot is a small tower where the aqueduct meets the new asphalt road. The course itself is well preserved, but the aqueduct structure survives only along a relatively short section (about 25 m). From here the aqueduct turns sharply to the south-east, reaching Qanat Musa Bridge 2.

2.3.6. **Qanat Musa Bridge 2** (Figs. 4.37-39) is much smaller than Qanat Musa Bridge 1. Its northern end is at coordinates 18788/14977 and the southern end is at coordinates 18790/14973. The total length of the bridge is approximately 25 m, and only two foundations on both sides of the stream channel survive. A large lump of stones, cemented together with chalky clay, resulting from the collapse of the bridge, remains in the streambed.

From the bridge the aqueduct continues generally south-east on the north-eastern slope of the spur (coordinates 18790/14974). The preserved aqueduct terminates at coordinates 18808/14966, after a section of about 150 m. From here onward only sections have been preserved, mostly as a ditch.

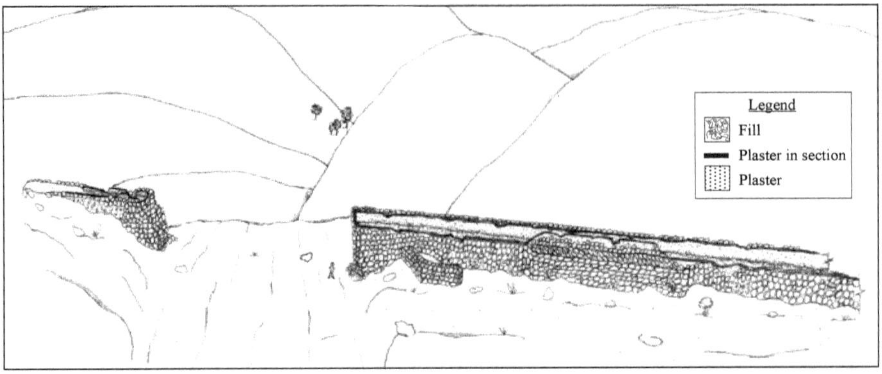

Fig. 4.34: The aqueducts to Jericho – the Qanat Musa 1 Bridge, perspective view west.

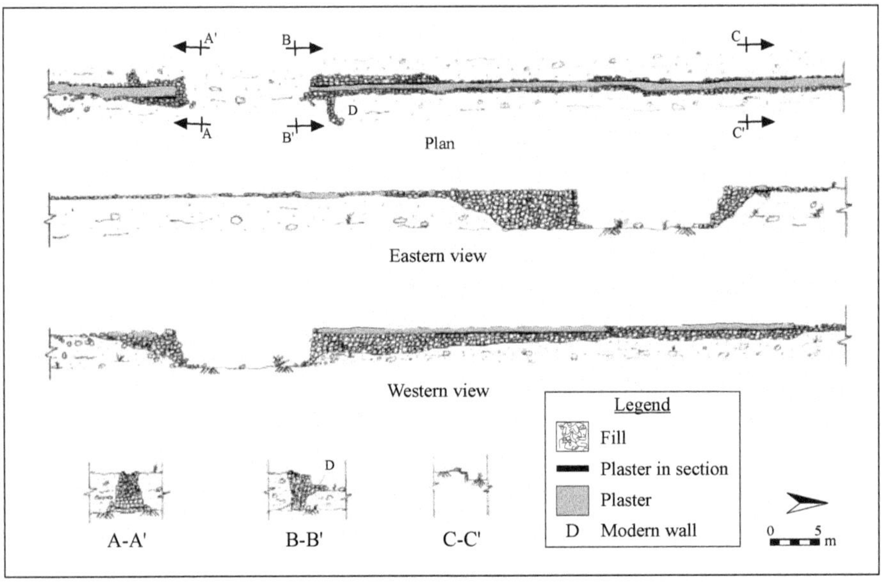

Fig. 4.35: The aqueducts to Jericho – the Qanat Musa 1 Bridge. Top – cross-sections, second from top – view east, third from top – view west, bottom – plan.

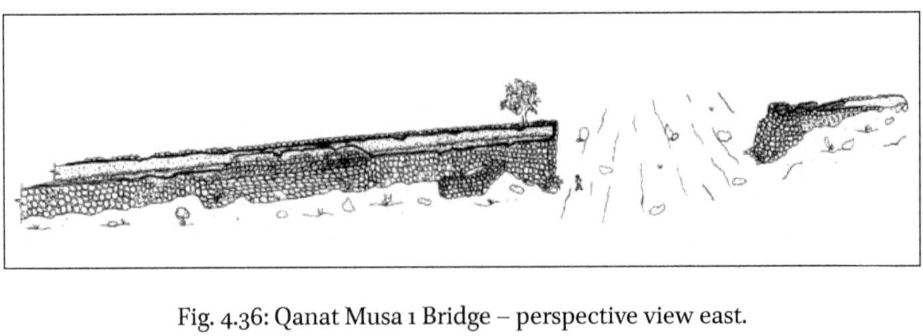

Fig. 4.36: Qanat Musa 1 Bridge – perspective view east.

2.3.7. **Description of Qanat Musa to the south:** From Qanat Musa Bridge 2 to Qanat Musa Bridge 4: the course of the aqueducts from Qanat Musa Bridge 2 and further east, down to Qanat Musa Bridge 4, was measured from December 2011 to January 2012 (Fig. 4.40). It is noteworthy that despite the mention of the

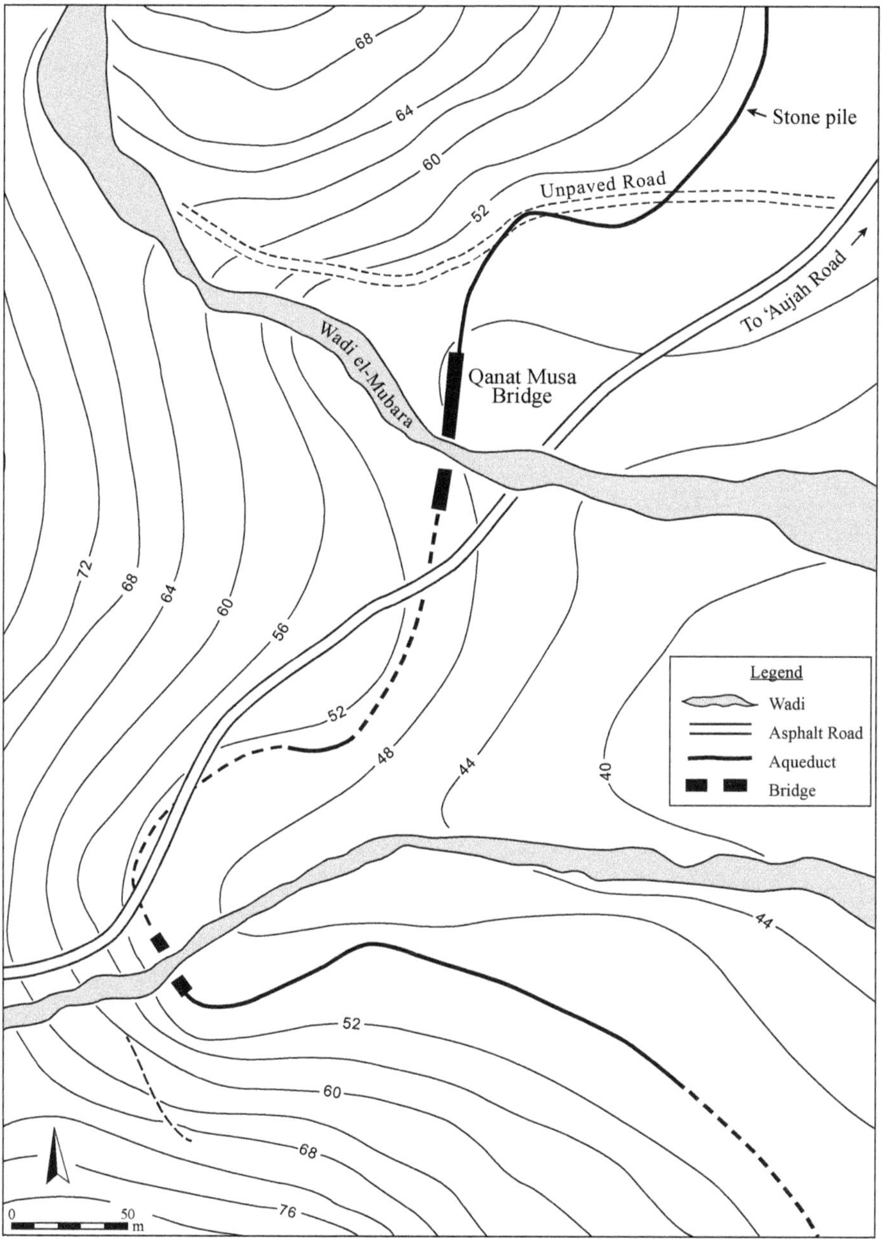

Fig. 4.37: Qanat Musa – plan of the aqueducts and the bridges of Qanat Musa 1 and 2.

Fig. 4.38: The aqueduct to Jericho: Qanat Musa – the bridge at Qanat Musa 2, view east.

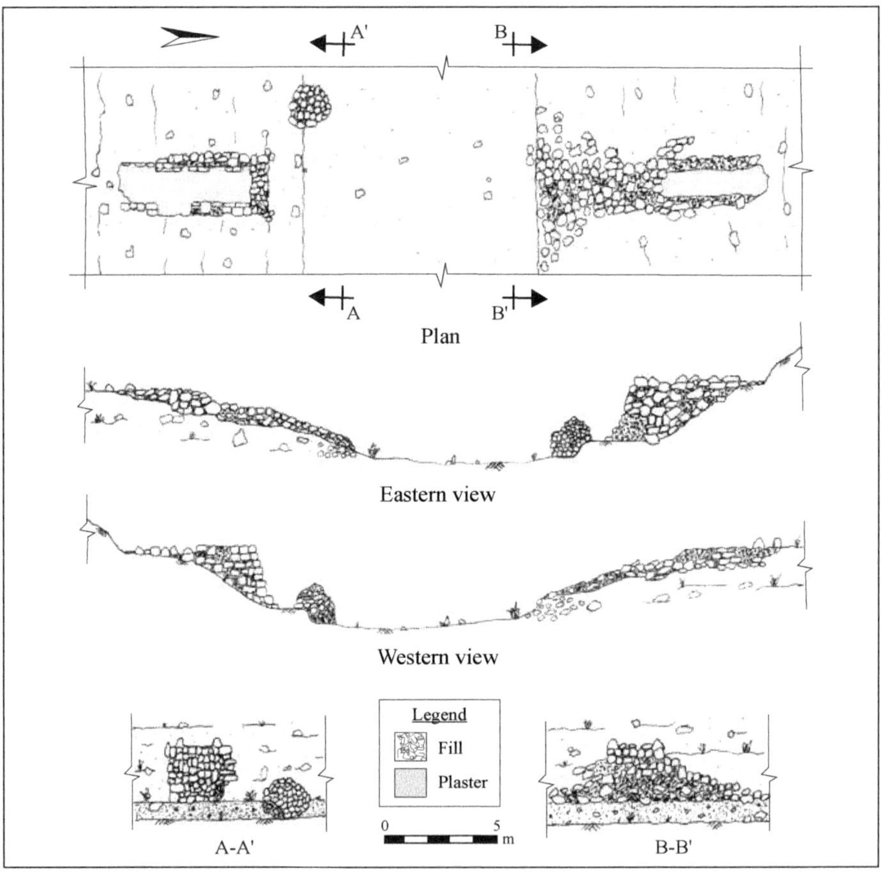

Fig. 4.39: 'Aujah aqueducts, Qanat Musa – the bridge at Qanat Musa 2, views and plan. Top – cross-sections (see plan). Centre – views east and west. Bottom – plan.

aqueducts in the British Survey, no thorough measuring was made in the past, and Conder and Kitchener, Porath and Garbrecht and Netzer only recorded the supposed courses of the aqueducts on an existing map without measuring them in the field, and without scrutinizing the topography. In our work we surveyed the aqueduct with the surrounding wadis and the terrain of the area, in order to show how the planners coped with the topography. Along the entire measured section the standard width of the aqueduct was approximately 1 m, and its features are similar to those listed above, in Porath (1985) and in the Wadi el-Makukh survey Map (Goldfus and Golani 1993). The description from north to south is as follows:

Section 1 – from Qanat Musa 2 to Qanat Musa 3: At the top of Fig. 4.37, the aqueduct terminates about 200 m east of Qanat Musa Bridge 2, and then, only the ditch of the aqueduct is visible over the spur. The aqueduct reappears at the beginning of Section 1, in the southern side of the spur. In this section a few remnants of the aqueduct have been found, and it is visible only next to the crossing of the first wadi – the northern tributary of Wadi Taiybet el-Ism (Point I in Fig. 4.40). From here the aqueduct turns south-east for about 250 m down to coordinates 18823/14931, and continues another 30 m and turns sharply west-south-west along the spur, the summit of which is Elevation Point -86. At this point the aqueduct reaches Wadi Taiybet el-Ism and the Qanat Musa Bridge 3. The estimated length of the aqueduct along Section 1 is about 500 m.

Qanat Musa Bridge 3 (marked II in Fig. 4.40; Figs. 4.41, 4.42): this bridge does not appear in the maps. It is not exactly a bridge, but actually a culvert, the southern end of which is at coordinates 18802/14920. The length of the structure is a little more than 25 m; its upper width is 2.2 m, and it is built of two rows of worked stones together with small ones, with chalky clay between them. In the central part the bridge now stands to a maximum height of 2.2 m, reduced towards the banks of the wadi. The culvert blocks the natural flow of the flood water, which is meant to flow above or perhaps alongside it. At the northern end of the culvert there is a breach about 2 m wide, and maybe here was a controlled passage of water. The structure stands, with holes and gaps resulting from the collapse of the worked stone outer wall and there are lumps of material which fell into the wadi. The top duct is well plastered, and its side walls, which are built of small stones, rise about 40 cm above the bottom of the duct.

In the channel of the wadi west of the bridge are stone walls, a sort of elementary dam, aimed perhaps to decelerate the flood. Along the north side of the channel is another wall, possibly designed to divert the flood water. In spite of lack of data regarding the date of these walls it can be surmised that they are later than the construction of the aqueducts.

Section 2 – from Qanat Musa 3 down to the southern tributary of Wadi Taiybet

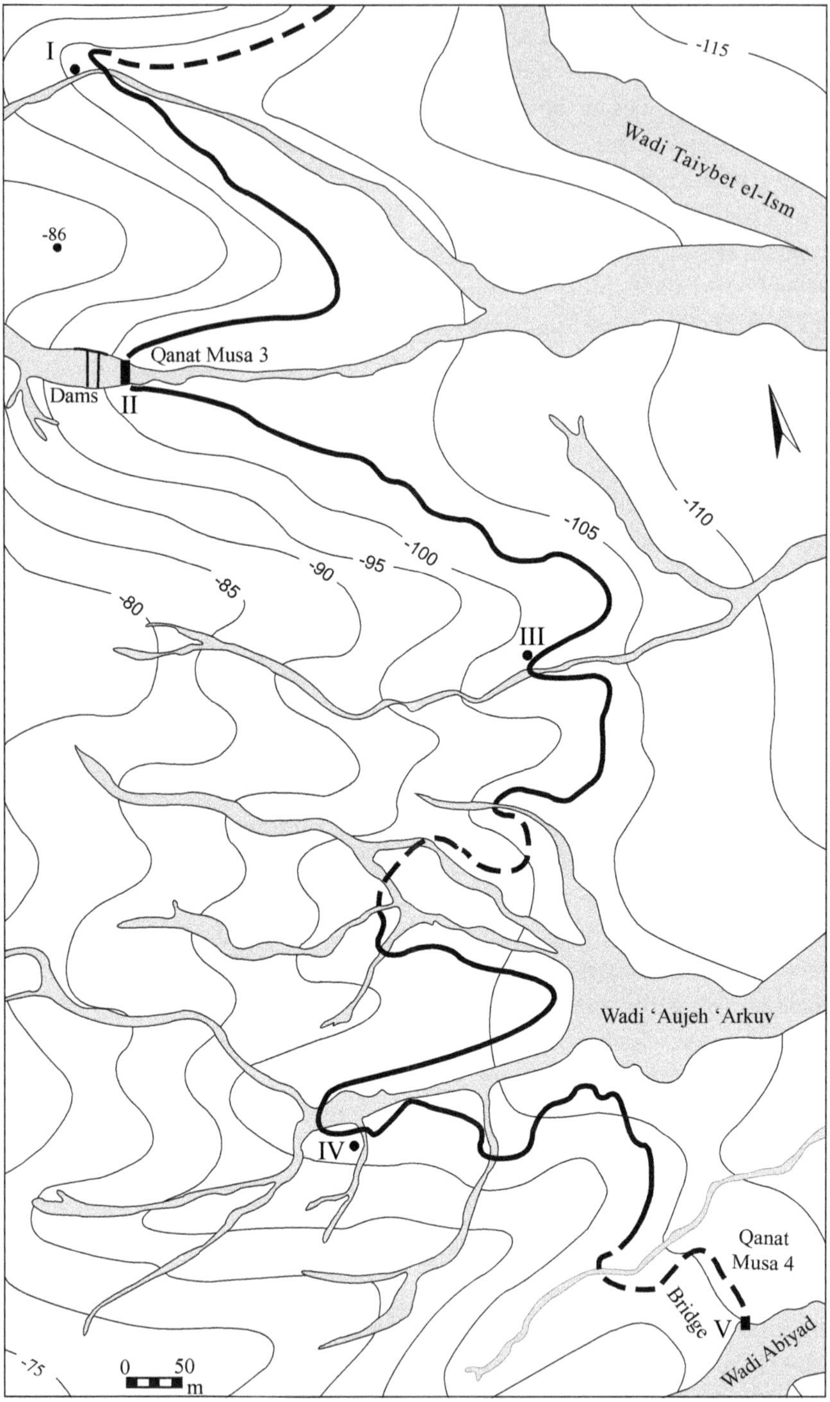

Fig. 4.40: Plan and topography of the aqueduct (Qanat Musa) between the bridges Qanat Musa 2 and 4.

el-Ism (marked III in Fig. 4.40): From Point II the aqueduct turns sharply to the south-east, between contour lines -100 to -105, and then turns south-west down to Point III. The length of this section is 1237 m, and apart from several curves it is relatively straight. At Point III the aqueduct leaves the drainage basin of Wadi Taiybet el-Ism, arriving at the next drainage basin, that of Wadi 'Aujah 'Arkuv.

Section 3 – Wadi 'Aujah 'Arkuv drainage basin (from Point III to Point IV in Fig. 4.40): This section is the most tortuous and intricate one of Qanat Musa. Here the planners were obliged to route the aqueduct across not less than seven tributaries of the main wadi. The drainage basin around here is rather flat, and therefore a network of shallow tributaries has been formed close to each other. The outcome is considerable meandering and ruined sections of the aqueduct, in place of crossing tributaries. The estimated total length of this section is 1200 m, and the distance between Points III and IV as the crow flies, does not exceed 400 m; a threefold elongation of the aqueduct.

Section 4: from Wadi 'Aujah 'Arkuv to Wadi Abiyad (Point IV to V in Fig. 4.40): In this section the aqueduct reaches into the drainage basin of the third wadi in the sequence from north to south, namely, Wadi Abiyad. Because the principal tributaries of the wadi are south of the wadi channel, the aqueduct leaves the former drainage basin and reaches the wide wadi channel with two short meanders. The length of this section is about 400 m, and the aqueduct reaches Qanat Musa Bridge 4 (Point V in Fig. 4.40) after a short gap.

Summary – Qanat Musa aqueduct: The aggregate length of the aqueduct between Qanat Musa 2 to 4 is estimated to be about 3500 m, although the actual distance does not exceed 1200 m. The planners of the aqueduct overcame many topographical obstacles en route, mainly the crossing of numerous tributaries in the drainage basins of the three major wadis. The method chosen was construction along a contour line, keeping the suitable moderate rate of descent for the water flow without straining the duct. In the wadi crossings the aqueduct was built in such a manner as to withstand average floods, allowing the water to go through it. Bridges and culverts were built across Wadi Mubara (Qanat Musa Bridges 1 and 2), Wadi Taiybet el-Ism and Wadi Abiyad (Qanat Musa Bridge 4). From the above it can be concluded that the number and power of the floods did not exceed today's, and the maintenance of the aqueduct could be achieved with small repairs every winter. Taking into account that the aqueduct functioned all year round and the average yearly rainfall in the region is not more than 150 mm, with two to three flooding events on average per year, one can conclude that an investment in the bridges in every wadi will not pay, and the solution adopted under the circumstances was the optimal one. However, it is obvious that there was a need for repair squads to maintain the aqueduct.

Qanat Musa Bridge 4 (Point V in Fig. 4.40; Figs. 4.43, 4.44): Wadi Abiyad[1] is one of the broadest and largest in the region; the width of the riverbed here is slightly less than 100 m, and it is about 5 m below the surface of the surrounding plain. The flood water flowing through it necessitated the construction of a

1 The source of the name is in the British Survey map, where the spelling is clear: Abiyad. In Israel's map 1:50,000 the name has been copied erroneously as "Abayed". After an additional check it came out that the original name of the wadi is Najmeh, as appears in the British Survey map.

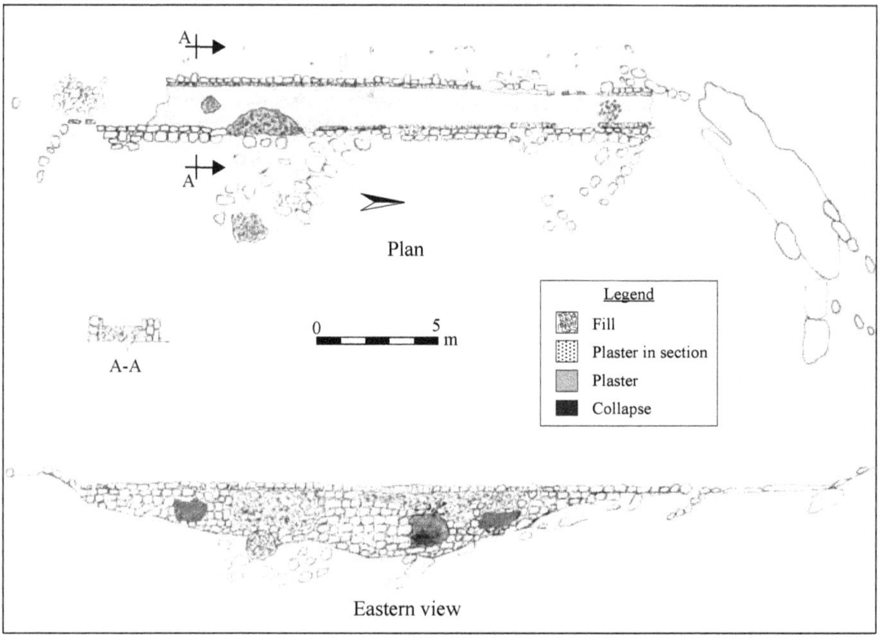

Fig. 4.41: The Qanat Musa 3 culvert – plan (top), view east (bottom).

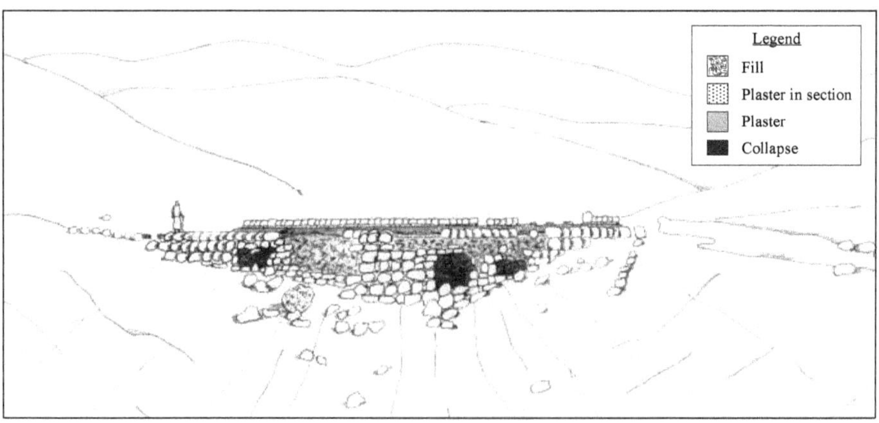

Fig. 4.42: The Qanat Musa 3 culvert – view west.

bridge to allow the crossing of the aqueduct. Porath (1985: 48 and drawing 30) calls it "An installation combining principles of under passage and solidly built wall" (translated from Hebrew). The present remains make it difficult to understand what exactly was the facility which once stood here, and what were the phases of its construction, but we shall try to reconstruct it.

Qanat Musa 4 is a stone structure, presently about 11 m long and 7 m wide. It is a wall, protruding into the wadi channel from the north, built of large and

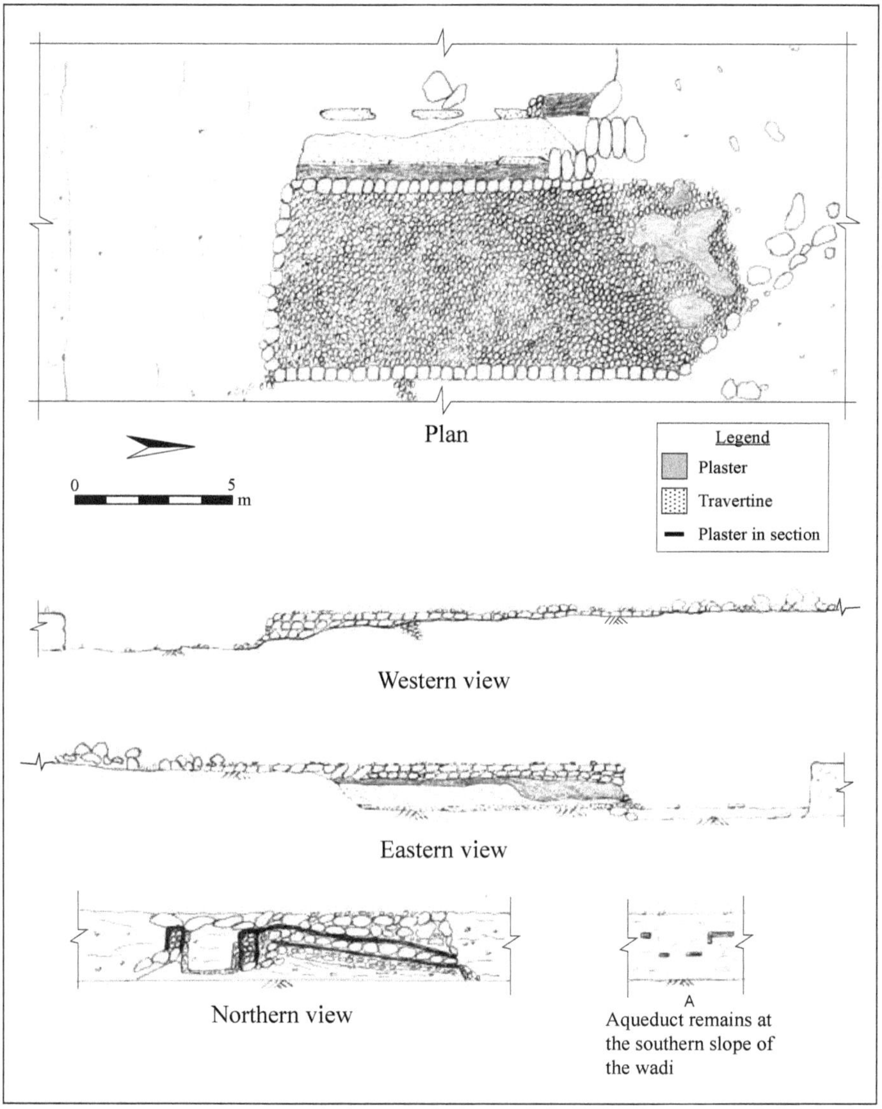

Fig. 4.43: The bridge at Qanat Musa 4 –plan (top) and views west, east and north (below).

Fig. 4.44: The bridge at Qanat Musa 4 – perspective view north-east.

medium-sized stones, some of them worked. To the western part of the structure is attached a plastered aqueduct constructed of small stones and plaster, 1.1 m wide and 60 cm deep, with layers of plaster covered by a layer of travertine. In the northern part, next to the bank of the wadi, several rectangular cover stones have been preserved, evidence that the duct was covered. The top of the aqueduct is slightly lower than the top of the bridge, although originally the levels were apparently the same. The western wall of the aqueduct facing the wadi is now ruined. The eastern wall which is attached to the bridge is intact, and from its upper part a strip of plaster slopes down eastwards. Beneath it is another strip of plaster, a relic of a former stage of the aqueduct. Above the plaster bands is a stone construction, part of the structure of the present bridge. Therefore we suggest construction in stages as follows:

Stage 1: The aqueduct crossed the wadi attached to a wall of some sort, maybe the type of wall of Qanat Musa 1 or 3? In order to adapt the structure to flood conditions, a diagonal plaster band was fixed over the carrying wall aimed at returning the surplus water to the wadi.

Stage 2: Apparently, this method proved inefficient; therefore the support wall was considerably widened, the plaster bands were covered, and a solid bridge was built, while the aqueduct was attached to its west side. The upper part of the newly built structure was lined with small stones, and sections of this structural bed were also plastered. Hence, it is probable that at this phase the aqueduct went out of use and the top part of the bridge itself became a new aqueduct. At this stage, the former aqueduct was converted to a protection element west of the newly built aqueduct. The latter was raised by about 1 m, requiring repairs and modifications along its course all the way from Qanat

Musa 1. The proof for the disuse of the aqueduct is its clogging at the time of the construction of the new stage. This is an assumption, based upon the scanty data in our possession. Other reconstructions are also possible.

The extension of the aqueduct south: In all the sources (the British Survey, Porath, Braunschweig) the aqueduct extends to Jericho. In Volume 8 of our survey we will deal again with our attempts to find and document these sections of the aqueduct.

Dating: While measuring the aqueduct, about 150 sherds were gathered along its various sections. Although this does not allow accurate dating, it should be remembered that in all cases these were mainly Early (Herodian) and Late Roman ceramics. There were almost no Byzantine and later ones (Moslem, Medieval).

2.3.8. 'Aujah aqueducts – Porath's description: This paragraph summarizes the details available when Porath (1985: fig. 28) worked at the site, but have since disappeared. Porath called the first part of the aqueduct, next to 'Ein 'Aujah, Qanat el-'Ein (Porath 1985: 46-47). He describes it as: "built of limestone held by chalky clay and plastered in and out. The duct is 120-130 cm wide, about 60 cm deep, and its sides are about 60 cm thick. The original plaster in the aqueduct is of type I1. During its use it was renovated twice by spreading a new layer of plaster over the accumulated travertine sediment. Type I1 plaster was used in the first renovation and Type II 1-2 in the second." (translated from Hebrew). In another place (Porath 1985: 47 and fig. 28) Porath calls Qanat Manil Na'aran aqueduct and follows it up to Diuk and Na'aran Springs, no. 61 in fig. 28. It seems that there has been some confusion with the names, because Porath also called the Archelais aqueduct Qanat Manil.

The advantage of Porath's work is the existence of the whole length of the aqueducts when his publication was written. According to him, from Qanat Musa Bridge 2 the aqueduct stretched in south-easterly direction for about 10 km connecting to Diuk Springs. Thus, a linkage of water sources was formed, finally reaching Jericho.

Porath continues his description thus:

"The aqueduct went south in a meandering route at the western edges of the valleys, according to the topographical conditions and the planning principles of ancient times, down to Wadi Nueimeh…the width of the duct was about 105 cm, the depth about 60 cm and the side thickness about 50 cm…in some damaged places repairs were executed in the walls of the duct, raising the sides, laying cover slabs, and even a change of route. The length of Qanat Musa, from its beginning in the north to the division in the south, is more than 10 km, while the distance as the crow flies is only 5 km. The route has been doubled in order to overcome many topographical obstacles, ravines and spurs…" (Porath 1985: 47).

2.3.9. The work of the Braunschweig expedition: In 1991 a German expedition from Braunschweig University published another survey of the Jericho aqueducts (Garbrecht and Netser 1991). This one deals with the ancient water supply to Jericho, and the survey is a part of the excavation project at the site. Chapter 9 deals with the survey of the aqueducts from Wadi 'Aujah and further south. After the assessment of the ancient water discharge of 'Ein 'Aujah to have been 3451 cu. m per second the writers suggested the existence of a branch in the direction of the village of 'Aujah et-Tahta from the main aqueduct to Na'aran. The photographs of the aqueducts are important because they show the situation nearly 30 years ago. Regrettably, there are few plans, and most of the drawings represent various cross-sections.

REFERENCES

Amit, D., Hirshfeld Y., and Patrich, Y., 1989. *The Ancient Aqueducts in Eretz-Israel*, Jerusalem (Hebrew).

Avitsur, S., 1976. *Man and his Work, Historical Atlas of Tools & Workshops in the Holy Land*, Jerusalem (Hebrew).

Bar-Adon, P., 1972. "The Survey in the Judaea Desert and in the Valley of Jericho", in Kochavi, M. (ed.), *Judaea, Samaria and the Golan, Archaeological Survey 1967-1968*, Jerusalem, 92-153 (Hebrew).

Conder, C. R., and Kitchener, H. H., 1882. *The Survey of western Palestine*, vol. 2: Samaria, London.

Garbrecht, G., and Netzer, E. 1991. *Die Wasservesorgung des geschitlichen Jericho und seiner koeniglichen Anlagen* (Gut. Winterpalaeste), Braunschweig/ Jerusalem.

Goldfus, H., and Golani, A., 1993. "Map of Wadi el-Makukh (Sites 322-428) ", in Finkelstein, I. and Magen Y. (eds.), *Archaeological Survey of the Hill Country of Benjamin*, pp. 265-338. Jerusalem (Hebrew).

Ilan, Z., 1973. *The Jordan Valley and the Samaria Desert*, Tel Aviv (Hebrew).

Porath, Y., 1985. *Ancient Irrigation Agriculture in the Arid Zones of Eretz Israel* (Ph.D. dissertation), Tel Aviv University, Tel Aviv (Hebrew).

Spanier, Y., 1993. "Water powered Flourmills in South-east Samaria", in Erlich, Z. (ed.), *Samaria and Benjamin*, vol. III, Ariel, 243-258 (Hebrew).

Yadin, Y., 1971. *Bar-Kokhba, The Rediscovery of the Legendary Hero of the Last Jewish Revolt against Imperial Rome*, Tel Aviv (Hebrew).

INDEX 1

LIST OF SPRINGS AND OTHER WATER SOURCES

No. in the Survey	Name	Israel Grid	Type
104	Wadi Far'ah	-	Stream
112	The Jordan River	-	River
171	Fasael Pool	1907/1614	Reservoir
178	'Ein Juheir	1860/1644	Spring
181	Wadi Fasael (Rashash)	-	Stream
182	Wadi 'Aujah	1849/1658	Stream
183	Fasael Springs	1883/1620	Spring
184	'Ein el-'Aujah	1867/1514	Spring

INDEX 2

LIST OF ROADS

Road no.	Origin and destination	Passing via
B10	Beit-She'an - Jericho	Tell el-Ḥammeh - Jiftlik Junction - Kh. 'Aujah - Jericho
C40	Phasaelis-Neapolis	Fasael - 'Ein Hafireh - Sahl Afjam - Ṭana - Neapolis
C41	Phasaelis-Neapolis	Fasael - Majdal Bani Fadel- Neapolis
C47	Phasaelis- Fasael Springs	Wadi Fasael
C48	Kh. 'Aujah-'Ein el-'Aujah	Wadi 'Aujah
C49	Jericho -Samaria Mountains	Jericho -Tariq Abu George- Rimonim Junction

INDEX 3

AGRICULTURAL INSTALLATIONS AND OTHER FEATURES

As in the previous volumes, a list of installations and other features is included. It has been suggested that settlement sites should be recorded separately from other features (Zertal 2004). The linkage of a site to its agricultural vicinity is clear, but it is difficult to relate an installation or agricultural area to a particular site with certainty. The difficulty is because of the large number of sites, the conservatism in using the facilities, and the fact that a particular facility could have been in use for centuries, and sometimes for millennia. Hence, relating features and facilities to a site, or dating them to a period, requires separate thorough research.

For a detailed description of the main different type of installations see Zertal and Mirkam 2016. In addition to the different features presented here we have also added sites that were reported by earlier investigations in the region and were not found by our team (probably due to their destruction by modern earth moving and construction activities).

The bibliography of this index was added to the general bibliography of the research in Part Two of the book.

Type	Location	Region	Description
Stone heap	1902/1608	Wadi Fasael	
Tumulus	1905/1613	Wadi Fasael	No finds
Tumulus	1903/1605	Wadi Fasael	No finds
Tumuli	1906/1606	Wadi Fasael	Two tumuli. No finds
Structure	1908/1601	Wadi Fasael	Muslim prayer niche
Cistern and tumulus	1912/1596	Wadi Fasael	No finds
Road	1937/1614	Wadi Fasael	Described by Bar-Adon (1972: site 14). Not found
Structure	1909/1616	Wadi Fasael	Sq. Two walls survived. No finds
Cistern	1917/1607	Wadi Fasael	
Cistern	1915/1604	Wadi Fasael	
Cistern	1931/1593	Wadi Fasael	
Structure	1911/1605	Wadi Fasael	EM, described by Porath (1985a: site 5a). Not found

Type	Location	Region	Description
Structure	1944/1599	Wadi Fasael	EM, described by Porath (1985a: site 5f). Not found
Structure	1943/1598	Wadi Fasael	Modern building. Few Pers sherds
Structure	1941/1590	Wadi Fasael	EM, described by Porath (1985a: site 5e). Not found
Wall	1919/1603	Wadi Fasael	East-west. 50 m long and 0.45 m (two stones) wide
Aqueduct	1917/1605	Wadi Fasael	No finds
Terraces	1917/1604	Wadi Fasael	
Sherd scatter	1917/1605	Wadi Fasael	50 dunames. Open area. Pottery from IA, Pers, Hel, Rom, Byz, EM. Chalc adze. Probably ancient cultivated area
Structure	1909/1611	Wadi Fasael	Round, 4 m diam. No finds
Wall	1908/1611	Wadi Fasael	East-west agricultural wall
Tomb	1909/1610	Wadi Fasael	Elliptical, possibly Bedouin tomb
Structure	1902/1609	Wadi Fasael	3×3 m rectangular. No finds
Structures	1911/1605	Wadi Fasael	Structures on ridges near E.P. -219. Rom-Byz sherds
Installation	1908/1601	Wadi Fasael	Mortar in rocky slope west of Fusayil
Walls	1909/1604	Wadi Fasael	Two parallel walls built of large stones
Stone circle	1908/1604	Wadi Fasael	2 m diam middle sized stone circle west of Fusayil. No finds
Aqueduct	1902/1605	Wadi Fasael	Lime pavement, probably of aqueduct west of Fusayil
Wall	1910/1608	Wadi Fasael	Agricultural wall abutted by small stone lunar shaped Structures. No finds
Walls	1912/1608	Wadi Fasael	3 middle sized stone field border walls
Wall	1911/1606	Wadi Fasael	Large stones. Near aqueduct
Wall and pavement	1911/1608	Wadi Fasael	Agricultural facility and field border wall. No finds
Walls and sherd scatter	1921/1600	Wadi Fasael	Walls in the plateau south of Fasael. ER sherds
Wall	1921/1602	Wadi Fasael	Middle sized stone field border wall
Structure	1921/1603	Wadi Fasael	4×12 m structure. Undatable finds
Tumulus	1922/1605	Wadi Fasael	Tomb south of Fasael. No finds
Cemetery	1920/1605	Wadi Fasael	Tombs, Bedouin?
Structure	1919/1605	Wadi Fasael	Small stones pavement, possibly part of a tomb
Aqueduct	1917/1605	Wadi Fasael	Stone built aqueduct near Fasael. No finds

Type	Location	Region	Description
Wall	1917/1604	Wadi Fasael	Small stones in two rows field border wall
Wall	1917/1604	Wadi Fasael	Double wall built of small stones
Wall	1918/1602	Wadi Fasael	East-west, small stones field border wall
Aqueduct	1921/1596	Wadi Fasael	No finds
Sherd scatter	1921/1594	Wadi Fasael	Rom-Byz sherds
Cistern	1922/1594	Wadi Fasael	3.5 m diam, 4 m deep, plastered
Wall	1913/1621	Wadi Fasael	Long terrace wall. Rom-Byz and MA sherds
Structures?	1904/1608	Wadi Fasael	Wall remains on a slope. IA I sherds
Structures	1904/1608	Wadi Fasael	Meagre architecture and a small non diagnostic flint Scatter
Tumuli	1905/1585	Jebel Fasil	On the summit of Jebel Fasil. No finds
Tumulus	1905/1589	Jebel Fasil	On the summit of E.P. -48. No finds
Enclosure	1906/1606	Jebel Fasil	Filled with erosion. Undated
Cisterns	1898/1594	Jebel Fasil	Two cisterns
Tumuli	1904/1575	Jebel Fasil	3 tumuli. No finds
Encampment	1901/1578	Jebel Fasil	Bedouin camp remains. Undated body sherds
Tumulus	1901/1565	Jebel Fasil	No finds
Cistern	1898/1563	Jebel Fasil	
Tumulus	1964/1595	Wadi Far'ah	Near E.P. -300. No finds
Well	1960/1597	Wadi Far'ah	Appears in the map as Bir Dasha
Cistern	1961/1589	Wadi Far'ah	
Cistern	1958/1602	Wadi Far'ah	
Cistern	1961/1589	Wadi Far'ah	
Tumulus	1977/1584	Wadi Far'ah	Small. Near E.P. -226. No finds
Tumulus	1975/1574	Wadi Far'ah	Near E.P. -324. No finds
Cistern	1945/1574	Wadi Far'ah	
Cistern	1983/1613	Wadi Far'ah	
Cistern	1984/1608	Wadi Far'ah	
Stone tools scatter	1985/1671	Wadi Far'ah	40 dunames. Basalt tools scattered. Some pottery and flint – probably Chal.
Sherd scatter	1993/1683	Wadi Far'ah	400 east of Damia army camp. IA II and Rom
Tumulus	1928/1577	Tomer	Near E.P. -265. No finds
Road	1913/1581	Tomer	Described by Bar-Adon (1972: site 16). Not found

Type	Location	Region	Description
Tumulus	1894/1564	Wadi Sha'ab el-Qubur	Large. On E.P. 93. No finds
Tumuli	1899/1558	Wadi Sha'ab el-Qubur	Two tumuli near E.P. 71. No finds
Tumuli	1907/1558	Wadi Sha'ab el-Qubur	6 tumuli near E.P. -11. No finds
Tumulus	1908/1550	Wadi Sha'ab el-Qubur	No finds
Tumuli field	1903/1555	Wadi Sha'ab el-Qubur	Large tumuli field on a spur. No related finds
Cave	1898/1562	Wadi Sha'ab el-Qubur	6X8 m in size. Plastered – possibly served as a cistern. In entrance lower crushing stone of an olive oil extraction installation (Spanier 1994: 69)
Structures	1915/1557	Wadi Sha'ab el-Qubur	On the southern bank of the wadi. No finds
Encampment	1909/1562	Wadi Sha'ab el-Qubur	Encampment remains on a moderate slope. Rom-Byz and MA sherds
Enclosure	1907/1563	Wadi Sha'ab el-Qubur	On a ridge above the southern bank of the wadi. Undated sherds
Tomb	1908/1563	Wadi Sha'ab el-Qubur	On the northern bank of the wadi
Encampment	1909/1563	Wadi Sha'ab el-Qubur	On the northern bank of the wadi. No finds
Encampment	1908/1568	Wadi Sha'ab el-Qubur	10 dunames. Rom, MA and modern sherds
Terraces	1912/1565	Wadi Sha'ab el-Qubur	
Structure	1911/1564	Wadi Sha'ab el-Qubur	4×6 m partly paved. No finds
Sherd scatter	1914/1565	Gilgal	In field. Rom and modern sherds
Structures	1915/1565	Gilgal	Possibly modern encampment
Tomb	1913/1564	Gilgal	1.5 m long. Elliptical shape. No finds
Wall	1912/1566	Gilgal	Two rows of small stones. No finds
Stone circle	1910/1567	Gilgal	1 m diam. No finds. Instalation?
Tomb	1909/1573	Wadi Abu Mahmud	
Tumulus	1909/1574	Wadi Abu Mahmud	No finds
Cemetery	1908/1574	Wadi Abu Mahmud	30 tombs on the southern bank of the wadi. Partly robbed. No finds
Tombs	1907/1572	Wadi Abu Mahmud	Bedouin tombs?

Type	Location	Region	Description
Cave	1892/1572	Wadi Abu Mahmud	3.5 m high and 7 m deep. Few Rom-Byz sherds
Tumuli	1954/1565	Wadi Malha	Small tumuli on a hillock. No finds
Tumulus	1977/1565	Wadi Malha	No finds
Structure	1966/1544	Wadi Malha	No finds
Structure	2003/1523	Wadi Malha	No finds
Tumulus	2011/1504	Wadi Malha	No finds
Cistern	1960/1544	Wadi Malha	Nowadays active and full with water
Cistern	1960/1588	Wadi Malha	
Tumulus	1988/1543	Wadi Malha	No finds
Tumulus	1999/1559	Wadi Malha	Near E.P. -310. No finds
Pool	1953/1587	Wadi Malha	Square and plastered. Built of stones and asphalt. Iron pipes. Apparently Ott or mod
Sherd scatter	1999/1544	Wadi Malha	Few Rom-Byz and modern sherds
Camp	2001/1537	Wadi Malha	WW1 military camp. Bullets, modern glass bottles (medicine?) and modern sherds
Structure	2008/1537	Qatrat ez-Zur	Destroyed stone structure. No finds
Stone circle	1908/1554	Tal'at Zagharah	Stone circle 5 m in diam. No finds
Tumuli	1900/1558	Tal'at Zagharah	Two tumuli on ridge end. No finds
Enclosure	1900/1569	Tal'at Zagharah	Meagre remains. No finds
Structures and enclosure	1906/1558	Tal'at Zagharah	Wall and enclosure meagre remains. No finds
Tumulus	1908/1554	Tal'at Zagharah	5 m diam. No finds
Tumulus	1908/1552	Tal'at Zagharah	6 m diam. No finds
Sherd scatter	1913/1552	Tal'at Zagharah	Bedouin encampment remains with Rom-Byz sherds
Stone circle	1907/1552	Tal'at Zagharah	Stone circle 6 m in diam. No finds
Stone circle	1907/1553	Tal'at Zagharah	Stone circle 5 m in diam. No finds
Structures	1930/1544	Netiv Hagdud	On ridge. Unidentified sherds
Tumuli	1913/1547	Netiv Hagdud	Few tumuli along modern road 5629. No finds
Tumuli	1903/1545	Netiv Hagdud	No finds
Tumulus	1892/1544	Netiv Hagdud	Near E.P. 60. No finds
Tumuli field	1900/1520	Netiv Hagdud	20 tumuli. No finds
Barns	1916/1541	Netiv Hagdud	Rounded, 2 m diam. No finds
Structure	1912/1556	Netiv Hagdud	2.5X6 m built of small stones. No finds
Stone circle	1913/1553	Netiv Hagdud	Very small, 2 m diam. Small stones and no finds

Type	Location	Region	Description
Structures	1914/1555	Netiv Hagdud	Structures on a plateau with adjacent meagre remains of enclosures. Bedouin tombs. Rom and Ott sherds
Built pit	1913/1559	Netiv Hagdud	2.5 m diam. Medium sized stones. Filled with soil up to the top. Maybe a *fugara*?
Walls and tombs	1912/1558	Netiv Hagdud	Terraces and a few Bedouin tombs
Engraved stone	1915/1548	Netiv Hagdud	Engraving of an arrow on a large boulder
Tombs	1923/1553	Netiv Hagdud	No finds
Sherd scatter	1922/1559	Netiv Hagdud	10×10 m in a ploughed field. Rom-Byz sherds
Tomb	1915/1558	Netiv Hagdud	Bedouin? Near a 4 m diam stone circle
Structure	1916/1544	Netiv Hagdud	2×3 m in size. Large stones. Nearby a few small stone circles. No finds
Structure	1915/1545	Netiv Hagdud	Square, of large stones. No finds
Wall	1933/1546	Netiv Hagdud	
Structure	1933/1548	Netiv Hagdud	Ancient meagre structure in a modern camp. No finds
Installations	1931/1543	Netiv Hagdud	Two hewn basins in separate large boulders
Enclosures	1938/1543	Netiv Hagdud	Two meagre remains of enclosures. No finds
Enclosure	1935/1540	Netiv Hagdud	Apsidal. No finds
Sherd scatter and walls	1935/1542	Netiv Hagdud	EM and MA near meagre structures remains
Stone circle	1934/1540	Netiv Hagdud	Large stones, 4 m diam. Unidentified sherds
Stone circle	1932/1541	Netiv Hagdud	1.5 m diam. No finds
Wall and installation	1933/1543	Netiv Hagdud	15 m east-west wall. At its end a rounded stone installation
Wall and installations	1925/1538	Niran	20 m wall. Adjacent to the south grouped cupmarks
Cupmark	1926/1537	Niran	
Tomb	1944/1532	Niran	Sheikh el-Hallali tomb. Nearby two ruined structures. No finds
Tumulus	1938/1540	Niran	On E.P. -191. No finds
Stone circle	1931/1531	Niran	4 m diam. Built of large stones. No finds
Stone circle	1929/1531	Niran	3 m diam. Built of large and medium sized stones. Maybe a tumulus? No finds
Structure	1928/1530	Niran	Large stones. No finds

Type	Location	Region	Description
Encampment and tombs	1931/1521	Niran	Bedouin
Tombs	1929/1523	Niran	Bedouin
Caves	1940/1538	Niran	Rom-Byz sherds in the slope below the caves
Structures	1942/1536	Niran	Two one row of large stones structures. No finds
Walls and sherd scatter	1941/1537	Niran	Two parallel walls of large boulders. Rom, Byz and MA sherds
Encampment	1931/1535	Niran	Bedouin encampment
Stone circle	1936/1536	Niran	2 m diam. Circle of large stones and an adjacent long terrace. Unidentified sherds
Wall	1931/1536	Niran	Field border wall built of one row of large stones
Walls	1930/1533	Niran	Two walls of small stones along wadi banks
Tumulus	1926/1534	Niran	2 m diam. Unidentified sherds
Stone circle	1927/1534	Niran	6 m diam. Only half of it survived. No finds
Cemetery	1927/1534	Niran	10 tombs spread on a 6 dunams area. Bedouin
Cupmark	1926/1532	Niran	
Wall	1938/1535	Niran	Meagre remains of a tomb or a small structure. No finds
Tomb	1938/1535	Niran	Modern?
Encampment	1937/1535	Niran	Meagre remains of ancient encampments. No finds
Tumuli	1905/1534	Wadi Hamam	10 tumuli on a large plateau. No finds
Walls and installation	1893/1532	Wadi Hamam	Few meagre walls and a small rounded installation. No finds
Tumuli	1899/1529	Wadi Hamam	Tumuli on a large plateau. No finds
Caves	1884/1530	Wadi Hamam	
Encampment and tombs	1890/1535	Wadi Hamam	Bedouin encampment and cemetery
Wall	1892/1527	Wadi Hamam	Large boulders agricultural wall
Cemetery	1890/1528	Wadi Hamam	A cemetery on a ridge above the wadi. No finds
Structure and walls	1890/1527	Wadi Hamam	4X4 m square structure of standing stones. Nearby agricultural wall and a possible dam in the wadi. No finds

Type	Location	Region	Description
Stone heaps	1899/1538	Wadi Hamam	Two large stone heaps on the end of a ridge
Tumuli	1917/1522	Wadi Maqor edh-Dhib	Two tumuli on a moderate slope above the wadi. No finds
Enclosure	1919/1523	Wadi Maqor edh-Dhib	Meagre remains of a rounded enclosure on a moderate slope above the wadi. No finds
Tumulus	1913/1527	Wadi Maqor edh-Dhib	Dismantled, probably robed. No finds
Encampment	1920/1523	Wadi Maqor edh-Dhib	Modern Bedouin encampment at a curve in the wadi. Small unidentified sherd scatter
Structures	1922/1522	Wadi Maqor edh-Dhib	Two structures. No finds
Stone circle	1925/1525	Wadi Maqor edh-Dhib	4 m diam. On a ridge above the wadi. No finds
Tumulus	1908/1524	Wadi Maqor edh-Dhib	No finds
Tumuli	1915/1525	Wadi Maqor edh-Dhib	5 tumuli on E.P. -101. No finds
Tumuli and pits	1912/1523	Wadi Maqor edh-Dhib	Scattered on the slope above the wadi. No finds
Stone circles	1929/1533	Wadi Maqor edh-Dhib	Two standing stone circles, 6 m in diam. No finds
Installations	1927/1532	Wadi Maqor edh-Dhib	Barns and quarried installations on a ridge above the wadi. No finds
Enclosure	1942/1523	Wadi Maqor edh-Dhib	Meagre remains of a rounded enclosure on a ridge to the west and above kh. Beiyudhat (Site 111). No finds
Cemetery	1927/1532	Wadi Maqor edh-Dhib	25 heaps of stones 1X1.5 m, on a 3 dunam area. These are probably tombs. Rom-Byz sherds
Enclosure and tombs	1525/1529	Wadi Maqor edh-Dhib	An oval 5X15 m enclosure of medium sized stones. On the nearby ridge Bedouin tombs. No finds
Encampment	1927/1532	Wadi Maqor edh-Dhib	3 oval structures, probably tent bases remains, on a 1 dunam area. No finds
Encampment	1929/1531	Wadi Maqor edh-Dhib	3 oval structures, probably tent bases remains. IA, Rom and Byz sherds
Encampment	1931/1537	Wadi Maqor edh-Dhib	A Bedouin encampment with a few 4 m diam, bases of tents. Modern sherds
Encampment	1938/1532	Wadi Maqor edh-Dhib	A Bedouin encampment with 2 bases of tents. No finds

Type	Location	Region	Description
Tumuli	1905/1530	Wadi Maqor edh-Dhib	Two tumuli. No finds
Stone circles	1888/1523	Wadi Nabiris	4 rounded stone circles 4 m in diam. No finds
Structures	1888/1524	Wadi Nabiris	On the ridge above the wadi. No finds
Cemetery	1890/1524	Wadi Nabiris	Bedouin
Structures	1891/1522	Wadi Nabiris	Enclosure and structures on a ridge. No finds
Tumulus	1888/1519	Wadi Nabiris	On E.P. 44. No finds
Cemetery	1893/1526	Wadi Nabiris	Bedouin
Tomb	1888/1528	Wadi Haiyat	Probably Bedouin on a ridge above the wadi
Tumuli field	1913/1515	Wadi Haiyat	10 tumuli spread near the wadi. No finds
Tumulus	1897/1532	Wadi el-Baqar	1 m high and 5 m in diam. No finds
Cemetery	1900/1547	Wadi el-Baqar	18 tombs on a ridge north of the wadi. Rom, Byz and MA sherds
Tumulus	1894/1544	Wadi er-Risha	On the ridge above the wadi. No finds
Cave	1890/1547	Wadi er-Risha	A 5 m deep and 15 m wide collapsed cave and an adjacent courtyard. Serving today as animal pen. Two Rom-Byz sherds
Sherd scatter	1892/1507	Wadi 'Aujah	EM sherds (Spanier 1992: site 174). Not found
Structure	1893/1502	Wadi 'Aujah	3×6 m structure. Adjacent stone heaps. Byz and MA sherds (Spanier 1992: site 176). Not found
Flint scatter and wall	1911/1493	Wadi 'Aujah	A small undated flint scatter and an adjacent, probably not connected, 3 m wall built of two rows of stones.
Wall	1919/1519	Wadi 'Aujah	On a ridge. Built of medium sized stones and survived only 2 m. no finds
Wall and tomb	1881/1505	Wadi 'Aujah	No finds
Walls and installation	1892/1506	Wadi 'Aujah	Meagre structure remains and a cupmark nearby. No finds
Wall	1893/1505	Wadi 'Aujah	On the bank of the wadi. No finds
Structure and cupmark	1893/1508	Wadi 'Aujah	A rounded 2 m in diam structure on hilltop. Nearby a cupmark. Few Rom-Byz sherds
Structure	1894/1508	Wadi 'Aujah	Rectangular structure on hilltop. No finds
Tumulus	1895/1510	Wadi 'Aujah	No finds

Type	Location	Region	Description
Tombs	1895/1511	Wadi 'Aujah	Tombs on a ridge. Probably Bedouin
Tumulus	1897/1510	Wadi 'Aujah	Robbed. In the center a cist burial chamber. No finds
Tumulus	1898/1510	Wadi 'Aujah	3 m diam. On hilltop. No finds
Tomb	1891/1507	Wadi 'Aujah	On low hilltop
Sherd scatter	1873/1512	Wadi 'Aujah	South of the wadi. Chal, EBA, IA II and Rom sherds
Tumulus	1907/1523	Wadi 'Aujah	No finds
Wall	1926/1514	Sahel 'Aujah	15 m long. On a slope. One large stone wide
Structure	1878/1498	'Aujah south	Two parallel walls. No finds

INDEX 4

SITE INDEX

INDEX 5

LIST OF SITES BY PERIOD

Persian period:

16, 23, 59, 71-72, 95, 107, 112, 116, 119, 131, 140.

Hellenistic period:

3-4, 8, 16, 23, 34, 51, 54, 58-59, 66, 71-73, 75, 89, 107, 111, 113-114, 116, 119, 131, 137(?), 140, 148.

Early Roman period:

3-4, 8, 10-13, 15, 17, 19, 23, 27, 29, 34, 36-38, 56, 58-61, 65, 71-73, 89, 91, 110-111, 113-115, 117(?), 124, 126, 131-132, 135, 138-141, 144, 146, 148, 149.

Late Roman period:

1-2(?), 4-8, 10-15, 17-19, 24, 28, 33-34, 37-38, 40-42, 44-45(?), 46-47(?), 49-62(?), 64, 66-69, 71-80, 83-90(?), 91-101(?), 103, 106-117(?), 118-119, 122-124, 126, 130(?)-138, 140-141, 143-149(?), 151, 153, 155, 157.

Byzantine period:

1-2(?), 4, 7-8, 10-17, 28-29, 34, 36, 38, 41, 44, 49-51, 53-54, 56, 59-59(1), 69, 72-73, 75-76, 78-80, 83-84, 86, 88, 94-95, 100, 105(?), 107-109, 111, 113, 115-116, 126,129, 132, 135-136, 138, 140, 142-146, 148, 150-151, 153, 155-157.

Early Moslem period:

8, 10, 12, 16, 26, 34, 36, 38-38(1), 50, 72-73, 84, 86, 95, 111, 126, 129, 132, 134, 138, 140, 142, 146, 148, 150-151, 157.

Middle Ages:

1, 4, 6-8, 10, 12, 14-16, 23, 26, 28, 41-42, 44-45(?), 46, 49-53, 56, 59(1), 61, 68, 71-73, 76-77, 80, 84, 86, 88-89, 92, 94-95, 101(?), 107, 109, 111, 113-114, 116, 122, 126, 129, 131, 135(?)-136, 140, 142-144, 146, 155.

Ottoman period:

1, 4, 8, 10, 12, 14-15, 18, 23, 28-29, 37, 46, 48, 51-53, 56, 61, 71, 73, 76, 84, 86, 89, 98, 107, 114, 116, 126, 129, 131, 140-143, 146, 149, 156-157.

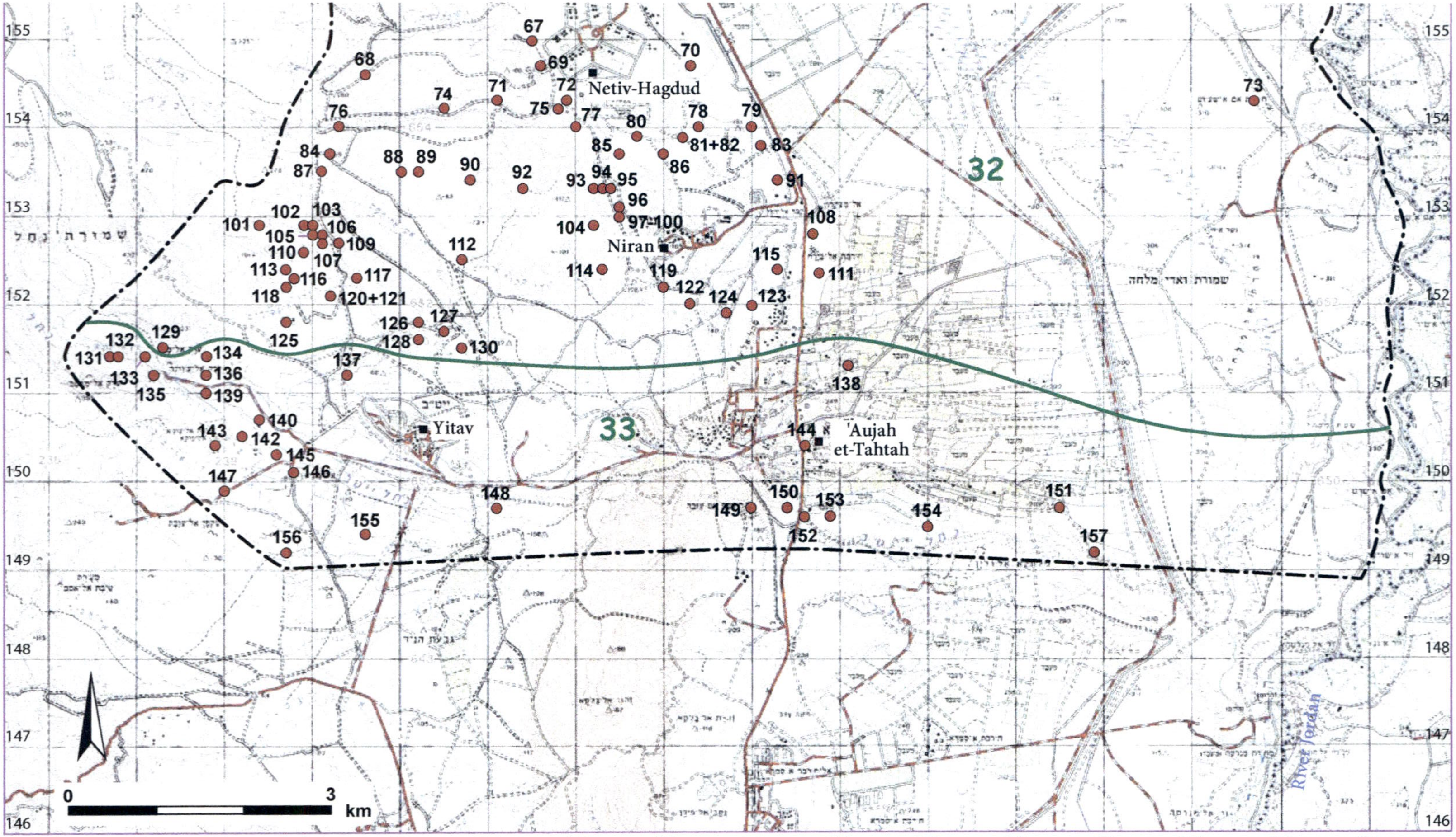

LEGEND: Survey boundary — 31 Landscape unit & number — 151 Site & its number

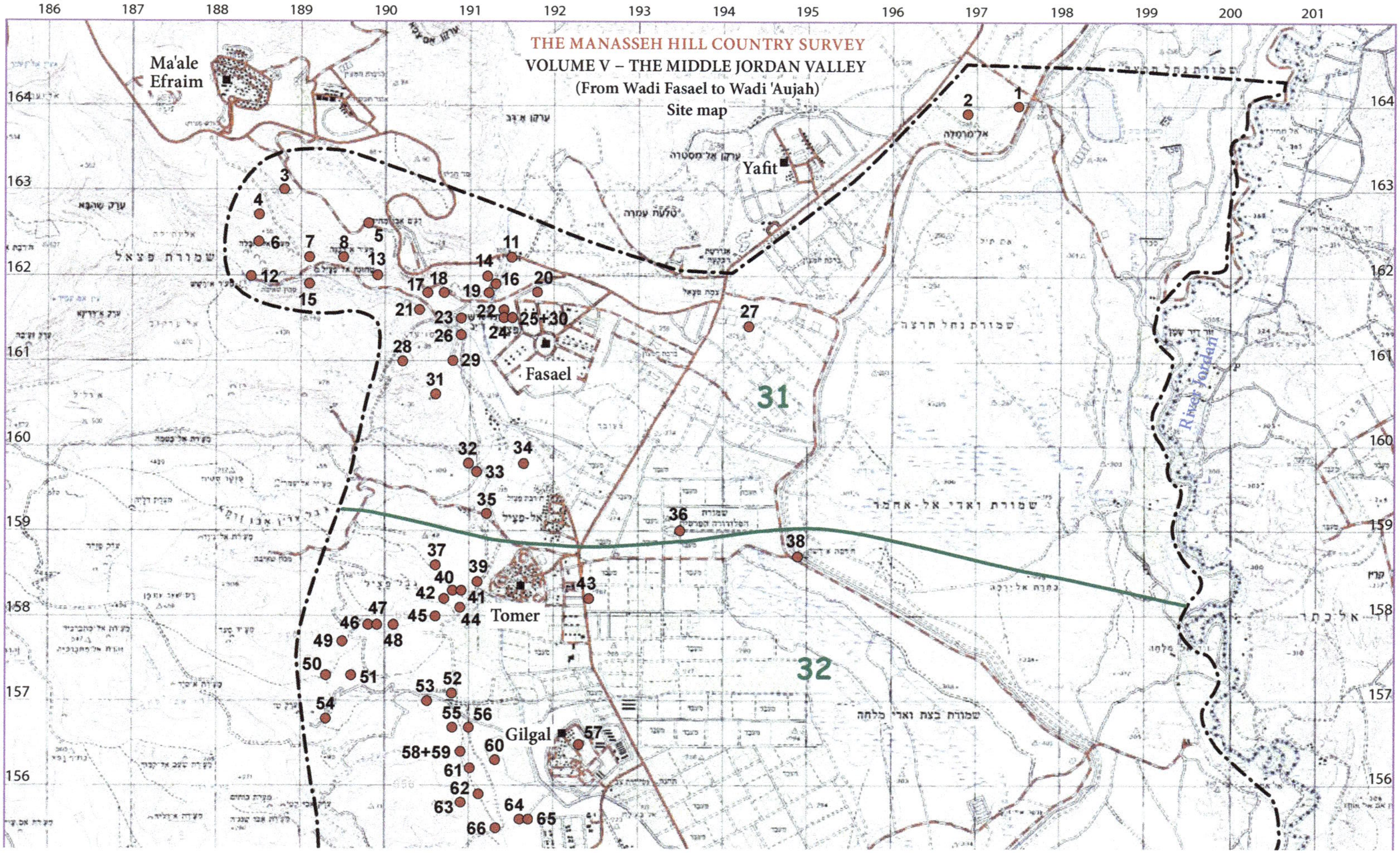
THE MANASSEH HILL COUNTRY SURVEY
VOLUME V – THE MIDDLE JORDAN VALLEY
(From Wadi Fasael to Wadi 'Aujah)
Site map
Ma'ale Efraim
Yafit
Fasael
Tomer
Gilgal
River Jordan
31
32

www.ingramcontent.com/pod-product-compliance
Ingram Content Group UK Ltd.
Pitfield, Milton Keynes, MK11 3LW, UK
UKHW022225051026
15624UKWH00002B/358

9 789004 400849